FOR GOD, COUNTRY AND
Coca-Cola

The Definitive History of the World's Most Popular Soft Drink

Mark Pendergrast

ORION
BUSINESS
BOOKS

This edition published in 2000 by Orion Business
a division of The Orion Publishing Group Ltd
Orion House, 5 Upper St Martin's Lane, London WC2H 9EA

*Unless otherwise stated, photographs are supplied
courtesy of the Coca-Cola Company.*

A CIP catalogue record for this book is available from the
British Library.

ISBN 1 84203 042 6

Typeset at The Spartan Press Ltd,
Lymington, Hants
Printed and bound in Great Britain by
Creative Print and Design (Wales), Ebbw Vale.

1916

Business has its Romance. The inner history of every great business success is just as stirring and fascinating as the most imaginative story ever told. Real success never comes easy ... Progress has been achieved only through continual struggle and hard, patient work. It has called for ingenuity and resource of the highest order, the courage that accepted no defeat, the endurance that wore down all opposition, the confidence that overcame every jealous libel.

And such has been the history of Coca-Cola.

—THE ROMANCE OF COCA-COLA (booklet)

May 21, 1942

Since 1886 ... changes have been the order of the day, the month, the year. These changes, I may add, are partly or wholly the result of the very existence of The Coca-Cola Company and its product ... They have created satisfactions, given pleasure, inspired imitators, intrigued crooks ... Coca-Cola is not an essential, as we would like it to be. It is an idea—it is a symbol—it is a mark of genius inspired.

—Letter from advertising man William C. D'Arcy

March 24, 1959

Please, Mr Kahn, you've written some excellent articles and profiles, but why all this effort spent on Coca-Cola? I can't conceive that it could be interesting to enough people to be worth your using all that paper, all those thousands of words, and hours of labor to write it. In addition, I consider it a most noxious drink.

—Letter to E. J. Kahn, Jr., in response to a series of articles on Coca-Cola in THE NEW YORKER

July 10, 1985

Why read fiction? Why go to movies? Soft drink industry has enough roller coaster plot-dips to make novelists drool.

—Jesse Meyers in BEVERAGE DIGEST special edition announcing reintroduction of original Coca-Cola

Dedicated to the memory of
Roberto C. Goizueta, Coca-Cola missionary,
and
E. J. Kahn, Jr., Coca-Cola chronicler

Contents

Notes on the Text

1. Virtually all of the main characters in this story are male, a commentary on American business for the past hundred years. Consequently, I have deliberately chosen to refer to Coca-Cola men or McCann-Erickson men, even though a few women have played vital roles in those organizations. As one Coke executive put it in 1957 with unselfconscious sexism, "Two things make this business great—one is the product Coca-Cola, and the other is *men*. We have the product but we shall need more and more good *men*. *Men* of character and intelligence. *Men* who are industrious and hard-working. *Men* of spirit and ambition. *Men* of dedication . . . I see a bigger future, with greater responsibility for more and more *men* [italics added].

2. Because this is not a Ph.D. thesis, I have not cluttered the text with numbered endnotes. Information sources are noted in the back of the book with appropriate page and text references. The reader will find some of the most entertaining Coca-Cola anecdotes and illuminating background material in the endnotes, since such juicy tidbits would have interrupted the flow of the main text.

3. The five mini dramas introducing the sections are fictional re-creations of likely events and should be taken as such.

4. All ungrammatical errors inside quotation marks are the mistakes of the original personage being quoted. I make this note here instead of putting [*sic*] into so many quotations. Until page 63, Coca-Cola is often misspelled or in lower case. After the text reveals that Asa Candler objected to such usage, I have corrected the spelling for ease in reading, and left out the quotation marks that Company men like to put around "Coca-Cola." In deference to historical company policy, I have used the entire name until page 192, when "Coke" became a recognized trademark. Thereafter, I have used either term interchangeably.

Preface to the First Edition

This book has been a kind of "Roots" project for me. Since both sides of my family lived in Atlanta from the late nineteenth century on, I suppose it was inevitable that Coca-Cola would intersect our lives many times. My paternal grandfather, J. B. Pendergrast, owned a drugstore at Little Five Points, where he regularly served the soft drink to Asa Candler, the first Coca-Cola tycoon, before investing in the Woodruff Syndicate's takeover of the company in 1919. Unfortunately, J.B. sold the stock a few years later in order to build a house. The most intriguing family story concerns the day young Robert W. Woodruff and his friend Robert W. Schwab discussed Helen Kaiser's allure as they sat outside her home. "Well," Woodruff said, "I think I'll go propose to her right now," awaiting a protest. "Go ahead," Schwab answered, feigning disinterest. When Woodruff returned a few minutes later, he said, "She turned me down. I guess you'll have to marry her." Schwab did, later becoming my maternal grandfather.

If Woodruff had married her, perhaps I would be a wealthy man today—or I might not be here at all, since Woodruff, who directed Coca-Cola's fortunes from 1923 until his death in 1985, had no children. It's just as well that things worked out the way they did, though, since I've enjoyed taking a more objective view of the Company and its entertaining role in world history. I hope you will, too.

Mark Pendergrast
August 1992

Preface to the Revised Edition

An old French adage goes, "*La plus ça change, la plus c'est la même chose*"—the more things change, the more they stay the same. That certainly applies to the subject of Coca-Cola, which remains as fascinating as ever. It has been a pleasure to follow the twists and turns of the ongoing saga of the world's most ubiquitous product as it breaks into the twenty-first century. Despite some rocky times during a global economic recession that hit hard in 1998, there is little doubt that Coke will continue its implacable quest for world domination.

I have altered little of the original first edition material, since I have not found much to correct or add. I did spice it with new tidbits such as the fact that Eddie Fisher was high on amphetamine when he sang for Coke in the 1950s, however. A year after my first edition appeared, Frederick Allen published *Secret Formula*, another excellent version of Coke history that I have mined in a few places (see the informational endnotes). Allen focused less on the international, cultural, and political implications of the drink's history, but he unearthed very interesting internal company lore, particularly regarding Robert Woodruff. I am also indebted to David Greising's 1998 biography of Roberto Goizueta, *I'd Like the World to Buy a Coke*. When I was originally researching Coke's history back in 1991, people asked me, "Can you really write a whole book about one soft drink?" Well, the answer is yes. In fact, it would take an encyclopedia to include everything. Thus, I am happy that there are other Coke books. The more, the better.

I repeatedly asked Coca-Cola Company spokesmen to let me know if there were inaccuracies in my first edition, but I did not receive a response. This time around, one Coke public relations man was kind enough to send copies of *Journey*, the company's internal magazine, as well as video clips with current ads. Unfortunately, I am afraid that the Company officially took a rather dim view of my first edition, which frankly surprised me. When I told the Company that I was providing commentary for a three-hour documentary, *The Cola Conquest*, it meant instant non-cooperation for the poor filmmakers (who produced a fascinating work anyway). Although I certainly didn't write a puff piece, it is not a hatchet job either, but a balanced and rather affectionate look at an American (and now global) institution and how it came to be. One of my friends inside the Company told me after reading it, "For a lengthy, well-researched history of a multinational corporation, I think we came off as well as could possibly be expected in your book." My impression, however, is that few inside the Coke culture have actually read the book. I wish they would. I think they would be surprised by what they found, and they might even learn something.

I am gratified to have heard from many Coca-Cola fans and collectors throughout the world who *have* read the book. "Your book has opened up a perception and appreciation of the Coke world around me," one typical respondent wrote. "I have always enjoyed Coke and remember the 5 cent bottles I obtained at the filling station in St Louis." Coke bottlers wrote, "Reading your book was a total immersion in Coca-Cola . . . a condition which held our interest most profoundly." (I hope they came up for breath occasionally.) While I appreciate favorable reviews in newspapers or periodicals, this kind of spontaneous response means more to me. Thus, when average readers wrote reviews on the Amazon.com web site, I was delighted to find comments such as: "Pendergrast tells the story of this amazing company in candid fashion. Highly recommended for Coca-Cola fans around the world!!" Another reader wrote: "Drink Coke and read this book! Both refresh your brain."

As those familiar with the first edition of this book know, the main storyline ended in November 1989 as the Berlin Wall fell, with Coca-Cola fizzing into the breach. In addition to a new appendix with thirty simple business lessons, I have added two new chapters (21 and 22) that chronicle the decade of the 1990s. The first is a tale of triumph for Coca-Cola and CEO Roberto Goizueta, capped by the 1996 Atlanta Olympics in Coke's home town. Goizueta died swiftly and tragically just shy of his 66th birthday in 1997, leaving Doug Ivester to face difficult economic times. Chapter 22 chronicles Ivester's troubled, brief reign, ending with his sudden resignation, as Doug Daft took over to guide the Company into the next millennium. As always, in this decade's story, readers will find high drama, corporate intrigue, and innovative ads that pluck the heartstrings. Always changing. Always the same. Always Coca-Cola.

Mark Pendergrast
September 1999

FOR GOD, COUNTRY
AND
Coca-Cola

Prologue: A Parable (January 1, 1985)

THE BOSS was a very old man, near death. Though his mind still ticked over a lifetime of executive decisions, it was trapped in a decaying body. All of his senses were shutting down. He could see only dimly, and his cigar, a trademark for most of his life, hung unlit from a slack mouth. His hearing, too, had nearly failed, and he seldom spoke in more than a monosyllable.

Robert Woodruff was ninety-five years old, four years younger than the soft drink he had made the world's most well-known, cherished product. For more than sixty years, Woodruff had steered the fortunes of Coca-Cola. Even in these last few years, as he and the drink approached the century mark, his approval had been sought for every major decision in the Company.

A younger man in a pinstripe suit approached the old man's bed. He had come alone to speak with the Boss, asking the attendants to leave the room. He sought the old man's blessing, looked for his benediction on the most revolutionary decision ever to be made at Coca-Cola.

Chemical engineer Roberto Goizueta, the Cuban native who had become the first foreign-born CEO of The Coca-Cola Company, planned to change the formula of the drink just a year short of its hundredth anniversary. Though the man in the pinstripes knew that tampering with the world's most closely guarded secret formulas was risky, he had sound business reasons for doing so. Now, he slowly and systematically laid them out for the Boss, practically shouting to make sure that he was heard.

Motionless, Woodruff listened.

The story the younger man told was full of statistics, percentage points, market share analysis, and talk of blind taste-tests. But the essential point was simple, and Goizueta repeated it loud and clear: Most soft drink consumers preferred the taste of Pepsi to that of Coke. It was a slim margin, but it was there. And no matter how much Coke outspent Pepsi on ads, no matter how great their distribution system, Pepsi's market share kept creeping higher. The competition already sold more in the supermarkets, and it was advancing on Coke's superior fountain and vending sales.

The time had come to modify the taste of Coca-Cola. The drink had been good in its time, but times change, tastes change, industries change, and nothing in the business world is sacred. The chemists at Coke had devised a new formula that consistently trounced Pepsi—as well as Coke—in blind taste-tests. Goizueta emphasized that the time was ripe, in fact overdue, for a New Coke. It simply had to be.

Finally, the younger man fell silent, intent on the old man's reaction. The cigar hung unmoved. The eyes glistened. Outside the window, a slight rain fell on the first day of the new year.

Woodruff's eyes slowly brimmed; the cigar trembled. In the silence, a grandfather clock ticked off fat, slow seconds. Finally, the Boss sighed. "Do it," he rasped, and his eyes overflowed.

Goizueta smiled. Woodruff had always liked him, had picked him as a successor. The two men used to lunch together; they had a special understanding, a bond. It was important that the Boss give his approval. People said the old man hated change, but Goizueta knew he just needed things explained in their simplest terms. This was just like diet Coke, and look at how well *that* had done. Goizueta thanked the Boss, said he would be back to see him soon, and left.

Roberto was convincing, not so much by his facts and figures, but by his earnestness. He must be right, but that didn't mean that the Boss had to live to see his sacred formula revised. The old man stopped eating. Two months later, a month before New Coke was made public, Robert Woodruff died. He never knew the uproar that the flavor change was to create. It is not beyond imagination, however, that somewhere in his steadily ticking brain, he guessed.

For three months, the stubborn management at Coca-Cola was besieged daily by thousands of phone calls and hundreds of pounds of letters, all begging for the old drink back. The press was full of outraged reports. While Goizueta waited for the uproar to subside, it only intensified.

It became clear that the Cuban and his management team, his marketing surveys, and his advertising men had miscalculated. Taste wasn't the issue. It didn't matter whether New Coke went down more smoothly.

The letters, oddly reminiscent of those sent to the company by GIs during World War II, clearly spelled out the real issue. Coca-Cola was an old friend, a piece of everyday life, a talisman of America, a kind of icon. But unlike the wartime letters, which expressed heartfelt gratitude, these contained feelings of betrayal:

"Changing Coke is like God making the grass purple."

"I don't think I would be more upset if you were to burn the flag on our front yard."

Roberto Goizueta and his cohorts were taught a quick, incisive business lesson, and they finally capitulated, bringing back the old Coke to a grateful world.

The issue was not taste. The issue was not marketing surveys or focus groups.

The issue was God.

The issue was Country.

The issue was Coca-Cola.

Part I

~

In the Beginning

(1886–1899)

A hot day in August, 1885.

The tall, bearded old man hesitated before crossing Marietta Street, one of Atlanta's busy thoroughfares. Horses and buggies clattered on the cobblestone; prosperous businessmen hurried past. Elegantly dressed women with parasols strolled to Jacobs' Pharmacy on the corner for an ice cream soda. Newsboys hawked the papers, screaming, "Read all about it! Whisky Ring Fights Sin Tax! Temperance Workers Meet! Anti-Prohibition Speech at Opera House a Flop! Read all about it!"

"I'll take a paper, son." Pursing his lips, temporarily forgetting the busy street, the man read. There was the usual sensationalism. A local suicide. An attempted lynching. The birth of triplets.

Impatiently, he rifled through the paper. Ah, here was an editorial laying into the liquor license. "It is guilty, at the bar of God and humanity, of this great crime: that it creates, fosters, solicits, incites, stimulates, and multiplies intemperance. The open barroom holds the whisky glass to every man's lips at every corner." No doubt about it. Atlanta would go dry, it was only a question of time.

The street cleared momentarily. Folding his paper under his arm, the elderly man crossed the street before another buggy bounced through the intersection. As he put his key into the lock at 107 Marietta Street, a young man briskly lifted his hat on his way by. "Good day, Dr Pemberton. Hot enough for you, sir?" The old gentleman nodded and smiled. Everyone in Atlanta knew and respected the kindly old patent medicine man, and most took one of his remedies for their cough, dyspepsia, headache, sexual debility, or whatever else ailed them.

As Pemberton entered his laboratory, he looked with satisfaction at his fresh supply of coca leaves, straight from Peru, and at the filtering system he had set up to produce coca extract. He was experimenting with a new concoction, one which he hoped he could sell as a temperance drink and medicine, since the town was in hysteria over the evils of alcohol.

Suddenly Pemberton doubled over with pain. It was his stomach again—heartburn or his ulcer flaring up. His bones ached with rheumatism. Still bent, he fumbled for his secret case in a false-bottomed drawer. Shaking, he filled the hypodermic needle, turned it to his arm, and slowly pushed the plunger. With a deep sigh, he carefully put the needle and materials away and prepared for his experiments.

Dr. John Stith Pemberton, as he began the experiments which would lead to the invention of Coca-Cola, was fifty-four years old. He looked at least ten years older. And he was addicted to morphine.

~ 1 ~

Time Capsule: The Golden Age of Quackery

I've been experimenting on a little preparation—a kind of decoction nine-tenths water and the other tenth drugs that don't cost more than a dollar a barrel . . . The third year we could easily sell 1,000,000 bottles in the United States—profit at least $350,000—and then it would be time to turn our attention toward the real idea of the business . . . Why, our headquarters would be in Constantinople and our hindquarters in Further India! . . . Annual income—well, God only knows how many millions and millions!
                    —Colonel Beriah Sellers, in Mark Twain's *The Gilded Age, 1873*

THERE'S NO QUESTION that The Coca-Cola Company loves its own history. As if to prove the point, in 1990 it spent $15 million on its Atlanta museum, which indoctrinates over 3,000 Coca-Cola-drenched tourists daily into the company's high-tech version of its past. The press release on opening day called the museum a "fantasyland." In more ways than one, it is just that. The red-clad, clean-cut young guides assure visitors, for instance, that Coca-Cola *never* had any cocaine in it.

The museum carries on a long-standing company tradition. The Coca-Cola saga has been reverentially preserved and nurtured over the years. In the official version, the story of Coca-Cola's 1886 creation has all the earmarks of the classic American success myth, as exemplified by the protagonists of Horatio Alger's novels. These heroes, who served as role models for hopeful young capitalists in the Gilded Age, catapulted to astonishing wealth from humble origins through perseverance, hard work, and an inevitable stroke of good luck.

Similarly, John Pemberton, Coca-Cola's inventor, has been depicted by the Company as a poor but lovable old Southern root doctor who stumbled upon the miraculous new drink. While Coca-Cola was supposedly born in a humble three-legged kettle in Pemberton's backyard rather than in a manger, the story is treated as a kind of Virgin Birth. Coca-Cola's first archivist, Wilbur Kurtz, described the moment: "He leaned over the pot to smell the bouquet of his brew. Then he took a long wooden spoon and captured a little of the thick brown bubbling contents of the pot, allowing it to cool a moment. He lifted the spoon to his lips and tasted." Pemberton's hard work and perseverance in finding just the right taste finally paid off, as in the Alger stories, with a stroke of luck, when the syrup was inadvertently mixed with carbonated rather than plain water. The customers loved the effervescent drink and smacked their lips in satisfaction.

From that point on, according to Company legend, the drink's future was assured. Of course, it needed a little help from Asa Candler, who purchased the formula as Pemberton was dying, advertised it widely, and quickly became the wealthiest man in Atlanta. By the early 1900s, the drink's phenomenal rise to fame was repeatedly called the "romance of Coca-Cola."

This official version of events is a myth, however. John Pemberton was not an uneducated, simple root doctor. He did not brew the drink in his backyard. More importantly, far from being a unique beverage that sprang out of nowhere, Coca-Cola was a product of its time, place, and culture. It was, like many other such nostrums, a patent medicine with a distinct cocaine kick.

One element of the myth rings true, however. The chances of Coca-Cola's success were about as remote as Colonel Sellers' "decoction." Twain's passage was an uncannily accurate prophecy of Coca-Cola's future, however. Today, Coke is the world's most widely distributed product, available in nearly 200 countries, more than the United Nations membership. "OK" excepted, "Coca-Cola" is the most universally recognized word on earth, and the drink it characterizes has become a symbol of the Western way of life. How, in the space of a little over a century, has a fizzy soft drink, 99 percent sugar water, attained such an astonishing status? Conditions in late nineteenth-century America largely determined its future.

A NATION OF NEUROTICS

During the Gilded Age, America's metamorphosis from a land of farmers into an urbanized society of mills and factories was arguably the most wrenching in its history. With the Civil War as a catalyst and turning point, industrialism and a virtual revolution in transportation marked the emergence of a distinctively American brand of capitalism—one which idealized individual hustle and relied heavily upon advertising and newspapers to spread its gospel. The railroad became the symbol and engine of powerful change, allowing the creation of national markets for goods.

The pace was so overwhelming that it generated concern over a new disease characterized by neurotic, psychosomatic symptoms. One writer of the era diagnosed it as the fruits of "an industrial and competitive age." We would now call it "Future Shock," but George Beard labeled the disease "neurasthenia" in his 1881 book, *American Nervousness, Its Causes and Consequences*.[*] Beard attributed the new malady to the dislocations wrought, both socially and economically, by "modern civilization."

The steam engine, he noted, which was supposed to make work easier, had

---

[*] Curiously, to be diagnosed as a neurasthenic was a sign of good breeding and high status. Only those with refined, delicate temperaments or highly charged brains were subject to the disease. Beard concluded that the blue-collar worker was too ignorant and full of robust health to be afflicted. The cure for neurasthenic men, such as Theodore Roosevelt, consisted of fresh air and physical activity, often on a dude ranch. Women such as Charlotte Perkins Gilman or Edith Wharton, on the other hand, were confined in utter passivity, spoon-fed milk in bed.

instead resulted in more frantic life-styles and in overspecialization, "depressing both to body and mind," according to Beard. He also pointed out that a more time-conscious America was becoming more obsessive: "Punctuality is a great thief of nervous force." In general, Beard noted, overwork, the strain of economic booms and busts, repression of turbulent emotions, and too much freedom of thought contributed to high states of nerves. Finally, "the rapidity with which new truths are discovered, accepted and popularized in modern times is a proof and result of the extravagance of our civilization."

Coca-Cola emerged from this turbulent, inventive, noisy, neurotic new America. It began as a "nerve tonic" like many others marketed to capitalize on the dislocations and worries of the day. After surviving an early history rife with conflict and controversy, this lowly nickel soft drink became so much a part of national life that by 1938 it was called "the sublimated essence of America."

The description is still apt. Coca-Cola remains emblematic of the best and worst of America and Western civilization. The history of Coca-Cola is the often funny story of a group of men obsessed with putting a trivial soft drink "within an arm's reach of desire." But at the same time, it is a microcosm of American history. Coca-Cola grew up with the country, shaping and shaped by the times. The drink not only helped to alter consumption patterns, but attitudes toward leisure, work, advertising, sex, family life, and patriotism. As Coca-Cola continues to flood the world with its determinedly happy fizz, its history assumes yet more importance.

During the late 1800s, however, no one, including the inventor of Coca-Cola, had such grand visions. Coca-Cola was just one in a flood of other patent medicines foisted upon the public by hopeful marketers during the golden age of quackery.

THE PATENT MEDICINE SHOW

Clever promoters made fortunes in patent medicines.[*] Popular since the Declaration of Independence, these nostrums were the pioneers in the field of advertising. Patent medicine ads paid for the rapid growth of the American newspaper, whose columns, even before the Civil War, were half filled by their claims. The period after the war saw an exponential growth in the industry, due partly to wounded veterans who had acquired a self-dosing habit out of necessity.

There were other reasons as well for the spectacular postwar success of patent medicines. The railroad, steamship, telegraph, and other communica-

---

[*] The term "patent medicine" was a misnomer, as many writers of the era pointed out. The more accurate term was "proprietary medicine," since a hopeful inventor would patent the label or trademark of his nostrum, but never its "secret formula." To reveal the ingredients would have ruined the mystique, opened the field for imitators, allowed the public to discover how cheaply the product was produced, and, perhaps most important, it would have revealed the amount of alcohol, narcotic, and/or poisons present.

tion revolutions made a national and even international market increasingly viable. Waves of immigrants brought new consumers to the country. The American population grew from 50 million in 1880 to 91 million in 1910—and 18 million of those were immigrants. The newcomers did not have much money, but they would often venture a dollar for a "cure."

Another reason for the boom in self-dosage was that the medical profession had not caught up with the industrial revolution. Many doctors killed as many patients as they cured, so cheap nostrums sometimes provided a safer alternative. Furthermore, there were few doctors in rural areas, forcing the country folk to use patent medicines. Finally, patent medicines were often taken to relieve the symptoms of overeating and poor diet, which went hand-in-hand in that period. Remedies for upset stomachs were the most common class of medicament during the late nineteenth century, which is not surprising, given the starchy diets and heavy meat consumption. Part of Coca-Cola's appeal to Asa Candler, for instance, was that it was supposed to relieve indigestion.

A TORRENT OF ADS

By the 1880s and 1890s, the amount spent on advertising such tonics and concoctions had reached stunning proportions, even in today's dollars. St. Jacob's Oil spent $500,000 in advertising in 1881. By 1885, some half-dozen nostrum-makers were spending over $100,000 annually on ads. Ten years later, *Scientific American* announced that some drug advertisers were spending a million dollars a year, adding that the creator of Carter's Little Liver Pills "cannot spend the money he is making" and that "judicious advertising has made it possible for . . . W. T. Hanson Company [to spend] $500,000 on Pink Pills for Pale People." One promoter noted that "without advertising, I might have made a living, but it was advertising that made me rich, and advertising a very simple commodity at that."

It is significant that the first national trade magazine for advertisers, *Printer's Ink*, was launched in 1888, just two years after the invention of Coca-Cola. In its fifty-year retrospective issue, the magazine credited the patent medicine industry with first recognizing the importance of trademarks and ubiquitous advertising, adding that "it was not until the twentieth century had fairly begun that manufacturers as a whole were inclined to listen to the broad proposition that advertising as such was a potentially profitable sales tool." One of the reasons that patent medicines could afford such extravagant advertising, of course, was their remarkable profitability. For a dollar, a manufacturer often sold a bottle which cost less than a dime to produce. It was easy for him to see the wisdom of spending another 10 cents a gallon on advertising. He had no major capital investment, little overhead, and few employees.

Besides, he knew that without extensive ads, few would buy his medicines, which were not essential products. He *had* to be a salesman. No wonder the nostrum-peddler dominated advertising expenditures during the Gilded Age.

Patent medicine makers were the first American businessmen to recognize the power of the catchphrase, the identifiable logo and trademark, the celebrity endorsement, the appeal to social status, the need to keep "everlastingly at it." Out of necessity, they were the first to sell image rather than product. At the same time, the stodgy producers of dry goods or sewing machines, with substantial capital investment and less margin, didn't see the need to advertise. It was beneath their dignity, a waste of good money. People needed what they had to sell, and if they advertised at all, it was simply to list their prices. Besides, the outrageous nostrum ads were giving advertising a bad odor, as *Printer's Ink* pointed out: "Most patent medicine advertising was shamefully and flagrantly disreputable in its fake selling claims. Absolute remedial powers for cancer, consumption, yellow fever, rheumatism and other afflictions were widely claimed for preparations that had no efficacy for even the mildest ailment."

The torrent of ads was not confined to newspapers, however. The cure-all makers flooded the marketplace with all kinds of novelties in order to keep their trademarks highly visible. They specialized in items which promised repeated use, such as clocks, calendars, matchbooks, blotters, pocket knives, almanacs, cookbooks, mirrors, or cards. Every time a consumer wanted to know the time or date, light a cigar, or look up a recipe, he or she was confronted with a reminder that Pale Pink Pills were good for the blood, or that Coca-Cola relieved fatigue and cured headaches.

Meanwhile, outdoor advertisers strove to outdo one another. Men with sandwich signs walked stiffly by on busy sidewalks. Banners were strung across Main Street. At night, the bill poster plastered every available surface with advertisements, layering over a competitor's work of the night before.

Sign painters were dispatched to paint huge trademarks where travelers were most likely to let their eyes wander. We tend to think of the Victorian era as a gracious period in which nature was unspoiled, but it wasn't unusual for a patent medicine advertiser of the era to clear-cut an entire mountainside so that he could erect a mammoth sign for Helmholdt's Buchu, visible from a train window.

In May of 1886, the very month that Coca-Cola was invented, one writer vividly described the desecration of the landscape, saying that a traveler might admire "the undulating country, breathing Spring from every meadow and grove and orchard"—that is, "if he could see a single furlong of it, without the suggestion of disease." It was not enough, he continued, that fences and sheds were defaced. "Enormous signs are erected in the fields, not a rock is left without disfigurement, and gigantic words glare at as great [a] distance as the eye is able to read them." Viewing "sign overlapping and towering above sign," the revolted traveler "turns away, shuddering, from the sight." Consequently, the critic concluded: "We cannot complain if the intelligent stranger from foreign lands should, instead of 'the scenery,' write 'the obscenery of America.'" One enterprising nostrum maker even offered to help pay for the Statue of Liberty, which was completed in 1886, in return for using the base as a gigantic advertisement.

William James, psychologist and philosopher, reacted violently to news-paper ads when he returned to the U.S. after several years abroad: "The first sight of the Boston *Herald* . . . made me jerk back my head and catch my breath, as if a bucket of slops had suddenly been thrown into my face." In 1894, he wrote a scathing letter to the editor of *The Nation* in which he spluttered in outrage at "this truly hideous feature of our latter-day life," complaining that "this evil is increasing with formidable rapidity . . . Now [these advertisements] literally form the principal feature of our provincial newspapers, and in many of the 'great dailies' of our cities play a part second only to the collective display of suicides, murders, seductions, fights, and rapes."

James tellingly added that "if a justification of these advertisements be sought, absolutely nothing can be alleged save the claim that every individual has a right to get rich along the lines of his own inventiveness." Most Americans were willing to put up with fraud and hype in the name of individual rights and democracy, particularly if there was money to be made. Even a scoundrel was admirable, if he was rich enough.

THE RIGHTEOUS PURSUIT OF WEALTH

The patent medicine tycoons, along with industrial titans like Andrew Carnegie and Cornelius Vanderbilt, stood at the apex of a new social order. By 1890, there were over 4,000 American millionaires, and the number was growing rapidly. Their greatest problem, with no income or corporate tax, became not how to make money, but how to spend it. The millionaire was the envied hero of the age, and the great new American religion had a fat dollar sign in front of it. Carnegie himself was busy spreading what he called the "Gospel of Wealth." Russell Conwell, a Philadelphia clergyman and the first president of Temple University, made a tidy living by delivering his "Acres of Diamonds" speech over 3,000 times, explaining that God loves those who produce wealth. "I say that you ought to get rich," Conwell told his audiences. "To make money honestly is to preach the gospel."

At the same time, the plight of the poor was becoming increasingly desperate. While the rich industrialists raked in the money, eight-year-olds labored in their factories for 10 cents a day. When confronted with the appalling gap between the haves and have-nots, men like Carnegie answered with a modified Social Darwinism, piously invoking the "survival of the fittest." Such were the unfortunate but inevitable results of progress. "The contrast between the palace of the millionaire and the cottage of the laborer with us today measures the change which has come with civilization," wrote Carnegie. This situation, he asserted, was "not to be deplored, but welcomed as highly beneficial. It is . . . essential for the progress of the race." Fortunately, Carnegie said, he regarded it as his Christian duty to help lift up the lower classes through wise philanthropy.

This attitude was not limited to Yankees. Mark Twain noted a new breed of Southerner—"brisk men, energetic of movement and speech; the dollar their god, how to get it their religion." Henry Grady, editor of the *Atlanta Constitution* and spokesman of this New South, informed the New England Club in 1886 that "we have wiped out the place where Mason and Dixon's line used to be," and that the "Georgia Yankee" was the equal of the Northerner. One Georgian of the period matched Conwell in exhorting his fellow Southerners to make money their priority: "Let the young south arise in their might and compete with [Yankees] in everything . . . Get rich! if you have to be mean! The world respects a rich scoundrel more than it does an honest poor man. Poverty may do to go to heaven with. But in these modern times . . . Get rich!"

Asa Candler, the man who would take Pemberton's Coca-Cola and parlay it into a fortune, was not so blatant, but in his speeches he clearly equated religion, capitalism, and patriotism. Candler's drink, Coca-Cola, came to symbolize that trio. In large measure, Coca-Cola's success stemmed directly from advertising which made it an emblem of the good things in America, a kind of secular communion drink. Like his brother Warren, a Methodist bishop, Asa Candler would send out his own brand of capitalistic missionaries.

The American penchant for associating God, country, and capitalism had been identified even before the Civil War by the observant Frenchman Alexis de Tocqueville, who noticed the phenomenon during his American travels in the 1840s: "Religious zeal is perpetually warmed in the United States by the fires of patriotism," he wrote. "If you converse with these missionaries of Christian civilization, you will be surprised to hear them speak so often of the goods of this world, and to meet a politician where you expected to find a priest."

By the 1880s, however, most who attempted to make a quick buck through patent medicines were disappointed. Fortunes had indeed been made, and "the spectacle of some of the medicine kings churning about the high seas in their palatial steam yachts" (as one contemporary writer put it) caused an inordinate number of would-be entrepreneurs to test the waters of the trade. In doing so, they usually lost whatever small savings they had.

On April 25, 1886, a *New York Tribune* reporter published a long article describing the saturated market for patent medicines. The "prevailing opinion," he said, was that the nostrum racket was "lucrative above all others," and that all who ventured into the field automatically became millionaires with yachts and race horses. On the contrary, he pointed out that only 2 percent of the latest patent medicines were even remotely successful. Thus, when Coca-Cola was first marketed a month after this article appeared, it clearly faced long odds.

THE SODA FOUNTAIN DURING THE GILDED AGE

Coca-Cola became the first widely available product that was at once both a patent medicine and a popular soda fountain beverage. In retrospect, it seemed a natural combination. After all, once Joseph Priestly learned to make what he called "fixed air" in 1767, artificially carbonated water was sold as a tonic and medicine, a cheaper form of naturally carbonated mineral water, which had been regarded as healthful since Roman times. An enterprising French immigrant, Eugene Roussel, first added flavors to his soda water at his Philadelphia perfume shop in 1839, and soon other soda fountains were serving orange, cherry, lemon, ginger, peach, and assorted other flavors. Because of the early medicinal legacy, the fountains formed a traditional part of drugstores, which in turn became social centers.

Soda fountains grew increasingly ornate throughout the 1870s and 1880s. They were "temples resplendent in crystal marble and silver," according to Mary Gay Humphreys, an 1891 commentator, and bore names such as Frost King, the Snow-drop, the Icicle, the Avalanche, or the Aurora Borealis to indicate the frosty nature of their beverages; the decor of others tried for a foreign flavor and were called the Persia, Ionic, Doric, Chalet, Arabia, Rialto, or France, while others, such as the Washington and Saratoga, were more patriotic. These monstrous affairs sometimes cost as much as $40,000 and offered over 300 beverage combinations. "To supply these," wrote Humphreys, "the entire side of the wall is dedicated and made glorious with California onyx, rare marbles, and plate-glass." Sophisticated, jaded consumers demanded an ever-greater variety of beverages. Most of these new flavors were recognizable combinations of old fruit drinks. Coca-Cola, however, was one of several unique blends offering something entirely new. All survived their early years as health boosters and nerve tonics to become recognizable national soft drinks. Unlike the regular run of fountain offerings or soda pop, these concoctions appeared modern and mysterious. Their ingredients were usually secret or came from some exotic country.

Coca-Cola was by no means the first of these drinks. Charles Hires, a Philadelphia Quaker, marketed Hires Root Beer in 1876 as a solid concentrate of sixteen wild roots and berries.[*] It claimed to "purify the blood and make rosy cheeks." Consumers mixed the 25-cent packets into five-gallon batches, making it the first drink to tap the home market. It was finally bottled in 1895.

Moxie Nerve Food was invented and bottled by Dr Augustin Thompson of Lowell, Massachusetts, in 1885. Thompson, who had a flair for promotion and strategic untruths, claimed that the drink was made from a rare, unnamed South American plant (said to resemble asparagus, sugarcane, or milkweed and to taste like a turnip) whose therapeutic powers had been discovered by a Lieutenant Moxie, Thompson's mythical friend. Moxie allegedly cured paralysis, softening of the brain, nervousness, and insomnia.

Charles Alderton created Dr Pepper as a Texas cherry soda fountain drink in 1885, but he soon bottled it as well. Early ads featured a naked, robust young woman cavorting in the ocean, her crotch teasingly covered by a wave, and asserted that Dr Pepper "aids digestion and restores vim, vigor, and vitality."

---

[*] At first, Hires called his drink Hires Herb Tea, in keeping with his pacifistic religion. Russell Conwell, the capitalistic evangelist who gave the "Acres of Diamonds" speech, advised him to change the name to "root beer" in order to appeal to hard-drinking Philadelphia miners.

With so many new drinks available, the soda jerks had to become virtuosos at mixing drinks with grace and speed. One of Coca-Cola's early selling points was that it could be so quickly prepared. As a contemporary article pointed out, "time is everything to the soda water man on a hot day. With new customers crowding and jostling each other to reach the counter, it is money in his pocket to get rid of consumers as quickly as possible." The busy late nineteenth-century soda fountain first satisfied the American demand for fast food and drink.

Nowhere were soda fountains more popular than in the South, particularly in the booming, busy, hot town of Atlanta. Though still opened only seasonally, generally from March to November, they garnered a huge business. The adventurous could order a drink called "don't care," a mixture of virtually every flavor, usually with a healthy splash of hard liquor to bind it together.[*] In the following 1886 Atlanta ad (one of the first to mention Coca-Cola), the proprietor specified that *his* "don't care" was nonalcoholic. The incredible range of choices ran from innocent fruit drinks to more stimulating "nerve tonics":

At the sodawater palace can be found the most cooling, delicious beverages—the ladies' favorite—ice-cream sodawater, any flavor that is desired.
  Syrups: Wine flavor—Claret, Catawba, grape, sherry, nectar, blackberry, ginger wine, oget, don't care, prohibition drink—great, everybody must try it to find out what it is—no whiskey . . . French wine of coca from Sinytis, coco-cola, French calisaya wine or nerve food, quiet the nervous system, ginger ale . . . lemons, chocolate, vanilla, cream, pine apple, raspberry, sarsaparilla, wild cherry, ginger, orange, blood orange, banana, coffee, ice tea, black gum, Beermann's egg phosphate, the most nutritious drink known, Maxey [i.e., Moxie] nerve food, milk shakes . . .

The soda fountain was a uniquely American phenomenon. In years to come, Coca-Cola would be advertised as the great national drink, a wholesome, enjoyable product which all classes of Americans could share. The seeds for that image were already germinating, as Mary Gay Humphreys (with no thought for Coca-Cola) pointed out in 1891: "Soda-water is an American drink. It is as essentially American as porter, Rhine wine, and claret are distinctively English, German, and French . . . The crowning merit of soda-water, and that which fits it to be the national drink, is its democracy. The millionaire may drink champagne while the poor man drinks beer, but they both drink soda-water."

The fountain owner, Humphreys explained, made a tidy democratic profit from rich man and pauper alike, selling a drink for a nickel that cost a cent and a half to produce. (Actually, she was overly generous to the fountain owner, since ingredients usually cost less than half a cent per glass.) Everyone was happy, since "for him who drinks it is small cost to see the 'bubbles winking on

---

[*] The "don't care" is the ancestor of the "suicide," popular at 1950s soda fountains. Using Coca-Cola as a base, a suicide called for the addition of every other flavor available.

the brim,' to feel the aromatic flavors among the roots of his hair and exploring the crannies of his brain, and to realize each fragrant drop as it goes dancing down his throat."

The competition among new soda fountain drinks equaled the cutthroat patent medicine field. One writer of the era estimated that less than one percent of all new drinks ever won a following. "The summer trade in soft drinks is . . . already so loaded down with different sirups and drinks that dealers will not take hold of a new thing unless it can be demonstrated to possess unusual virtues, or the inventor of it is willing to put a lot of money into advertising it."

John Pemberton's Coca-Cola had little chance. In 1886, the inventor did not have much money to put into advertising, but he struggled to demonstrate his drink's "unusual virtues." Pemberton, a perennial optimist despite the many disappointments in his life, clearly believed in his own product. Certainly, much of the credit for Coca-Cola's survival has to go to Asa Candler, who eventually acquired the product (in an exceedingly questionable manner) and pushed it aggressively. But an equal measure of credit must go to Pemberton and the time and place in which he found himself.

What Sigmund Freud, Pope Leo, and John Pemberton Had in Common

> *The use of the coca plant not only preserves the health of all who use it,*
> *but prolongs life to a very great old age and enables the coca eaters to*
> *perform prodigies of mental and physical labor.*
> —Dr. John Pemberton, 1885

JOHN PEMBERTON was obsessed: he wanted to invent the ultimate medicine and the perfect drink all rolled into one. With it, he would make enough money to fund his dream laboratory, with plenty to spare for his family. He could even donate to worthy charitable organizations. After all, other inventors with far less education or dedication had made fortunes from their patent medicines, most of which cured nothing except imaginary illnesses. But the Georgia pharmacist knew that he was running out of time. By 1879, he was forty-eight years old. The average life expectancy for men was only forty-two, and Pemberton had suffered from bouts of debilitating rheumatism and a mysterious stomach ailment even before he was wounded in the War Between the States. At least he was sure now that he was on the right track, having just read about a wonderful new medicine—a plant with magical properties that grew high in the Peruvian mountains.

AN ECLECTIC EDUCATION

Pemberton's entire life had led to his pursuit of the perfect medicine. Born in 1831 in the tiny town of Knoxville, Georgia, he had attended the nearby Southern Botanico Medical College of Georgia when he was just seventeen, where he discovered the wisdom of Samuel Thomson, an unlettered New Hampshire herbal practitioner whose teachings formed the basis for the college curriculum. In 1822, Thomson had published his *New Guide to Health; or Botanic Family Physician, Containing a Complete System of Practice, On a Plan Entirely New.*

Thomson's "complete system" consisted primarily of repeated steam baths and massive doses of lobelia (aptly nicknamed "screw auger" and "hell-scraper"), an herb which caused violent vomiting. While this sounds horrific, it was actually an improvement over the "heroic" measures (as they were then known) of the period. Doctors generally prescribed a combination of three therapies: bleeding to the point of unconsciousness with a lancet, intentionally raising and then popping huge blisters, or dosing with calomel, whose principal ingredient was mercury. Thomson called these doctors murderers who attacked patients with "their instruments of death—mercury, opium, ratsbane, nitre, and the lancet." Almost single-handedly, Thomson fomented a revolt of the masses against traditional medicine that one medical expert called "a second American revolution."

Even before Thomson died in 1843, however, splinter groups had formed. The egotistical rebel abhorred all formal education, preferring to keep himself as the sole font of wisdom. Nonetheless, various botanico colleges sprang up despite his resistance. Thomsonianism was particularly popular in the South. When the Georgia school was opened in Forsyth, Georgia, in December of 1839, the college president declared that "the eyes of the world are upon us" because they were ushering in "an era in the progress of civilization and a triumph for suffering humanity."

By the time Pemberton attended college, most Thomsonian schools had modified their reliance on lobelia and become more "eclectic," emphasizing other herbal remedies and some traditional medical study. At the age of nineteen, Pemberton graduated in 1850, and after a brief stint as a traditional Thomsonian "steam doctor," he went to Philadelphia for another year of schooling as a pharmacist before beginning his real career as a druggist in Oglethorp, Georgia. There, he met Anna Eliza Clifford Lewis, called "Cliff," whose father was a prominent local plantation owner and dry-goods merchant. They were married in 1853, and the following year, Cliff gave birth to her first and only child, Charles Ney Pemberton. Charley was a beautiful, precocious child, but neither of his parents could bring themselves to discipline him, and he was spoiled. For a minimal sum, Cliff's father "sold" two slaves to the young couple to help care for the infant.

In 1855, Pemberton moved to the larger town of Columbus, where he built a thriving practice for the next fourteen years with a number of different partners. While primarily a druggist, he also practiced some medicine, including eye surgery. His main income, however, came from the sale of various proprietary products with names like Dr. Sanford's Great Invigorator or Eureka Oil, and the occasional medicinal wine, such as Southern Cordial.

By the spring of 1861, Pemberton wrote Cliff's mother that business was booming, and six-year-old Charley was "learning fast, you would be surprised to hear him spelling and I teach him his Sabbath School book every week." In urging his mother-in-law to visit, Pemberton described their "delightful home" and the twenty acres of corn, potato, sugarcane, and watermelons they had just planted. He also revealed his love of nature, referring to "the sweetest of all times below, a Sabbath Eve in the Springtime," adding that "the trees and flowers are blooming in our yard and the air is fragrant with the sweet perfume from them."

Less than a month after he described that peaceful scene, Fort Sumter was attacked, and the Civil War began. Pemberton enlisted as a first lieutenant in May of 1862 and eventually organized a home guard of the overaged and exempt into Pemberton's Cavalry. When the Yankees attacked on April 16, 1865, a week after Lee's surrender at Appomattox, Pemberton was shot and cut with a saber while defending the bridge into town, in one of the final skirmishes of the war. This brush with death left him with an impressive scar across his abdomen and chest; his life was apparently saved by the money belt he wore.

SWEET SOUTHERN BOUQUET AND CARBUNCLE CURES

Pemberton must have recovered quickly. By November of 1865 he was industriously promoting his drug business again, having just returned from a buying spree in New York City, where he purchased "the largest and most complete stock of European and American drugs, medicines, and chemicals." Like many hustling Georgia businessmen, he resolved to put the war behind him and didn't mind seeking the help of Yankees. Later, when his nephew pestered him to tell him how he got his scar, Pemberton refused, telling him he wanted to forget all about the war.

For the next five years, Pemberton's partnership with Dr Austin Walker, a wealthy local physician, allowed him to thrive. He could never save money, however. What he didn't spend on his laboratory and research, he gave freely to family and friends. During the late 1860s, Pemberton began to experiment, creating his own proprietary items, including Globe Flower Cough Syrup, Extract of Stillingia, a "blood purifier," and Sweet Souther Bouquet, a perfume—all made from locally gathered herbs.* An 1867 visitor was so charmed by Pemberton's business, and by the inventor himself, that she wrote a long letter of praise to the local paper. "I confess I was astonished at the extent of the laboratory," she noted, "for I did not know there was such an establishment in the South." Pemberton, "every inch a gentleman," had presented her with an elegant wicker-covered bottle containing what she described as "the most delightful and delicate perfume that ever regaled my olfactories."

LIFE IN THE PHOENIX CITY

In 1869, Pemberton abandoned his well-established Columbus business and moved to Atlanta to make his fortune. Atlanta had begun as a collection of shanties, whorehouses, and saloons simply called Terminus, since it happened to be the site where the railroad stopped. While there was a prewar "Moral Party," the opposing "Free and Rowdy Party" had more attraction for the denizens of Snake Nation and Murrell's Row. Even so, there were enough

---

* Globe Flower Cough Syrup was a big seller over the next two decades, purportedly curing consumption, bronchitis, asthma, croup, bleeding of the lungs, pleurisy, and laryngitis. According to another ad, Extract of Stillingia cured "ulcers, pustules, carbuncles, scald head, salt rheum, and the 88 different varieties of skin affections."

banks and railroads in Atlanta before the war to give the city a "progressive" reputation.

In the wake of the Civil War, Atlanta, calling itself the Phoenix City, rose with a dynamic vengeance from the ashes to which William Tecumseh Sherman had reduced it. "The one sole idea in every man's mind is to make money," wrote one observer of the Atlanta scene just after the war. A visitor from the country wrote in 1866 that "Atlanta is a devil of a place," adding that "the men rush about like mad, and keep up such a bustle, worry, and chatter, that it runs me crazy. Everybody looks as if nearly worked to death." Atlanta was a whirling, self-important, frenzied vortex for Southern business after the Civil War. To this wild, wide-open city, John Pemberton brought his wife and child for a new life.

At first, he was a great success. With his partners, he established the largest drug trade in the city at the elegant Kimball House, a luxury hotel with six floors and over 300 rooms featuring elaborate furnishings and gold ornaments, complete with steam-powered elevators, fountains surrounded by tropical plants, and its own French chef. But by 1872, he had slipped into bankruptcy. He and his partners, an R. G. Dun credit man noted, were "honorable & industrious but lack good management." Pemberton never quite recovered from this bankruptcy, though he continued to experiment with new medicines and to attract moneyed partners through the years. He suffered through two major fires, in 1874 and 1878. After the second fire, in which $20,000 worth of stock was destroyed (covered for half that amount by insurance), the Dun man described Pemberton as "a broken down merchant"—surely an unfair description, but understandable under the circumstances. In 1879, he finally paid off the bankruptcy debts and was free to devote more time to creating and manufacturing new products.

In subsequent years, he invented Indian Queen Hair Dye, a rheumatic remedy called "Prescription 47–11," Triplex Liver Pills, Gingerine, Lemon & Orange Elixir, and probably a few other now-forgotten patent medicines and drinks. In his endeavors through the last years of his life, he met with "varying success," as the newspaper politely put it in 1886.

Despite his adversities, Pemberton remained the perfect Southern gentleman, receiving customers with old-fashioned courtesy. Perhaps because his son, Charley, was a difficult child, Pemberton always found time for his sister's children. "One of my earliest memories," recalled his niece, "is of the chewing gum Uncle John always had in his pocket, but was forbidden in my home as not lady-like . . . I enjoyed visits [there], where I received more attention than at home." Pemberton's nephew, Lewis Newman, portrayed the busy doctor as an obsessed, secretive inventor with "a laboratory in a back room to which but few were given admittance." Pemberton would forget mealtimes and work far into the night. Another visitor remembered Pemberton as having "more energy than anybody. His chemical laboratory was a very busy place; he was always getting up something."

In addition to his two degrees as a doctor and pharmacist, Pemberton was a lifelong scholar who not only kept up with the current drug journals, but read widely in the increasingly international pharmaceutical literature. For years, he labored over a master reference work on drugs. In a December 1886 interview, he showed his work-in-progress to a reporter, who described it as containing "about 12,000 chemical tests." Though the inventor died before publishing his book, its existence attests to the breadth of his knowledge, far beyond the accomplishments of the simple country root doctor of the Coca-Cola myth. It is not surprising, then, that in creating new patent medicines, he stopped limiting himself to locally grown plants such as stillingia and globe flowers and began to experiment with more exotic substances. One of these imports, initially hailed as a cure-all—but soon to be assailed as the source of an addictive drug—particularly fascinated Pemberton.

COCA COMES INTO ITS OWN

In the late 1870s, Pemberton first read about this miraculous new substance. Chewed by native Peruvians and Bolivians for over 2,000 years, coca leaves acted as a stimulant, an aid to digestion, an aphrodisiac, and a life-extender, giving the mountain-dwelling Andeans remarkable endurance during long treks with little food. The Incas had called it their "Divine Plant," and it was central to every aspect of their political, religious, and commercial life. The *cochero* was never without his *chuspa*, or coca pouch.

Around 1876, Pemberton read an article by Sir Robert Christison, seventy-eight-year-old president of the British Medical Association. Fortified by chewing coca, the elderly doctor reported that he climbed Ben Vorlich, a 3,224-foot mountain, skipped lunch, and "at the bottom I was neither weary, nor hungry, nor thirsty, and felt as if I could easily walk home four miles." Intrigued, Pemberton began reading everything available on the coca plant. And he was not the only one. By the early 1880s, doctors and pharmacists were reporting on the use of coca and its principal alkaloid, cocaine, as a possible cure for opium and morphine addiction. Cocaine had first been isolated in 1855 by the German Gaedeke, but it was Americans who pursued active experimentation.

In the cosmopolitan cross-fertilization typical of the time, a young Viennese doctor named Sigmund Freud read one of these articles in an 1880 Detroit drug journal, and, like Pemberton, was excited by the possibilities. In 1884, Freud first tried cocaine himself. It seemed the perfect antidote to his periodic depressions and lethargy; he also clearly thought it increased his sexual potency, writing to Martha Bernays, his fiancée: "Woe to you, my Princess, when I come. I will kiss you quite red . . . and if you are forward you shall see who is the stronger, a gentle little girl . . . or a big wild man who has cocaine in his body."

Later that year, Freud published *Über Coca* (About Coca), "a song of praise to this magical substance," as he wrote to his fiancée. In that same year, 1884, an associate of Freud's, young Carl Koller, found that cocaine could be successfully used as an anesthetic in eye surgery. This discovery, still used, quickly made Koller famous and revolutionized surgery. It also caught the attention of John Pemberton, who had once performed painful eye surgery without benefit of painkiller.

By the mid-1880s, one drug journal accurately described a "veritable *coca-mania*" as a result of the "crusade against the enormously increased use of alcohol and morphine." It was impossible to open a drug journal without finding numerous articles about new uses for the leaf and its principal alkaloid. In response, manufacturers produced coca tablets, ointments, sprays, hypodermic injections, wines, liqueurs, soft drinks, powders, and even coca-leaf cigarettes and cheroots. Coca-Bola, a popular masticatory that came in plugs similar to chewing tobacco, was extensively advertised in 1885.

VIN MARIANI: THE DIVINE DRINK

The coca leaf found its most famed commercial use in a now-forgotten drink called Vin Mariani, invented by Angelo Mariani, an enterprising Corsican who in 1863 began selling the Bordeaux wine with a healthy infusion of coca leaf. Pemberton's French Wine Coca, first advertised in 1884, was a direct imitation. Since Pemberton then modified his Wine Coca to create Coca-Cola, Vin Mariani is, in effect, the "grandfather" of Coca-Cola.

Mariani's coca-laced wine became wildly successful not only throughout Europe, but in the United States, where his brother-in-law, Julius Jaros, opened a New York branch. A marketing genius, Mariani specialized in testimonials from an incredible array of notables, including Thomas Edison, Émile Zola, President William McKinley, Queen Victoria, Sarah Bernhardt, Lillian Russell, Buffalo Bill Cody, and three Popes. Leo XIII went so far as to give Mariani a gold medal bearing Leo's likeness "in recognition of benefits received from the use of Mariani's tonic." The Pope apparently bore out Mariani's claims that coca extended life, since he died at ninety-three in 1903. According to an 1887 biography of Pope Leo, he took "the simplest food, a little wine and water." Looking at the Pontiff's frail body, the author wondered "how the lamp of life is fed," particularly when his face was "of alabaster whiteness," his eyes "all-radiant with the fire of piety and fatherly kindness." In fact, the Pope's lamp of life was fed by Vin Mariana, and the "all-radiant" eyes may have taken their fire as much from coca as from piety.

Mariani also collected glowing words from "kings, princes, potentates, the clergy, statesmen, artists, and from a host of people eminent in a high degree" around the globe. Only half in jest, an admirer once told Mariani he had forgotten to solicit a testimonial from God. His two major production laboratories were in Neuilly-Sur-Seine in France and New York City, but Mariani had principal distribution centers in London, Strasbourg, Montreal, Brussels, Geneva, Alexandria (Egypt), and Saigon.

Just how much of a kick did Vin Mariani deliver? Fortunately, we can hazard a good guess, since a chemist studying various wine cocas reported in 1886 that Vin Mariani contained 0.12 grain cocaine per fluid ounce. The dosage on the wine's label called for a "claret-glass full" before or after every meal (½ glass for children). Assuming the wineglass to hold six fluid ounces, three daily glasses would amount to a full bottle of 18 ounces, or 2.16 grains of cocaine per day—enough to make someone feel very good indeed.

Mariani's most important market outside Europe was the United States, and he took advantage of any opportunity for publicity there. During President Ulysses Grant's final illness in 1885, his physicians administered Vin Mariani, which soothed the pain of his throat cancer and was credited with extending his life so that he could finish his *Memoirs*. In the midst of Grant's travail, Angelo Mariani traveled to New York City "at the request of a number of prominent physicians who desired to get from him personally a better understanding of . . . this wonderful medicine." Mariani subsequently advertised the general's use of his product before the body was cold in Grant's Tomb.

The overwhelming popularity of Vin Mariani naturally spawned imitators, particularly in the intensely competitive American patent medicine market. The drug journals of the 1880s were full of recipes for wine of coca. Most were poor copies containing straight cocaine mixed with cheap wine, resulting in a bitter taste but greater effect. By 1885, Vin Mariani ads warned against over twenty *ersatz* wines, and Mariani himself groused about "the many worthless, so-called Coca preparations [which are] nothing more than variable solutions of Cocaine in inferior grades of wines or other liquids, shamefully prepared by unscrupulous or ignorant persons [serving to] bring into discredit a really useful drug." In 1887, one cynical writer, describing Vin Mariani and its illegitimate spawn, referred to "the famous, expert-indorsed, world-renowned coca wine, made now by everybody and his relatives, from the skilled chemist to the mackerel and sugar handlers."

PEMBERTON'S FRENCH WINE COCA: A SUPERIOR IMITATION?

Pemberton's French Wine Coca appeared as one of the legion of imitators, though his product was probably far superior to most on the market. In a March 1885 interview, it was obvious that Pemberton had read the Mariani testimonials for the "intellectual beverage." Like Mariani, he espoused his wine's beneficial effects on the educated, professional upper crust of society. The new disease, neurasthenia, had arrived as a status symbol which afflicted only the most refined, mentally active people. Pemberton not only acknowledged his debt to Mariani, but claimed somehow to have seen his formula.

"Scientists, scholars, poets, divines, lawyers, physicians, and others devoted to extreme mental exertion, are the most liberal patrons of this great invigorator of the brain," Pemberton told the spellbound reporter, explaining that "Mariani & Co., of Paris, prepare an exceedingly popular Wine of Coca . . . I have observed very closely the most approved French formula, only deviating therefrom when assured by my own long experimentation and direct information from intelligent South American correspondents that I could improve upon [it]." Modestly, he concluded that "I believe that I am now producing a better preparation than that of Mariani."

Pemberton advertised that his wine contained "the medical virtues of the Erythroxylon Coca plant of Peru, South America—the African Cola Nuts —true Damiana, with pure Grape Wine." These two additional ingredients must have constituted the improvements he felt he had made on Mariani's drink. The kola nut quickly followed the coca leaf as a new medicinal rage. Grown in West Africa, primarily in Ghana, kola nuts were used by the natives in a manner similar to coca. Chewed for extra energy, identified with local dieties, and taken as an aphrodisiac, the nuts had been a major part of the fabric of African life for centuries. Like coca leaves, kola nuts had a potent alkaloid—caffeine—in greater proportions than either tea or coffee.

By the mid-1880s, long articles on kola nuts were running in all the drug journals, praising the nuts as a hangover cure and stimulant. Many articles explicitly compared kola to coca. "Like Coca, Kola enables its partakers to undergo long fast and fatigue," read one 1884 article. "Two drugs, so closely related in their physiological properties, cannot fail to command early universal attention." In its 1883–1884 catalog, Frederick Stearns & Company featured Coca and Cola Nut on the same page in parallel columns, with a common headline running across the top: "For the Brain and Nervous System."

The second ingredient was damiana, defined by a vintage Webster's as "the dried leaf of *Turnera diffusa* of tropical America, California, and Texas, used as a tonic and aphrodisiac." An 1885 advertisement for "The Mormon Elder's Damiana Wafers" leaves little doubt that it was indeed regarded as a sexual stimulant: "The Most Powerful INVIGORANT Ever Produced. Permanently Restores those Weakened by Early Indiscretions . . . A positive cure for Impotency and Nervous Debility." Thus, all three ingredients of Pemberton's tonic were considered aphrodisiacs.

Pemberton's ads for his coca wine featured an Americanized, supercharged version of Mariani's claims. He minimized the artistic, gentle aspects while emphasizing his drink as an aggressive cure for nervous disorders, disturbances of internal plumbing, and impotency. He also appropriated Mariani's testimonials for his own, asserting that "French Wine Coca is indorsed by over 20,000 of the most learned and scientific medical men in the world." Enthusiastic and wordy, if not completely grammatical, here is an ad Pemberton ran in 1885:

> Americans are the most nervous people in the world . . . All who are suffering from any nervous complaints we commend to use that wonderful and delightful remedy, French Wine Coca, infallible in curing all who are afflicted with any nerve trouble, dyspepsia, mental and physical exhaustion, all chronic and wasting diseases, gastric irritability, constipation, sick headache, neuralgia, etc. is quickly cured by the Coca Wine. It has proven the greatest blessing to the human family, Nature's (God's) best gift in medicine. To clergymen, lawyers, literary men, merchants, bankers, ladies, and all whose sedentary employment causes nervous prostration, irregularities of the stomach, bowels and kidneys, who require a nerve tonic and a pure, delightful diffusable stimulant, will find Wine Coca invaluable, a sure restorer to health and happiness. Coca is a most wonderful invigorator of the sexual organs and will cure seminal weakness,

impotency, etc., when all other remedies fail. To the unfortunate who are addicted to the morphine or opium habit, or the excessive use of alcoholic stimulants, the French Wine Coca has proven a great blessing, and thousands proclaim it the most remarkable invigorator that ever sustained a wasting and sinking system.

THE MORPHINE ADDICT

Pemberton had a personal reason for his interest in coca as a cure for morphine addiction: he was probably using French Wine Coca in an attempt to break his own habit. Three people associated with him in the final year of his life stated categorically that Pemberton was an addict. J. C. Mayfield recalled under oath that "Dr Pemberton was in bad health. We did not know at the time what was the matter with him, but it developed that he was a drug fiend." Mayfield's ex-wife wrote that Pemberton was "for years addicted to the morphine habit." Finally, another partner, A. O. Murphy, said that when he discovered the doctor's addiction, he found it "distasteful."

"Morphinism," as it was then called, was increasingly prevalent, particularly among physicians and pharmacists. The importation of opium to the U.S. had increased dramatically, from almost 146,000 pounds in 1867 to over 500,000 pounds in 1880. Advertisements purporting to offer cures for the habit appeared frequently in Atlanta papers. Addiction was so common among veterans of the Civil War that it was called "Army disease." Pemberton may have first resorted to morphine to ease the pain of his own war wounds, continuing its use throughout his periodic illnesses.[*]

It may seem odd that Pemberton was able to hide his habit so well, but many addicts did. "Few of those addicted to the drug for years are suspicioned even by their most intimate friends," wrote one physician in 1890. Opium, he said, allowed the habitué to "engage in his daily business pursuits with renewed energy for the time being. The opium eater's mind seems clear, his thoughts are well directed, his general appearance is above suspicion."

At least temporarily, Pemberton must have felt that he was beating his addiction, because he told a reporter in 1885 that "I am convinced from actual experiments that [coca] is the very best substitute for opium, with a person addicted to the opium habit, that has ever been discovered. It supplies the place of that drug, and the patient who will use it as a means of cure, may deliver himself from the pernicious habit without inconvenience or pain."

EARLY WARNING SIGNALS

While patent medicine suppliers and physicians were generally euphoric about coca and cocaine, some doctors and publications were already sounding the

---

[*] As an inventor and pharmacist, Pemberton had ready access to drugs. His formula book included recipes using not only cocaine and morphine, but cannabis.

alarm that cocaine might indeed free addicts from morphine—only to enslave them on the new drug. Freud's friend Fleischl, for instance, to whom he introduced cocaine as an antidote to his morphine, died horribly in 1891 after years as a cocaine addict.* A German doctor published a scathing and widely translated attack on cocaine in 1886, calling it "the third scourge of mankind," and American colleagues soon took up his cause.

As early as June 1885, Pemberton was defending himself against a short piece published in the *Atlanta Constitution*, which warned: "The new drug cocaine will do almost anything . . . on the other hand, the injudicious use of cocaine will make a man more brutal and depraved than either liquor or morphine. Herein lies a new danger. Before long a remedy will be demanded for the cocaine habit." Pemberton refused to believe it. Most likely fortified with Wine Coca, in a rambling interview a few days later he dismissed the charges as predictable prejudice against anything new.

Pemberton granted that cocaine, if misused, could be dangerous, but the same could be said for any effective medicine. "I wish it were in my power to substitute the Coca and compel all who are addicted to the use of opium, morphine, alcohol, tobacco, or other narcotic stimulants to live on the coca plant or any of its true preparations," he said. "It is perfectly wonderful what coca does." Explaining that "we [Americans] are a great army of nervous invalids," he espoused coca as a universal panacea that promoted robust health, prodigious physical and mental activity, and long life.

Sales of French Wine Coca were extremely encouraging. Exactly a week after that peroration on the wonders of coca, Pemberton took out a large ad in the paper announcing that "888 BOTTLES OF PEMBERTON'S COCA WINE SOLD SATURDAY! IT SELLS AND PROVES A LIVING JOY To all who use it. Read what is said by others about this WONDERFUL TONIC AND INVIGORANT." The inevitable testimonials followed, one by a Bremen, Georgia, doctor who cured himself of "Insomnia, Melancholia, Hypochondriasis, and all the other foul fiends that haunted my mind and body." He had also treated twenty patients successfully with Wine Coca—"all of them bona fide ladies and gentlemen of high reputation." He asserted that the tonic acted quickly on the "great Ganglionic Centers."

PROHIBITION PROBLEMS

Pemberton's fortunes were finally on the upswing. Perhaps he would join that band of patent medicine millionaires plying their steam yachts. But just when sales of French Wine Coca were booming, the Reverend Sam Jones and his temperance movement nearly ruined him.

Jones was a popular, roughhewn, fast-talking Georgia evangelist, a reformed

---

* "Addiction" is difficult to define; cocaine apparently is not physically addictive, since habitual users do not exhibit the classic withdrawal symptoms, but there is no question that the drug is *psychologically* addictive.

drinker, the darling of the press because he was at the same time pious, earthy, witty, and imminently quotable. One critic dubbed him "the Cracker Evangelist." Jones made much of his rural, homespun origins, making forays from his Cartersville home to blast the sins of big-city Atlanta, while at the same time carefully flattering the city's fortunes and future. Actually, it was all an act, since the minister was quite well educated and capable of refined speech. For years, Jones had led the fight for Prohibition, slamming the "red-nosed whisky devils" and complaining that legislators were unable to pass anything—"not even a cheap bar room."

"How he did hammer the brethren!" one survivor of a Jones revival meeting recalled. "He raked us fore and aft. He gave us grape and canister and all the rest. He abused us and ridiculed us; he stormed at us and laughed at us; he called us flop-eared hounds, beer kegs, and whisky soaks. He plainly said that we were all hypocrites and liars . . . For six weeks [work was] neglected, and Jones! Jones! Jones! was the whole thing."

The accumulation of his wit and abuse had its effect. By a slim margin, on November 25, 1885, encouraged by the local option bill recently enacted by the state legislature, Atlanta and Fulton County voted to go dry. In order to give saloonkeepers a chance to close shop, the ban on liquor would begin seven months later, on July 1, 1886, for an experimental period of two years.

Pemberton could see the handwriting on the wall, and not only in Atlanta. The national temperance movement had been gaining momentum for several years. The saloon, found on almost every streetcorner in America's cities, offered an all-male bastion where the lower and middle class could repair for whiskey, beer, and a free lunch. The Women's Christian Temperance Union, founded in 1874, promoted the notion that virtually all crimes—murder, child abuse, political corruption, industrial accidents—resulted from demon rum or German beer. The emotional attacks of the WCTU polarized entire communities, so that by 1886, a Methodist minister in favor of temperance was murdered in Sioux City, Iowa, while driving his team through a pro-liquor crowd.

The days of a wine-based medicine appeared doomed, though it depended, of course, on what the law interpreted as alcohol. Pemberton frantically experimented with modifications of the Wine Coca formula. Convinced of the virtues of the coca leaf and kola nut, he removed the wine and started testing an assortment of essential oils, primarily distillations of fruit flavors. But they all tasted too bitter to him. Adding sugar masked the bitterness but made for a sickly sweet drink. To counteract that, Pemberton added citric acid. Throughout the winter of 1885, he continued to search for a satisfactory formula.

FRANK ROBINSON ARRIVES

In December, Frank Robinson and David Doe, two Yankees, appeared on Pemberton's doorstep trying to peddle a machine they called a "chromatic printing device," capable of producing two colors at one impression. Both were Maine natives but had lived for the past few years in Iowa, sprawling farm country that didn't offer much market for a slick publishing device. Touring the South, Robinson and Doe landed in Atlanta, where the booming patent medicine industry would presumably pounce on a novel advertising opportunity. Asking around for likely prospects, they were told to try old Doc Pemberton, who seemed always to be looking for new partners and ideas.

After Pemberton talked it over with his old partner, Ed Holland, the four men shook hands on a deal and agreed on a new corporate name, the Pemberton Chemical Company. Holland was the only one who had much capital to invest, but they went in as equal partners. Pemberton contributed his talents and laboratory, and Robinson and Doe put in their printing machine. The firm's letterhead soon bragged that "the great wonder of the world is printing two colors in a newspaper at one impression," but Atlanta publishers never responded favorably to the novelty.

THE COCA-COLA LABORATORY

Throughout the winter and early spring of 1886, Pemberton obsessively experimented with his new coca and kola "temperance" drink, sending it down to Venable's soda fountain at Jacobs' Pharmacy for repeated trial runs. Pemberton's nephew, Lewis Newman, visiting from college, was one of the errand boys:

> My last visit to Auntie's was when Uncle John was giving cococola a try out and he was even more glad to see me than usual. He was eager to show me through his "factory" and to tell me that he had begun selling "my temperance drink," as he called it . . . Uncle John sent me with an order for a drink and [told me] to wait in Jacobs Pharmacy to hear comments of those who came for Coca cola when it was first introduced. [It sold about] 3 to 5 gallons per day.

Both Newman and John Turner, who apprenticed with Pemberton around the same time, remembered being sent down to the drugstore to get a drink of Coca-Cola for Pemberton, since there was no carbonated water at the laboratory. This contradicts the Company dogma that Coca-Cola was accidentally mixed with soda water about a year later.

Lewis Newman described his uncle's 1886 laboratory, revealing how the myth of the root doctor stirring his kettle probably began:

> The remodeling and equipment of the Marietta Street house absorbed all the money Uncle John had or could get . . . The wonderful part of the equipment, to me at least, was the enormous filter made of matched flooring, wide at the top and narrowing to the base. It was built through the floor of a second story room and the ceiling of the room below. This big hamper-like receptacle was filled with "Chattahoochee River* washed sand," Uncle John explained . . . The prepared ingredients of coca cola were poured into the top

---

* The Chattahoochee River runs near Atlanta.

of this filter and treacled through the several wagon loads of washed sand into a metal trough.

My best recollection is that this process was for the purpose of "ripening" the mixture by [letting it] filter through without access of air. There were two large kettles such as sorghum and sugar cane juices were boiled in . . . Paddles of ash similar to those used in propelling canoes stirred the liquid while it was boiled . . . before [being] taken through the filtering and fermentation process.

This cumbersome method of making Coca-Cola was later abandoned, but Pemberton's laboratory certainly consisted of more than his kettles. Unfortunately, there is no way of knowing what this original Coca-Cola tasted like after it had been slowly "ripened" through the enormous sand filter.

A PAPER IS READ IN SAVANNAH

In April of 1886, Pemberton was scheduled to deliver a major speech to the annual convention of the Georgia Pharmaceutical Society, but he was too close to a satisfactory formula to tear himself away and travel all the way to Savannah. Instead, he sent the text of the speech to be read aloud. In the paper, he gave a detailed, scholarly account of caffeine and cocaine, including the history of both drugs' isolation and use. He noted that "caffeine, as obtained from tea and coffee in this country, is inferior to that manufactured from the kola nuts by Merck, of Darmstadt."

Pemberton's real passion, however, was obviously the coca leaf. "All of the medical journals are full of its praises and I am perplexed to know where to begin and how to end so interesting a subject," he wrote. "Never in the history of the medical world has a remedial agent, within so short a space of time, risen from comparative obscurity to such practical . . . importance. The article went up like a rocket amidst the universal plaudits of the medical profession all over the world." The veteran pharmacist then enumerated the many benefits of coca, including an account of Koller's experiments with eye surgery. Interestingly, he made the same point as Mariani—that the Peruvians did not value the coca leaf with the largest amount of cocaine, preferring a milder leaf with a better blend of alkaloids. Pemberton obviously had conducted extensive experiments with the coca leaf by this time: "I must say, after considerable experience, that of many samples sent me by reputable houses, only about one out of one dozen samples proved to be of any value, many of the samples containing no Coca whatever."

A HISTORIC NAMING CONTEST

At almost the exact moment this speech was being read in Savannah, Pemberton finally pronounced himself satisfied with his new product, but he was still calling it simply "my temperance drink." He needed a good name. All four of the partners brainstormed and submitted potential titles. It would be interesting (and amusing) to hear what they were, but all we know is that Frank Robinson came up with Coca-Cola. Everyone agreed it was the best name, not only because it described the two principal ingredients (damiana having fallen from the formula), but because it had an alliterative ring.

Triple (and sometimes quadruple) alliterations were in vogue, particularly in Atlanta, allowing a tongue-twisting tour of the alphabet: Botanic Blood Balm, Copeland's Cholera Cure, Goff's Giant Globules, Dr Jordan's Joyous Julep, Ko-Ko Tulu, Dr Pierce's Pleasant Purgative Pellets, Radway's Ready Relief, Swift's Sure Specific. Robinson later wrote that he created the name "Coca-Cola" not only to indicate the key ingredients, but "because it was euphonious, and on account of my familiarity with such names as 'S.S.S.' and 'B.B.B.'." Robinson and The Coca-Cola Company later had good reason to emphasize the poetic rather than descriptive character of the name. For over seventy years, the fact that the name clearly stemmed from its ingredients would inspire harried Coca-Cola lawyers to write tortured legal briefs arguing just the opposite. By 1959, the president of The Coca-Cola Company was referring to it as a "meaningless but fanciful and alliterative name."

EARLY SUCCESS

At first, the new drink sold moderately well, at least in Atlanta. Pemberton, who had worked so hard on the formula, now turned the manufacture over to Robinson and took a rest. Busy brewing the stuff, Robinson soon devoted all of his time to the one drink. He made it, promoted it as best he could on a limited budget, and sold it. Further, he recognized that Coca-Cola could be marketed as a dual-purpose product. It was a stimulating medicine to cure headaches and depression, but it was also a new soda fountain drink with a unique taste. In his first ad, which ran in the *Atlanta Journal* on May 29, 1886, he emphasized its qualities as a beverage: "Coca-Cola. Delicious! Refreshing! Exhilarating! Invigorating! The new and popular soda fountain drink containing the properties of the wonderful Coca plant and the famous Cola nut." While this first effort featured "Coca-Cola" in block letters, Robinson worked on the script logo over the winter, introducing the familiar Spencerian handwriting for the first time in a June 16, 1887, ad.

Compared with most promotions of this period, the first Coca-Cola ad was remarkably brief, pointing the way to modern advertising. It first used the adjectives, "delicious and refreshing," which would become virtually synonymous with Coca-Cola. Unlike Pemberton's tours de force of the past, Robinson avoided lengthy Victorian perorations, nor did he mention the doctor by name. Robinson apparently wanted the drink to be set apart, not just another of Pemberton's preparations. The inventor himself used Robinson's adjectives when he wrote the label for his new syrup, but otherwise the prose was vintage Pemberton:

COCA-COLA SYRUP AND EXTRACT For Soda Water and other Carbonated Beverages. This Intellectual Beverage and Temperance Drink contains the valuable Tonic and Nerve Stimulant properties of the Coca plant and Cola (or Kola) nuts, and makes not only a delicious, exhilarating, refreshing and invigorating Beverage (dispensed from the soda water fountain or in other carbonated beverages), but a valuable Brain Tonic and a cure for all nervous affections—Sick Head-Ache, Neuralgia, Hysteria, Melancholy, etc. The peculiar flavor of COCA-COLA delights every palate.

There was, of course, another good reason for the brevity of Robinson's original ad: it was cheaper. Because Pemberton and his partners had limited funds, their newspaper ads were sporadic. During the first year of the drink's existence, total advertising expense amounted to around $150. While that was not a great deal of money, it bought a sizable amount of exposure for Coca-Cola. Large banner-style oilcloth signs cost a dollar apiece, streetcar signs a little over a penny, and posters about a third of a cent. A thousand coupons for sample drinks could be printed for a dollar.

Robinson soon arranged for an oilcloth sign to be pinned to the awning of Jacobs' drugstore—the drink's first point-of-purchase advertising, with red lettering on a white background ordering patrons to "DRINK COCA-COLA 5¢." Within a year, there were oilcloth signs advertising Coca-Cola at fourteen Georgia soda fountains. Thousands of Coca-Cola posters were distributed, while every streetcar in Atlanta carried an ad for the drink.

Only two days after the drink's introduction, Pemberton had written an arch note to Jacobs' Pharmacy complaining that "a certain individual, best remaining unnamed," had refused to sample Coca-Cola. "Do not give him a *free* sample," Pemberton wrote, since "profits will not permit such extra-vagance." He did, however, promise a refund if the drink failed to satisfy. Soon, however, Robinson convinced the doctor that he had been wrong to think that profits wouldn't permit the "extravagance" of giving away a nickel glass of Coca-Cola. On the contrary, future profits *demanded* it. Robinson had tickets printed up, to be redeemed at local soda fountains, offering free drinks and, using the Atlanta city directory, mailed them to prospective customers as well as giving them to traveling salesmen to distribute. Once they tasted Coca-Cola, new patrons were sure to come back for more, Robinson reasoned. He promised the soda fountain owners that he would redeem their tickets.

Meanwhile, the dreaded onset of local Prohibition arrived on July 1, 1886. In an orgy of self-congratulation, Atlanta pioneered as the first major city in the United States to swear off liquor. "ATLANTA DRY" the front page of the *Constitution* announced, "The First of July Marks a New Era." It is unclear, however, just how dry the city actually was. In the same paper there appeared an ad for "Duffy's Pure Malt Whiskey for Medicinal Use, Absolutely Pure and Unadulterated. In Use in Hospitals, Curative Institutions, Infirmaries. Cures Consumption, Hemorrhages, and all Wasting Diseases." Prohibition appar-ently did not affect the Kimball House, whose liquor license didn't run out until October 9. The crowds there became so rowdy that the management no longer allowed drinking on the premises, forcing consumers to take their booze with them. A Kimball House ad in the October 5, 1886, *Constitution* warned buyers that they'd better stock up: "Will sell in quantities."

Not surprisingly, then, Pemberton was advertising French Wine Coca again soon afterwards, now claiming extraordinary longevity for those regular coca users: "Instances are recorded of persons who have lived over 120, 130, 140, and even over 150 years." Pemberton also began calling his Wine Coca "the Great 'EuBion' and Temperance Drink." If he could really get away with selling Wine Coca as a temperance beverage during Prohibition, sales should rise dramatically.

They did. Though Prohibition was resoundingly voted out on November 26, 1887, sales of French Wine Coca and Coca-Cola were booming long before that. On May 1, 1887, an article in the *Constitution* stated that "the daily sales are five gross for the wine coca. The sales within the last few weeks for the coca-cola syrup amounted to six hundred gallons. Both the coca-cola syrup and the wine coca are being sold throughout the United States, and everywhere are coming orders for the goods, and testimonials unsolicited pouring in on all sides." While the paper undoubtedly exaggerated the national market for the hometown products, these figures are still impressive. "The goods manufactured by this firm," the article bragged, "are not 'nostrums' by any means but are pharmaceutical preparations and are recognized as such by the elite of the medical profession everywhere."

At 720 bottles a day, French Wine Coca sales still far outstripped those of Coca-Cola. Nonetheless, considering that the soda fountain season had only just begun, Coca-Cola's 600-gallon sale was a considerable achievement. Since each gallon of Coca-Cola syrup ideally yielded 128 drinks (one ounce per drink), the 600 gallons translated to 76,800 drinks. Frank Robinson later downplayed the first year's sales, testifying under oath that "from May 1886 until May 1887 . . . he [Pemberton] sold twenty-five or thirty gallons, maybe, something like that." Either his memory was faulty or he was lying. At any rate, the twenty-five-gallon figure for that first year has become part of inaccurate Company lore.

The spring also brought changes in personnel. The shadowy Mr Doe withdrew from the partnership, taking the printing machine with him as his share. He was replaced by M. P. Alexander, a Memphis pharmacist described in the same article as "an energetic, thorough business man [who] will reflect credit upon any business with which he is connected." Since the stock of Pemberton Chemical Company had been increased by $10,000, it is reasonable to assume that Alexander brought cash as well as energy to the partnership, which is probably why he immediately assumed the presidency. At the same time, Woolfolk Walker, "a young man of fine business tact," joined the firm as a salesman. A Columbus native, Walker had served as a private in Pemberton's Cavalry during the Civil War. Probably as a result of war wounds, Walker had a pronounced limp; he was to play a key role in the early history of Coca-Cola.

Finally, though he was not mentioned in the article, Charley Pemberton appeared on the payroll for this period and learned to make Coca-Cola, freeing Robinson for more concentrated promotion. Dr Pemberton's only child was thirty-three years old and, according to all accounts, womanized and drank too much. The young Pemberton had been a gifted athlete, the champion catcher for a local baseball team back in 1872, but somehow he had gone sour (his friend Lewis Newman wrote of a failed romance). Now Charley's talents were directed at the pool room in the local saloon. Concerned about his son's future, Dr Pemberton hoped Charley would eventually take over his business.

Pemberton must have been optimistic and full of new schemes. As usual, he had spent the winter working on new formulas and was preparing to unveil his latest. He told the reporter that it was called Phospho Lemonade & Phospho Ironade (renaming it Lemon & Orange Elixir later); it would replace beer and wine, he asserted, comparing the new drink favorably to the finest imported champagne. The inventor appeared to be, as the paper had predicted in 1886, "on the high road to fortune." He had two best-selling drinks, with more on the way. "The success of this company has been something phenomenal," the *Constitution* reporter concluded on that May Day of 1887, and it must have seemed that nothing could go wrong.

On June 6, to assure his legal claim to the popular new drink, Pemberton applied for a Coca-Cola trademark patent. On June 28, it was granted. A week later, all hell broke loose.

~ 3 ~

The Tangled Chain of Title

*It is always a relief to believe what is pleasant, but it is more important
to believe what is true.*

—Hilaire Belloc

*All truth—and real living is the only truth—has in it elements of battle
and repudiation. Nothing is wholesale.*

—D. H. Lawrence

IN THE MIDDLE of July 1887, John Pemberton initiated a series of transactions that would lead to the most confused, convoluted genesis of a successful corporation that the world could ever have witnessed. In a little over a year, the formula for Coca-Cola would be subdivided and passed from hand to hand like the proverbial hot potato. The story resembles a Shakespearean play in which subplots weave among themselves before reaching a final resolution. None of the main characters emerged a real hero; each engaged in some form of subterfuge, deceit, or scheme.

On July 8, John Pemberton sold two-thirds of his Coca-Cola rights to Willis Venable and George Lowndes for the grand sum of one dollar, though for the time being he kept the sale a secret from his partners in Pemberton Chemical Company. Actually, Lowndes, who supplied the money, paid Pemberton $1,201, but $1,200 of it was considered a no-interest loan to be paid back out of future profits. The inventor, who retained a third interest, would also receive a third of the profits. In return, he sold Venable and Lowndes all of the necessary equipment and supplies at cost ($283.29), as well as providing a copy of Coca-Cola's formula.

Why did Pemberton sell? According to Lowndes, it was because he had fallen ill again and was worried about where money would come from—both for his family and his morphine, which he must have needed more than ever to kill pain. Pemberton and Lowndes had been close friends since sharing a boardinghouse in 1869; now the inventor wanted his old friend to buy his greatest creation. "Lowndes, I am sick," he began, "and I don't believe I will ever get out of this bed. The only thing I have is Coca-Cola." Urging Lowndes to buy it, Pemberton told him that "Coca-Cola some day will be a national drink. I want to keep a third interest in it so that my son will always have a living." Shortly before the sale, the ailing doctor confided to his nephew Lewis that if only he had the proper capital, he could make a fortune from Coca-Cola: "If I could get $25,000, I would spend $24,000 advertising and the remainder in making Coca-Cola. Then we would all be rich." With the profits, he envisioned endowing "a great hospital for impecunious sons and daughters of Confederate soldiers." Now, however, he thought that he was dying and would never see the fulfillment of his dream.

An additional motivation for the sale can be found in a small item in the *Atlanta Constitution* recounting local court news of July 9, 1887, the day after the contract was signed: "Mssrs. J. S. Pendleton, F. M. Robinson and C. A. Robinson [presumably Frank's brother] allege that the president of the [Pemberton Chemical Company], M. P. Alexander, has taken full possession of the books, papers, etc, and is so conducting business as to seriously prejudice their interests. They say that Alexander and other persons have formed a conspiracy to ruin the business." The judge granted a temporary restraining order and set the case for July 13.

Alexander drops entirely from any records beyond this point. The "energetic, thorough business man," as he was described just two months before, must have absconded with the books *before* Pemberton sold to Venable and Lowndes, since it would presumably require more than one day to obtain a lawyer and court date. Where did Alexander go, and who were the "other persons" with whom he had "formed a conspiracy"? There is no way of knowing. It is conceivable that Alexander got wind of Pemberton's filing for sole proprietorship of Coca-Cola in June and decided to take drastic measures to ensure that he got his money out of the partnership. If so, he apparently didn't tell poor Frank Robinson, who appeared in court that day without knowing that a second bombshell was about to drop.

FRANK ROBINSON'S SURPRISE

Two tense weeks passed. On July 21, Pemberton wrote out an inventory of materials he was selling to Venable and Lowndes and received a check for $150 with a promissory note for the balance of $133.29 to be paid in thirty days. Pemberton then calmly informed Robinson that he had obtained a patent for the Coca-Cola label as sole owner and had, in addition, sold most of the rights.

Robinson, who had named Coca-Cola, written out the Spencerian-script logo, manufactured it, and masterminded the advertising and promotion, was in shock. Because Coca-Cola was created while Pemberton was a partner in the Pemberton Chemical Company, Robinson had assumed that each partner owned a fourth interest in the formula. After all, the company letterhead specifically stated that the Pemberton Chemical Company was the "sole proprietor" of French Wine Coca, which Pemberton had invented *before* the partnership commenced. Now, however, the company was a mere shell, with Alexander (and his money) on the lam and Coca-Cola sold.

The next day, July 22, 1887, Robinson carefully reconstructed a financial statement for Coca-Cola, probably from memory, since Alexander had the books. With fitting irony, he wrote it out on Pemberton Chemical Company letterhead which proclaimed Alexander the president of the firm. The stationery listed all of Pemberton's proprietary medicines, including Coca-

Cola. Robinson's figures showed that 990 gallons of Coca-Cola syrup were sold for $1,500 from March 1 to July 14, 1887. He estimated the cost of materials at a dollar per gallon, leaving a $510 profit. Then, however, he listed salaries and expenses for the same period amounting to $1,459.78. The resulting balance sheet was decidedly in the red. Still, he was sure that in time the drink would pay handsomely.

He persuaded partner Ed Holland to accompany him to consult John Candler, who had recently represented the partners against Alexander, "to see if he didn't think [we] could have [our] rights maintained." Candler, an ambitious twenty-six-year-old prosecuting attorney, agreed to look into the matter, and paid a visit to Pemberton, still bedridden in what the lawyer described as "a small cheap house." Pemberton denied any wrongdoing. "They are mistaken," he said. "They have got no interest in [Coca-Cola] whatever; I have done what they say, but I never did give them any rights in it, nor their company." He sighed. "It don't make much difference, though, even if they did have any rights. I don't know how you would get anything out of me." The lawyer decided not to take the case, since neither Robinson,

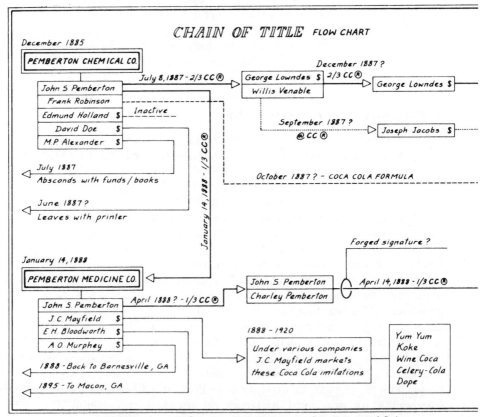

Holland, nor Pemberton had any money. "I laughingly told [Mr Robinson] I didn't see much chance," Candler recalled. "I didn't care for his case on any contingent fee . . . and that was the end of it."

As far as independently wealthy Ed Holland was concerned, perhaps the lawyer was right. But Frank Robinson had worked hard for Coca-Cola and believed in the future of the product; he wasn't about to let the matter drop, nor did he feel it was a laughing matter. Robinson cast about for another plan. Pemberton may have sold the *rights* to the formula, but Robinson still had a *copy* of it, and he must have felt legally entitled to it. He needed to find someone to purchase the rights to Coca-Cola and promote it properly, someone with vision and capital.

VENABLE AND LOWNDES SELL OUT

Meanwhile, Willis Venable and George Lowndes had carted their inventory from 107 Marietta down the block to the corner of Marietta and Whitehall, where they dumped it in the basement of Jacobs' Pharmacy. Venable, who as

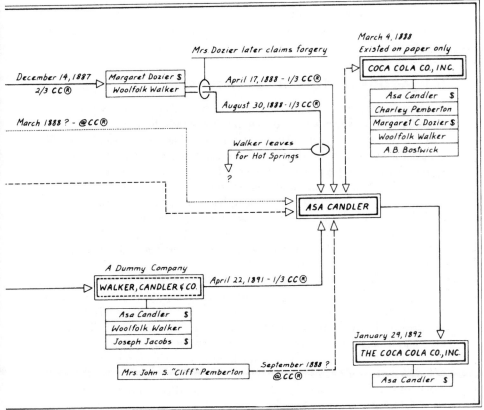

the self-proclaimed "soda fountain king" of Atlanta had written a glowing testimonial to Coca-Cola in April, agreed to manufacture the product as well as market it. The first man to sell a glass of Coca-Cola, Venable was a well-respected businessman, dispensing a standard array of drinks at his twenty-five-foot soda fountain. Lowndes, who worked for another patent medicine house, simply supplied capital. Busy at the soda fountain, Venable couldn't spare the time to promote Coca-Cola, much less make it. After several months, Lowndes forced a change. "We did very little business, that's the truth," he later testified, "and it went into the concern to pay the expenses . . . I found he wasn't handling it as a thing of that sort should be handled, and I told him we had best separate—he buy or sell to me."

According to Lowndes, Venable did indeed sell to him, but Lowndes couldn't find the time to promote the drink either. "I realized that Coca-Cola would die if it did not receive immediate attention. Consequently, I resolved to sell it." On December 13, 1887, Pemberton signed a note authorizing the sale, and the next day, Lowndes (with Venable's signature, since it had been on the original sales document) sold to Woolfolk Walker and Mrs. M. C. Dozier, for $1,200 plus the cost of the manufacturing inventory. Walker persuaded his younger sister, Margaret Dozier, to supply the $1,200 for the purchase. The ownership of Coca-Cola had become yet more fractured, with Mrs. Dozier owning two-ninths and Walker four-ninths of the total formula rights.

JOE JACOBS MUDDIES THE WATERS

To confuse matters, however, Venable somehow disposed of his portion of Coca-Cola *twice*. At some point during the fall of 1887, he apparently gave his share of the drink to Joseph Jacobs, the owner of Jacobs' Pharmacy. As the druggist later recalled it, "thru some business deal, I acquired Mr. Venable's share [of Coca-Cola] in lieu of some money I had loaned him in completing his beautiful home in the West End." Jacobs did not sell to Walker and Dozier, keeping his share well into 1888, though his memory was frustratingly hazy and contradictory. He later testified that "at the time we bought [Coca-Cola], Moxie had a large sale and we thought we would make a big thing out of [Coca-Cola] . . . Dr. Pemberton put this on the market and I took a part ownership and I think finally all of it."

Soon after acquiring his share in Coca-Cola, Jacobs became annoyed with both the drink and its inventor. By his own admission, he didn't know much about the soda fountain business, which he left entirely to Willis Venable. While Venable had continued to make Coca-Cola "in a small way," Pemberton kept harassing Jacobs for advances on his share of the sales. "There was a clause in the original agreement," wrote Jacobs, "in which Dr. Pemberton was to have a royalty of 5 cents a gallon. He seemed to be pressed for money pretty much all the time and was having money advanced constantly, based on the potential royalty. This did not please me."

PEMBERTON REVIVES

In addition to plaguing Jacobs, the ailing Pemberton was not idle. Although virtually bankrupt, he placed a misleading ad in the *Atlanta Constitution* on October 2, 1887:

> WANTED: An acceptable party with $2,000.00 to purchase one-half interest in a very profitable and well-established manufacturing business, absolutely no risk, and guaranteed a 50 per cent profit on investment, with possibilities of much larger profits and rare opportunity to right party.

To avoid his creditors, Pemberton's blind ad did not give his correct address, but another house on Marietta Street, presumably a friend's. With this bait, he snared three eager entrepreneurs, so he graciously allowed all three of them to pitch in $2,000, thus buying what would logically be 150 percent of his business.

J. C. Mayfield, an Alabama chemist, was reassured when Pemberton answered his response to the blind ad, since he had previously sold Pemberton's concoctions. A. O. Murphey and E. H. Bloodworth, from Barnesville, Georgia, had no experience with patent medicines but were impressed with the records Pemberton showed them. After much correspondence throughout October, November, and December, the three new partners finally moved to Atlanta in late December, ready to produce all of Pemberton's wonderful medicines, including Coca-Cola. The good doctor had neglected to tell them that he had sold off any of his formulas.

ASA CANDLER MAKES HIS ENTRANCE

With the Christmas season of 1887 about to commence, the fortunes of Coca-Cola were quite uncertain. The formula was officially owned by John Pemberton, Woolfolk Walker, and Mrs. Dozier. In fact, it is clear that several others had some interest in it, including Charley Pemberton, Joe Jacobs, Frank Robinson, J. C. Mayfield, A. O. Murphey, and E. H. Bloodworth.

One more person had almost certainly entered the picture by this point—Asa Candler, the older brother of lawyer John Candler. In his search for a savior, Frank Robinson had found his well-capitalized, industrious businessman. The epitome of the ambitious Atlanta druggist, Candler was always looking for a likely new product, but he was cautious about spending money. Robinson had a difficult time convincing Candler that Coca-Cola was a worthwhile venture, finally galvanizing him by conjuring a prophetic vision: "See that wagon going by with all those empty beer kegs? Well, we are going to push Coca-Cola until you see the wagons going by with Coca-Cola just like that."

Though Asa Candler does not appear in any Coca-Cola documents until 1888, he insisted in later testimony that he had become involved the previous year: "I had the whole control of it [Coca-Cola], as far as the business was concerned, in 1887." Curiously, however, he added, "I don't know whether I had bought it or not at that time," explaining that he acquired the drink in return for debts owed him by certain "gentlemen." Later, he "intervened into the affairs of this Pemberton Chemical Company." While vague about exactly how he became involved with Coca-Cola, Candler was positive about one thing: "Robinson had manufactured it, collected it all, and did everything else before 1888. Robinson might have been called my agent."

Candler's muddy statement becomes clearer when we compare it with his last courtroom testimony in 1924. In it, he said he *thought* he had purchased the Coca-Cola formula from Joe Jacobs, but added "I am not certain about it." What he *was* absolutely clear about was that Frank Robinson had given him the actual formula. Obviously, after Robinson brought him the directions for manufacturing Coca-Cola, Candler then had to obtain legal possession—a process that would be not only confused, but highly suspicious.

With the opening of the soda fountain season in March of 1888, Candler officially began to take control of Coca-Cola. During that spring, Joe Jacobs complained to his friend Asa Candler about Pemberton's constant requests for money. Candler, without appearing too eager, offered to take the drink off his hands in return for some stock in a glass factory and "odds and ends such as bed pans, pewter syringes, wooden pill boxes, and empty bottles." The uninsured glass factory burned soon afterward. Though Jacobs kicked himself for the stupid barter in subsequent years, he remained lifelong friends with Candler.

CHARLEY PEMBERTON STAKES HIS CLAIM

Meanwhile, Mayfield, Bloodworth, and Murphey had settled in, and on January 14, 1888, had formed a copartnership with Pemberton which they called the Pemberton Medicine Company, in which Pemberton specifically gave them the rights to all of his patented products, including Coca-Cola and his new Lemon and Orange Elixir. After moving to a better location on Pryor Street, the partners commenced production, naively unaware of the disintegration of the Pemberton Chemical Company or the sale of Coca-Cola. Mayfield ran the laboratory, Bloodworth took to the road as a traveling salesman, and Murphey kept the books. The only discordant note seemed to be Mayfield's rather stormy marriage—Diva Mayfield often helped her husband in the laboratory, and their arguments made Murphey and Bloodworth uncomfortable.

Within a few months, however, trouble appeared in the person of Charley Pemberton, who had returned from a drug firm in Louisville, Kentucky, to claim his birthright. He demanded that Mayfield relinquish the manufacturing job to him. Mayfield refused. Charley was "disgruntled, dissatisfied and made it up for the old man, Dr. Pemberton," Mayfield said later. "The doctor came to us and told us that he would have to give—that the son contended that he had promised him the Coca-Cola business. Of course, it was a bomb in our camps."

Charley, whom Mayfield regarded as "disagreeable, a drinking kind of boy," began throwing tantrums, boozing, wheedling, and putting his father in an awkward position. Dr. Pemberton finally told the partners he had signed the rights to Coca-Cola over to Charley some time previously but hadn't remembered it until then. He blamed his lapse of memory on his morphine habit. For a while, there was no resolution to the matter. "We ran along there quite a little while thereafter undecided just what to do," Mayfield remembered. As matters simmered, the partners were further disillusioned with Pemberton when they discovered that Asa Candler had quietly maneuvered to gain legal control of Coca-Cola, forming a new company with Charley Pemberton and Dr. Pemberton's former salesman, Woolfolk Walker. In addition, as the soda fountain season opened, Candler's company was brewing Coca-Cola faster than they were and pushing it hard.

THE UNKNOWN COCA-COLA COMPANY

On March 24, 1888, Asa Candler, Charley Pemberton, and Woolfolk Walker and his sister filed in Fulton County Superior Court for incorporation of the Coca-Cola Company. Candler soon regretted both the incorporation and the partnership with the immature Pemberton, who proved to be more a liability than a help. While much of the wording was probably "boiler plate" for such documents, it is nonetheless instructive to see what they planned:

> The purposes of this Company . . . will be the manufacturing of Coca-Cola Syrup; the buying of ingredients and appliances necessary therefor, and the sale of the manufactured article, as a syrup in bulk, bottled, as a medicine, and as a nerve tonic; And they desire the privilege of extending such manufacturing to other specialties of like kind . . . The Capital Stock of said Company shall be twelve thousand dollars; more than ten percent of which has already been paid in . . . The principal office and place of business . . . shall be . . . Atlanta . . . but petitioners desire the privilege of establishing branch offices or factories elsewhere.

Like all other incorporations, this one would last for twenty years before renewal. The petition stated that over $1,200 had already been paid in. Presumably some of this was Walker/Dozier money, with the rest coming from Candler. Charley Pemberton probably paid nothing for his share.

This "first" Coca-Cola Company is not a part of the official chain of title, nor is it ever mentioned in any corporate history. Asa Candler didn't file for incorporation of *The* Coca-Cola Company (the legal basis for the current company, always spelled with a capital T) until 1892. He must have been extremely nervous about the existence of this prior company and its partners, any of whom could have caused considerable trouble for him, at least until the charter expired in 1908. The existence of this early version of the Coca-Cola Company explains some myserious endorsement letters addressed as early as 1888 to the "Coca-Cola Company." In an 1898 pamphlet announcing the grand opening of his new Coca-Cola factory, Candler slipped, asserting that the company had begun in March 1888, a clear reference to this otherwise well-buried legality.

ASA WRITES TO WARREN

On April 10, 1888, shortly after incorporating the company, Asa Candler wrote to his younger brother Warren, a Methodist minister then editing a religious journal in Nashville. After advising Warren not to accept the presidency of Emory College because it didn't pay enough (Warren ignored him, establishing an important link between Emory and the Candlers), Asa went on:

> You know how I suffer with headaches. Well some days ago, a friend suggested that I try Coco-Cola. I did & was relieved. Some days later I again tried it & was again relieved. I determined to find out about it—investigation showed that it was owned by parties unable to put it fairly before the people. I determined to put money into it & a little influence. I put $500.00 of the first & am putting a goodly portion of what I have of the last.[*]

Clearly, Candler was certain he had a winning drink, and he was prepared to promote it. In the remainder of the letter, he asked brother Warren to find a fountain outlet in Nashville for Coca-Cola, saying he would send two free gallons of syrup as an introductory offer. While adopting Robinson's idea of giving out free tickets, he aimed to build up a direct mail list by soliciting customers' addresses from Tennessee druggists. "I don't want to make a merchant or peddler out of you," Candler explained, as he did just that. "I enclose circulars. It is a fine thing—certain."

Just days after writing to his brother, Candler's "influence" bore fruit. Eager to dispense with Charley Pemberton, Candler arranged to buy him out. On April 14, 1888, Charley Pemberton (with his father as cosigner) sold the remaining third of the Coca-Cola title to Walker, Candler & Company for $550 ($50 to be paid down, and $500 due in thirty days). Walker, Candler & Company comprised Woolfolk Walker, Asa Candler, and Joe Jacobs, though Jacobs and Candler later insisted that it was a "dummy" corporation, since Candler supplied all of the money.[†]

Three days after putting $50 down on the Pembertons' third of Coca-Cola, Candler added to his legal rights, buying out half of the Walker/Dozier title for $750 on April 17, 1888. Frank Robinson witnessed the document. Around this time, Candler rented Pemberton's vacant old site at 107 Marietta Street, and the original apparatus for preparing Coca-Cola was once again trundled

---

[*] It appears that although Candler had exercised full control over Coca-Cola since late 1887, he was only now getting around to tasting it, and he still couldn't spell it correctly. Or perhaps he was only now trying it as a cure for his perennial headaches. It is likely that the $500 referred to Candler's contribution to the Coca-Cola Company capitalization.

[†] If Candler was really the sole buyer, why would he bother to camouflage it? John Pemberton probably bore a grudge against Candler for buying out his entire stock of drugs and lab equipment five years earlier, when Pemberton was too sick to protect himself from predatory partners. The sick inventor had sued Candler along with everyone else involved. In a bitter affidavit, Pemberton wrote that he was "now lying perfectly helpless and utterly dependent upon the proceeds of the partnership." If allowed to proceed, the sale would be his "present and utter ruin." Nonetheless, Pemberton lost the suit and his lab.

down Marietta Street from Jacobs' basement to its old home, where Frank
Robinson began producing Coca-Cola in earnest.

THE FINAL ACT

The hot Atlanta summer arrived in full force. John Pemberton lay dying of
stomach cancer. Asa Candler pushed Coca-Cola, with Woolfolk Walker on the
road for him. At this point, Candler must have cursed the incorporation with
Charley Pemberton, who was now marketing a competing drink and had
proved anything but a stable stockholder in the Coca-Cola Company. On June
2, 1888, Asa again wrote to brother Warren in Nashville. "We are doing
moderately well with Coco Cola. Its only obstacle is that [Charley] Pemberton
is continually offering a very poor article at a less price & the public who pay
for Coco Cola & are not benefitted erroneously decide that it is a fraud."

At about this time, Dr. Pemberton, in an attempt to make everyone happy,
told his partners that while the *name* Coca-Cola belonged to Charley, they
could continue to use the same formula but sell it under a different trademark.
When the uninspired title of Yum Yum failed to catch on, they switched to
Koke (already a nickname for Coca-Cola). Murphey, disgusted with the whole
scene and his discovery of Pemberton's morphine addiction, withdrew from
the partnership and went back to Barnesville.

Thus, as the muggy heat of Atlanta turned oppressive in July and early
August, three varieties of Coca-Cola were competing to assuage thirst, cure
headache and hangover, and relieve that tired feeling.

Even as he was dying, Pemberton struggled to continue his work. Several
times in his final months, he staggered to his laboratory, attempting to perfect
his last drink, a modified cola with celery extract. "He did not care anything
about what he had already accomplished," J. C. Mayfield said. "He wanted
something new." He never finished. On August 16, 1888, John Pemberton
died at the age of fifty-seven, leaving behind a legacy of hard work, sound
scholarship, poor business sense, shattered dreams, drug addiction, lawsuits,
and a few patent medicines with quaint names that would be forgotten within a
few years—Extract of Stillingia, Globe Flower Cough Syrup, Indian Queen
Hair Dye, Triplex Liver Pills, French Wine Coca. His beloved and only child
was an alcoholic who would die an apparent suicide six years later, and his
widow would end her life a pauper. Still, Pemberton was, above all else, a
gentle man, an obsessed scholar, a creative genius. He did not know it as he
died, but his principal legacy was Coca-Cola, the drink that would make him
famous and might have made him wealthy, had he lived long enough.

The newspaper notice of Pemberton's death called him "the oldest druggist
of Atlanta and one of her best-known citizens . . . an especially popular
gentleman." Asa Candler, weeping fat crocodile tears, called all the druggists
of the city together at his store to suggest they close their establishments for
the day of his funeral. "Mr. Candler paid Dr. Pemberton a beautiful tribute of
respect, speaking of his lovable nature and many virtues," the newspaper
reported. "He voiced, he said, the feelings of all present that 'our profession

has lost a good and active member.'" Candler served as a pall-bearer at the Atlanta funeral ceremony, before the casket was whisked to an unmarked grave in Columbus. Years later, Candler protested, "Why, I suppose Dr. Pemberton felt I was one of his best friends in this town." If the doctor did, he was deceived.

Candler wasted no time consolidating his claim to Coca-Cola. Exactly two weeks after Pemberton's death, on August 30, 1888, he bought the remaining interest of Woolfolk Walker and Margaret Dozier for $1,000, payable in a series of notes. Now, except for the technicality of the Walker, Candler & Company ownership, Asa Candler had staked a solid legal claim to Coca-Cola. He had paid a total of $2,300, according to the official chain of title. By May 1, 1889, he was calling himself the drink's sole proprietor.

FORGERY AND OTHER JUICY TIDBITS

There are, however, weak links in the chain Candler forged. Even Candler's son, in the official biography of his father, noted that "this is the factual chain of title, established by attorneys and accepted by the courts, of the ownership of Coca-Cola. Behind these bare facts, there are probably others which would be interesting to know . . ." Mrs. M. C. Dozier would have agreed.

Margaret Dozier showed up in 1914 at the age of sixty-five, insisting that she had never sold her share of the formula. A dithery witness on the stand, she nonetheless appeared quite certain about the vital issues: "I did not sign any paper at all conveying any interest to Asa G. Candler or anyone else. Most positively I never received a cent." Her brother Woolfolk had "charge of the whole thing," she said, complaining that he told her nothing; "in fact, when he got control of it he never came near me at all."

Two handwriting experts who have looked at Mrs. Dozier's signatures on the questionable chain of title documents (those of April 17 and August 30, 1888) agree that the April Dozier signature is a forgery.[*] The August signature may be authentic, but at least one of the experts couldn't be sure. It seems likely that Woolfolk Walker, perhaps with Asa Candler's knowledge, forged his sister's signature, at least on the April document.

Walker himself vanished immediately after signing over the rights to Candler at the end of August. His sister testified that he left town without even saying goodbye, and though she wrote repeatedly to Hot Springs, Arkansas where he was rumored to reside, he never answered her. His disappearance was suspiciously providential for Asa Candler.

---

[*] Three handwriting experts were each given three genuine signatures—the December 14, 1887, sale to Walker/Dozier and two Fulton County Superior Court documents now in the author's possession. Using those three signatures as a standard, George Pearl of Atlanta, Georgia, stated that the April 17, 1888, signature was a forgery, though he was uncertain about the August signature. John Brullmann of Jackson Heights, New York, pronounced the April signature a forgery. Charles Hamilton of New York City felt that "all are by the same person. Differences of letters like the capital M or slight alterations in the C are not important."

But that's not the end of the forgery. John Pemberton's signature on the crucial April 14, 1888, sale to Walker, Candler & Company is a fake. According to handwriting expert George Pearl, the writing is "way, way out of natural variation for this signature to be genuine. The writing is not smooth and fast but rather slow and unsure, wondering where to go next . . . This is a simulated signature and not a very good one at that."

Though there is no way to know with any certainty, Charley Pemberton is the most likely one to have forged the signature. At the same time, he tried to contrast and obscure his own handwriting by signing with a large flourish and much spilled ink. But why would Charley Pemberton have committed the forgery? Did he really need the resulting $550 that badly? It is more probable that he had made some kind of deal with Asa Candler. Candler apparently wrote the body of the contract itself in his distinctively hasty script.

Although it is difficult (and presumptuous) to play armchair detective over a hundred years later, it seems likely that Candler was the shadowy figure behind both the Pemberton and Dozier forgeries, which occurred within three days of one another in April of 1888. Both forgeries were committed within a week of Asa Candler's admission to his brother Warren that he was exerting "a little influence" to gain full control of Coca-Cola.

The other jarring note in the chain of title stems from Mrs. Pemberton's family. Her sister Elberta was convinced that Asa Candler had bought the formula, not from Pemberton or Walker, but from Mrs. Pemberton soon after the funeral. Elberta Newman taught her grandchildren never to drink Coca-Cola, since she did not want them to contribute even a nickel to Candler's ill-gotten fortune. "Your Auntie sold the Formula to Asa Candler in his own hand," she later wrote to her son, "and he remarked to her, he was making a risk, but if he made any thing from it he would give her a home and she would never want. He never gave her a cent. She believed to her last day that he would keep his promise."

Elberta's daughter Mary overheard Mrs. Pemberton telling her father of the transaction. When her father found that Candler had paid only $300 for the formula, he told her she should have had a lawyer. "Oh! Asa said he would give me a fine home and handsome income *if* he made anything out of it," Mrs. Pemberton said. "My aunt was a devoted Methodist," Mary explained, "and as Asa Candler taught in the Methodist Sunday school she felt sure he would keep his word."

Other versions of the family story place the blame for the sale of Coca-Cola on the dissolute Charley Pemberton, who was supposed to have sold the formula while drunk, or in return for being bailed out of jail, where he was languishing for disorderly conduct. Yet another relative said that Charley had cajoled his mother into selling to Candler for $600, which he soon spent on drink. Regardless of the exact story, the entire clan was convinced, along with nephew Wilson, that "there was some crookedness about the deal."

On June 23, 1894, Charley Pemberton was discovered unconscious, lying flat on his face in a tiny bedroom above the Oriole Restaurant. A stick of crude opium was found on a chair nearby. The incident was fully reported in the sensation-loving Atlanta newspapers: "Whether the opium was taken with suicidal intent is not known, but for three hours Pemberton was walked, rubbed, beaten, and dosed." The reporter went on to comment that Charley was the son of "one of the most noted physicians Atlanta has ever had. He was the discoverer of the famous Coco-Cola and left his son in charge of the patent when he died."

After ten days of "intense suffering," Charley Pemberton died at Grady Hospital at the age of forty. His mother remained by his side during the ordeal. The notice of this death said that "Charley Pemberton was well known in Atlanta," that his father was "a physician of learning and distinction," and repeated that Charley had inherited the formula, which "he afterwards disposed of . . . for a comparatively small sum." While Charley was an acknowledged alcoholic, this is the first indication that he took opium. His death could have resulted from an accidental overdose, suicide, or murder. A cousin later wrote that "there was something mysterious about Charley's death." Monroe King, a Pemberton expert, believes that suicide was unlikely: "Remember that Charley Pemberton had worked for years with his father and knew the drug trade intimately. He would have chosen a much more effective way to kill himself had he chosen to do so. Taking raw opium instead of a massive dose of morphine makes no sense." At any rate, Asa Candler must have been relieved that the unpredictable, unstable Pemberton was gone.

The allegations of *some* sort of questionable activities were verified by Price Gilbert, a lawyer who apparently did a good deal of work for Asa Candler. Gilbert told a friend that "if I told what I knew about the early days of Coca-Cola, what I said would be very embarrassing," adding that "I'm not going to tell the maneuvering we did to keep afloat in the early days of the company." In 1910, during one of the Company's moves to larger quarters, Asa Candler, over the objections of his nephew, ordered that the earliest records of The Coca-Cola Company be burned, leaving only the official chain of title intact. Beyond that, only circumstantial evidence and rumor remained to haunt him.

As rusty and weak as the chain of title may be, though, it is quite likely that we would view Coca-Cola Extract and Syrup as just one more quaint creation of Dr. Pemberton if Asa Candler had not taken control of it. In the end, Rob Stephens, yet another relation of Mrs. Pemberton, was probably correct when he wrote:

> Coca-Cola became a go because it was pushed and pushed by an energetic man. If the Pembertons had not sold the formula it probably would have stayed in an old drink somewhere and been lost in time. I think Cousin Cliff always thought Mr. Candler robbed her and Charley, but I doubt if it can be said he did. He paid them for something of no use to them and he made it a go by his own efforts.

~ 4 ~

Asa Candler: His Triumphs and Headaches

If people knew the good qualities of Coca-Cola as I know them, it would be necessary for us to lock the doors of our factories and have a guard with a shotgun to make the people line up to buy it.
—Asa G. Candler

I don't know a single day in my life when I have been moved by a desire to make money.
—Asa G. Candler, aged sixty-four

ASA CANDLER, a short bantam of a man with a high, squeaky voice, may not fit the ideal image of the Big Business Man, but even as a youth he was the quintessential capitalist. Born on December 30, 1851, the eighth of eleven children, Candler liked to paint a log-cabin portrait of his poor-but-happy rural youth. In fact, Sam Candler, his father, was a well-to-do planter and merchant who founded the town in which Asa was raised.

A gold prospector, the elder Candler named Villa Rica ("Rich Town" in Spanish) to attract others who had the gold bug. He must have passed on this spirit of enterprise and promotion. Despite his relative wealth, however, Asa Candler's father did not believe in spoiling his children—they earned every penny of their spending money. Asa soon proved that he would do almost anything for a dollar. He once chased down a wild mink, which bit him severely when he finally caught it. As Candler told the story,

> I hadn't heard of people selling mink skins, but it seemed to me it might be a good idea and I decided to try. Atlanta was thirty-six miles away and there was no railroad, but that seemed to be the best possible market, so I sent the skin in to town by wagon, and I said to myself, "Maybe I'll get twenty-five cents!" I got a dollar—the first I had ever made.

Thrilled, the young Candler soon organized other children to do the mink-trapping for him, and he established a regular Atlanta trade. On the return wagon, he purchased straight pins for resale in Villa Rica and learned a lesson he would later apply to Coca-Cola: there was good money to be made from penny and nickel sales. "Seems you couldn't make anything off pins, doesn't it? But when I went away to school, I had more than $100 saved up through the sale of mink skins and speculation in pins."

Asa Candler received little formal education, since the Civil War closed schools when he was ten. After the war, he managed to complete two years of high school before quitting to apprentice as a pharmacy clerk. Candler undoubtedly received a proper Christian home education, however, from his strong-willed mother, Martha Beall Candler.

Married at the age of fourteen, the diminutive Mrs. Candler, who rose ramrod straight to less than five feet and never weighed a hundred pounds, dominated the family. Though her husband wasn't a churchgoer until his later years, Martha Candler belonged to the Primitive Baptist Church, whose members were more descriptively known as Hardshell Baptists. And woe unto the child who crossed her. "She tried to boss everybody in sight and came very near doing it," one of her grandchildren recalled. Martha Candler's imprint on her seven sons is quite apparent in an 1891 photograph which shows the indomitable matron surrounded by her grown male offspring. All in the picture—mother and children—display the solemn downturned mouth characteristic of the Candlers.

A YOUTH'S APPRENTICESHIP

When he abandoned his schooling in 1870, Asa Candler went to Cartersville, northwest of Atlanta, to apprentice in a drugstore run by two physicians, friends of his family. He lived in the rear of the store and studied Latin, Greek, chemistry, and medicine at night. As a child, he had dreamed of becoming a doctor—"I would concoct imaginary potions and doctor sick pigeons, hogs, dogs, and cattle"—but after two years of working in the drug business and observing the doctors' country practice, he changed his mind. He would remain a druggist, but not in small-town, small-pay Cartersville, where after two years he was earning only $25 a month. "I think there is more money to be made as a druggist than as a physician," he wrote in the fall of 1872, "and I know it can be done with a great deal less trouble of soul and body."

At the age of twenty-one, Candler arrived in Atlanta with his trunk on January 7, 1873. In later years, he liked to tell the story of how he came to the big city looking for work, wearing homemade clothes and carrying only $1.75 in his pocket, but he told a reporter in 1909 that he had been "promised a place with a wholesale druggist." While he only had $2 in cash, he told the journalist, he also had a note for salary due him from his old job.

Even if Asa Candler's rags-to-riches fable doesn't ring quite true, he displayed unusual fortitude once he discovered there was no job waiting for him that chilly day, applying at virtually every drugstore in Atlanta (including Pemberton's establishment) for work. Finally, at 9 P.M., he tried George J. Howard's drugstore, where he encountered a bored prescription clerk, sitting on a counter. The clerk interrupted Candler's recitation of his résumé to ask, "When can you go to work?" When Candler said he could start right away, the clerk led him into the back room, introduced him to Dr. Howard, and tendered his resignation, effective immediately. Asa Candler had a job. He also found a boardinghouse that was willing to wait for his first paycheck.

Howard owned stores at several Atlanta locations. In March of 1877, he took John Pemberton as a partner—an arrangement that lasted only a few months —simultaneously selling one of his stands to his two young clerks, Marcellus Hallman, twenty-eight, and Asa Candler, twenty-five. The Dun credit agent was impressed, noting that Hallman and Candler were "clever young men . . . economical & reliable." They had saved $3,000 to begin the business. "They are very energetic," wrote the credit rater. "Have no pending debts hanging over them & will no doubt be successful."

The Dun man proved to be a good prophet. Two years later, he wrote that the partners were carrying a full stock, had an active trade, paid their bills promptly, and claimed to be worth $10,000. In addition, he added that they were "correct reliable young men, close in business matters, addicted to no extravagant habits." This description was an understatement, as far as Candler was concerned. He was a workaholic, never touched liquor, and was tightfisted with his money.

THE OVERWORKED BOSS'S DAUGHTER

In the meantime, Asa Candler had gotten married. Lucy Howard, only eighteen, must have seen more in the small, determined young man than her father, who was violently opposed to her marriage to his former clerk. Grudgingly, George Howard finally wrote a curt note to his son-in-law in November of 1878: "I am disposed to 'bury the hatchet' and to be friendly in the future—if this should meet your approval you can let me know." Eight days later, Lucy gave birth to Charles Howard Candler, who was always known by his middle name. Asa and Lucy Candler appear to have had a genuinely happy marriage, eventually producing four boys and one girl. Howard later wrote, however, that "my Mother's patience was tried by household responsibilities with which she had to cope with little help from her husband, engrossed in the perplexities and problems of a growing business."

While Asa was thus engaged, Lucy was "superintendent and well-nigh slave" to a household of his relatives. Her mother-in-law, the imperious Martha Candler, moved in after her husband's death, along with Asa's retarded older brother Noble and his youngest brother, John. At various points, Asa's brother Warren (with his family) and sister Jessie (who gave birth to a third child shortly after arriving) also moved in for a while. Little wonder, then, that Asa and Lucy Candler bought a home in 1879, then a larger one three years later. Lucy must have been quite relieved when her flint-willed mother-in-law finally moved to a home of her own two doors away in 1882. For the next fifteen years, until her death, Asa Candler visited his mother every day before and after work, anticipating "her every need and . . . wish," as Howard Candler recalled.

In 1881, Asa Candler bought out his partner, Marcellus Hallman, and the next year formed a partnership with his father-in-law and former boss, George Howard. Soon afterward, the pair purchased Pemberton's drug business while he lay sick in bed, then survived a disastrous fire. In 1886, Candler bought

Howard's interest in the partnership, renaming the firm Asa G. Candler &
Company.

ASA AND ATLANTA ARE WIRED

That spring, as Pemberton was perfecting Coca-Cola, Asa Candler cast around
for a ticket to wealth. Thirty-four years old, he felt that he had served his
apprenticeship in the drug trade. It was time to make some real money, and he
knew that fortunes were building all over the country. As the patent medicine
capital of the South and the home of major successes such as B.B.B. and
S.S.S., Atlanta exceeded all cities in the country in the proportion of
manufacturing income derived from the questionable drugs.

The city may have been hustling to recover from Sherman's devastation
when Pemberton arrived on the scene back in 1869, but by 1886 Atlanta was
booming. It had become the capital of the state in 1877 and was, according to an
observer of the 1880s, a "great, populous, and thriving metropolis . . . famous
for the greatness and brilliancy of its enterprises." The Atlanta newspapers of
the period were awash with boosterism and particularly delighted in quoting
praise from Yankees. The city, noted a Massachusetts visitor in 1886, "has all
the push and energy of the North coupled with a most delightful climate . . .
Atlanta has become one of the best advertised cities in the United States.
People have come here to settle from all parts of the Union."

In their pursuit of everything they considered progressive, Atlantans
naturally were fascinated by the newly invented electric generator, even
though it had few practical applications. Direct current, which could travel a
mile or less, was considered the only safe form of the new energy source. Still,
in the mid-eighties, one innovative Atlanta druggist was advertising his
electric doorbell, which rang in his residence to summon him "at all hours
during the night." Another ad featured "Dr. Dye's Celebrated Voltaic Belt
with Electric Suspensory Appliances" for the speedy relief of impotence. An
1885 Atlanta editorial used electricity as a metaphor for the kind of businessman the city needed. In retrospect, it appears an apt description of Asa
Candler, who fairly bristled with nervous energy: "What we now need is a few
electric men—men who will put their electric shoulders to the great wheel of
Southern progress." Their "electric brains" would crackle with "electric
ideas" which would "induce capital in abundance and immigration of an
acceptable class to come southward."

In his 1886 ads, Candler described himself as "active, pushing, and
reliable." His new patent medicine was appropriately called Electric Bitters,
only 50 cents a bottle. Candler's ad, like many others, obviously aimed to
induce the symptoms he claimed to cure:

> You are feeling depressed, your appetite is poor, you are bothered with head-
> ache, you are fidgetty, and nervous, and generally out of sorts, and want to *brace*
> up . . . What you want is an alterative that will purify your blood, start healthy
> action of liver and kidneys, restore your vitality, and give renewed health and
> strength. Such a medicine you will find in Electric Bitters.

ASA'S AILMENTS

If Candler's copy sounds convincing, it is because he often experienced all of those symptoms himself. His son recalled that "many times when Father got home at the end of a day of hard work at the store or the office he was miserable and exhausted, suffering intense headache"—often exacerbated by eyestrain. In addition, if he were living today, Candler might be diagnosed as a manic-depressive. While he normally functioned at a manic, high-energy level, he was periodically morose, even at the peak of his success. He also suffered from dyspepsia, caused in part by his irregular eating pattern and his tendency to bolt his food. He often skipped lunch and came home for dinner long after the rest of his family had eaten.

This impressive list of ailments was magnified by Candler's hypochondria. His letters to family members were filled with complaints and health concerns. "Do not allow yourself to get billious or to feel in a drowsy, sleepy state," a typical message read. "Such symptoms generally indicate miasma." He sought cures for his afflictions in patent medicines (no doubt sampling the products he pushed), as his son Howard recalled: "He knew in a general way the properties of drugs and believed in and practiced self-medication, which was not only unwise but fraught with some danger," given the sometimes lethal ingredients with which he must have dosed himself.

THE ROAD TO COCA-COLA

Unlike John Pemberton, Asa Candler was no brilliant inventor. Instead, he specialized in hard-sell copy, offering a moneyback guarantee if customers were not satisfied, knowing that few would take advantage of it. In addition to Electric Bitters, Candler bought the rights to a number of other proprietaries before finding Coca-Cola. These included Everlasting Cologne (presumably a perfume with an alarmingly permanent odor), Bucklen's Arnica Salve ("for cuts, bruises, sores, ulcers, salt rheum, fever sores, tetter, chapped hands, chilblains, corns, and all skin eruptions, positively cures piles"), King's New Discovery ("for consumption, colds and coughs, will surely cure any and every affection of throat, lungs, or chest"), and De-Lec-Ta-Lave ("will whiten the teeth, cleanse the mouth, harden and beautify the gums").

Even after he purchased the rights to Coca-Cola in 1888, Candler continued to look for other likely patent medicines. In 1890, he bought the venerable Botanic Blood Balm (B.B.B.), which had been a big seller for its inventor, Dr. J. P. Dromgoole. A landmark Georgia Supreme Court case in 1889 had considerably reduced the value of the company, however, when the court ruled against the Blood Balm Company in favor of a Mr. Cooper, who had taken three bottles to cure a rash on his leg. He would have been better off settling for the rash, according to the court records, since by the time he'd consumed the recommended dosage, "his head, neck and breast were covered with red spots and the inside of his mouth and throat filled with sores." Eventually, "a large part of the hair fell from his head." It is easy to see why

Candler may have picked up B.B.B. at a bargain-basement price after that lawsuit.

ASA'S 1889 EMPIRE

As active and pushy as Candler may have been, there was nothing particularly unusual about him in 1888 when he finally gained complete legal control of Coca-Cola. To a casual observer of the Atlanta scene, he was just one more enterprising businessman. No one would have guessed that by the turn of the century, he would be one of the wealthiest men in Atlanta, and Coca-Cola would be the most popular soft drink in America.

In an interview, Candler later said that at the beginning of 1889, he was "in bad health, $50,000 in debt and Coca-Cola on [my] hands." But in the next months, he overcame his headaches, stomach problems, and dour outlook enough to impress an *Atlanta Journal* reporter, who described the Peachtree Street facilities of the "enterprising druggist" that May. Frank Robinson supervised the manufacturing in the basement, while Asa Candler's "private sanctum" took up the rear of the first floor, which housed the retail outlet. The shipping department, on the second floor, was "practically packed" from floor to ceiling (14 feet high) with $10,000 worth of various Atlanta patent medicines. Finally, on the top floor, a group of young women bottled "extracts, medicines, oils, etc."

Candler, "a continuous worker, always confined in his office," relied on Frank Robinson and one other full-time salesman to hawk his products, including Coca-Cola, identifed as "one of their leading specialties."[*] Another salesman joined the small firm soon afterward. Sam Dobbs, who would play a key role in the company's early history, arrived as a seventeen-year-old to ask his Uncle Asa for a job. At first he was refused, but the black porter, a former Candler family slave, died the following day, and Dobbs got his position, soon proving himself as a salesman—the first of many Candler relations to find work through Coca-Cola.

Traveling salesmen in those days were known as drummers, since they drummed up trade, and the Atlanta variety already had a reputation for hustle, as an 1881 observer noted: "The trade of Atlanta is rapidly extending into wider and more distant territory. The drummers . . . for Atlanta houses swarm over Georgia and surrounding States." Candler's men must have followed the pattern, since the testimonial letters for Coca-Cola printed in the May 1889 article came from Mississippi, Alabama, and Virginia in addition to Georgia. By 1890, only 40 percent of Coca-Cola sales were made at Atlanta

---

[*] Candler told the reporter that "Coca-Cola was introduced to the public a little over a year ago in a modest way. Its inventor was unable to devote to it the means necessary to its general introduction to the public . . ." It is interesting that Pemberton's name is carefully avoided here, though he had been dead less than a year and was well known in Atlanta. Candler was already minimizing the inventor's contribution. Note, too, that he moved the introduction of Coca-Cola to "a little over a year ago" (1888) rather than 1886.

soda fountains, and by the following year, the figure had shrunk to 27 percent.

A few months later, veteran fountain man Foster Howell described Coca-Cola as "one of the most popular drinks ever sold in Atlanta." Howell was less circumspect than Candler in explaining Coca-Cola's popularity as a hangover cure: "Men who get on a razee the night before come up in the morning and drink . . . coca-cola . . . one of the finest nerve tonics in the world." He then recounted how one of Pemberton's employees, a "long-headed chemist," had introduced him to the new headache cure in 1886, appearing early one morning carrying a syrup bottle with "Coca-Cola scribbled on the label." Just then, a badly hung over customer staggered in, so Howell tried the "new discovery" on him. "It worked like a charm. He came back in a few minutes and in an hour he had swallowed four glasses." Howell described another customer who drank five glasses straight, then "went away with a regretful look, seeming to feel unhappy because he could hold no more."

The combination of cocaine and caffeine must have induced repeated calls for Coca-Cola, and we have here the first indication of habitual users, soon labeled "Coca-Cola fiends."[*] Nonetheless, Howell insisted that there was no danger of addiction; people would not become "soda drunkards." But he added that "if you drink it of a night you don't go to sleep."

Throughout 1889, without much advertising, Candler saw sales of Coca-Cola mushroom. He personally went back to Cartersville to ask his first employers to stock Coca-Cola. Total sales for 1889 amounted to 2,171 gallons of syrup. Since each drink called for one ounce of syrup, that meant that almost 61,000 drinks were sold.

1890: YEAR OF DECISION

On January 1, 1890, Asa Candler took stock of his financial situation, writing out a personal balance sheet. He was no longer in debt, showing a net worth of $17,326, although this included his house. One of the entries shows "Coca-Cola Patent Trade Mark etc . . . $2,000," which is presumably what Candler figured he had paid for it. At the same time, he downgraded DeLec-Ta-Lave

---

[*] The actual amount of cocaine in original Coca-Cola has been the subject of much speculation. According to a formula in possession of Frank Robinson's great-grandson (apparently in Robinson's handwriting), 36 gallons of syrup called for 10 pounds of coca leaf. That translates to about 0.13 grain of cocaine per drink, or 8.45 milligrams, which is a tiny amount of the drug. Recent studies, however, suggest a symbiotic relationship between cocaine and caffeine. "Our research [with rats] indicates that caffeine primes brain systems—it increases the effects of cocaine," Dr Susan Schenk says. Consequently, even the negligible amount of cocaine in original Coca-Cola could have had an effect when combined with the 80 milligrams of caffeine. A normal "dose" of cocaine snorted on the street today contains 20 to 30 milligrams. The gentleman who drank five straight glasses of Coca-Cola at Foster Howell's soda fountain received over 40 milligrams of cocaine—quite a jolt, although the drug is more efficient when inhaled rather than ingested.

to $1,000, though he had purchased it for almost $4,000. He did not list any other patent medicines by name.

That January, in the drab coolness of an Atlanta winter, Coca-Cola continued to sell, an unprecedented feat for a soda fountain drink, normally confined to summer sipping. By the month's end, Candler had sold 168 gallons of syrup. Inspired by these figures, he wrote a form letter that he sent to druggists in February, promoting Coca-Cola as "a delightful summer and winter soda fountain beverage." Candler asserted that "the genuine merit and deserved popularity" of the drink was proved by "a reputation that now extends all over the states of Georgia, Alabama, Florida and Tennessee, and to numerous localities in many other States."

Candler clearly had been reading Pemberton's old notes and ads, praising the "medical properties of the Coca Plant and the extract of the celebrated African Cola Nut," adding that "the best physicians unhesitatingly endorse and recommend [Coca-Cola] for mental and physical exhaustion, headache, tired feeling, mental depression, etc." Finally, Candler emphasized that "the principal customers for Coca-Cola are business and professional men, who do not generally spend their money for that which gives them nothing in return." Coca-Cola was, he implied, a practical pick-me-up for the harried man of business, a theme he would stress repeatedly in the ensuing years.

While he promoted Coca-Cola as a soda fountain drink, Candler also advertised the straight syrup as a patent medicine, which he sold for 25 cents a bottle—about a quarter of the going rate for most medicines—in grocery and drug stores. In almanacs distributed throughout the Southern states, Candler suggested that Coca-Cola syrup "should be kept in every house to cure headache and tired feeling," as well as to "overcome depression and languor." The suggested dosage was a tablespoonful to a wineglass of water.

Sales for 1890 amounted to 8,855 gallons, over four times the previous year's record. By the end of the year, Asa Candler realized that if he could pay sufficient attention to Coca-Cola, it might well make his fortune. He finally decided to abandon the drug business and devote all of his time to Coca-Cola. Careful as always, he remained diversified for the moment, retaining the rights to B.B.B. and De-Lec-Ta-Lave. A January 1891 newspaper piece, titled "Going Out of Business," noted that Candler's trade in the three proprietary medicines had "grown to be immense and all of his time is required to look after them."

Convinced that Coca-Cola was his future, Candler decided to create a solid chain of title, and on April 22, 1891, he persuaded Joe Jacobs, as the only other remaining member of Walker, Candler & Company (Woolfolk Walker having conveniently disappeared in 1888) to sign over that company's Coca-Cola rights to Candler individually. Then, on June 5, Candler deposited all of the relevant documents with the U.S. Patent Office.

Having sold his drug business, Candler sought to economize by moving that fall to 42½ Decatur Street, where he manufactured Coca-Cola above a pawnshop, secondhand clothing store, and black saloon. He was not a popular tenant, since the forty-gallon kettle of brewing syrup periodically boiled over.

The sweet, sticky mixture would ooze through the floorboards and drip into the establishments below.

As the money from Coca-Cola rolled in, Candler spent more on advertising his product throughout Georgia and, to a lesser extent, the rest of the South, using the now-familiar Coca-Cola script logo originated by Frank Robinson. He soon hired a black man, George Curtright, and another nephew, Sam Willard, to make Coca-Cola, freeing Robinson to market the drink full-time.

ROBINSON: THE UNSUNG HERO

If anyone can be called the unsung hero of Coca-Cola, it is certainly Frank Robinson. A small, unassuming man—even shorter than Asa Candler—with a bushy mustache, Robinson never demanded attention or fame. Although stark contrasts, he and Candler made a complementary team. While Candler was driven, high-strung, and temperamental, always on the verge of cracking, Robinson remained calm, deliberate, and unflappable in the face of the worst controversy. Following Candler's example, Robinson taught Sunday school. But while Candler's pre-pubescent students poked fun of him behind his back, Robinson studied the Bible with a devoted flock of young women in their twenties. One photograph of the period shows Robinson, looking quietly pleased with himself, seated on a stool surrounded by fifty of his female students.

A 1917 biographical sketch correctly noted that "while Mr. Robinson's modesty would not permit him to make any such claim, many knowing friends do not hesitate to say that it was Frank M. Robinson who made Coca-Cola and gave it its worldwide reputation." Indeed, Robinson's behind-the-scenes creation of Coca-Cola advertising over the next twenty years would catapult the drink to fame. The mastermind of this most Southern soft drink was a native of Corinth, Maine. His father had been severely wounded in the battle of Cold Harbor during the Civil War, and Frank Robinson himself had served in the Maine Volunteers. Despite his accomplishments with Coca-Cola, one of his greatest sources of pride in later years was his election as county auditor of Osceola County, Iowa, in 1872, before he came to Atlanta.

Candler, however, probably devised some early ads himself. Written in the first person, they bear his rather idiosyncratic stamp. "IT MAKES FRIENDS RAPIDLY. IT DOES WHAT IS CLAIMED FOR IT. MERIT SELLS IT," one such ad proclaimed. His statement in an early ad was, in light of Coca-Cola's subsequent history, ironic: "I challenge the world to show an article of its kind as popular as Coca-Cola, for which so little advertising has been done." In the same ad, Candler explained that he had been "a great and almost daily sufferer" of headaches before trying Coca-Cola. "In offering it to the public," he added, "I feel I am a public benefactor."

When that first year of full-time devotion to Coca-Cola, B.B.B., and De-Lec-Ta-Lave was over, Candler had sold 19,831 gallons of syrup, more than double the previous year's record, and he had done it with a relatively small amount of promotional budget. What would happen if he *really* funneled money into advertising? Sure that there was more money to be made from Coca-Cola, a boon to suffering mankind, Candler determinedly put all of his effort behind the single product. He soon sold De-Lec-Ta-Lave to Joe Jacobs and B.B.B. to J. B. Brooks, one of his part-time traveling salesmen, and on December 29, 1891, Candler filed for incorporation of The Coca-Cola Company.

COCAINE BLUES, AGAIN

Even as Coca-Cola was rocketing to fame, however, rumors of its cocaine content were stirring. As they would for many years to come, patrons calling for Coca-Cola usually asked for a "dope," a practice which infuriated Candler. On June 12, 1891, just a week after depositing his chain of title with the Patent Office, Candler opened the *Atlanta Constitution* and read the headline, "WHAT'S IN COCA COLA? A Popular Drink Which Is Said to Foster the Cocaine Habit." His stomach churning and a headache rolling like a thunderclap up the base of his neck, Candler read what a "thoughtful citizen" had told a reporter.

Coca-Cola drinking was, the indignant citizen said, "a very vicious and pernicious thing," and asserted that "people are drinking it a dozen times a day." The informer stated that "the ingredient which makes coca cola so popular is cocaine. There is evidently enough of it in the drink to affect people and it is insidiously but surely getting thousands of people into the cocaine habit." He then related the story of his friend who, in despair over his inability to shake the cocaine habit, had shot himself. The implication, of course, was that drinking a Coca-Cola was the first step on the road to self-destruction.

Candler responded by taking out an ad in which he challenged anyone to prove a case in which Coca-Cola had led to cocaine addiction. "If I thought it could possibly hurt anybody," he asserted, "I would quit the manufacture of Coca-Cola instantly." He stated that the formula for Coca-Cola called for only a half-ounce of coca leaf per gallon of syrup and that "no sensible man would undertake to say that this quantity in a gallon would hurt a person taking a glass of the beverage." If Candler was giving accurate information, he was certainly correct that a glass of Coca-Cola had a negligible amount of cocaine in it, amounting to a little over a hundredth of a grain. Either Candler was lying, however, or he had substantially reduced the amount of coca leaf in the formula, since the Pemberton formula called for ten times the amount Candler claimed to use.[*]

The controversy died down, and Coca-Cola drinkers indulged their nefarious habit with no visible ill effect. Nonetheless, rumors about Coca-

---

[*] Drug experts, beginning with Angelo Mariani and John Pemberton, have drawn a legitimate distinction between coca and cocaine. The Peruvian Indians valued the milder forms of the leaf, disdaining the bitter variety with a higher cocaine content. As cocaine got a bad name, Mariani, Pemberton, and then Asa Candler fought to maintain a distinction between the "natural" use of coca leaves, which produced mild stimulation from a mixture of fourteen alkaloids, and the more drastic effects of the pure alkaloid, cocaine.

Cola's drug content would continue to haunt Candler and the drink in the years to come. It is likely, in fact, that these rumors helped more than hindered sales. People were intrigued by the stigma associated with the drink and felt a sinful thrill when imbibing it.

THE MAGIC FORMULA

The mystique of Coca-Cola was also enhanced, of course, by its secret formula, whose blend of flavors was code-named 7X.[*] Soon after Frank Robinson brought him the formula, Asa Candler changed it. His son said that he did so because "the Pemberton product did not have an altogether agreeable taste; it was unstable; it contained too many things, too much of some ingredients and too little of others . . . the bouquet of several of the volatile essential oils previously used was adversely affected by some ingredients." The main reason that Candler modified the formula, however, was to distinguish it from all of the other recipes floating around. At least ten people had access to the original Pemberton formula. In addition, as Coca-Cola achieved universal popularity, versions of the formula were offered by imitators, druggists, and charlatans for varying amounts, ranging, according to Joe Jacobs, "from $1,000 down to a bottle of Whiskey."

In order to protect his valuable secret, Candler engaged in an elaborate ritual whenever he received a shipment of ingredients. Either he or Robinson would remove the labels immediately, instead adding a number code, from 1 to 9 (the essential oils for 7X were left entirely unlabeled). Candler opened all of the Company mail, so that he could intercept invoices for secret ingredients before anyone in the accounting department saw them.

At first, only Candler or Robinson mixed the precious 7X. Later, when Howard Candler joined the business, he was taught the solemn ceremony as a rite of passage. "One of the proudest moments of my life," he remembered, "came when my father . . . initiated me into the mysteries of the secret flavoring formula, inducting me as it were into the 'Holy of Holies.'" No formula or instructions were ever written down. The containers, labels removed, were identified "only by sight, smell and remembering where each was put on the shelf." Finally, either Candler or Robinson sampled each batch of syrup before it left the factory. Robinson had a particularly keen nose and palate and could detect even a trace of an off-flavor.

INCORPORATION (RE-INCORPORATION)

The Coca-Cola Company was granted its corporate charter on January 29, 1892. Candler must have breathed a sigh of relief when no bureaucrat noticed that there was already a Coca-Cola Company on the books from 1888. The

---

[*] For a detailed description of the formula and the ingredients in 7X, see Appendix 1, "The Sacred Formula," p. 456.

charter for the new company called for a capitalization of $100,000, to be divided into a thousand shares at $100 each.

In February, Candler transferred his rights in Coca-Cola to the corporation in return for 500 shares, while giving Frank Robinson only ten. Candler intended to raise money for his business in 1892 by selling the other 490 shares to investors, which explains two unfamiliar names: J. M. Berry of Virginia, and F. W. Prescott of Massachusetts. While Berry soon dropped out of the picture, Prescott, an entrepreneur "well posted in the different markets" according to one newspaper account, actively tried to market shares in the Boston area. Candler also contacted stockbrokers and venture capitalists in New York and Baltimore. Despite the demonstrated profitability of Coca-Cola, Candler located few backers for his relatively unknown proprietary medicine. Candler granted the Darby Manufacturing Company of Baltimore the exclusive Maryland territory for Coca-Cola for ten years; as an added incentive, they received a share of Coca-Cola stock for every 500 gallons of syrup they bought (up to fifty shares). They had earned eighteen shares by 1899, when they sold back to the Candler family.

F. W. Prescott found better investors in Boston. The firm of Seth Fowle & Sons, already in the proprietary drug business, bought fifty shares and the exclusive rights to the New England trade for twenty years. The two Fowle sons became dedicated Coca-Cola men, issuing the first newsletter to boost the product. *The Coca-Cola News* of the 1890s, aimed at the retailer, emphasized the profits to be made from the soft drink, calling it a "restorative, a blessing to humanity." Recognizing the new national rage for bicycling, the Fowle brothers urged the drink upon "wheelmen" and other athletes. The ever-increasing sales of Coca-Cola soon gave Candler all the capital he needed—there were never more than 586 shares outstanding at any one time.

RUNNING AFOUL OF KENT'S COCA-COLA

As business gathered momentum, in May of 1892, Candler decided to patent the trademark Coca-Cola script. What he thought would be a routine matter threatened to destroy his business before it fairly got off the ground. He was denied the registration; incredibly, someone else had already invented and trademarked a product called Coca-Cola. This was cause for another Candler headache, a bona fide migraine.

It shouldn't have shocked Candler. By the mid-1880s, the coca leaf and kola nut were frequently mentioned in conjunction; it appeared inevitable that someone would put the two ingredients together. It is not too surprising, then, that two men not only had the same idea, but the same name.* A Paterson, New Jersey, druggist named Benjamin Kent had seen the 1883–1884 Frederick

---

* Indeed, in 1885, Sigmund Freud playfully inscribed one of his papers to Carl Koller, "To my good friend, Coca Koller."

Stearns catalog with parallel columns on coca and kola[*] and, inspired by the juxtaposition, named his new tonic Kent's Coca-Cola in late 1884, over a year before Frank Robinson named Pemberton's drink.

Like Pemberton's formula, Kent's Coca-Cola was imbibed mainly as a hangover remedy, the label, eerily similar to Pemberton's, calling the medicine "a panacea for all those tired, worn out, exhausted mental and physical conditions that require a frequent tonic." Unlike Pemberton's drink, however, Kent's contained not only caffeine and cocaine, but a healthy dollop of whiskey, euphemistically called "spirits of frumenty." The bitter syrup was taken with soda water and became quite popular in Paterson.

In 1888, Kent approached John Kerr, a Paterson lawyer, about registering his Coca-Cola as a trademark, which Kerr did on January 22, 1889. The application stated that Kent had used the trademark "continuously in the business since June 1, 1888." Kerr later testified that he advised Kent to use the 1888 date, since a U.S. trademark required that the article be sold outside the United States. Consequently, he had told Kent to sell his Coca-Cola through a friend in Canada, which he had accomplished in June of 1888. Due to this technicality, Atlanta's version of Coca-Cola was eventually given precedence. Pemberton had registered the Coca-Cola trademark a year earlier, on June 28, 1887, and in Interference Procedure No. 15,753, the Patent Office ruled that only the official dates given in the applications were relevant. In 1894, Candler quietly bought out Kent for $400, though the hopeful New Jersey druggist had asked for $10,000.

COCA-COLA TAKES OFF

With all major obstacles removed, properly incorporated, and duly trade-marked, Candler's Coca-Cola was poised for a period of phenomenal growth. From almost 20,000 gallons in 1891, sales shot up to 35,360 gallons in 1892, then (during a nationwide depression) to 48,427 in 1893, 64,333 in 1894, and 76,244 in 1895. All of this was accomplished with a tiny home office staff, never more than thirty in the first two decades of the Company. The key, as Candler and Robinson soon demonstrated, was advertising. In his first annual report, covering the ten months after incorporation in 1892, Candler reported that the firm had spent almost $22,500 on ingredients for Coca-Cola and over half of that amount ($11,400) on advertising. He commented that "we have done very considerable advertising in territory which has not as yet yielded any returns. We have reason to believe that it will show good returns during the ensuing year."

The majority of the advertising budget was spent on point-of-purchase signs, calendars, novelties, and newspaper ads, all of them prominently displaying the Coca-Cola script. Candler, who at first had misspelled his own product, became very touchy about the correct spelling of Coca-Cola—not

---

[*] See page 24.

coco-cola or cocoa-cola, it must also be capitalized and hyphenated.[*] His concern, while sometimes petulantly expressed, was justified, since variant spellings and lower-case usage would have made it easier for the drink to become a generic term open to any competitor.

The early ads were almost universally medicinal. Curiously, this was a turn away from Pemberton's first ad for Coca-Cola, which called it "Delicious and Refreshing." While the firm letterhead did proclaim that Coca-Cola was "Delicious, Refreshing, Exhilarating, Invigorating," Candler's early ads failed to use those adjectives. Instead, Coca-Cola was "Harmless, Wonderful, Efficient, Quick . . . Relieves Headache . . . Gives Prompt Rest." It was the "Ideal Brain Tonic and Sovereign Remedy for Headache and Nervousness. It makes the sad glad and the weak strong." Clearly, Candler believed in the drink's beneficial effects, even if he denied they were due to cocaine.

While the ads were primarily aimed at businessmen, a few addressed women: "The ladies are taking it right along. They find it relieves headaches and exhaustion, besides it's a tonic and a pleasant beverage." Another sought to attract smokers, who presumably could wash away that stale tobacco taste. Finally, Candler recognized that children, who could wheedle a nickel from their parents, were prime customers. An early trade card showed three small boys in sailor suits holding a sign proclaiming, "We drink Coca-Cola."

In 1894, free sample coupons were again issued. Over $7,000 in tickets was redeemed that year and the next, amounting to over 140,000 free drinks each year. Promising to bring in new business, a salesman would ask a dispenser for the names and addresses of a hundred regular customers. Then free tickets were mailed, along with a cover letter, timed to reach the potential consumer just as the fountain received its Coca-Cola order and a supply of point-of-purchase advertising. This system was an ingenious, effective way to build new outlets. It made it easy on the fountain owner, who could dispense free drinks and mount attractive posters to brighten his store. In addition, "premiums"—serving urns, scales, cabinets, cases, and clocks —were offered to encourage sales. All, of course, prominently displayed the Coca-Cola logo.

CANDLER AND SONS

As Candler started to make money from Coca-Cola, it was not reflected in his largess to his children. Like his father, he did not believe in spoiling his children, repeatedly stressing economy in letters to them at Emory College, then located in Oxford, Georgia. Ever the careful businessman, Candler kept a running account of every cent his son Howard spent. In 1894, apparently in response to his son's request for money, Candler wrote out a balance sheet showing Howard's expenses, including 10 cents for bananas and 25 cents for a

---

[*] Candler was equally irritated when his own name was misspelled Chandler. As his fame spread and ego inflated, Candler refused even to open mail which spelled his name incorrectly.

toothbrush. Underlining the balance of $15.40 in red, the strict father told his son that he *should* have that much money left.

At the same time, Candler exerted enormous pressure on his children to excel. "My boy, you cannot know how anxious I am about you," he wrote to Howard in 1894. "I do so greatly desire your *Success*. I hope you will *fully* appreciate . . . my efforts to aid and care for you . . . [so] as to improve your *chances*. I expect you to be first in your class." Candler made it clear that he expected Godliness to accompany Success; many of his letters resembled sermons: "Don't be religious in word only, but in your life . . . Let your life constantly *exhibit Christ*. We live for Him."

Asa Candler was capable, however, of jumping from the most sentimental platitudes to hard-nosed business matters, in the next sentence asking Howard to help with the local Coca-Cola business: "I am sending by Express today . . . some advertising matter for your careful distribution to the fountains in Oxford." He also asked Howard to look into "empty bottle troubles" and to spy on a druggist he suspected of offering Wine Coca in place of Coca-Cola.

GOING NATIONWIDE

While not the best child-rearing traits, Candler's obsessions with detail, frugality, and achievement worked well for Coca-Cola. So did its location in Atlanta, the center of a web of rails carrying the recycled whiskey barrels full of sweet syrup across the country. By the end of 1895, Candler could proudly report to his stockholders that "Coca-Cola is now sold and drunk in every state and territory in the United States." In the four years since incorporation, the company had achieved nationwide distribution, even though the vast majority of sales were still concentrated in the South. "The great American Eagle—that discriminating bird of freedom—is passionately fond of Coca-Cola," *The Coca-Cola News* proclaimed, "because Coca-Cola has become a National drink."

A close look at 1895 company finances reveals how money was spent and made. Candler paid $44,247 for the ingredients of the 76,244 gallons of syrup he sold—58 cents per gallon, or less than half a cent per drink. At the same time, he spent $17,744 on advertising (23.3 cents per gallon) and $12,054 on "expense, discount & interest." That last figure included salaries, which were, as Howard Candler later admitted, "moderate and in some instances inadequate."

If Candler could have effectively retailed his drink directly to consumers, his profits would have been incredible, since his total disbursements came to just under $1 for a gallon of syrup selling for $6.40 (128 drinks at a nickel apiece). Rather than expand his work and sales force, however, he chose to spread the profit among distributors and fountain owners, who would sell for him. In each territory, he sought out jobbers (usually candy or drug wholesalers) with whom he could set up a long-term, trusting relationship. He sold the syrup to them at an average cost of $1.29 per gallon in 1895, leaving himself a profit of 30 cents a gallon and allowing a whopping markup for both jobber and retailers. That smaller profit margin translated into huge influxes of cash as the total gallonage sales rose steadily. By the beginning of 1896, the Company had a surplus cash war-chest of almost $50,000.

By the end of that year, the Company needed new quarters, and there was plenty of money to build them. In 1893, to the relief of the pawnshop and saloon, Coca-Cola had moved to larger rented space at Ivy and Auburn Avenue, where a 100-gallon copper kettle replaced the old 40-gallon affair, and a 1,500-gallon holding tank was installed. But this space was also soon inadequate. Thus, at the December 9, 1896, annual meeting, $10,000 was allocated to buy a lot and begin construction.

The pulse of Coca-Cola beat faster with every year, as an 1896 jingle asserted: "Stronger! stronger! grow they all, / Who for Coca-Cola call. / Brighter! brighter! thinkers think, / When they Coca-Cola drink." While others might grow stronger from the beverage, however, Asa Candler was on the verge of a complete mental and physical collapse. He had overworked himself to the point of exhaustion, and even repeated glasses of Coca-Cola were not having the desired effect. Consequently, the annual report recorded that "the President was requested to take an extended vacation during the year 1897."

"AS LONG AS SIN ABOUNDS"

Another sign of the company's coming-of-age that year was the need for lawyers. Candler had complained of "bogus substitutes" in his 1894 annual report. As Coca-Cola's success grew, so did its hangers-on. As a prelude to a century of court battles, in 1896 "the President was requested to consult an Attorney in reference to the advisability of bringing a suit, or suits, against parties who are selling substitutes for . . . COCA-COLA." It is, of course, ironic that the makers of Coca-Cola should have been so self-righteous about *ersatz* colas when their drink was derived from a Vin Mariani clone.

The host of imitators was led by J. C. Mayfield, who had re-incorporated the Pemberton Medicine Company as the Wine Coca Company in 1894. After trying Yum Yum and Koke, he now reverted to Pemberton's well-known Wine Coca, but he modified it to copy Coca-Cola, so that Howard Candler identified it as the "deceitful" product which "cut most seriously into our business." Through the years, Mayfield would continue to be a thorn in the Company's side and would later play a crucial role in its history.

Mayfield's wife, now divorced and remarried, also made a career out of selling Coca-Cola substitutes, calling herself Diva Brown and marketing My-Coca. She too claimed to have Pemberton's recipe, though her ex-husband disputed it. In fact, he complained that she had tried to steal *his* formula. Diva Brown was "demented," according to Mayfield, although she had "rational intervals" during which she was "very grasping," demanding his copy of the Coca-Cola formula. When he refused, she threatened to kill him, unsuccessfully trying to carry out her threat on several occasions. Demented or not, Diva Brown, "the Original Coca-Cola Woman," was shrewd and determined, portraying herself on her bottle labels as a pleasant-looking woman with short, dark hair. She sniffed righteously at the numerous frauds on the market: "I have seen dozens of formulas purporting to be mine, which were not even similar."

Candler had to contend not only with these fake Coca-Cola products, but with the dilution of his own syrup. Since one universal characteristic of the imitation syrups was their lower price, it was tempting for drugstore owners to add the cheaper syrup to the real thing, hoping no one would know the difference. At the turn of the century, Candler commented on diluters and frauds: "We have them all over the country, and will have them, as long as sin abounds—where they adulterate good things." He must have been pleased when a prominent trade journal editor responded to an 1899 request for the Coca-Cola formula by protesting, "I do not know the formula, or anything near it. It has defied all attempts at imitation. Even if it could be done you could not get the result."

THE TRANSITION FROM MEDICINE TO BEVERAGE

In 1895, Frank Robinson told Asa Candler that women and other consumers frequently wrote to object to the medicinal image of Coca-Cola. They didn't want to feel guilty for taking doses of a medicine when all they wanted was a bracing soft drink. Prompted by these complaints, Robinson made a brilliant tactical move with Coca-Cola advertising. He realized that there was more future in Coca-Cola as refreshment than medicine. After all, everyone got thirsty. As Robinson put it, "We found that we were advertising to the few when we ought to advertise to the masses." By promoting Coca-Cola as a beverage, they reached thousands rather than "one man in a hundred."

Consequently, he published more ads that simply said, "Drink Coca-Cola. Delicious and Refreshing." Instinctively, Robinson understood that the older ads were too long and too negative. With a larger budget, he flooded the market with his succinct message, not only in newspaper ads, but with posters, streetcar signs, calendars, serving trays, thermometers, clocks, pencils, book-marks for schoolchildren, and glass plates for fountains. By 1898, Robinson was distributing over a million items per year.

Since 1891, the annual Coca-Cola calendar had featured attractive young women. Appealing but suitably modest, the "Coca-Cola girls" would stir male fantasies for years to come. The Company's Philadelphia lithographer made an annual pilgrimage to Atlanta with posters displaying a new crop of young beauties. With a salacious twinkle in his eyes, Robinson would select a likely candidate, saying, "I think Mr. Asa will like this one." By the turn of the century, the Company pioneered celebrity endorsements from actress Hilda Clark, a soft-featured blonde singer, and the more imposing opera star Lillian Nordica.

The advent of the Spanish-American War indirectly gave the Company more reason to shy away from medicinal claims. In 1898, Congress passed a special war tax on proprietary medicines, but not on beverages. The

Commissioner of Internal Revenue ruled that Coca-Cola was a drug, not a drink, and ordered the Company to pay the tax. Furious, Candler sued the government. The case dragged on until 1902, when it was finally decided in Coca-Cola's favor, but it marked the beginning of Candler's disaffection with the U.S. government.

The Company did not abandon medicinal claims altogether, however. The 1899 Hilda Clark calendar stressed the "delicious and refreshing" qualities of the drink, but it also maintained that Coca-Cola "relieves mental and physical exhaustion" and "cures headache." About 10 percent of the ads in 1899 still talked about headache relief and benefits for brain workers, while others emphasized the use of the coca leaf by Andeans and the kola nut by Africans. But an important corner had been turned, and the future of the entire enterprise hung in the balance. If Robinson had not promoted Coca-Cola as a socially acceptable drink, imbibed by the best people, it is likely that the patent medicine would not have survived the early part of the twentieth century, which saw a dramatic backlash against such nostrums.

GROWING AND BRANCHING OUT

As a new century loomed, the well-honed young company fizzed with profits and enthusiasm for the future. Despite the pending government suit and the omnipresent imitators, Candler's annual reports sounded as self-satisfied as the dour little man ever became. "Prosperity has been with the Company during the year just closed," he wrote in January of 1899. "At this rate of increase," reported *The Coca-Cola News*, "how long will it be before enough Coca-Cola will be sold in one year to make a river as large as the Mississippi?"

Candler had opened branch offices and syrup factories in Dallas (1894), Chicago (1895), Los Angeles (1895), Philadelphia (1897), and plans were under way for an office in New York (1899). Whenever possible, Candler sent nephews to assume command of these branches. Dan Candler ruled in Dallas, Sam Candler in Los Angeles, Sam Willard in Philadelphia. Yet another nephew, Sam Dobbs, had worked as a salesman since 1888 and now served as a clerk and bookkeeper in the main office. As his sons reached maturity, Candler sent them to branches as well—Asa Jr took over in California, and Howard went to New York. At the same time, he was looking beyond U.S. borders. In his 1897 annual report, he noted that the drink was being sold in Canada and Hawaii, with an eye toward Mexico. "We are firmly convinced," he wrote, "that wherever there are people and soda fountains, Coca-Cola will, by its now universally acknowledged merit, win its way quickly to the front of popularity."

To encourage his jobbers, Candler had instituted a rebate plan in 1897, so that the more Coca-Cola a dealer sold during the year, the more he would get back as a bonus. While the list price was $1.50 per gallon, there was a nickel rebate for every hundred gallons sold, up to a maximum of 25 cents for 2,000 or more gallons. "At the close of his business year," Candler said, "when actual results are still somewhat in doubt, it greatly enthuses a dealer when we hand him a [rebate] check," causing him to increase his sales efforts the following year.

COCA-COLA MEN

By 1899, fifteen Coca-Cola drummers rode the country's rails, pushing the drink as early as February. Most salesmen bought cotton during the winter, since selling soft drinks was still a seasonal occupation. Nonetheless, they thought of themselves as Coca-Cola men, a distinctive breed. Before they were sent out on the road, Asa Candler fully indoctrinated them into the religion of Coca-Cola, often having them work in the manufacturing department briefly, and stressing the purity of the ingredients, the sanctity of the secret formula, the extraordinary qualities of the product.

When Asa Candler believed in something, he often reacted with extreme emotion. A fundamentalist Methodist, he would get so worked up at revival meetings that, according to his son, he would become physically ill. "His eyes would shine, his body become tense, and his whole being pulse with . . . exhilaration." Candler communicated this kind of fervor for his product to his impressionable salesmen. Howard commented that his father had "an almost mystical faith" in Coca-Cola. A small man, Candler also had a bit of a Napoleon complex. He delighted in wearing his elaborate uniform for the Georgia Horse Guard, and he continually exhorted his children and salesmen to be *men*. While Candler was "in no way . . . an imposing person physically," his son wrote, "his anger and impatience could, on occasions, be monumental." None of his employees cared to cross him.

There were many temptations for young drummers on the road, spawning the innumerable jokes about traveling salesmen, farmers' daughters, and the like. Asa Candler was determined that his salesmen would be enthusiastic, morally upright representatives for Coca-Cola, and he kept tabs on them as much as possible. He wrote to reprimand one salesman, for instance, because "you have been on *sprees* to the detriment of The Coca-Cola Company's good name." By 1898, Candler reported with satisfaction that "our salesmen have become known every where in this Union as gentlemen in every respect, and have not only maintained the good name of the Corporation, but have succeeded in making Coca-Cola a familiar and gracious name in all the land."

Candler convinced Coca-Cola men that "theirs was the greatest product and the greatest company on the face of the earth," as his son recalled. Because of their deep belief, these proselytes were motivated to overcome every obstacle. Like the early Christians, Candler's salesmen often faced hostility, rumor, and indifference—and, like those early martyrs, they maintained their faith against all odds.

HOWARD HITS THE ROAD

One of Candler's drummers in 1899 was his twenty-year-old son Howard, on summer vacation from medical school and armed with a letter of introduction from his Uncle Warren, by then a Methodist bishop and president of Emory University, to the Governor of Missouri, the cleric's close personal friend. Asa wrote frequently to his son on the road; the letters paint a revealing portrait of the business as a new century loomed. Many are concerned with petty details, worrying over "substitutes and frauds," emphasizing thrift and caution, and advising how to handle local businessmen. The overall impression, however, is that the Coca-Cola boom nearly overwhelmed a frantic Asa Candler, who struggled to coordinate his increasingly national enterprise.

April 13, 1899: I am just as busy as it is possible for me to be . . . God bless my "Wandering Boy."

April 19, 1899: We are very busy here. It takes every moment of our time looking after traveling men. We now have 12 working from this office. Bradley leaves tomorrow. We will go into Ohio & Indiana . . . I hope you remained in Wichita long enough to do business that ought to be done there and to let us catch up with you.

May 6, 1899: You are making a fine record in business . . . We are 5000 gallons behind with orders, notwithstanding we are turning out above 3000 gallons [of] goods daily.

May 8, 1899: Demand for goods has been in excess of our ability to supply since about the 20th of April.

May 9, 1899: There is so much territory and so few of you men to work it that it seems imperative that we do a little work in a great many places.

May 12, 1899: Sales averaging 2000 gallons daily of which Atlanta does about 1000.

May 19, 1899: We are now throwing men into various large Western cities where there seems to be fine opportunity for work.

June 13, 1899: Our business this week is simply immense.

June 19, 1899: We have so much territory that must be looked after within the next 60 days that we can't give to any territory as much time even of one man as that territory seems to deserve . . . We are inclined to furnish you with all the material, both of Coca-Cola and advertising matter that you need . . . and would prefer that you have a surplus than that you should have none.

As the summer wore on, Howard Candler proved to be the best salesman of the lot. In August, his father wrote him a thoughtful letter of praise in which he pondered the future. Could things really go on like this indefinitely? The letter also revealed Candler's inner doubts about the ultimate worthiness of his enterprise, despite the missionary zeal with which he sent out his salesmen:

August 10, 1899: I feel quite proud of your summer campaign . . . I don't know whether I can let you be a doctor or not. If I felt sure that this business would hold out perpetually, I believe I would resign to give you the place. But my boy I can't take such risk on your future. I have no right to limit your usefulness to the narrow compass of a 5 *cent* Soda Fountain Beverage. You are capable of grander achievements . . .

Candler needn't have worried. Howard quit medical school of his own volition the next year.

ON THE EVE OF THE TWENTIETH CENTURY

On December 28, 1899, about twenty people met at 10 A.M. in the Atlanta headquarters. For the first time, all of the salesmen, branch managers, and home office personnel assembled in one place. Other "intimate and helpful friends" were also invited to give advice. Probably half of those present were related to Asa Candler. They talked for four hours.

We do not have the minutes from that historic meeting, only days away from the new century, but we can reconstruct a scenario. First, Asa Candler outlined the firm's financial position. "Few corporations can show a more satisfactory financial condition,"[*] he began, pointing out that sales had exceeded 280,000 gallons of syrup for the year. "That's almost 36 million drinks of Coca-Cola that we sold this year, gentlemen. We have over $200,000 in cash, and we own real estate worth some $50,000. We have accomplished this while spending over $48,000 this past year on advertising, $38,000 in rebates, and $11,000 in extorted taxes for war revenue. I should add that we hope to get those unjustified taxes back and have gone to court to do so."

Candler expressed particular satisfaction that February volume (over 11,000 gallons) demonstrated the drink's growing winter strength. He summarized the activity around the country, then announced that he had just hired a man in Havana, recently liberated from Spanish rule. This new Coca-Cola man would build the fountain business in Cuba and Puerto Rico. Already, over a thousand gallons had been sold on the islands. After a round of applause, Frank Robinson quietly displayed the new advertising for the year, explaining how the outside signs would be mounted, how many complimentary tickets would be disbursed, and why they were keeping Hilda Clark on the calendar for a second year.

The meeting was then thrown open to general comment. After an initial awkward silence, people began to talk about their daily concerns. The branch officers wanted more responsibility; the home office wanted the branches to be more profitable, particularly the New York and Los Angeles outlets, which were losing money. The traveling salesmen wanted better direction; Asa might tell them one thing, Frank Robinson another, and Sam Dobbs something else. Sometimes the home office was too busy, and no one told them anything. This matter was resolved when Asa declared that Sam Dobbs would be responsible for the sales force, allowing Frank Robinson to concentrate on advertising.

Then there was the cocaine issue. Everywhere they went, the salesmen were encountering more and more rumors about how Coca-Cola led to cocaine addiction. Even the temperance women, who should have been on Coca-Cola's

---

[*] This is actually a quote from the 1899 annual report, issued on January 11, 1900. The following scene is based primarily on this annual report.

side, were turning against the drink. Finally, someone asked the heretical questions: "Couldn't we just take out the cocaine? Does it really make that much difference?"

The room hushed as Asa Candler tapped his fingers on the desk. Finally, he spoke. "So you want me to change the formula of the country's favorite beverage because of some hysterical women? Do you really want us to change Coca-Cola, the purest, most healthful drink the world has ever seen?" His voice rose higher and cracked as he began to shout, "Never! There is *nothing* wrong with Coca-Cola." He took a deep breath and continued, more calmly. "If there was anything the matter with it, do you think we would have such a problem keeping everyone supplied with it? No, Coca-Cola has been good to me, and I will not change it. That's the end of this discussion."

When the meeting adjourned, the group enjoyed a catered dinner in the Coca-Cola building, with boxes of chocolate from Nunnally's passed out to everyone. The employees were surprised at the sumptuous spread, since it was common knowledge that Asa Candler never spent a dime he didn't have to. The company must have been doing very well, indeed.

AN OMISSION

There was one item of business that appeared too trivial to mention at this meeting. Back in July, two Tennessee lawyers had come to Atlanta to see Asa Candler about a business proposition. They wanted to bottle Coca-Cola.

～ 5 ～

Bottle It: The World's Stupidest, Smartest Contract

Yes, these early bottlers of Coca-Cola have been a hardy, a rugged, and a determined lot . . . They had the faith, and the courage, and the dedication, and the determination to lay the road, build the bridges and weather the storms, and solve the problems that have brought this business to the position of eminence which it enjoys today.
—Lee Talley, President, The Coca-Cola Company, 1959

"Ben," he said, "I wonder how they happened to get together all the dumb sonsuvbitches in the world and put 'em in this goddam bottling business."
—*Big Beverage,* by William T. Campbell

BENJAMIN FRANKLIN THOMAS, a lawyer and businessman, came to Chattanooga, Tennessee, in 1887, attracted by the little town where the "drive to make money . . . almost permeated the . . . air," as one historian put it. Not content with a simple practice, Thomas had already operated a stone quarry, hosiery mill, and paving brick company, as well as selling Sofas, a patent medicine whose key ingredient was baking soda. Still, he wasn't satisfied. Sam Erwin, a friend at his boardinghouse, recalled how Thomas "used to come in every few days with a new scheme to make a million dollars."

When the U.S. went to war with Spain in 1898, Thomas became a clerk in a Cuban commissary, where he was impressed by the popularity of a carbonated pineapple drink called Piña Frio. Upon his return to Chattanooga the following year, he decided that perhaps his fortune lay in bottling the popular soda fountain drink, Coca-Cola. When Thomas told his fellow boarders his latest plan, Sam Erwin laughed at him as usual, but said that he actually might help with this one, since it happened that Asa Candler was Erwin's first cousin. He soon arranged an introduction for the eager lawyer.

Although Candler didn't appear interested, Thomas repeatedly took the short train trip to Atlanta to talk with the Coca-Cola magnate, all to no avail. Thomas decided he needed a partner to convince Candler that he was serious. Sam Erwin, his first choice, wasn't interested in his friend's cockeyed idea. Finally, after much discussion. Thomas persuaded another boardinghouse friend and fellow lawyer, Joseph Brown Whitehead, to join him in the tentative venture. Both men enjoyed baseball, and Thomas painted a glowing picture of the potential bottled soft drink sales at double-headers. He also noted that the soda fountain drinks they brought back to their offices went flat while they talked to clients. "Wouldn't it be great if a fellow could put this stuff in a bottle and stop it up so the gas wouldn't get away, and he could drink it whenever he wanted?"

Armed with a few samples of bottled Coca-Cola, the two men met with a harried Asa Candler in mid-July 1899. He was annoyed to find Thomas pestering him again. In addition, he wasn't particularly impressed with anyone from Chattanooga, which he considered a hick town. "I went up there once to bring back a fugitive nigger," Candler later said, "and I didn't think there was anything up there." His initial impression of Thomas and Whitehead must not have been favorable either. Thomas, thirty-eight, was a heavyset man with a florid, sweaty face. Whitehead, though a few years younger, walked with a pronounced waddle, carrying nearly 200 pounds on his 5'4" frame.

Besides, Candler was wary of the bottling business; he remembered that Woolfolk Walker had already bottled Coca-Cola briefly back in 1888, and that the product had been, to use nephew Sam Dobbs' term, "putrid." At that time, Candler had vehemently forbidden Dobbs to sell Coca-Cola in bottles. He already had enough problems defending his drink without allowing the promotion of an inferior product. Mostly, though, he was simply too busy to think about bottling Coca-Cola. As he recounted the conversation years later, Candler told them, "Gentlemen, I don't think we want to have it bottled; we can't handle it ourselves; there's too much detail about the bottling business." In summary, Candler said he had "neither the money, nor time, nor brains, to embark in the bottling business, and there are too many folks, who are not responsible, who care nothing about the reputation of what they put up, and I am afraid the name will be injured."

While Thomas and Whitehead may not have been impressive at first, they were born salesmen, friendly and jovial. They listened to everything Candler said, nodding with understanding. Then, speaking easily and well, they described their plans, assuring Candler that they would maintain the purity and integrity of Coca-Cola, no doubt making it the best-known bottled drink in the United States, the same way that he, Candler, had so brilliantly made it the most famous soda fountain drink. Warming to their subject, the men concluded with a sincere burst worthy of their best courtroom oratory: "We promise and guarantee to you, Mr Candler, that in all the business we do in the bottling of Coca-Cola, we will make the name better every day we conduct this business." They weren't trying to rush him, though; he should take the matter under advisement, sample their bottled product and think it over. They would be in town a few days.

Candler, his ego flattered and interest piqued, visibly softened. He had to admit that Thomas was persistent, a good trait for a Coca-Cola man. "That's a big contract you have taken on your hands; I have already spent all the money I have trying to make it respectable." He told them he would have to look into their backgrounds and would let them know his decision in a few days. In the meantime, they should prepare a suitable contract.

Candler must have been pleased that both men were lawyers; he was increasingly coming to rely on men of their profession. Thomas also had a varied entrepreneurial background, including experience with patent medi-cines. With satisfaction, Candler noted that Whitehead's father was a Baptist minister; hopefully, Whitehead would bring a religous fervor to the Coca-Cola business. In addition, it didn't hurt that he specialized in tax law, in light of the pending litigation over the war tax. Finally, Whitehead, too, was already involved in patent medicines as the vice-president of the New Spencer Medicine Company.

GIVING AWAY THE BOTTLING RIGHTS

On July 21, 1899, Asa Candler called the men back into his office to approve their plan. Casually, the partners handed him the 600-word contract they had prepared and signed. After carefully reading it over, Candler also signed the document. Clearly relieved, Thomas and Whitehead assured Candler that he would not regret it and turned to go before he changed his mind. Candler called after them: "If you boys fail in this undertaking, don't come back to cry on my shoulder, because I have very little confidence in this bottling business."

Candler must have felt he had everything to gain and nothing to lose under the contract's terms. It bound the bottlers to use only Coca-Cola syrup, banning any substitutes, and it expressly excluded the soda fountain business, which would remain the sole province of The Coca-Cola Company. In addition, the contract specified that if the bottlers failed to "supply the demand in all territory embraced in this agreement," the contract would be forfeited. It is little wonder that Candler had told them they had a "big contract" on their hands. The territory included almost the entire United States, excluding only New England (held by Seth Fowle & Sons, though they never bottled there) and Texas and Mississippi, where noncontract business-men were already putting the drink in bottles.

If Thomas and Whitehead succeeded, Candler stood to sell more syrup. If they failed, he would not have put up any capital or had to spend time on the fruitless venture. Why not let them have a go at it? He agreed to sell them syrup at $1 a gallon and to provide their advertising needs. Candler was right that the contract would result in his selling more syrup, though he obviously didn't realize the enormous implications. This simple contract was to revolutionize the Coca-Cola business, giving birth to one of the most innovative, dynamic franchising systems in the world.

At the same time, however, it virtually assured conflict within the Coca-Cola family of the future. Candler set no term on his contract. As long as Thomas and Whitehead fulfilled their end of the deal, it was permanent, and they could pass it along to the bottling companies they created.[*] In addition,

---

[*] In later years, Candler denied that he intended it to be a permanent contract. Only months earlier, when Seth A. Fowle had suggested that his twenty-year contract be made perpetual, Candler responded that "the laws of Georgia would not permit us to give you the extension of terms that you wish."

the agreement did not include a provision for modifying the price of syrup, should the cost of ingredients increase. These two jokers in the contract would haunt The Coca-Cola Company in the next century, resulting in numerous lawsuits.

Coca-Cola folklore relates that an anonymous tipster offered to give Candler invaluable advice in return for an unspecified sum. After Candler paid, the informant leaned over and whispered two words in his ear: "Bottle it." The story is, of course, pure fiction. In fact, no money changed hands when the contract was signed. Candler literally gave away the bottling rights. Subsequent histories say that a token dollar was exchanged, but there is no mention of it in the contract. In the years to come, The Coca-Cola Company would pay millions of dollars to buy back piecemeal what Candler so casually signed away for nothing. At the time, however, Candler did not regard the contract as worthy of note. On the same day he signed it, he wrote a letter to his son Howard, talking mostly about how to sell special fountain glasses for Coca-Cola. He did not mention the two Chattanoogans or their bottling deal.

BOTTLING AT THE TURN OF THE CENTURY

Coca-Cola historians have treated the subsequent success of the Thomas/ Whitehead venture as if it were the real genesis of bottled soft drinks. On the contrary, the bottling business was booming even as Pemberton first experimented with Coca-Cola in 1885. In that year, one bottler was interviewed at his factory, a "wilderness of bottles and machinery," revealing a snapshot of the contemporary industry. "Ten years ago I did a large business," said the bottler, "but my customers were exclusively saloons. Now my trade is five times larger, but nine-tenths of it are groceries and private families." He produced root beer, sarsaparilla, ginger ale, raspberry, pop, mead, and plain beer—in descending order of popularity. Sometimes the extracts underwent "some funny change and taste horrible," the bottler complained. "Raspberry and pop are affected by sunlight, and their flavor changes to that of turpentine."

The "raspberry" went bad because it had no raspberry in it, but cheap chemical ethers. The main reason the bottler had such trouble, however, was the uncertain seal, a problem widely recognized within the industry, resulting in a scramble to patent a better stopper. The *National Bottlers' Gazette*, a trade magazine, portrayed an amazing array of fifty stopper designs for patents issued in 1885, all purporting to solve the problem. The devices usually featured elaborate wire-and-cork contraptions, although a few elegant designs used internal balls, held in place by the pressure of the carbonation.

The industry standard throughout the late 1880s was the Hutchinson stopper, a cumbersome, unpredictable seal with an internal rubber disk pulled up into place by a wire loop. To open the bottle, a consumer knocked the loop down, releasing the pressure with a sudden "pop," which gave soda pop its name. The Hutchinson stopper was relatively inexpensive, but workers or consumers often jarred the loop accidentally, spilling the bottle's sticky contents. In addition, the Hutchinson bottles were difficult to clean because of their internal mechanism, and the acidified drinks ate away at the rubber gasket.

Nonetheless, by 1890, over 3,000 American bottlers used Hutchinson stoppers. With an industry that large, the question isn't why two lawyers got the notion to bottle Coca-Cola in 1899, but why no one had thought of it sooner. In fact, they had. Sam Dobbs remembered that there were at least a dozen pre-1899 Coca-Cola bottlers in Florida, Colorado, Georgia, South Carolina, Texas, Mississippi, and New England. Two of those pre-1899 bottlers successfully continued into the twentieth century. Joe Biedenharn, a Vicksburg, Mississippi, candy manufacturer with a sideline in bottled pop, was one of the early jobbers for Coca-Cola syrup, which sold well at the city's soda fountains. Biedenharn was convinced that it would do equally well in rural areas, which had no fountains. Consequently, in 1894, he began bottling carbonated Coca-Cola for sale to the country trade. As a courtesy, he sent one of the first cases to Asa Candler, who wrote back that it was "fine," and thought no more about it. The Biedenharn brothers—all seven of them—created a Coca-Cola bottling dynasty. Similarly, the Valdosta Bottling Works of Valdosta, Georgia, started selling bottled Coca-Cola in 1897. Describing their early Coca-Cola experience, a partner said that the Hutchinson bottles caused trouble: "The rubber washer on the stopper caused a not-too-wholesome odor in the drink after it had been bottled for a period of ten days . . ."

In April of 1892, at exactly the same time as The Coca-Cola Company, the Crown Cork and Seal Company was incorporated. Though the crimped crown bottle cap solved all of the Hutchinson problems, its acceptance was glacially slow, since it required a new stock of bottles and a special machine to attach the crown caps. By 1900, however, the change was well under way. Thomas and Whitehead were entering the business at the right time. Other innovations in the next few years made mass-produced bottled soft drinks an increasingly attractive field.

CARVING UP THE U.S.

Thomas and Whitehead wasted no time in setting up their first plant in Chattanooga. Bottling in that era was a dangerous, makeshift affair which necessitated face masks and heavy gauntlets. The foot-powered machines allowed only one bottle to be capped at a time. Recycled bottles were hand-washed, with metal shot shaken inside in a vain attempt to flush out the accumulated crud. The ten-gallon syrup keg was hoisted aloft so that syrup could flow into bottles by gravity, but the hose often came loose, with sticky results. It is little wonder that Thomas and Whitehead quickly decided to leave the actual bottling to others.

On November 12, 1899, they placed their first small ad in the *Chattanooga*

Times: "Drink a *bottle* of Coca-Cola, five cents at all stands, grocers and saloons." The ad may have been short, but it spoke volumes for the future of the drink. The "stands, grocers and saloons" were revolutionary new outlets for Coca-Cola, allowing the drink to reach a completely different class of consumer. At the time, no one in Chattanooga paid much attention. An article running adjacent to that first ad carried a detailed account of business activity in town, including a section on various new companies and their products. The bottling concern wasn't even mentioned. The partners officially incorporated as the Coca-Cola Bottling Company on December 9, 1899.

Within a year, the partnership shattered. Thomas and Whitehead disagreed about almost everything except the desirability of bottling the soft drink. Thomas wanted to use brown bottles, while Whitehead favored clear or light green. Thomas thought each bottle should contain eight ounces; Whitehead opted for a little over six ounces. But the more serious conflict began when the time came to execute additional contracts with other bottlers. Thomas believed in two-year contracts so that he could replace a poor bottler if there were problems. Whitehead wanted to give permanent contracts to reinforce loyalty and enthusiasm. Finally, the two men agreed to split their territory. To assure an equitable division, Whitehead created the two territories, while Thomas chose the one he wanted. He must have enjoyed a challenge, because he picked the heavily populated Eastern seaboard and the West Coast, in addition to Chattanooga and a fifty-mile radius around it. That left Whitehead with the Coca-Cola heartland of the South, plus much of the West.

Whitehead may have had the prime territory, but he had no money. Looking for capital, he found J. T. Lupton, who had married into the wealthy Patten family, owners of the Chattanooga Medicine Company. Lupton had given up his law practice to join the family business, helping the Pattens market their two popular proprietary medicines, Wine of Cardui and Black Draught. Lupton saw the future in bottled Coca-Cola and agreed to back Whitehead in return for half interest in his territory, paying him $2,500. Whitehead relocated to Atlanta and incorporated The Coca-Cola Bottling Company, using a capital T to differentiate his company from the Chattanooga concern. Since this led to inevitable confusion, the two firms were more commonly called the Thomas Company and the Southeastern Parent Bottler.

It was obvious from the beginning that neither concern had the money or manpower to open bottling plants all over the United States. Instead, both companies began looking for prospective bottlers with a little money and a lot of hustle. In those days, it cost a bit over $2,000 to buy the necessary bottling equipment, which included a carbonator, bottling table, washing machine, settling tanks, washing tubs, bottles, and cases. In addition, a horse and wagon were recommended, as well as $2,000 working capital. Thomas and Whitehead signed contracts with these bottlers to sell them syrup and provide an expert bottler, caps, and advertising. In return, they would garner half of the plant's profits. Consequently, the Thomas and Whitehead/Lupton firms became known as the "parent bottlers," while the manufacturing plants were called the "actual" or "first-line" bottlers.[*]

Whitehead ran the day-to-day side of his operation, aided by his young bookkeeper, Charles Veazey Rainwater. As his guardian angel, Lupton supplied about half of the start-up capital for most bottlers. Even with his help, however, a substantial number of early bottlers failed, and the partners had to find someone else to take over the territory, portraying a glorious future that, at the time, seemed highly unlikely. To induce the "right man" to tackle the business, Lupton would explain that, "while the business was new, the beverage was new, yet it was rapidly acquiring a good standing with the public, and that in the years to come there would be a large profit to be made out of it."

Lupton was right, particularly with regard to himself. Because he wound up with a substantial investment in most of the bottling plants, he raked in fantastic amounts of money in the next few years, making him the wealthiest man in Chattanooga. "His entire business life," Sam Dobbs later noted cynically, "has been spent in getting all that he could put his hands on. In a great many bottling plants, he has demanded certain interests for which he paid nothing and then as fast as they were able to make a little money he insisted on dividends." In addition, Lupton installed many of his innumerable relations as bottlers all over the Whitehead/Lupton territory. They too became wealthy, establishing the Lupton name as a fixture in the Coca-Cola bottling firmament.

Ben Thomas didn't have the Lupton resources and had more difficulty contracting bottlers, but he was also to become a wealthy man. In the process, he and Lupton transformed Chattanooga into as much of a Coca-Cola town as Atlanta. In seeking bottlers, Thomas often relied on city acquaintances, later joking that he had single-handedly depopulated Chattanooga of its young men.

Like Whitehead, Thomas had a difficult time finding and keeping bottlers, particularly in the northern territories. His contract specified that bottlers should only use crown caps and should handle Coca-Cola exclusively, giving up other soft drinks. But he really couldn't stick to those provisions and was forced to grant contracts to veterans who kept using their Hutchinsons and pushing their old line of flavors. Many of these older bottlers were men of limited vision and capital, putting out a shoddy fruit drink on a seasonal basis for the local market. In *Big Beverage*, a thinly fictionalized narrative of the early days of Coca-Cola bottling, William T. Campbell portrayed one such bottler, Pop Butts, a Coca-Cola millionaire despite himself. Butts resented the

---

[*] As time went by, and the business grew larger, other parent bottlers split off from the original two. In 1903, Texas and the Indian territories were ceded to Whitehead/Lupton, who incorporated what became known as "the 1903 Company," or the Southwestern parent bottler. In 1905, the Western parent bottler, headquartered in Chicago and covering a huge area, was split from the Whitehead/Lupton territory. In 1912, the Seth Fowle contract in New England expired, allowing bottling franchises to begin in New England, where the New England parent bottler was formed in 1916. Finally, in 1924, the Pacific Coast parent bottler was split off from the Thomas Company.

incursion of Coca-Cola on his own drinks. He *knew* what was in his own mix, while the mysterious syrup from Atlanta came ready-made in barrels. Besides, he objected to the higher price of Coca-Cola, which ran nearly twice what it cost him to produce his own drinks.

Describing Butts and his kind, a *Big Beverage* salesman gives one intriguing explanation for Candler's doubts about bottling:

> Those are the kind of men who got the Coca-Cola franchises—little guys that thought little, and still think little . . . They were the only ones Thomas and Whitehead could get—*they didn't know any better!* Mr Candler told me that he couldn't find a real business man who would even consider bottling Coca-Cola, and he was afraid the pop bottlers would ruin his product. That's why he waited over ten years before he let the bottle franchise. He knew the average druggist was sanitary and careful, but he was scared to death of the pop bottler.

While there were many who resembled Pop Butts in the early industry, there were an equal number of bright men who saw the future in Coca-Cola and fought hard for their franchise. Even for them, it was not an easy task. Take, for instance, the cases of William Heck and Arthur Pratt.

HECK AND PRATT: GERMAN TURNCOAT AND CONVERTED SINNER

Thomas had high hopes for the Nashville trade, telling Candler in 1900 that William Heck was a "sober, honest, hard-working, economical German who has had a long experience in the bottling business." Based on that experience, Heck insisted on using an eight-ounce bottle, even though Candler and Whitehead wanted a six-ounce size. Thomas supported him, pointing out that soda pop was "almost universally" sold in eight-ounce bottles. While White-head might be content with a smaller bottle in Atlanta, where demand for Coca-Cola was higher, Thomas and Heck were dealing with a highly competitive situation. They were not primarily trying to sell to the "high-class" establishments where dainty sips would do. Many of their consumers were blacks, who demanded volume. "We have a customer—a firm composed of two negros who run a barber shop in a small town near here—who sold 27 cases of Coca-Cola last week," Thomas wrote. Another outlet on the road to Nashville sold eighteen cases to black factory workers. During the same period, Thomas said, the high-tone local saloon sold only three cases.

Regardless of the bottle size, Heck's main headache was Celery Cola, one of J. C. Mayfield's drinks. Thomas advised Heck that "an effectual way to kill [Celery Cola] off" was to prompt a local consumer "to talk it among the people that it was nothing but a cheap rubbish and the only reason that the dealer had for wanting to foist it off on them was that he made more off of them every time he sold a bottle." Although Thomas assured Heck that he was "absolutely certain" that he would eventually succeed, his lieutenant Henry Ewing, lacking the Thomas tact, bluntly wrote in the summer of 1901 that "we are not doing this thing for pleasure; we want some profit."

In desperation, Heck sold out, only to bottle his own *ersatz* version of Coca-Cola, using surplus labels he had taken with him. By the end of 1903, Thomas reported with considerable satisfaction on Heck's demise. Undaunted, Heck surfaced the next year in Indiana, marketing Heck's Cola as a suitable substitute for the real thing. Thomas wrote to the Evansville, Indiana, bottler to assure him that Heck was ultimately harmless. "Heck's Cola is not Coca-Cola and all the lying that the man who puts it up can do will not convince anyone that it is."

While the case of William Heck was not an isolated incident, the majority of Coca-Cola bottling plants eventually flourished, although it was never an easy proposition, especially in the North. Arthur Pratt, who was to become a legendary Coca-Cola bottler, reversed the Heck pattern. Pratt began as an unsuccessful Coca-Cola imitator in Huntsville, Alabama. Failing to unseat the genuine drink, he and his brother Russ bought out the local Coca-Cola operator in 1901 and built a thriving business, operating four simultaneous bottling machines, each capable of producing fourteen cases an hour.

Reasoning that he could do "big things if we had more people," Arthur Pratt tried to persuade Ben Thomas to give him the New York City territory. Thomas told him he was reserving that "golden nugget" for whoever proved to be his most successful bottler, but offered him Newark, New Jersey, instead, where Pratt's 1902 plant was uncomfortably wedged between a saloon and a Women's Christian Temperance Union fanatic. "It was no easy job to start from scratch and introduce a new drink in this hard-boiled territory."

Despite some hard-earned sales, Pratt found that the Northern winters killed his trade: "Nobody thought very much of selling soft drinks during zero weather." He swung a deal with a local jam-maker to promote their products along with Coca-Cola, hoping to supplement the winter trade. It drove Pratt crazy that a 10-million-person market lay fallow in nearby New York City. He developed a single outlet there at a downtown Broadway cigar stand, delivering two dozen bottles at a time in an old suitcase. Telling the Thomas board of directors that he was already servicing the New York market (but neglecting to inform them of his single cigar store outlet), Pratt bluffed his way into the entire New York City territory, opening a plant there in 1904. Despite the enormous potential, Pratt didn't make much headway in the big city until he broke into the Italian neighborhoods, where he was at first mystified by the large turnover at vegetable stores, barbershops, undertaking establishments, and harness makers. He soon discovered that all of these stores were fronts for illegal gambling tables in the rear. The Italians had found that by mixing Coca-Cola with their Chianti wine, they could drink all night—taking longer to get drunk and keeping alert with caffeine.

EARLY STRATEGIES

With enterprising bottlers like Arthur Pratt, as well as a ready-made Southern market, the parent bottlers realized that soon they would be overseeing a huge business. In the spring of 1901, Thomas wrote to Whitehead to congratulate him on his "phenominal" sales, at the same time reporting that the Thomas territory would soon reach 3,000 cases a month. Shortly after that, the Louisville, Kentucky, plant opened with a distribution of 10,000 tickets for free drinks. It soon showed a healthy profit.

Thomas was convinced that offering free coupons was the fastest way to build trade, but to hold it he needed massive advertising, including streetcar placards, calendars, change plates, trays, posters, and steel, muslin, and oilcloth signs. Pleading with Frank Robinson for more point-of-sale advertising for Louisville, Thomas wrote that "this is the first real large city that we have operated in." The hundred signs he had were inadequate, since "we expect to have 400 or 500 places started up there within a very short time." After all, he already had 200 stands in Chattanooga, which was less than a sixth as large as Louisville.

Thomas was equally enterprising during the slower winter months, when he urged his bottlers to infiltrate elementary schools and hand out free blotters as the children were dismissed. Thomas also advertised extensively in newspapers, after bottlers informed him which local paper had the highest circulation. Finally, the parent bottler solicited testimonials from major outlets, explaining that "an expression favorable to Coca-Cola's selling qualities will be of great assistance in a new field." While they did not agree on everything, Whitehead and Thomas kept in touch, sharing strategies. Both men sought out railway employees, hiring them on commission as part-time Coca-Cola salesmen. Cases of bottled Coca-Cola were thus sold on trains and at depots before the advent of the delivery truck.

AMENDING THE CONTRACT

In 1901, Thomas sold his plants in order to concentrate on administering his growing bottling empire. Whitehead followed suit two years later by selling a third of his Atlanta plant to Arthur Montgomery, a railroad express agent impressed with the amount of Coca-Cola he was shipping. Montgomery took over the plant management. By that fall, the original 1899 contract was already causing problems for the bottlers as well as The Coca-Cola Company. Candler regretted his promise to provide free advertising, since Frank Robinson was deluged with requests for streetcar signs, expensive German lithography, blotters, novelties, and all the other available items. At the same time, the parent bottlers were frustrated by delayed shipments from the Company. In a testy letter to Atlanta in June of 1901, Henry Ewing complained that "we have to do business with you, certainly for this summer," adding that "I do not need to explain how a business like ours with established customers will suffer if we cannot supply them . . . We are in a fair way to do a very large business and make you valuable customers."

The parent bottlers were also unhappy with their arrangement with the actual bottlers. It was obviously going to be impractical to hire a supervisor for every bottler. In addition, these direct employees of the parent bottlers caused bad feeling with the actual bottlers, who felt there was a spy in their midst. Or, like the Memphis bottler, they complained that this special employee was a slob who didn't show up for work on time. Finally, the parent organizations realized that by insisting on a return of half of the profits, they might well bankrupt their bottlers.

For all of these reasons, Whitehead and Thomas came to a new arrangement with The Coca-Cola Company in November of 1901. In an undated amendment, the 1899 contract was changed to allow a 10-cent-per gallon rebate to give the bottlers responsibility for their own advertising. In effect, the syrup price was set at 90 cents a gallon, with the parent bottlers paying 10 cents a gallon for advertising—an expense they immediately passed through to their actual bottlers. At the same time, Thomas and Whitehead abandoned their obligation to place an employee/spy with each actual bottler. Rather than taking half of the bottlers' profits, they now switched to a straight royalty of 6 cents per case, or a quarter cent per bottle. Given the increasing demand, this seemingly small levy would make the parent bottlers millionaires within a few years, while permitting a nice profit for the actual bottlers, jobbers, and retailers of the drink.

CHILD LABOR AND ADULTERATED SYRUP

The actual bottlers replaced the supervisor as cheaply as possible, often with child labor. Thomas helped to find responsible, inexpensive help for his bottlers, in 1902 recommending a "negro boy" who would work for $4 a week. While wages would rise somewhat in the future, the tedious manual labor in Coca-Cola bottling plants never commanded a decent salary. In later years, because of the noise and monotony, many plants hired deaf employees at minimum wage.

After the contract amendment, Thomas cut corners in other ways as well. He began to adulterate his own syrup, the same practice that all good Coca-Cola men professed to find so evil. In September of 1901, he rush-ordered ten pounds of saccharin (trade-named "garantose") from Merck & Company for experimentation. In January, Thomas sent a coded recipe for "simple syrup" to his bottlers. By adding caramel coloring, phosphoric acid, and saccharin in the right proportions, bottlers stretched a gallon of Coca-Cola syrup so that it would yield 144 bottles. In the ensuing months, Thomas engaged in considerable correspondence about the proportions of this saccharin mixture, since it resulted in slight variations in color, acidity, and sweetness. Writing to his Pittsburgh bottler, Thomas said, "I do not think that you can make a mistake in having your Coca-Cola too sweet . . . I am sure that it takes better than that which is not so sweet." He went on to say that "tastes vary" regarding the proper amount of acidity.

In Thomas' defense, he was probably adding saccharin not only because it was cheaper than sugar, but because it acted as a preservative. From the outset, he had been plagued by a cloudy drink that deposited an unpleasant sediment. At first he blamed the Hutchinsons' faulty seal. When the problem continued with the crown cork, he decided that polluted water must be the cause. An amateur chemist, Thomas tinkered with pasteurization of Coca-Cola, but it killed the taste. Eventually, he devised a system of cleaning the water with alum, and recommended filtering the syrup before use as well.

PARENT BOTTLERS: PIONEERS OR PIRATES?

The efforts of Thomas have been emphasized here simply because no similar records have survived from Whitehead and Lupton. It is obvious from the correspondence between Thomas and Whitehead that both men deserve full credit for building the Coca-Cola bottling business. Whitehead, frazzled by overwork, died of pneumonia in 1906 at forty-two, and Thomas followed at fifty-two in 1914. They had seen the future far more clearly than Asa Candler, and their protean efforts paid off quickly. They were at the same time salesmen, cheerleaders, advertising agents, bottlers, lawyers, negotiators, venture capitalists, chemists, and accountants. They created the prototype of the American franchise system, and they brought Coca-Cola to the masses.

Years later, during a bitter court battle between the bottlers and The Coca-Cola Company, Company officials would denigrate the accomplishments of the parent bottlers, accurately pointing out that the parent organization never even saw the Coca-Cola syrup which was shipped directly to the actual bottlers. Why should they have a perpetual right to their royalty? In later years, there was certainly some validity to those arguments, and The Coca-Cola Company eventually bought back the parent bottlers to avoid this unnecessary tithe. But in these early years, there is no doubt that the parent bottlers performed the essential job of recruiting, coordinating, and training legions of small bottlers, all with growing capital expenditures. Without lifting a finger or investing a penny, Asa Candler and his Company saw their business mushroom and reach into untapped rural areas. Coca-Cola advertising, already extensive, gained added momentum as parent and local bottlers covered their territory with the Coca-Cola logo.

By 1902, Whitehead, even with his smaller bottle, was doing an "enormous business" of 2,400 cases a week in Atlanta alone. At the same time, Thomas observed that bottles didn't have to piggyback on an existing fountain trade. "In Charleston, where Coca-Cola had practically no [fountain] business, the bottling plant is running considerably over an average of 100 cases a day. It has been a great surprise to every one."

Some fountain operators felt threatened. "We predict the *death* of your specialty—which has had so many years of success," wrote an indignant Indiana fountain man in 1904. He complained that the bottled drink came in a motley assortment of containers, "as pleases the whim, ignorance or averice" of the local distributor, thus "throwing down the Bars for the many imitators of your drink" and "destroying Fountain trade." While sales might initially be "immenseily increased," the angry owner predicted that the inevitable result would be that "any old thing with an amber color" would soon pass for Coca-Cola. A Company official reassured the apoplectic druggist that, far from hurting the trade, bottlers would help the fountain in the long run. "The bottled goods are as a rule so uniform and satisfactory that it stimulates the dispensers to give a better glass of Coca-Cola in order to hold their trade," wrote the Company man. "In this city the matter has been tested for years, and the dispensers are doing more business now than ever before."

By 1904, no one at The Coca-Cola Company would say anything against the bottlers. Where five years before, there had been only sporadic, informal efforts to bottle Coca-Cola, now there were over 120 manufacturing facilities covering almost every state. By the end of the year, the Company published a booklet showing the sales of the bottled drink, asking readers to consider the import of this growing branch of the business, with its "remarkable, and in many cases phenomenal" growth. Pointing out that every gallon of syrup represented about ten dozen bottles of Coca-Cola, the spokesman urged the reader to "use your pencil, make a few calculations and see what an enormous business has been done in nearly every place where a bottling plant has been established."

While at first it had been difficult to lure anyone into the bottling business, the parent bottlers were soon turning away droves of eager entrepreneurs. In 1912, one self-promoting Texas owner had stationery printed up depicting a Coca-Cola bottle spewing dollar signs instead of a beverage. "THERE IS MONEY IN IT" the legend below bluntly stated. By 1919, there were 1,200 plants; virtually every town in America had a Coca-Cola bottler. Asa Candler was delighted but still mystified by the bottlers' success. One day in 1904, Candler ran into Veazey Rainwater, who operated the booming Athens, Georgia, plant at the time. "Veazey," Candler said, "what are you doing with all of that syrup, pouring it into the Oconee River?" Rainwater just smiled, but later, when he had taken over the Atlanta parent bottler administration following Whitehead's death, he accurately summed up the bottlers' accomplishments. Coca-Cola, he said, had been put into the hands of "thousands of merchants in the suburbs and outlying districts of every city, in the stores of every country town and village, and in the homes of thousands of people where it had not been possible to put Coca-Cola before." As a result, "an enormous field was opened up . . . and hundreds of thousands of individuals who had never before tasted or seen Coca-Cola were introduced to this product first in bottles."

THE COCAINE KICKER

The bottling business had one unfortunate, unforeseen consequence, however. No longer simply a soda fountain drink for upper-class urban white professionals, Coca-Cola was increasingly consumed by blacks. Sensational stories of "Negro coke fiends" attacking whites caused many to fear the widespread availability of Coca-Cola. As the century turned, so did public opinion, and in 1900 Candler found himself under intensified pressure to reform his "dope."

Part II

~

Heretics and True Believers
(1900–1922)

Asa Candler could no longer stand it. His younger brother John, the lawyer, had told him to stay away from the trial, but it was more than he could bear. He had endured enough, reading the outrageous lies every day in the Georgian. *What possible difference could it make if he just went and sat quietly in the back?*

And so, on a rainy April morning in 1911, the president of The Coca-Cola Company snuck quietly into the back of a Chattanooga courtroom. Glancing around, he quickly found that all the Coca-Cola men, including his son Howard, sat on the left. He joined them. Putting his finger to his lips, he warned Howard not to make an issue of his father's presence. Hunching inconspicuously in his seat, he fidgeted with repressed rage, listening to government witnesses malign his drink. He recognized that great tub of lard, Harvey Wiley, nodding sagely on the other side of the courtroom.

At the noon recess, Candler had just stepped outside and was about to hurry away when a hand pulled at his elbow. "Mr Candler, I believe." That voice! It was Kebler, the government spy he'd caught skulking around the Atlanta syrup plant two years ago. Turning around, Candler turned a shade of Coca-Cola red. "Ah, I thought it was you. Mr Candler, I'd like to introduce Dr Wiley." And Kebler gently pushed Candler toward the imposing chemist, who reached out a massive hand. "I'm pleased finally to meet so worthy an opponent," Wiley boomed.

"You, sir, are a hypocrite to offer your hand," Candler said. "I won't take it. You are persecuting and attempting to ruin a beneficial beverage, a boon to mankind. Well, you won't succeed." Candler was just building to one of his explosive, high-pitched climaxes when his brother John grabbed him by the arm. "Asa!" he hissed, pulling him away, "I thought you agreed not to come. You're causing a scene. Please, please, go back to Atlanta."

Asa Candler shook himself loose, straightening his tie. He took a deep breath. "Johnnie, you're right. I'd better go before I do bodily harm, sure enough. But you know that God watches over His own, and we will prevail." And reassuming his dignity, the gray-haired little man walked away.

~ 6 ~

Success Under Siege

It is only since the rising tide of Coca-Cola's popularity has grown to the extent of attracting general public attention that this fire has been directed to it . . . Now that everybody drinks it, a certain coterie, composed mostly of disgruntled competitors and misguided fanatics, have discovered that it is more seductive than opium, more injurious than tobacco and more pernicious than whisky.

—Judge John S. Candler, 1909

ASA CANDLER had a problem: by 1900, Coca-Cola was already not simply a soft drink, but a phenomenon. With success, however, came increased notoriety and controversy. The drink's cocaine content had been a source of trouble from the beginning, but it was also a major selling point. Without the benefit of the coca leaf's small kick, how could Coca-Cola survive? Also, if Candler took it out, how could he legally defend his trademark? It would be like jettisoning the first half of the name. Candler was determined not to tamper with the formula. In 1898, a zealous Oregon evangelist named Lindsay had arrived in Marietta, Georgia, near Atlanta, as the minister of the local Baptist church. From the pulpit, Reverend Lindsay soon launched a hellfire attack on Coca-Cola, the ingredients of which were, he asserted, fully two-thirds cocaine; imbibing would lead to "morphine eating." His accusations made good newspaper copy, prompting a quick Candler response: "I do not propose to vend a poison or be instrumental if I know it of doing harm to anybody." By righteously denying that his magical drink had any harmful effects, Candler hoped to defuse any controversy.

The 1898 incident was a local disturbance and faded away, but cocaine was soon making national headlines, in part because racism was on the rise along with the Ku Klux Klan, in the North as well as the South. In September of 1906, a major race riot occurred in Atlanta, though it primarily involved whites attacking blacks rather than vice versa, caused by inflammatory newspaper accounts of black "brutes" attacking white women. Long before the riot, cocaine, the 1885 wonder drug, had become the 1900 scourge of humanity, and in the South it allegedly caused crazed Negroes to attack their bosses and rape white women. There may have been vestiges of truth behind the sensational headlines, since many farmers were giving cocaine to their black sharecroppers in lieu of food, and cocaine in the city, where 50 cents bought a week's supply, was a cheaper high than alcohol.

Whatever the reason, the papers were filled with black cocaine fiends. A white Georgian complained to a *New York Tribune* reporter that "in Atlanta, cocaine sniffing has grown to such proportions that some of the keepers of saloons patronized by the colored people are going out of business," adding that Coca-Cola produced "similar effects to cocaine, morphine, and such like. Men become addicted to drinking it, and find it hard to release themselves from the habit." The *Atlanta Constitution* wrote in 1901 that "use of the drug among negroes is growing to an alarming extent . . . It is stated that quite a number of the soft drinks dispensed at soda fountains contain cocaine, and that these drinks serve to unconsciously cultivate the habit."

During his testimony in the trial against the IRS, Candler admitted that there was a "very small proportion" of cocaine in Coca-Cola. With mounting frustration, he listened to physicians testify on the effects of the "Coca-Cola habit." One Atlanta doctor cited the case of a thirteen-year-old boy who usually drank ten to twelve glasses per day, but who lost his job and was suddenly unable to buy Coca-Cola: "He came to my office the day after in a very nervous, almost collapsed condition, stating to me that he could not get his Coca-Cola and that he knew something was the matter with him." Another doctor said that his neurasthenic partner was "very strangely affected" by drinking Coca-Cola: "If he takes a glass, he can't find his way home." Perhaps the poor man drank a double or quadruple dose, since Atlanta druggists were in the habit of using anywhere from one to four ounces of syrup per glass, according to one witness.

All of these statements come from the 1902 trial, but Candler had already heard similar testimony during the *first* IRS trial, which had ended in July of 1901 with a hung jury. At some point during the first trial, the accumulation of such testimony, combined with adverse press coverage and the spread of bottled Coca-Cola among black consumers, forced him to remove the cocaine. His first attempt was only partially successful, which explains why a chemist found four-hundreths of a grain of cocaine per ounce of syrup in 1902. It also accounts for Candler's curious, stumbling answer at one point when he was asked how much cocaine was in Coca-Cola: "If we got all of it—but we don't treat it—" Unfortunately, the lawyer saved him by interrupting with another question. No wonder Candler was smitten with severe headaches while on the witness stand.

Soon afterward, in August of 1903, Candler contracted with the Schaefer Alkaloid Works of Maywood, New Jersey, to decocainize the coca leaves before sending "Merchandise No. 5" on to Atlanta. The exact date of Candler's first attempt to remove cocaine cannot be pinpointed, but it was probably in 1901. That January, Coca-Cola distributed a defensive pamphlet, *What Is It? Coca-Cola, What It Is* in which Candler admitted a small amount of cocaine. The pamphlet contained an 1891 analysis which said "it would require about thirty glasses . . . to make an ordinary dose of the drug." The text also praised the coca leaf, which "makes one active, brilliant, vigorous, and able to accomplish great tasks easily." It seems clear, then, that at the beginning of 1901, cocaine was still in the drink, but most of it had been removed by the following year.

The removal of the cocaine presented a delicate public relations problem. If the company responded to attacks by telling the truth, they would be admitting that the drink *did* once have cocaine in it. The implication would be that they had removed it because it was harmful, which might even open the door to lawsuits. Besides, it was unthinkable to admit that Coca-Cola had ever been anything but pure and wholesome. Finally, of course, they didn't want the public to know that one of the drink's more enticing ingredients was now missing.

Consequently, Candler orchestrated a mighty revision of Coca-Cola history, perhaps convincing himself in the process. In later years, he repeatedly denied, under oath, that the drink had ever had cocaine in it. Even today, the Company feels compelled to deny it, though there has been no cocaine whatsoever in Coca-Cola since 1903. After 1900, instead of bragging about the removal of cocaine, the Company poured on the advertising, stressing the soft drink's healthful qualities. In December of 1902, the Georgia legislature made the sale of cocaine in any form illegal. By luck, grace, or good judgment, Coca-Cola once more narrowly escaped disaster, though the controversy over the drink had only begun.

AN ADVERTISING BLITZ

When John Candler was asked during the IRS trial what sort of vehicles The Coca-Cola Company used for its advertising, he answered, "I don't know anything they *don't* advertise on." By the turn of the century, Frank Robinson was annually sending out over a million pieces of advertising in some thirty forms. In 1900, the firm spent almost $85,000 on advertising. By 1912, that figure was well over a million dollars a year, and Sam Dobbs could accurately claim that Coca-Cola was the single best-advertised product in the United States. Wherever Americans looked, they could not avoid seeing the Coca-Cola script. During 1913, the company advertised on over 100 million items, including thermometers, cardboard cutouts, and metal signs (50,000 each); Japanese fans and calendars (a million each); 2 million soda fountain trays, 10 million matchbooks, 20 million blotters, 25 million baseball cards, and innumerable signs made of cardboard and metal. The novelties distributed in that one year alone could have supplied every man, woman, and child who had lived in the continental United States since 1650.

It is little wonder that Coca-Cola had begun to permeate every aspect of American life. Horses were named Coca-Cola; bears at Yellowstone drank it.[*]

---

[*] Over the years, the Company received innumerable letters and photographs testifying to the love of the animal kingdom for Coca-Cola—including horses, bees, goats, elephants, and monkeys, but mostly dogs, so that wearied Company men called them all "bow-wow letters." Those sending the photos received a stock response: "While pets drinking Coca-Cola usually make for an appealing picture, we have always thought it a sound policy to depict our product being consumed by human beings." The Company was not above taking advantage of one clever myna bird, however, who shouted at conventions: "Won't you have a Coca-Cola, huh?"

Coca-Cola chewing gum, cigars, and candy were marketed to take advantage of the popular trademark.[*] Because of the stigma attached to the drink, Coca-Cola added a deliciously sinful note to lyrics of popular songs. In one ditty, a young man enjoying his first debauch in the big city wrote home to say, "Oh! mother, you wouldn't know your child / Oh! mother, I'm getting awfully wild / I am drinking Coca-Cola now / On the level, I'm a little devil." In "Follow Me, Girls, to the Fountain, and Be My Coca-Cola Girl," the drink was used as a seductive lure. The composer dedicated the song to The Coca-Cola Company, "whose delicious drink has wet the whistle of countless thousands and made 'HIGH LIFE' possible even in a dry town."

The young film industry, too, had begun its love affair with the soft drink. Asa Candler bragged that "a moving picture cannot be taken in the open air . . ., but what it is likely to catch a Coca-Cola [sign]." Buster Keaton drank it on screen. Popular silent film stars such as Pearl White and Marion Davies appeared in Coca-Cola ads. The drink even found its way into an early Hollywood sex scandal, when comedian Fatty Arbuckle was rumored to have utilized a Coca-Cola bottle during an orgy.

Asa Candler was undoubtedly as unhappy about the Arbuckle publicity as he was with the unauthorized advertising of the Western Coca-Cola Bottling Company. In 1905, this third parent bottler, owned by J. T. Lupton, had split from the Southeastern Parent Bottler. Based in Chicago, it faced stiff competition from the breweries and Northern winters. S. L. Whitten, who ran the organization, wrote to Asa Candler at the beginning of 1907 that "not a single Coca-Cola bottling company in our territory . . . made money last year," but added that "we are working along lines somewhat differing from our work of last year."

Whitten's "somewhat differing" approach used overtly sexual advertising for Coca-Cola. One of his 1908 trays featured a bare-breasted young woman holding a Coca-Cola bottle. The surrounding text suggested trying "Coca-Cola High Balls," and "Coca-Cola Gin Rickies." Another ad showed a young woman in black lingerie reclining on a tiger-skin rug with an expression of exhausted bliss. She held an empty glass, a Coca-Cola bottle on the table beside her. The caption: "Satisfied." The viewer could easily deduce that she was satisfied in more ways than one.

While the sanctimonious Candler was appalled by Western's ads, the beautiful young women used in authorized ads were suggestive in their own ways. The wholesome-but-sensuous models specialized in come-hither looks

---

[*] Coca-Cola chewing gum had a long and checkered history. Like many of the early trademark spin-offs, it was never officially sponsored by the Company. In later years, when protection of the logo became a crusade, the Company was embarrassed by the gum, which had deteriorated in quality. Through an intermediary, the Company bought out the nearly bankrupt firm in 1924. According to a persistent piece of Company folklore, the Coca-Cola chewing gum trademark was then "protected" once a year when a salesman delivered a carton to a rural South Carolina store, walked around the block, bought a piece of gum, chewed it, purchased the entire carton, and left.

from the corner of the eye while they sipped their drinks demurely through a straw. One contemporary critic described the "bewitching sirens who lure us to Coca-Cola, with their display of charms," but were ready to flee in "innocent alarm at the possibility of spectators." Men fell in love with the millions of pictures of Betty, the 1914 calendar girl, while women made every attempt to look like her.

The most visible, widespread advertising for Coca-Cola, however, were hand-painted signs. One thirty-two-foot-high effort featured a soda jerk drawing a glass with real water flowing from the spigot. Most signs weren't so elaborate, but many were as large, taking up entire sides of buildings. The first wall turned red for Coca-Cola in Cartersville, Georgia, in 1894. By 1914, the Company had over 5 million square feet of painted walls, enough to give one unfortunate consumer nightmares, as a salesman reported in 1906. "Hounded almost to a state of imbecility with Coca-Cola signs," the poor man would "wake up at night with big white devils with a red mantel chasing after him screeching 'Coca-Cola! Coca-Cola!' until he made up his mind that he would have to go in somewhere and get a glass of Coca-Cola or part with his reason."

THE COCA-COLA INSTITUTE

Backed by such effective advertising, the small band of Coca-Cola men invaded the cities and towns of America in the first decade of the century. In December of 1903, the twenty-nine salesmen were summoned to Atlanta for a four-day pep rally and sales meeting grandly called The Coca-Cola Institute. As Candler noted in his annual report, "some of these men had never before been seen by the officers of the Company. They were brought into personal contact with each other and have returned to their various fields of work greatly enthused."

Sam Dobbs had taken firm charge of the sales force, traveling extensively to supervise his far-flung team. At the 1903 meeting, he praised them as "splendid men," gentlemanly and high-toned. "Never be ashamed to say you are a traveling salesman," Dobbs urged. Thoroughly aroused, the salesmen burst out with cheers of "HURRAH for Coca-Cola, the drink that strengthens but does not inebriate—Coca-Cola, the drink of the age!" Throughout the rest of the week, they shared tips with one another on how best to spread the gospel, such as rigging a "mechanical attachment" to a man in a window display so that he moved a Coca-Cola glass to his lips while rolling his eyes, or putting large thermometers in a sunny window, accompanied by an offer of a free fan with every glass of Coca-Cola.

Salesmen discussed the proper distribution of free tickets, counseling one another to avoid residential neighborhoods, where most of the tickets would end up with children, and to stick to the business districts, office buildings, and college campuses. "Don't cast [tickets] before swine or small boys. [But] do not be stingy. Let the public feel that The Coca-Cola Company is the most liberal Santa Claus in the world." Though one salesman noted that "female stenographers and bookkeepers are good Coca-Cola drinkers," no one identified women as a major market for Coca-Cola other than in the work force. In order to avoid counterfeits, the tickets were lithographed by a German firm in lots of 2 million. Even so, many soda fountain operators redeemed Coca-Cola tickets for other soft drinks. Salesmen could best prevent such practices by bribing the soda jerk with novelties such as pocket-knives or watch fobs.

Frank Robinson spoke at the 1903 meeting, too, but he lacked the inspirational tone of Sam Dobbs, stressing small matters such as urging the salesmen to note the name of imitation colas. Robinson said that he ordered "high class, artistic and expensive advertising matter" which should be carefully placed: "A large lithograph costing $1.00 should not go into an obscure place or be left with a dispenser to do with as he pleases." His warnings were understandable, since the gorgeous sixteen-color artwork puts modern prints to shame. Robinson betrayed some emotion when he pointed out with pride that he had just placed 650 large lithographs in railway stations and that "in Philadelphia and Chicago the large oilcloth signs are so conspicuous and so numerous . . . as to give the impression that The Coca-Cola Company owns the town."

By the end of the week, the salesmen were well indoctrinated. Coca-Cola was "a thirst-quenching, heaven-sent drink," one employee glowed, "a blessing to this sun-parched earth." Another speaker advised salesmen to think of themselves as bearers of a secular religion. Like "the missionary going into a foreign field" to teach the "rudiments," the Coca-Cola man must be "a live one, [a] practical, hustling man." Bishop Warren Candler visited the Institute several times to open the meetings with a morning prayer. Together, Warren and Asa led the group in a rousing rendition of "Onward Christian Soldiers" to end the week. As the printed report of the meeting stated, "the Convention . . . was carried on from beginning to end with a very unusual degree of earnestness and enthusiasm."

THE BISHOP'S BLESSING

The Bishop wasn't simply doing his brother a favor. Asa's younger brother truly believed in the twin virtues of capitalism and religion. In 1888, he had helped Coca-Cola gain its first foothold in Nashville, and he owned Coca-Cola stock. Warren and Asa Candler were extremely close, sharing religious values and monetary advice throughout their lives. The Bishop was by far the greater intellect, dominating the Southern branch of the Methodist Church for over thirty years with the force of his character, writings, and sermons. Howard Candler described his uncle as "a short, barrel-shaped man" with "quick passions and doggedly stubborn prejudices." The Bishop's son compared him to a bulldog. A contentious, pompous little man, he relished good fights, and his conservative views guaranteed he would find them—often with Tom Watson, the Georgia populist-turned-demagogue who called Bishop Candler "a Coca-Cola lobbyist . . . unctuous, self-righteous, [and] self-complacent."

Warren Candler believed deeply in the superiority of what he called Anglo-Saxon culture. In his 1904 book, *Great Revivals and the Great Republic*, he asserted that the United States was destined to lead the world because of its revivalistic religion: "Romanism has made South America and Southern Europe what they are, and Protestantism has made England, Germany, Holland, and North America what they are." In other words, God was on America's side; at the least, He smiled as Americans made money.

One of Bishop Candler's strongest arguments in favor of revivals was that they helped maintain the status quo and avert labor unrest. He pointed out that "disturbances between labor and capital have been most frequent in those industries in which the laborers have been brought from the unevangelized masses of Continental Europe." He ended by emphasizing that the efforts of ministers were essential in an industrial age: "What they [have] accomplished in the way of soothing the irritations of the social system, and of postponing if not preventing the worst industrial disorder, can scarcely be overestimated." Warren Candler's paternalistic, conservative views were echoed by his brother Asa, who set the pattern of anti-unionism at The Coca-Cola Company, whose Atlanta employees have never organized.

Naturally, the Bishop thought it essential for missionaries to disseminate the Protestant gospel and the virtues of industrial harmony. "The missionary enterprise must go in advance of international commerce," Bishop Candler wrote, "to secure justice in trade and safety for the merchantmen." He personally spread the Word to China, Korea, and Mexico, but his great love was Cuba. The Spanish-American War of 1898 opened the perfect target for the Methodist missionary—a country full of poor, oppressed Catholics.

The war was scarcely over when, in late 1898, Warren Candler sailed for Cuba, the first of twenty such visits. Upon his return, he enthusiastically reported that Cuba was "our nearest, neediest, ripest missionary field." The next year, he helped to found Candler College, a Cuban Methodist mission school which Asa founded substantially, explaining: "We may be sure that commercial currents will follow the channels which education opens and deepens . . . Herein our duty and our interest coincide." After hearing about this "ripe field" from Warren, Asa promptly enlisted José Parejo, a wine merchant, as a Havana wholesaler for Coca-Cola in May of 1899.

Cuba was not the first foreign country to be invaded by Coca-Cola. It had been sold in Canada, Hawaii, and Mexico by 1897. When Howard Candler went to England during the summer of 1900, he took along a gallon of Coca-Cola syrup and was delighted to find John Ralphs, an American, running one of the new London soda fountains. Ralphs used up the gallon and ordered more from Coca-Cola's Philadelphia branch.

ASA'S UPS AND DOWNS

In one of his manic moments in 1900 Asa Candler wrote to Howard in London, envisioning Coca-Cola's world dominion. While his fantasies would not come true during his tenure at the Company, Asa Candler wasn't a bad prophet. "I propose to put you and your brother in charge somewhere in some of the important places," he wrote, asking Howard to "critically observe conditions in Europe" while Buddie (Asa Jr.), presumably from his vantage point on the West Coast, would plot strategy for Asia. "Together we must map out for great conquests." The next year, Candler bragged to a reporter that "Coca-Cola is now being shipped to London and to Berlin, to Canada and to Honolulu, and it is being sold in large quantities in Cuba, Puerto Rico and Kingston, Jamaica." In fact, outside of Canada and Cuba, the amount sold was negligible. It was primarily distributed through New York and Philadelphia brokers who wouldn't even tell Coca-Cola officers who their customers were, for fear the Company would sell to them directly.

Asa Candler enjoyed picturing these "great conquests" for his children, but he was becoming increasingly morbid about his own life. In 1901, Candler wrote that "I realize with almost crushing disappointment that I can only be of importance to the interests of my generation through the good that I may bring to it in my boys. I pray constantly that my boys may be *men*." The following year, when he was only fifty-one, Candler sounded as if he were dying of old age. "Only a few years at best and I will have to sit down and wait for the *Reaper* to *carry* me off like the streetcleaner the trash," he moaned. "I have not felt well for two weeks. My head aches now."

Candler's business was outgrowing him. He was appalled at the amount of money that was being spent on advertising and labor, even though the dollars were accruing faster than he could spend them. At the beginning of 1901, he complained that "we have grown so large and so many to be paid, and with that, money goes out in great torrents." At that moment, there was a cash surplus of nearly $200,000 and the Company owned $71,000 in real estate free and clear.

Similarly, he wasn't keeping up with his drink's potential market. He continued to harbor the Victorian illusion that Coca-Cola must remain a high-class fountain drink, fighting the democratic tide that bottling had unleashed. "We must not cater to *dives* and cheap places." Nor was he eager to embrace the automobile. Complaining about mechanical difficulties plaguing the New York office's Locomobile in 1902, he expressed no confidence in "such machines," adding that "like the Bycicle I have looked upon them as a fad only."

The horseless carriage was no fad. In fact, it was a fitting symbol for the restless age that Candler himself represented. In 1901, an *Atlanta Constitution* journalist wrote that "our new friend, the automobile, [is] a striking exemplification of this queer spirit of unrest which seems to have become an heritage of our national life." Everyone in America appeared to be "incessantly searching for some new method of economizing time and condensing life into the briefest possible compass. Even our pleasures are taken in that same forceful, strenuous, nerve-straining manner."

If Candler read this editorial, he must have recognized himself in it. "I am so habituated to hurry," he wrote, "that I seem to be unable to *stay* in *one place*." When someone politely asked Candler for his ear when he next found a leisure moment, he snapped, "I am never at leisure; what will you have while I am busy?" Finding no peace in his triumph, Candler was as much a victim as a hero of his age. Coca-Cola brought him no relief, though its advertisements promised quick new energy, instant relaxation. In fact, Coca-Cola was emblematic of the modern American attempt to package pleasure. As the editorial implied, even leisure had become strenuous. Candler's nephew wrote that the "fever heat" of American civilization, characterized by "rushing and striving," accounted for the growing demand for Coca-Cola, an instant pick-me-up. But for harried businessmen, including his uncle, the drink provided only temporary respite. Candler could not cope with membership in the leisure class, comprehending only the virtues of work. Years ago, he had clipped a poem which advised: "It is *hustle* that will *tell*; / It is Godlike to excel. / Have you work? Do it well." Though he had excelled, Asa Candler did not feel godlike. His stomach hurt. Searching for solace, he carefully typed out a quotation from Hawthorne: "The world owes all its onward impulses to men ill at ease."

Still, the money poured in. He created the Candler Investment Company and began to buy Atlanta real estate. In August of 1904, he watched the foundation being laid for the Candler Building, a seventeen-story skyscraper that rose above Atlanta, a talisman of the New South. On January 4, 1906, elegantly gowned women and men in three-piece suits entered to admire the nearly completed showpiece, with its six elevators, artistic gargoyles, polished marble, mahogany and brass, and glittering crystal chandeliers. On the first floor was Candler's newly formed bank, the Central Bank and Trust Corporation. Here was permanence. Here was immortality. In the building's cornerstone Candler placed a copper box containing his picture and a bottle of Coca-Cola.

The next month, as if God were mocking Asa Candler, a heavy wind-storm tore a huge plate-glass window from the building and smashed it in the middle of Peachtree Street. Candler fretted. "*My friends* too often are *my enemies*," he wrote. If that were so, even God might turn on him. "He has given me so many unmistakable evidences of His ability to carry me safely over dangerous places—yet I do not trust Him and may be lost." Still seeking immortality, he spread his name and presence across the United States, paying for skyscrapers in Kansas City, Baltimore, and New York City, all named the Candler Building. The New York effort, fronting on West 42nd Street near Times Square, cost $2 million and soared to twenty-five stories, with the Candler coat of arms cast into the doorknobs, elevator doors, and mailboxes. With an obsessive attention to detail and petty economy, he specified the wattage of light bulbs.

In the first twenty years of the century, Asa Candler invested in virtually every aspect of Atlanta's life. "It would literally be impossible," wrote Howard Candler, "to describe all my father's business interests." Through his railroad holdings, he traveled gratis on any line and insisted that Coca-Cola be sold in dining cars. When the bottom dropped out of the cotton market, he built a huge warehouse and bought the surplus cotton at low prices, making a tidy profit when the market improved. During the "panic of 1907," Candler bolstered real estate prices, snapping up hard-hit properties. For most of these profitable activities, he was hailed as a hero even as he raked in more money. To radicals and labor leaders, however, Candler was a villain. A 1908 political cartoon criticized the wealthy banker, showing his support of vested interests while saying "Nothin Doin" to the poor.

Indeed, Candler's money did not make him generous. When a personal friend owing him money reminded him of their longtime relationship, Candler cut him off, saying that while he appreciated all that, "We are not talking friendship now; we are talking business." An indigent missionary once begged Candler for money to support his wife and five children, explaining that it was "humiliating in the extreme" but that he would starve otherwise. Candler sent him $10, along with a note: "You realize I am sure that such calls as yours are frequent on me." He wasn't even that generous with Cliff Pemberton, the impoverished widow of Coca-Cola's inventor. When a group of women approached Candler to ask that he give her $50 a month, he refused. In July of 1909, as Mrs. Pemberton lay dying of cancer, a relative wrote that "if someone would present her case properly to the rich man who purchased the Coca-Cola formula, his heart, if he had one, would be moved." Two months later, she was dead.

The year before Mrs. Pemberton's death, another unpleasant side of Candler was revealed. In 1908, the fourth annual convention of the National Child Labor Committee met in Atlanta, principally to protest the horrific conditions in cotton mills, where women and children worked over sixty-hour weeks, breathing cotton motes for 50 cents a day or less. Georgia would be the last Southern state to pass child labor legislation. As president of the Atlanta Chamber of Commerce, Candler gave an almost unbelievable opening speech, considering his audience. "Child labor properly conducted, properly surrounded, properly conditioned, is calculated to bring the highest measure of success to any country on the face of the earth," he began. "The most beautiful sight that we see is the child at labor." In fact, the younger the boy began work, "the more beautiful, the more useful does his life get to be." Candler ended by asserting that the proper function of the Committee was to assure that the child's work turned him into "a noble, useful, competent laboring grown person."

In commenting on this performance, a committee official chose to interpret Candler's speech as "subtle humor," a character trait no one else ever accused Candler of possessing. He was clearly serious, perhaps recalling his own youthful entrepreneurial days, but more likely defending the widespread use of child labor in Southern cotton mills—including his own in Hartwell, Georgia, which he sold two years later—and, of course, at The Coca-Cola Company and bottling franchises.

During the summer of 1913, Candler, sixty-one, took his wife on the Grand Tour of Europe, as befitted the wealthy of that era. He granted an interview just before leaving in which he was "altogether optimistic and cheerful as to the business outlook," surveying a horizon "abundantly rainbowed and promising nothing but good things." The interview was a fraud. The real motivation for Candler's trip was flight from a breakdown, as he admitted to his brother Warren: "I left home to try to recover my nerve steadiness." As usual, he hated the enforced idleness, writing that while his wife enjoyed Paris, "I do not but will tough it through."

He only parted with substantial sums of money when he felt it would add to his greater glory. While Candler was in Europe, Andrew Carnegie offered a million dollars to Vanderbilt University, which had always been a Methodist institution, on the condition that it become nondenominational. Faced with losing Methodist influence in higher education because of the godless Yankee capitalist, the religious leadership naturally turned to Asa Candler, Carnegie's Southern equivalent. Candler was embarrassed and angered by a rumor that he would give $2 million to Emory College to transform it into a fine university. He wasn't at all sure he wanted to give *any* money to Emory, which he called "a crumbling castle." Goaded by Warren, rumor, and his belief in religious education, he eventually awarded *one* million to Emory in July of 1914, noting testily in announcing the gift that "I do not possess by a vast deal what some extravagantly imagine and confidently affirm." Emory subsequently moved from Oxford, Georgia, to Atlanta. Before his death, Candler would lavish over $8 million on the college.

COCA-COLA IN COLLIER'S

While Candler spent more time caring for his other business interests and agonizing over philanthropy, Coca-Cola advertising guaranteed that he would never have to worry about poverty. Though a few years older than Candler, Frank Robinson had none of his misgivings about spending money to attract new consumers. He had always bought ad space in major U.S. newspapers, but in the first years of the 1900s, the new popularity (and circulation figures) of magazines attracted him. He placed the first Coca-Cola ad in a national periodical in 1904, spending just over $4,000 for the year. The next year, however, he boosted the budget for magazines to over $56,000, hiring Atlanta's Massengale Advertising Agency to create the national spreads. Almost all Massengale ads featured long, curved arrows pointing toward a glass of Coca-Cola—clearly an early, awkward effort to induce an automatic psychological response. "Whenever, you see an Arrow," read typical copy, "think of Coca-Cola."

At the beginning of 1906, Robinson added another $25,000 to the budget, earmarked for religious and literary publications in an attempt to sway Coca-Cola's critics. Such magazines had "a powerful influence," he argued, certain that ads there would convince "the very best people in this country that Coca-Cola is not only perfectly harmless, but . . . helpful and health-giving." Robinson promised that when publications such as *Collier's Weekly*, *The Saturday Evening Post*, or *The Christian Herald* were "flooded with letters" objecting to the Coca-Cola ads, the magazines would leap to the drink's defense.

Unfortunately, the flood of such protest letters had the opposite effect on *The Wesleyan Christian Advocate*, a Methodist magazine, which in 1906 refused to accept any more Coca-Cola ads. Reluctantly, Bishop Candler sold his Coca-Cola stock to avoid controversy. Asa Candler was infuriated, particularly since the *Advocate* continued to accept advertising from obviously fraudulent patent medicines, electric belts, and weight reducers. "Cut to the quick," as son Howard put it, Candler forthwith canceled his subscription.

The defensive Coca-Cola ads of this period continued to mix messages. True, the drink was delicious and refreshing, but its medicinal, bracing qualities were also stressed. A 1905 Massengale ad in *McClure's*, for instance, portrayed a young man in a darkened room, reading a book in an armchair. The lamp threw light onto the book and the glass of Coca-Cola he was about to drink. The text, a handwritten mock prescription, read: "Rx for *Students* and *all Brain Workers.* Take one glass Coca-Cola at eight to keep the brain clear and mind active until eleven." By 1907, however, Coca-Cola spreads no longer stressed *only* brain workers. Uncle Sam himself served as a soda jerk in one ad, which depicted him drawing a glass of Coca-Cola from a spigot attached to the front of the White House. The "Great American Beverage" was for "All Classes, Ages and Sexes." While an ad in *The Saturday Evening Post* featured a businessman in the foreground, women and children drank Coca-Cola at the soda fountain behind him.

Other ads targeted specific groups, the first efforts at "market segmentation." By 1907, the advertising finally recognized that women were major consumers, calling Coca-Cola "the shoppers' panacea." Here the medicinal claims were particularly strong. In one ad, Mrs. Blue exclaims: "Oh My, how tired I am! Nothing wears me out so completely as an afternoon's shopping." Mrs. Cheerful tells her the "wonderful secret" of how she remains so bouncy: "When I start out I get a glass of Coca-Cola; that keeps my nerves quiet. On the way home I get another. This relieves that headachy feeling and I return home as fresh as when I started out." Ads in theater magazines explained that "Coca-Cola is just as enjoyable as the play itself," while the *Scientific American* showed a man slumped over a drafting board *before* he had a drink and explained pseudo-academically that Coca-Cola soothed the "Rattled Nerves" and restored "Wasted Energy to both Mind and Body." Other efforts simply attempted to make readers hot and bothered. "When the Sun is Red Hot, and you and your collar are limp as rags; when your mouth and throat are the only dry spots on you and you are very, very thirsty, there's just one thing to do—Drink Coca-Cola."

Many of the 1905–1907 ads contained celebrity endorsements by movie stars or athletes. Coca-Cola gave Eddie Foy "vim, vigor, and go" on stage, while Ty Cobb and many other baseball players found it put the zip back into their games. "On days when we are playing a double-header," Cobb testified in a 1906 ad, "I always find that a drink of Coca-Cola between the games refreshes me to such an extent that I can start the second game feeling as if I had not been exercising at all."

All of the advertising of the period addressed the urban consumer, calling

Coca-Cola a "metropolitan beverage." Even those with a country setting stressed the sophistication of the consumers, such as two well-dressed couples served drinks in their automobile at a roadside stand. While most soda fountains were in the city, Coca-Cola had many rural customers. The Massengale men must have thought that snob appeal worked for the farmers and country folk who wished they were more cosmopolitan. Another explanation for the up-scale image, of course, was the Company's effort to disassociate the drink from cheap soda pop.

It is surprising that there was no mention of bottled Coca-Cola in this ad, or those featuring baseball. After all, a bottle would be more logical for these mobile consumers in the country or for sports fans. Even though bottle sales grew enormously in the first decade of the 1900s, the Company resolutely ignored them, presumably because the bottler would advertise his own product. There was more to it than that, however. Since there was virtually no mention of the bottle in annual reports of the period, Candler must have felt that *real* Coca-Cola was served at the fountain to upper-class people, and he resisted giving credit or exposure to the bottled drink.

BOTTLING BOOM COMES OF AGE

Nonetheless, the bottling industry had come of age by 1913, when the Coca-Cola Bottlers Association was formed. By that time, technology had revolutionized the young industry. While some plants still used the horse and wagon, many had bought trucks, allowing for more efficient and widespread delivery to a growing variety of outlets, including bowling alleys, barbershops, billiard rooms, fruit stands, and cigar stores. The New Orleans bottler, A. B. Freeman, used the most innovative modern delivery system, servicing the bayous with his motor launch, *Josephine*. Automated bottling, soaking, and washing machines made it possible to produce a more uniform drink at higher speeds.

The Coca-Cola bottler was now one of the wealthiest men in town. He sponsored elaborate floats covered with American flags and Coca-Cola signs for the local Fourth of July parade, gave to charity, and owned a prestigious automobile—though a true Coca-Cola man wasn't too high and mighty to ride his delivery trucks to "jolly the trade" or to promote Coca-Cola through "under-the-crown" contests. The typical bottler was a true believer even more than the fountain man, since Coca-Cola had made him rich. In addition, the widespread plants meant that wherever he traveled, a Coca-Cola man could count on an instant enthusiastic friend who spoke the language of refreshment.

The quirky bottling industry soon had its share of dynamic Coca-Cola *women*, however, who proved their mettle over the years. The first was Joseph Whitehead's widow, Lettie Pate Whitehead Evans (she remarried a Colonel Evans in 1913). In 1906, when Whitehead died, she pondered selling her share of the parent bottler, which John Candler advised her to do, since the business was "like a big balloon—punch a hole in it, and it is gone." Wisely, she decided to retain control, which she quietly exercised until her death in 1953. Other women took direct charge of bottling plants, usually as widows. Arthur

Pratt's sister-in-law Julia didn't wait for her husband, Russell, to die, however. She despised Los Angeles (and must not have been particularly fond of her husband, who remained there), returning to Florence, Alabama, where, from 1911 on, she ran an extremely profitable bottling operation.

BUGS IN THE BOTTLES

But the 500 bottlers who formed an association in 1913 weren't banding together out of sheer love for Coca-Cola; they also needed protection from lawsuits. From the very first, the bottled soft drink had caused problems. Since a wide array of bottles and carbonation were used, the finished product sometimes exploded in the consumer's hand. Returnable bottles arrived at plants with slugs, roaches, mice, cigarette butts, slime, and other unmentionable items; frequently the rinsing machinery of the day didn't entirely remove these "foreign ingredients," and they became a part of the delicious and refreshing drink sold to the public.

One of the early "exploding bottle" cases, involving a grocer named Hudgins, made it to the Georgia Supreme Court in 1905. Hudgins lost, as did most of the plaintiffs in cases against Coca-Cola. The law put the burden on the consumer to *prove* negligence—virtually an impossibility. It couldn't have hurt, however, that Judge John Candler sat on the Georgia Supreme Court bench at the time. The "foreign ingredient" cases made for good newspaper copy. In one early suit, Mrs. Mattie Allen, having discovered "a large number of bugs and worms" in her bottle of Coca-Cola, couldn't return to work for a week due to "untold mental agony from fear that an untimely death might result from said poisoning drink."

Wealthy bottlers attracted fraudulent charges. Often, they preferred to settle out of court for sizable sums rather than risk the adverse publicity of a court trial. In 1913, two bottlers in adjacent states discovered that they had paid the same woman hush money. Upon further investigation, they discovered that she routinely located dead bugs in her Coca-Cola as she moved around the country. And she was not the only one. When the associated bottlers finally located an insurer, they had to write their own policy, the first liability insurance in the United States. In the ensuing years, Coca-Cola bottlers generally refused to settle out of court. In 1913, they even won a case in which a deaf-mute had lost one of his remaining senses when blinded by shards from an exploding bottle.

The court cases, in conjunction with the concern about newly discovered "germs," led the bottlers to emphasize Coca-Cola as a clean, pure product. "Just now a wave of sanitary ideas [is] blowing over the country," a bottler wrote in 1909. "If the boards of health and the various pure-food committees of your vicinity get on the rampage, it is a very good advertisement for you if they find your place in a first-class, spotless condition." When salmonella-tainted milk made headlines, one bottler advised, "Tell your customers to cut out the milk diet and drink Coca-Cola. They are reasonably certain to get a pure drink prepared in a sanitary way."

THE LOATHSOME FOLLOWING

While imitators had plagued the Company when it offered only a fountain drink, there were now literally hundreds of bottled drinks cashing in on Coca-Cola's fame. Candler's nephew contemptuously described them as "little mushroom beverages that rise up at every morning's milestone," lamenting that it was impossible to escape such a "loathsome following."

The Company's efforts in the first few years of the century to squelch imitators yielded frightening results. In 1901, the Company had sued John B. Daniel, one of Pemberton's former partners, over his Passiflora Koko-Kolo, a drink which added maypop, or passionflower (yet another supposed aphrodisiac), to the standard coca and kola. In the suit, John Candler alleged that Daniel was "deceiving and misleading the public" by selling it in red five-gallon kegs for 25 cents a gallon less than Coca-Cola. Daniel's lawyers argued that he was not infringing on the name because the words "coca" and "cola" were descriptive and not subject to copyright. Coca-Cola lost the case. The next year, John Candler instituted a similar suit in New Jersey against Oscar Grenelle and Charles Schanck, who brazenly sold drinks they called Coco-Cola and Kola-Coca. Without denying their actions, Grenelle and Schanck mounted the same defense as Daniel: Coca-Cola was a purely descriptive term. Afraid to press the explosive issue, Candler dropped the prosecution.

Other Atlanta syrup manufacturers and bottlers declared open season on Coca-Cola imitation. One such firm, Afri-Kola, had the gall to open a factory just down the street on Edgewood Avenue. In 1903, John Candler arranged for a Washington law firm to send a threatening letter to the Atlanta imitators, hoping to frighten them off, and Sam Dobbs followed with a personal visit. The owner of Kola-Ade admitted to Dobbs that he had received the letter. "Why did you go so far from home to get a lawyer?" he sneered, insolently adding, "Suppose I am substituting, what are you going to do about it?"

Pemberton sold his formula to a few different people, but his ghost must have kept busy selling the secret wholesale, given the host of colas claiming to be as good as the original. Among others, these included Afri-Kola, Cafe-Coca, Candy-Cola, Carbo-Cola, Celery-Cola, Celro-Kola, Charcola, Cherry-Kola, Chero-Cola, Citra-Cola, Co-Co-Colian, Coca and Cola, Coca Beta, Coke Extract, Coke-Ola, Cola-Coke, Cola-Nip, Cold-Cola, Cream-Cola, Curo-Cola, Dope, Eli-Cola, Espo-Cola, Farri-Cola, Fig-Cola, Four-Kola, French Wine Coca, Gay-Ola, Gerst's Cola, Glee-Nol, Hayo-Kola, Heck's Cola, Jacob's Kola, Kaw-Kola ("Has the Kick"), Kaye-Ola, Kel-Kola, King-Cola, Koca-Nola, Ko-Co-Lem-A, Koke, Kola-Ade, Kola-Kola, Kola-Vena, Koloko, Kos-Kolo, Lime-Cola, Lemon-Ola, Loco-Kola, Luck-Ola, Mellow-Nip, Mexicola, Mint-Ola, Mitch-O-Cola, Nerv-Ola, Nifti-Cola, Noka-Cola, Pau-Pau Cola, Penn-Cola, Pepsi-Cola, Pepsi-Nola, Pillsbury's Coke, Prince-Cola, QuaKola, Revive-Ola, Rococola, Roxa-Kola, Sherry-Coke, Silver-Cola, Sola-Cola, Standard-Cola, Star-Cola, Taka-Kola, Tenn-Cola, Toka-Tona, True-Cola, Vani-Kola, Vine-Cola, Wine Cola, Wise-Ola. It is little wonder that one Coca-Cola man referred to the lot as "Fake-Colas."

HAROLD HIRSCH TO THE RESCUE

The situation became intolerable, but a St George was at hand to take on the imitation dragons. Harold Hirsch, a Columbia Law School graduate, was twenty-two when he joined the Candler law firm in 1904. The next year, the Trademark Law of 1905 was passed, and Coca-Cola registered under the Ten-Year Proviso, a grandfather clause giving legal status to *any* trademark, descriptive or otherwise, which had been in continuous use since 1895. Encouraged by the trademark's secure status, Hirsch decided to do something about the imitators. In 1909, he assumed full charge of Coca-Cola legal affairs, beginning a dogged courtroom pursuit of the "loathsome following." By the beginning of 1913, John Candler could write with satisfaction that "we have brought and tried within the last twelve months at least ten infringement cases where we brought one in 1906."

Not simply a lawyer representing a client, Hirsch was a true Coca-Cola man, inspiring bottlers, company officials, and other lawyers to defend the sacred trademark. "I have known every human emotion that the soul can know in connection with The Coca-Cola Company," he once said. "I have spent my nights and my days in thinking Coca-Cola." In 1914, sounding more like a hellfire evangelist than a lawyer, he dramatically urged a convention of bottlers to use the Coca-Cola name only on the genuine product. "If you fail us, if you do not stand back of us, the trade-mark 'Coca-Cola' is doomed," he warned. "No one, the great God Almighty Himself could not save you from final destruction. " Hirsch paused to let his words sink in. "But if you aid us with your work, this Coca-Cola becomes sacred."

In court, many defense laywers argued that substitution was legal when customers requested a "dope" or "coke." Consequently, Coca-Cola advertisements begged consumers to "demand the genuine by full name—nicknames encourage substitution." Asa Candler offered $100,000 to anyone who could curtail the widespread habit. When one of his bank employees asked the elderly entrepreneur to join him for a dope, Candler exploded: "It is not dope! There is no dope in it! It is Co-Ca-Co-La!" It was "blasphemy and treason," one salesman recalled, to utter a nickname. "To me 'Coke' was a dirty word, just like the other four-letter . . . words."

Hirsch hired Pinkerton detectives to go to soda fountains, ask for Coca-Cola, and take samples of bogus drinks served, which were then chemically analyzed to prove they were not the genuine product. In 1915, he persuaded the Company to form the Investigation Department and hire full-time spies. The parent bottlers agreed to pay for a portion of the detectives' salary and to share legal expenses.

By 1923, Hirsch had won enough cases setting different precedents to fill a 650-page Bible of Coca-Cola law, followed in later years by two more volumes. The Company graciously distributed these volumes to lawyers and libraries, reasonably assuming that potential infringers would be intimidated. By 1926, one reporter estimated that there were more than 7,000 "burials" in the Coca-Cola "copy-cat" mausoleum.

Hirsch won his cases on various grounds. He sued any cola drink that dared to use a script logo, a diamond label like Coca-Cola's, or red barrels. If the name was too similar, such as Chero-Cola, he objected on those grounds. He even attempted to claim the dark caramel color for Coca-Cola alone. Fighting his battles in city, county, state, and district courts, Hirsch appealed adverse decisions all the way to the Supreme Court. He opposed the registration of many colas at the U.S. Patent Office, effectively nipping them in the bud. During the course of his career, spanning three decades, Harold Hirsch virtually created modern American trademark law, filing an average of one case per week.

CREATION OF THE PERFECT PACKAGE

The Coca-Cola bottle frustrated Hirsch. Ben Thomas had tried to standardize it by blowing the logo into the glass on the bottle's shoulder. If an imitator ran its name in a similar location, Hirsch attacked it as an infringement. But he wasn't satisfied. The straight-sided bottles looked just like any other soda pop. In addition, imitators almost universally adopted the same diamond-shaped labels. Coca-Cola needed a unique bottle which required no paper label at all.

At a 1914 bottler convention, Hirsch cajoled the small bottler to look beyond the short-term expense of implementing a new bottle. "We are not building Coca-Cola alone for today. We are building Coca-Cola forever, and it is our hope that Coca-Cola will remain the National drink to the end of time." He called for a "bottle that we can adopt and call our own child." Before his death that same year, Ben Thomas had also begged for a package so distinctive that people could recognize it by feel and instantly identify even a broken bottle.

In June of the following year, the company asked several glass works to create prototypes of a distinctive bottle. Root Glass Company employees sought inspiration from the drink's ingredients. At the Terre Haute, Indiana, public library, the company auditor failed to find any pictures of the coca leaf or kola nut resembling a bottle. But the illustration of the cocoa bean pod, near the coca entry in the *Encyclopaedia Brittanica*, caught his eye. He may, in fact, have mistaken cocoa for coca. If so, it was a fortuitous error. Using the cocoa bean's fluted contour as his starting point, Earl Dean, the company machinist, produced a few sample bottles only minutes before the furnace cooled for the summer season.

Dean had designed what subsequently became known as the hobbleskirt bottle, named after a dress in fashion around 1914. Understandably, the skirt didn't stay in vogue long, since it was so narrow below the knee that it "hobbled" women before spreading wider at the ankles. These first few bottles had quite a bulge in the middle, later reduced to fit standard bottling equipment. Someone looking at this bosomy first effort called it a Mae West bottle, a nickname that stuck for many years. At the 1916 Coca-Cola Bottlers Convention, a seven-man committee overwhelmingly approved the design, though it took a few years before most bottlers accepted the more expensive container.

The new bottle eventually came to symbolize Coca-Cola as much as the script logo. Solidly built, it had a nice heft in the hand, although part of its weight was added to make the consumer forget that it held only six and a half ounces. Industrial designer Raymond Loewy waxed lyrical about the package, calling the "perfectly formed" bottle "aggressively female," while another authority maintained that it had "twenty cleverly concealed devices . . . to lure and satisfy the hand."

Harold Hirsch had no such grandiose ideas when he suggested the bottle, however. As the first ads made clear, the bottle was intended to stop fraud. "We've Bottled Up the Pirates of Business," one ad bragged. "They have imitated the [old] Coca-Cola bottle and label . . . but they cannot imitate the new [one]—it is patented."

DOBBS VS. ROBINSON

Harold Hirsch was not the only rising star in these turbulent years. Sam Dobbs, whom one observer called the "brains and beauty of the family," was eager to fill his uncle's shoes. Ever since Candler elevated his nephew to sales manager at the end of 1899, a power struggle between Sam Dobbs and Frank Robinson had been brewing. The brash, good-looking, self-assured Dobbs boasted that his sales force was "working like one great machine, without friction anywhere." As he gained power within the Company, Dobbs chafed at what he considered the old-fashioned approach to advertising that Robinson represented.

By 1906, the simmering personality conflict came to a head. Dobbs attacked one of Robinson's pet projects, a booklet showing the annual Coca-Cola gallonage of individual jobbers and bottlers. In a memo to Uncle Asa in February 1906, Dobbs, thirty-eight, wrote that "I have always opposed the publishing of inside facts of our business," and recommended that the booklet's publication cease. He explained that the widely distributed booklet furnished "*facts* and *figures* for the horde of imitators who are springing up over the country," handing them a gift-wrapped list of potential customers. In addition, he said, the impressive sales figures invited attack by hostile legislators who could manipulate the statistics to prove how widespread the "evil" of Coca-Cola really was. Dobbs certainly had a point; in 1905, sales had exceeded a million and a half gallons, a 37 percent increase over the previous year.

Robinson, then sixty years old, countered with a dignified rebuttal pointing out that the booklet's "great mass of evidence" of the "never-ending increase" in Coca-Cola's popularity encouraged dealers to compete with one another for yet greater sales. More important, he had a fundamental philosophical objection to Dobbs' suggestion. He didn't want to scheme or hide. "We have always conducted our business in the open," he wrote. "Our flag floats from the mast head. We are far, far beyond all competitors and this fact has been established by our statements." To kill the booklet would be "equivalent to pulling down the flag, wiping out the figures on our monument, covering up our tracks and crawling into a hole and refusing to show ourselves. Clouds of doubt and distrust would be hanging over us."

Robinson lost his fight, in more ways than one. The booklet was terminated, and Dobbs took over advertising as well as sales in 1906. He moved quickly to make changes. Jealous of St Elmo Massengale, who had been managing the Coca-Cola account, Dobbs hired his personal friend William D'Arcy and his St Louis agency. Dobbs threw huge amounts of money into full-page magazine spreads in the summer. Robinson watched in horror while Dobbs impetuously spent most of the ad budget by the fall. In November, the older man called for a "calm, deliberate, carefully considered, conservative, continuous campaign," spreading the same amount of money over the entire year with a slight increase during the summer months, allocating $3,000 to January and $8,000 to July. He called Dobbs' approach "flash advertising" which was planned at the last minute and resulted in a flurry of telegrams and confusion.

Robinson continued to plug away in his methodical, dedicated fashion until his retirement in 1913, but he was increasingly taken for granted. Dobbs claimed full credit for Coca-Cola advertising, becoming the darling of the press. After his election as president of the Associated Advertising Clubs of America in 1909, he promoted the "Truth in Advertising" campaign, gaining public acceptance of his profession—and, of course, distinguishing Coca-Cola (truthful and good) from patent medicines (fraudulent and bad).

When Dobbs talked about his profession and its importance, his self-confidence verged on arrogance. "The advertising man of today is a school-master," he asserted. "The world is his schoolroom and the people are his pupils." Some, he noted, were "unwilling pupils," but what of it? They would learn anyway. The advertiser spoke in a universal tongue that recognized "no politics, no creeds or hobbies." Dobbs compared an advertising campaign to a military action, speaking of the big guns of outdoor display and the small arms of metal signs.

For all of his braggadocio, Dobbs had a singularly limited vision. In 1908, for instance, he advised against the use of a large electric sign, which he considered too dangerous. Nor did he think it worthwhile to implement special Yiddish signs for Jewish districts. He saw no future in pushing Coca-Cola overseas, though by 1909 bottling plants were operating in Cuba, Hawaii, and Puerto Rico. Two years later, a British advertiser eloquently urged England as a market featuring "forty-five million people, with plenty of money to buy, compactly settled in a country little larger than Kansas." Dobbs wasn't interested, answering that "the old USA is keeping us fairly busy." In 1915, Dobbs wrote that "the foreign field is not a very attractive one," rejecting repeated entreaties from foreign firms.

Along with his friend D'Arcy, Dobbs stressed the beneficial qualities of Coca-Cola over the objections of parent bottler Ben Thomas. Advertised as a simple beverage, Coca-Cola attracted "every man, woman and child" as potential consumers, Thomas asserted. Calling it a tonic would create "the impression that it is a strong . . . stimulant" and would "create a prejudice in the minds of those people who think young children at least should not be given such a drink." Dobbs reacted defensively to the criticism, noting that he and D'Arcy had met six times and had "hammered and pounded on this stuff until it looks to me like it is about just right." True, he said, Coca-Cola was a beverage, but wasn't it more than that? "If simply a beverage, we have no grounds for claiming any excellency or special merit for it." Dobbs also disagreed with Thomas about the advisability of advertising to children, saying that he had to restrain his own children from drinking too much Coca-Cola. "Children are so apt to abuse a thing like Coca-Cola."

THE HARVEY WILEY THREAT

When Dobbs wrote that sentence in April of 1907, he unwittingly echoed the thoughts of Dr. Harvey Washington Wiley, whose name would soon cause Coca-Cola men to shudder as if confronted with the Anti-Christ. Early that year, the pure food reformer turned his intense gaze toward the soft drink industry and its most famous beverage. Over the next decade, Wiley nearly destroyed Coca-Cola.

～ 7 ～

Dr. Wiley Weighs In

Wiley is now made chief inspector, chief examiner, instigator of the charge, prosecutor, jury and judge; and if any manufacturer dares cry out against such an unjust condition he is met with the cry from Wiley and the Wiley press: "He is an adulterator and a dopester . . ." And all this power in the hands of a man who says: "I am the spirit and essence of the pure food law, and without me there would be no law."

— *The American Food Journal*, February 15, 1912

SINCE HIS ARRIVAL in Washington in 1883, Dr. Harvey Washington Wiley, the first head of the U.S. Bureau of Chemistry, had steadfastly fought against food adulteration; but it was only in 1902 that Wiley became a household name when he inaugurated his "poison squad," a group of twelve young men who were human guinea pigs for food additives Wiley suspected were health hazards. The "experiments" proceeded without scientific controls and ignored volunteers' expectations that their diet would make them ill; but what the investigations lacked in rigor, they supplied in publicity, inspiring satirical journalistic doggerel:

> *We're on the hunt for a toxic dope that's certain to kill, sans fail,*
> *But it is a tricky, elusive thing and knows we're on its trail.*
> *For all the things that could kill we've downed in many a gruesome wad,*
> *And still we are gaining a pound a day, for we are the Pizen Squad!*

The next year, Wiley used his new public status to attack the patent medicine industry and to demand passage of a pure food and drug bill. All such proposed legislation—almost 200 bills in the thirty previous years—had been killed by the combined lobbying efforts of the Proprietary Association of America and the whiskey and food industries. "There seemed to be an understanding between the two Houses [of Congress]," Wiley recalled, "that when one passed a bill . . . the other would see that it suffered a lingering death." The tide of public opinion, however, had begun to turn, in large measure because of the press. The ads of the nineteenth-century patent-medicine maker had been largely responsible for the growth of national magazines. Now, ironically, it was those same magazines which gave men like Harvey Wiley and journalists Samuel Hopkins Adams and Mark Sullivan the platform from which to blast the overblown claims and narcotic contents of the nostrums. In October of 1905, *Collier's* published the first in a series titled

"The Great American Fraud"—blistering, well-researched pieces by Adams which galvanized public and legislative opinion.

In his first article, Adams exposed the "red clause" used by patent medicine men to blackmail publications into favorable editorial positions. Printed in red in advertising contracts, the paragraph voided a contract if hostile state legislation were passed. "Tyrannical masters, these heavy purchasers of advertising space," Adams commented, commending William Allen White, editor of the *Emporia Gazette* in Emporia, Kansas, for refusing to bow to such pressure.

What made it possible for White and other editors to be so courageous was the growth of other advertising revenue from more savory products. Patent medicines had led the way, but now manufacturers of breakfast foods, sewing machines, farm implements, and other mass-produced items were finding that advertising paid. Following Adams' 1905 praise, editor William Allen White, using his small-town Kansas paper as a platform, became the conscience of America's heartland for the next forty years.

When William McKinley was assassinated in 1901 and an unpredictable but pugnacious Theodore Roosevelt replaced him as president, the Gilded Age gave way to the Progressive Era. Reform, a natural consequence of the rapid change and industrialization of the late 1800s, suddenly achieved a respectable status. Now members of the previously docile urban middle class demanded assurance of the safety and purity of the foods and drugs they bought. They began to suspect the worst of impersonal, powerful corporations, whose beguiling advertising often promoted adulterated products. Goaded by the muckrakers, consumers clamored for change on all fronts. Upton Sinclair's *The Jungle* was published in February of 1906, revealing the revolting conditions in Chicago's meat packing houses. A socialist, Sinclair had written his book primarily as an indictment of working conditions, but it was his graphic description of laborers falling into vats and becoming part of the lard sold at the corner store that had an effect. "I aimed at the public's heart, and by accident I hit it in the stomach," he lamented.

In the new muckraking atmosphere, Coca-Cola was the unhappy object of multiple assaults. "In the past years," J. J. Willard wrote in *The Coca-Cola Bottler*, "we have seen a great, cyclonic wave of reform sweeping over the country, pretending, upon its face, to correct all manner of evils and remedy many defects . . . Very few of the successful industrial concerns of the country have not felt its sting." Coca-Cola, he noted, was certainly no exception, finding itself vilified by "the man who has excess zeal and little knowledge, the professional boozer, the original teetotaler, and the man with his upturned palm." Willard's list aptly summarized the drink's enemies. Reformers possessed, in his opinion, "excess zeal" and insufficient knowledge. The brewers ("boozers") were convinced that Coca-Cola was providing secret funds for the Prohibition lobby and resented the *soft* drink which claimed to be a temperance beverage but still provided a kick reputed to be as substantial as alcohol's. Coca-Cola was also denigrated by the temperance forces ("teetotalers") because of its caffeine content and rumors of cocaine. Finally, lawmakers (with "upturned palm") saw the wealthy bottlers and the Coca-Cola Company as a convenient source of special sin taxes.[*]

THE PURE FOOD LAW IS PASSED

In 1906, with Adams continuing his series in *Collier's* and Sinclair's book a best-seller, the time was finally ripe for passage of strong national legislation. Wiley stumped the country tirelessly, lobbying the legislatures, advising sympathetic journalists. He wrote to state chemists, talked to women's clubs, addressed trade associations. He seemed to be everywhere at once. When the Pure Food and Drugs Act was passed in June of 1906, it was almost universally known as Dr. Wiley's Law.

Asa Candler and everyone else at The Coca-Cola Company were, of course, well aware of the pure food movement. Sam Dobbs archly referred to "pure food cranks," while John Candler complained of "misguided fanatics." On the state level, Coca-Cola had been fighting adverse legislation since the turn of the century, enlisting the help of local bottlers to kill bills to tax or ban Coca-Cola in virtually every Southern state. It became clear to Judge John Candler, however, that some form of national legislation was inevitable. Although appointed to the Georgia Supreme Court in 1902, he still devoted almost half of his time to Coca-Cola's legal affairs, and, as the pure food movement gained momentum, the judge realized that the Company needed a full-time lawyer. Assessing his priorities, he resigned from the bench in January of 1906. Ever politically astute, John Candler convinced his older brother Asa that the impending pure food law could actually work to the Company's benefit. By supporting it, Coca-Cola would appear virtuous and set itself apart from the "bad" patent medicines. Besides, the law could be used to Coca-Cola's advantage; it would probably put imitators with cocaine content out of business.

Consequently, John Candler traveled to Washington in the spring of 1906 to testify in favor of the Pure Food and Drugs Act. When it passed, the Company ran ads prominently declaring that Coca-Cola was *pure* and wholesome, the Great National Temperance Beverage. "Refreshing as a Summer Breeze," one late 1906 ad soothingly began, "it aids digestion and is genuinely good to the taste, gives a zest for additional labor and a keener enjoyment of recreation. Guaranteed under the Pure Food and Drugs Act." Coca-Cola fountain salesmen used the new law to threaten those who were diluting or substituting, saying they would send samples to the Pure Food Commission.

As a result of the law, The Coca-Cola Company also changed the formula, apparently to take saccharin out of both bottle and fountain syrup. Wiley was known to object to saccharin as an adulterant. Exactly when and why the

---

[*]Attempts to levy special state taxes on Coca-Cola became a national pastime for local legislators over the next eighty years, though many bills were thinly disguised shakedowns by predatory politicians who wanted bottlers to make it worth their while to drop the tax effort.

artificial sweetener had been added is a matter of conjecture, but it was probably after consultation with Benjamin Thomas, who convinced Candler that it would be cheaper and would act as a preservative. Since the changed formula cost more, Asa Candler attempted to raise the price of bottlers' syrup by 10 cents a gallon. Thomas objected, referring pointedly to his fixed-price contract, eventually compromising at a 2-cent-per-gallon hike. Though no Coca-Cola publicity called attention to the changed formula, it was soon common knowledge. In Emporia, Kansas, William Allen White reported that "a number of the drinkers of this beverage do not think the new kind is as good as the old, but the fountains have their usual run of regular customers."

WILEY TAKES ON DOPE

For a few months, it appeared that all would be well. But early in 1907, Asa Candler picked up a paper and read the headline: "Dr. Wiley Will Take Up Soda Fountain 'Dope.'" Clearly, Wiley was referring to Coca-Cola. Although its producers had *claimed* to remove the cocaine, he said, Coca-Cola's caffeine content was subject to investigation. Candler wrote to Wiley on February 25, 1907, to complain that his statement would "work vast deteriment" to his drink's sales and offered Wiley the "plain facts" that Coca-Cola was a harmless nonalcoholic beverage. "It contains *no* cocaine, nor any deleterious drug," he stressed, adding that a serving of the soft drink contained about as much caffeine as a weak cup of tea. "There can be no more objection to the consumption of caffeine in the form of Coca-Cola than there is . . . to the importation of tea and coffee and their use," Candler concluded. "We therefore ask you most respectfully to give your endorsement to the meritorious cause to which we have devoted our energy."

Candler may be forgiven for believing that this would resolve the matter, but he didn't understand how Harvey Wiley's mind worked. In many ways, Candler and Wiley had similar backgrounds. Both were imbued with a strong religious fundamentalism and grew up on antebellum country farms. Wiley was raised in Indiana, suffering through strictly observed Sundays during which, he recalled, fishing was considered a "heinous sin." Where Candler had thought of becoming a physician before turning to pharmacy, Wiley had actually earned a medical degree but never practiced, instead becoming a chemistry professor. Their most important similarity, however, was an almost fanatical belief in the righteousness and correctness of their respective causes. Wiley took his father's advice seriously: "Be sure you are right and then go ahead."

In almost every other way, Wiley and Candler were opposites. A Yankee whose father read *Uncle Tom's Cabin* aloud and made his home a station on the Underground Railroad, Wiley served in Sherman's Army, though he saw limited combat. Physically, Wiley dwarfed not only Candler but most men. He was a solid six-footer, "tall and massive of stature," as one journalist put it, "with a big head firmly posed above a pair of titanic shoulders." His "penetrating glance" unnerved opponents, but, unlike Asa Candler, he possessed a sense of humor and ready wit, taking robust pleasure from life. Wiley's humor left him, however, when he thundered from the pure food pulpit; he was repeatedly mistaken for a clergyman because of his dress and demeanor, earning the nickname Father Wiley. In fact, he was a professed agnostic, but all of Wiley's childhood religious training was channeled into his work. He was, as his admirers called him, a "preacher of purity," or, as his critics preferred, a "zealot." One historian has aptly described him as a "chemical fundamentalist."

Above all else, Wiley mounted a *moral* crusade against fraud and vice. "The injury to public health," he said, "is the least important question . . . [and] should be considered last of all. The real evil of food adulteration is deception of the consumer." Wiley's obsession with deceit rather than health issues was reflected in his law. The Pure Food and Drugs Act of 1906 did not make poisonous substances illegal; it simply said that they had to be stated on the label. Logically enough, Candler felt that he was safe under the new pure food law. Caffeine (unlike cocaine) was not on the list of poisonous substances and consequently did not have to be listed on the label. Candler was merely using common sense when he said that Coca-Cola was no more harmful than a cup of tea.

For Wiley, however, there was a clear difference. Everyone *knew* that tea contained caffeine, but Coca-Cola purported to be a wholesome drink and was sold to children as such. Also, caffeine was a natural constituent of tea and coffee, but not of Coca-Cola. Candler could hardly have been happy with Wiley's reply of February 28, 1907: "I have heard many complaints of the Coca-Cola habit . . . You might as well say that hydrocyanic acid is harmless because it occurs in peaches and almonds." Ominously, Wiley ended by reassuring Candler that "the Department will not do anything that is hasty or illegal . . . and when we come to the examination of your product, you shall have full opportunity to be heard."

In July, the Acting Secretary of Agriculture (no doubt prompted by Wiley, whose Bureau of Chemistry was part of the Agriculture Department) wrote to The Coca-Cola Company, threatening to cancel its serial number if it did not stop claiming in ads to be "guaranteed" under the pure food law. As the Company's attorney, John Candler wrote a polite response asking how the guaranty was being abused; he was told that the Agriculture Department objected to ads claiming that Coca-Cola was "pure." The Company agreed to drop the offending word from future ads.

THE WCTU ENTERS THE FRAY

Meanwhile, Wiley plotted against Coca-Cola behind the scenes, enlisting the aid of Mrs. Martha M. Allen, chair of the Medical Temperance Department of the Women's Christian Temperance Union and the wife of a Methodist minister. A formidable opponent, Mrs. Allen had written a book about hidden alcohol and narcotics in medicines and had been elected to membership of the American Association for the Advancement of Science. Somehow, she and

Wiley found old testimony from the 1901 IRS mistrial which showed that Coca-Cola contained a small amount of cocaine and 2 percent alcohol. Using the old trial testimony, Wiley and Allen elicited support from the Surgeon General of the Army, who wrote in May that "a soldier drinking a half dozen bottles of this preparation during the day would get an indefinite quantity of cocaine . . . and the same amount of alcohol [as] in an equal quantity of beer." Based on this assessment, the U.S. Army banned Coca-Cola in June of 1907—quite a blow for the Company that was trying to position its product as the patriotic National Temperance Beverage.

Coca-Cola did, in fact, have a tiny amount of alcohol, less than one percent of the syrup, a residue from the essential oils and extracts. The 2 percent figure apparently came from an assay of adulterated syrup. To persuade the Army to remove the ban, Coca-Cola braved the lion's den, and asked Wiley's Bureau of Chemistry to analyze samples of the drink, probably hoping to convince Wiley of its harmlessness at the same time. In September of 1907, John Candler sent Wiley a chemical analysis of Coca-Cola made by an independent pharmacist, showing 1.25 grains of caffeine, compared with 2 grains in the average cup of coffee. "Tests for cocaine failed to respond," the pharmacist wrote. Wiley sent back a curt note of thanks.

Influential politicians, obviously seeking to please their powerful Coca-Cola constituents, besieged the Army with requests for reconsideration of the ban, among them Henry Cabot Lodge of Massachusetts and Georgia congressman Leonidas Livingston. At the same time, sensationalist newspaper coverage broke the story nationwide. "COCAINE IS SERVED AT SODA FOUN-TAINS," blared one New Jersey headline. "War Department Bars It from Army Canteens—Concoction Asserted to Contain Not Only Cocaine and Caffeine, but Also as Much Alcohol as Beer—South Has the Habit." As a result, the Army received letters of inquiry from alarmed organizations whose executives had read the newspaper stories. The International Sunday School Association, the Illinois Board of Health, and the Chautauqua Institution wanted to know if Coca-Cola was injurious. It was a public relations disaster for the soft drink company.

Once it became clear that there was no cocaine and negligible alcohol in Coca-Cola, the Army rescinded the ban in November of 1907, but not before substantial damage had been done. Sales weren't materially affected in the United States, but the incident nearly ruined the Cuban business. The Coca-Cola Company had opened its own bottling plant in Havana in 1902 and built a thriving business, based on sales to Cubans, tourists, and the U.S. Army, which had intervened a second time since the Spanish-American War to crush a revolt. When local competitors found that Coca-Cola had been banned on Army bases, they distributed handbills proclaiming that the drink was a "subtle poison." Cuban sales plummeted. "Our competitors considered us dead," the plant manager later wrote. For the first but not the last time, Coca-Cola became the symbol of American imperialism; it took years to rebuild the Cuban trade.

SAM DOBBS MEETS MRS. ALLEN

Mrs. Allen was intent on mobilizing the mothers of America against Coca-Cola. With Wiley's help, she published a pamphlet implying that the drink still contained cocaine and asserting that its caffeine, combined with the alcohol content, was a health hazard, particularly to children. In an attempt to placate the feisty WCTU leader, Sam Dobbs proceeded north where, as though taking part in a duel, he and Allen each brought a "second" to the Yates Hotel in Syracuse, New York, near Mrs. Allen's home. Dobbs opened the debate by praising his Uncle Asa. "It would be impossible for so high-minded a man to make and sell a beverage that contained the least possible danger of a drug-habit," he explained. "Why, he gives largely to missions and schools."

Mrs. Allen remained unimpressed, calmly commenting that the British tyrant Charles I had been noted for his kindness to children. "Giving to missions, Mr Dobbs, is small atonement for years of advertising a coca beverage." At this, Dobbs lost his temper and waved the defamatory WCTU pamphlet in her face, screaming, "Do you suppose we would give *poison* to our own children? My children drink Coca-Cola; if it had *poison* in it, do you think I would let them have it?" When he sputtered into silence, Mrs. Allen replied that the pamphlet never used the word "poison," but that she believed the drink to be harmful. "I know of a lad who has become worthless in school or anywhere else because of his addiction to Coca-Cola." As a finale, Dobbs countered by invoking the patron saint of the muckrakers, Samuel Hopkins Adams, asserting that when *Collier's* had sent Adams to Georgia to investigate Coca-Cola, he had been unable to find anyone injured by the drink.

It was clear when the two parted that neither duelist had changed the other's mind, but Martha Allen subsequently wrote to Adams to ask about his trip to Georgia. "Mr. Dobbs has used my name not only without authority," Adams replied, "but in a way to produce a false impression. What I reported to *Collier's* was that I was convinced that coca cola does not contain cocaine. I do most emphatically believe that it produces a habit . . . baneful and difficult to break. There is too much smoke not to indicate some fire, and I hear from all parts of the South, both by letter and personal interview, of cases where the addict must have his fifteen or twenty [daily] glasses of 'dope.'"

Coca-Cola was the subject of an increasing amount of gossip in those years. Growing up in Asheville, North Carolina, Thomas Wolfe heard most of the rumors, but they only increased his taste for Coca-Cola. He immortalized the Great American Drink in this passage from the Great American Novel, *Look Homeward, Angel*: "Drink Coca Cola. They say [Candler] stole the formula from old mountain woman. $50,000,000 now. Rats in the vats. Dope at Wood's [Drug Store] better. Too weak here. [Gene] had recently acquired a taste for the beverage and drank four or five glasses a day."

DEPUTY KEBLER TOURS THE SOUTH

Adams was not the only one who went south during the fall of 1907 to investigate Coca-Cola. Going considerably beyond the simple sample analysis requested by the Army, Wiley sent his drug deputy, Lyman F. Kebler, for an extended jaunt through Coca-Cola heartland, where he visited Army bases as well as major cities and Coca-Cola bottling facilities. Kebler's report reads, one commentator aptly observed, as if he were a "stranger in an alien and hostile land, appalled by the odd and dangerous customs of the natives."

The drug deputy characterized Atlanta as "the home of coca cola and . . . the city of fountains," observing that there was a soda fountain on almost every street corner and in all major office buildings. He noted that Coca-Cola was drunk by people "in all walks of life, but most abundantly by office workers and . . . brain workers," who, he noted with horror, took a glass before work, another at lunch, and several more in the evening. Soda jerks informed him that "Coca-Cola fiends" drank ten to twelve glasses a day. "We personally saw the beverage consumed by children of four, five and six years of age," he wrote, adding that Coca-Cola was often brought home in pitchers to be guzzled by the entire family.

Kebler inspected the Coca-Cola plant itself and was disgusted by what he observed: "The kettle in which the sirup was made appeared to boil over occasionally, and it was surrounded with filth of every description, including sticks, dirt, straw, and all sorts of debris." He noted that, although the filling area in the cellar was cleaner, the containers were not. "Dead mice and similar things have been found in the sirup barrels and kegs after they have been emptied."

Visiting bottling plants in Chattanooga, Kebler was equally offended by the "slovenly and unhygienic manner" in which Coca-Cola was bottled. "If, for example, some foreign material is present in a dark bottle," he wrote, "it is likely to be overlooked and left inside, and the bottle filled with the beverage. The cleaning, as a rule, is very superficial, and only a small portion of filth is removed." At nearby Fort Oglethorpe, Kebler learned that Coca-Cola had served primarily as a hangover cure before the ban, but a local saloon proprietor said that soldiers drank "Coca-Cola high-balls"—the soft drink mixed with whiskey—which made them "wild and crazy."

Kebler finally returned to Washington late in the fall of 1907, convinced that Coca-Cola was a habit-forming menace, confirming Wiley's worst fears. At the end of October, Wiley announced that he was forming a new Poison Squad specifically for soft drinks. Newspapers reported that his twelve brave volunteers, young men in their twenties, would test 100 different drinks "widely advertised as invigorators, nerve-restorers, and brain stimulants" and known to contain "cocaine, caffeine, chloral hydrates, or opium."

WILEY'S FRUSTRATED OFFENSIVE

When 1907 finally ended, Sam Dobbs noted in the annual report that "during the past year, we have not only had to work to get new business, but we have had to fight to keep the business we already had. Throughout the year we were constantly engaged in combating prejudice, ignorance and graft." Having weathered the multiple onslaughts of 1907, Asa Candler must have been relieved when the following year passed relatively uneventfully, with sales nearing 3 million gallons annually and a cash surplus of $1.2 million.

But Wiley had not retreated: he was only preparing for a massive frontal assault which he would have launched in November of 1908 except for bureaucratic interference. George McCabe, the department's solicitor and a member of the Board of Food and Drug Inspection, repeatedly refused to approve Wiley's recommended seizures, since caffeine had not been proven harmful. On February 8, a frustrated but resigned Wiley wrote to Adams to assure him that "I am going to stay by the ship until I am court-martialed and put under arrest." The next month, Wiley located an interstate shipment of Coca-Cola in New Orleans and recommended its seizure. Worn down, McCabe finally referred it to Dr. Dunlap of the board for a decision. Dunlap pointed out that "if the data are so strongly against caffeine," he would logically have to ban the importation of tea and coffee—an impossibility—and he too countermanded the chief chemist.

Infuriated, Wiley dismissed the comparison to tea and coffee, claiming that the matter did not "merit discussion." His anguished memos make it clear that his main concern was that children drank Coca-Cola. In May, he tried again, writing that a woman on a local board had objected to Coca-Cola signs erected near schools, luring students to imbibe. "If their parents knew they were drinking caffeine," Wiley asserted, "they would be horrified. I again renew my request, which has been denied on several occasions, to institute proceedings." Again, he was denied. This time, James Wilson, the Secretary of Agriculture, personally told Wiley to lay off Coca-Cola. Wiley was "surprised and grieved," he wrote later, but "as usual I could see behind it the manipulation of powerful hands." He must have reflected bitterly that while he was lionized by the public, nominated that year for the Nobel Prize in Chemistry, his opinions held no weight with his superiors.

Even though Secretary Wilson had ordered him to leave the Atlanta beverage king alone, Wiley sent Inspector J. L. Lynch to look over the main factory in July, where Lynch observed a black man "cooking" the huge kettle of Coca-Cola, reporting that the cook's dirty undershirt was soaked with sweat, his feet poked through his broken shoes, and he shot wads of chewing tobacco indiscriminately onto the platform next to the mixing kettle. When sugar spilled onto the platform, the employee shoved it into the vat with his feet.

As if to taunt Wiley, Asa Candler hired a dirigible with a gigantic Coca-Cola logo to float above Washington in 1909. At the same time, Sam Dobbs and William D'Arcy were writing *The Truth About Coca-Cola*, a defensive tract which opened with the words: "This is a book of information—not of defense." During the strife of the next few years, the Company distributed millions of these pamphlets, despite Ben Thomas's objections to defensive strategies.

FINALLY GETTING THE GO-AHEAD

In August of 1909, John Candler could still boast that "not once . . . has there been a single State or Federal prosecution against . . . Coca-Cola." But two months later, that all changed. While in Washington, Fred L. Seely, editor of the *Atlanta Georgian*, asked Harvey Wiley why Coca-Cola had not been prosecuted under the pure food law. Unlike the *Constitution* and *Journal*, the *Georgian* wasn't part of the Atlanta business establishment. Seely, a New Jersey native, had founded the paper in 1906 and was considered radical for his opposition to child labor and chain gangs. The crusading editor and Asa Candler were already antagonists. In May of 1909, Seely had threatened to publish photos of the appalling conditions at the Decatur Orphans' Home, where Candler was a trustee.

Stung by Seely's question, Wiley poured out his frustrations to the editor, brandishing his file of Coca-Cola memos. Seely immediately went to Secretary Wilson and told him that unless he allowed Wiley to go ahead, he, Seely, would make trouble for him in his paper. As Wiley put it, "It is remarkable what the fear of publicity will do." The next day, Wiley was given the go-ahead.

On October 19, 1909, Drug Deputy Kelber and Inspector Lynch traced a shipment of syrup bound for Chattanooga. The next day, they made yet another unannounced inspection of the Coca-Cola factory. Howard Candler was startled to find them sneaking around in the cellar, but he remained polite and provided them with a sample of Merchandise No. 5, the coca and kola mixture. When Howard's father found out the government agents were once again snooping about, he flew at them like an enraged hornet, "very excited and very much worked up and very nervous," as Lynch recalled. "By God," Candler said, "if I had been here you would not have got [that sample]." Lynch was baffled when Candler called Kebler "a God-damned carpenter." In fact, the Yankee inspector obviously misunderstood the epithet. In his outrage, Candler had labeled the government agent a God-damned *carpetbagger*.

Two days later, Inspector Lynch seized thirty-seven barrels and twenty kegs of Coca-Cola syrup in Chattanooga, though somehow three more barrels must have been added later. The case was officially called *The United States vs. Forty Barrels and Twenty Kegs of Coca-Cola*. Although ludicrously named, the case promised to be a fierce legal battle between formidable opponents. It was only the second case under the new pure law to go to court. Now that Wiley finally had the Agriculture Department's support, no effort or expense was spared.

SPY/COUNTERSPY

It took almost a year and a half for Coca-Cola and the government to prepare the case for trial. After Wiley's investigators found that Coca-Cola intended to call famous scientists to testify that caffeine was not harmful, Wiley lined up his own expert witnesses. He also ordered his spies to dig up dirt on the opposition scientists, although nothing came of it. Over his strong objections, the trial was held in Chattanooga, site of the seizure, rather than Washington. As Wiley was aware, Chattanooga was a Coca-Cola town; the jury was likely to favor the defense. "It was equivalent . . . to trying the case in Atlanta," Wiley complained.

As the trial geared up in March of 1911, seven government spies infiltrated Chattanooga to keep an eye on jurors, trying to prove they were incompetent, immoral, or associated with Coca-Cola. Meanwhile, Candler had hired his own counterspies to keep an eye on the government agents. The entire affair started to resemble a Keystone Kops film. One juror, it transpired, had once been arrested for horse stealing, while another frequented saloons. The agent dismissed the rest as "very low class men" who seemed "entirely incompetent to try a case of this nature." In unearthing such information, one government spy complained that they were "watched, followed and pointed out by agents of the defense . . . This makes us almost useless now." He also noted that rooming at the downtown Hotel Patten, owned by Coca-Cola's J. T. Lupton, was a mistake.

Just before the trial commenced, Wiley, sixty-six, a lifelong bachelor, married Anna Kelton, a librarian less than half his age. Giving her a taste of what her marriage would be like, he took her on their "honeymoon" to the Coca-Cola trial, where everyone expected him to be the star witness. The Chattanooga papers and high society were thrilled to have the famous Dr. Wiley in their midst, even though he was on the wrong side, and the Wileys were treated like visiting royalty.

THE TRIAL

From opening day on March 13, 1911, the Barrels and Kegs trial attracted national attention, making daily headlines in Chattanooga and Atlanta for its nearly month-long duration. The two main charges were that Coca-Cola was adulterated and misbranded. According to the pure food law, a product was adulterated if it had a deleterious added ingredient. Consequently, the government had to prove that caffeine was both harmful and an "added" ingredient under the law. Coca-Cola was misbranded, the charge stated, because it did not in fact have the whole coca leaf in it (i.e., cocaine was removed), and it had only an infinitesimal amount of kola nut. The misbranding charge was somewhat ironic, of course, because if the drink *had* contained cocaine, it would have been illegal as well.

For Chattanoogans, the trial provided ample entertainment. Lynch and Kebler repeated their observations on the filthy Coca-Cola plant, appealing to racist sentiment by dwelling on the black cook's sweat and expectorations. Kebler testified that Coca-Cola was not only poisonous, but had made one deceased victim's heart so hard that it was impossible to cut with a knife. At that point, Judge Edward Terry Sanford had to reprimand Coca-Cola's expert witnesses, who couldn't contain their audible amusement. Another government witness reported that he had found straw, part of a bumble bee, and other insect fragments in the seized syrup.

Well-known Methodist evangelist George Stuart took the stand briefly. Unfortunately for those eager for real sensation, he didn't get far before the prosecution had to bow to defense objections and withdraw him. Stuart had thundered against Coca-Cola from an Atlanta pulpit, then written Bishop Candler a long public letter in which he said that excessive use of Coca-Cola at a girls' school led to "wild nocturnal freaks, . . . violations of college rules and female proprieties, and even immoralities." Coca-Cola also kept boys awake, Stuart said, inevitably tempting them with the evils of masturbation.

Most of the trial, though, was taken up with expert witnesses. Whether the jurors were "low class" or not, it is doubtful they understood a fraction of the scientific jargon that the doctors and pharmacologists unleashed in the courtroom. The caliber of the witnesses was beyond reproach. All three co-editors of the 1905 edition of *The National Standard Dispensary* testified at the trial—Henry H. Rusby for the government, Charles Caspari and Hobart A. Hare for Coca-Cola. Near the end of the event, when the jurors were already dazed, Coca-Cola lawyers triumphantly unveiled a massive deposition from world-renowned German pharmacologist Oswald Schmiedeberg, delaying the trial because of the need for translation.

Despite their impressive credentials, most expert witnesses relied on flawed experiments highly colored by their own opinions. Harry and Leta Hollingworth's ground-breaking double-blind experiments on caffeine's effects on humans, still-cited classics of the literature, were the exception. Harry Hollingworth, a young psychology professor at Columbia, took the job—considered "a somewhat shady business"—only after his seniors rejected the research. Leta directed the actual experiments, which indicated that caffeine, in moderate amounts, improved motor skills while leaving sleep patterns relatively unaffected. Awaiting his turn to testify, Harry Hollingworth found the proceedings "a most interesting and often amusing conflict." Appalled by the "anecdotal and misguided testimony that appeared on both sides," Hollingworth was particularly dismayed by one scientist's conclusion that caffeine caused congestion of the cerebral blood vessels in rabbits, whom he had dispatched by a club to the head.

Neither of the principal antagonists testified, which in Asa Candler's case was easy to understand. His lawyers didn't want the volatile owner anywhere near the courtroom. Candler stayed in Atlanta for most of the trial, firing off dyspeptic letters to Chattanooga calling Lynch a perjuring liar and expressing outrage over the *Georgian*'s sensationalistic coverage. He can scarcely be blamed. At one point, Seely's newspaper ran the headline "EIGHT COCA-COLAS CONTAIN ENOUGH CAFFEINE TO KILL." Candler concluded, "It is outrageous that our government is disposed to harass us, but I feel that right will eventually prevail." The government's scientists spent days describing the effects of Coca-Cola on various animals. When defense attorney J. B. Sizer complained that injecting frogs with Coca-Cola hardly constituted viable evidence, Harvard professor Dr William Boos countered, "It is a difficult thing to feed a frog. Have you ever tried it?" With relief and some contempt, Asa Candler wrote on March 21, that "U.S. has almost exhausted its rat rabbit & frog evidence."

The papers repeatedly anticipated that Wiley would take the stand, but he never did. While masterminding the prosecution, Wiley apparently preferred to let the specialists testify, telling the lawyers that he did not qualify as an expert in any specific area. Surely, however, Wiley would have testified if he had had strong evidence of Coca-Cola's negative effects on his poison squad, but apparently the young men must have thrived on the beverage.

Coca-Cola eventually won the case, though not on any scientific grounds. All of the testimony and spying on jurors proved irrelevant. Judge Sanford (who was appointed to the United States Supreme Court in 1923) issued his opinion from the bench, ordering the jury to return a verdict in favor of Coca-Cola. He ruled that the product was not misbranded, since it did contain coca and kola, even though in tiny amounts. Without deciding whether caffeine was a poison or not, Sanford said that it was *not* an added ingredient under the law, but had been an integral part of the formula since the drink was invented.

WILEY'S CRUSADE

Jubilant, Company officials publicized this victory widely. The trial did, nonetheless, cause an immediate change in Coca-Cola advertising. The most compelling case against the drink in the trial had been its consumption by children. Defense lawyers hadn't contested caffeine's bad effects on youngsters; instead, they had denied that children drank Coca-Cola at all. This assertion was somewhat awkward, since many contemporary ads showed children drinking right along with their parents. "Father likes it. Son likes it," crowed one 1907 ad which depicted a five-year-old happily imbibing. After 1911, an unwritten law stated that no one under twelve years old would be shown drinking in a Coca-Cola ad—a dictum enforced until 1986.

Because of adverse publicity from the trial, two bills were introduced to the U.S. House in 1912 to amend the Pure Food and Drugs Act, adding caffeine to the list of "habit-forming" and "deleterious" substances which must be listed on the label. Coca-Cola successfully fought to kill the bills, the first of many such efforts to keep its caffeine content out of the public eye.

The trial had an impact on Dr. Wiley as well. His superiors, looking for any excuse to ditch the bullheaded chemist, accused Wiley of having illegally paid Dr. Rusby too much for his testimony. A special Senate investigation was launched, and the papers were filled with cartoons and editorials about Wiley. He was finally cleared, but by 1912, he realized that he would always be frustrated in the government bureaucracy. He resigned in March of 1912, at the height of his national popularity. It is impossible to overestimate Wiley's fame and influence, which was far greater than his modern counterpart, Ralph Nader, ever attained. The Wiley seal of approval was all-important, even after he left the Bureau, which explains why the president of Dr Pepper sent him the drink's formula (since it contained no caffeine), invited him to visit the Waco, Texas, plant, and assured the chemist that he was behind Wiley all the way. When the sixty-seven-year-old Wiley became the father of a boy in May of 1912, the infant was promptly labeled the Pure Food Baby.

If the Candlers hoped that the elderly gentleman would quietly retire, they were soon disappointed. Wiley commenced a grueling regimen of speeches all over the country. It must have galled Candler no end when Wiley delivered a speech on "The Advantages of Coffee as America's National Beverage," considering all his experts' recent insistence on caffeine as a poison. At the same time, Wiley joined *Good Housekeeping* as a regular columnist, using the magazine as a national platform to assail Coca-Cola. In September of 1912, he published "The Coca-Cola Controversy," in which he recounted his version of the trial. He portrayed the scientists for Coca-Cola as mercenaries whose opinions had been purchased. An accompanying cartoon showed a smiling scientist observing Coca-Cola through a magnifying glass emblazoned with a dollar sign. Another portrayed the good Dr. Wiley warning a gullible public against gremlins—labeled *nervousness*, *habit*, and *indigestion*—crawling inside a giant glass of Coca-Cola.

Even though Coca-Cola had won the case, the national publicity hurt the drink, attracting the attention of a moralistic young filmmaker named D. W. Griffith. In 1912, Griffith's enormous success with *Birth of a Nation* was three years away, and he was still working anonymously at the Biograph studios in New York, churning out two short silent films every week. One of these was an anti-Coca-Cola epic called *For His Son* in which the inventor of "DOPO-KOKE" watched his son fall prey to the drink's cocaine. "The drink no longer satisfies," read one caption, as the young man went on to hypodermic injections, eventually dying of an overdose. It didn't concern Griffith that Coca-Cola no longer contained cocaine. He delighted in creating a soda fountain scene in which his nervous, addicted heroine, played by Biograph regular Blanche Sweet, pushed a young boy aside to get her Dopokoke, then smiled and sighed in relief. Instructed by her boyfriend, she learned to doctor her drink by pouring cocaine powder into it (a common practice then, even with dopeless Coca-Cola).

RENDERING UNTO CAESAR

The Barrels and Kegs Case was appealed to the district court level. Before a decision was handed down, though, the U.S. government struck from another direction. The first corporate tax had been passed in 1909, but it hadn't amounted to much. Reformers cried for more: "The corporation is becoming more and more a centralized industrial power," wrote one critic in 1909. "It must therefore more and more be regulated by a centralized political power." In 1913, the reformers' prayers were answered by the accumulated earnings tax, a penalty tax imposed on corporations that hoarded cash "beyond the reasonable needs of the business." In effect, the law forced corporations to pay dividends, which were then taxable to the individual stockholders, but were not deductible at the corporate level, amounting to double taxation.

The new tax law meant that harried accountants had to separate Asa Candler's personal affairs from his Company's—not an easy task. "In a very real sense," Howard Candler wrote, "The Coca-Cola Company *was* Asa G. Candler and the line between his personal property purchases and those of the company was frequently thinly defined." By the time the law went into effect at the end of 1914, The Coca-Cola Company showed a surplus of over $10 million. Candler deeply resented the tax. He had earned the money, he reasoned, and it was his to spend or keep as he pleased. Besides, he regarded a "war chest" as a necessity for any unforseen contingencies, particularly given the hostile environment of that time. "He felt strongly on this point," his son remembered, "and often remarked that Moses . . . had tried such a [tax] system in Biblical times and saw it fail."

Nonetheless, Candler was forced to declare whopping dividends, disbursing over $10 million in cash and $6.4 million worth of real estate to shareholders in the next two years. There were about 530 shares outstanding, of which Asa Candler owned 400. Consequently, Candler's taxes must have been staggering for those years. The 1914 million-dollar gift to Emory University was undoubtedly a partial attempt to reduce his tax burden.

JUSTICE HUGHES' LAST ACT

After the government had lost its district court appeal in 1914, it took the case to the nation's highest court. Two years later, on May 22, 1916, Charles Evans Hughes reversed the decision at the Supreme Court level, in his last opinion before leaving the bench to run for president against Woodrow Wilson. Hughes, the son of a Baptist pracher, had thought of entering the ministry himself; his decision in the Barrels Case reflected his puritanical attitude. To the government's delight and Coca-Cola's chagrin, Hughes said that the word "Coca-Cola" was not a distinctive name, but simply the conjunction of two common words. More important, he ruled that caffeine was indeed an added ingredient, and he sent the case back to Sanford in Chattanooga for a retrial to determine whether caffeine was harmful or not.

As soon as the Hughes decision was issued, Harold Hirsch commenced negotiations to avoid a new trial. Both the Company and the Bureau of Chemistry frantically experimented—Coca-Cola's scientists assessed the drink's taste and flavor with reduced caffeine, while Dr. Alsberg, the government's chemist, attempted to prove that caffeine was harmful. Failing to come up with anything definitive, Alsberg asked for more time.

In the final event, the case was settled out of court on November 12, 1917. Coca-Cola consented to a plea of "no contest," allowing the government a technical victory. In return, the Company agreed to reduce the caffeine content by half, to no more than 0.61 grains per ounce of syrup, while doubling the amount of decocainized coca leaf and kola nut that went into Merchandise No. 5. Though Judge Sanford's notice of settlement did not specify it, there was a tacit agreement that the government would now leave Coca-Cola alone. Wiley was no longer at the Bureau to push the issue, and everyone was sick of the case by this time, eight years after the initial seizure. In later years, however, Howard Candler implied that a federal attorney had accepted a bribe in return for the settlement.

Having spent over $250,000 on the case, The Coca-Cola Company apparently got nothing out of it other than a reduced kick and the return of forty barrels and twenty kegs of very stale syrup. But all of that was beside the point. As Harold Hirsch later wrote, "It was a serious litigation and involved the possibility of the entire destruction of the company's business." In essence, Hirsch had won a major victory: Coca-Cola had survived.

INTERNECINE STRIFE LOOMS

The settlement of the Barrels and Kegs Case did not, however, signal the end of Coca-Cola's troubles in the courts or tangles with government bureaucrats. The turmoil took its toll on an aging Asa Candler, who regarded it as unjust persecution. When he left the Company in the care of his children, Candler set off a chain of events that led to a graver threat to the Coca-Cola system. It did not come from a competitor, politician, or reformer. This time the trouble, like a latent virus, came from within.

~ 8 ~

The Sinister Syndicate

Complainant now shows to the Court and avers that some time in the summer of 1919 a number of promoters conceived a plan to get control of the stock of said Georgia corporation. By reason of the inflated condition of the currency growing out of the war and the willingness of the people to speculate . . . said promoters did so get control . . .
     —Bill of Complaint, *The Coca-Cola Bottling Company* vs. *The Coca-Cola*
                                                                      Company

WHEN CHARLES EVANS HUGHES delivered his devastating opinion in the Barrels Case in May of 1916, it was just one more indication to sixty-four-year-old Asa Candler that the United States government was persecuting him. It would bleed him with taxes, pursue him in court, plague him with inspectors.

In addition, J. C. Mayfield, Pemberton's last partner, had reappeared as a thorn in Candler's side. As much of a hustler as Candler, Mayfield never quite succeeded in his numerous ventures. Besides soft drinks, he had speculated in real estate, oil wells, and a vinegar factory. In 1909, his Celery-Cola was seized under the Pure Food and Drugs Act for containing cocaine. Nothing kept the irrepressible Mayfield down for long, however. He resurrected Koke, one of the first names he had used, bought the rights to another Coca-Cola imitation called Dope, and was soon selling both drinks across much of the U.S. as the Koke Company of America. In 1914, as part of his crusade to protect Coca-Cola's trademark, Hirsch had sued. Unlike most imitators, however, Mayfield had enough money to hire lawyers for a rigorous, prolonged court fight.

In Koke Case testimony, many of the questionable activities during Coca-Cola's early years came to light. On the stand, Mayfield told the story of John Pemberton's morphine addiction, the reappearance of Charley Pemberton, and his own 1888 days of manufacturing Yum Yum and Koke. He asserted, with some authority, that he had the original formula for Coca-Cola, legally and directly, from its inventor. In addition, his lawyers found Mrs. Dozier, who insisted that her signatures on two crucial chain-of-title documents were forged. Asa Candler must have been extremely disturbed to have all of this material re-emerge after it had been buried for over a quarter of a century.

The Koke Case was replete with ironies. While Candler and Hirsch had fulminated for years against the use of slang terms for Coca-Cola (particularly those that implied cocaine content), now they found themselves calling pharmacists to the stand to prove that "Koke" and "Dope" were universally recognized calls for Coca-Cola, not Mayfield's drinks. One Atlanta druggist, J. B. Pendergrast,[*] testified that "when a man asks for 'dope' at my soda-fountain I understand that he means 'Coca-Cola.'" Pendergrast also served Coca-Cola in response to an amusing array of nicknames, including A-Shot-in-the-Arm and Another-Brick-in-the-Candler Building.

While the decision on the Koke Case was pending for most of 1916, Mayfield stirred up more trouble for Coca-Cola by complaining to the Federal Trade Commission, created in 1914, that Coca-Cola's harassment of imitators constituted an illegitimate business practice. A special agent for the Department of Justice asked pointed questions of Coca-Cola bottlers and their competitors in the fall of 1915 and the following spring. That summer, Asa Candler received a letter from the chairman of the FTC officially notifying him of complaints and asking for a response. When irritated, Candler often scribbled his rebuttals on letters, and he wrote "not so" next to most of these 1916 allegations:

1. Refusing to sell Coca Cola to dealers who handle competing cola drinks.

2. Intimidating customers of competitors by threats of legal suits.

3. Maliciously instituting litigation against competitors.

4. Using rebates based on total annual purchases combined with excessive advertising, thereby, it is alleged, in practical effect compelling dealers to purchase exclusively of your company.

5. Slandering the character and business of competitors.

6. Using premiums in the sale of Coca Cola, such premiums being given only to customers who will handle no other cola drink.

7. Shutting off competitors' supplies of bottle caps by threats of litigation against bottle cap manufacturers.

8. Maintaining a system of espionage to discover names of customers and other business secrets of competitors.

9. Procuring cancellation of orders and breach of contracts secured by competitors.

Candler can hardly be blamed for feeling persecuted. He must have felt that the American government had gone mad, abusing him for being an astute businessman who employed aggressive promotion and reasonable concern to protect his product's good name and integrity.

ASA CANDLER, MAYOR

At almost the exact moment that he received the FTC's official notice, Candler was approached by a group of Atlanta businessmen and politicians, urging him

---

[*] J. B. Pendergrast was the author's grandfather.

to run for mayor. The city was in poor financial shape, with impoverished schools, a $150,000 debt, and streets badly in need of repair. The police chief had been fired and was suing for his job back, and the streetcar conductors were threatening a strike. At first, Candler refused to run—he was a businessman, not a politician—but his ego soon overcame his doubts, and on July 19, 1916, only four days after he received the letter from the FTC, he agreed to become a candidate. The mayoral race clearly gave him an excuse to retire—Candler had a "willingness, sometimes amounting almost to anxiety, to get out of Coca-Cola," according to his son.

Having declared his candidacy, Candler promptly departed for a mineral springs spa in Michigan, intending to remain there until the election was over, but his political advisers finally convinced him that it appeared arrogant for the multimillionaire to remain in Michigan without even pretending to mount a campaign. With only eight days left before the primary, he returned to Atlanta for a vigorous week of stump speeches. "I am not here to tell you I think so little of this office as not to want it. I do want it," he told his supporters. "If I can discharge my duty to all of you, I will get a crown that will reach far beyond the grave." His opponent, a union linotype operator, was not interested in immortality as much as appealing to the poor as "the people's candidate," calling Candler "capitalism personified."

Capitalism personified is apparently what Atlanta wanted. Easily nominated, Candler was swept into office in the December 6 election. Most citizens of Atlanta rejoiced, regarding "Uncle Asa" as the savior whose millions would solve the city's problems. When he donated his $4,000 annual salary to charity, they were heartened, but aside from that, Candler spent none of his own money during his term except for an improved waterworks. One cynic commented after the election: "Seems funny that as soon as some ordinary gink makes a fortune out of flivvers, soft drinks, liver pills or safety pins, he is always right in line for political office."

As the mayor-elect, Candler served as the head of the Law and Order Committee, which helped to break the streetcar workers' strike. Atlanta's first serious labor unrest, with its dynamited trolleys, gunshots, and cries of "Scab! Scab!," unsettled the status quo. The workers demanded union recognition, shorter hours, and higher pay. In the end, the remaining drivers were granted a slight pay increase, but the union was disbanded and its organizers fired. Now the man of the hour, Candler waxed eloquent in his condemnation of labor unrest: "The demagogue whose radical measures threaten the stability of the commercial system . . . is a political parasite sprung from the feculent accumulations of popular ignorance and fattened upon the purulent secretions of popular prejudice." He went on to defend the capitalist system, explaining that "commerce is not the selfish and groveling thing which many esteem it. On the contrary, it is the means of the world's progress and the instrument of boundless blessing to the race of man."

After a year of Mayor Candler, many of his supporters were disillusioned. His cabinet had suggested raising water rents, which would have hurt the poor. Others wanted to impose higher taxes on the rich, which Candler rejected out of hand. "Did the Asa boomers last fall really think that the old gentleman would furnish the money as a free gift gratis for nothing to pay the town's deficits?" asked one editorial. *Atlanta Civics*, a tract written and published by Mrs. Bessie Linn Smith, appeared briefly in the fall of 1917 and was devoted almost exclusively to Candler-bashing. "During Candler's campaign," wrote Mrs. Smith, "we were promised . . . almost that our souls would be purged of sin, our debts wiped away with a stroke of his genius hand . . . To date, if he has accomplished a thing for the betterment of Atlanta, a single thing except Candler glory and profit, our highest powered microscope fails to see it." Mrs. Smith pointed out that while Candler urged civic-minded citizens to declare high property appraisals to swell the city's tax coffers, the mayor himself reduced his personal tax returns by $108,000. She also gleefully reported that Candler was so cheap that he had taken a paper from a newsboy, scanned the headlines, and then given it back instead of paying the three cents.

Candler's parsimonious ways did have some positive effect, however. By the time he left office, he had balanced the city's budget. On the whole, he appears to have been a conservative, decent, honest mayor, even if his priorities sometimes seemed odd. One of Mayor Candler's accomplishments was to pass an "Ice Cream and Soft Drink Ordinance" to make sure that soda fountains were "properly lighted, ventilated, and kept free from rats, flies, or other insects." He also insisted on the virtue of idle Sundays, the violation of which was "a more alarming peril," he wrote, "than the success of the German Kaiser in the pending war struggle." Of course, his critics had a ready answer for that: what about the soda jerker who dispensed Coca-Cola during the Sabbath?

A TIME OF TRANSITION

Howard Candler had officially taken over as president of The Coca-Cola Company at the January 21, 1916, board meeting, but his father still owned most of the stock. Although busy with his new political office, Asa Candler soon made it clear that he had no intention of relinquishing his power over Coca-Cola—at least not yet. The battle came over the family's plans to sell the company. Two New York lawyers, Bainbridge Colby and Ed Brown, represented a syndicate which proposed to purchase Coca-Cola for $25 million. Besides netting a huge profit, the sale would have major tax benefits: the accumulated earnings tax on $25 million in invested capital would be minor compared to the huge amount then being paid, and the firm would no longer have to pay such extraordinary dividends. The details of the proposed deal were outlined in a January 15, 1917, letter.

A tumultuous Coca-Cola board meeting took place three days later. By the time the minutes were demanded in court in 1920, they had conveniently disappeared, along with the Colby/Brown letter. The surviving annual report contains only the cryptic statement, "Asa G. Candler made a verbal report." It is fairly safe to conjecture that his "verbal report" was a blistering attack on the planned sale of his company. As *The New York Times* later reported, "the deal fell through when one of the chief stockholders, a member of the Candler family, declined to sell." At board meetings, Candler would typically sit silent, listening to suggestions and presentations. If he disagreed, he would become increasingly agitated, often twiddling his thumbs. Then, speaking in his high-pitched, jerky, emphatic way, he would say: "I, Asa G. Candler, owner of 90% of the stock of this corporation, vote against the proposition of Mr. Howard Candler."

Although the planned recapitalization hung fire for the rest of the year, a real reorganization of the Company never took place. According to the minutes of a June 4, 1918, meeting, "it is now deemed better policy not to abandon the old corporation." Instead, "beneficial ownership certificates" for $25 million were issued in return for the stock. Colby & Brown threatened to sue for breach of contract and received a million dollars' worth of stock certificates as a settlement. By the time that decision was made in the summer of 1918, the Candler children had complete legal control of The Coca-Cola Company. On the heels of the settlement of the Barrels and Kegs Case, Asa Candler had turned over all of his real estate holdings to his children, and as a Christmas present in December of 1917, he gave all but seven shares of stock to his family.

SUGAR AT WAR

By the summer of 1918, other major changes had been thrust upon the Company. The United States' entrance into World War I had resulted in sugar rationing. Coca-Cola took out ads proclaiming that "sugar enlists for war," asking the public's patience with reduced supplies. Another patriotic spread showed a hand holding a glass of Coca-Cola with a shadow of the Statue of Liberty grasping the flame behind it. For the first time, the Company found itself actually begging its bottlers not to seek new markets, since it couldn't provide enough syrup.

Sugar was by far the most costly ingredient of Coca-Cola. For many years, its wholesale price had hovered around 5 cents a pound. By May of 1917, the price had gone to 8 cents, which required a 5-cent-per-gallon price hike. Sam Dobbs wanted to *order* the parent bottlers to pay more. Harold Hirsch disagreed, pointing out that the bottling contract called for a flat price. He advised diplomacy rather than strong-arm tactics. Consequently, Sam Dobbs traveled to Chattanooga to discuss it with George Hunter, who had taken over the Thomas Company when his Uncle Ben died in 1914. Hunter agreed to a temporary price hike only as long as he deemed necessary because of "the abnormal conditions" of the war.

By the following January, Howard Candler decided to abandon the rebate program, partly to discourage volume and partly to dodge the FTC litigation that he knew was coming.[*] The same month, he issued a statement that plants

---

[*] On February 15, 1918, the FTC case finally went to trial. Even to the FTC commissioners, the evidence against Coca-Cola appeared too flimsy, and the case was dismissed on November 17, 1919.

would begin to shut down until the new crop of sugar came in. At government request, soft drink manufacturers had halved their output. "But we can't get the sugar just now for even half our supply," he concluded.

The effect on Coca-Cola's business wasn't as dramatic as might be expected. In 1916, sales didn't quite reach 10 million gallons of syrup. In 1917, this figure jumped to over 12 million and then fell back to 10 million gallons the following year. The total demand for cola drinks was rising substantially, however, and Coca-Cola clearly lost business because it couldn't obtain enough sugar. Soda fountains displayed signs such as: "COCA-COLA being unobtainable we are serving AFRI-KOLA The Next Best." Many other fountains and bottlers weren't so honest; substitution was rampant.

The war also meant more taxes. John Candler testified before the U.S. Senate Committee on Finance, arguing against a special 10 percent tax on soft drinks. "My clients," he said, "are willing to pay a tax, they expect to pay a tax, they have no desire to dodge a tax." But slim profit margins wouldn't absorb the proposed levy. "All that we ask is that we be not destroyed," Candler begged the politicians, explaining that the Company couldn't pass the tax on to the bottlers, who had perpetual contracts at fixed prices. Nor could the bottlers or soda fountains boost the price beyond the traditional nickel, or the public would rebel. In short, Candler argued, the soft drink business would be decimated, and the government would receive *less* rather than *more* revenue.

The senators passed the 10 percent tax anyway. To no one's surprise, the soft drink industry survived. The Coca-Cola Company *did* charge part of the tax to the parent bottlers, who in turn gave it to their actual bottlers, causing considerable dissatisfaction. Under intense pressure from the Candlers and parent bottlers to maintain the nickel retail price, many bottlers decided it was economic suicide and charged the wholesaler more, resulting in 6-cent and 7-cent retail sales. One bottler wrote, "I *must* make a profit this year or I will be in bad shape. I have bought an ice machine for $3000, trucks for $6000 and have about $6000 taxes to pay on last year's profit."

Other desperate bottlers resorted to use of sugar substitutes such as corn syrup, beet sugar, and saccharin in order to stretch their syrup supply. After the war ended in November of 1918, Coca-Cola proudly advertised that "nothing changed, cheapened, nor diluted, Coca-Cola remained 'all there' from the beginning of the war to the end," but the statement clearly bent the truth.

With the war behind, 1919 promised to be a banner year for Coca-Cola. "Those returning soldiers will be mighty dry," one bottler anticipated, "and they will remember what it was that hit the spot." Demand for Coca-Cola syrup would soon outstrip production capacity, and at a February 12 board meeting, Howard Candler recommended the purchase of land on North Avenue for a huge new manufacturing plant, to include an office building, factory, cooperage, and sugar mill, at a cost of almost $850,000.

It must have taken a leap of faith to continue with plans for the new factory. Two weeks later, on February 24, the Court of Appeals ruled in favor of J. C. Mayfield, citing the doctrine of "unclean hands." The decision held that

Coca-Cola had no rights whatsoever, since it had once contained "the deadly drug cocaine." In addition, most of the caffeine in the drink had always come from tea leaves, not the kola nuts. Thus, the court found that Coca-Cola had engaged in "such deceptive, false, fraudulent, and unconscionable conduct as precludes a court of equity from affording it any relief." As a writer in *The National Bottlers' Gazette* pointed out, "under this decision the Coca-Cola Co. is utterly helpless against imitators, no matter how bold they are," adding that it put the Company in an uncomfortable and possibly "fatal" position. Coca-Cola immediately appealed the Koke Case to the Supreme Court, where the outcome was far from certain, since the same body had ruled against the Company only three years previously in the Barrels and Kegs Case.

THE WOODRUFF SYNDICATE

On July 1, 1919, with the ultimate outcome of the Koke Case looming over the Company's future, Sam Dobbs met with Ernest Woodruff at the Waldorf Hotel in New York City to discuss the sale of The Coca-Cola Company. Woodruff, the president of the Trust Company of Georgia, had numerous New York contacts and was probably behind the original attempt to buy the Company in 1917. He now stated that "certain interests" would offer the same price of $25 million. Besides the threat of the Koke Case, Dobbs realized there were powerful tax incentives favoring a sale, which would greatly reduce the accumulated-earnings tax and, as important, the excess-profits tax which had arrived with the war. The government taxed the company on "excess" earnings above a "reasonable" percentage of its tiny capitalization. Enthusiastically, Dobbs agreed to take the Woodruff proposition back to Atlanta.

The stocky, jut-jawed son of a wealthy flour miller, Woodruff had, like John Pemberton, come to Atlanta from Columbus, Georgia. Unlike Pemberton, he had prospered in the Gate City, putting together a string of deals which made him a much envied (and feared) power. Woodruff sought out small, struggling companies, merging them to form major corporations such as the Atlantic Ice and Coal Company, Atlantic Steel, Empire Cotton Oil Company, Pratt Laboratory, and the Continental Gin Company. But the coup of his career was the negotiation of the Coca-Cola deal, by far the biggest transaction ever to hit the South.

Careful to hide his involvement in the process, he knew that the Candlers, particularly rival banker Asa, would prefer selling their Southern business to anonymous New York interests than to Ernest Woodruff, who was universally despised. Despite his wealth, Woodruff was so tight with money that he made Asa Candler look like a spendthrift. Notorious for his petty frugality, Woodruff saved hotel soap and strapped bulky bonds under his clothes to avoid paying freight charges on them. Once, while a porter awaited a tip, Woodruff fished unproductively through his pockets. "I have a quarter here somewhere," he muttered. "Mr. Woodruff," the porter said, "if you ever had one, you still got it." Even normally respectful newspaper columnists acknowledged Woodruff's unpleasant nature, while praising his financial wizardry. "Nobody knows just how much he is worth," a 1919 Atlanta editorial stated. "Nobody knows much about his personal business. He is a silent man, and not companionable, [with] few intimate friends. But when he calls for the dollars, they come."

Woodruff's Syndicate included officers from the Chase National Bank and the Guaranty Trust Company of New York, though neither of the banks was officially involved. To conceal the potential buyers, the option Dobbs brought back to Atlanta was left blank. Soon, however, Eugene Stetson, vice-president of the Guaranty Trust Company, abandoned his anonymity and arrived in Atlanta to negotiate the deal, while Ernest Woodruff remained in New York in temporary offices, with a direct phone link to Atlanta. After a flurry of meetings, with Dobbs acting as the go-between, most of the options were signed by July 26, giving the Syndicate until August 28 to buy all of the $25 million in beneficial ownership certificates.

At the August 2 meeting of the Trust Company's board of directors, there was "considerable discussion" about the option on Coca-Cola. Sam Dobbs, now a member of the Trust Company board, took part. Woodruff presented his case: here was a hugely profitable enterprise run on a shoestring, essentially still a small family business. With proper management, it could explode exponentially, particularly in foreign operations. Also, with the Volstead Act just passed, Prohibition would commence on January 16, 1920, substantially boosting Coca-Cola sales.

Of course, the purchase was a gamble, dependent on a favorable ruling in the potentially disastrous Koke Case. Finally, it was resolved to exercise the option only if the bank's lawyers reported positively on Coca-Cola's odds before the Supreme Court. By August 13, the legal department must have given the green light: "Be it resolved," the minutes read, "that this company do enter into a Syndicate for the purchase of the participation certificates representing the shares of The Coca-Cola Company." Twenty thousand shares were voted to Ernest Woodruff personally "in consideration of the time and services given by him in connection with this transaction."

In effect, Woodruff had accomplished what would now be called a friendly leveraged buy-out. The Coca-Cola Company of Georgia would be sold to a new corporation, The Coca-Cola Company of Delaware (a state famed for lenient corporate taxes). The stockholders (i.e., the Candlers) were to receive $15 million in cash and $10 million in preferred stock yielding 7 percent interest. In addition, 500,000 shares of common stock would be offered to the public at no set par value, in an attempt to avoid taxes. The Trust Company was to raise $4.5 million of the necessary $15 million in cash. Presumably, the rest would come from other members of the underwriting Syndicate.

The Trust Company did not have that kind of money readily available. With deposits of only $1.8 million, it was by far the smallest of Atlanta's seven banks. Nonetheless, Woodruff was confident that he could pull it off. On August 22, the day he publicized the deal, the *Atlanta Constitution* ran a banner headline across the top of the entire front page: "COCA-COLA BOUGHT BY ATLANTANS: Trust Company of Georgia Gets National Drink." The same day, the bank mailed a letter headed *Strictly Confidential* to its shareholders, who must have been contacted individually with an explanation of what was really happening, since the letter itself was quite confusing. Trust Company stockholders were given the opportunity to buy one Coca-Cola share for each of their bank shares *if* they deposited $195 per share within five days. The letter promised that when the Syndicate was dissolved, by October 1, a "distribution" would be made. The vague language veiled the behind-the-scenes reality. Those who came up with the money to help fund the buy-out wound up purchasing Coca-Cola for only $5 per share, receiving a $190 refund in October. When the shares were made available to the public at 9 A.M. on August 26, they sold for $40 a share. By 3:45 P.M. that day, the stock was oversubscribed by 140,000 shares, assuring the sale. Almost half of the shares were bought by Atlantans.

Once the dust had settled, the ramifications of the completed sale became clearer. The Candlers were suddenly very wealthy indeed, and in the next few years their mansions would spring up all over Atlanta. Sam Dobbs was repaid with the presidency of the new company, while Howard Candler was kicked upstairs as chairman of the board. The real power, however, rested with a "voting trust" of three men: Woodruff, Stetson, and Dobbs. The shareholders had no voice in the running of the company, and Dobbs, the only Candler kin, could be outvoted by the bankers.

It is not at all clear how much money the mysterious "Syndicate" made out of the deal. Insiders apparently bought 83,000 shares at $5 per share, while there is no record that Ernest Woodruff paid anything for his 20,000 shares. The Trust Company wound up with an option to purchase 24,900 shares at $5, and would never struggle for money again. Estimates of the immediate profit ranged from $2 million to $5 million. The bottlers later complained bitterly of the back-room "manipulations" of nefarious speculators, but there is no indication that any laws were broken, other than a lingering IRS suit over taxes.

The most important change was reflected in the bottom line of the new Delaware corporation. The beginning balance sheet showed real estate, buildings, machinery, and equipment worth less than $2 million, but the "intangible assets" were valued at $24.96 million. These intangibles formed the heart of Coca-Cola, including the formula, trademark, and "good will." Never had an accounting term been so apt. What the Woodruff Syndicate had purchased was, indeed, not primarily a syrup factory, but the good will of the American consumer. In the years to follow, it would grow considerably stronger, with tangible financial results. One share of original 1919 Coca-Cola stock had split into 4,608 shares by the year 2000. If the dividends from that one original share had been reinvested in Coca-Cola stock, the $40 (or $5 for insiders) investment would be worth nearly $7 million. Using the same scale, if a great-grandparent had purchased one of Asa's $100 shares in 1892, it would bring approximately $7.34 *billion*.

ASA'S BITTER CUP

Asa Candler learned nothing of the proposed sale until his children had signed the option. He was, according to his biographer son, "profoundly shocked," refusing to attend the Georgia corporation's final board meeting at which the sale was approved. For the old man, the timing couldn't have been worse. Candler's wife, Lucy, had died of breast cancer in March of 1919, just after her husband's term as mayor had ended. Now, having given away his Company, the tycoon felt betrayed and powerless—King Lear at the beginning of the storm. Bereft of Coca-Cola, Asa Candler quickly became a pathetic figure who, when most honest with himself, wrote: "I can't bring myself to a frame of mind that causes this life to be really joyous."

His accomplishments, he said, amounted to "ashes, just ashes." He began to live increasingly in a mythical past. His rural youth took on the patina of an irretrievably lost Eden. "When I think of those golden days amid these parched years of care and distraction," he said, "I sometimes think that once I lived in Heaven and, wandering, lost my way." In 1921, Candler plaintively wrote to Howard that "I was once counted with Atlanta's builders, Georgia's active sons—your advisor—now I am companionless, not needed nor called to any service." Awash with self-pity, Candler resolved to find a new wife.

The next year, Candler, seventy, informed his family that he intended to marry a Catholic divorcee, Onezima de Bouchel of New Orleans. His brother the Bishop, embarrassed and appalled, did everything in his power to stop the match. Knowing that Asa would not listen to him, Warren persuaded a mutual acquaintance to write a "friendly" letter of advice. Candler scribbled "Et tu Brute" and "Why the stab" on the letter and mailed it back. When Asa finally caved in to family pressure and called off the marriage, Ms de Bouchel sued him for breach of promise, causing one of the Bishop's friends to write that "I am more and more convinced that your brother's whole trouble comes out of a Jesuit plot to get his millions for the Catholic Church."

Only a few months later, Asa Candler married Mae Little, a thirty-seven-year-old stenographer in the Candler Building. "Tomorrow I am taking to my self a life companion," he wrote Howard, "one I believe who is interested in me and will be a comfort to me." With her ten-year-old twin daughters, the new Mrs. Candler moved into the mansion on Ponce de Leon Avenue, but eight months later, she made the *New York Times* when she was caught sharing a quart of bootleg liquor with two men. "We're just having a little party," she informed the police. In June of 1924, a year after his wedding, Candler filed for divorce, writing that "from the very first" his wife had ignored his "comfort and convenience," leaving the house early every morning to seek "the company of a man, driving out into the Country." In October of that year, weaving on the wrong side of the road, Mrs. Candler ran over and killed a five-year-old girl.

By the end of 1924, Asa Candler was a beaten man. Called to testify in court one last time (as a defense witness in a My-Coca case), he lamented that Frank Robinson was gone. "Everybody is dead but me, and I ought to be dead but I just won't die. I have lived too long. There are too many days between my cradle and my grave now." He spent Christmas Day alone in a Biltmore hotel room in New York City, writing that he would "dislike to go out of it at all," since the room was warm. "Try to think of me as I *was*," he pleaded with his children. Candler never rallied. His mental and physical health failing, he died in 1929 at the age of seventy-seven.

It is tempting to regard Asa Candler's life as a morality play, to think of him as a kind of Willy Loman, obsessed by a success which continually seemed to elude him, even as he brilliantly created its illusion. Fundamentally insecure, he desperately sought bedrock beliefs and found them in American capitalism, a Methodist God, idealized women, and Coca-Cola, the drink that was a blessing to humanity. Without Asa Candler, Coca-Cola would never have become the world's best-advertised single product; it would never even have attained national distribution. He wanted immortality, and in his drink he achieved it.

Candler had hoped to live on through the grand enterprises of his children, but they suffered from the curse of a domineering, teetotaling father, easy wealth, and fate. Asa Jr., known as Buddie, became an engaging alcoholic who kept a public swimming pool, laundry, and zoo in his front yard. He named his four elephants Coca, Cola, Refreshing, and Delicious and was sued when one of his baboons climbed over the fence and ate $60 out of a neighbor's purse. Walter was involved in a notorious lawsuit when he was caught attempting to rape another man's wife at 3 A.M. on a cruise ship. William, who built the elegant Atlanta Biltmore, was killed on a south Georgia road when his car ran into a stray cow. Lucy Candler Owens Heinz Leide lost her second husband in a bloody murder for which a black burglar was jailed, though rumors persisted that Heinz had been done in by a relative.

Only Howard, the oldest, always seemed to live up to his father's expectations. Yet in his own way, it was Howard who resented Asa the most. It was Howard, as president of the Company, who sanctioned the secret sale to the Woodruff Syndicate, knowing it would kill his father. Driven by a mixture of guilt, love, and repressed rage, it was Howard who wrote the curious book about his father which has been quoted in these pages. On the surface, the biography is an almost nauseatingly adulatory portrait of Asa Candler. Nothing is said of his breach-of-promise suit or his failed second marriage. But Howard managed to get back at his authoritative father subtly, between the lines, and the portrait is often devastating, particularly in the story of Frank the pony:

> Many times, after harnessing and hitching this little horse to the buggy, and after taking his seat, clucking the go-ahead with a tap of the lines on the horse's back, Father would be unable to get Frank to go ahead or to do anything but spread his feet apart, squat, and tremble. At this Father would unhitch, grasp the lines in his right hand near the bridle bit, and in a towering rage administer a vigorous lashing with a long, willowy whip with his left hand, admonishing the horse in his high-pitched, excited voice to go to work—all to no avail.

In his heart of hearts, Howard Candler often must have longed to balk like

Frank the pony. In the battle between man and beast, it is clear where his sympathies lay. Whatever his resentments, though, Howard kept them well buried. When Sam Dobbs was made president in 1919 after the Woodruff takeover, he did not complain. And when, the next year, the bottlers rose up against the new owners, he proved that he was a good Company man.

PREFACE TO REVOLT

The parent and actual bottlers knew almost nothing about the Syndicate maneuvers. Back in Chattanooga, George Hunter heard rumors about ominous New York meetings, however, and wired Harold Hirsch to "take a few minutes and write me what is actually coming off." Hirsch, at the heart of the negotiations, wrote back on August 8, 1919, to reassure the parent bottler: "Powerful interests are taking this proposition over and will make a big go of it," Hirsch wrote, "but the bottlers' rights will be absolutely protected without any thought of annulling the same."

Hirsch was wrong, and he was soon forced to choose sides in a bitter battle between the new management and the bottlers.

~ 9 ~

Coca-Cola's Civil War

Family quarrels are bitter things. They don't go according to any rules. They're not like aches or wounds; they're more like splits in the skin that won't heal because there's not enough material.
—F. Scott Fitzgerald, *The Crack-up*

When you get right down to it, we all really hate each other.
—Sebert Brewer, Jr., former Coca-Cola bottler

AFTER THE SYNDICATE'S TRIUMPH, Ernest Woodruff's glee soured over the contract locking him into a perpetual partnership with the bottlers. The inflexible agreement had already caused trouble in 1917, when the bottlers granted the first temporary price hike. Now, though World War I was over, the sugar situation proved even more threatening. The U.S. Sugar Equalization Board, created in July of 1918 to assure a supply at 9 cents a pound, expired at the end of 1919. Even before then, the government lost control over prices, which doubled by the fall. The new president, Sam Dobbs, wrote to the parent bottlers in November, asking for permission to purchase "all the sugar [we] can at such a price as Mr [Howard] Candler elects to pay." Dobbs stated that the Company was making no profit under the current arrangement and asked for a sliding scale on the basis of the sugar price, stressing that this was a "temporary proposition." The bottlers agreed readily enough. In December, they also acceded to the Company's request for what amounted to a temporary loan. Howard Candler wrote to George Hunter that he was "truly grateful . . . for this further evidence of your liberal policy."

What Rainwater and Hunter did *not* know, however, was that even while Dobbs and Candler acted so ingratiating, they were plotting against the bottlers. A week before Dobbs' November letter, a committee to "investigate the status of the bottling contracts" was formed, and at a December 15 board meeting, W. C. Bradley, a Columbus mill owner brought into the Syndicate and onto the board by his former neighbor Ernest Woodruff, announced a "proposed plan of readjustment" with the bottlers.

The Christmas season passed in peace. In the January 1920 issue of *The Coca-Cola Bottler*, Howard Candler sent his New Year's greetings to the bottlers: "May we join with you in hearty fellowship and accord and face the new day together: FRIENDS." In the same issue, Harold Hirsch wrote that "the new management appreciates to the fullest extent . . . the bottlers and has the greatest confidence in this branch." Veazey Rainwater reciprocated with a message to "HAVE FAITH!" Less than two weeks later, Rainwater's faith was shattered when he discovered the Company's hypocrisy.

Hirsch requested another conference with the parent bottlers over the sugar situation, which was not particularly alarming. When Veazey Rainwater and George Hunter got together to read over the meeting agenda, however, they could hardly believe it. "We saw," Rainwater said, "that it was not an amendment for relief as we had supposed it would be, owing to unusual conditions . . ., but it was a proposal to change our whole method of doing business." Refusing to attend the scheduled conference, they wrote to Hirsch offering to consider another temporary price hike. After a few more days of increasingly agitated correspondence, Harold Hirsch called Rainwater and Hunter to his office. "Boys," he said, "I have called you up here to tell you bad news." He informed them that the Coca-Cola board of directors had ruled "that your contracts are contracts at will, and can be canceled on reasonable notice." Hirsch asked the parent bottlers whether they had any suggestions to "prevent the thing from going that far." The two men were, as Rainwater recalled, "completely dumbfounded." When they recovered, they asked Hirsch what he thought of the Company position. "I think," the uncomfortable lawyer answered, "I will eliminate myself from the proposition."

HIRSCH IN A BIND

Of course, Hirsch could not "eliminate" himself, but he did find himself in an extraordinarily awkward position. For years, he had been co-counsel to the Company and the bottlers, successfully defending their joint use of the Coca-Cola trademark. The bottlers had trusted him completely, in part because Hirsch owned a bottling plant himself. Now, it seemed that Hirsch had been bought. A central figure in the Syndicate buy-out, he was rewarded with a seat on the board of directors, while his annual salary jumped to an unheard-of $37,500.

Yet Hirsch actually had little choice in the matter. In vain, he argued with Ernest Woodruff that abrogating the contracts would cause irreparable damage within the Coca-Cola "family." Woodruff was appalled at the unbusinesslike situation he had inherited. From his vantage point, the parent bottlers weren't bottlers at all, but leeches. Besides, Sam Dobbs, Howard Candler, and Asa Candler agreed that the contracts were terminable at will. The elder Candler insisted that he had never intended to give away the bottling rights in perpetuity.

Rainwater and Hunter immediately sounded the battle cry among their actual bottlers who, already anxious about the changes taking place in faraway New York and Atlanta, sided with the parent bottlers, apparently their sole protection against the ruin of their "little shops," as Sam Dobbs contemptuously called them. When Hirsch reported to the board that all parties refused to attend a conference, he was authorized to commence legal proceedings. Instead, the tortured lawyer conferred with Veazey Rainwater in a final effort to reach some compromise. In a February 12 joint letter, Hirsch and Rainwater proposed a complicated sliding scale for syrup, along with the Coca-Cola formula in a sealed envelope to be opened "in case of dispute involving proportions" of ingredients. Dobbs vehemently rejected the proposal. "We will not under any consideration, or in any way, disclose or place in anybody's hands the proportion of ingredients," Dobbs wrote. "Some things must be taken upon faith."

In the final event, both sides lost faith in the other's integrity. On March 2, 1920, Howard Candler, as chairman of the board of The Coca-Cola Company of Delaware, notified the parent bottlers that their contracts would be terminated as of May 1, 1920. In response, Rainwater and Hunter immediately insisted on the old agreed-upon price of 97 cents per gallon for syrup. Forced to comply, the Company watched the price of sugar spiral over 20 cents a pound in April, by which time the Company was losing $20,000 a day.

King and Spalding, the Atlanta attorneys for the bottlers, wrote a stinging denial of the Company's right to cancel the contract. The lawyers specifically blamed the Woodruff Syndicate for the action and promised that "our clients . . . will not submit to any such outrage, but will fight in every lawful way to protect and defend their property." One last-ditch compromise proposal looked promising, but it too fell through. On April 16, the parent bottlers filed suit against the Company in Fulton County Superior Court. "The fight is on," wrote Sam Dobbs, "and we are determined to see it through." Coca-Cola's Civil War had officially begun.

LOVE FEAST TURNS TO HATE ORGY

The parent bottlers won the first skirmish, obtaining a temporary injunction preventing the Company from supplying the actual bottlers with syrup after May 1. Attempting to turn this injunction to the Company's advantage, Sam Dobbs wrote to the actual bottlers, explaining that "your welfare will be materially affected" if the Company could not supply syrup. Although furious at the parent bottlers, Dobbs felt powerless, as he wrote to his friend Bill D'Arcy a few days later: "The Chattanooga crowd are moving heaven and earth to prejudice the actual bottlers against us."

Rallying the troops, Hunter and Rainwater called for a mass bottler meeting on April 22 in Chattanooga. Though Harold Hirsch was pointedly excluded, he wrote plaintively that he had always tried to encourage a "spirit of cooperation in the Coca-Cola Family," but had failed. He stressed that both sides had the same basic goal—"a continuous and ever-free flowing supply of bottlers' Coca-Cola syrup." In the bitterness of the fray, however, "this particular purpose has, to some extent, been lost in the shuffle." The angry bottlers assembled in Tennessee preferred emotional condemnations of the Company to Hirsch's plea for sanity. "If I go down," George Hunter declared, "I'm going to pull the whole business down with me."

The Company and parent bottlers backed away from their vindictive game of "chicken" before the syrup spigot was actually cut off. They compromised on a temporary solution just before the May deadline, allowing the Company to supply the actual bottlers at $1.72 a gallon with an adjustment for the volatile price of sugar (much to the relief of the Company). As the courtroom filled for what Atlantans knew would be an entertaining trial, sugar still cost over 20 cents a pound as a result of stockpiling by a consortium of sugar interests in Cuba, whose economy boomed along with Coca-Cola sales. In Atlanta, however, the cost of a fountain Coca-Cola rose to 8 cents a glass.

COURTROOM DRAMA

The trial quickly degenerated into a literal tug-of-war. Ben Phillips, the lawyer for the bottlers, grabbed the Coca-Cola minutes book, reading the contents into the record over the opposing counsel's repeated objections. Finally, Harold Hirsch physically wrenched the minutes away from Phillips. Normally composed, Hirsch sounded more like a petulant schoolboy than a lawyer: "It is not going in the record and I demand the book back. Give me my book back." Once order was restored, Hirsch and his colleagues argued convincingly that the parent bottlers were parasites, middlemen "who serve no useful purpose, simply buying the syrup at a fixed price and reselling same at a profit—not even seeing the syrup." During Veazey Rainwater's cross-examination, he admitted that the parent bottlers took a 25 percent profit on advertising provided by the Company. With hardly any investment, the Southeastern Parent Bottler had made $2.5 million in twenty years.

The parent bottlers responded, with equal justice, that without them, there would have *been* no bottling business. Hunter and Rainwater chronicled the difficult early years, the failed bottlers, the fights against imitators. The actual bottlers had invested over $20 million in real estate, plants, and equipment. The Coca-Cola Company had not had to lift a finger or spend a cent on the entire venture. Far from being leeches, the parent bottlers were constantly training and exhorting their bottlers to put out a uniform, high-quality product. They sponsored conventions and training seminars, arranged for bulk buying, secured the most modern equipment. As for the $2.5 million in profits over a twenty-year period—what about the Syndicate's one-day earnings of *twice* that figure, accomplished by financial sleight-of-hand instead of hard, prolonged work?

The truth of the matter lay somewhere in between these two positions. By 1920, the bottling territories were nearly blanketed. The number of franchises peaked at 1,263 in 1928 (the same year the volume of bottled syrup finally surpassed fountain), slowly consolidating in the following decades. While the parent bottlers had unquestionably performed a valuable service in the formative years of the bottling industry, their role had diminished by the time of the trial. They had a sweet deal and they knew it—which is why they weren't about to give up their contract.

In the midst of the testimony, the city of Atlanta exacerbated the situation by suing The Coca-Cola Company for the names of its stockholders, in order to tax them. But that was nothing compared to the daring new tactic of the

bottlers' lawyers. "BOTTLERS SUE FOR COCA-COLA RECIPE," headlines blared on May 15. Deliberately attacking the Company where it was most
paranoid, the bottlers insisted that the original contract granted them the right
to the formula. If they lost the first suit, they would at least be able to supply
their own syrup if they won the second.

As a finale, the bottlers unexpectedly withdrew their Fulton County suits on
May 31, simultaneously filing the same suits in Delaware federal court. "It
came as a thunderbolt out of a clear sky," Dobbs wrote. "This infernal lawsuit
hangs over me like the Sword of Damocles." The public explanation for this
move was that "federal questions" were involved, but the lawyers probably
wanted to find a more impartial judicial climate than Atlanta. The Delaware
case, which got under way in June, was argued for the bottlers by John Sibley
from Atlanta and J. B. Sizer from Chattanooga. Having worked effectively
alongside Hirsch in the Barrels and Kegs Case, Sizer now found himself on the
other side, becoming so emotionally overwrought during his opening
arguments that he fainted.

The quibbling over the relative merits of the parent bottlers was really
extraneous to the main question—was the 1899 contract permanent? The
contract had been modified in 1915 at Hirsch's suggestion, to avoid possible
prosecution under the Clayton Act for restraint of trade. One Florida bottler
had refused to sign the amended contract until Hirsch specifically reassured
him that it was indeed permanent. Sizer and Sibley triumphantly produced
this 1916 letter. "Above all and beyond question," Hirsch had written, "the
new contract is perpetual and even more binding and stronger than the original
contract along that line."

On the stand, Hirsch tried to weasel his way out, asserting that "I did not
write this letter as counsel for The Coca-Cola Company [but as] counsel for
the bottlers." Nonetheless, he admitted that he had always considered the
contracts to be permanent until he "re-examined" the subject in 1919 and
decided he had been wrong. Other testimony revealed that Asa Candler, Sam
Dobbs, and Howard Candler had repeatedly begged the Thomas Company to
abandon its two-year contracts, pointing to the successful Whitehead/Lupton
operation. The Coca-Cola Company officials had insisted, Rainwater testified,
that permanent contracts with bottlers gave them "the greatest incentive to do
their best at all times," and made them feel "absolutely safe" in making
necessary capital improvements.

THE SUMMER OF '20

On June 23, 1920, the testimony concluded, and Judge Hugh Morris was left to
mull over some 2,500 pages of transcripts before issuing his verdict, which was
expected in the fall. Around this time, Howard Candler committed a terrible
purchasing blunder. Unable to obtain Cuban sugar at a reasonable quantity or
price, he ordered a gigantic shipment from Java at 20 cents a pound. During
the summer, one of Cuba's sugar plantations broke ranks and offered to sell at
a cut rate, triggering a steep drop from the artificially high price. By

September, the price had fallen from its May high of 27 cents a pound to 15 cents, continuing to drift down below 9 cents in December.

Candler and other Company officials prayed that the boat from Java would be caught in a tropical storm and sunk, but it arrived as scheduled on December 15 with 4,100 tons of high-priced sugar, the largest single shipment of sweetener ever received in Georgia. One unsympathetic wag said that The Coca-Cola Company had a "terrible case of diabetes." While most other soft drinks lowered their prices, Coca-Cola bottlers could not, and they were blamed for what was beyond their control. "It is very hard for the public to realize that we are NOT manufacturers of our syrup," wrote bottler Crawford Johnson. In response to pleas to lower the syrup price, the Company actually *boosted* it in November, provoking an outraged letter from Rainwater.

Tempers must have flared at the Company offices during that summer and fall of 1920. The Bottler Suit was pending, as was the Koke Case. The sugar decline spelled disaster for the next year's syrup price. Discouraged shareholders sent the price of the stock steadily down. Under these circumstances, the personality clash between Sam Dobbs and Ernest Woodruff came to a boil.

Dobbs had quickly developed a distaste for the obstreperous Woodruff. At the onset of the litigation, Dobbs had written to D'Arcy that "our friend Woodruff is in no way helping by his constant butting-in and interfering . . . He seems too disposed to tell us all what we ought to do and is very much outraged when we don't agree with him." In the midst of the trial, Woodruff further annoyed Dobbs by suggesting what might have been the tycoon's most brilliant amalgamation: "Woodruff is as busy as a mangy dog with fleas, with a great scheme of consolidating The Coca-Cola Company, the parent bottlers and all of the actual bottlers into one big corporation, with the bottlers to take Coca-Cola stock for their holdings and plants." Dobbs dismissed the idea; he would be damned if he would agree to coexist with both Woodruff *and* "Lupton and his bunch."

Now, at a July meeting of the executive board in New York, Dobbs finally blew up. Woodruff insisted on spending no more than $1.2 million for the year in advertising, despite inflated postwar prices. Wall painters, for instance, were demanding twice the previous year's wages. Dobbs had to inform the board that he had already paid $1.1 million and needed to spend considerably more by year's end (in fact, the final advertising expense for 1920 was $2.3 million). After the meeting, Dobbs took Woodruff aside and blistered him with an unaccustomed lecture. "I asked him pointedly what he knew about Advertising and Advertising costs," he recounted to D'Arcy. "I then asked him what his opinion was worth on a question of advertising about which he was densely ignorant."

From that moment on, of course, Dobbs' fate was sealed. Harold Hirsch met the president when he returned from a Western trip, explaining that Woodruff had the board's solid support in demanding that Dobbs step down. Dobbs was blamed not only for the overspent advertising budget, but the Java sugar debacle. On October 4, he tendered his resignation, agreeing to keep silent about it until the board meeting in November, when it would become final. He noted to D'Arcy that "Woodruff, through his confidential conversations with everybody that comes into his office, will soon have it all over town." He was right. Rumors of dissension within the Company plummeted the stock $5 in one day. To no one's satisfaction, Howard Candler was installed as president for the second time. As dividend payments were postponed, the stock dropped to a new low of $25 a share.

Beset by management woes, loaded down with overpriced sugar, and threatened by pending lawsuits, the new Coca-Cola Company appeared to be floundering. On November 3, the Fulton County Superior Court ruled that Coca-Cola had to reveal stockholders' names to the city of Atlanta. Five days later, Judge Morris finally announced his decision. The contract, he held, was indeed permanent. "I never read a more forceful and conclusive opinion in any case," Sizer exulted. "This is a golden opportunity for The Coca-Cola Company to make a fair and reasonable settlement of this litigation." At first, he seemed to be correct. While filing an appeal, the Company asked for negotiations. W. C. Bradley and Veazey Rainwater were chosen to represent either side and commenced a protracted series of meetings.

A RAY OF LIGHT

While Bradley and Rainwater sparred, Supreme Court Justice Oliver Wendell Holmes, Jr., delivered an opinion which redeemed the otherwise miserable year that had almost passed. In his decisive ruling, Holmes reversed the Court of Appeals, favoring Coca-Cola over Mayfield's Koke Company of America. In words lovingly quoted by Company officials in years to come, he wrote that Coca-Cola was "a single thing coming from a single source, and well known to the community. It hardly would be too much to say that the drink characterizes the name as much as the name the drink." In other words, it didn't matter that the drink was originally named for its primary ingredients or that it had once contained cocaine. The judge ruled that Koke was an infringement on the trademark, but that Dope was a generic term which Mayfield was free to use.

Finally, the wrangling bottlers and Company officials could rejoice over a mutual triumph. If the opinion had gone the other way, it would have rendered their bickering meaningless, since Coca-Cola itself would have been badly damaged. "The decision is of the utmost importance," Hirsch told a reporter. "It establishes beyond all question the validity of The Coca-Cola Company's trademark and trade name, and will forever protect the company against infringement." In his temporary euphoria, Hirsch may be pardoned for overstatement. He would prosecute plenty of cases in the future, but they would be substantially easier to win.

Meanwhile, Howard Candler continued to price syrup on the inflated 20-cent sugar in his storehouse. Bottler Crawford Johnson moaned that his consumers could not understand "why we are compelled to sell our product on a basis of 20¢ sugar when the market price today is 8¼¢." Rainwater and Bradley remained deadlocked over the Company's right to inspect bottling plants, and the bottlers' demand to examine the Company's books. The new year dawned with no settlement in sight. In February, the bottlers instituted yet another suit against the Company, charging Howard Candler with using fraudulent sugar prices.

A few days later, *The Wall Street Journal* embarrassed the Company by implying that its annual report was hiding something—which, of course, it was. "The report of the Coca Cola Co. leaves plenty to the imagination. It is unlike any annual statement that has made its appearance since the first of the year." The stock took yet another dive, and Howard Candler hurriedly filed a profit and loss statement showing a 1920 loss of over $2 million from sugar. In April, in an all-out effort to woo favorable press, The Coca-Cola Company threw a bash at Atlanta's Capital City Club to unveil big new ads to editors and publishers.

On May 4, 1921, after only two days of hearings, the Court of Appeals judge in Philadelphia virtually affirmed Judge Morris' opinion from the bench. In an unusual procedure, he called the attorneys to the bar and suggested that they agree on a sliding scale for their mutual benefit. Afterward, Hirsch and Sizer agreed it would be best to leave it up to a court-appointed official, since Rainwater and Bradley were at an impasse. By the end of June, the war within the Coca-Cola family was resolved. The contracts were permanent—even the contracts of the Thomas Company with its bottlers. Beginning on November 1, the price of syrup would be set at $1.17 ½ per gallon for the parent bottlers, and $1.30 to the actual bottlers, both of which included a 5-cent allotment for advertising. For every cent that sugar rose above 7 cents a pound, the price of syrup would increase by 6 cents. The bottlers dropped their other suits.

Coca-Cola had weathered its worst crisis. The overpriced sugar was almost exhausted, and sales continued to increase, despite a national economic slump. A jobber explained the drink's depression-proof status: "It is a business in innumerable articles of comparatively small cost that have a universal demand." In June, another major infringement suit against Chero-Cola—a drink which had dominated its home territory of Columbus, Georgia—came down in favor of Coca-Cola.

HARRISON JONES INTO THE BREACH

The internecine struggle may have been over, but it left deep psychic wounds which would never fully heal. The bottlers would never again truly trust the Company. But one man who had joined The Coca-Cola Company managed single-handedly to bridge the gap between the two parties. Harrison Jones soon achieved mythic stature among the bottlers. A solidly built 6'2", Jones was an imposing man, his curly hair boiling from an oversized head, while his booming voice dominated any conversation. A timid journalist, still recovering from an encounter, described him as "a very large gentleman who masks a kindly and patient disposition with a slightly ferocious exterior and a vocabulary more graphic than recordable . . . Mr Jones appears forever to be about to hit something with an ax." Jones had joined the firm of Candler,

Thomson & Hirsch in 1910 and was involved in the 1919 buy-out. Perhaps recognizing that he was more suited to sales than the law, Hirsch suggested that Jones transfer to the Company to reorganize its sales force. The new employee split the country into ten sales territories, installing a manager in each, and instituted annual meetings. In 1921, Jones published the first newsletter for Coca-Cola fountain salesmen, which he called *The Friendly Hand*. He even managed to pry money out of Ernest Woodruff for thirty brand-new cars.

At the same time, he recognized that the bottlers, too, badly needed a friendly hand from the Company. As a first act of reconciliation he planned a huge convention for all of the bottlers in 1923—a first-time event, since previous conventions had been sponsored by the separate parent bottlers. He enlisted veteran salesman Ross Treseder to assist him. According to Treseder, Jones became "all steamed up" over the need to make the convention a memorable, effective affair which would inaugurate "permanent closer cooperation" between the Company and the bottlers.

Jones wanted the bottlers to feel that it was *their* convention and traveled to solicit their suggestions. Ross Treseder's description of the men he and Jones visited reveals the Coca-Cola bottler in his kingdom. Mobile, Alabama, bottler Walter Bellingrath was eager to talk, since Coca-Cola was "his religion morning, noon and night," punctuating his advice on Coca-Cola with Biblical quotations. He used much of his wealth to create elaborately landscaped gardens. From Mobile, Jones and Treseder traveled to Memphis to see "Uncle Jim" Pidgeon, the premier U.S. bottler, who used 100,000 gallons of syrup annually. A white-haired dynamo, Pidgeon was another true believer. "By the time you left [him]," Treseder wrote, "any misgiving or doubt you had about Coca-Cola and its potential success would have vanished completely."[*] In Paducah, Kentucky, they found Luther Carson, who periodically leaped up in church to testify to Coca-Cola's wonders. Carson had good reason to praise the Lord, since he owned the best car and biggest home in town; he delighted in showing off his oriental rugs.

Armed with plenty of ideas, Jones and Treseder returned to Atlanta and prepared a complete stage set of "Typical Town," with Mom and Pop stores, barbershops, haberdasheries, and shoe stores. On the "wrong" side of the street, Coca-Cola displays were put in out-of the way places or the logo was misspelled. On the "right" side, appropriately placed signs announced the drink's superiority. The 1923 spring program appealed particularly to the route salesman, who shouldn't consider himself merely a delivery man. "If a man thinks he's a salesman, he is a salesman," Jones said. "If he thinks he is a truck driver, he is a truck driver." Taking the drivers down "Brass Tacks Lane," the seminars covered every aspect of a typical day.

---

[*] Unlike most Coke bottlers, Pidgeon paid top wages and attracted loyal employees. Every morning as his loaded Coca-Cola trucks rolled out, he shouted after his drivers: "Give 'em hell, boys—give 'em hell!"

Harrison Jones grew positively lyrical in his grand address of reconciliation to the bottlers: "This is a great day! It is a day of reunion, a day of family unity, when the stalwart sons of Coca-Cola . . . meet together in the old homestead . . . to give inspiration and to gain it." He proceeded to give it, emphasizing the indissoluble bond between the Company and the bottlers: "You, the bottlers of Coca-Cola, and we, the manufacturers of Coca-Cola, are interlocked, interlaced and interdependent one upon the other in a way that injury cannot be done to the one without the other, and that the progress of one must inevitably be the progress of the other. Men, we are one."

Jones called the bottle and glass "the Siamese twins" of the Coca-Cola industry and summoned "men with guts . . . whole-souled, red-blooded he men" to go out and find consumers "at the crossroads country store, at the filling station, at the ball game, at the skating rink, on the trains, at the clubs—literally, anywhere and everywhere." On the bottler's heart and mind, Jones wanted the message imprinted: "Let's make it impossible for a consumer to ever escape Coca-Cola."

Treseder was awestruck. "He was the best speaker I ever listened to . . . capable of inspiring any audience." In fact, Harrison Jones spent most of his life talking nonstop, retailing anecdotes liberally spiced with creative obscenities. Thomas Wolfe, in a lyrical passage about a salesman, could easily have been describing Harrison Jones: "He had . . . a wild energy, a Rabelaisian vulgarity, a sensory instinct for rapid and swingeing repartee, and a hypnotic power of speech, torrential, meaningless, mad, and evangelical. He could sell anything." Jones often called Coca-Cola "holy water"; once, however, carried away at a bottlers' convention, he declared more truthfully, "Hell, I could sell bottled horse-piss."

In his travels around the country to boost his salesmen's morale, Jones was equally enthusiastic. The Canadian business was thriving, despite the long, cold winters. One day in St. Louis, Harrison Jones launched into a vivid description of the Canadian enterprise, explaining that, in the winter, the denizens of the frozen North kept their houses toasty warm and practically lived on Coca-Cola. "Wait," one of the salesmen interrupted. "Is there any chance for me to get the bottling franchise for the North Pole?" Given Jones' persuasive powers, the eager potential bottler may not have been kidding. As another Coca-Cola man noted, "Harrison Jones could sell you a snowball in Alaska."

ARCHIE LEE SEEKS FAME AND FORTUNE

As Harrison Jones was rejuvenating the Company, Archie Lee, the man who would revolutionize Coca-Cola's advertising, was planning his first campaigns at the D'Arcy agency. Unlike most Coca-Cola men, Lee was an introspective, quiet sort who had been seriously questioning the meaning of his life before he joined D'Arcy. Just after America had entered World War I in 1917, young Archie Lee penned a long, soul-searching letter to his parents. "The doctrines of our churches are meaningless words," he wrote. "Whither we are bound no one seems to know." Still, he said, "Ah what a loss it is when we contemplate the Garden of Eden. There is something deep in our hearts that tells us life was meant to be beautiful, peaceful and joyous. All our actions lead to turmoil and strife. Where is there a man today who is holding out a genuine and satisfying hope?" Perhaps, he wrote, "some great thinker may arise with a new religion."

Lee went on to say that he wanted to "do something really worth while. I would die happy if it should be just one recognized and lasting thing." The "great ambition" of his life was to write wonderful books. Of course, it would be nice if he earned decent money while he was at it. "Fortune and fame! They make a lot of difference." Two years later, at D'Arcy, he was indeed on the road to fame and fortune, though not as a novelist. He had, however, found something that held out a "genuine and satisfying hope." Coca-Cola, his new religion, offered a brief illusion of Eden to a world full of "turmoil and strife." Archie Lee would translate the fundamental human longings into some of Coca-Cola's most powerful ads.

"It is hard work," Archie admitted to his parents in 1920, "giving a different dress to many stories about the same thing." In Coca-Cola, however, he felt that he had found the key to his fortune as well. He borrowed $1,000 from his father to invest in Coca-Cola stock at its lowest ebb in 1920, accurately noting that "there is a big chance that it will net a good profit, perhaps leading the way to a real fortune." The next year, he wrote that he was creating "the best work I have ever done." He had designed the year's entire Coca-Cola campaign and was growing closer to Bill D'Arcy. "I feel confident that my reward will not be inconsiderable." He hadn't given up his goal of writing fiction—"at least one novel and some stories"—but he couldn't find the time. Later in 1921, he described an Atlanta presentation, where they displayed over fifty pieces of ad copy, most in color. Lee basked in Howard Candler's praise of "the best material that had ever been presented." There was no more mention of writing fiction. Archie Lee had found his calling.

Lee was probably responsible for several changes in Coca-Cola's ads in his first few years. By the time he joined the agency in 1919, the D'Arcy approach had grown more sophisticated than the wordy "reason why" ads of 1907. A full-color 1916 design, for instance, featured two women, one with tennis racquet, the other with golf clubs, drinking Coca-Cola, with minimal copy and dramatic use of white space. Women were wholesome, active, full of life, as opposed to the harried, neurotic shoppers pictured a decade before. A 1917 ad stressed Coca-Cola as "a favorite friend . . . a bond of mutual enjoyment." Medicinal claims and negative advertising had been nearly abandoned.

In 1920, the D'Arcy agency took the trend to minimal copy to its extreme, possibly at the suggestion of the creative Archie Lee. A *Life* ad simply depicted a busy street corner dominated by a huge wall painting which read "Drink Coca-Cola, Delicious and Refreshing." Another copyless ad featured the New York City skyline and harbor, with a hand holding a glass of Coca-Cola in the foreground. In 1921, ads showed a clean-cut young soda jerk who dispensed "with a deft, sure hand," emphasizing superb, uniform service and product.

Lee also assisted with a project to help the bottlers find new markets, sending out a packet of advertising and direct mail letters that could be tailored for varying circumstances. Aimed at retail dealers and women, the letters focused on the take-home market for the first time, urging them to request delivered cases from their local grocer. While the twenty-four-bottle case was awkward, the inventive D'Arcy approach tapped a huge potential market.

Archie Lee's real talent, however, lay with the perfect, gracious slogan, and in 1922, he devised his first big winner, "Thirst Knows No Season," which ran for several years. February and December ads using the slogan portrayed Coca-Cola in lively ski scenes. The phrase was repeated again and again at a 1922 Atlanta convention, where fountain salesmen were delighted with its message. While the Company had always pushed Coca-Cola as an all-season drink, this was the first really sustained winter campaign.

ROBERT WOODRUFF TAKES OVER

In July of 1923, Archie Lee wrote that he was busy with a major new client—the White Motor Company of Cleveland, Ohio. D'Arcy had won the account because the new president of Coca-Cola, a former White executive, had made the connection. Lee and the new Coca-Cola head were destined to become the symbiotic team that guided the company into a golden age. Lee introduced the man whose name would become synonymous with Coca-Cola:

> A fellow about my age and the son of a prominent banker in Atlanta, a fellow I met when I first went to Atlanta years ago, started selling White trucks about the time I went to work on a newspaper in Atlanta. He did remarkably well, and after the war he was taken to Cleveland and soon became General Manager of The White Company . . . Although he was making lots of money in Cleveland, he went back in Atlanta a few months ago as president of The Coca-Cola Company. This man is Robert Woodruff.

Part III

~

The Golden Age
(1923–1949)

Georgi Zhukov was exhausted. He still hadn't finished briefing his officers for the next day, and the sun had set hours ago. With a sigh, he asked his aide to bring him something to eat. The Russian general hadn't paused once since he had defended Moscow against Hitler's crack troops, then broken the German resistance at Stalingrad, lifted the siege of Leningrad, and championed the triumphant Russian advance from Warsaw to Berlin. Pushing his troops unmercifully to get there before the Americans, he had yearned to settle a personal score. "Soon I'll have that slimy beast Hitler locked up in a cage," he had promised his friend Khrushchev. Though Zhukov accomplished everything else, he was thwarted when Hitler shot himself.

Now, bogged down in the kind of administrative tasks he loathed, the general oversaw the Russian-occupied zone of defeated Germany. Even though he despised the enemy, he pitied the starving, pathetic Germans who begged for food. While Zhukov felt contempt for most American troops—those braggarts who had entered the war late and considered themselves the world's saviors—he had found a fellow soldier in Dwight Eisenhower, and the two had become friends at the Potsdam Conference.

Thinking about Ike reminded Zhukov of the American's favorite drink. To the Russian, it had looked evil—a dark, fizzy potion—but he couldn't offend his new acquaintance when Ike offered it to him. Smiling, he tossed off the drink as he would a shot of vodka, then felt it explode up his nose. Spluttering, he thought he'd been the victim of a practical joke until Eisenhower, laughing, told him to sip it more slowly. "It'll still give you gas," he said, "but back in Kansas they say a healthy belch is good for your digestion." Zhukov liked it the second time, subsequently developing quite a taste for the beverage.

That was what he needed to brace him for the rest of the evening. "Nikolai!" he shouted. "Bring me one of those special Red Star drinks with my food." Eager to enjoy the new drink, Zhukov had asked General Mark Clark, commandant of the American-occupied zone, if he'd arrange for a supply of Ike's drink. "But it must not look like the American product," he cautioned. "Don't put it in that funny-looking bottle. And make it a different color." Zhukov knew that Stalin, that jealous madman, would be only too delighted to have an excuse to liquidate the people's hero. The general couldn't be caught with the capitalist soft drink.

Ah, here it was. His aide brought borscht and what looked like a bottle of mineral *water. Snapping the red-starred cap, the hero of all the Russias tilted his head back and drank deeply, then emitted a small burp. "Ahh," he said under his breath. "Coca-Cola!"*

Robert W. Woodruff: The Boss Takes the Helm

Great things are done by devotion to one idea; there is one class of geniuses, who would never be what they are, could they grasp a second.
—John Henry Cardinal Newman

IN 1923, when Ernest Woodruff's dynamic son Robert became president of The Coca-Cola Company at the tender age of thirty-three, most people assumed that the crusty old banker had willed the appointment. In fact, Robert Woodruff, the youngest executive of a major corporation at the time, was hired over the initial objections of his father. Ernest Woodruff was consistent in his business and family activities—he was a bastard in both. As Robert Woodruff's official biographer noted, his relationship with his father was "a never-ending pattern of affection, rebellion, respect, defiance, devotion, tolerance, and admiration." According to the younger Woodruff, his "dictatorial" father never approved of anything he did. "He was much harder on me than on his other sons."

If Robert Woodruff was born on December 6, 1889, with a golden spoon in his mouth, his father had promptly confiscated it and melted it down for the bullion. As the oldest of three sons, Robert received no allowance and was expected to live in the Spartan manner of his father. Though he grew up with numerous servants in a suitably ostentatious house in Atlanta's Inman Park, he was in many ways a poor little rich boy. The household's atmosphere was serious, constrained, and severe; the three boys were never allowed to rough-house or chase one another through the echoing halls. Childhood pictures of Robert Woodruff, even at the age of two and a half, reveal a preternaturally calm, adult face—contemplative, serious, calculating, self-conscious, and deeply melancholy. His deepset eyes seem to assess a grim world, but show no sign of fear. The world had best watch out.

As one of Asa Candler's Sunday school pupils, Woodruff received a dose of Candler's fervent Methodism along with his father's Puritanical influence. While not overtly rebellious, the young Woodruff undoubtedly delighted in joining his fellow students in mocking the Coca-Cola magnate behind his back. It must have given him great pleasure to bilk both Candler and his father at the same time. Ernest Woodruff gave his son 50 cents a week to feed the pony the boy rode to school. The resourceful student befriended the groom behind the Coca-Cola factory near his school and left his pony there all day to munch on Candler's oats, allowing young Woodruff to pocket the money.

He was a uniformly poor student. At thirteen, he attended a summer school run by Mrs. W. F. Johnson, who liked the awkward, serious boy. With her encouragement, he blossomed. "I have been greatly pleased," she wrote, "to note the effort you have made since coming to my little summer school, and if you will only continue in this line, some day you will be a man to whom your parents will point with pride." Woodruff cherished this note, keeping it among his mementos. When he later became president of Coca-Cola, he sent Mrs. Johnson a small monthly stipend, explaining that "You had a great many pupils, lots of whom were much better than Robert W. Woodruff, but I had only one Mrs. Johnson."

Woodruff's response to this kind woman was probably related to his devotion to his mother, Emily Winship Woodruff, by all accounts a saint. Gentle and understanding, she served as a foil for her domineering husband and encouraged a love of music and poetry in her children. Throughout his life, along with the gruff manner inherited from his father, Robert Woodruff displayed a sentimental side, and he always sought out nurturing women in addition to his manly sporting and gambling companions.

Despite his summer school efforts, Woodruff quickly flunked out of Boys' High School and was shipped to Georgia Military Academy, where he remained a poor student but found his niche as a leader. Because of his gruesome dental braces, Woodruff couldn't take part in sports. Instead, he managed virtually everything at GMA—the football team, the school publication, the dramatic club—while putting his natural charm to good use as a salesman. Of course, it didn't hurt to be Ernest Woodruff's son. Raising money for the school band, he went straight to his father's banking cronies. Woodruff's arts of persuasion, coupled with his last name, also saved the school from bankruptcy. The brash young man visited James S. Floyd, the vice-president of the Atlanta National Bank, which was about to foreclose on GMA's mortgage. The lanky sixteen-year-old fixed the bank executive with his rather intimidating stare and told Floyd to "go easy" on the school. When Floyd found the interloper was only a student at GMA, the executive started to throw him out—until Woodruff told him his name and implied that Tom Glenn, one of the Trust Company's officers, would endorse the GMA note. Suddenly Floyd was more than cooperative, and the school was saved.

Once out of GMA, Robert Woodruff caved in to his father's demands that he go to college, and in the fall of 1908, he departed for Emory College at Oxford, Georgia, where he excelled at cutting classes, spending money, and writing home with multiple complaints—his eyes bothered him, he didn't have enough ready cash, the dormitory roof leaked and he caught a cold. He paid other students to do his math homework, remaining unrepentant about it even in later life. One of his widely quoted dictums was: "If you can get somebody to do something better than you can do it yourself, it's always a good idea." By the end of the semester, even Ernest Woodruff had to admit defeat when James Dickey, the president of Emory, wrote a devastingly direct letter:

"I do not think it advisable for him to return to college this term . . . He has never learned to apply himself, which together with very frequent absences, makes it impossible for him to succeed as a student."[*] Furious, Woodruff's father insisted that he get a job and pay him back for the wasted tuition, room, and board.

AN INAUSPICIOUS EARLY CAREER

Robert Woodruff harbored two adolescent fantasies about his adult life—he would either make a million dollars or hunt big game like Buffalo Bill Cody, whom he had once met. He eventually achieved both goals, but they must have seemed far away to the nineteen-year-old who went to work in February of 1909 at the General Pipe and Foundry Company as a general laborer shoveling and sifting sand. That lasted only a week, after which he became a machinist's apprentice, learning to work a lathe and other machinery. After a year, he was fired for no apparent reason, but was rehired by the parent corporation, the General Fire Extinguisher Company, as an assistant stock clerk, soon shining as a salesman. Or so it seemed. Again, he was inexplicably fired.

After bouncing from one manual job to the next, Robert Woodruff received a magnanimous offer from his father: a position as purchasing agent at the Atlantic Ice and Coal Company. He was about to marry Nell Hodgson, who came from a prominent Athens family, and he needed steady work. Still cocksure despite his checkered career, Woodruff soon horrified his father by purchasing a fleet of White motor trucks to replace the horses and wagons which had been delivering ice and coal. Ernest Woodruff nearly collapsed when he heard of this extravagance, and he vetoed a promised pay raise.

When Robert Woodruff found, through his immediate manager, that his father was behind the decision to deny him a raise, he became suspicious and discovered that his father was also responsible for having him fired from his previous jobs. Ernest Woodruff wanted to impart a lesson in hard knocks, proving that life wouldn't automatically be easy as a rich man's offspring. The angry son promptly quit, vowing never to do business with his father again—a vow he later broke.

While an underpaid salesman at the ice company, Woodruff had joined the Norias Shooting Club, a southwestern Georgia game reserve where wealthy executives from all over America came to hunt, drink, play poker, and conduct discreet business. He recognized that membership would allow him to brush shoulders with "mighty important men." Many years later, he advised his nephew that "it is just as easy to make your friends among people of consequence as among people of no consequence. I don't mean just people

---

[*] Robert Woodruff probably retained a feeling of defensive inferiority about his brief college stint. He eventually resumed Asa Candler's tradition of Coke philanthropy toward Emory, the "Coca-Cola School." Even the college song asserts, "We were raised on Coca-Cola, no wonder we raise hell."

with money, I mean people that have amounted to something in the field that they operate in." Woodruff lived by this precept his entire life, surrounding himself with famous businessmen, writers, politicians, entertainers, and athletes.

Walter White, a Norias member, was impressed with the way Woodruff had negotiated for his trucks as well as with his conduct at the club. He now offered the young man a job as southeastern salesman for the White Motor Company. Almost overnight, Woodruff created a sensation as a truck salesman, with his unerring way of nosing out the right contact, the "man of consequence." Unlike many salesmen, Woodruff was direct, honest, and relaxed, radiating confidence and stability. He represented a quality product which he was graciously offering to a needy public. He rose quickly through the ranks, becoming sales manager of the southeastern region. During World War I, he left White to serve in the U.S. Ordnance Department, developing a troop transport carrier that gave the White Motor Company considerable business, then rejoined the firm after the war. Ernest Woodruff, who had counseled his son against the "terrible mistake" of selling trucks, must have decided that his son was worthy after all, inviting him to join the board of the Trust Company of Georgia, where Robert participated in the Syndicate's scheme to buy The Coca-Cola Company in 1919. He purchased a substantial chunk of insider stock at $5 a share, and also persuaded his hunting buddy, Ty Cobb, to buy Coca-Cola stock, laying the foundation for Cobb's fortune.

As vice-president of White, Woodruff was riding high, with a huge salary of $75,000 a year plus commission. He also *lived* high, much to his father's disgust, borrowing heavily to finance a luxurious life-style and further investments. During the recession of 1921, he narrowly avoided having his notes called in, and he watched his falling Coca-Cola stock with dismay. Although by the end of 1922, the stock had turned and sales had improved, the soft drink's future was still uncertain. The Coca-Cola board was unhappy with Howard Candler at the helm. He lacked any real drive or leadership ability and had been responsible for the disastrous sugar purchase. There was considerable discussion about bringing in a more aggressive president who would provide much-needed direction. Robert W. Woodruff was a natural choice. Initially reluctant, Ernest Woodruff finally had to admit that Robert was a gifted salesman, and offered the presidency of Coca-Cola to his son at a salary of $36,000 a year.

The young executive wasn't eager to leave White for a $39,000 pay cut. Complicating his decision further, Walter Teagle had tendered him the presidency of Standard Oil for a salary of $250,000. Woodruff was tired of New York, however, and longed to return to Atlanta. He also saw an enormous potential for increased sales of Coca-Cola, both domestically and overseas. The 3,500 shares of Coca-Cola stock he owned ultimately motivated him: "The only reason I took that job," he later said, "was to get back the money I had invested . . . I figured that if I ever brought the price of stock back to what I had paid for it, I'd sell and get even. Then I'd go back to selling cars and trucks."

Woodruff made a counteroffer: he would take the presidency for a base salary and 5 percent of any annual increase in sales. His father rejected that idea. Finally, Woodruff agreed to take the job with the proviso that he be given free rein, making it clear that he would brook no opposition from his father. With the Standard Oil offer in his pocket and a promise of his old job at White if things didn't work out, Robert Woodruff assumed the presidency of Coca-Cola. For over sixty years, the charismatic leader would guide the soft drink's fortunes, making it the world's most famous product.

THE BOSS

Even to his closest associates, Robert Woodruff remained an enigma. He stood an even six feet tall, but his commanding presence made him seem much larger, as he chewed his ever-present cigar and silently assessed a room he had just entered. "You knew when the Boss had arrived," one acquaintance recalled, "even if you were facing the other way. You could feel it. He had an indescribable presence, a magnetism." Coca-Cola men would do anything to win his favor and demonstrated fanatical loyalty to him over the years. Yet, on the surface, Woodruff was a singularly uninteresting man. He didn't read. Several of his intimates swore that he never finished a book in his life, and he refused to look at any correspondence that went beyond a single page, relying on aides to digest material for him. He didn't appreciate culture, history, or art. When stuck in traffic only minutes from St. Peter's in Rome, he impatiently ordered his driver to turn around. "But Mr. Woodruff, we're only five minutes away!" his secretary exclaimed. "That's close enough," Woodruff snapped.

Although Woodruff was a poor speaker who avoided the limelight, many of his sayings were more widely quoted by Coca-Cola men than Biblical verse. Woodruff's simple pronouncements, such as the dictum that "everyone who has anything to do with Coca-Cola should make money," often cut to the heart of the obvious. Others were trite generalizations, such as: "There is no limit to what a man can do or where he can go if he doesn't mind who gets the credit."

While the gregarious Harrison Jones held forth in the company cafeteria with the common man, Woodruff had a private elevator installed so that he could go directly to his office, where he ate in his private dining room with a select group. Prowling bearlike through the halls at Company headquarters, Woodruff chomped on his cigar, passing most people as if he didn't know they were there. When someone had the temerity to accost him with, "Good morning, Mr. Woodruff," he would often growl back, "What's so good about it?" The Boss could, however, suddenly turn friendly and charming, putting his arm around an ecstatic employee while he talked.

Phobic about being alone, Woodruff made sure that he was always surrounded by people. It was common for him to call at 5 P.M. and say, "Come over for dinner tonight." Regardless of what the employee or acquaintance might have planned, he would obey the summons. Likewise, if the Boss couldn't sleep, he would wake up someone for company. The groggy friend was often baffled about why he was there, however, because Woodruff had little to say. He preferred to sit in companionable silence, dismissing company when he felt sleepy again. "Being too close to Mr Woodruff was dangerous," recalled one Company man. "It was like being a moth near a flame."

In some ways, Woodruff resembled Asa Candler. He was intensely restless, constantly on the move. He once invited a group of friends to a Florida resort for a week's relaxation. After two days, he abruptly announced he was leaving, but of course everyone else should stay and have fun. He had accomplished whatever he had come for, and he had to move on. "The world belongs to the discontented," was one of his maxims, echoing Asa Candler's Hawthorne quote. Woodruff seemed truly at home only at Ichauway, the 30,000-acre plantation he bought in southwest Georgia in 1929, where he replicated the old Norias hunting club on a grander scale—with the Boss in definite command. Otherwise, he frequently moved from his home in Atlanta to his penthouse in New York, or, later, the T.E. Ranch in Wyoming, where he pursued big game on Buffalo Bill's former spread.

The favorite poem of both Candler and Woodruff was Rudyard Kipling's "If," though Woodruff managed to live by the poem's injunctions better than Candler had. Through the years, Woodruff did indeed keep his head while others were losing theirs. Woodruff also resembled Candler in never paying exorbitant salaries, though he at least understood the value of nicely timed bonuses. Finally, both men demonstrated a devotion to Coca-Cola which approached idolatry. Even in his old age, the multimillionaire would squat next to a rural gas station's vending machine and count the number of bottle caps to see which percentage belonged to Coca-Cola.

Notoriously competitive as an outdoorsman, crack shot, and fine horseback rider, Woodruff proved mediocre at golf, which his friend Ralph McGill called his "hair shirt." Still, Woodruff never lost, even on the links. He would set a high enough handicap for himself so that he even beat his friend Bobby Jones, Jr. More often, he snagged Jones—who owned Coca-Cola bottling plants throughout the United States, South America, and Scotland—as his partner. Likewise, Woodruff never lost at poker, keeping the game going into the early hours of the morning if necessary. In one famous instance, he insisted that the Company plane fly in a holding pattern over the airport until he won at gin rummy.

Above all else, Robert Woodruff valued *control*, which he exercised even over himself. One acquaintance praised him for "the capacity of becoming angry and not revealing it." Instead, the Boss moved to deal with his enemies quietly but effectively, assuming natural command in virtually any situation. He rarely attended social functions. "I give parties," he said, "I don't go to them." Early on, he realized that those who wielded the greatest power often remained in the background, and so he became a master of subtle influence, of exercising velvet-gloved authority.

But Woodruff didn't use that power in a vacuum. A superb listener, he constantly questioned and asked advice. Often, he had already made up his mind about a course of action, but he asked for opinions anyway—to verify that he was right, and to make everyone feel a part of the action. His advisers ran from his top executives down to his servants. At one point, a vice-president asked Woodruff's chauffeur whether the Boss had sought his input on an important matter. "No, sir," the driver answered, "but he will."

CHANGES IN THE TWENTIES

Though Robert Woodruff is usually given credit for "saving" the Company, he actually took over a well-managed business that had already weathered its most difficult period and was well on the way to recovery. The annual report for 1922 proudly noted that a whopping loan of $8.4 million (due to sugar losses) had been paid in full over the last two years. Harrison Jones had effectively restored morale while dividing the country into more efficient sales districts. Archie Lee and Bill D'Arcy had begun to refine Coca-Cola advertising. Sales were booming. Inflation and sugar prices had moderated, assuring a nickel drink for decades to come.

More important, Woodruff inherited the corporate culture of Coca-Cola, a drink which already had a semi-mystical aura. Company men cherished a deep-seated belief in the product itself, regardless of whether Candlers or Woodruffs were shaping its future. The real protagonist of the drink's history would be Coca-Cola itself. Woodruff's genius lay in recognizing this fundamental principle and building on it, resisting all efforts to diversify. As Justice Holmes had said, Coca-Cola was a single thing coming from a single source, and Woodruff fiercely adhered to his solitary product in the standard six-ounce bottle until he was literally forced to change it decades later.

In some ways, Coca-Cola typified major corporations in the twenties—the era of the first professional managers, who relied increasingly on lawyers, public relations experts, market researchers, psychologists, and advertisers. Woodruff, a consummate manager, brought an almost military precision to what had essentially been a family business, run in a brilliant but amateurish fashion by Asa Candler and his relations. The Boss insisted on procedure manuals for every aspect of the Company.

Even better than his father, Robert Woodruff understood how to manipulate corporate structure to maximize profits, privacy, and control while minimizing taxes and governmental scrutiny. Early in 1923, when he was first elected to the board, Woodruff supervised the creation of Coca-Cola International. Despite its name, this holding company had nothing to do with foreign sales; it simply replaced the awkward three-man voting trust. Its purpose was the same—to assure that Woodruff and his friends retained control of the corporation. Common stock in Coca-Cola (over 251,000 shares) was traded on a 1-to-1 basis for International shares, although the New York Stock Exchange initially balked at listing the new issue, objecting to holding companies that conducted no actual business.

Generally, circumstances in the 1920s favored Woodruff. With economic recovery following the brief postwar recession, the U.S. entered the free-swinging, self-confident Jazz Age, and Coca-Cola fizzed along as a vital part of the times. The muckraking Progressive Era was essentially over, and Coca-Cola emerged from its cloud of controversy to match the image it had always sought—a wholesome family drink, a temperate alternative to bootleg liquor. Those who continued to attack the soft drink now appeared old-fashioned holdovers from a prior era.

Tom Watson, in his last hurrah as a U.S. senator in 1921, the year prior to his death, excoriated Coca-Cola from the floor of the Senate. "An addict who consumes from fourteen to twenty bottles of the stuff every day is no uncommon case," he thundered. "I have had the best doctors in the State of Georgia tell me that Coca-Cola destroys . . . the brain power and the digestive power and the moral fabric and that a woman who becomes an addict to it loses her divine right to bring children into the world." But no one paid attention to him any more than they did to the predictable ravings of octogenarian Harvey Wiley. Though Southerners continued to call for their "dope" with a shot of lime, cherry, or ammonia, it was just a nickname. Coca-Cola did retain a vaguely risqué mystique, but that only led to greater consumption, not persecution.

By 1929, a WCTU campaign against Coca-Cola was ripe only for ridicule. "At the spectacle of men returning home, sodden with Coca-Cola, to beat the wives," William Allen White wrote sarcastically, "the sight of little children tugging at their fathers as they stand at the Coca-Cola bars long after midnight, . . . we remain unmoved." Another journalist commented that the WCTU might as well wage a campaign against using toothpicks in public. The same year, *The New York Times* formally announced the end of Coca-Cola's public persecution, noting that a future "studious historian" would find the assaults on the soft drink worth only an interesting paragraph. Ultimately, however, the drink "gently took its place in Big Business, where it now is."

While Woodruff may have inherited a going concern, he had a positive genius for locating the heart of its strength. He may not have saved the Company, but he unquestionably catapulted it to a higher level. Involved in all aspects of the Company from the beginning of his reign, he approved every major decision, while his own snap judgments, based on a simple philosophical framework, proved uncannily on the mark, time after time.

Part of Woodruff's ability lay in picking the right men, those he esteemed as the best in their respective fields. "He can take a man's measure so rapidly," wrote one Woodruff-watcher in 1930, "that the man does not realize he is being observed." Many of the men who would guide the destiny of the Company came on board during the twenties: Eugene Kelly, who took over the Canadian operation; Lee and John Talley, who would rise to executive levels; Al and John Staton, Georgia Tech football heroes and scholars; William "Pig Iron" Brownlee, a determined, fair, but tough manager. Many of Woodruff's recruits were Georgia natives whose soft-spoken Southern drawl charmed clients wherever they went—whether in New York, Montreal, or Paris—while their quick eyes missed no business opportunity.

If Woodruff was impressed with an opponent, he often hired him. Arthur

Acklin, a Georgia-born IRS agent who tried to pry back taxes out of Coca-Cola, soon joined the Company to do battle from the other side. John Sibley, the aggressive young attorney for King & Spalding who had fought Coca-Cola in the recent Bottler Case, soon began to work for the Company he had so bitterly opposed. Sibley became a lifelong Woodruff friend and adviser, gradually accruing power as Harold Hirsch's authority diminished. Sibley realized that Woodruff's strength lay in an intuitive grasp of the business, as he once wrote to the Boss:

> In directing a sizable business engaged in national and international operations, there are two basic things that need to be watched . . . The first I term day-to-day and year-to-year operations, consisting of sound production and merchandising methods, proper financial control, and the ability to handle men from an administrative and an executive viewpoint. The second I term sound general policy, which involves keeping all relationships right; that is, steering the business in the proper course . . . At any given time, the balance sheet should reflect the state of operations, but may not tell the story of the strength or weakness of the general policy pursued; this may be seen only from the inside or culminate later in a disaster.

ADVERTISING FOR THE ROARING TWENTIES

One of the reasons that Coca-Cola was no longer maligned by the end of the twenties was that Woodruff immediately recognized that a defensive, negative posture was poor policy and forbade any further pamphlets quoting Dr. Schmiedeberg on caffeine. The Boss set a modest, gentlemanly tone that is still echoed at the Company. The drink, he said, had no earthshaking importance —a small thing, really, serving to make life a bit more relaxed and pleasant, that's all. By such aw-shucks false modesty, of course, he assured Coca-Cola more importance; the stress on taking a moment for a pleasurable, sociable drink fit the hedonism and energy of the times.

Archie Lee and Robert Woodruff, who shared the same attitude toward the drink, quickly became close friends. Lee was one of the few people besides Sibley who actually dared address Woodruff as Bob. The ad man had the talent to translate Woodruff's groping thoughts into gracious, unassuming slogans—direct contrasts to most period advertising, which utilized wordy negative copy as never before, playing on consumers' fears. A hand cream featured "The Tragedy of Nan—Domestic Hands." Hoover Vacuum ads proclaimed that "Dirty Rugs Are Dangerous." Ads for Gillette Blue Blades showed a man with stubble admitting, "I was never so embarrassed in my life!" Postum depicted a boy tutored after school who was "Held Back by Coffee." The prize for the genre, however, went to a Scott Tissues ad featuring a surgeon and nurse bent over an unseen patient. The copy read, " . . . and the trouble began with harsh toilet tissue." In an era increasingly concerned with outward appearances and social status, most ads exploited a fear of appearing a misfit—unless, of course, the ad's particular product was used.

Coca-Cola advertising must have been a refreshing change for the harassed, anxious consumer of the 1920s. No longer did the ads show a tyrannical sun beating down on despondent, wilted shoppers. Instead, Archie Lee's message in 1923 was to "enjoy thirst at work or at play." Coca-Cola was "always delightful" and was found in a "cool and cheerful place." Copy was kept to a minimum, while pictures conveyed the message that active, contented, good-looking, successful young men and women enjoyed the drink.

The D'Arcy agency hired some of the best artists of the day—N. C. Wyeth, McClelland Barclay, Fred Mizen, Haddon Sundblom, Hayden Hayden, and Norman Rockwell, among others. Their oil paintings for Coca-Cola were often genuine works of art, but the illustrators were never stupid enough to put their egos above the product. "The idea in an illustration," McClelland Barclay said in 1924, "must hit [the viewer] like a shot. It ought to force the exclamation from them—What a peach of an idea! Not only that, but they must remember that it was Coca-Cola that was refreshing and good to drink." Barclay was particularly pleased with his *Ladies' Home Journal* ad of that year, a well-dressed socialite standing at a soda fountain, lifting her veil to sip a glass of Coca-Cola. Everything about the picture denoted classy restraint—the woman in white, the clean-cut soda dispenser, the understated copy which appeared underneath: "Refresh Yourself. The Charm of Coca-Cola is proclaimed at all soda fountains."

Woodruff and Lee continued the tradition of avoiding overt sexuality in ads while remaining suggestive. A 1923 effort verged unusually close to outright sex appeal, showing a pretty blonde with a low-cut white dress and an almost sultry look. "There's nothing like it when you're thirsty," the double-entendre caption proclaimed. In the ensuing years, however, more brunettes than blondes were portrayed, and while they were undoubtedly buxom, they weren't nearly so blatantly sexual. "We used to call the Coca-Cola girls the Atlanta Virgins," one ad man recalled. "They were sexy only above the hips, offering sex without sweat."

In 1923, Archie Lee first toyed with the phrase that would be his greatest creation. "Pause and Refresh Yourself," he wrote. "Our nation is the busiest on earth. From breakfast to dinner there's no end of work." This ad was actually a throwback to the negative hurry-hurry, worry-worry, ads of 1905, and Lee soon abandoned it. But the idea of a magical way to stop time, to take a breather in a hectic day, was valid and useful if divorced from its negative connotations.

Already hectic at the turn of the century, the pace of life in America now appeared downright frantic. "Talk about the tempo of today!" wrote one twenties commentator, describing a typical office worker's schedule. He suffered from "speed-desire-excitement," an endless cycle that "whirs continuously in his brain, his blood, his very soul." Everything had to be accomplished in a huge hurry, according to another writer, with "quick lunches at soda fountains . . . quick cooking recipes . . . quick tabloid newspapers." In 1929, Lee first coined the phrase "The Pause that Refreshes." Over the next twenty years, this "pause" became synonymous with Coca-Cola, as harried businessmen made the luncheonette a standard part of their day.

Another interesting motif entered advertising in the 1920s: a nostalgic appeal to rural America. "Every day in every way life is getting speedier, jazzier," wrote one commentator in the twenties, calling for a return to "the simple life." In response, a 1923 Coca-Cola *Ladies' Home Journal* spread portrayed a down-home girl in sharp contrast to the upper-class models usually found in the ads. A fresh-scrubbed rural beauty with boyishly short hair and a straw hat around her neck enjoyed her drink from a bottle through a straw. "You'll like it as surely as sunshine and fresh air make you thirsty," Lee wrote. Soon, subscribers enjoyed Norman Rockwell's ads with freckle-faced boys at the old fishing hole, complete with dog and Coca-Cola bottle, just as the United States increasingly industrialized. These clever appeals to a mythical peace back on the farm have continued to produce some of Coca-Cola's best advertising.

Lee's slogans and Coca-Cola's fine new artists soon were on display along the 600,000 miles of new highways built in the twenties. On twenty-four-poster billboards, the first of which went up in 1925, the "Ritz boy," a white-clad bellhop, held a tray with a single bottle of Coca-Cola and a glass. The simple caption read: "6,000,000 a Day." The billboard was joined by the "Spectacular," the name Coca-Cola men applied to huge electric signs strategically placed in the heart of a city. The first neon extravaganza was created in 1929 in New York's Times Square, which one Coca-Cola man gleefully reported to be "the busiest spot in the world . . . the mammoth parade ground of the universe." Researchers estimated that over a million pairs of eyes saw the signs there every twenty-four hours. The same writer noted that Times Square was "plebeian to the core. The masses flock to the Main Stem. They eat more, talk more, see more, dress better . . . than anywhere else." Presumably, they also drank more Coca-Cola.

Finally, in an ingenious effort to attain "scientific" advertising, the Company initiated the "Six Keys to Popularity" contest. A variety of ads stressed different reasons to buy Coca-Cola: Taste, Purity, Refreshment, Sociability, Price, and Thirst-Satisfaction. Consumers could win one of 635 prizes by writing in to explain why their favorite "key" was the most important. The 1927 campaign was in reality a massive market research tool, but it also allowed consumers to participate and feel part of the advertising itself. The $10,000 grand prize was not coincidentally given to a perfect representative of middle America: Mabel Millspaugh, a stenographer in Anderson, Indiana.

DESCENT OF THE SURVEY CREWS

In 1923, Robert Woodruff had expanded the former Information Department into the Statistical Department, which soon performed what would now be called pioneering market research. During the decade's last three years, this department frenetically laid the foundation for a scientific approach to selling more Coca-Cola. By that time, there were practically no new outlets. There was a bottling plant in nearly every town. Coca-Cola was sold in each of the

115,000 soda fountains in the United States. In the title of a 1929 article, one of the few he wrote, Woodruff posed the question, "After National Distribution—What?" Could it be that the drink had reached its saturation point?

Of course, Woodruff didn't want to answer that question affirmatively. In 1927, he assigned Turner Jones,* the head of advertising, to oversee a massive survey. Over a three-year period, Coca-Cola's field workers studied 15,000 retail outlets to determine whether there was a relationship between traffic flow and sales volume. Sure enough, the dealers with highest sales turned out to have the largest number of potential passing customers. They also tended to pay the highest rents, since they were in desirable locations. Roughly a third of the outlets accounted for 60 percent of the sales volume, while the bottom third sold only 10 percent of the total. The survey revealed that many of the high-volume outlets had few Coca-Cola signs either outdoors or inside the store. As a result, salesmen began to visit these dispensers four times a year (twice had been the standard), offering special service, aids, and encouragement. After this initial effort, the survey crews followed up with observations of 42,000 drugstore customers across the country. They discovered that 62 percent of all shoppers made purchases first at the soda fountain. Of those, 36 percent asked for Coca-Cola. Twenty-two percent of customers sipping the right soda went on to a secondary purchase at some other counter.

Armed with this information, Woodruff not only directed a more intelligent distribution and sales effort, but an innovative public relations campaign based on a series of soft-sell movies with names like *Soda Fountain Service, Come In, Customer*, and *These Changing Times*, using professional actors in the role of druggist and dispenser. The films were shown to retail dealers and chain store managers, who learned the benefits of serving the drink correctly. Coca-Cola was best served at 34 degrees with perfectly chipped ice in a thin-sided bell-shaped Coca-Cola glass, which had a convenient mark for the appropriate syrup level. Coca-Cola men came equipped with special thermometers to take the temperature of a possibly ailing drink. They also gave away six-pronged ice forks, explaining that the single pick was clumsy and that an ice shaver was out of the question. Finally, the carbonated water should be poured down the side of the glass to avoid losing fizz, and the drink shouldn't be overstirred. The films also emphasized methods of maximizing profit and reducing overhead. Soda fountain items offered fast turnover, low inventory costs, and a high profit margin. As a finale, the Coca-Cola representative handed out a free manual to help individual outlets estimate a storewide departmental breakdown in gross sales and costs.

This kind of effort did not go unnoticed. Trade associations, other corporations, and the press were impressed with the quality of Coca-Cola's research and the way the Company used it. "COCA-COLA GETS UP AND GOES TO BED WITH THE CONSUMER," one headline asserted. While

---

* The Coca-Cola Joneses—whether Turner, Harrison, Bobby, or others yet to come—were not related to one another.

such behavior would probably be somewhat sticky, there's no question that the devoted soft drink man would do almost anything to get his drink down one more throat. "Follow the crowds" became the Coca-Cola battle cry, and with the new surveys, those crowds were easy to find.

SERVICE STATIONS, SIX-BOXES, AND BLACK WIDOWS

One of Woodruff's earliest decisions was to push the bottle. Woodruff had none of the Candler defensiveness about this separate wing of the business, and it was clear to him that the future lay in the portable green bottles. As a former White salesman, he more than anyone knew that Americans were more restless and mobile as paved roads and highways crisscrossed the country. It was Woodruff who insisted that Coca-Cola be available literally anywhere in the United States and identified the service station as a major new outlet. Company dogma asserted that the soft drink should always be "within arm's reach of desire." By 1929, one and a half million American filling stations offered perfect outlets for soft drinks. These "elaborate, attractive oases for the motorist," a Coca-Cola journalist pointed out, provided a golden opportunity to snag the driver who has "paused for an interval and is gazing leisurely around with ready cash in hand."

In 1924, the Company publication sponsored a contest with a small cash prize for anyone who sent a picture of bottled Coca-Cola being served in a new outlet. The contest was a real challenge, given the alphabetical list of already discovered outlets: Bakery, Barber Shop, Bowling Alley, Café, Cigar Stand, Club, College, Confectioner, Construction Job, Dairy Depot, Dancing Academy, Delicatessen, Fire Station, Fish-Game-Poultry-Meat Store, Five and Dime, Fraternal Order, Fruit Stand, Garage, Grocery, Hat Cleaning & Shoe Parlor, Home, Hospital, Hotel, Ice Cream Parlor, Military Organization, Manicure Parlor, Market, News Agency, Park, Place of Amusement, Police Station, Pool Room, Railroad Office, Railroad Train, Restaurant, Tea Room, Telegraph Office, Telephone Office, Wiener Stand.

At many retail outlets, Coca-Cola was hidden off to the side or in the rear. Some enterprising merchants cut the red syrup barrel in half, filling one half with ice and using it as an attractive cooler. Woodruff saw the need for an inexpensive, standard cooler. In 1928, John Staton, a young Coca-Cola executive, was assigned the task. Staton disassembled all available models, testing them for durability and efficiency, then designed his own cooler and put it out for bid. After extensive negotiations, the square metal box on a stand was manufactured by the Glascock Brothers of Muncie, Indiana, for only $12.50. Within a year, 32,000 had been sold.

Woodruff encouraged bottle sales in other ways as well. In 1923, Harrison Jones sponsored the development of the first six-pack (called a "six-box" until the fifties) in a self-contained cardboard box with a "handle of invitation." It really wasn't promoted until late in the twenties, however, when Coca-Cola appealed to dealers with a picture of an attractive woman holding a carton in one hand while seductively pulling her dress above her knee with the other.

The caption below read, "My Six Appeal." Even so, the six-bottle carton failed to gain momentum until well into the next decade, when refrigerators became more common in the American home.

Meanwhile, nuisance suits continued to plague bottlers. In 1923, the Bottlers' Association was a nearly bankrupt shoestring operation with a part-time secretary working out of Harold Hirsch's office. When Hirsch resigned as the organization's legal counsel that year to devote full time to the Company, the bottlers hired Ralph Beach, a large, humorless, bespectacled man with close-cropped hair who injected new energy into the organization. Realizing that he needed legal grounding, Beach studied for a law degree at night. Frustrated by the increasing number of foreign-ingredient suits, he created a massive filing system to catch repeaters. To defend exploding-bottle cases, he devised a demonstration to be used in court, dropping ball bearings from varying heights onto innocent Coca-Cola bottles.

But the real star of the foreign-ingredient cases was Perry Wilbur Fattig, an Emory biology professor who studied the results of ingesting insects thoroughly marinated in Coca-Cola. In a 1933 article, Fattig wrote majestically in the royal we, noting that "all of the most poisonous insects and small animals that we have been able to obtain have been used. We have tested the Black Widow Spider (Latrodectus mactans) not only upon ourselves but upon thirty-nine other people." Not surprisingly, he wrote with evident frustration that "it was not so easy to get volunteers."

Coca-Cola lawyers claimed, of course, that the bugs *couldn't* have gotten into the drink until after it was opened. Even if by some miracle a bug *had* invaded the bottle, however, they called Fattig for the defense. He explained that the carbonated water in soft drinks acted as a germicide, rendering any bugs harmless. He then proceeded to give a personal demonstration. Juries must have been fascinated, if appalled, by Fattig's culinary habits, as he calmly munched lizards, scorpions, blowflies, cockroaches, spiders, caterpillars, fleas, roaches, grasshoppers, beetles, snails, frogs, bees, praying mantises, centipedes, worms, and stink bugs, chased down by a black widow or two. While an undoubted phenomenon in court, Fattig was not quite so popular socially. Ralph Beach's wife, for instance, refused to attend Fattig's dinner parties, where he often spiked the drinks with roaches.

STANDARDIZING COCA-COLA

One of Robert Woodruff's bedrock tenets was that Coca-Cola should be standardized. Every bottle and fountain drink should taste exactly the same across the United States. He knew from experience that the drink's quality varied considerably from place to place, depending on the water, carbonation level, ratio of syrup to soda, and cleanliness. That, he declared, would change. In 1929, he established a Fountain Training School, where salesmen learned exactly how to mix the perfect drink, check carbonation levels, and the like. They were to convey this information to the dispensers, along with the all-important lesson of proper temperature. Coca-Cola had to be sold *ice-cold* or it didn't taste good. Lecturers coined homilies to help salesmen remember: "It's gotta be cold if it's gonna be sold."

In a brilliant psychological move, Woodruff summoned his entire fountain sales force for a special meeting in 1926. He informed them that they were all fired. Coca-Cola didn't need salesmen, since the drink was now selling itself. However, if they cared to return the next day, he was forming a new department and they might be interested. When the shaken men came back the following day, they were rehired as "servicemen" who would no longer "sell" Coca-Cola, but offer their free advice and repair service. To assure a new outlook and to emphasize change to the dealers, each man's territory was reassigned.

Woodruff also preached standardization to the bottlers, a more delicate task given their recently bruised feelings. Through Veazey Rainwater, he implemented the bottlers' Standardization Committee in 1924. At first, this group dealt primarily with appearances rather than product, issuing decrees on appropriate uniforms and truck colors. Initially, they chose a white and green striped cotton suit which some Coca-Cola men complained resembled jail outfits. Trucks should be yellow and red with black hoods and fenders. The real issue, of course, was whether Coca-Cola was being bottled at each of the 1,200 plants under hygienic conditions, with uniform carbonation and syrup throw. The bottlers' contract unfortunately left the matter of quality up to the individual bottler, specifying only that each drink should contain at least an ounce of syrup per eight ounces of carbonated water at more than an atmosphere of pressure.

The contract did not prevent Woodruff from exerting his considerable influence. He was horrified when visiting one bottling plant early in his presidency. Dust caked the machinery, broken bottles were piled in a corner, and everywhere spilled syrup attracted flies. The Boss summoned the owner and told him he'd better clean up his operation by the next day, or he would soon find himself in some other line of work. "But Mr Woodruff," the bottler protested, "it don't do no good to clean up. The next day it'll just look like this again." There was a moment of tense silence as Woodruff slowly and deliberately took his cigar out of his mouth, his eyes boring holes into the bottler. "You wipe your ass, don't you?" Woodruff said. With that, he replaced the cigar and left.

While this piece of Company folklore may be exaggerated, there is no question that Robert Woodruff could and did make the bottlers acutely uncomfortable, notably by manipulating the amount of advertising "cooperation" he extended beyond the minimal amount specified in their gallonage allowance. The bottlers soon got the message: if you played ball with Woodruff, if you were a good boy, you were rewarded with more advertising support, more encouragement, more perks. If you didn't, you suddenly found yourself with virtually no support, ostracized by many members of the Coca-Cola family.

Woodruff found another solution for failing bottlers during the twenties: he bought them out. By the end of the next decade, The Coca-Cola Company owned twenty-five bottling plants, most in major cities. In the ensuing years, these plants served as training grounds for new employees and future managers. Independent bottlers loved to point out that the Company-owned plants never did particularly well, largely because of management turnover.

THE SEEDS OF FOREIGN CONQUEST

As impressive as all of these changes were, none could compare to Robert Woodruff's greatest contribution to Coca-Cola's future. He applied his energy and organizational skills to opening overseas markets. It is a tribute to his independence and foresight that he did so against the express wishes of his board.

The old men on the Coca-Cola board—Ernest Woodruff and his cohorts—had initially regarded an invasion of Europe as one of their principal tasks. The last sentence in the Syndicate's official press release announcing the 1919 buy-out said that the new management would "extend the operations . . . more widely than heretofore, not only in the United States, but in foreign countries." For years, Sam Dobbs had resisted every effort of eager would-be European entrepreneurs, insisting that the time was not yet ripe for real expansion beyond the United States. Under direction from the new owners, however, Howard Candler finally agreed to a European venture. "Our Sales Department is being deluged with applications to handle Coca-Cola throughout the world," Candler noted in his 1921 annual report. "We believe the foreign field should be occupied by direct representation, owning plants, manufacturing and bottling our own product." In 1922, with an expenditure of some $3 million, bottling franchises were started all over Europe, largely funded by Coca-Cola and run by locals.

The new outlets were an immediate and unequivocal disaster. For six months, Coca-Cola "teaser" advertising had stimulated curiosity and anticipation for a grand introduction of the drink. Crowds assembled in cafés, restaurants, and stores to try the new bottled beverage. After they snapped the crowns, their curiosity was soon overcome by nausea. The American drink made them sick. The cafés and bars, covered with caramel-colored vomit, soon emptied.

What had happened? Although the bottlers had religiously followed instructions, putting the proper amount of syrup into each bottle and adding sufficient carbonated water at the correct pressure, no one had bothered to make sure the water was clean and nonalkaline. And no one had told them that the crown corks had to be sterilized. The bacterial Coca-Cola quickly reacted with the germ-infested corks to produce a poisonous brew. Only one French bottler persisted. Georges Delcroix solved his sanitation problems, then overcame a governmental ban on importation of a "medicine," but his sales, primarily to American tourists at Harry's Bar and the Eiffel Tower, remained quite small.

With the European disaster fresh in their minds, the board members responded negatively when young Robert Woodruff told them he intended to see whether only Americans could develop a taste for the soft drink. Thwarted once again by his father, Woodruff took matters into his own hands, sending Colonel Hamilton Horsey to England in the fall of 1924 for a thorough survey. Long-term prospects, Horsey reported, were good. Over 10 million people lived within a fifty-mile radius of Trafalgar Square, compared with only seven and a half million within a similar compass of New York City. Transportation and communication facilities were excellent. British advertising was similar in character to that in the United States. Nonetheless, Horsey noted serious obstacles. The drab year-round weather encouraged hot drinks, though mineral waters and ice cream were becoming more popular. The soda fountain was a new phenomenon in England; there were only some thousand in the entire country. The British resented any "show of pomp [or] braggadocio," Horsey observed; Coca-Cola would have to go slow, avoiding "crashing through" methods.

Horsey's final recommendation was to commence bottling in the London area, committing $500,000 to a three-year introductory period. He suggested importing syrup from Canada for political and tax purposes, since it was a member of the Commonwealth. In addition, a separate British corporation, entirely under control of The Coca-Cola Company, should be set up. Since a prospective consumer "does not become enthusiastic when he first tastes it," Horsey predicted that "the work of the English Company, in the beginning, will be similar to the pioneer work . . . done in American forty years ago."

Woodruff did not actually implement Horsey's suggestion in England until 1932, probably because he failed to secure sufficient funds from his board. Instead, in 1926 he founded the Foreign Department and sent Horsey back to the Continent to rekindle the business there on a limited budget. At the same time, he sent other emissaries to Central America and China, and the following year himself embarked on a three-month trip throughout South America.

Woodruff regarded continental Europe as a vital area, placing it directly under Gene Kelly, who ran the Canadian operation. A native Georgian and former White employee, Kelly was the only truck salesman Woodruff hand-picked for work at Coca-Cola. Even more than Woodruff, he was a stickler for detail, writing trunk-filling manuals to cover every conceivable aspect of the Coca-Cola business. He had brought the per capita consumption of the soft drink in Montreal near that of New Orleans. If anyone could salvage the European trade, it was Kelly. Woodruff also put Cuba under Canadian supervision, which resulted in some overbuilt bottling plants on that tropical island—the roofs were designed to hold heavy snow.

By the end of the twenties, Coca-Cola's missionaries had installed bottlers throughout the world, and Woodruff had secured adequate advertising for the new ventures. Because the soda fountain was a uniquely American institution, sales of foreign fountain Coca-Cola were meager. Rather than ship bulky syrup containers overseas, Woodruff had his chemists develop a special powdered concentrate with no sugar, which made it doubly useful for the Company. Foreign bottlers would supply their own sugar so that, if the price went up again, it wouldn't affect The Coca-Cola Company.

Woodruff did not make the mistake of locking himself into a perpetual overseas contract, leaving him free to change the price of concentrate and to replace weak bottlers. In other ways, however, he used the domestic bottlers as a model, insisting that the Company wouldn't suffer from the stigma of being an intrusive American product. Instead, the business would use local bottles (all made in the hobbleskirt shape to Coca-Cola specification), caps, machinery, trucks, personnel. Wherever it went, Coca-Cola would benefit the economy. Everyone would make money. Everyone would be happy.

The systematic creation of a worldwide industry posed unforeseen difficulties, however. Coca-Cola had to rely either on already established local bottlers, who might not push the product properly, or on wealthy entrepreneurs who knew nothing about soft drinks. In the latter case, the Company preferred to deal with prominent locals, but it often wound up using American corporations. In Guatemala and Honduras, for instance, the United Fruit Company, which dominated the local economy, took the franchise. An Illinois flour concern owned the bottling rights for Haiti, Puerto Rico, and the Dominican Republic.

In other countries, government regulations presented major problems. In Amsterdam, health officials forced the Company to label the drink "limonade gazeuse," despite objections that "lemonade," the European term for soda pop, implied a cheap, common drink. In Rome, a tax was levied on all advertising signs, and the city had to approve each type of display before it was erected. That was better than Bermuda, where no large outdoor billboards were allowed at all.

In each new country, the Company hired local lawyers to handle the delicate matter of registering the trademark, a process occasionally complicated by someone who had arrived first. The American achievement of Coca-Cola had already resulted in a flurry of imitators. One British firm, Duckworth & Company, concocted an *ersatz* Coca-Cola syrup which it exported widely to South America and elsewhere. In 1928, The Coca-Cola Company filed its first overseas suit in Britain's Chancery Division to cut off the Duckworth syrup. As a more direct expedient, Coca-Cola simply bought out some prior registrants, such as Toni-Kola in Holland and Peru. In neighboring Mexico, the trademark situation was a complete disaster, spiced by political unrest and revolving governments. There were already four pirated registrations for the identical "Coca-Cola" name, as well as a host of registered imitators. In 1925, Harrison Jones, accompanied by company chemist W. P. Heath and a lawyer, drove to Mexico to untangle the situation, but even the redoubtable Jones left without accomplishing anything. Cuba, too, hosted innumerable imitators, but the legal system there, swayed by American intervention over the years, proved more malleable.

Different languages and cultures also caused problems. The Company developed one universal ad for distribution showing only the torso of a man in a tuxedo drinking from the trademark glass and featuring the hobbleskirt bottle. "Coca-Cola" was the only word in the ad. But even that wouldn't have worked in China. The Chinese characters which most closely reproduced the sound of "Coca-Cola" translated roughly to "bite the wax tadpole." Finally, an alternative that meant "can mouth, can happy," had to suffice.* In Dutch, the slogan "Refresh Yourself With Coca-Cola" meant "Wash Your Hands With Coca-Cola," so in Holland another phrase was devised.

In Cuba, an unfortunate wind blew one day as the soft drink manufacturer tested the new art of skywriting. "Tome Coca-Cola" (Drink Coca-Cola) was blurred so that the crowds below received the message, "Teme Coca-Cola" (Fear Coca-Cola). Even the Company's most earnest efforts to adapt advertising to local culture provoked trouble. An elegant lithograph showing a bullfight was prepared for Cuba, but since the sport was illegal there, it proved unusable.

Even though the overseas business didn't bring in much immediate revenue, Woodruff knew that it had great public relations value. He sent photographers around the world to take snapshots of Coca-Cola's new presence and, apparently with the board's approval, he published them in a special edition of the *Red Barrel* at the beginning of 1929. The copy accurately pointed out that

> few Americans realize that Coca-Cola is now found within the bull fight arenas of sunny Spain and Mexico, at the Olympic Games Stadium below the Eiffel Tower above "Gay Paree," on the holy pagoda in distant Burma, and beside the Coliseum of historic Rome. For many years Coca-Cola has been a national institution of the United States with widespread popularity throughout Canada and Cuba. But during the past three years it has been extended beyond national borders and its sales are now international in scope. At present Coca-Cola is sold in seventy-eight countries.

While it was no doubt true that *some* Coca-Cola fountain syrup and special gold-foiled export bottles were shipped to seventy-eight countries, the drink was actually only bottled in twenty-seven nations—and the volume was pathetic, the drink's quality often disgraceful. Nonetheless, Woodruff legitimately considered it a remarkable achievement in a short time. A world map appeared at the end of the *Red Barrel* article, with the countries where Coca-Cola was sold shaded in black. It clearly challenged any self-respecting Coca-Cola man to fill in the taunting white spaces.

AN ILL-ADVISED SHORT SALE

By the end of 1927, Robert Woodruff could look back on his first five years at Coca-Cola with satisfaction. Sales had climbed steadily from a little over 17 million gallons a year in 1923 to nearly 23 million in 1927. With the money

---

*Coke never actually went public with its tadpole-biting title. Many years later, however, Pepsi's "Come Alive with the Pepsi Generation" *was* literally translated in Taiwan, where it meant "Pepsi will bring your ancestors back from the dead." The nearest Coke ever came to such a public faux pas was with its French version of "Have a Coke and a Smile," which, when heard as lyrics in a song, could easily be misunderstood as "Have a Coke and a Mouse."

pouring in, Woodruff had retired all of the preferred stock in 1926, leaving the Company free of debt. There was a contingency reserve of $5 million in addition to a $10 million surplus. From a low of $65 in 1923, Coca-Cola stock had stormed to just under $200 in 1927, when Woodruff had declared a 2-for-1 stock split.

The Boss knew that the entire stock market was due for a fall, and he was sure that it would take his overvalued Coca-Cola stock with it. This runup had been too quick, too easy. Of course, he had faith in the ultimate future of the soft drink, but no stock soared up forever. Consequently, in October 1927, Robert Woodruff quietly sold short his 4,600 shares of Coca-Cola stock. In other words, he bet half his personal fortune against his own company, planning to use the proceeds of his gamble to help his former boss and good friend, Walter White, take the troubled White Motor Company private.

As anyone who lived through the stock market crash of October 29, 1929, knows, Woodruff was absolutely right about the market in general. But he was wrong about Coca-Cola. After the stock had split in 1927, it was worth $96 a share. The day of the crash, it stood at $137. During the day, it slipped to just above $128 and by the end of the year had recovered to $134, continuing to rise steadily in the following years. By the time he actually covered all his shorts, Woodruff had lost nearly $400,000. In the future, his belief in Coca-Cola would be unshakable, but he had earned that faith the hard way.[*]

Even though Woodruff failed to raise the cash to take the automotive company private, he and Walter White didn't give up. They spent a great deal of time together on a 30,000-acre plantation they had bought in southwestern Georgia and christened Ichauway, an Indian word meaning "where deer sleep." Then, in late September 1929, Walter White was killed in a car crash, and all plans to take the company private were abandoned. The Boss stepped into the breach, serving simultaneously as the president of White Motor Company and The Coca-Cola Company, an unheard-of feat which garnered much admiration and publicity. For over a year, Woodruff lived on a Pullman car, conducting business for both companies on the train between Atlanta and Cleveland. Few knew that one of his primary motivations was his "serious and critical financial condition," a phrase culled from a secret memo detailing his disastrous short sale. Nonetheless, Robert Woodruff and Coca-Cola faced the Great Depression in remarkably good shape. Over the next decade, virtually every company in America would languish as the economy was cut in half. But

---

[*] Woodruff dreaded the negative publicity that would ensue if it became public knowledge that he had shorted his own company's stock—other chief executives caught doing the same thing were pilloried in the press. To hide the affair, he maneuvered funds between the Blue Ridge Investment Company (a front for his investments) and The Coca-Cola Company. The net result: the IRS refused to allow Woodruff to take the loss on his taxes. The disastrous short sale very nearly led to the sale of the Company. In an apparent attempt to help his son, Ernest Woodruff and other major Coca-Cola shareholders tried to drive the stock down through more short sales, but aggressive investor Lindsey Hopkins stepped in to cover them. Ernest Woodruff's attempt to pool shares and sell out completely was thwarted by Hopkins and board chair W. C. Bradley.

the Coca-Cola cover girls smiled through it all, for good reason. The only cloud on the horizon was an imitator that had nearly died several times already. The upstart would prove a worthier opponent than anyone at Coca-Cola could have foreseen in 1929.

A Euphoric Depression and Pepsi's Push

That merry symphony of nickels and dimes rolling into the myriad cash registers across the nation and eventually into the Coca-Cola Company's treasury has meant a remarkably steady income . . . both in good times and bad. You could have bought Coca-Cola stock at the top price of 154½ in 1929, carried it through a major depression and the latest business recession, sold it at the low this year and you would have had, including dividends, a profit of approximately 225%.

—*Barron's*, November 7, 1938

Pepsi-Cola hits the spot,
Twelve full ounces, that's a lot.
Twice as much for a nickel, too,
Pepsi-Cola is the drink for you.
Nickel nickel nickel nickel,
Trickle trickle trickle trickle.

—Radio jingle, 1939

"BY WHAT MAGIC does Coca-Cola make its universal appeal? There surely must be something, for the demand grows and grows," wrote an awestruck journalist in 1932. By the beginning of the 1930s, the Coca-Cola business had become an astonishing avatar that left business observers admiringly bewildered. "Regardless of depression, weather, and intense competition Coca-Cola continues in ever-increasing demand," another investment analyst wrote, adding the caveat that "Coca-Cola is after all [only] a specialty product." The "specialty," however, seemed to be everywhere. In the spring of 1931, when the Empire State Building broke through the New York skyline, it nearly did so in the form of a gigantic Coca-Cola bottle. Douglas Leigh, who had created the Spectacular billboard in Times Square, suggested the bottle's familiar contours as a fitting cap to the new skyscraper.

The same year, Coca-Cola's popularity was proved in an entirely different way in the streets below, as police finally caught up with a huge Coca-Cola counterfeiting operation in a Bronx loft, complete with a 200-gallon vat, chemical laboratory, printing press, and fake labels. The elusive "bottling ring," as *The New York Times* called the five men who perpetrated the fraud, had managed to stay one jump ahead of the law in twenty-five cities over the past year. Their Bronx operation had 6,800 gallons of syrup ready to go when the police closed in.

When alcoholic beverages were finally legalized again in December of 1933, many stock analysts predicted doom for Coca-Cola. "The repeal of prohibition," a journalist wrote a year after the event, "would deal The Coca-Cola Co. a staggering blow, for who would drink 'soft stuff' when *real* beer and 'he-man's whiskey' could be obtained legally? Why, the case was an open and shut one: The Coca-Cola Co. was on the skids." Of course, nothing of the sort occurred. "While the advent of legal beer gave Coca-Cola a little jolt for a time, the novelty soon wore off and Coca-Cola addicts turned *en masse* to their old habits." In 1932, the soft drink company's stock had been added to the Dow Jones Industrial Average. By 1935, selling at over $200, Coca-Cola had become the highest-priced industrial stock in the U.S. before splitting that November, 4-to-1. Writing to a Company official that year, one observer commented that the stock had shot up so quickly that "you must have placed a sack of Vigero under it." As the Company approached its fiftieth anniversary in 1936, it appeared unstoppable.

THE GREAT FIFTIETH ANNIVERSARY CELEBRATION

When over 2,000 Coca-Cola men assembled in Atlanta for a three-day bash to celebrate the fiftieth birthday of Pemberton's drink, they looked back from a very satisfactory promontory. The strife between the bottlers and the Company now seemed minor, in light of the enormous success under Robert Woodruff's guidance. Veazey Rainwater referred to it only briefly as a "family quarrel," adding that since they were "dependent upon each other," they could "under no circumstances . . . afford to fight among ourselves."

Wealthy bottlers of the 1930s had little to worry about. They owned a simple, profitable business. As one Company veteran recalls, "The plant foreman would flip a switch and those hobbleskirt bottles would fill up, then he'd turn the switch off." Many of the Coca-Cola plants constructed during that time were monuments to their owners' wealth, stability, and vanity, complete with murals, gold inlay, sculptures, and domes. One bottler built his plant as a miniature Taj Mahal in honor of his wife.

Many of the pioneer bottlers were still active, including Joe Biedenharn, the much-celebrated Mississippian who had first bottled Coca-Cola in 1894. As a tribute to these men, a play titled *Pioneer Days* depicted the "Podunk Coca-Cola Bottling Company," with scenes of reluctant retailers finally appreciating the new drink. As good clean fun, Coca-Cola men and their wives were treated to boxing and wrestling matches in the evening, where the wives screamed for their favorite wrestler to tear his opponent apart. Elsewhere in the convention hall, antique machinery reminded bottlers of how far they had come, and a "Visomatic" display room illustrated the technological training of future employees. While watching filmstrips, a new soft drink man could be indoctrinated with the winning Coca-Cola attitude. By the time he had seen each of the Visomatics, he had received his first transfusion in a career-long process. In his veins, Company men laughingly acknowledged, a Coca-Cola man had not blood, but syrup.

Robert Woodruff didn't address the bottlers at the convention, but he did deliver a short speech at a special dinner for fountain men, the elite cadre he often called his Marine Corps. "We are still pioneers," he said, noting that Coca-Cola's success tended to promote "ease and financial independence" which would "soften too many of us too soon." He warned that "there are hazards in this talk of success . . . In the long life of Coca Cola, this half century is hardly more than a flicker; but we can use it, if we will, to light a beacon that will be a guide to us and those who follow."

Woodruff's quiet cautions were drowned out in a wave of optimism. As the convention finale, Harrison Jones delivered a speech entitled simply "Tomorrow": "There will be trials and tribulations. Men will be sorely vexed and their souls will be tried . . . There may be war. We can stand that. There may be revolutions. We will survive. Taxes may bear down to the breaking point. We can take it. The Four Horsemen of the Apocalypse may charge over the earth and back again—and Coca-Cola will remain!" The motto to live by, Jones concluded, was that "Coca-Cola is not *yesterday*; Coca-Cola is *tomorrow*." With a smug look backward, then, Coca-Cola men left the 1936 convention secure in their hopes for the future.

TAKING ADVANTAGE OF THE DEPRESSION

The men leaving the convention had ample reason to gloat. By 1936, it was clear that Robert Woodruff and his men had managed to turn the Depression on its head by deliberate, determined, multiple attacks on consumers. As a *Fortune* reporter observed two years later, the Statistical Department's punch cards recorded "the precise state of Coca-Cola affairs on its far-flung capillaries" and could forecast sales and profits for the following year within a 2 percent margin of error.

Increasingly, for a public prodded by the Company's calculated advertising, Coca-Cola not only quenched thirst but performed a social function, as a contemporary observer noted: "Everywhere, but in the South particularly, it seems to be taking the place of coffee—or other liquids—as the something over which men must sit to talk." Imbibing also began earlier in the day. Sam Dobbs had remarked in 1910 that Coca-Cola had found a place everywhere except the breakfast table. By 1932, there was even fizz in the A.M.: "Pay a visit to one of Schrafft's stores in New York in the early morning and note the number of people breakfasting on Coca-Cola and rolls or even Coca-Cola alone."

The soda fountain proved a magnet for all ages. Coca-Cola was the approved beverage over which teenagers mooned and spooned. In common jive parlance, the soft drink was also known as "heavenly dew," while water was called "sky juice." In the evening, working men and neighborhood women congregated under the ceiling fans to sip communally, while privileged children perched on the high stools with their own glasses, listening to the adults' idle gossip. No one was more aware of the importance of placing the soft drink at the heart of America's social activity than the Company itself. "Play up the soda fountain as an institution, a gathering place," advertising department head Turner Jones advised Archie Lee in 1934. The D'Arcy man did highlight the soda fountain, but he didn't stop there in his Depression-era efforts.

Lee was one of the first advertising men to realize that a product's image was actually more important than the product itself. During a beach vacation, Lee noticed that his four-year-old daughter lavished such attention on her Pooh bear that other children fought over it, though other toys appeared more attractive. Lee took the incident as a parable. "It isn't what a product is," he wrote to Robert Woodruff, "but what it does that interests us"—and set out to plant the proper thoughts about Coca-Cola, which he wanted to make as popular and well-loved as the Pooh bear. Extensive Depression-era advertising presented the drink as a pleasant, inexpensive time-out from an increasingly difficult reality. Everyone could find a nickel to "bounce back to normal," as Archie Lee's slogan promised. A historian looking at Coca-Cola ads of the thirties would be hard-pressed to find any evidence that the United States was suffering through hard times. Promotions for the soft drink portrayed people enjoying Coca-Cola at work and play with no hint of the Depression—exactly what people wished to see. They needed no reminders of their daily reality. Coca-Cola ads, as well as the drink, provided a temporary escape, showing happy-go-lucky tourists at the Kentucky Derby, Mardi Gras, Carlsbad Caverns, or Old Faithful enjoying themselves with the pause that refreshed.

COCA-COLA GOES TO THE MOVIES

Movies provided a similar escape, thriving along with the soft drink. Archie Lee dispatched photographers to Hollywood with expense accounts to buy Coca-Cola for movie sets. Throughout the thirties, movie stars appearing in Coca-Cola ads included Wallace Beery, Joan Blondell, Claudette Colbert, Jackie Cooper, Joan Crawford, Clark Gable, Greta Garbo, Cary Grant, Jean Harlow, Carole Lombard, Fredric March, Maureen O'Sullivan, Randolph Scott, Johnny Weissmuller, and Loretta Young. "Movies have a wider appeal than any other thing in this country," Lee wrote to Turner Jones in 1935. In the same letter, he crowed over the "free advertising that we are getting . . . in recent movies." *Imitation of Life* was "very popular," Lee said, and was "really based on Coca-Cola." *Broadway Bill* mentioned the soft drink several times, and Dizzy Dean gulped it in a film while announcing baseball games. Lee liked these movie advertisements immensely, noting that they made "many people so actively conscious of it that they subconsciously buy it."

By the end of the decade, businesses were hiring specialized agents to arrange film placements for their products. Coca-Cola's infamous Barbee brothers,[*] who had built their Los Angeles bottling plant in the shape of an

---

[*] Stanley and Al Barbee, identical twins and Lupton relatives, operated Los Angeles Coca-Cola Bottling Company with their older brother Cecil. Both manic-depressives, the twins were obsessed with sex and the glitzy Hollywood life-style, while Cecil was all business. Stan collected art (original Delacroix, Picasso, Renoir, Degas, Chagall, Van Gogh) while Al spent his money on world travel and huge boats.

ocean liner complete with portholes, hired J. Parker Read to hand out Coca-Cola on Hollywood back lots—two cases every month to major stars, five cases a day to all current productions. For Read, a movie mogul in the era of silent films, it was a humiliating job, but he performed it with style. In 1939, when Spencer Tracy called for "two Coca-Colas, please," in *Test Pilot*, 60 million adoring fans watched him enjoy his soft drink. "The movies," noted a *Business Week* reporter, "combining sight and sound, can boast a marked advantage over either magazines or radio when it comes to showing a product in use." This "low-pressure selling" was effective, the writer asserted, because of its "subtle suggestion."

Most of the female movie stars in Coca-Cola ads were clad in bathing suits more revealing than the modest swimming dress worn twenty years before. In fact, one series of Depression-era spreads contrasted two Coca-Cola beauties, one in the demure costume of the past, one in a skimpy modern suit. Treading the fine line between overt sexuality and wholesome allure now posed a real challenge, and without saying so in public, some Coca-Cola men clearly came down on the side of sex. Writing to Archie Lee in 1934, Turner Jones suggested his Hollywood photographer be on the lookout: "Why shouldn't he take pictures of any stars he can get in bathing suits, in some good sexy poses?" A Portland, Oregon, bottler took the theme further. He built a huge billboard at a busy intersection, leaving a cutout section in the middle for a simulated beach scene in which Miss Oregon and another beauty queen lolled on the sand for three hours nightly, making oral love to Coca-Cola bottles. "On some nights it has been necessary to have a traffic officer present to keep the traffic moving," the local bottler gleefully reported.

AT HOME WITH IDA BAILEY ALLEN

Aside from going to the movies for escape and sexual fantasy, though, most Americans found few social outlets. With less money to spend, more families entertained and ate at home. At the same time, it was much simpler to keep soft drinks ice-cold with the new technological wonder of the refrigerator. Consequently, the Company planned major campaigns to persuade women and children to drink more Coca-Cola at home.

The Company recognized "the tremendous importance of that veritable army of women shoppers," said one journalist, noting that they bought "daily supplies for some 25,000,000 American homes." With the new carton, Coca-Cola was available for the first time in thousands of Piggly Wiggly and A&P stores. Housewives were urged to grab a six-box for the fridge, and the home market blossomed almost overnight. To ensure its growth, Woodruff sent bands of women from house to house to install the familiar Coca-Cola bottle opener and to offer coupons for free cartons.

At the same time, in 1932, the Company gave away millions of copies of a booklet, *When You Entertain: What to Do, and How*, by Ida Bailey Allen, whose cookbooks and syndicated show, "The Radio Home-Makers Club," made her the last word on the etiquette of entertaining at home. Desperate to avoid embarrassing faux pas in front of neighbors or the husband's boss, housewives sought the advice of the redoubtable Mrs. Allen, whose matronly profile graced the frontispiece. She promised to help them craft the correct meals, right down to the doilies. Nor did she press the Coca-Cola bottle too firmly to her readers' lips, holding herself back until page 26, when she first mentioned that "Coca-Cola or tomato juice cocktails are delightful with canapes." Once having suggested the soft drink, however, she soon lost all restraint, mentioning it as an accompaniment for every meal, including "Dramatizing the Breakfast Occasion," a meal which she graciously allowed could be "charmingly served with or without a maid." The recipe called for Eggs Benedict, Crisp Rolls, Crullers, and Grape Fruit Sections in Coca-Cola.

To promote the idea of buying cartons for the home, Coca-Cola ads featured food for the first time along with the soft drink, a "natural partner of good things to eat." The hot dog or hamburger with chips, washed down by a Coca-Cola, were presented as the typical American meal.

SANTA WEARS COCA-COLA RED

Coca-Cola bottlers had always known that they had to snare the next generation of drinkers early, regardless of the taboo on direct advertising to those below twelve. Now that children could find Coca-Cola in their refrigerators, the Company went after the school-age market as well, though it took care never to show anyone of elementary age actually drinking the beverage. One approach directed at children wound up reshaping American folk culture through the art of Haddon Sundblom.

A hard-drinking Swede whose work was brilliant but usually late, "Sunny" made himself indispensable, regardless of his habits, by creating the classic Coca-Cola Santa Claus in 1931. Sundblom's Santa was the perfect Coca-Cola man—bigger than life, bright red, eternally jolly, and caught in whimsical situations involving a well-known soft drink as his reward for a hard night's work of toy delivery. Every Christmas, Sundblom delivered another eagerly awaited Coca-Cola Santa ad. When his first model, a retired Coca-Cola salesman, died, Sundblom used himself. While Coca-Cola has had a subtle, pervasive influence on our culture, it has directly shaped the way we think of Santa. Prior to the Sundblom illustrations, the Christmas saint had been variously illustrated wearing blue, yellow, green, or red. In European art, he was usually tall and gaunt, whereas Clement Moore had depicted him as an elf in "A Visit from St Nicholas." After the soft drink ads, Santa would forever more be a huge, fat, relentlessly happy man with broad belt and black hip boots—and he would wear Coca-Cola red.

The Company produced a series of miniature scenes for window displays also primarily aimed at children. The charming cardboard cutouts could be assembled to create, in successive years, a miniature circus, a tiny town, an airport, the Olympics, a corner drugstore, and the cast of Uncle Remus animals.* Millions of children took free smaller versions of each scene home, where parents helped put them together—all part of the Company's devious calculations. Similarly, a house-to-house sampling campaign made "a tremendous impression upon the younger generation," a bottler noted with pride. The kids "gathered around the truck in swarms."

The Company helped bottlers invade public schools by offering a series of Nature Study Cards along with a booklet, placing the Coca-Cola logo in classrooms across the country. Some local businessman went much further, though. In 1931, a Texas bottler wrote with pride that "the kids play basketball at recess on Coca-Cola goals, use Coca-Cola blotters to blot out their troubles, consult a Coca-Cola thermometer, and write their notes on Coca-Cola tablets. Can you beat that?" Some school administrators were not so amenable to free advertising, however. One Georgia bottler found that an open house at his plant provided the "opening wedge," as he put it. "We make an appeal to the children in the form of a useful toy, forcing the parents to attend by not allowing children admission" without an adult. "Heretofore," he wrote, "it has been strictly against the rules of the school authorities" to allow the Company to pass out materials. Once he gave away the pencils, sharpeners, and tablets at his plant, however, they found their way into the schools anyway, and the financially strapped district caved in. "Due to the general economic conditions, we have received requests from practically every school in the community," the bottler smugly concluded.

Other bottlers didn't wait until children had reached school age. N. A. Lapsley, a hustling Kansas owner, scoured local papers for birth notices, mailing a little poem in honor of the birth along with a coupon for two free bottles of Coca-Cola. "Toast your own health from the cheering bottle," Lapsley rhapsodized, "Tilt back your heads, then open the throttle." Presumably, most parents appropriated the coupons for their own use, but some undoubtedly put a feeding nipple right onto the bottle, as did James Durkin, a Rhode Island serviceman. "I have a baby boy 15 months old," he wrote, "who will drink nothing but Coca-Cola . . . I feel so proud of my son saying Coca-Cola almost as soon as he learned to say 'Da-Da.'"

RADIO COMES OF AGE

By the end of the 1930s, families were listening on the average to over four and a half hours of radio programming daily. "No medium has ever captured the imagination—not to mention the leisure time—of the public with the speed of radio," commented one historian. Identifying the wave of the

---

*The Uncle Remus display caused quite a stir, though not, as it might today, because of racial stereotyping. Blacks never appeared in Coca-Cola ads of the period except as servants, though they were already a major consumer group. The 1930s flap was over copyright: Joel Chandler Harris' widow sued the Company and lost.

future, The Coca-Cola Company firmly committed itself to radio in 1930 with a budget of almost $400,000. Grantland Rice, one of Woodruff's buddies and a well-known sportswriter, went on the air with a sports program, beginning with interviews of Ty Cobb and Bobby Jones, Jr. Leonard Joy conducted an all-string orchestra, introducing each show with a special Coca-Cola anthem he initially wrote as a tango, but Woodruff hated it. Slowed to a stately waltz time, however, the theme, played by a sweeping string section, charmed the radio generation, providing the signature for every company-sponsored show.

Coca-Cola's radio programs gave Archie Lee headaches, caught as he was between the artists, Woodruff, and the audience. Woodruff insisted that shows associated with Coca-Cola be as wholesome and upbeat as the product, employing a gracious soft sell rather than the sirens, gongs, and pistol shots that often announced commercials for other products. He vetoed any news coverage as too negative to warrant sponsorship. There would be no controversy. Lee carefully instructed a comedian to avoid not only off-color jokes, but "any remarks about politics, religion, prohibition, and so forth"— anything that might even remotely "arouse antagonism."

Woodruff's favorite radio personality was "Singin' Sam," born Harry Frankel, a country smoothie from Indiana (Archie Lee called him the "homey hoosier") who crooned for the soft drink from 1937 until 1942. Lee, though, preferred the silken sounds of André Kostelanetz. Unfortunately, the conductor was a prima donna of sorts, insisting on a full orchestra of forty-five men. Kostelanetz even refused to play in a new million-dollar studio because the sound didn't suit him. By 1940, Archie Lee looked back on the decade as his "years of struggle and grief with radio," but he felt that Coca-Cola programming had achieved a decent balance. Singin' Sam appealed to rural, blue-collar types, while the temperamental orchestra leader attracted most other adults. For the bobby-soxers, there was a new program featuring the swing and jazz bands of men such as Tommy Dorsey and Jimmy Lunceford, whom Lee referred to as a "darkey" who "shrieks and howls through his trumpet."

The great irony of the thirties was that technological innovations such as radio and refrigeration were revolutionizing American domestic life at the precise time the country suffered through its first protracted economic disaster. As technology advanced, the iced Coca-Cola cooler of the twenties evolved into an electrically chilled unit with a sliding lid. Westinghouse introduced a Standard Electric Cooler for only $76.50 in 1934. The next year, 75,000 coolers, quickly dubbed "Red Devils" by competitors, were sold to dealers. Three years later, the Mills "47," a coin-operated cooler with a capacity of over a hundred bottles, hit the market.

"The Coca-Cola cooler," wrote one bottler, "is advertising manager, salesman, clerk, delivery boy, warehouseman, and sometimes even the cash register all at the same time." A Jumbo unit, introduced at the 1936 convention by a talking cooler, solemnly proclaimed, "I am the bottler's friend." Factory workers, too, soon regarded the Red Devils with affection, using their share of the soft drink profits to buy team uniforms or to fund social clubs. In 1937, 8,000 coin-operated coolers were installed in public areas.

Coca-Cola took advantage of yet another technological innovation in the 1930s, as air travel matured from the biplane into a reliable mode of transportation. Robert Woodruff's friend Eddie Rickenbacker started Eastern Airlines, whose stewardesses served the ice-cold soft drink aboard all flights on the eighteen-passenger Condors. The Biedenharn and Freeman families, both bottling dynasties, helped C. E. Woolman expand Delta Airlines from a Mississippi crop-dusting outfit to a passenger service offering free Coca-Cola. The soft drink also took to Georgia airways via a Fokker airplane named "The Voice of the Sky" whose oversized wings bore the famous logo on their underside. Citizens of Atlanta were subjected to "strange music and voices in the air" as three amplifiers blared the Coca-Cola theme song from on high. To attract airborne consumers, the Birmingham Coca-Cola Bottling Company created a hundred-foot logo in the back court of the plant, easily visible to American Airways passengers en route to and from the Alabama city.

PRESSURE ON THE D'ARCY MEN

As Coca-Cola's advertising diversified through young technologies, the D'Arcy Advertising Company involved itself in virtually every aspect of the Coca-Cola business. The agency men performed an astonishing number of tasks for The Coca-Cola Company during these years, going well beyond the creation of advertising. In 1934, for instance, the Company was frustrated by its inability to place coolers in a Chicago office building owned by a printer named Donnelly. "Why can't you get some of the magazines in which we advertise . . . to hit Donnelly?" Turner Jones inquired of Archie Lee. The agency also conducted consumer and dealer surveys for the Company. The harried advertising men even had to organize crown cap counts, a particularly offensive survey in which used bottle caps were collected from coolers to see what percentage belonged to Coca-Cola.*

Almost everyone, one Coca-Cola ad man once concluded in frustration, was an expert on his subject. "Even morons have ideas and opinions about advertising," he noted sourly. Archie Lee must have entertained similar thoughts when Turner Jones complained, "This is not simple and clear writing—it is most hopelessly confusing." If so, Lee kept them to himself. The Coca-Cola Company was too important a client to offend in any way. Of course, that didn't mean that ad men couldn't complain to one another. Jack Drescher, a fellow D'Arcy employee, wrote to tell Lee of an illustration that had to be changed: "[Ralph] Hayes and [Robert] Woodruff say that if the

---

* A greenhorn Coca-Cola rep's first "crown count" often commenced as a nasty practical joke. His supervisor handed him the bag of used bottle caps, telling him to spread them out on his motel bed, where assorted roaches and silverfish hiding in the caps darted for cover. The sidewalk was a more appropriate place for crown counts.

attached man had about ten years taken off of him and he was made a little more cheerful, that he would be right for the poster. I say that if you do this, you would have what we have now."

In December of 1934, Robert Woodruff wrote a letter to William D'Arcy which must have ruined Christmas for the advertising mogul. In no uncertain terms, Woodruff suggested that D'Arcy augment his staff to handle increasingly diverse Coca-Cola advertising more effectively. At the same time, Woodruff advised D'Arcy to "freshen the viewpoint of your agency . . . by throwing it more closely in contact with advertising and business thought . . . in the East." Clearly, Woodruff thought St Louis was too isolated; he wanted a branch on Madison Avenue, emphasizing that the need was "urgent." The following year, D'Arcy opened a New York office.

By the end of the thirties, the beleaguered D'Arcy agency was almost an extension of The Coca-Cola Company, resulting in cumbersome, pedantic rules to prevent ruffled executive feathers. At the beginning of 1938, Jack Drescher wrote a memo to other D'Arcy men specifying thirty-five different commandments for Coca-Cola advertising. Among the charges were:

• Never split the trade mark "Coca-Cola" in two lines.

• The phrase "trade mark registered" must always appear in the tail of the first "C" even though it is illegible.

• When the cooler is shown *open*, the *righthand* side which shows the bottle opener should be opened if possible.

• The trade mark must never be obliterated so that it is not perfectly legible.

• The circular sign should carry the phrase "Delicious and Refreshing."

• On oil paintings or color photographs be inclined to show a brunette rather than a blond girl if one girl is in the picture.

• Adolescent girls or young women should be the wholesome type; not sophisticated looking.

• Never refer to Coca-Cola as "it."

• Never use Coca-Cola in a personal sense—such as, "Coca-Cola invites you to lunch."

• Never show or imply that Coca-Cola should be drunk by very young children.

PROTECTING THE SACRED TRADEMARK

Most of those rules actually originated in the Coca-Cola Trademark Protection Department. By the late thirties, Company efforts to prevent substitution and infringement were standardized and sophisticated. The soft drink lawyers were keenly aware that they could quickly lose their trademark by letting it slip into common usage. That fate had already befallen aspirin, cellophane, and the escalator. References to "cola" drinks were anathema, as were calls for dope.

In 1938, fresh out of law school at the University of Georgia, Jasper

Yeomans nervously sat through his interview for a job as a Coca-Cola investigator. "When you were a law student, how did you order a Coca-Cola at the local soda fountain?" Yeomans had not prepared for this particular question. "Dope with cherry, sir." His interviewer grimaced. "Jasper, that's the last time that you will call Coca-Cola 'dope.' Also, Coca-Cola is a product that cannot be improved upon; therefore, it needs no additives." That night, when Yeomans' girlfriend asked how the interview had gone, he answered, "You can't have any more dope with lime."

Yeomans was one of a cadre of "investigators" kept busy checking out substitution rumors. The Coca-Cola spies, mostly young lawyers trying to save money to begin a practice, were given strict orders to remain anonymous. Entering a suspect soda fountain, a hot water bottle hidden in his trench coat, the agent would order a Coca-Cola, then surreptitiously pour a sample for later analysis. Immediately after a foray, he would write detailed notes with time, place, and description of the soda jerk. The samples, sealed in small vials with hot wax, were shipped for lab analysis. "We used to call it the Gumshoe Department," one veteran Company man recalls. "Those guys were the closest thing to the FBI you ever saw."

If the fountain was indeed serving fake Coca-Cola, it received a warning letter. If two subsequent samples revealed continued substitution, *two* agents were sent at the same time—one as a witness for the impending lawsuit. Few such suits ever reached the bench, since most offenders chose to settle out of court. In the case of the minority that did go to trial, Coca-Cola never lost, but the Company sought no monetary damages, only the judge's orders that such derelict behavior cease forthwith.

WOODRUFF'S QUIET MANEUVERS

Robert Woodruff himself remained in the background, constantly maneuvering to outwit the bottlers, the government, and the competition. Woodruff bought back the parent bottling organizations one by one. He had purchased the weak New England organization when he first took the helm in 1923. Ten years later, he absorbed the Southeastern region, followed by Western in 1935. In 1940, he purchased the Texas territory known as the 1903 Company. And, in 1942, Woodruff nearly achieved his goal of acquiring the last two parent bottlers. By that time, Arthur Pratt owned the Pacific Coast, which he had purchased from George Hunter, who still ran the original Thomas Company. Pratt sold, but Hunter backed out of the deal at the last minute, remaining loyal to his Uncle Ben's memory. As the last parent bottler, the Thomas Company continued to irritate Woodruff for another thirty years.

With Coca-Cola's continued growth came predictable attention from the tax man. In 1933, Georgia governor Eugene Talmadge announced his intention of enforcing an old tax law on intangibles. This "ad valorum" tax on stocks and bonds appeared an easy way to raise desperately needed money at the Depression's nadir. Because of the county unit voting system, poor rural areas dominated Georgia politics, and the soak-the-rich tax was passed with an even higher rate for all "foreign" corporations—firms like Coca-Cola that were technically incorporated out of state—taxing them on *all* their profits, even if they were made outside of Georgia.

Woodruff warned the governor that he would move the firm rather than submit to the tax. Each believed the other was bluffing, until Coca-Cola made good on its threat by reincorporating on January 1, 1934, as a holding company. The timing was so tight that the Coca-Cola staff finished packing and fled the tax assessor just before midnight on New Year's Eve, setting up administrative headquarters in Wilmington. While the syrup was still manufactured in Atlanta, Woodruff and his administrative staff stayed in Delaware for a decade, until the Georgia laws were amended. Harold Hirsch, however, refused to budge from Atlanta. As a result, in 1935 John Sibley replaced him as the Company's general counsel. Though Hirsch remained an important legal adviser, his domination of Coca-Cola policy was effectively ended. He died five years later.

How Woodruff maneuvered the reversal of the ad valorem tax is a telling example of his patient, unrelenting strategy. While the Boss took care to avoid any illegal activity, he used every other means of influence and persuasion at his disposal. In this case, he assigned Atlanta lawyer Hughes Spalding the task of securing a constitutional amendment to remove the ad valorem tax. In 1937, Spalding hired journalist Frank Lawson to crank out two weekly columns arguing against a pending Georgia soft drink tax. One of these, aimed at the rural farmer, copied Tom Watson's hysterical, inflammatory style, utilizing boldface, italics, multiple exclamation points, and every conceivable propaganda tactic. The other, far less strident in tone, offered a more balanced, editorial tone. Both were printed in almost a hundred rural Georgia papers eager for filler. Copies were also sent to influential businessmen and members of the General Assembly.

As a result, the soft drink tax was voted down in December of 1937. In the early 1940s, Georgia governor Ellis Arnall asked the legislature to grant soft drink companies special tax treatment, pending the passage of a constitutional amendment permitting foreign corporations exemption from the intangibles tax. By unanimous vote, it was passed. "What's good for Coke," the governor pointed out, "is good for Georgia."

Another result of Woodruff's repeated tax tangles was his 1939 decision to give the Coca-Cola presidency to Arthur Acklin, the former IRS man. Acklin wasn't eager to take the job, particularly since Woodruff clearly had no intention of relinquishing any of his control, which he would exercise as chairman of the executive committee. That way, Woodruff could remain out of the public eye, which was how he liked it, letting the bureaucrat handle routine administration. Besides, Woodruff, peering over the horizon as usual, probably suspected that the U.S. would eventually enter World War II, and Acklin's governmental contacts would be essential.

Even as president, Woodruff had moved swiftly and secretly to assure a steady flow of Coca-Cola's most controversial ingredient. The U.S. legislature had passed a bill in 1927 to prohibit the importation of coca leaves for all but medicinal purposes. That did not necessarily incommode Coca-Cola, since the Company could take the decocainized leaf after the cocaine had been extracted. The trouble was that Coca-Cola consumption mandated more leaf than the doctors needed for cocaine. By 1931, Coca-Cola was using 200,000 pounds of coca leaf annually. With pressure from Woodruff, Georgia's U.S. senator Walter George hammered out a bill allowing the importation of extra coca leaf if the resulting cocaine was destroyed at Coca-Cola's expense.

In the early 1930s, however, the United States was considering joining the Geneva Convention, which required the importation of coca leaves *only* for medicinal and scientific purposes. In addition, Harry J. Anslinger, the head of the FDA, was a militant antidrug chief who was suspicious of Merchandise No. 5. The situation was too uncertain to let it rest with politicians. Robert Woodruff secretly flew to Peru, where he made arrangements for a plant to decocainize the leaves in Lima. The facility was ready to go by the fall of 1937, although it never proved necessary.

Woodruff had another reason, related to his overseas operation, for concern over the coca situation. In 1930, he had formed the Coca-Cola Export Corporation to replace his Foreign Department. Throughout the following decade, Coca-Cola's already-established overseas outpost gradually grew, while new countries were added—small islands like Curaçao, Java, Trinidad, and Jamaica as well as major territories such as England, Scotland, Ireland, Norway, Denmark, Hong Kong, Peru, Bolivia, Chili, Switzerland, Austria, Australia, New Zealand, and South Africa. As sales increased abroad, Woodruff decided to build plants worldwide to manufacture concentrate. That way, only the secret flavoring ingredient, 7X, and Merchandise No. 5 (the coca and kola extract) would have to be exported. In 1935, with logic only a government bureaucrat could comprehend, the U.S. Narcotics Bureau ruled it illegal to *export* No. 5, even though it was perfectly all right to *import* the whole coca leaves and to decocainize them under direct governmental supervision. Through delicate lobbying (including discreet monetary support for antinarcotics organizations), the Company maneuvered a reversal in 1937. Otherwise, Woodruff's Peruvian facility would have become indispensable.

In 1932, Woodruff was searching for someone with connections to help with the importation of coca leaves, negotiate with Washington officials, and advise him on the most appropriate (and useful) targets for Coca-Cola philanthropy. He found Ralph Hayes. Courteous, resourceful, and infinitely tactful, Hayes, a former aide to Secretary of War Newton Baker, was regarded as one of the few men in Washington who could keep a secret. After Baker's retirement, the accomplished young man headed the New York Community Trust, one of the first nonprofit foundations, and, by cultivating the right people, he built its coffers to over $175 million before retiring in 1967.

When Woodruff approached Hayes in 1932, the lonely, urbane bachelor was immediately attracted to the charismatic Coca-Cola boss, who replaced Newton Baker as his surrogate father. Hayes and Woodruff were an odd couple. While the Boss was taciturn and almost illiterate, Hayes was a voracious reader who wrote long, witty, insightful letters replete with

Shakespearean quotations. He loved to give after-dinner speeches and enjoyed attending all of the parties that Woodruff shunned. For the next thirty-five years, Hayes would work behind the scenes as Woodruff's diplomat, lobbyist, and occasional spokesperson and speechwriter.

STUBBS AND FARLEY HIT THE ROAD

Hayes could cope with the American government's minor irritants, but fighting the same battles in every nation around the world caused massive headaches by the late thirties. The Cubans impounded a major caffeine importation, while the German health authorities protested the coca leaf content. Mexican officials demanded the formula before allowing the concentrate into the country. In Peru, the Coca-Soda people protested an American company attempting to monopolize the word "Coca" when the leaves themselves were actually Peruvian. The list of foreign woes appeared endless.

To help combat them, The Coca-Cola Export Corporation retained Stephen P. Ladas, a Greek native specializing in foreign patents and trademarks in New York. For the next twenty-five years, Ladas, in conjunction with Coca-Cola's legal counsel, masterminded worldwide strategy. In 1940, Coca-Cola lobbyist Ben Oehlert, who, along with Ralph Hayes, would surface repeatedly in the next three decades wherever quiet pressure and diplomacy were necessary, suggested the firm find a seasoned lawyer to travel for the Company, putting out fires where necessary. As a result, Coca-Cola hired Roy Stubbs, a small-town Georgia country lawyer.

For the next fifteen years, Stubbs crisscrossed the globe for Coca-Cola. "I became a sort of legal journeyman," he wrote, "from one trouble spot to another in Latin America, Australia, Europe and the Middle East." Already fifty-five when he started his new career, Stubbs proved to be an invaluable employee who recorded his sharp observations and research in an impressive series of bound "compilations," one for each country.

It took Stubbs a year to guide Coca-Cola's registration through the Mexican government without revealing the formula, during which time he taught himself Spanish. He then embarked on a whirlwind tour of Latin America, where he made careful observations of potential markets and interviewed local patent lawyers, seeking competent and politically well-connected retainers.

Stubbs found that he had to adapt himself to the lethargic pace of Latin life, where the lawyers customarily strolled into their offices around eleven, departed soon for long lunches at home, worked a desultory hour or two, then left for the day. Though frustrated, Stubbs, like many of Woodruff's Georgia emissaries, was remarkably sensitive to other cultures. "It takes an interminable time to get things started here," Stubbs wrote to a Coca-Cola lawyer in 1941. "Interminable red tape and delay—delay—about matters that would be wound up in our country in twenty minutes . . . You have to catch [someone] in the right frame of mind, and catch him at the right place and at the right time, and rub him the right way—and above everything else—take your time. They have no appreciation of our notion of getting it done. And don't think anybody can change it."

Americans, Stubbs recognized, were often perceived by foreigners as arrogant and obnoxious—for good reason. "An American generally rears back on his hind legs and skids along on his ignorance," he wrote, "thinking all the time what a smart fellow he is." Stubbs did not make that mistake, and he soon came to have genuine respect for his Latin American colleagues, who valued tradition, culture, and style, finding time for "the protocol of amenities."

At the same time Stubbs was combing Latin America for legal talent, James Aloysius Farley was making *his* first goodwill trip for Coca-Cola through the same territory. "Big Jim" Farley, the imposing postmaster general who had masterminded Franklin D. Roosevelt's brilliant 1932 campaign, publicly split with FDR when the President ran in 1940 for a third term. Smelling opportunity, Robert Woodruff hired Farley as the chairman of the board of The Coca-Cola Export Corporation, a position created for the occasion, and promptly dispatched him to Latin America, where he was received as a visiting dignitary rather than a Coca-Cola executive. His daily itinerary made the pages of *The New York Times*. For the next thirty-five years, Farley, friend of every subsequent president, would represent Coca-Cola's interests around the world.

DEAR FDA

While Stubbs and Farley combated health issues in foreign countries, similar problems had cropped up in the United States with a resurgent consumer movement. "The tide has turned against us," W. C. D'Arcy gloomily told his fellow ad men in 1934. Rumors about the soft drink's cocaine content and effects on health surfaced with the regularity of the tide. Aside from health issues, the thirties and the New Deal also brought criticism of big business opportunism. The authors of *Partners in Plunder*, a 1935 book whose subtitle warned against "business dictatorship," heaped abuse on Coca-Cola, pointing out that the ingredients of the nickel drink cost a bit over one-half cent.

Members of the harassed FDA Food Control Division had to answer quite an array of letters in the FDR years. School officials and concerned parents asked whether the drink harmed children, who quaffed it with "fanatical zeal." An elderly woman inquired in a shaky hand whether Coca-Cola contained narcotics, since it increased the irritability of her grandson, a divinity school student with "a most Hypersensitive Nervous system." A Mormon wrote from Salt Lake City urging that Coca-Cola be banned and, incidentally, wondering whether FDA officials might consider a course in "the Word of Wisdom." Several writers wanted to know whether Coca-Cola was made with guano, a question that was not quite as wacky as it sounds, since caffeine could be synthesized from bird or bat dung. Others inquired about the effect of taking Coca-Cola with aspirin, which was persistently rumored to create a "high" or act as an aphrodisiac. Among the complaints about foreign ingredients was one from a North Carolina woman who found a large spider in her drink. "I have had a Poison Stomach every since," she wrote plaintively. In the end, however, one letter stated the case more accurately than any of the others: "Everybody says, 'don't drink it,' but I notice everyone does just the same. I like it."

FDA officials, prodded by suspicious legislators and public demand, periodically traveled to Maywood, New Jersey, descending on the Maywood Chemical Company, which was the same old Schaefer Alkaloid Works under a different name, still producing the only decocainized coca leaf in the United States—all for Coca-Cola. Each time, rigorous chemical analysis of Merchandise No. 5 failed to find even a hint of cocaine, though it did locate the equivalent of .0012 milligram of ecgonine per drink. This alkaloid, an obscure cocaine derivative with no known toxic effect, was not deemed to be a problem, certainly not in such a minute quantity.

While Coca-Cola officials had always been overly cordial to the FDA, in 1939 they became downright obsequious. The year before, during a New Deal wave of consumer consciousness, the Congress had passed a tougher Pure Food, Drug and Cosmetic Act which required that all foods and beverages list ingredients on the label, throwing the entire soft drink industry into an uproar. Coca-Cola was particularly averse to the idea of labeling, since it would mean revealing its caffeine content, a subject tabooed by Robert Woodruff.

After a friendly visit from Ralph Hayes and Ben Oehlert failed to sway Dr Dunbar of the FDA, the Company rallied its bottlers, who formed a well-organized local lobby. Letters poured in to the FDA from legislators and state health officials requesting that soft drinks be exempted from the new labeling requirements. In November, nine members of the American Bottlers of Carbonated Beverages (ABCB), including Harrison Jones, met with FDA officials, complaining that enforcement of the law would cost their industry some $80 million just in bottle stock replacement.

Predictably, Harrison Jones dominated the meeting. He claimed that the labeling requirement would lead to increased unfair competition and fraud, since an imitation cola could legitimately claim to have the same basic listed ingredients. Warming to his subject, Jones explained that the contour Coca-Cola bottle was practically a sacred object and must remain unchanged—and unlabeled. "It is grasped 18 million times a day," he intoned dramatically. "Even a blind man can recognize a Coca-Cola bottle."

The FDA caved in, granting a temporary exemption from labeling to allow the soft drink industry time to arrive at a suitable "standard of identity." Once such a standard was in place—specifying allowable amounts of carbonation, caffeine, acid, and sugar—labels would be unnecessary, since consumers could refer to the regulations. Loath to submit to such an iron-clad standard, the industry managed to stretch the "temporary" exemption, at first using the advent of World War II as an excuse. For years, though consumers continued to complain to the FDA about the unspecified caffeine content of Coca-Cola, they failed to get a satisfactory response. When a standard of identity was finally established in 1966, the public saw no difference, since Coca-Cola remained unlabeled.

THE RESURRECTION OF PEPSI

Bureaucratic tangles weren't the main problem Coca-Cola faced during the Depression, however. Surviving several near-deaths, Pepsi-Cola emerged for the first time as a serious competitor during the 1930s. Coca-Cola, the undisputed king of soft drinks, suddenly found itself coping with an aggressive young contender. Pepsi's roots went back almost as far as Coca-Cola's, to 1894, when Caleb Bradham, a North Carolina pharmacist, developed a variant cola drink with pepsin, selling it as a tonic to relieve dyspepsia. Known merely as "Brad's Drink," its popularity grew until Bradham renamed it Pepsi-Cola in 1898. By World War I, the drink had achieved modest success, with franchised bottlers in some twenty-five states. Unfortunately, Bradham was caught in the same wildly swinging sugar market that trapped Coca-Cola. In 1920, when the price spiraled over 20 cents a pound, Bradham bought heavily. When the bottom fell out of the market, his business went bankrupt.

In 1922, Bradham tried to sell Pepsi to The Coca-Cola Company, but the Woodruff Syndicate wasn't interested in the ailing soft drink. A Wall Street speculator named Roy Megargel bought Pepsi from Bradham in 1923, only to flounder two years later. Still hoping for some return on his investment, Megargel reorganized the company and limped through until 1931, when only two bottlers remained. On the edge of a second bankruptcy, he offered Pepsi to Coca-Cola. For the second time, the Company refused to buy the nearly defunct competitor.

At this point, there is little doubt that Pepsi would have gone the way of most Coca-Cola imitators if it hadn't been for Charles Guth's temper. Guth, a New Yorker long known as the "stormy petrel" of the candy business, had taken over the Loft chain of candy stores in 1929, purchasing the Happiness and Mirror stores the following year. Through the three chains' soda fountains, Guth sold quite a bit of Coca-Cola—enough, he thought, so that he should receive a bulk discount. The Company thought otherwise. Infuriated with Coca-Cola's inflexibility, Guth called Atlanta one Friday in 1931 and left a message with a secretary. "We are not going to buy through any jobber. We are going to buy direct or not at all. Unless I hear from Mr Judkins [in charge of fountain sales] before this evening, I will issue orders that not another drop of Coca-Cola will be served in any of the Loft stores. And once out, it will stay out." He repeated himself to make sure she wrote every word.

In the meantime, Guth swung a deal with Megargel in which he maneuvered Pepsi's third bankruptcy in return for a chunk of stock in the "new" company, which Guth would buy out of receivership. Megargel was also to receive a royalty of 2½ cents per gallon for six years. In July of 1931, the new Pepsi-Cola Company was born. Guth's chemist dropped the pepsin and tinkered with the formula to duplicate Coca-Cola as closely as possible. Guth then ordered that all of his soda fountains serve only Pepsi-Cola, which he proclaimed to be "the best 5¢ drink in America. It is a real bracer." The wily Guth was perfectly aware that Coca-Cola would be trying to prove substitution; in October, he advised his employees in writing: "Under no circumstances is Pepsi-Cola to be offered for Coca-Cola or compared with it," and offered $10,000 to anyone who found one of his outlets substituting Pepsi for another soft drink.

Coca-Cola's diligent investigators soon descended on Loft stores and found at least some employees who gave them a Pepsi in response to a call for Coca-Cola. In the spring of 1932, Coca-Cola sued. At the same time, Harrison Jones wrote to Guth claiming $30,000 as Coca-Cola's prize for having proved substitution in Loft, Happiness, and Mirror stores. Guth responded with a barrage of seven countersuits. Four, filed individually by Pepsi-Cola and the three candy stores, claimed that Coca-Cola had interfered with sales and harassed their staff. The other three suits were for libel, claiming that the Harrison Jones letter was "defamatory."

Guth soon sent The Coca-Cola Company a defamatory letter of his own. In July of 1932, he mailed a cartoon to the Company's Atlanta headquarters, depicting a Pepsi bottle overturning a cart containing "Coke" and "Dope" apples, which were being eaten by "Coke" pigs. Underneath, Guth had written: "Pepsi-Cola will soon be the largest selling 5¢ drink in your city both in bottles and at the soda fountain." While Coca-Cola executives must have been outraged at Guth's gall, they had no evidence that he posed a serious threat in Atlanta or anywhere else. Pepsi's sales were dismal, even with a guaranteed outlet at the candy stores. When Guth approached Coca-Cola the following year offering to sell Pepsi for $50,000, the soft drink behemoth refused for the third and final time.

Desperate now, Guth took an unexpected tack: he decided he had nothing to lose by promoting a twelve-ounce bottled drink for the same nickel Coca-Cola got for its six-ounce container. In 1934, he test-marketed the oversized drink in Baltimore, putting it up in used beer bottles. It immediately scored in blue-collar neighborhoods where a Depression-era nickel buying twice the drink made Pepsi the obvious choice, regardless of Coca-Cola's ubiquitous advertising. Soon, Pepsi was selling nationwide in a motley assortment of recycled beer bottles, and Guth was turning a profit, with net earnings in 1934 of $90,000 on gross sales of $450,000. The additional cost of the actual twelve-ounce drink was minimal, since most of the expense involved bottling machinery, bottles, distribution, and advertising. By 1935, Guth realized that there was more future in Pepsi than in Loft, and he resigned from Loft to devote full-time to the Pepsi-Cola Company, where his field was clear, since Megargel had died two years earlier.

The Loft directors, led by new president James W. Carkner, realized they were left holding an almost bankrupt candy bag and decided to sue Guth for using Loft funds and personnel to develop the soft drink. They knew, however, that without a quick infusion of capital, they might well lose a proxy fight with Guth at their 1936 meeting. Phoenix Securities Corporation, which specialized in saving troubled companies, jumped in with the necessary funds at the last minute. Phoenix head Walter Mack, who had an unerring way of diagnosing a firm's critical problem, usually assumed management responsibilities. In Loft's case, he decided that going after the up-scale market was a mistake, redirecting sales efforts at 5-cent candy. He knew that the real future of the company, however, lay in winning the court case with Guth. As Loft struggled, Phoenix continued to lend the candy firm money. In September of 1938, the case was decided almost completely in Loft's favor. Guth had to turn over his 91 percent share of Pepsi.

WALTER MACK INHERITS WORLDWIDE LITIGATION

For six uncomfortable months, as the case remained on appeal, Walter Mack served as the president of Pepsi while Guth, as general manager, made Mack's life as unpleasant as possible, locking him out of the men's room and sticking him in a cubbyhole office above the boiler room. Finally, in April of 1939, Guth lost his appeal and Mack assumed full charge of the soft drink's future. He found himself knee-deep in litigation with The Coca-Cola Company in twenty-four countries, the result of John Sibley's master strategy.

When Sibley had officially replaced Harold Hirsch as general counsel in 1935, he had conducted an intensive, year-long study and decided that Coca-Cola was in jeopardy from "an organized and insidious effort . . . to seriously impair or ultimately destroy this company's trade-mark." Half of the logo, he said, was in peril. "Cola" was well on its way toward becoming a generic part of the language. In the past, Harold Hirsch had attacked only those imitators which most closely resembled Coca-Cola—usually, like Chero-Cola, beginning with "C" and mimicking the familiar script. Sibley felt that such a lax attitude was a huge and perhaps fatal error. He believed in "the ultimate . . . assertion," that "Coca-Cola" was "an aggregate word consisting of two inseparable parts, and that each part is so linked and riveted to the other part in the public mind that when one is used the other is drawn to it." In other words, said Sibley, *all* other soft drinks using the word "Cola" should be regarded as infringers. He was particularly alarmed that a judge had ruled Roxa-Cola a valid trade-name in 1930. Also, Nehi had recently come out with the twelve-ounce Royal Crown Cola and was doing very well with it. As his final recommendation, Sibley, regarding it as too dangerous to sue Pepsi in the U.S., proposed aggressive litigation in foreign countries while instituting domestic suits against RC Cola and "the most flagrant infringers" with similar names such as Cleo-Cola.

In 1938, The Coca-Cola Company simultaneously brought suit against Pepsi all over the world, with the most conspicuous case right across the border in Canada. In July, the Canadian Exchequer Court found in favor of Coca-Cola. Still in charge at that point, the embattled Guth immediately appealed and launched a two-pronged counterattack in the United States. In a bold stab toward the heart, Guth filed an interference suit in the Patent Office, claiming that "coca" and "cola" were descriptive terms and could not be trademarked. At the same time, he sued in Queens, New York (Pepsi headquarters), charging that Coca-Cola had resorted to "illegal and fraudulent" methods, including intimidations, threats, and "trap orders" to deter Pepsi sales in New York City and elsewhere.

Goaded into action, Sibley took the Queens bait and countersued Pepsi for trademark infringement. The circle of worldwide litigation was complete. With so many lawsuits hanging fire, it is little wonder that one of Sibley's colleagues, considering the coming year, wrote that "1939 may well be the most critical year to date in the history of the Legal Department." Sparing no expense, Sibley sought the best trademark lawyers in the country, including Edward S. Rogers and Harry D. Nims, to defend the sacred name of Coca-Cola. He also hired Judge Hugh Morris, who had ruled in the Bottler Case and had now returned to private practice. Such was the volatile legal situation that Walter Mack inherited.

Described by a contemporary journalist as "a long-limbed, sad-eyed man who in looks, zeal, and tenacity bears a . . . resemblance to a bloodhound," Mack immediately set about mastering the far-flung court cases, as well as plotting the further sales of his soft drink. He forced himself to attend the pre-trial hearings every day at the Queens courthouse when they started in 1941. "Every morning," he remembered, "a big Coca-Cola truck would pull up in front of the courthouse and all these Coca-Cola men in livery would march in carrying volumes of books showing all the court cases they had won. It seemed overwhelming."

One morning, Mack received a phone call from Mrs. Herman Smith, a Coca-Cola imitator widow. She wanted to commiserate. "Coca-Cola is going to put you out of business . . . My husband thought he was right too, but they still put him out of business. And I still have a photograph of the check they gave him." His bloodhound pulse quickening, Mack asked if he could borrow the picture, which indicated that Coca-Cola had bribed its way to victory to the tune of $35,000. Confronted with this evidence in court, Coca-Cola's lawyers hastily requested a three-day recess.

The next day, Robert Woodruff phoned Mack, asking him to lunch at Woodruff's apartment in the Waldorf Towers. The two had become friendly acquaintances in 1934, before Mack had ever heard of Pepsi, when they happened to share the same transatlantic ocean liner. Now, after a few drinks, the Coca-Cola magnate said, "You know, Walter, I've been thinking. This lawsuit between us isn't doing anybody any good . . . Don't you think we ought to settle it?" On a piece of Waldorf stationery, Mack penned an agreement stipulating that Coca-Cola would henceforth agree to acknowledge Pepsi's trademark in the United States, and Woodruff signed it. When Sibley found that Woodruff had agreed to settle, he felt betrayed and attempted to quit the case. Woodruff refused to hear of it. At the end of 1941, Sibley wrote a bitter memo outlining his "fundamental disagreement" with Woodruff. "The responsibility of the position I occupy is heavy and the work is very taxing. Under the existing situation, I am unwilling to continue except on a temporary basis." In 1943, he finally relinquished his position as general counsel to Pope

Brock, a fellow King & Spalding lawyer, but Sibley remained concerned with Coca-Cola matters for the rest of his life.

Sibley was even more unhappy when the British Privy Council ruled in favor of Pepsi-Cola in March of 1942 (the Canadian trademark case had ended there after the Canadian Supreme Court reversed the Exchequer's ruling of 1939). The poor Coca-Cola lawyer must have been nearly suicidal two months later, when Woodruff and Mack settled *all* litigation over the trademark forever. Coca-Cola promised never to assail Pepsi's trademark rights again, dropping suits worldwide. Coca-Cola had irrevocably lost the exclusive right to "cola." Afraid of this possibility, Sibley had decided in 1941 to protect the *first* part of the name. In the Koke Case decision, Oliver Wendell Holmes had virtually ruled that "Coke" belonged to the Company. Now, in a deliberate campaign, Coca-Cola reversed its long-held policy and actually encouraged the use of the nickname "Coke," intending to patent that trademark after establishing use.

While the court battles raged, Walter Mack arranged for the Pepsi-Cola Company to swallow Loft. In order to spread Pepsi bottling franchises, he hit upon an ingenious system. "In my travels around the country," he wrote, "I found that there was always a wealthy bottler in each area, and that was the Coca-Cola bottler . . . So I went out and found the best of the little bottlers and tried to seduce them into taking Pepsi-Cola." Mack bought a huge quantity of secondhand beer bottles and sold them to franchise owners for a quarter cent per bottle. Filled with Pepsi, the bottles brought a 2-cent deposit, providing instant start-up capital. Later, when his franchises were established, Mack designed standard bottles which cost 4 cents each but could be amortized over many refills. Baked onto the new bottles, the Pepsi logo was red, white, and blue, making blue the distinctive color in contrast to Coca-Cola's red and white.

With a minuscule advertising budget, Mack achieved maximum impact. While Coca-Cola had been permanently soured on skywriting by the Cuban fiasco of the twenties, Mack had no such reservations. He sent pilot Sid Pike up and down the Eastern Seaboard, starting in Florida in the winter and slowly moving north. With a patented mechanism, Pike scripted the Pepsi logo over city skies, prompting one cartoonist to draw Coca-Cola antiaircraft gunners trying to shoot the skywriter out of his Pepsi cloud.

Mack's real triumph, however, was the jingle. Two offbeat writers named Alan Bradley Kent and Austen Herbert Croom Croom-Johnson played a phonograph record for Mack one day in 1939. To the tune of "Do Ye Ken John Peel," they had written lilting doggerel. "Pepsi-Cola hits the spot," Mack heard, and began to tap his toes. "Twelve full ounces, that's a lot. / Twice as much for a nickel, too, / Pepsi-Cola is the drink for you." Mack liked the jingle so much that he ordered his advertising agency to cut the surrounding hard-sell verbiage and run it alone as a thirty-second radio spot. Although no major radio station would accept his jingle—too short in an era when ads lasted at least five minutes—Mack found small New Jersey stations that needed money badly enough to run anything. The jingle, the first of its kind, was an immediate hit. Soon the big stations were begging for it. When Mack pressed an orchestrated version, it sold 100,000 copies. The music was adapted as a march, waltz, rumba, and country song, becoming "the scourge of the continent," according to one disgusted commentator. In 1941, the jingle played nearly 300,000 times over the airwaves. Mack had started a trend.

THE DIE IS CAST

While Robert Woodruff constantly warned against becoming too rigid to shift with the times, he refused to abandon his single-size drink in the face of the twelve-ounce colas. In public, Harrison Jones loudly defended this official viewpoint, but in private, he urgently confronted Woodruff with the need to act. "Every day's delay . . . aggravates the situation and makes the fort harder to hold," he wrote in an August 1941 seven-page memo reviewing the situation. Although Coca-Cola retained 46 percent of the entire soft drink market, other colas, which he designated "X drinks,"[*] had climbed to 14 percent, while ginger ale, grape, orange, root beer, and the rest had the last 40 percent. "The bed has been erected by us," Jones said, "and the bed-bugs just crawl in." The solution, according to Jones, was to give the bottlers "a definite revelation . . . of the true picture," which "should have been done long ago instead of now, and it is not being done now." He recommended a daring diversification in which the Company and the bottlers would set up a separate corporation to produce a twelve-ounce cola, under a completely different trade name, and to experiment with other flavors as well. Ultimately, Jones hoped, the competition would be "snuffed out or eliminated."

Woodruff ignored the warning. Instead, he tried in vain to bribe Walter Mack away from Pepsi by offering him the White Motors presidency at $250,000 a year. But it was too late to buy off Pepsi, setting the pattern for what Walter Mack termed "a fundamental American struggle." The competition ultimately benefited Coke, however, as one prophetic journalist observed in 1938: "Pepsi, if it survives the courts, may prove to be a good thing for Coca-Cola; the latter's sales have surged ahead in the places where Pepsi's campaigns have been the hottest."

Pepsi posed as the brash upstart, willing to indulge in questionable taste in order to grab attention. As if to prove the point, Walter Mack attempted to buy the rights to Popeye so that he could replace that hero's magic spinach with magic Pepsi. Failing that, he created "Pepsi and Pete," two cops who careened through adventures in a comic strip, always overcoming evil by drinking the right stuff at the last moment. Implicit in all Pepsi advertising was a

---

[*] Even as Harrison Jones issued a clarion call to face reality, he refused to designate Pepsi or Royal Crown by name, a practice common to Coca-Cola men for years. In a form of magical thinking familiar to anthropologists, the Company men apparently thought on some level that if they didn't *name* Pepsi, it would go away and leave them alone.

competitive jab at Coca-Cola; otherwise, "twice as much" would mean nothing. Coke remained the measure of success.

As proof of the soft drink giant's central place in American culture, Coca-Cola was the first firm awarded a contract for the 1939 New York World's Fair, where the public could view a real bottling operation, a huge mural, and a color version of the film *Refreshment Through the Years*. The next year, a bottle of Coke was interred in a Georgia "crypt of civilization" to be exhumed (and presumably drunk) in the year 8113. Even a woman complaining about the drink's health effects to the FDA wrote that "'Coke' nowadays is synonimous with a 'Date.'" When veteran editor William Allen White, the voice of Middle America, was featured in *Life* on his seventieth birthday in 1938, he insisted on having his picture taken sipping a Coke at a soda fountain in Emporia, Kansas. "Coca-Cola," he wrote soon afterward, "is . . . a sublimated essence of all that America stands for, a decent thing honestly made, universally distributed, conscientiously improved with the years."

Coca-Cola men might display a sense of humor about other things, but never about their sacred drink. On the brink of World War II, Robert Woodruff addressed his own troops just before Pearl Harbor. "We have the greatest product in the world," he said. "I can never divorce myself, my affections, my life from Coca-Cola, and neither can any of the rest of you." He warned against complacency, reminding the men of Sapolio, once a household word as a cleaner and now forgotten. "Whom the gods would destroy they first make fat . . . Never let it be said of our business, 'This is a Nice Highclass Old Business.'" The Boss called for "young, virile, ambitious men" to spread the Coca-Cola gospel.

Woodruff couldn't have known it at the time, but the Japanese were about to give his virile young men the chance for the Coca-Cola adventure of their lives.

~ 12 ~

The $4,000 Bottle: Coca-Cola Goes to War

*Today was such a big day that I had to write and tell you about it.
Everyone in the company got a Coca-Cola. That might not seem like
much to you, but I wish you could see some of these guys who have been
overseas for twenty months. They clutch their Coke to their chest, run to
their tent and just look at it. No one has drunk theirs yet, for after you
drink it, it's gone; so they don't know what to do.*
  —Private Dave Edwards, 1944, in a letter to his brother from Italy

BY THE TIME America entered World War II, Coca-Cola was over fifty
years old, so well-entrenched in the nation's culture that a 1942 ad for the U.S.
Rubber Company asserted that among "the homely fragments of daily life"
American soldiers fought for were "the bottles of Coke they'll soon be sipping
in the corner drug store." Outside the U.S., however, was a different story.
True, Woodruff had tried to spread the drink worldwide, but in most places, it
was quite *thinly* spread. While Coca-Cola had established a strong presence in
Canada, Cuba, and Germany, it barely had a toehold elsewhere. The Japanese
didn't realize that by bombing Pearl Harbor, they were indirectly giving The
Coca-Cola Company a worldwide boost that would ensure the soft drink
company's unquestioned global dominance of the industry. It's likely that the
Japanese weren't thinking about soft drinks at all, though four Hawaiian Coke
coolers were in fact martyred that day at Hickam Field. Nonetheless, the war
would be a pivotal point for Coca-Cola, validating the wartime claims for the
drink as "the Global High-Sign." Already sacred to Coke men, the fizzy drink
would assume an almost religious significance to the American soldier as well.

ESSENTIAL MORALE-BUILDING FOR THE BOYS

Shortly after Pearl Harbor, Robert Woodruff issued an extraordinary order:
"We will see that every man in uniform gets a bottle of Coca-Cola for five
cents, wherever he is and whatever it costs our company." Woodruff's gesture
was undoubtedly a genuine act of patriotism, but his shrewd business sense
and eye for publicity also prompted his magnanimity. Certainly he was aware
that young soldiers had an unquenchable thirst for beer and Coke. Well before
Pearl Harbor, he had assigned George Downing (later to set up bottling plants
in Europe behind the lines) to supply Coca-Cola to troops in the United States
during war games. Late in that summer before Pearl Harbor, during sweltering
Army maneuvers in Louisiana, Coca-Cola proved predictably popular. "One

military unit came right into a small local bottling plant to get some Coke," Downing recalls. "Their supply was gone, so the soldiers literally bought the bottles off the line before they were capped." Requests for Coca-Cola from the military were almost pathetically urgent, even before America's entry into World War II, as demonstrated by rafts of letters in the Coca-Cola Archives. In September of 1941, for instance, a base surgeon begged for adequate provisions, explaining that "I cannot conceive of any greater calamity than a loss of the base supply of Coke."

After Pearl Harbor, the trickle of letters swelled to a deluge, pouring into Coca-Cola's mailroom in response to sugar rationing. In January of 1942, an exchange officer wrote to his local bottler:

> Very few people ever stopped to consider the great part Coca-Cola plays in the building and the maintenance of morale among military personnel. Frankly speaking, we would be at a loss to find as satisfying and as refreshing a beverage to replace Coca-Cola.
>
> Accordingly, we sincerely hope that your Company will be able to continue supplying us during this emergency. In our opinion, Coca-Cola could be classified as one of the essential morale-building products for the boys in the Service.

Ben Oehlert shifted into high gear as Coca-Cola's Washington lobbyist. Already sophisticated in weaving his way through the halls of Congress and the FDA, Oehlert now moved effortlessly through the political jungle, unctuously and persistently presenting the case for Coca-Cola. He urged the Company to sell its 23,000 bags of stockpiled sugar to the military as a goodwill gesture which would put the Company in "a better psychological and public relations position." At the same time, Oehlert offered to "aid the policy-making" of the War Production Boards' Sugar Section, helping it to "formulate the proper orders" in administering the available supply. He forwarded market surveys showing the flood of Coca-Cola drunk on military bases, following up with a hundred sample letters from Army and Navy units, USO branches, Red Cross chapters, and defense industries, all "stressing the importance to them of our product." Oehlert added that "there may be a thoughtless tendency . . . to regard the soft drink industry as being somewhat non-essential in a period such as this." Nothing could be further from the truth!

To prove it, Oehlert and the D'Arcy agency created a 1942 masterpiece of pseudo-science entitled "Importance of the Rest-Pause in Maximum War Effort." The first eight pages, simply quoting various authorities to show that factory workers and military men performed better if given periodic breaks, didn't mention Coca-Cola. Then, of course, the ninth page revealed a huge illustration of a tilted Coke bottle with a pointed text: "Men work better refreshed. Time rules the present as never before. A nation at war strains forward in productive effort in a new tempo . . . In times like these Coca-Cola is doing a necessary job for workers."

As part of his "aid," Oehlert managed to get Coca-Cola executive Ed Forio appointed to the sugar rationing board; the Company granted the soft drink executive an extended leave so that he could serve his country's sweet tooth. Meanwhile, James Farley, new head of The Coca-Cola Export Corporation, engaged in his special variety of quiet back-room politicking, along with Washington tax lawyer Max Gardner, who was urged to render the bureaucrats "docile, receptive, tractable, malleable."[*]

All of the lobbying paid off. By the beginning of 1942, Coca-Cola was exempted from sugar rationing when sold to the military or retailers serving soldiers. Finally, in June, Brehon Somervell, the Army's quartermaster general, asked the head of the Sugar Board for an extension of the exemption, specifically naming Coca-Cola. The Army's attitude toward the soft drink had dramatically shifted since it banned Coca-Cola on its bases thirty-five years before. Harrison Jones, who had burst into creative obscenities when sugar rationing commenced, was ecstatic. While the rest of the soft drink industry suffered from an 80 percent quota (based on prewar figures), Coca-Cola readied for an all-out effort to send its sweet beverage fizzing down as many GI throats as possible. At its worst, U.S. sugar rationing dipped to 50 percent, but only domestic Coca-Cola bottlers unfortunate enough not to have any military base nearby were ever seriously affected.

COCA-COLA COLONELS

At first, the Company attempted to ship already-bottled Coca-Cola abroad. But despite its privileged status, Coca-Cola ran afoul of military shipping priorities. In a 1942 NBC radio broadcast, Martin Agronsky criticized a massive Coke transport to Australia when there was a critical need for guns and planes. With logistics and the media against them, Company officials devised another plan, copying the Army's use of dehydrated food. Why not ship only Coca-Cola concentrate and bottle the stuff overseas? And where a bottling plant wasn't feasible, why not import portable soda fountains to the front lines?

The Company actually began experimenting with these ideas only a month or so after Pearl Harbor, sending Albert "Red" Davis to Reykjavik, Iceland, to bottle Coke for the air base under construction. Using sign language, Davis demonstrated the clunky mysteries of an antiquated Dixie unit, and the local bottler sold his first carbonated drinks to the military in May of 1942, the same month Agronsky's complaint aired on NBC. Nazi sympathizers and locals were initially skeptical of the American drink, since they resented the sexual exploits of the occupying GIs, but Coca-Cola quickly demonstrated its

---

[*] At the same time, former Coca-Cola advertising director Price Gilbert joined the Office of War Information (OWI) along with a swarm of other ad men who were soon "happily painting the war in glowing terms," according to Henry Pringle, whose parting shot upon his departure from the OWI was a mock poster of a Coca-Cola bottle wrapped in the American flag, with the legend: "Step right up and get your four delicious freedoms. It's a refreshing war." Another jaded journalist inquired, "What do they think this war is—the cause that refreshes?"

universal appeal. Previously unknown in Iceland, the drink achieved such popularity that the Prime Minister demanded that half of the sugar ration sweeten beverages for civilians, who agreed that Coke was "*Heilnaemt og Hressandi*" (delicious and refreshing). Today, Iceland's annual per capita consumption of 446 exceeds that of any country in the world, including the United States.

Davis was the first of 248 Coca-Cola employees who followed the soldiers, serving them 10 billion Cokes in the process, from the jungles of New Guinea to officers' clubs on the Riviera. During the war, sixty-four bottling plants were established on every continent except Antarctica—largely at government expense. The adventures of the overseas Coca-Cola men would become legendary within the Company, while the fruits of their labor would yield a postwar Coke marketing explosion.

In a remarkably cozy arrangement, the U.S. Army gave the Coca-Cola representatives the pseudo–military status of "technical observers," a designation invented during World War I for civilians needed in the war effort—those servicing military machinery, for instance. Charles Lindbergh for a time served as a technical observer during World War II for United Aircraft Corporation. Incredibly, it appears that technicians who installed Coca-Cola plants behind the front lines were deemed as vital as those who fixed tanks or airplanes. The Coke representatives wore Army uniforms with "T.O." as a shoulder patch. Each Coke man received military rank commensurate with his Company salary, leading some wags to nickname them "Coca-Cola Colonels."

Though the Coca-Cola Technical Observers were exempt from the draft, rarely were in any real physical danger, and often led soft lives compared with the common soldier, no one resented them or the profits they garnered from a captive market. Rather, the soldiers were grateful that The Coca-Cola Company cared enough to send representatives to bring them a taste of home in the midst of the hell of war. An anecdote related by T.O. Quint Adams illustrates how they were treated. North of Naples, Adams and an officer were stopped by a guard who demanded to see a Fifth Army pass, which they hadn't brought. The guard was insistent. The officer obediently backed up, telling Adams that the bottling plant would have to wait. "Why the hell didn't you say he was a Coca-Cola man?" the guard complained, stepping aside to let them proceed.

A GENERAL FONDNESS

It was not only common soldiers who liked Coca-Cola: generals seemed particularly fond of the drink. Patton reputedly regarded a cache of Coke as a necessity, making sure the T.O.s transported a bottling plant wherever he went, perhaps because of his well-known thirst for rum and Coke. He once suggested, not altogether facetiously, a way to end the war more quickly: "Hell, we ought to send the Coke in first, then we wouldn't have to fight the bastards." MacArthur autographed the first bottle of Coke produced in the Philippines after his famous return. General Wainwright, the hero of Bataan, combined three American symbols when photographed after the war at Yankee Stadium: baseball, a half-eaten hot dog, and an uplifted bottle of Coke.

General Omar Bradley suffered from a double weakness: ice cream and Coca-Cola. "Even in Britain, where the climate encourages the drinking of more warming beverages, the general keeps a case of Coca-Cola in his office," a journalist reported. Even non-U.S. Filipino General Carlos Romulo wrote "with trembling hands" of the important day during the Battle of the Philippines when he had a Coke. He added, apparently without a trace of irony: "That day I had seen men blown to shreds; I had seen white-faced nurses drag themselves from the bloody debris of a bombed hospital. All this paled and was forgotten before the miracle of a five-cent drink any American can buy at his corner store."

But the real Coca-Cola addict was Eisenhower, who would become a close personal friend and golfing buddy of Robert Woodruff after the war. "MILLIONS CHEER IKE AT PARADE HERE," a Washington, D.C., paper headlined its front page of June 19, 1945, while commenting on the hero's taste in beverages:

> After feasting copiously at the Statler luncheon yesterday, Gen. Eisenhower was asked if he wished anything else.
> "Could somebody get me a Coke?" he asked.
> After polishing off the soft drink, the General said he had one more request. Asked what he wanted, he answered:
> "Another Coke."

It is not surprising, then, that Eisenhower sent an urgent cablegram from North Africa on June 29, 1943, which threw the T.O. program into high gear:

> On early convoy request shipment three million bottled Coca-Cola (filled) and complete equipment for bottling, washing, capping same quantity twice monthly.
> Preference as to equipment is 10 separate machines for installation in different localities, each complete for bottling twenty thousand bottles per day. Also sufficient syrup and caps for 6 million refills. Syrup, caps and sixty thousand bottles monthly should be an automatic supply. Monthly shipment bottles is to cover estimated breakage and losses. Estimate ship tons initial shipment 5 thousand. Ship without displacing other military cargo. Data available here very meager as to these installations and operations. Request they be checked by fully qualified sources and this Headquarters advised promptly recommended installation to meet the two hundred thousand bottle daily demand and when same can be shipped.

Eisenhower's request that the plants arrive "without displacing other military cargo" was clearly intended to placate anyone who might object, though certainly no one was going to countermand the general. And so the man who years later was to warn the American public of the dangers of the "military-industrial complex" implemented an openly cooperative arrangement between the U.S. Army and The Coca-Cola Company.

Army Chief of Staff George C. Marshall quickly validated the Eisenhower telegram in an innocuously worded War Department order: "Articles of necessity and convenience will be made available to troops overseas in adequate quantities." Early in 1944, after Company lobbying for stronger language, Marshall issued Circular No. 51, specifically allowing commanders to requisition Coca-Cola plants by name, along with the Technical Observers to install and operate them.

RIDING THE RED BALL EXPRESS

Woodruff hurriedly dispatched T.O. Albert Thomforde to Africa by high-priority military air transport to satisfy Ike's troops. Thomforde arrived ahead of his supplies and encountered the same difficulties which most T.O.s would confront: antiquated native bottling plants, polluted water, and a frustrating relationship with the Army Exchange Service. Nonetheless, by Christmas of 1943, the first Coke was rolling off the line in Oran. Once Coke had established a beachhead, the Company quickly mobilized its bottling forces for every available front. Thomforde flew to Italy to commence bottling there, followed by other Observers shadowing the U.S. military up the Italian boot. From England, they crossed the Channel just after D-Day.* T.O. Paul Bacon rode in the first "red ball express" (an open Army jeep) that jounced into Paris after its liberation. As the Allied forces pushed the Germans back toward Berlin, the Coca-Cola men surged into Germany along with their bottling plants, refurbishing European mineral water operations and continuing to serve the troops their favorite beverage.

Meanwhile, T.O.s were also flooding into the Pacific theater, but because of the war's geography and the quickly shifting front, bottling was not nearly as feasible as in Africa or Europe. Consequently, thirsty Pacific troops drank cups of Coke dispensed from portable "jungle fountain units." In the wilds of New Guinea, black and white soldiers were at least temporarily integrated, drinking from the same Coke fountain, unlike the segregated soft drink spigots on American bases.

"THE TECHNICAL OBSERVERS ARE WINNING THE WAR"

By and large, the Technical Observers took their jobs seriously, attempting to produce an adequate supply of their drink under difficult circumstances. Some of their exploits were truly Herculean, such as John Talley's retrieval of a filler

---

* Coke didn't actually hit the beaches with the boys, though shortly after the Normandy invasion, GI Mike Barry wrote a humorous letter to his sister about "the most important question in amphibious landings: Does the Coke machine go ashore in the first or second wave? I've told you before what a problem this is. If you send the Coke machine in with the first wave, future waves come pouring in without enough nickels. Obviously, getting change for a dime or a quarter on an enemy beach is quite difficult. On the other hand, if you hold the Coke machine up until the second wave, the men of the first wave wait on the beach for it to come in, instead of driving forward to attack the enemy."

dropped into the LeHavre harbor, or Fred Cooke's 1,300-mile trip "over the Hump" of the Himalayas to bring a bottling plant to China. The day-to-day life of the T.O. involved more prosaic battles with Rube Goldberg contraptions. "It will long be a mystery to me," wrote one Coke man of another, "how Bill Musselman keeps that hunk of junk he calls a bottling machine in continuous operation a full seventeen hours a day. Bailing wire seems to be his main support plus weld upon weld for practically every moving part."

Military personnel supplied most of those welds, as well as other repairs. The line between private industry and government forces was, to say the least, blurred during the war, so that T.O. Gene Braendle could write from New Guinea that "the one most important thing in our favor is the fact that everyone from the Base Commander down to the lowly private are vitally concerned in the Coke situation and go all out to help us all they possibly can." Another Observer happily remembered that "the first thing we did [at a new location] was make friends with either a port construction battalion or the Seabees. You could get anything done with those fellows. They would forge a new piece of machinery or do anything else." GIs also worked in bottling plants, presumably on Army rather than Coke pay. One T.O. bragged of his eighteen-hour work days, explaining that "both the Quartermaster and the Army Exchange Service were kind enough to furnish the night labor gang for this work. All of the Army personnel assigned to the plant have been very cooperative."

If they *hadn't* been cooperative, they would have been in deep trouble, according to war correspondent Howard Fast, who nearly died as a result of a pilot's fear of offending Coca-Cola. At first, Fast couldn't fathom why his transport plane landed at a remote Saudi Arabian Army outpost where the thermometer read 157 degrees Fahrenheit. They were there to pick up thousands of empty Coca-Cola bottles. When the overloaded C46 lumbered off the desert runway, it failed to gain altitude, barely clearing the sand dunes. The writer logically suggested jettisoning bottles. That, he was told, was impossible. "Guns they could dump, jeeps, ammo, even a howitzer . . . but Coca-Cola bottles? No way. Not if you wanted to keep your points and not become a PFC again." The pilot summarized the well-learned moral: "You don't fuck with Cola-Cola."

Prisoners of war were also assigned to work in Coke plants. The Coca-Cola men preferred diligent Germans and Japanese POWs to locals whose work ethic was not so strong. One Observer complained that French workers had "very little conception of what is meant by the words cleanliness and sanitation. They are not too much concerned whether they work or not, and when they work they are indifferent, to put it mildly, toward the kind of work they do." On the other hand, the German POWs "make very good labor and are easy to handle. When you show them what you want done, they go ahead and do it, and do it well."

Just as the soldier's life consisted of danger, fear of death, long periods of boredom, and occasional binges, the Coca-Cola T.O. led a roller-coaster existence, a mixture of harsh conditions and a life of ease. In the unpublished

Company history of the period, James Kahn waxed poetic about the hard life of the T.O., who often suffered from poor, inadequate rations and uncomfortable sleeping arrangements. "They got malaria and frostbite and jungle rot," he wrote, "and came home yellow from the endless capsules of atabrine they took." Three of them, he concluded, never returned, "killed in plane crashes as they made their determined rounds."

While Kahn's account may be overdramatized, it is essentially true, as far as it goes. He neglected, however, to mention the soft side of the Coca-Cola men's overseas life. T.O.s reported game hunting, sitting around in officers' clubs drinking and playing poker, buying sailboats, and spending weekends in the Alps with Red Cross nurses. "You express solicitations for my personal comfort," one Observer wrote from Italy. "In this regard I am almost ashamed to report." He went on to describe his luxurious Mediterranean villa, complete with servants' quarters.

Though the Coca-Cola men often lived the good life in the midst of war, poverty, and starvation, they could console themselves with the knowledge that their jobs were actually important and meaningful. They saw ample daily evidence that many soldiers regarded the drink as a miracle. Though The Coca-Cola Company had abandoned its medicinal claims long ago, the drink's placebo effect was revitalized during the war. An Observer commented on "one poor devil with one leg and one arm gone" who had given up on life until he was offered a Coca-Cola. "He told the nurse not to kid him. When he really did get a drink he cried like a baby because it reminded him so much of home." Another Observer from New Guinea, recounting how wounded soldiers limped to obtain their drinks, could have been describing a scene with a faith healer: "Men on crutches, in wheelchairs, men with bandaged hands, some who cannot see—all lined up by the hundreds to get their Cokes. It makes you feel all tied up inside and long for just one more carbonator . . ." At such moments, the T.O.s must have felt that they really *were* dispensing a morale-boosting beverage, rendering "The T.O. Theme Song" somewhat more understandable:

> *The Technical Observers are winning the war, Parley Vous.*
> *The Technical Observers are winning the war, Parley Vous.*
> *The Technical Observers are winning the war, so what do*
> *The Heinies keep fighting for? Hinkey, Dinkey, Parley Vous.*

THE HOME FRONT AND THE HIGH SIGN

Back in the United States, Coke's ad campaigns exploited the drink's patriotic presence abroad. To avoid paying more excess profits taxes, the Company poured money into wartime promotions. One showed sailors bellying up to a ship's bar for the soft drink, with the caption: "Wherever a U.S. battleship may be, the American way of life goes along . . . So, naturally, Coca-Cola is there, too." Set in exotic locales such as Hawaii, Great Britain, Russia, Scotland, Newfoundland, and New Guinea, Coke's ads carried the new catchphrase, "the global high-sign," and introduced American readers to a few foreign phrases. The Russians, for instance, reacted to Coke by saying "*Eto Zdorovo*," translated as "How grand!" The ad men continually touted the soft drink's status as an American icon: "Yes, around the globe, Coca-Cola stands for **the pause that refreshes**—it has become a symbol of our way of living."

These international ads were balanced by scenes from the home front, where Coca-Cola was shown assuaging the thirst of busy Victory gardeners, war bond salesmen, and returning soldiers, whose doting wives and children plied them with soft drinks while listening wide-eyed to their war stories. As with Depression-era efforts, the wartime ads avoided unpleasant reality. There were no gory scenes, just good-looking WACs and whole-bodied veterans. According to a 1943 survey, these ads were the most effective with both men *and* women: "Feminine readership went up when personalized copy of people on the battle line and home front replaced the story of gleaming planes, tanks, and jeeps."

Other products also sounded patriotic themes but were roundly condemned for their efforts. One soldier penned a "Memorial to the Great Big Beautiful Self-Sacrificing Advertisers" in which he pilloried "four-color-process hypocrisy" that portrayed "not so much blood and filth, of course, as to offend good taste . . . Some day somebody will fracture an arm thus publicly waving a flag." Although Coke's ads were guilty of just such "hypocrisy," no GI criticized them. The most popular, widely quoted ad during the war, "The Kid in Upper 4," was produced by a railroad and featured a soldier lying in his berth "wide awake . . . staring into the blackness," thinking about "the taste of hamburgers and pop, [and] a dog named Shucks, or Spot." Coca-Cola was such an imbedded part of the American Dream that its advertising *couldn't* be offensive.

Consequently, the Company ferverishly boosted its patriotic image during World War II. For a dime, the Company sold thousands of copies of a "Know Your War Planes" booklet—an ingenious appeal to war-happy kids. The "Our America" pamphlet series, designed for junior high students, told the story of the U.S. steel, lumber, coal, or agricultural industries with minimal advertising. Coca-Cola distributed cribbage boards, playing cards, Chinese checkers, dominoes, dartboards, Bingo, table tennis sets, and comic postcards illustrated with military themes. As sponsor of the popular radio series "Victory Parade of Spotlight Bands," Coca-Cola hired over a hundred name bands to play concerts and drink Cokes at bases around the country. Irish tenor Morton Downey, destined to play a postwar role in the Company's affairs, sang on his own Coca-Cola-sponsored radio show.

Despite Oehlert's attempts to persuade the War Production Board that Coca-Cola was essential for civilian morale, too, the general public's supply was severely rationed. A Kansas editor wrote that the Coke shortage really brought home the *seriousness* of the war, while Texas Coca-Cola addicts were particularly upset by rationing, according to one journalist, who feared protestors "swinging a six-shooter in one hand and a Coke bottle filled with TNT in the other." One customer, rushing to pull a warm bottle of Coke out of a cooler just after it was stocked, explained it all: "Those people have spent twenty years making a drinker out of me and [they] can't shut me off this easy."

ACKLIN'S AGONIZING WAR

The tall, frail, gentle man responsible for the daily management of the Company during World War II, Arthur Acklin assumed the Coca-Cola presidency just before the war began, apparently because Robert Woodruff no longer wanted to be in the spotlight or to deal with mundane matters. Acklin hated pressure; he had already broken down once in 1934, and he begged Woodruff not to make him president in 1939, but to no avail. As he put it himself, Acklin possessed a "temperament that takes seriously any problem with which I am confronted." He found it difficult to cope with day-to-day decisions—and there were enough during the war to rattle any executive. He worried over buying Peruvian sugar for the domestic business at inflated prices. He had to negotiate with Monsanto Chemical Company, encouraging them to build special plants to manufacture caffeine in Brazil and Mexico. He contracted for recycled bottle caps because of metal short-ages. Monthly, Coke consumed 25,000 gallons of vanilla extract; annually, the drink needed a million pounds of Merchandise No. 5, the coca leaf and kola nut extract. Shortages loomed for both ingredients.

The pressure started to tell on Acklin, who grew gaunter by the day. He asked Woodruff to form a "working policy committee" to help him, but the Boss refused. Coca-Cola's mismanaged baseball team, the Atlanta Crackers, lost money. The government froze wages and prices. The Thomas Company wanted everything for nothing. Over half of the Company personnel were drafted. Three weeks after the Germans surrendered, Acklin cracked. "Naturally you cannot be conscious of the multitude of problems with which I have been confronted," Acklin wrote plaintively. "The strain has taken a rather heavy toll." Woodruff had to assume the presidency again as an interim measure. Acklin managed to steer domestic Coca-Cola through the war in good shape, but he himself was a casualty.

WALTER MACK MAKES HIS MOVES

In the meantime, Pepsi president Walter Mack thrived on the same pressure that undid Acklin. Complaining that Coke had "an inordinate amount of political influence," Mack attacked Ed Forio's position on the Sugar Rationing Board, telling the head of the War Production Board that Forio was a "phony" and threatening to cause a public stink unless he was replaced within a week. Three days later, the Coca-Cola man resigned.

Regardless of who was in charge of sugar rationing, however, Pepsi was in trouble. Desperate for sweetener, Mack pursued every conceivable avenue. Initially, he bought a Cuban plantation but was unable to export anything until after the war because of Cuban regulations. Mack then went to Mexico and cemented a deal with the government to purchase 40,000 tons of sugar a year at slightly above the top asking price. That didn't really help, though, since Mexican law prohibited the export of sugar and U.S. law forbade its importation. Undaunted, Mack incorporated the Mexican-American Flavors Company in Monterrey, where he converted the sugar into a syrup he called "El Masquo" and legally transported it over the border to his Pepsi bottlers. Coca-Cola dubbed Mack's syrup "El Sneako" and eventually pressured the government into closing the loophole in 1944. The unstoppable Mack then turned to a New Jersey condiment maker and bought a million and a half gallons of sugarcane juice, which he clarified into 12 million pounds of sweetener before the government again foiled his strategy.

Although his aggressive style didn't help when he protested Coca-Cola's virtual monopoly on bases, Mack was determined to attract military business anyway, opening three huge Pepsi-Cola Servicemen's Centers in Washington, San Francisco, and New York, where soldiers could find free Pepsi, nickel hamburgers, and a shave, shower, and free pants pressing. And in 1942, Pepsi invaded military installations to offer another free service. GIs could record greetings and send them anywhere they chose. For tongue-tied soldiers, Mack even provided sixteen boiler-plate messages addressed to Mom, Dad, or the girl back home. "Let me tell you," thousands of these ghostwritten messages sincerely commenced, "Uncle Sam is doing a good job keeping me in the pink of condition for you, honey, so don't be worrying about me." By the end of the war 3 million personalized Pepsi recordings had been delivered to loved ones. To further cheer the lowly private, Mack dispatched professional wrestling troops to perform in Army camps.

Nor did Mack neglect the civilian population. Taking advantage of Coca-Cola's scarcity at the soda fountain, Mack pushed into this traditional Coke stronghold with syrup for a ten-ounce fountain drink selling for the same nickel as Coke's six-ounce glass. Pepsi sponsored national softball tournaments, huge square dances, and clubhouses for teenagers. While Pepsi couldn't match Coke's presence in Hollywood, it did garner a plug on Broadway. In 1943's *Something for the Boys*, Ethel Merman, playing a woman whose tooth fillings brought in radio broadcasts, tuned in her incisors to the famous jingle. As the orchestra played the opening bars, Merman loudly announced: "Pepsi-Cola!"

Through such shenanigans, Walter Mack made inroads on Coca-Cola's American empire during World War II, securing a place in the postwar market. Nonetheless, despite his showman's flair, Mack could do nothing about Coca-Cola's monopoly overseas, where sipping a Coke in his foxhole was a minor miracle to the war-weary GI.

WARTIME TESTIMONIALS

The triumph of Coca-Cola during the war was in many ways due to its relative scarcity, which enhanced its value and desirability. One young soldier, writing from New Guinea to his parents, described his home-brewed Coke. "The syrup is old and the [carbonated] gas low, but it's still our greatest luxury. The syrup is dipped with a tin spoon into an aluminum canteen cup and stirred with a stick and we still love it." He concluded that American ingenuity could accomplish wonders. "This war should be a cinch now." His attitude was echoed by many other letters from homesick young Americans for whom Coca-Cola assumed an astonishing significance:

> It's the little things, not the big, that the individual soldier fights for or wants so badly when away. It's the girl friend back home in a drug store over a Coke, or the juke box and the summer weather.

> I always thought it was a wonderful drink, but on an island where few white men have set foot, it is a Godsend. I can truthfully say that I haven't seen smiles spread over a bunch of boys' faces as they did when they saw Coca-Cola in this God-forsaken place.

> . . . one real bottle of Coca-Cola, the first one I have seen here. It was pulled out from under the shirt of a pilot . . . He caressed it, his eyes rolled over it, he smacked his lips at the prospect of tasting it. I offered him one dollar for half of it, then two, three, and five dollars.

> You will probably think your son has had his head exposed to the sun too long. But the other day, three of us guys walked ten miles to buy a case of Coca-Cola, then carried it back. You will never know how good it tasted.

> The crowning touch to your Christmas packages was the bottled Coca-Cola. How did you ever think of sending them? To have it here and turn up the bottle and see "Ronceverte, W. Va.," on the bottom was an added thrill.

> This week, Coca-Cola came to Italy. Seemingly everyone had heard the rumor, but no one put much faith in it. How could it be true? Coca-Cola is some vaguely familiar nectar, reminiscent of some far-off paradise land. Italy is a land of C-rations and Spam and dehydrated food.

> To have this drink is just like having home brought nearer to you; it's one of the little things of life that really counts. I can remember being at Ponce de Leon Park, watching the [Atlanta] Crackers play baseball as I filled up on Coca-Cola and peanuts. It's things such as this that all of us are fighting for.

One soldier summarized the sentiments: "If anyone were to ask us what we are fighting for, we think half of us would answer, the right to buy Coca-Cola again." Letters such as these poured into Company offices, though they were publicized only to Company employees. Consequently, the Company was delighted when Colonel Robert L. Scott, in his best-seller *God Is My Co-Pilot*, explained that his motivation to "shoot down my first Jap" stemmed from thoughts of "America, Democracy, Coca-Colas." Before World War II, Coca-Cola men had been taught to have faith in their drink, to hustle and sell every day, to proclaim the virtues of their product everywhere they went. Certainly, here was the proof that Coca-Cola *was* America, at least by 1945. George Brennan, a corporal, wrote back to his old boss at Coca-Cola that his wartime experience had given him a new appreciation for the drink: "In civilian life, when there is an abundance of Coca-Cola, you feel convinced that it is good and more or less let it go at that. But you have to experience the scarcity of

Coca-Cola or suffer its absence to acquire a full appreciation of what it means to us as Americans."

OPENING CEREMONIES, CARBONATED RAFFLES, SACRAMENTAL WINE

Given the depth of the feelings expressed in those letters home, it is understandable that the downing of a Coke overseas often became a matter of considerable ceremony. One soldier wrote that "I have seen four high-ranking officers opening a bottle of Coca-Cola as if it were a magnum of Cordon Rouge 1929." Another soldier, with tongue somewhat in cheek, wrote:

> The pop, as you open it; with some pomp and a good deal of ceremony you bring open bottle to within 3 inches of your nose. No mistaking now, it is; it is Coke. The urge now is to quaff the whole thing in one gulp, but if you have the least bit of the esthetic in you, you don't. One more sniff, and, deftly holding the bottle between thumb and two middle fingers, small finger slightly raised, you bring bottle to eager lips and straining, impatient tongue. Then—this takes a lot of will-power and self-control—you don't take a full swig, but just a wee bit of a sip, and smartly roll the liquid on your tongue. A fraction of a fraction of a moment you hesitate and pause. By golly! Coke, all right! Finally, what the hell, down goes the entire contents of the bottle in one gulp.

Given the popularity and symbolic weight Coca-Cola achieved during the war (and the lack of GI spending outlets), it was predictable that Coca-Cola would bring a considerable amount of money on the black market and the informal commerce common to soldiers. One bottle was reported to sell for anything from five to forty dollars. In an auction in Iran, a bottle went for $1,000. The most famous (and expensive) bottle was sold on Italian auction for $4,000.

Coca-Cola developed a psychological significance akin to an icon or rare religious relic; many bottles remained unopened after the war, kept hidden away as sacred mementos. It seemed fitting that Mary Churchill, Winston's daughter, should christen a new destroyer with a bottle of Coke. During the war years, explicit treatment of Coke-as-religion cropped up. Since the notion of a soft drink being worshiped was disconcerting, these references were often humorous. Corporal Frank Hardie, for instance, wrote a parody of Jesus' parable of the foolish and wise virgins: "But the wise converted their quarters into nickels when he who filleth the Coca-Cola machine passed through. And lo, there came a time when the red light disappeared from the face of the machine, and the machine was filled . . ."

T.O. Maurice Duttera recalled dining at the officers' club in Cannes with two Catholic priests, who frequently kidded him about the soldiers' attitude to Coca-Cola, urging him to requisition a plane, fly to Rome, and obtain the Pope's blessing on Coke as holy water. Those clerics were joking, but during the Battle of the Bulge, Ken Hogan, an Observer, really *did* supply a priest with Coca-Cola in lieu of sacramental wine.

INSULATORS, SHANDIES, AND URINALS

The near-religious awe with which many soldiers regarded Coca-Cola did not prevent others from putting the ubiquitous bottle to other uses. Coke bottles were drafted as emergency electrical insulators in the Pacific, dropped on Japanese airfields in "Coke runs" to puncture tires, wielded by sailors in life rafts to kill sea turtles for food. The British scandalized GIs by mixing Cokes with beer and calling the result "shandies," while another groggy soldier brushed his teeth with the soft drink every morning. Coca-Cola cases were much in demand as portable mailboxes and stools. "Coca-Cola" was the battle password while crossing the Rhine.

Other alternative utilizations were more risqué. Like the boys back home, many soldiers advised their girlfriends to douche with the fizzy drink. Perhaps the most inventive recycling of bottles, though, combining nostalgia with irreverence, concerned a Navy officers' club men's room in the New Hebrides. Hundreds of Coke bottles embossed with local franchises' locations were embedded, bottom out, in the concrete urinal wall, with varicolored lights behind them providing an eerie glow to a continual wash of water. "It was something to see," one nostalgic veteran recalled. "People came from long distances 'just to piss on the old home town.'"

THE GERMS OF THE DISEASE

Coca-Cola's symbolism and its insidious infiltration were not lost on the Axis powers. Otto Dietrich, the Nazis' press chief, declared in 1942 that "America never contributed anything to world civilization but chewing gum and Coca-Cola." Japanese radio proclaimed that "with Coca-Cola we imported the germs of the disease of American society. These germs, however, were introduced in such a pleasant way that we failed to realize it." The "pleasant way" worked all too well, despite the propaganda. German, Japanese, and Italian soldiers all knew and enjoyed the taste of Coca-Cola. A photo of a U.S. captive aboard a German sub showed him drinking—of course—a Coke. Nor were the Japanese immune. When a luxurious Japanese "jungle city" was captured in western New Britain, it disgorged cases of captured Coca-Cola. And on one hot summer day, Italian prisoners of war refused to continue working until they had been given the pause that refreshes. The Technical Observers were well aware of the possible markets they were opening. "I'm sure that many of the smaller children had never tasted Coca-Cola before," wrote one T.O. from New Guinea, "but they'll certainly be steady customers from now on."

Coca-Cola men also discovered a potential market in more primitive cultures, joyfully reporting that Zulus, Bushmen, and Fijians relished the drink. Even making allowances for the time, their attitude was often racist, condescending, and ethnocentric, such as a New Guinea T.O.'s description of a native's first encounter with a Coke, which he downed too quickly. "Then the fun began. He belched, the gas went up his nose and brought tears to his eyes. He was a scared native for a few minutes. So now it can be said that we have sampled and opened up a new outlet—the Fuzzy Wuzzy market." Another Coke man snapped a photo of a Polynesian king sitting on a wheelbarrow throne, prophesying that he would soon be sitting "on one of those famous Red Barrels and surrounded by full and ice-cold Coca-Cola bottles, and be wearing crowncorks with the 'trademark registered' in his ears." One soldier, writing home from India to say he was getting Coke at his PX, went on to describe Kayo, a six-year-old Indian boy who had learned the American way—soft drinks, popular tunes, and obsessive hygiene—all too well. "He brushes his teeth three or four times a day and takes showers regularly. They told him that if he washes frequently he will become white like us, and he certainly tries hard."

PROFITABLE PATRIOTISM

As the war wound to a close, the fervor of the Coca-Cola Technical Observers in selling their product only increased. The T.O. program continued for another three years before a graceful transition to a civilian operation, symbolized by the death in 1948 of one publication, *T.O. Digest*, and the birth of another, *Coca-Cola Overseas*. The pseudo-military Coke men were in a delicate position. While they were acutely aware of the potential profits and future markets they were creating, they had to moderate their sales pitch. With selling, sampling techniques, and catchy slogans drilled into their heads, however, they found it difficult to be circumspect about pushing the product. In a series of unpublished notes written while he served as a Technical Observer in Germany in 1946, George Downing explained that "the T.O.'s only merchandising tool was a friendly spoken word. No profit, no increased sales, no rapid turnover, no small investment could be stressed. Ours was to be a giving of service in making Coca-Cola available to GIs wherever they might be." Then, in two columns, Downing listed the way Coca-Cola language had to be translated for the patriotic war effort:

Regular Coca-Cola Language (accustomed to)	Lingo Due to Military Necessity
"If we are gonna make sales rise, boys, we gotta merchandise."	"Fellows, as representatives of the Army Exchange Service in charge of soft drink production and distribution, we would like to help you with any problems that you have."
"If they are gonna be sold, they gotta be cold."	"We have learned that people prefer their Cokes below 40 degrees and we would like to show you how it can best be done."
"Mr Dealer, in order for you to capitalize on advertising, we would like to place this attractive custom built sign to identify your business as one having Coke for sale."	"Fellows, we can make lithography available to you that would add a touch of home to your soda fountain, Coke bar, etc."

Because Downing and his cohorts had virtually a captive market, the euphemisms and appeals to the "fellows" worked—so much so, that when Jim Farley and other Coke executives came for a tour of inspection, they were embarrassed by the extent of blatant advertising at the PX and urged the T.O.s to "soft pedal it a bit." Despite Company protestations that the war effort was a purely philanthropic gesture, it was, on the contrary, clearly a profitable operation in the postwar environment. As their wives and children flew over to join them, American servicemen brought home cases of Coke, much to the delight of the T.O.s, who competed fiercely for the highest sales figures.

WHITE COKE FOR A RED RUSSIAN

One of those Technical Observers was Mladin Zarubica, sent to Austria in 1946 to install a gigantic bottling plant. He went at the direct request of President Truman, who was concerned by the number of green troops who were drinking poisonous schnaps and going blind. Zarubica, a wartime PT boat commander, all-American football player from UCLA, and son of a Yugoslav immigrant, threw himself into his new job with exuberance, helping to construct thirty-eight Coke plants in southern Europe within two years. He also purchased as much warehouse space as possible, in part to keep Pepsi out, in part to stockpile materials while the Army was still paying for transportation. His largest plant, in Lambach, Austria, was four city blocks long and ran continuously, bottling 24,000 cases of Coca-Cola every twenty-four hours. "I had a railroad siding that I had midnight requisitioned [i.e., stolen] out of the Russian Zone," Zarubica recalled. "I even built my own CO_2 plant because I couldn't count on the purity of the local gas." To protect shipments from black market bandits, 500 American soldiers guarded his sugar train on its way to Austria.

Zarubica was flying high, with a huge expense account. At James Farley's suggestion, he refurbished a huge villa near Berchtesgaden into a hunting lodge for influential visitors from Paris, London, and New York who were met at the airport and escorted to the beautiful lodge overlooking a mountain lake. "We had waiting lists to come there—senators, potentates, you name it."[*]

The White Coke episode was, however, the most astonishing coup Mladin Zarubica pulled off. When Dwight Eisenhower introduced the American drink to his new friend General Georgi Konstantinovich Zhukov, head of his country's occupied zone, the Russian liked it. He asked General Mark Clark, in charge of the American zone, for more, with one proviso: it couldn't look anything like Coke. As the central Russian war hero, Zhukov knew he couldn't be seen drinking an American imperialist symbol. Clark passed the request up the line to President Truman, who summoned Jim Farley, and soon the word

---

[*] It was at this lodge that Zarubic claimed to have met Hitler's right-hand man, Martin Bormann, posing as Carlo, one of the hunting guides. Zarubica based his 1964 thriller, *The Year of the Rat*, on the incident.

filtered back to Zarubica, who found a chemist to take out the caramel coloring. Then the Coca-Cola man had the Crown Cork and Seal Company in Brussels make a special straight, clear bottle and a white cap with a red star in the middle. "My first shipment to Zhukov was fifty cases," Zarubica said. "White Coke for Red Russians. That was a deep, dark secret." The subterfuge was worthwhile, though. The regular Coke supply from Lambach had to pass through the Russian zone to reach its Vienna warehouse. While others often waited weeks for the Russian bureaucracy to allow them through, the Coke shipment was never stopped.

SWASHBUCKLERS, SAMPLING, AND SEX

Zarubica called the T.O. program "the greatest sampling program in the history of the world," during which the drink practically sold itself, not only to Americans (and the occasional Russian general), but Germans and Austrians.[*] The order forbidding GIs to fraternize with Fräuleins was impossible to enforce. "So every time a soldier would take two cases home, the girl and her kids drank it all up, and they transferred to drinking Coca-Cola without even a blink."

The soldiers weren't the only ones fraternizing with Fräuleins. Some T.O.s took advantage of their position to trade Coca-Cola for sex or money. "Anything with sugar in it was currency on the black market," recalled one Observer. "It was a joke that you could give a woman a Hershey bar and she was yours. And Coca-Cola was a close second." Another T.O., a lover of literature who felt out of place in the world of gung-ho Coke men in postwar Germany, recalled one of his cohorts as "the horniest individual" he ever knew. "I never did understand why they sent over the shabby people they did. The black market was just rampant. The opportunity was almost laid out in front of you." Zarubica verified that there were some bad apples, hired as friends of friends with little training. "We had a lot of alcoholism there," he acknowledged. There were also the swashbucklers and soldiers of fortune, as T.O. Don Sisler called them. "I'd say these adventurers made up about 20% of us," he recalled. "They liked the excitement of being in an unusual place at an unusual time. They had no intention of taking this whole thing seriously. They were great womanizers, but that was just part of the whole stew and added a little spice."

UNIVERSAL ACCEPTANCE

Swashbucklers and serious Coke men alike could read the writing on the wall

---

[*] The Japanese also offered a gigantic potential market. "We are casting covetous eyes towards the civilian population out here—some 18 million potential Coca-Cola customers on Kyushu alone," wrote one T.O. "The transition period from a Military to a Civilian market will be very interesting." In this instance, however, Coke would be frustrated by governmental regulations which effectively prevented the sale of the drink to the Japanese until the early 1960s.

by 1947, when the military presence in the occupied zones was dwindling, along with soft drink sales. By the end of the following year, the Technical Observers would hang up their military uniforms, but the plants and goodwill they had established remained. Everyone wanted to try the American soldiers' soft drink. The GIs were heroes, liberators with seemingly endless supplies of chocolate bars, cigarettes, and Cokes in the midst of a bombed-out world. Admiration was often mixed with envy, but even envy was easily converted to emulation. The world was primed for Coca-Cola. As a postwar Coca-Cola official acknowledged, World War II resulted in "the almost universal acceptance of the goodness of Coca-Cola . . . Anything the American fighting man wanted and enjoyed was something [others] wanted too."

And Coca-Cola was even more popular on the home front, where the returning veterans brought a decided preference for the drink that had meant so much to them overseas. This result was anticipated by at least one soldier. "Personally, I think that The Coca-Cola Company's cooperation with the Army in getting Coca-Cola to the men in the field is the best advertisement that Coca-Cola has ever had," he wrote to his former Company boss. "The things that are happening to these men now will stick with them for the rest of their life."

He was right. In a 1948 poll of veterans, conducted by *American Legion Magazine*, 63.67 percent specified Coca-Cola as their preferred soft drink, with Pepsi receiving a lame 7.78 percent of the vote. In the same year, Coke's gross profit on sales reached a whopping $126 million, as opposed to Pepsi's $25 million; the contrast in net after-tax income was even more telling, with Coke's $35.6 million towering over Pepsi's pathetic $3.2 million. As the Company's unpublished history stated, the wartime program "made friends and customers for home consumption of 11,000,000 GIs [and] did [a] sampling and expansion job abroad which would [otherwise] have taken 25 years and millions of dollars." The war was over, and it appeared, at least for the moment, that Coca-Cola had won it.

~ 13 ~

Coca-Cola Über Alles

Ein Führer [ist] ein Mann, der Anhänger hat. Ein Führer verdient, dass er Anhänger hat. Er hat sich Anerkennung erworben ... Ein Führer vervielfacht sich in anderen. Er ist ein Menschenbildner ... Er ist ein Mann des Geistes und der Tat—Sinnender und Schaffender zugleich.

[Translation] A leader is a man who has followers. The leader deserves to have followers; he has earned recognition ... The leader duplicates himself in others. He is a manbuilder ... He is a man of thought and a man of action—both dreamer and doer.

—1963 Tribute to Max Keith

One man must step forward in order to form, with apodictic force, out of the wavering world of imagination of the great masses, granite principles, and to take up the fight for their sole correctness.

—Adolf Hitler, *Mein Kampf*

IN EARLY 1945, a group of German prisoners of war debarked in Hoboken, New Jersey, apprehensive and lonely in a foreign land. When one of them pointed to a Coca-Cola sign on a nearby building, the prisoners began excitedly gesticulating and talking among themselves. Taken aback, the guard yelled for order, demanding an explanation from a prisoner who spoke English. "We are surprised," he answered, "that you have Coca-Cola here too."

Coca-Cola executives love to retell this anecdote as proof that Coke is a native product wherever it goes, but the story's real significance can only be understood in the context of Hitler's Third Reich. In order to thrive inside Nazi Germany, its Coca-Cola franchises had waged a rigorous campaign to disassociate themselves from their American roots. While the soft drink came to symbolize American freedom—all of the good things back home the GI was fighting for—the same Coca-Cola logo rested comfortably next to the swastika. The drama of German Coke's survival before, during, and after World War II swirls around one central figure—Max Keith, at once the quintessential Coca-Cola man and Nazi collaborator.

In 1933, the same year that Hitler came to power, thirty-year-old Keith (pronounced "Kite") went to work for Coca-Cola GmbH. Like many Germans, Keith desperately sought financial security as well as something to believe in. Whereas others embraced the Fatherland and Aryan Supremacy, Max Keith found Coca-Cola. "I was full of activity and enthusiasm," he recalled thirty years later, "and the thing which then took possession of all that was in me and which . . . has never lost its hold on me, was Coca-Cola. From then on, and to all eternity, I was tied to this product for better or for worse."

The German soft drink business was in its infancy. Ray Rivington Powers, an American expatriate, had started bottling German Coca-Cola in 1929 after a colorful, if shady, career in post-World War I Europe. A huge man—almost six and a half feet tall and nearly as wide, with a personality to match—he enjoyed playing the part of the American buffoon, speaking tortured German mixed with English, even though he was perfectly fluent in German. But Ray Powers had the gift of creating believers through his hyperbole. "One day," he would tell prospective Coca-Cola men, "you will have a villa in Florida and you will be one of the richest men in the world."* During the first four years of the business, he boosted Coca-Cola sales from just under 6,000 cases to over 100,000 in 1933.

A great salesman but a terrible manager who couldn't be bothered with financial details, Powers had just persuaded Woodruff to give him the franchise for the entire country, when his German partner pulled out, demanding his money back late in 1929. Frantic, the American fled to New York in a vain attempt to raise capital, then tapped Woodruff for over $100,000. There ensued a tangle of incorporations and mergers in an attempt to replicate the structure of the American business. The auditors sent to examine the Essen books found them "in a state of chaos," according to an internal memo by Hamilton Horsey. The auditors and lawyers, wrote Horsey, "advised us to have nothing to do with Mr Powers' company in Essen," so an entirely new corporation was formed to purchase its assets.

In the final event, two primary entities emerged from the mess. Coca-Cola GmbH would manufacture the syrup and own the trademark, while the Deutsch Vertriebs GmbH für Naturgetränke, commonly known as Deverna, would act as the parent bottler. Powers, running Deverna, was supposed to live off the royalties of the bottlers he found. Unfortunately, he couldn't find anyone to risk bottling, which required too much cash. Instead, he sold through "concessionaires," distributors who picked up cases of the soft drink and sold them in exclusive territories near Essen.

When Keith opened Powers' desk drawer and found unpaid bills and unopened bank statements, the former bookkeeper recognized a satisfying challenge. He soon put Coca-Cola GmbH's finances in order and turned his formidable organizational skills to promoting the business. While he lacked the American's winning personality, he more than made up for it with a forceful style. Men laughed with Ray Powers, but they trembled before Max Keith.

---

*Not surprisingly, Powers admired a fellow propagandist: Adolf Hitler. In 1930, Powers defended Hitler to Robert Woodruff, and in the spring of 1936, the American closed a letter to the Boss with the salutation, "Heil Hitler." Three years later, a swastika was prominently displayed on Atlanta's Peachtree Street during an international Baptist convention. It was not particularly unusual at the time for some Americans to admire Hitler, but the fact that Woodruff was a Baptist doesn't tell us how he felt about the Führer.

Keith was an imposing man, over six feet, with high Teutonic cheekbones rarely dimpled by a smile, and a little whisk-broom mustache which, like the Führer's, quivered alarmingly when he was enraged. In several other ways, Keith's mannerisms and leadership style resembled the dictator's. His high-pitched voice proved hypnotic when raised in anger. "Max Keith could chew you out like you've never been chewed out before," one of his aides recalled, "but he could also build you up again." He could be charming, gentle, and conciliatory when it suited him. Once he decided something, Keith never changed his mind, and he brooked no opposition in public. It was suicidal to espouse a conflicting point of view in a staff meeting. "He was a born leader, a very charismatic figure," according to Klaus Pütter, a longtime employee. "You liked to work for him although he was almost a slave driver . . . Oh, yes, I was scared of him. We *all* were, even aides who were older." Still, Pütter said, most of his followers "would have died for this man."

Keith's tactics could be brilliant. Against enormous odds, including near disaster at the hands of both the Nazis and the American conquerors, he built the Coca-Cola business into a thriving enterprise. Through cunning, bluff, intimidation, wheedling, influence, marketing, and sheer willpower, Max Keith survived along with his beloved drink. For Keith, as one aide put it, the ruling thought was not "Deutschland Über Alles," but "Coca-Cola Über Alles."

BOOM YEARS WITH MAX AND ADOLF

As Hitler had collected ragtag malcontents to form his Brown Shirts, Keith too looked for lost souls who would become true believers. "They were mostly people who had almost tried everything in their life and failed," Keith remembered in an interview near the end of his life. "They thought that by taking Coca-Cola, what could they lose more?" The Coca-Cola manager had little choice in employees, since there was virtually no German soft drink business. Nonalcoholic beverages were considered a syrupy concoction for children, not for robust beer-drinking adults. It was also widely believed that cold beverages (with the exception of beer) caused stomachaches.

Determined to alter that attitude, Keith forced himself and his men to work twelve-hour days and more, sometimes collapsing at 2 A.M. before rising early to start all over again. On foot, bicycles, pushcarts, three-wheeled motor scooters, and one old Chevrolet truck, Keith's concessionaires delivered the goods. In 1934, he added a bottling plant in Frankfurt, with warehouses in Cologne and Koblenz. He forged ahead despite the stingy Canadian super-vision of Gene Kelly, who refused to buy a second truck until Keith had accrued over 600 retail accounts.

At least Kelly provided as many small point-of-purchase signs as the Germans could nail up, and he allowed Keith to print millions of leaflets titled *Was ist Coca-Cola?* ("What Is Coca-Cola?"), which his men would distribute at sporting events and restaurants. "We went to restaurants on weekends [and] put this prospectus on every table," Keith remembered, and when distraught proprietors threw them out, the Coke men doggedly replaced them. Many who picked up the folder expected to find an analysis of the ingredients and were angered when it simply said that Coke was a refreshing drink, but the endless repetition of the product name had its intended effect.

To encourage his distributors, Keith initially hired three field men to demonstrate proper sales technique and open new outlets. These overworked salesmen had to lug around a large briefcase dubbed the *Seufzertasche*, or the "case of sighs." It contained a tin lining, ten Coca-Cola bottles, and ice. Entering a tavern, early field men such as Joe Knipp opened markets by persistent sampling, offering ice-cold (*eiskalt*) drinks. "Ja, Blah! I've had it before, I would not touch it," the owners would say, but once they tasted a cold drink, they would often exclaim that it was an altogether different taste when properly chilled.

Once a retailer was convinced that Coca-Cola might make money for him, he often had to hide the bottles under beer in the ice, since over half the pubs and restaurants were owned by local breweries who forbade the sale of another drink. At times, Keith's personal presence alone solved the problem; ten minutes of Keith was enough to cow most brewers. Other times, Keith brought in Walter Oppenhoff, the attorney who had incorporated the Company in 1930 and who took an almost daily part in the business. The lawyer usually procured a satisfactory out-of-court settlement. With Keith's guidance and Powers' continued sales efforts, Coca-Cola sales grew quickly throughout the decade. In 1934, they doubled to 243,000 cases and, two years later, broached a million cases for the first time. By the time war broke out in 1939, the Coca-Cola men were selling almost four and a half million cases inside Germany.

While Keith deserves much of the credit for this phenomenal growth, he himself recognized that "the time marched with us." As in America, refrigeration invaded the home during the 1930s, while automobile travel was facilitated by the Autobahn system, dotted with its Coke-supplied filling stations. Even as the first concentration camps were opened by the Nazis in 1933, Germany was experiencing the onset of relative prosperity. By 1937, the German national income had doubled. "Germany in the mid-Thirties," wrote William L. Shirer in *The Rise and Fall of the Third Reich*, "seemed like one vast beehive." The busy workers needed the pause that refreshed. "The requirements of the people were much higher than in the past," Keith said. "They had to work harder, had to work faster, the technical equipment they had to handle required soberness."

Of course, the "technical equipment" was part of the vast military machine that created new jobs. And while unemployment shrank to almost nothing, workers were little more than serfs forbidden not only to strike, but to change jobs. The employer became a kind of mini-dictator, a *Geschäftsführer*, or "leader of the enterprise." Wages were deliberately set quite low, but most workers were happy just to have jobs and to believe Hitler's propaganda that the Teutonic "Volk" would overcome all obstacles. Far from being resentful of a brutal dictatorship, most workers, Shirer noted, were imbued with "a new hope and a new confidence and an astonishing faith in the future of their country." No wonder Max Keith's faithful workers labored so diligently. By 1939, forty-three German plants bottled Coca-Cola, with nine more under construction. Over 600 concessionaires, independent franchisees making considerably more money than most German workers, distributed the drinks. Each was his own mini-Führer, though bowing ultimately to Max Keith, who had made it all possible for them.

COKE AT THE BERLIN OLYMPICS

The 1936 Summer Olympics in Berlin marked a moment of triumph for Max Keith, who provided enormous quantities of Coca-Cola for athletes and visitors. That August in Berlin was equally satisfactory for Hitler, proud host to the nations of the world, showing off his blond Aryan athletes and his revitalized Germany. Just before the Olympics, Max Schmeling had proved that a white German could beat an inferior black American when he knocked out Joe Louis in the twelfth round in Madison Square Garden. Arriving in Germany, Schmeling was welcomed by a huge crowd as he stepped off the zeppelin *Hindenburg*, then whisked to lunch with Hitler, who slapped his thigh in appreciation every time he saw Schmeling hit Louis in the film of the fight. A prominent Nazi publication gloated that "Schmeling's victory was not only sport. It was a question of prestige for our race. With his hard fists he has won the respect of the world for the German nation."

German athletes dominated the Olympics, winning thirty-six gold medals while America took home only twenty-five first-place finishes. Although Hitler seethed over black superstar Jesse Owens' four gold medals, on the whole he was smug about his Berlin charade. Signs such as *Juden Unerwünscht* (Jews Unwelcome) had been quietly removed for the duration while the country put on its best behavior. Max Schmeling, viewing the games with Hitler in his private box, summarized the feelings of most Germans when he told a U.S. reporter, "We have no strikes in Germany. Most everybody has a job. Times are good. We have only one union. We have only one party. Everyone agreeable. Everybody happy."

Göring and Goebbels hosted elaborate parties for foreign guests, most of whom were suitably impressed by what they saw. One of those guests was Robert Woodruff, who had brought over an entire Coca-Cola entourage. Woodruff, however, was not taken in by Hitler's façade. His finely tuned antennae felt the rumbles that could destroy a business. True, Woodruff approved of the modern Berlin bottling plant with its forty-spout filler. But while pleased to see Coca-Cola prominently on sale at the Olympics, he was most unhappy with the wrapper around the neck of every bottle, which read *Kaffeinhaltung* (Caffeine-Containing). The Nazi health ministry, perhaps prodded by the Führer's food faddism, insisted that the caveat be placed on the bottles. For many German consumers, however, the wrapper served more as an advertisement than a deterrent, since coffee was a rare commodity.

Nonetheless, the label violated one of Woodruff's sacred tenets, and he ordered his high-powered chemists and lawyers to write affidavits in an attempt to undo the damage. Referring to this incident, John Sibley wrote to Woodruff in November of 1936: "That country is feeding itself on prejudice and this is just another evidence of this fact. I hope that we get through without getting scarred up." In his meeting with Max Keith and Walter Oppenhoff, Woodruff refused to allow them to combat the rumors about caffeine. When Keith pressed the issue, Woodruff dramatically banished the visiting Americans from the room so that he could be alone with the Germans. "I am not accustomed to giving my American people explanations," he said, "but I will break the rule for you. You must *never* engage in defensive advertising. It simply gives dignity to your opponents and prolongs the issue."

For once, Keith had met his match. Without ever raising his voice or displaying irritation, Robert Woodruff had exercised steely command. "When Max Keith met Robert Woodruff," one of his aides remembered, "he was overwhelmed. That was the man he worked for, the only man in the world he really deeply respected." For his part, Woodruff recognized in Keith a potent personality who could build the German business. The two men remained lifelong friends.

While in Berlin, Woodruff also dealt with the Ray Powers situation. Deverna as a parent bottling company hadn't worked out, and Powers had failed to make any money from his contract arrangement. After a lengthy meeting, company lawyers agreed to dissolve Deverna, to make Max Keith the official *Geschäftsführer* of Coca-Cola GmbH, and to give Powers a flat royalty fee for all the drinks sold in Germany until 1950.

In September of 1936, a month after the Olympics, Hermann Göring, Hitler's designated successor and head of the Luftwaffe, took charge of a new Four-Year Plan which stressed German self-sufficiency in preparation for war. The Nazi leader cut imports to a bare minimum and discouraged foreign businesses. In a letter to the German Revenue Office, Oppenhoff had taken pains to present Coca-Cola GmbH as a *German* business, despite the fact that The Coca-Cola Company owned most of it (Oppenhoff called the foreign capital a "loan"). Under Göring's iron rule, such prevarication was useless, and the supply of U.S. concentrate appeared doomed until Robert Woodruff pulled his magic strings.

Woodruff belonged to a network of corporate executives, many of whom were worried about their German subsidiaries and interests. With war clouds darkening, these titans of American industry quietly maneuvered to protect themselves against all contingencies. Some, like Henry Ford, were in fact Nazi sympathizers, while others, such as Walter Teagle of Standard Oil, avoided taking sides but saw nothing wrong with doing business with the Nazis. Like his friend and hunting companion Teagle, Woodruff practiced expediency. His politics were Coca-Cola, pure and simple.

Through his New York banking connections, Woodruff moved behind the scenes to influence Göring. In 1936, he enlisted the aid of Henry Mann, a German agent for several American banks, who convinced Göring to permit the importation of Coca-Cola concentrate. "He accepts gifts," one acquaintance had murmured helpfully to a favor-seeker early in Göring's career. In order to reduce the imports to a minimum, Keith began making his own concentrate so that he needed only Merchandise No. 5 and 7X from America. Woodruff toyed with the idea of producing even these ingredients inside Nazi Germany if war broke out. "Some consideration should probably be given to the . . . possibility of having Number 5 manufactured in Germany in case developments should make that desirable," he wrote to Sibley, but he finally abandoned the plan as impractical.

The correspondence between Robert Woodruff and John Sibley during this crucial 1936 European trip reveals that Woodruff, while outwardly calm in the face of any adversity, was actually high-strung and restless. Writing from London before his German visit, Woodruff said that he was "nervous and lonesome" but that he was at least sleeping well for a change.* Despite the problems facing him in Germany, he wrote that his five-day visit would "pass fairly quickly (I hope)." Recognizing Woodruff's tension, Sibley expressed the hope that his friend would get a "complete rest" while playing golf in Scotland.

FIGHTING THE "JEWISH SLANDER"

Woodruff may have helped Max Keith by interceding with Göring, but he was unable to control other looming problems. The caffeine rumors were only the beginning of controversy. As Coca-Cola became a big seller in Germany, the mineral water interests, breweries, and cola imitators used every smear tactic available. Phosphoric acid, they claimed, ate the lining of the stomach, demonstrating that a piece of veal left overnight in Coke was leached white. Some competitors complained that Coca-Cola was misnamed because it had no cocaine; others spread the rumor that it *did* contain the "poison," which had a "stimulating effect on the brain." As an "artificial coloring," even the caramel coloring caused problems. The sacred hobbleskirt bottle itself was maligned because it held 0.192 liters rather than the German standard of 0.2.

But the most devastating threat to Coca-Cola's future in Germany came from one Herr Flach, who manufactured an imitation drink called Afri-Cola. Flach belonged to the so-called Labor Front, the Nazi organization which had replaced unions in 1934. In 1936, Flach and other Labor Front representatives visited the United States on a goodwill tour of American industries. Ray Powers arranged for a visit to a New York Coca-Cola bottling plant, where Flach scooped up a handful of bottle caps with Hebrew inscriptions indicating that Coca-Cola was kosher—not a big surprise, since the huge New York

---

*Woodruff was traveling with his wife, Nell, but though a devoted husband, he apparently derived little comfort from her company. He rather plaintively asked Sibley to sail across the Atlantic, spend less than a week with him in Germany, then accompany him back on the cruise ship. Sibley politely declined. Woodruff apparently preferred the company of close male friends to the somewhat rarified company of "Miss Nell," who frowned on cigar smoke and poker games.

Jewish population comprised a ready market. Back in Germany, Flach distributed thousands of flyers featuring photographs of the bottle cap. Coca-Cola, he claimed, was a Jewish-American company, run by Harold Hirsch, a prominent Atlanta Jew.

Sales plummeted. Nazi Party headquarters hastily canceled their orders. The entire business was in jeopardy, and Keith, forbidden to print defensive literature, could do little about it. Walter Oppenhoff fought for a preliminary injunction in Cologne against the "Jewish slander," but F. A. S. Gwatkin, Coke's London counsel, and Sibley prevented further court proceedings, fearing the consequent publicity. The independent bottlers and concessionaires felt betrayed and instituted their own lawsuits, sometimes defiantly naming Coca-Cola GmbH as co-plaintiff. Oppenhoff wrote to Gwatkin, explaining that no one living outside Germany "could have any conception" of the scope of the problem. Desperate for relief, Keith begged Woodruff to remove Harold Hirsch from the Coca-Cola board or at least to clarify that he did not own the company. Woodruff stood by Hirsch, but he did ask the legal department to draft a notice verifying the large number of shareholders, proving that no one person "owned" the Company. In the face of Flach's jubilant defamations, however, the list of shareholders was a blunt weapon.

INTO THE HEART OF NAZISM

Ultimately, Coca-Cola weathered even this fiasco, though pictures of the kosher bottle cap kept surfacing for years. As Woodruff had done in America, Keith zeroed in on "special events," such as patriotic mass meetings, realizing that sampling was the best way to build the business. Coca-Cola appeared at bicycle races, emphasizing its wholesome refreshment for athletes. As young men goose-stepped in formation at Hitler Youth rallies, Coca-Cola trucks accompanied the marchers, hoping to capture the next generation.

In 1937, the year after Flach's initial accusations, Keith placed Coca-Cola at the heart of the Nazi industrial renaissance. That year, the Reich "Schaffendes Volk" ("Working People") Exhibit opened in Düsseldorf, displaying the accomplishments of the German worker during the first five years of Hitler's rule. A functioning bottling plant, with a miniature train carting *Kinder* beneath it, bottled Coca-Cola at the very center of the fair, adjacent to the Propaganda Office. Touring the Düsseldorf fair, Hermann Göring paused for a Coke, and an alert Company photographer snapped a picture. Though no such picture documented the Führer's tastes, Hitler reputedly enjoyed Coca-Cola, too, sipping the Atlanta drink as he watched *Gone With the Wind* in his private theater.

In March of 1938, as Hitler's troops stormed across the Austrian border in the *Anschluss*, Max Keith convened the ninth annual concessionaire convention, with 1,500 people in attendance. Behind the main table, a huge banner proclaimed, in German, "Coca-Cola is the world-famous trademark for the unique product of Coca-Cola GmbH." Directly below, three gigantic swastikas stood out, black on red. At the main table, Max Keith sat surrounded by his deputies, another swastika draped in front of him.

Although acknowledging glorious past efforts, Keith urged his workers to forge onward into the future, never to be content until every German citizen was a Coke consumer. "We know we will reach our goal only if we muster all our powers in a total effort," he said. "Our marvelous drink has the power of endurance to continue this march to success." If he sounded like Hitler, it was probably deliberate. The meeting closed with a "ceremonial pledge" to Coca-Cola and a ringing, three-fold "Sieg-Heil" to Hitler.

Far from expressing horror at Nazi aggression, Keith and his men swiftly followed the troops into Austria, establishing a Vienna branch in September. Keith registered no protest a month later when, on November 10, 1938, *Kristallnacht*, the Night of Broken Glass, heralded a new level of terror for Jews, whose Austrian businesses were demolished and synagogues set on fire. Nor were Woodruff or Powers disturbed, though the *Anschluss* did cause friction between the two men. Powers felt that his royalty should cover all Coca-Cola sold within German borders, wherever they might extend due to Hitler. Woodruff demurred, saying the contract specified the borders as they existed when it was signed. Shortly after the argument was settled, Powers was killed in an automobile accident, and Keith was left the undisputed leader of the German Coca-Cola business.

Keith presided over the tenth anniversary of the German Coca-Cola business in April of 1939, lavishing praise on the recently deceased Ray Powers, though Keith's joy at achieving control could scarcely be concealed. The past year, he gloated, had been historic because Hitler had annexed Austria and the Sudetenland, bringing those lands back into the German fold. The phenomenal spread of Coca-Cola during 1938 was a close second, however. Then Keith ordered a mass Sieg-Heil for Hitler's recent fiftieth birthday, "to commemorate our deepest admiration and gratitude for our Führer who has led our nation into a brilliant higher sphere."

BOMBED-OUT BOTTLING PLANTS

On September 1, 1939, when Hitler's troops rolled into Poland, and England and France finally declared war, Max Keith realized he was in trouble. While Göring may have previously permitted the flow of 7X, it was only a matter of time before the supply was severely curtailed or cut off altogether by the exigencies of war. Not only that, Keith feared that as a "foreign" business, Coca-Cola GmbH might be nationalized and its leaders imprisoned. Quickly, he moved on two fronts to forestall disaster.

First, he maneuvered to become a part of the vast German bureaucracy. Hitler may have had ultimate power, but he was bored with the details of governing, leaving much of it to old-line civil service men, many of whom were quite sympathetic with the plight of businessmen. Fortunately for Keith, Walter Oppenhoff was good friends with the head of the Ministry of Justice. Oppenhoff managed to get himself and Max Keith appointed to the Office of

Enemy Property to supervise all soft drink plants, both in Germany and captured territory. As German troops overran Europe, Keith and Oppenhoff followed, assisting and taking over the Coca-Cola businesses in Italy, France, Holland, Luxembourg, Belgium, and Norway.

Keith's second move was to find another product. While rationing Coca-Cola carefully to the different plants, he asked his chemists to invent an alternative drink which would see the Company through the war. They created a fruit-flavored drink. Like Coca-Cola, it was a unique caffeinated blend not readily identifiable as orange, grape, or lemon. Relying on available ingredients—often the leavings from other food industries—the new drink used whey, a cheese by-product, as well as apple fiber from cider presses. Keith later commented that the drink was made of "left-overs from left-overs." The mix of fruit ingredients shifted, depending on the availability of Italian produce. At first, the drink had to be sweetened with saccharin, but in 1941, it was exempted from sugar rationing and allowed to use 3.5 percent beet sugar, resulting in a beverage far better than any wartime competitor's.

In a christening contest, Keith asked his assembled employees to let their fantasy—*Fantasie* in German—run wild, and veteran salesman Joe Knipp immediately blurted the winning name, Fanta. Walter Oppenhoff registered the new trademark in Germany as well as all occupied countries, though in Belgium, manager Carl West opted for the name Cappy, thinking that Fanta sounded too Germanic for angry Belgians. A new, distinctive bottle was created, and Fanta sold well enough to keep the business alive during the war, even after the U.S. entered late in 1941 and all Coca-Cola supplies ceased. In 1943, Keith sold nearly 3 million cases of Fanta. Many bottles weren't drunk, but were used to add sweetness and flavor to soups and stews, since wartime sugar was severely rationed.

At the same time, Max Keith did everything possible to keep the name Coca-Cola before the German public. The Nazis outlawed "reminiscent advertising" for products no longer available. Still, in all Fanta advertising, he included the phrase, "a product of Coca-Cola GmbH." Before the supply of Coca-Cola itself ran out at the end of 1942, he reserved his German supply only for hospitals with wounded Nazi soldiers, though branches of the German military also managed to snag a few cases.

When the Army requisitioned his best trucks, Keith's mechanics nursed the old ones with constant repairs. Ford Motor Company also continued to do business inside Nazi Germany, supplying the *Geschäftsführer* with special coal-fueled trucks. To ensure that his remaining trucks weren't confiscated, Keith (like Woodruff) rendered his business "essential" to the war effort by capping carbonated water in his now-idle Coca-Cola bottles and storing them in mine shafts, safe from air raids. His trucks then became emergency vehicles to distribute free "catastrophe water"—and to maintain goodwill.

Keith could hide his bottles from the bombs, but not his plants. All forty-three Coca-Cola plants were bombed at some point during the war—a few on several occasions. The Company's Essen headquarters and plant were hit more times than any other. Located in Germany's industrial heartland, the town was completely demolished by the end of the war, not one building left whole. Nonetheless, Keith continued to bottle both Fanta and water, even at the height of the bombing. "I arranged for so-called siding plants on the outskirts of the cities where we had our bottling plants," he explained. Housed in old farmhouses or dairies, the makeshift operations kept the Fanta supply steady while the main plant in the city was repaired.

When his employees were drafted, Keith replaced them with ex-convicts unacceptable to the Army. "One of our best salesmen in Essen," Keith proudly remembered, "had killed his father and was imprisoned for twenty years." Later in the war, Keith used Chinese labor and "people who would come from anywhere in Europe—the war brought them from everywhere." For Keith to say blandly that "the war brought them" implies that they were willing refugees, which is somewhat misleading. In fact, the wartime railroads not only carried Jews, Gypsies, and others to concentration camps, but some 9 million *Fremdarbeiter*, or foreign forced labor, who accounted for a fifth of the German labor force by 1944.

Clearly, Max Keith was willing to do almost anything to keep the Coca-Cola business going, including collaborating with the Nazi government. His associates later excused his behavior, asserting that he had no other alternative. "Yes, Max Keith tried not to offend those in power," Klaus Pütter admitted. "He was a very skilled negotiator, a cautious man. You know, when you live in a country governed by a dictatorship, you have to watch your tongue and be very careful. If your neighbor heard you say anything against Hitler, they came at night and fetched you and off you went. It's impossible for you here in the United States to understand." As a result, Keith honed a fine-tuned diplomacy while representing a foreign company. "One false step, one false remark would have been fatal."

When his loyalty to Coca-Cola came under fire, Keith proved himself willing to die for his drink rather than submit to the Nazis. By the beginning of 1945, it was clear to everyone except Hitler and his fanatical followers that the war was lost. In reaction, devoted Nazis turned paranoid, looking for an enemy within to blame. Keith and Oppenhoff were summoned that January to report to the general in charge of the Ministry of Commerce and told to nationalize their company. "Change the name to anything else," the general ordered. "Call it Max Keith GmbH if you want, but change it within two days, or you will be placed in a concentration camp."

Keith remained obdurate. He and Oppenhoff went to see their old friend at the Ministry of Justice, who was afraid that if he interfered, he too might be imprisoned. Unsure what would happen, the two Coca-Cola men prepared for the showdown the next day, but it never came. The general was providentially killed in an air raid, saving the business. Three months later, in a Berlin bunker, Hitler shot himself through the mouth. The war was over.

INVASION OF THE TECHNICAL OBSERVERS

Max Keith had prevailed. "Coca-Cola GmbH still functioning," he tele-graphed to Woodruff. "Send auditors." Astonished, Woodruff promptly dispatched Stephen Ladas, the New York lawyer for Coca-Cola Export, to try to locate Walter Oppenhoff in his home city of Cologne, whose bombed-out population of a million people had been reduced to only 35,000. Ladas couldn't find Oppenhoff, but he did learn from neighbors that he was alive. Leaving an encouraging note, Ladas returned to America.

In the meantime, the Technical Observers poured into Germany just behind the liberating American troops, quickly commandeering a mineral water plant at Niedermendig and bottling Coke there by April, just before the German surrender. The three top T.O.s hopped in a jeep and set out to find Max Keith and "whatever remnants of our pre-war German company we could," as one later remembered. When they found Keith, he was busily bottling Fanta in a half-destroyed plant.

To the Company executives back home, Max Keith was a hero. Harrison Jones, in his 1946 speech to the newest batch of Technical Observers headed for Germany, told them that Max Keith was "a grea-a-t, grea-a-t man" who had united the bottlers during the war. At the time, however, such praise rang hollow for Keith, who felt betrayed and angry. He had survived the war, keeping his little bottling kingdom intact, only to have it usurped by the American T.O.s. Later, he called this postwar period an "even worse breakdown" for him than he had suffered under the Nazis.

Keith's distress was understandable, but so was the attitude of the Technical Observers in their U.S. military uniforms, ordered not to fraternize with Germans. Eisenhower had ordered that industry be "de-Nazified." Together with Walter Oppenhoff (who had surfaced intact), Keith attempted to negotiate with Army officers and the American Coke men. "We had quite some discussions," Oppenhoff remembered later. T.O. George Downing, who flatly called Keith "a second Hitler," was appalled at his effrontery. "Could you imagine a German in a defeated Germany coming and telling Americans how to do something?" Downing was sure that Keith planned to take over Coca-Cola's worldwide operations if Germany had won the war. Those might well have been Keith's aspirations, but he was well schooled in patient diplomacy, and he now tried to ingratiate himself with the victors. At first, the Americans not only refused to give Keith any Coke syrup, but curtailed his Fanta production. They eventually compromised, allowing Coca-Cola GmbH to bottle Fanta while the T.O.s monopolized the American drink for GI consumption.

In the uneasy truce, the Technical Observers bottled Coke on one side of the Frankfurt plant, while Keith capped Fanta in the other half. But in the devastated postwar economy, he couldn't scrounge enough sugar or fruit—nor could most Germans afford to buy his drink. Sales fell from over 2 million cases in 1944 to a half million in 1945, even though he also started bottling soda water and a new flavor called Rosalta.

Keith was determined to take over the business when the American soldiers eventually left. He instructed his men to infiltrate the T.O. operations, and the Americans were more than happy to find experienced help. "As life around this plant took shape," reported the T.O. in Stuttgart in August of 1945, "native Coca-Cola men became once again part of a great business. From the fields and prison camps old employees returned to the business. Good machinists and diligent effort have made what first appeared to be a hopeless mess a shining success." No wonder one T.O. said, "I couldn't teach myself to hate the Germans—they were so *industrious.*" No one seemed unduly concerned that these "native Coca-Cola men" were ex-Nazis or collaborators, partly because a magical transformation had taken place overnight with the Allied victory. "It was amazing," one naive Technical Observer subsequently noted, "but not one member of the populace was a Nazi, all were anti-party members and were definitely against Hitler and his objectives."

Despite his precarious position, Max Keith tried to keep in touch with these former employees while offering his "help" to the T.O. operations. In Augsburg, Cliff Johnson explained to his assistant Don Sisler that "this Kraut, Max Keith, is coming to visit, and we've got orders to be nice to him." When Keith arrived, clad in a huge fur coat, his former employees, now working at Augsburg, were "practically fainting with ecstasy," as Sisler recalled the scene. "Elsie was swooning because Herr Keith was there, and Herr Kohler was bowing all over the place." Sisler himself was impressed with Keith's "regal presence."

Finally, Keith seized an opportunity to outwit the Americans in 1949, when he discovered that a large supply of stale Coke syrup, shunted around the world during the war by the military bureaucracy, had arrived in Germany. He persuaded Paul Lesko, then in charge of the German Technical Observer operation, to sell him the syrup so that he could extract sugar from it for Fanta. To guard against its being reused, Lesko nearly dyed the syrup green, but Keith convinced him that such precautions were unnecessary. Putting his chemists to work, Keith clandestinely filtered and reworked the syrup, then hastily bottled his first Coca-Cola since 1942. Lee Talley, head of Coke's operations in Europe, happened to call Keith to say he was planning to visit Frankfurt. "That's wonderful," Keith said, "because I want you to cut a ribbon tomorrow morning. We are starting with the Coca-Cola business again." On October 3, Talley, who was quite surprised that Keith had all that syrup, nevertheless snipped the ribbon, and Keith's trucks ventured forth with huge signs proclaiming "*Coca-Cola ist wieder da!*" ("Coca-Cola is back again!"). Lesko was infuriated at being hoodwinked, but with Talley tacitly approving the operation, he was powerless to do anything about it.

Keith's timing was perfect. As the American military presence and T.O. operation dwindled, Woodruff decreed that the bottling should be returned to natives, and Lesko suddenly found himself having to answer to Keith, who was once again in command. To make peace with the American, Keith allowed him the Bremen bottling rights. It didn't take Max Keith long to rebuild the German industry, now that he had free access to Coca-Cola concentrate. It was impossible to find Germans who had the capital requirements set down by the Export company—$1 per capita for every person in the franchise territory. Keith arbitrarily reduced that amount, demanding one Deutschmark per capita, the equivalent of a quarter. Still, few had such resources, so Keith had to cosign loans for many of them, extorting oaths of lifelong fealty. "I pick you," he told his bottlers, "and I will make you rich, but you do what I tell you."

Keith was true to his word. When former T.O. Don Sisler returned to Germany many years later, he found that Elsie and Herr Kohler owned the Augsburg bottling plant and were "rolling in wealth." They treated him at the town's best restaurant and laughed tolerantly at memories of those difficult days just after the war. One thing had not changed, however: they still groveled before Max Keith, now Coca-Cola commander throughout Europe. Braver bottlers, in hushed tones, called him "Super-Führer."

THE GREAT WHITE ARYAN HOPE BECOMES A COCA-COLA MAN

Even Max Schmeling showed proper obeisance to Keith when he became a Coca-Cola bottler in 1957. The German hero contacted James Farley, New York's boxing commissioner in the prewar years, when the Coke executive came to Essen in 1954 to celebrate the twenty-fifth anniversary of Coca-Cola in Germany. Farley immediately recognized that Schmeling would be a real catch. Down on his luck, the boxer jumped at the chance to bottle Coke in Hamburg and would serve as a goodwill ambassador for the drink in Germany for years to come. Once the personification of Nazi superiority, the man who kept a signed autograph of Hitler in his study joined the *gemütlich* Coca-Cola family.[*]

---

[*] It is only fair to note that Schmeling was always uncomfortable as a symbol of Nazism, insisting that he was only a professional boxer—with a Jewish manager for a while. After World War II, Schmeling made a point of befriending Joe Louis and escorting him on a tour of his Coca-Cola bottling plant.

Part IV

~

Trouble in the Promised Land (1950–1979)

"Into the Eighties With Coke!" The flashing red signs in the great empty hall, once so comfortably familiar, appeared bizarre and disorienting to Paul Austin. Why were they so bright, so much like an incandescent bloodletting? His heart pounded irregularly; he felt dizzy.

Stumbling toward the bar at the side of the amphitheater, Austin confronted a huge photograph of a beautiful woman's head, her gigantic teeth bared in a ferocious grin. "Have a Coke and a Smile!" she ordered. He leaned against the counter, steadying himself. "I'll have a Scotch on the rocks," he heard himself say, his voice sounding unreal and distant to his ears, as if it echoed from a corner of the hall. The technicians scurried purposefully around the room while a few bottlers and their wives strolled among the displays. Mumbling his thanks, Austin gulped his drink.

A man hurried toward him, deferentially nodding his head and holding out a hand. "Oh, there you are, Mr Austin," he said. "Would you mind coming up on the podium for a sound check, sir?" Refilling his glass quickly, the tall Coca-Cola executive moved toward the stage. Perhaps another drink would calm him, ease the confusion. Deliberately, heavily, he ascended the steps and stood behind the microphone. His hand quivering slightly, he carefully placed his glass on the table beside him, as he had done countless times in the past. He leaned over the podium, grasping both sides.

Paul Austin stared into the pulsing red space before him. Sucking in a deep breath, he leaned further forward, and, his speech slightly slurred, asked a question which reverberated throughout the hall. "Excuse me, but could anyone tell me why I'm here?"

~ 14 ~

Coca-Colonization and the Communists

Apparently some of our friends overseas have difficulty distinguishing between the United States and Coca-Cola. Perhaps we should not complain too much about this.

—One Coca-Cola executive to another, 1950

IN APRIL OF 1945, representatives of fifty countries converged on San Francisco for a conference with the idealistic mission of creating the United Nations, a postwar organization to maintain the peace. Sensing a pivotal moment in history, Robert Woodruff promptly dispatched James Farley to San Francisco with an unlimited entertainment budget to wine, Coca-Cola, and dine the powerful delegates so conveniently assembled in one town. "The relationships I established," Farley later wrote with characteristic under-statement, "might be helpful in our efforts to establish Coca-Cola bottling companies" around the world.

Farley was the consummate politician, famous for his prodigious memory for names and his paper flood of polite correspondence signed in green ink. He once explained that "it's the little things that cause trouble, it's the little sores that cause bitter feelings." Consequently, he vowed early in his life to be a consistent friend to everyone; no detail was too minor, no gift too small to be acknowledged. During the 1932 Democratic Convention, a journalist wrote that wherever Farley appeared, "rainbows flashed and quivered," perhaps reflected from his enormous bald pate, a beacon at the top of his burly 6'2" frame. "Give him time," noted the reporter, "and he will call everybody in the United States by his Christian name."

As a Democrat, Farley stressed loyalty above policy. Naturally gregarious, he neither drank nor smoked and needed only six hours' sleep a night. He loved to travel, meet new people, and exert subtle influence—in short, he was the perfect Coca-Cola man. In 1941, Ralph McGill, the famed Atlanta journalist and friend of Robert Woodruff, wrote solemnly that Farley's new job with Coca-Cola "entirely divorced him from politics." Far from being divorced from the process, Farley's diplomatic missions for his soft drink in the postwar world required every ounce of his skill. Increasingly, Coca-Cola *was* politics, particularly to the Communists.

For a brief moment near the war's end, it appeared that the traditionally antagonistic relationship between the USSR and the U.S. would give way to the friendship of victorious allies. But Stalin's purges, power hunger, and rebuffs to tentative American feelers soon led to the Cold War's first chill.

That spring of 1945, while Farley hobnobbed with Faisal of Saudi Arabia, Lord Halifax of Great Britain, and representatives from Egypt, Mexico, Brazil, and many other countries, he pointedly avoided Andrei Gromyko, the Russian delegate. Within a few years, American hostility to the Soviets would turn to paranoia, as Richard Nixon prosecuted Alger Hiss, the State Department member accused of being a Communist. Ironically, Hiss arranged Farley's San Francisco meetings with foreign delegates.

Farley proved as loyal to Coca-Cola as he had been to the Democratic Party. Indeed, he delighted in the product which made him a nonpartisan goodwill ambassador and gave him entrée to the rich and powerful. After a three-month trip around the world in 1946, Farley confidently told the press that the countries of the world "look to the American nation to lead them out of their difficulties," adding that "there isn't any doubt of the affection" these foreigners felt for Americans. The Coca-Cola ambassador was equally certain that the Chinese, torn by a civil war between Chiang Kai-shek and Mao Tse-tung, could "work out a solution to their problems."

Building on the goodwill fostered by the American soldier and his soft drink, The Coca-Cola Company swiftly licensed bottling plants in new countries and held its first international convention at Atlantic City in 1948, clearly intending to impress its newfound overseas bottlers. "When we think of Communists, we think of the Iron Curtain," a placard at the convention read. "BUT when THEY think of democracy, they think of Coca-Cola." At the convention, an executive prayed fervently: "May Providence give us the faith . . . to serve those two billion customers who are only waiting for us to bring our product to them." By the end of 1950, the business had started in Egypt, Morocco, Barbados, Liberia, Rhodesia, Guadeloupe, Algeria, Gibraltar, Kenya, Thailand, Tunisia, India, Congo, Iraq, Lebanon, Cyprus, and Saudi Arabia. Meanwhile, additional plants and aggressive marketing in countries where the industry was already established—primarily Europe and South America—substantially increased per capita consumption around the world.

The first step when entering a country was to locate a wealthy, socially prominent, politically influential bottler. Key employees were then brought to the U.S. for an extensive eight-month indoctrination—working in plants, riding the trucks, putting up advertising, properly icing coolers, enduring endless Visomatics in the appropriate language. By the time they went home, the new Coca-Cola men had received multiple syrup transfusions. "They are linked," wrote one Company man, "by a common faith in Coca-Cola, their belief in the honesty of the product and its value to mankind."

Giovanni Pretti, a thirty-year-old Italian salesman, was typical of the new international Coke man in 1950. Bounding from bed, he confronted a bathroom mirror whose signs inquired: "Hair Combed? Shaved? Uniform Clean and Neat? Shoes Shined? Friendly Smile?" Properly clothed and brimming with enthusiasm, he lovingly polished his shiny red and yellow truck and drove through Milan, explaining to a journalist that because of his "responsible position," he was now known as *Signor* Pretti.

As part of morale-building continuing education, Coca-Cola Export field men staged skits for bottling plant workers. In Cairo, for instance, the assembled employees watched a morality play about Barsoum, a mustachioed Egyptian bottler who, failing to apply proper ice to his Coke, lost sales. Taking advantage of this lapse, a nefarious salesman for a competing drink convinced Barsoum to push the inferior product. Fortunately, the wise Coca-Cola salesmen arrived just at the crucial moment, booted the imitator, and restored refrigeration and the proper soft drink.

As an epilogue, one of the Coke field men, extolling the virtues of the Coca-Cola cooler, was interrupted by a loud voice. "Stop talking! I can speak for myself," the machine shouted. "I'm a twenty-four-hour salesman," it explained to the rapt Cairo audience. "I advertise the product, I cool the product, I present your product attractively." In another overseas presentation, a giant Coke bottle proclaimed: "I am Coca-Cola, vigorous with life and more than a mere shape," immodestly calling itself "a royal bottle . . . the object of your strivings." This sort of hokey presentation, standard since the 1930s in America, created a sensation abroad. By 1950, sales in the six Egyptian bottling plants, owned by the four Pathy brothers, mushroomed, reaching 350 million drinks annually only five years after the first Coke rolled off the line there.

The growth of the business overseas fascinated American media. Henry Luce, the anti-Communist publisher of *Time* and a Woodruff hunting companion, featured the company in his May 15, 1950, issue. When Robert Woodruff refused to allow his portrait on the cover, Luce commissioned a classic painting in which a smiling red Coca-Cola disk with a skinny arm held a Coke bottle to the mouth of a thirsty globe. The legend underneath read, "WORLD & FRIEND—Love that piaster, that lira, that tickey, and that American way of life." The article pointed out that the "gentle burps" evoked by the drink could be heard amid "the bustle of Parisian sidewalk cafes" and "the tinkling of Siamese temple bells." By that time, a third of the Company's profits came from abroad. The *Time* reporter noted that "to find something as thoroughly native American hawked in half a hundred languages on all the world's crossroads from Arequipa to Zwolle" was strange—"like reading Dick Tracy in French." Nonetheless, he concluded, it was rather reassuring.

James Farley agreed. In a speech to the American Trademark Association, Farley pointed out that the American flag itself was "the most glorious of all trademarks," representing the "greatest tide of products and services in the history of mankind." As an example of America's contribution to global progress, Farley cited the Philippines, where at first he had been disturbed by the primitive conditions—homes of bamboo and grass raised on stilts, with shabbily dressed natives and naked children wandering along mud streets. "But you turn a corner in all this poverty," Farley said, smiling at the memory, "and suddenly you catch sight of a beautiful Coca-Cola bottling plant." In the midst of the squalor, here was a well-constructed, sparkling white factory equipped with "the latest and most modern bottle fillers, bottle cleaners and water treating equipment." The floors, Farley noted, were meticulously clean.

The local employees, despite their unsanitary regular lives, showered at the plant daily and wore freshly laundered uniforms. If they were sick, there was a plant doctor. In conclusion, Farley bragged that Coca-Cola plants had "raised the standard of living in each of these islands."

Naive and thoroughly ethnocentric, Farley blindly accepted the poverty he saw around him, easily condemning native culture, and assuming that the American way of life, represented by Coca-Cola, was the *only* way of life. He added that the soft drink was effective in "influencing" favorable attitudes toward America and would eventually embrace all nations in "a brotherhood of peace and progress." It was true, however, that Coke often brought much-needed technology for cleaning water, that Coca-Cola employees were paid decent wages by local standards, and that the bottling plant was usually owned and run by natives. In 1950, only one percent of Coca-Cola Export employees were Americans. As one Coke executive pointed out, "in Germany it is a German business; in France, it is a French business; in Italy, it is an Italian business." Local industries to produce glass, carton, crown, and bottling equipment started in each new country. The Coca-Cola Company even supplied specifications, blueprints, and economic advisers.

NOT EVERYBODY LOVES US

Nevertheless, the result of Coca-Cola's postwar onslaught was not a "brotherhood of peace and progress." The fate of China proved symbolic of Coca-Cola's new woes. Farley's optimistic prediction that the opposing factions would "work out a solution" amicably was dead wrong, and in 1949 Mao Tse-tung founded Communist China, while Chiang Kai-shek fled to Taiwan. All of Coca-Cola's Chinese bottling plants were nationalized, except for the British outpost in Hong Kong.*

Traveling a barren road next to the barbed wire fence separating Hong Kong from Communist China in 1950, a Company man braked impulsively before a huge, bright red billboard with the single word "Coca-Cola" in English and Chinese characters. Only feet from the Bamboo Curtain, it faced Mao's regimented realm. Inspired, the Coke executive reflected that the sign painter had been "a man with a soul" who created the sign "to breathe its defiance of communistic doctrine." The Communists, too, viewed Coca-Cola as the fitting symbol of "degenerate capitalism." In countries around the world, they defamed the American soft drink in the press, lobbied against it in legislatures, and whispered of its vile effects in back alleys.

The Communists were not the only ones concerned about Coca-Cola's postwar expansion, however. While the native bottlers may have been happy,

---

* When China disappeared behind the Iron/Bamboo Curtain, it caused a panic at Coca-Cola, since one of the key ingredients of 7X was cassia, otherwise known as Chinese cinnamon. Through a London intermediary, however, Coke continued to do business with the Chinese, who willingly sold the secret ingredient of the capitalist beverage.

many of their countrymen were not, particularly if they sold competing beverages such as wine, beer, mineral water, or soft drinks. Many citizens across the Atlantic also resented the brash, aggressive Americans and their powerful new position in the world. This was particularly true of Europeans, whose love/hate attitude toward Americans was easily transferred to Coca-Cola.

Under the Marshall Plan, named for Coke's old friend George C. Marshall, Europe was rebuilt with massive infusions of American capital. The aid was not altogether altruistic, however, but intentionally gave American multi-national corporations such as Coca-Cola a mighty boost. A bitter Englishman observed in the 1950s that "victory brought an intensification of the state of siege" for his country, while it triggered "a paradise of consumption" in the United States. The lavish spending and infantile behavior of American soldiers who remained on huge bases (sneeringly called "Coca-Cola towns" by locals) didn't alleviate this resentment. Thrifty Germans were appalled by GIs who left lights on all night, opened windows in winter, and never turned off the radio.

In 1949 and 1950, the French and several other nationalities, afraid of the imminent "Americanization" of their cultures, blindly fought back at the most convenient, blatant symbol of American hustle, a product which threatened to alter consumption patterns and attitudes of the next generation—Coca-Cola, the drink with the singsong name, the alluring poster girls, and the low cost. "There are many Europeans," commented one journalist, "who genuinely believe that the object held aloft by the Statue of Liberty is a Coke bottle."

THE UNHOLY FRENCH ALLIANCE

In planning for Coca-Cola's return to the French civilian market, Company executives made a valiant effort at cultural harmony, worrying over issues such as the gender of their drink. The French-Canadian ads were masculine, but in all other Latin languages, such as Spanish, Italian, and Portuguese, it was a less aggressive female. After considerable discussion, they decided to skirt the issue with simple "Buvez Coca-Cola" signs, dropping "le" or "la." The ploy backfired when grammatically punctilious Frenchmen complained about the lack of the proper definite article. The American company, they said, tortured their language.

Such niceties were lost on the French Communists, who howled in 1948 when Coca-Cola applied to the authorities for permission to bottle in France. Forced out of the governing coalition in 1947, the Communists still remained the largest party in the French National Assembly, where they raged against "American imperialism" and the Marshall Plan. Throughout 1949, using smear tactics and whipping up the wine and mineral water interests, the Communists warned against the "Coca-Colonization" of Europe. When the first bottles were sold in Paris in December of 1949, their propaganda intensified, insisting that the Coca-Cola distribution organization doubled as a spy network. Skull and crossbones appeared overnight on Parisian Coke signs. In the Assembly, the Communists pressed unsuccessfully for a bill to ban Coca-Cola as a poison.

Coke's man on the scene was Prince Alexander Makinsky, a suave, multilingual White Russian émigré. The French-educated anti-Communist had worked for the Rockefeller Foundation in Paris before joining Coke in 1945. He now quietly conferred with the U.S. ambassador and French officials to calm the waters and prevent revelation of Coke's ingredients. He diplomatically pointed out the "innocent error" of a French analytical laboratory which had found cocaine in the drink, but he couldn't prevent a furor over the phosphoric acid and caffeine. The matter reached a head at the end of February in 1950, when the Communists formed what Farley called "a strange alliance" with the wine and mineral water interests, supporting a bill introduced by Paul Boulet, the deputy mayor of Montpellier and spokesman for many winegrowers. Boulet proposed a general measure against all nonalcoholic beverages with vegetable extracts—a thinly veiled assault on Coca-Cola. On February 28, it passed one house of the French legislature. Soon afterward, a suit was filed charging Coca-Cola with violation of a 1905 law prohibiting the sale of pharmaceuticals without ingredients on the label.

There was actually no immediate cause for concern, since the bill, even if passed by both houses, only made it *possible* for the Health Ministry to ban Coca-Cola. The lawsuit, which took years to drag through the courts, would at worst change the labeling. The moderate coalition government, led by Premier Georges Bidault, wasn't eager to offend the Americans, who might cut off the financial spigot. Secretary of State Dean Acheson fired off a memo to David Bruce, the U.S. ambassador to France, asking him to inform Bidault that the State Department was "disturbed" by legislation that was "prejudicial to legitimate American interests," asking Bruce to "emphasize unfavorable . . . U.S. public opinion" which would inevitably result. Bidault, anxious and conciliatory, assured the American ambassador that he wouldn't stand for "discrimination against the product" and would prevent the Health Ministry from taking any adverse action. He was powerless, however, to control the Communist propaganda, which he described as "widespread and effective."

Acheson's prediction of American outrage was accurate. Billy Rose banned French champagne from his New York nightclub. The *New York Daily News* suggested that "France would be smart to watch her chic little step. Should worse come to worst, we could lop off Marshall Plan aid." The *Philadelphia Inquirer* commented that "this is worse than Marie Antoinette. The Commies won't even let 'em drink Coke." A Denver paper complained of the French habit of "snooting our beverages, soft and hard, as so much dishwater."

Atlanta's mayor William B. Hartsfield, preparing for a European tour, declared his intention of bringing two cases of Coke along. "I'm going to offer myself as a living example of what happens to a lifetime drinker of Coca-Cola," Hartsfield told reporters, though the dumpy, bespectacled politician may not have helped his cause once the French saw him. Georgia legislator Prince Preston read his concern into the *Congressional Record*, suggesting retaliatory laws again French wine, champagne, and perfume. It was ridiculous to pretend that Coca-Cola was a health hazard, since "doctors prescribe it for babies." Besides, Preston said, the French were entirely too prissy. Drinking Coke would give them a much-needed "good belch." James Farley described the French legislation as "the weirdest bit of political shenanigan I have ever encountered," pointing out that "Coca-Cola was not injurious to the health of the American soldiers who liberated France from the Nazis . . . Benevolent Uncle Sam, after his usual pause to refresh, may think this is one straw too much."

The French press jumped to the defense. The moderate *Le Monde* denounced "dangers that Coca-Cola represents for the health and civilization of France," comparing the Company's advertising with Nazi propaganda— both "intoxicated" the masses. "The moral landscape of France is at stake," the paper concluded. French intellectual Raymond Aron foresaw the destruction of his culture, with "Coca-Cola substituted for the noblest product of the soil (I mean, of course, wine)." Some of the anti-American French statements were classic for their hyperbole: "The Yankee, more arrogant than the Nazi iconoclast, substitutes the machine for the poet, Coca-Cola for poetry." A Frenchman at the zoo, watching a panther having diarrhoea, told his son, *"Voilà la production de Coca-Cola!"* Encouraged, Communist deputy Gérard Duprat led a spontaneous seven-hour filibuster in the French Assembly, breaking out into impassioned oratory, waving his hands and decrying warmongers and Coca-Cola.

Mobs overturned Coke trucks, the bottles broken and trampled as a brown stream fizzed into the gutters. At a French bicycle race sponsored by Coca-Cola, angry spectators protested by throwing debris on the track. The level of hysteria reached such a pitch that Alexander Makinsky's wife feared the Communists might bomb their home. It was, Makinsky said, "McCarthyism in reverse," philosophically commenting that "the best barometer of the relationship of the U.S. and any country is the way Coca-Cola is treated." Time and patience, as Woodruff and his cronies knew, would ultimately solve their problems. In the meantime, they rushed to establish new bottlers throughout France as quickly as possible.

Stephen Ladas, the Export Corporation's trademark lawyer, writing in July of 1950, noted that "when Frenchmen place their millions into plants and factories and trucks, etc., they will see to it through their deputies and friends that any interference with their business is avoided." The lawyer suggested signing bottling contracts with wine, beer, fruit juice, and soft drink interests. That way, he said, "we will bore into the enemy from within." Ladas was correct. Through bottling contracts with Pernod and other French concerns, Coca-Cola won a few friends inside the country. In addition, a Parisian temperance leader favored the American drink, claiming that half of his countrymen were alcoholics. The Health Ministry never enforced the Boulet law, and the lawsuit was finally dropped in 1953.

The French controversy may have helped rather than hindered Coca-Cola sales. "Probably no other product in the world," observed one Company executive, "has received such an extensive amount of gratuitous editorial mention." It was, as Milton Bellis, an American living in Paris, noted, "a press agent's dream." The Communists' claim that Coca-Cola would poison innocent French men, women, and children with its mysterious 7X formula only piqued the native curiosity, rendering Coke "an enchanting, exotic temptation: THE FORBIDDEN DRINK!" Watching a belly dancer in a French dive redolent with hashish smoke, Bellis noticed that Coca-Cola constituted a third of the drinks. Makinsky, too, realized that the younger generation viewed Coke as an "emancipation" from parental authority.

Nonetheless, the French fears of Coca-Cola's domination of their country proved, at least in the short term, ill-founded. For decades, the Gallic per capita consumption would lag behind most other countries. As one American journalist correctly commented in 1950, "The Frenchman replace wine with a soft drink? Fantastic!" Not even Coca-Cola, he wrote, could "wean the Frenchman away from the grape."

AGITATION AROUND THE WORLD

While the French uproar captured all the headlines, Coca-Cola faced similar threats and rumors at midcentury around the world, particularly in neighboring European nations.[*] In Italy, the Communists asserted that Coca-Cola turned hair white and caused the dread disease, Coca-colitis. "Tremble!" advised an Austrian newspaper. "Coca-Cola is on the march!" Alarmed Viennese were informed that the American soft drink company intended to market cuckoo clocks whose birds announced the hour by chirping, "Coca-Cola! Coca-Cola!" Another Communist-inspired story claimed that the huge Lambach bottling plant was actually manufacturing atomic bombs. Soviet guards in Austria clutched their stomachs, exclaiming "Coke nix gut, make kaput." Belgian brewers urged their association to buy Coca-Cola franchises and then refuse to bottle the soft drink, which their health ministry declared a harmful laxative. In Morocco, Pepsi-wielding Francophiles attacked Coke drinkers, and vice versa, since Coca-Cola represented the independence movement. In Cyprus, vandals defaced Coca-Cola signs with the hammer and sickle. Even the British became concerned when a female Labour Party member vilified Coca-Cola in the House of

---

[*] In 1951, British satirist Nancy Mitford drew a deliciously nasty portrait of Hector Dexter, the quintessential ugly American blowhard. In order to spread the "American way of living," he said, "I should like to see a bottle of Coca-Cola on every table in England, on every table in France, on every—" He was interrupted by his British hostess. "But isn't it terribly nasty?" Not at all, Dexter said. It tasted good. But that wasn't the point. "When I say a bottle of Coca-Cola, I mean it metaphorically speaking. I mean it as an outward and visible sign of something inward and spiritual, I mean it as if each Coca-Cola bottle contained a djinn, and as if that djinn was our great American civilization ready to spring out of each bottle and cover the whole global universe with its great wide wings." Though Mitford was clearly spoofing the hectoring American (who turned out to be a Communist agent), Robert Woodruff apparently loved this passage and clipped it. Years later, Coke historian Frederick Allen came upon it in Woodruff's papers and quoted it, in all seriousness, at the conclusion of his book, *Secret Formula*.

Commons, asserting that her countrymen shouldn't waste money on the American drink.

In Switzerland, Company men waged a bitter battle against health legislation which would have prohibited the drink because of its phosphoric acid. As in other countries, the mineral water, fruit juice, and beer industries lobbied hard against Coca-Cola. Burke Nicholson, Jr., the Coke executive sent to Switzerland to douse the flames, found that "we had some people who had talked rather big," bragging of the advertising avalanche about to descend on the Alpine valleys. In reality, he said, the Coke business was a tiny infant. "It was like people climbing up on furniture and yelling 'Snake! Snake!' and a tiny little worm would come out." The Defense Center Against Coca-Cola, which printed its own magazine and placed defamatory articles in other local media, initiated a well-coordinated Swiss campaign against Coca-Cola. While the Communist press was predictably rabid, the Defense Center material complained only of Coca-Cola's "loud propaganda and the free distribution of products," aggressive American tactics "unknown in the Swiss sector of beverages." Unless such promotions were stopped, Switzerland would become Americanized by Coca-Cola, ballpoint pens, and nylon stockings.

Eventually, by maintaining a low profile, remaining patient, and promoting the drink more subtly, the Company prevailed. Coke's public relations firm, Hill & Knowlton, arranged an "educational" tour of bottling plants for Swiss hairdressers and barbers, assuming that they gossiped with their customers. The Company sponsored a contest, consisting of carefully tailored queries about Coca-Cola—i.e., Question: "For every Swiss franc spent on Coca-Cola, what percentage stays in the country?" Answer: "94.2%." The winner, who just happened to be the son of a prominent Swiss brewer, received a free trip to the United States.

In Germany, the brewers, winegrowers, and soft drink manufacturers formed the Coordination Office for German Beverages, which the Coca-Cola men saw as a "mastermind of conspiracy." All of the familiar stories surfaced, along with defamatory pamphlets entitled, "Coca-Cola, Karl Marx, and the Imbecility of the Masses," asserting that Coke, not religion, was the opiate of the people. Walter Oppenhoff finally convinced Pope Brock, the Company's Atlanta general counsel, that he should sue for libel, and the German court ordered the campaign stopped.

Coca-Cola's battles against slanderous stories weren't limited to Europe, however. Around the world, wherever the new drink appeared, so did outrageous rumors. In Egypt, Coke sales temporarily plummeted when a Moslem demagogue asserted that the drink was made with pig's blood—not only disgusting but against his religion's prohibition against pork. In the Philippines, word spread that Coca-Cola made teeth fall out and that a San Miguel Coke employee had fallen into a vat of syrup, the dissolved body adding flavor to the drink. Company men quickly started a counterrumor: the story was true, but it was a *Pepsi* vat.

In Japan, where Coke was only available to the U.S. military, the drink reputedly sterilized women. In Brazil, on the other hand, Coca-Cola supposedly caused cancer and rendered macho Latin men impotent—such a serious charge that Coke men, winking knowledgeably, whispered that the drink was an aphrodisiac. In fact, the negative stories often backfired on the drink's opponents. An inadvertent message conveyed that the mysterious drink had strange and magical powers. Spontaneous myths surfaced in Barbados that Coke would turn copper to silver. In Haiti, an old woman was reportedly revived with the drink—long enough to rewrite her will to include her grandson, at any rate—and in Russia, women used smuggled syrup to smooth wrinkles.

In Trinidad, however, the association of Coca-Cola with the American soldier hurt more than helped. Before World War II, native sentiment had favored an American takeover from the hated British, but by the end of the war, locals were infuriated by American racism and conspicuous consumption. The song "Rum and Coca-Cola" originated in Trinidad and, with its bouncy Calypso beat, achieved enormous popularity in the United States. The lyrics, however, clearly indicated the islanders' bitterness. While the men got drunk on rum and Coca-Cola, "both mother and daughter" were "working for the Yankee dollar."

Coca-Cola, the overseas men soon learned, generally required repeated sampling before people found it palatable. Predisposed by Communist propaganda, first timers vied to outdo one another with disgusting similes to describe the taste. A Tokyo shoeshine boy commented that it resembled dog medicine, while a Brazilian maintained it had the bouquet of a burnt comb. A poetic Irishman, thoughtfully swirling the liquid in his mouth, described the flavor as "foot's asleep." More graphically, Italians asserted that drinking Coca-Cola was like "sucking the leg of a recently massaged athlete." One sentimental Japanese waitress, however, described it as "the sweet-and-bitter taste of first love."

Philosophical about the Communist antagonism, Woodruff said that it was natural for the Reds to resent Coca-Cola, since it was "the essence of capitalism." Another executive explained that "with Coca-Cola, every shopkeeper makes a profit and becomes a member of the bourgeoisie. That's why the Commies are anti-Coke." In America, the Reds recognized a losing battle, advising fellow travelers that they shouldn't antagonize the American proletariat by disparaging the workers' drink. After a leftist meeting filled with valiant speeches against the imperialistic American beverage, Italian Communists retired to a café, where they all quaffed Coca-Cola. Even in France, one of the Communist deputies, holding up a half-empty Coke bottle, complained, "Isn't it a tragedy? I drink it and I have to vote against it."

BLESS THIS BOTTLE, OH LORD

Company men prudently adapted themselves to local cultures, particularly where religious leaders acknowledged the sacred nature of the drink. When Jim Farley attended the Cork, Ireland, plant opening, he prayed right along with the Catholic priest who blessed the plant. Similarly, nine orange-robed

Hindu priests walking barefoot through the new Bangkok bottling plant sanctified it by dabbing gold paint on the equipment and workers' foreheads. Coke officials made sure that governmental Muftis officially announcing the month-long fast of Ramadan all held Coke bottles, and there were plenty of bottles to quench thirst after dark.

Since "everybody is a customer for Coca-Cola," explained a Company executive, "we just can't be offensive and stay in business. We can't offer a measure of hospitality with a drink and be inhospitable ourselves." Consequently, Coca-Cola representatives were determinedly good-natured and malleable as long as people imbibed their brown liquid. They hoped to make Coca-Cola an "integral part of every community . . . woven into the pattern and customs of every land."

Devout Company men who had been trained never to dilute their drink with any other substance soon learned that in the overseas business, it was best to look the other way. Signor Pretti told skeptical Italians, "Ah, but you must try Coca-Cola in the wine." In the Caribbean, of course, rum and Coca-Cola was known as a Cuba Libre. In Bolivia, locals mixed the American soft drink with *pisco*, a native brandy, to produce a Poncho Negro. The Austrians liked it with schnaps, while the British diluted their beer with the soft drink. Filipinos mixed their Coke with a potent native corn liquor, selling the concoction in jelly jars. Finally, as the Cold War thawed somewhat at the Geneva summit conference in 1955, some Soviets suggested mixing a "Coexistence Cocktail" of vodka and Coke.

Once past initial resistance, Coca-Cola representatives pushed their product in every conceivable way, including Tasmanian car trials, Brazilian waiter races with open bottles, Peruvian home delivery, and a white South African anniversary celebration of the Zulu defeat. In some well-established overseas businesses, bottlers could act out what remained tantalizing fantasies for their American counterparts. In the Philippines, for instance, where the United States had dominated since military intervention at the turn of the century, refreshment stands and Coca-Cola coolers were routinely installed in schools, while Company men blanketed Manila with neon Coca-Cola signs and twenty-four-sheet posters. The worldwide signs looked nearly identical, since the Company inaugurated "pattern advertising," using the same illustrations and message—all portraying middle-class white Americans.

To combat allegations that the drink was a health hazard, the Company sponsored numerous sporting events, identifying Coke with robust bikers, soccer players, and boxers. At the 1952 Helsinki Olympics, Coca-Cola donated a cooler to the Russian compound, snapping photos of the Soviet athletes drinking the imperialistic American soda. Four years later, at the Melbourne Olympics, Russian and Czech participants downed 10,776 bottles of Coke— Company representatives, of course, keeping careful records of each Communistic gulp.

OUR LATIN AMERICAN NEIGHBORS

During World War II, Coca-Cola had made substantial strides in South America, a major untapped market in the Western Hemisphere unaffected by the war overseas. After the war, business south of the border boomed, despite the widespread rumors about Coca-Cola's health effects. As a counterpart to the European Marshall Plan, the World Bank, which emerged in the postwar world as another American-dominated institution, promoted projects in Latin America and worked sympathetically with Coca-Cola. Mladin Zarubica's continuing saga illustrates the tight military/government/business network. Eugene Black, new head of the World Bank, was the former chief disbursement officer for the Army in Italy. Impressed with Zarubica's handling of the huge Austrian Coke plant, Black asked Export president James Curtis if he could "borrow" the Coke man. Curtis was only too glad to comply, since Zarubica could perform double duty. While on salary from Citibank in Montevideo, he conducted surveys of potential bottling franchises, with the full knowledge of the bank. "Don't forget that Coke was a major customer for Citibank," Zarubica recalled years later. The detailed surveys covered every aspect of a territory, including age and sex distribution, natural resources, the water situation, cultural prejudices, available refrigeration, and weather.

As a result of Zarubica's surveys, Robert Woodruff's nephew Morton Hodgson opened and operated a chain of South American bottling plants in Uruguay, Argentina, and Chile. These plants were partially owned by the Joroberts Corporation, a syndicate of forty Augusta National Golf Club members put together by golfer/investor Bobby Jones and Cliff Roberts, a New York investment banker. Most members of the Georgia club were well-connected corporate giants who flew from New York for a few rounds of golf and business. Joroberts investors thus included the heads of U.S. Steel and General Motors.

At the same time, Bill Bekker, a Dutchman who had pioneered the Italian and Spanish bottling industries, was establishing a Coca-Cola kingdom in Argentina, where he ruled with the same iron will exercised by Max Keith in Germany. An astute but stingy businessman, Bekker resented intrusion or advice from the New York Export office, simply throwing directives in the trash if he considered them nonsense. All who worked for Bekker lived in fear of his tread. Sweltering in cubbyhole offices above the bottling plant's din, they also worried about Bekker sneaking around to catch them sluffing off. The great man himself had a red light outside his door which, when lit, indicated that he was deep in thought and not to be disturbed. He drove himself as hard as he did his employees, often working late into the night.

Despite his tyrannical ways—or perhaps *because* of them—Bekker effectively fostered the business in a difficult territory. For years, the profit margin for Coke in South America was quite thin, due not only to the poverty of the people, but to government-imposed price controls. At the same time, Bekker had to contend with a well-entrenched trucking union. He solved that problem by abolishing regular Coca-Cola vehicles and hiring *fleteros*, independent truckers who would work for less money and make multiple daily trips without complaint. The main offices in New York demanded that Bekker send his profits back north, but he refused, plowing the money back into his Argentine trade.

While the South American business may not have been terribly profitable, it overcame most prejudice against Coca-Cola. By 1953, a Brazilian intellectual identified the drink as a symbol of the "complete overthrow of the gloomy concepts of a dark, mouldy past." On the contrary, he said, Coca-Cola was emblematic of "light, health, air, frankness, simplicity, strength and hope for a better future for Brazil." Coca-Cola, he asserted, meant progress and was opposed to diverse ills such as corrupt politicians, bad roads, gangsters, malaria, yellow fever, and bare feet.

THE ROYAL SOFT DRINK

To promote Coca-Cola as a high-status product, Company photographers loved to catch snapshots of the rich and famous drinking it. King Farouk reportedly had such a love for Coke that every restaurant in Egypt kept an iced supply in case the monarch should arrive unexpectedly. Two boy kings, Hussein of Jordan and Feisal of Iraq, sipped Coke together, as did four Dutch princesses. Batista drank it in Cuba, while Nixon and Eisenhower upended bottles in the U.S. The sultan of Morocco kept his palace supply well-chilled, while all elegant foreigners with fine sensibilities treated Coca-Cola as if it were the rarest champagne—or so Company executives claimed.

Many of the potentates who drank their Coke so religiously had an economic incentive. "The leading commercial, social and government leaders in all countries of the world wish to become associated with our product," one Coca-Cola man bragged, and he wasn't far off the mark. Like the American government, The Coca-Cola Company was perfectly happy to conduct business with dictators, as long as they were professed anti-Communists. Several ministers serving Franco, Spain's fascist ruler, doubled as Coca-Cola bottlers. James Farley met and befriended Getulio Vargas, the Brazilian dictator; while in Nicaragua, he solicited Anastasio Somoza's autograph for his daughter. Big Jim was, of course, always lavishly entertained in Taiwan by Chiang Kai-shek and his wife. He even unsuccessfully wooed Portugal's autocratic ruler, Antonio de Oliveira Salazar, undeterred by the fact that Salazar ran a police state. In 1954, the United Fruit Company, Coke's Guatemalan bottler, helped overthrow the democratic leftist government, replacing President Jacobo Arbenz with a series of strong-arm dictators. In a *Coca-Cola Overseas* feature three years later, the Company blandly ignored the overthrow, praising United Fruit for supplying workers on its banana plantations with Coca-Cola, their favorite soft drink.

In India, the Maharajah of Patiala oversaw his Coca-Cola holdings from his huge, ornate palace, complete with golf course, tennis courts, four swimming pools, gardens, and lakes—all maintained in manicured splendor by hundreds of servants. Coca-Cola Export representative Frank Harrold, who traveled the world to encourage local bottle sales, was awed by the Maharajah's opulent life-style. "His jewels have been estimated at one hundred million dollars," he wrote, casually adding that "outside the palace walls and so on for three thousand miles is the worst squalor and filth and poverty in the world."

THE ADVENTURES OF FRANK HARROLD

Harrold kept a diary of his world travels in the early 1950s which paints a fascinating portrait of the business. Riding the Coca-Cola trucks for two days in Bombay, he saw "a seething, boiling mass of humanity striving to survive from one day to the next." Despite their wretched lives, they still managed to purchase a miraculous amount of Coca-Cola. By the end of the day, Harrold had an overwhelming desire to lock himself into the Taj Mahal Hotel to "shut away all the misery." The next day, with no apparent sense of irony, Harrold described the "perfectly gorgeous" Coca-Cola bottling plant, surrounded by five acres of grounds. "There is nothing else like it in Bombay, so I am told," he noted with pride. At a party one night, he met several Indian movie stars. "Coca-Cola has a marvelous tie-up with the moving picture industry here," he wrote, explaining that the actors felt a part of the Coca-Cola family. This was fortunate, since the movie industry in India was second in size only to that of the United States.

Wherever he went, Frank Harrold found that "the best way to feel a city is to put on a Coca-Cola uniform" and follow the local route salesmen for a day. "A Coca-Cola truck goes anywhere and everywhere," he wrote, "to the finest cafes and hotels as well as to the lowliest dumps in the slums." His uniform gave him entrée where no other white men dared go, such as Algiers' infamous Casbah, a "criss-cross puzzle of crooked alleys" where desperate hands grabbed at anything.

In Hong Kong, Harrold saw rickshaws, tattoo artists, and little Buddhist shrines in local groceries. He later marveled at the Filipino women and children who carried Coca-Cola on their heads in "buckets, cases, baskets, chamber pots." In Marrakech, he met Malika, a renowned high-class prostitute, "the most beautiful creature of color" he'd ever seen. He was taken by "the flickering flames, the tinkling bells, the shouting showmen, the smell of smoke" of Casablanca. He posed for a photograph with Iola the Coca-Cola lion, who rode as a mascot on a Kenyan delivery truck. In Cairo, Harrold socialized with King Farouk, who told him dirty jokes.

"How did you ever get here?" the man from Americus, Georgia, frequently asked himself. The answer, of course, was Coca-Cola, the former patent medicine, now seasoned world traveler. Spurred by foreign growth, sales volume soared. While it took until 1944 to sell the first billion gallons of Coca-Cola syrup, the second billion had gurgled down thirsty throats by 1953.

THE LIMITS OF CIVILIZATION

Coca-Cola men loved to point out that wherever they went, they boosted the beverage market for *everyone*. Once local competitors were faced with Coke's sampling and advertising campaigns, they usually rose to the challenge, resulting in a more competitive but larger market. People drank less water and milk, lured by sugary drinks. In fact, one Coca-Cola president bragged in the 1950s that Coke was often imbibed by people who had never drunk milk.

Unfortunately for the Coke men, Pepsi representatives could attest that Coca-Cola did indeed open up attractive new markets. Following on the leader's heels, Pepsi salesmen soon claimed an alarming share of the market, particularly in poor areas such as Egypt, Thailand, Mexico, and the Philippines, where the sweeter, bigger drink made heavy inroads. Nonetheless, in 1950, Coca-Cola enjoyed a 5-to-1 worldwide dominion over Pepsi. As in the United States, Pepsi suffered from a downscale image. It was, according to one Coca-Cola representative, "like the difference between an orchid and a bunch of wild daisies."

By the early fifties, travelers couldn't avoid the cheery red Coke signs, which appeared, as one British writer put it, "like a measles rash over scores of countries." While Coke men might not like the analogy, they appreciated the thought. "No matter where one goes, cool, refreshing Coca-Cola is near at hand," a Company publication crowed. "No other soft drink has ever enjoyed such world-wide popularity. None has been so enthusiastically accepted by so many different races in so many different climes." As proof, Company officials loved to tell the story of the Mexican Indian who had never heard of World War II but broke into a grin at the mention of the soft drink. "*Sí, sí, Cola-Cola es perfecto, es magnifico!*" he exclaimed.

Halfway around the world, an American traveling across the Sahara asked his driver when they would leave civilization behind. The native asked for a definition of the term. "Well, when will we reach the point where there won't be any Coca-Cola?" The driver shrugged. "Never," he answered, pointing to a billboard emerging from behind the next sand dune.

～ 15 ～

Breaking the Commandments

Any change, even a change for the better, is always accompanied by drawbacks and discomforts.

—Arnold Bennett

It may be mere sentimentalism, but there are some of us who can never see an old way of doing things passing without regret.

—Robert Lynd

AT THE ONSET of the fifties, Robert Woodruff exercised unprecedented power on the local, state, and national level. Known affectionately by employees as the Old Man, he was a vigorous sixty years old in 1950, reveling in his established life-style. Woodruff's tenure as president had lasted only briefly when Arthur Acklin fell apart in 1945. The next year, the Boss appointed Bill Hobbs, a former government functionary, as his chief executive. Freed of day-to-day responsibility, Woodruff resumed his comfortable nomadic existence, hunting quail at Ichauway in the fall and winter and stalking big game at his Wyoming ranch during the summer. He visited Europe once a year, usually finding time to golf at Scotland's Gleneagles. In between, he nested briefly at his Atlanta and New York homes. Woodruff often hit New York bars with singer Morton Downey, who served as a kind of court jester there and at Ichauway. The Boss put away an astonishing amount of Scotch without any apparent effect on his athletic constitution.

Everywhere he went, Woodruff conducted business, facilitated by an eager staff who jumped at his every command. His Man Friday from 1943 until the end of Woodruff's life was Joseph W. Jones, a quiet, tactful Delaware native who arranged the Woodruff itinerary, bought his custom-made clothing and cigars, handled correspondence, and served as gatekeeper to the Boss. Joe Jones' work was unremittingly demanding, a twenty-four-hour-a-day, seven-day-a-week project without vacation. As Woodruff's virtual slave, Jones lost two wives, but he remained the faithful retainer to the end.

Woodruff's power base unquestionably lay in Atlanta, where the Coca-Cola magnate's influence was subtly omnipotent. When Woodruff got an idea, "you can depend upon it, others will get the idea," lawyer Hughes Spalding explained in 1950, because the Boss would summon a few of the inner circle and tersely introduce it, sometimes at 3 A.M., when the restless Woodruff often had his brainstorms. "We do not engage in loose talk about ideals and all that other stuff. We get right down to the problem. All of us are assigned tasks to carry out." Spalding amiably admitted that, like many others, he was a "stooge" for The Coca-Cola Company. "I guess I'm a *top* stooge," he said. "When Mr Woodruff wants something done, and if I can possibly do it, I do it!"[*]

Similarly, Mayor Bill Hartsfield, who first worked with Woodruff at the fire extinguisher company, told an interviewer that "I never made a major decision, that I didn't consult Bob Woodruff." The mayor periodically hunted as an Ichauway guest and kept a prominently framed picture of Woodruff in his office. He invariably offered visitors a Coke as his first gesture of Southern hospitality. Without any apparent anxiety over conflict of interest, Hartsfield accepted a $6,000 annual retainer from The Coca-Cola Company while he served as mayor.

In sociologist Floyd Hunter's classic 1950 "sociogram" of the Atlanta power structure, Hartsfield and Spalding nested obviously in the center, while Woodruff, hovering to the side, was attached by strategic lines to important points, like a spider monitoring its web from the fringes. "The actions of the top leaders who may attend meetings of the lower echelons are watched with acute attention," Hunter wrote. "Even grunts of disapproval are carefully recorded." In fact, as Woodruff grew older, he seldom spoke, and his minions became adept at deciphering his rumblings, which could either indicate approval, indecision, or absolute disagreement, depending on their inflection.

By this time, Woodruff had added two other soubriquets to his nicknames. At meetings, he was sometimes called "the Consensus," ever since one memorable moment when the Coca-Cola board had convened, only to find that Woodruff was absent. The chairman had banged his gavel and declared, "This meeting is cancelled for lack of a quorum." In Georgia, Woodruff was also known as "Mr Anonymous," since his enormous gifts to Emory University, cancer research, and other charities were never attributed to him—partly because Woodruff was genuinely reclusive, but mostly to avoid beggars. In 1941, Ralph McGill wrote an article on his friend Woodruff for *The Saturday Evening Post*, entitled, "The Multimillionaire Nobody Knows." The Boss was annoyed, since it prompted an onslaught of money requests.

The Atlanta realm over which Woodruff ruled in 1950 featured a meticulously balanced, graciously administered, smoothly functioning "old boy" network. Nonetheless, there were signs of friction. Floyd Hunter was dismayed to find that no blacks were part of the official Atlanta power structure, though he could construct a separate (but unequal) sociogram for them. When Hunter interviewed Benjamin Mays, the distinguished black president of Morehouse College, the educator told him that "the first thing I

---

[*] Robert Woodruff sometimes abused his extraordinary power. When he was annoyed with one of his managers, he might summon him to Atlanta, keep him waiting for a week, then summarily fire him. When Woodruff decided that Bill Hobbs was not an effective president, he let him know in the rudest possible manner—one Monday morning, Hobbs found his office door locked and was informed that his possessions would be sent to his home. Woodruff could be, as one source put it, "ruthless as hell."

can remember is a white mob looking for a Negro to lynch." Significantly, Hughes Spalding called segregation *the* major issue facing Atlanta. The 2,000 annual Atlanta black college applicants were shunted North. "Maybe it is not what the Negroes want," Spalding said, "but it is what they are going to get!"

Woodruff wasn't involved with such petty details of Atlanta life, however, but rather devoted his energy to a national and international vision, informing Hunter that he wanted to "put Atlanta in the center of the world." In reality, of course, the Boss himself resided at the hub of the action. "How is policy really developed?" Hunter asked him. "Is it made in board rooms, or where?" Unblinkingly, Woodruff told him, "It's made wherever I am. I may be at Ichauway, on a boat, anyplace I call it." Alexander Makinsky once compared Woodruff to a Russian Czar who, when asked to identify the important people in his court, replied that "they're the people to whom I talk—and only while I'm talking to them."

THE BOSS LIKES IKE

One indication of Woodruff's awesome power, which reached well beyond Georgia, was a casual remark he made to Floyd Hunter in 1950 when the sociologist asked why General Eisenhower's picture hung on the wall. "Some of us want to see him made president," Woodruff said. "We sent him overseas to give him an international flair, then we made him the president of Columbia so the eggheads would like him." No one had decided just yet, Woodruff concluded, whether Eisenhower should run as a Democrat or a Republican.

The popular general had resisted a movement to draft him as a candidate in 1948, but by 1952, he had been thoroughly prepared by his "gang," as he called them—a group of calculating, high-powered businessmen, all of whom played golf with Ike at Augusta National.[*] Aside from his demonstrated wartime fondness for Coca-Cola, Eisenhower had other qualities that endeared him to Woodruff and his cronies. For one thing, he wasn't a business-bashing New Dealer. Instead, Ike genuinely believed in the partnership of free enterprise and moderate government. He was also the perfect leader to calm the country's postwar anti-Communist jitters and usher in a decade of good feeling and conspicuous consumption.

An astute investor as well as military man, Eisenhower kept close tabs on his portfolio. In October of 1951, for instance, he wrote from Paris to Cliff Roberts, his (and Woodruff's) financial adviser, asking whether he should consider moving some bonds into stocks because of increased inflation. By that time, the general and his son had invested in the Joroberts Corporation, which owned Coca-Coca bottling plants in South America. Morton Hodgson, who managed the plants from his Montevideo office, invited Eisenhower to

---

[*] Eisenhower and Woodruff were close enough friends for Ike to twit the Boss about his golf game. When the two were playing as partners one day, someone asked Eisenhower what his handicap was. "Woodruff," he promptly responded.

Uruguay to see the Coke operations in person, and though Ike never ventured there, as President he routinely sent aides to assess the progress of his South American Coca-Cola plants.

For the Coca-Cola executives, Eisenhower was the perfect antidote to Franklin Roosevelt's legacy. Ike believed in "reasonable protection for American industry," declaring that an explicit purpose of foreign policy should be the encouragement of a hospitable climate for U.S. investment abroad. Not only that, he emerged from World War II as a popular symbol on a par with Coca-Cola, with a boyish grin that was a public relations man's dream. "Ike, with that puss you can't miss being President," one of his friends told him. With Woodruff and his gang behind the popular candidate, his election was assured. Eisenhower's presentation to the public was as carefully packaged as a bottle of Coca-Cola. Ike appeared as a somewhat naive, straightforward guy, not really a politician, but representing all of the American virtues. In reality, Eisenhower carefully calculated every move he made. "Frankly," he wrote to Cliff Roberts, "my discard of manuscript at Detroit was on the unanimous advice of everybody around me" in order to produce "an atmosphere of complete spontaneity."

In 1952, Eisenhower was elected in a landslide, and Robert Woodruff had placed an intimate friend in the White House. As a benign, ironic gesture, Woodruff now prefaced letters to the president with "Dear Boss," but there was never much question about who was really the dominant character. During the fifties, Eisenhower hunted with Woodruff several times at Ichauway, as well as joining him for lunch or golf elsewhere. In 1959, Woodruff scolded Eisenhower for a photo in which the President sipped from a Coke bottle through a straw—a sissy way to imbibe. Ike responded that "when I tip up a bottle of Coca-Cola for a good drink it lasts only seconds—with a straw, a lot of talk and more walking, I was able to contact more photographers and newspaper correspondents."

FIGHTING FOR THE NICKEL COKE

Despite Woodruff's immense influence and a Coca-Cola investor in the White House, the fifties brought a maze of woes for the soft drink company and its bottlers, starting with postwar inflation. The United States had spent its way out of the Depression during World War II, and many economists expected a postwar recession once the war ended. They were wrong. Instead, Americans released their pent-up savings in an orgy of spending. Besides, the war never really ended, since the Korean conflict soon flared. Even when that war was over, the arms race with the Soviet Union resulted in an ever-increasing defense budget. In 1945, America began a steady inflationary spiral that would cut the value of the dollar in half by 1970.

At first, increased costs worked in favor of the Coca-Cola bottler, since they played with a bigger profit margin than their Pepsi and Royal Crown counterparts, who were trying to eke out a living while selling their twelve-ounce drinks for a nickel. Within two years of the war's end, Walter Mack had to modify his popular jingle to "twice as much for a penny more," since Pepsi bottlers could no longer afford to sell their drink for a nickel. Some bottlers raised the price to 6 cents, 7 cents, or a dime, while others reduced the bottle size to ten or eight ounces. Chaos reigned. A new slogan promising "more bounce to the ounce" didn't help. Pepsi's profits plunged from over $6 million in 1946 to just over $2 million in 1949. During the same period, its stock dived from $40 to $8 a share.

Meanwhile, Robert Woodruff was determined to hold the traditional 5-cent price, even when exorbitant sugar costs triggered the 1921 Consent Decree's automatic jump in syrup cost to the parent and actual bottlers. The 5-cent Coke had become, as Woodruff's crony Ralph Hayes put it, "a national expectation and an American institution," and neither he nor the Boss sanctioned deviation from the sacred price. Hayes noted that with the proper "evangelical zeal" any potential backsliders might be held in check.

Of course, Company men could easily toe the line, since it was the bottler who actually felt the low retail price's squeeze. In 1950, Coca-Cola accounted for half of all U.S. soft drink sales, and those associated with the drink were accustomed to the good life. "Coke bottlers," commented a financial journalist, "have had two Cadillacs in their own and their children's garages for so long that they think their rights are being trifled with when the profits don't just roll in." By 1950, inflationary pressures had intensified, and many Coca-Cola bottlers nudged their wholesale prices above the traditional 80 cents per carton. In turn, most retailers in the area then bumped prices above a nickel for a bottle.

While the situation was merely uncomfortable for Coke bottlers, it was killing the opposition. The soft drink trade journals clamored for Coca-Cola to let go of the nickel price, hailing every defection with loud hurrahs. An executive for Bireley's Bottling Company plaintively begged Coca-Cola for "some relief" for "those who would like to stay in business." The situation grew so desperate that some competing brands actually lobbied in favor of state soft drink taxes, which would force even Coke bottlers to abandon the nickel.

Dr Pepper tried a different tactic, suing Coca-Cola in 1951 for $750,000 damages for "restraint of trade," accusing the soft drink giant of monopolizing the market. The rival drink company claimed that Coke threatened to cut off supply to retailers who sold for over a nickel. At the same time, a Senate committee investigating the "Crisis in the Soft Drink Bottling Industry" accused Coca-Cola of the same ploy, asserting that Company officials should "release their stranglehold on the industry and let bottlers set their own price on a competitive basis." The media and general public rallied to the nickel drink's support, however. "It is true that the price of nearly everything has gone up," wrote an editor for the *Pittsburgh Post-Gazette*, "but should this company be penalized if its bottlers can still undersell their competitors?" Coca-Cola deserved "a medal instead of a lawsuit," he concluded.

The abandonment of the nickel price was inevitable, however, as the Chicago sales representative recognized when he beseeched the Company not to add a huge neon "5¢" to the local Spectacular. As costs of labor, transportation, energy, bottles, and ingredients rose steadily throughout the fifties, even the die-hard bottlers were forced to disregard the Boss. By the beginning of 1951, the Company ceased mentioning the 5-cent price in national ads, and by mid-decade, the nickel drink was all but dead.

As Woodruff attempted to hold the line on price, Coke stock fell for the first time in years, and a few disgruntled bottlers felt that the Boss had lost his leadership ability. Veazey Rainwater, Jr., planned a daring insurrection in April of 1951. Renting a huge hall in Florida, he invited major bottlers and other stockholders to a banquet to plot strategy. His father, getting wind of Junior's efforts, sent telegrams urgently advising bottlers *not* to go. The next day, only one curious stockholder appeared, and Veazey Jr.'s abortive coup attempt flopped.

PARABLE OF THE NEW SHOES

The price debacle was the first in a string of unwanted changes forced on Woodruff. The Coca-Cola magnate had led the Company with uncanny brilliance through the Roaring Twenties, the depths of the Depression, and a tumultuous world war by adhering to several simple iron-clad principles. Coca-Cola was the greatest soft drink in the world. No human market should remain untapped. The 6.5-ounce hobbleskirt bottle for 5 cents offered the drink in the perfect container at the optimal price. With quality control, efficient distribution, and massive advertising, everyone associated with the drink would make more and more money. There was no need to market any other drink. There was no need to diversify into other businesses.

Although he guarded against it, Woodruff was a victim of his own success. "Flattery is like chewing tobacco," Woodruff liked to say. "It tastes sweet, is very satisfying, and does no harm unless you swallow it." Inevitably, however, the Boss was surrounded by toadies who, as Ralph Hayes put it, chanted "an everlasting litany" of "yessir, yessir, thatsrightsir, yousaiditsir." Lawyer Hughes Spalding, for instance, told Woodruff that "more depends on you than any other man in the Southeast." Woodruff naturally assumed that he was infallible. In addition, the sentimental Coca-Cola man hated change. He saved knickknacks to such an extent that his office resembled a rummage sale. Once Woodruff found the right way to do something, he stuck to it unless absolutely compelled to do otherwise. Joe Jones illustrated the point with the story of Woodruff's hand-tooled British shoes. The Boss complained that a new pair didn't fit as well as the old ones, which he had worn for twenty-five years. "Well, Mr Woodruff," Jones said, "you wear these new ones for twenty-five years and then we'll return them if you don't like them."

While Woodruff may have been forced to admit defeat over the drink's price, that seemed a small matter compared with the beloved little bottle that fit the hand so neatly. In 1948, Cecil Barbee, the oldest of the California bottling brothers, shocked his fellow Coca-Cola men at a convention by directly defying Woodruff. "Men," he said, holding up a brown parcel, "I have here the answer to all our troubles." As he spoke, he removed layer after layer of paper, finally holding up a specially made carton of twelve-ounce hobbleskirt bottles. It took more than a renegade bottler to change Woodruff's mind, though. In the end, that job fell to a traitorous Coca-Cola executive named Alfred N. Steele.

PALLY STEELE'S CIRCUS

Steele, a D'Arcy advertising man, joined The Coca-Cola Company in 1945 at the age of forty-three as vice-president in charge of bottler sales. A large man with tortoiseshell glasses and wavy iron-gray hair—a younger, less profane version of Harrison Jones—Steele brimmed with energy and big ideas. "Call me Al," he bountifully ordered subordinates, whom he routinely accosted with "Hey, Handsome," or "Let's try this out, Pally," accompanied by a robust slap on the back. Consequently, he himself soon earned the nickname of Pally Steele.

The new Coca-Cola salesman had once run a circus, where his favorite act had not been the trapeze artists or lion tamers, but the sideshow barkers. Like them, he could "talk the horns off a brass bull," as Delony Sledge, Coke's advertising director, put it. He could also outspend anyone else at the Company. In 1948, Steele went all-out to create the most elaborate pep skit ever seen at a bottlers' convention. Unfortunately, the sound system failed, and the drama flopped as actors flailed and jumped about without being heard, while bottlers tittered nervously.

Steele's personality irritated Woodruff, but the Boss could have tolerated the flamboyant salesman's excesses if they had yielded results. Unfortunately, this disastrous convention was soon followed by an unforgivable incident at the Atlanta Biltmore. Steele, unhappily married for the second time, brought a call girl with him to Atlanta and had her publicly paged as Mrs. Steele. Word of this behavior reached the Boss. Typically Southern, the Coca-Cola moral code forgave adultery but punished anyone stupid enough to get caught, and Steele soon found himself in a new office, Woodruff's version of Siberia—no mail, no phone calls, no meetings, no responsibilities. The Boss disliked firing his people, but he didn't mind humiliating and boring them into quitting. For a man like Steele, who could never sit still behind a desk anyway, such treatment was torture. In 1949, he joined Pepsi as a vice-president under Walter Mack. Along with him, he took a group of daring Coke men who believed Steele when he told them that at Pepsi they wouldn't be stifled by tradition—and it didn't hurt that he doubled their Coca-Cola salary.

But Walter Mack wasn't ready to relinquish power to Steele, and he had his own traditions—promoting square dances, sky-writing, and art exhibits while his demoralized bottlers were bailing out in droves. Steele informed the Pepsi board that he would quit unless he was given complete control of the company. Consequently, at a dramatic March 1, 1950, board meeting Mack was booted upstairs as board chairman, and Al Steele became president of the Pepsi-Cola Company. Mack quit a few months later.

Pepsi, Steele recognized, was plagued by its past image as a lot of drink for little money—oversweet bellywash for kids and poor people. In the South, racist whites considered it a "nigger drink," and even in the rest of the country people preferred to pour Pepsi into glasses and serve it as Coke. Steele recognized the need, as he put it, to get Pepsi out of the kitchen and into the living room. To revitalize the drink's advertising, he lured his old friend John Toigo away from D'Arcy and installed him at Pepsi's agency, the Biow Company. At the same time, Steele's chemists reformulated the drink, lowering the sugar content to approach Coca-Cola's tartness.

In the calorie-conscious fifties, Toigo touted Pepsi as "the Light Refreshment" which would "refresh without filling." Svelte socialites drank from the bottle, redesigned with elegant swirls. On television, the new American craze, classy Faye Emerson hosted a fifteen-minute Pepsi show, leaning in her low-cut dress over iced bottles. When Al Steele saw that the studio was using a plain container, he rushed to Tiffany's, bought an ornate silver champagne cooler, and placed it in the shot. "Pepsi-Cola's up to date / With modern folks who watch their weight," perky Polly Bergen sang in TV spots.

At the same time, Steele penetrated the vending market, which Mack had abandoned to Coke because the twelve-ounce bottle wouldn't fit the standard machine. It was clearly impossible to hold the line on a 5-cent drink in the big container anyway, so he created an eight-ounce bottle (still offering more for the money than the tiny Coke) which fit vending machines. He then arranged low-interest loans for the machines with payment to begin six months after purchase. That way, poorer bottlers could buy the $1,000 units on credit and pay for them out of profits. He also spearheaded paper cup vendors, correctly surmising that Coke bottlers, trapped by their own history and contract, wouldn't compete, since they could not use fountain syrup.

The flamboyant Steele knew that none of his innovations would matter unless he could instill new confidence and pride in his bottlers. Undeterred by his disastrous experience at the 1948 Coke convention, he threw huge bashes for Pepsi franchisees, urging them to plow money back into their businesses and local advertising. "You can conserve yourself into bankruptcy," he told them, "or you can spend your way into prosperity." Steele demonstrated his belief in this maxim by plunking down a cool $6 million for 1952 advertising. He assigned his right-hand man, Herb Barnet, to copy Coca-Cola tactics—insisting on quality control, standardized blue uniforms, shelves of procedural manuals, and military organization. Steele built a coterie of managers in his own image. "The whole trick in hiring executives," he told a subordinate, "is to find a good man and turn him into a prick. A good man will be able to stand the course, but if the guy was a prick to begin with, he'll crumble along the way."

Steele's charismatic exhortations also inspired his syrup salesmen. "I don't care if the consumer wants carbonated sweat in a goatskin pouch," he told them. "If so, this side of the room go looking for goats and this side start running fiercely in place." Pepsi men targeted twenty-five metropolitan areas for particularly heavy sales efforts. Spending $13 million, Steele bought out key Pepsi bottlers who were failing to push the product and installed his own men. Unlike Coca-Cola, which had sold most of its ailing Company-owned plants after World War II, Pepsi's directly managed plants turned a profit quickly. Steele even dared to invade the fortress of Coca-Cola's virtual monopoly on the fountain trade. For $30,000, he placed Pepsi in 600 Fox theater outlets on the West Coast. Finally, leaving the domestic business in Barnet's hands, Steele commenced globe-hopping to jump-start the Pepsi trade overseas.

The radical Pepsi overhaul proved incredibly effective. As Coke's Delony Sledge put it, Pepsi's sales jumped "like a scalded cat." In less than five years, Coke's worldwide lead dwindled from 5-to-1 to 3-to-1, with Pepsi's share of the domestic cola market rising from 21 percent to 35 percent. Even in Atlanta, the Mecca of Coca-Cola, Pepsi's sales increased 30 percent a year. Al Steele, back in his competitor's hometown to open a new Pepsi bottling plant, had the gall to inform Atlanta journalists that Coca-Cola was not Pepsi's biggest competitor—tea and coffee were. Rubbing salt into the wound, he added, "It's a tribute to The Coca-Cola Company that a number of its former employees are on the management team that is helping Pepsi-Cola move up."

COCA-COLA ENTERS THE TELEVISION AGE

While Pepsi roared to life under the direction of Al Steele, a Coca-Cola shareholder wrote that the Company "slumbers peacefully, self-satisfied with all of its past progress." Coke's public relations consultant compared Coke to a frumpish housewife, "modest, sedate, pretty for a long time," while Pepsi was the Marilyn Monroe of the business. "Lots of people think she's too common. But they look—and a lot who won't even admit it want to feel." Momentarily rising above his "stooge" role, Hughes Spalding was also alarmed, writing to Woodruff that his executive board was aging. "Pardon me for saying so," he wrote, "but I just have a hunch that when a fellow has his prostate removed he has lost his ambition, certainly in some respects." Coca-Cola was, in some ways, growing old and fat, just as Woodruff had feared. Bottling plants were celebrating their fiftieth anniversaries; many of the third-generation bottlers took profits for granted. They lacked the fire in the belly that characterized their hungry Pepsi counterparts, and they hated change as much as Woodruff.

During the early fifties, The Coca-Cola Company could hardly be accused of standing still, however. Aware that television was revolutionizing home entertainment even more than radio had in the thirties, Coca-Cola sponsored a 1950 Thanksgiving special in which the Company's radio stars, Edgar Bergen and his dummy, Charlie McCarthy, debuted on TV. The dummy amused audiences by complaining about the wooden nickels he received as pay, demanding real money so he could buy Coca-Cola. A month later, Bergen also starred in a Christmas Day special, *One Hour in Wonderland*, which marked the first association of Coke with Walt Disney's animated characters. Later in the decade, Coca-Cola sponsored *The Mickey Mouse Club*.

The advent of television steadily changed America's leisure habits, along with other trends of the 1950s. Soda fountains at the local drugstore went into a long, slow decline, as people clustered around the TV set instead of gathering in public places. The take-home market, where Pepsi was scoring its greatest gains, now accounted for two-thirds of all soft drink sales. To worsen matters, the corner grocery stores where Coca-Cola was so well entrenched folded as chain supermarkets sprouted in the young suburbs.

While the Company had always targeted children, they now had an added incentive because of the postwar baby boom. *The Adventures of Kit Carson*, starring clean-cut, well-spoken Bill Williams—the star never uttered "He went that-a-way"—lit the TV screen in 1951. Delony Sledge, the Company's in-house advertising chief, studied demographic figures closely, though his attitude toward life and death was somewhat skewed by his devotion to Coca-Cola. "In 1951," Sledge told one audience, "1,535,406 people died in the United States. In spite of our best efforts, this large group has been eliminated as consumers of our product." Fortunately, he observed, almost 4 million potential Coke guzzlers had been born during the same year.

Sledge recognized that Coca-Cola advertising had to reach virtually every consumer group. "Our product appeals to the entire population without consideration for race, color, economic status, geographical location or religious preference," he said. "We believe to the depths of our collective hearts that Coca-Cola is the best beverage buy in the world. Our work is a religion rather than a business." Consequently, "anybody, anytime, anywhere, is a fruitful prospect for Coca-Cola." The trouble with such a messianic, universal approach, Sledge noted ruefully, was that it made specific campaigns aimed at particular consumer groups impossible. The Company continually searched for a spokesperson to appeal to all age groups. In 1953, with Eddie Fisher, they thought they had found him.

Twice a week, the twenty-four-year-old Fisher sang hits such as "Oh! My Papa" and "I'm Walking Behind You" to adoring living room audiences composed of toddlers to grandparents. The boyish crooner had "the sort of face that middle-aged ladies want to put through college," according to one critic, but his artfully tousled hair particularly appealed to the bobby-soxers, who were "swooning for Eddie, not Frankie"—and who were an increasingly distinct market for soft drinks and other consumer products. On *Coke Time*, Fisher personally praised Coca-Cola in soft-sell commercials. His handsome likeness appeared in life-size cardboard cutouts, holding out the hobbleskirt bottle and coaxing shoppers to "Have a Coke." In drugstores across America, teenagers began to order "Eddie Fishers" when they wanted a Coke. No one knew that Fisher's effervescent personality was fueled not only by Coca-Cola—he really did drink 20 Cokes a day—but by hypodermic shots of vitamins and amphetamines, administered by Dr. Max Jacobson, otherwise known as Miracle Max, Dr. Needles, or Dr. Feelgood.[*]

---

[*] Jacobson turned many celebrities and politicians into speed freaks, including Alan Jay Lerner, Tennessee Williams, Yul Brynner, Zero Mostel, Nelson Rockefeller, and Marlene Dietrich. Eddie Fisher later met President John Kennedy, another Jacobson addict. Kennedy didn't question what was in the shots. "I don't care if there's panther piss in there," he said, "as long as it makes me feel good."

Like Morton Downey, the Irish tenor who had just retired from his professional career in order to devote the rest of his life to Coca-Cola, Fisher and his new wife, Debbie Reynolds, attended Company conventions as part of the Coca-Cola family. In 1955, they spent their honeymoon at an Atlanta bottlers' convention, where fresh-faced Debbie Reynolds, holding her new husband's hand, stepped to the microphone and announced, "I don't drink Coke. It's bad for your teeth. I drink milk." And she smiled beatifically. After a moment of stunned silence, the bottlers burst into laughter. They thought Reynolds was just being funny. It was inconceivable to them that anyone would seriously make such a statement in such a place. (She was serious, and she didn't like Fisher's amphetamine addiction either. They divorced a few years later, after Fisher's Coke contract ran out and in the wake of his affair with Elizabeth Taylor.)

Nor did Coca-Cola's Hollywood agents neglect the movies, though it was no longer simply a matter of supplying the back lots with soft drinks. Now a "buried plug," as it was called, cost $250 per mention for most companies. To avoid such expense, Coca-Cola arranged for payment through "reciprocal publicity," as with the 1950 film, *Destination Moon*, which featured four astronauts drinking Coca-Cola in their spaceship.

Such efforts were augmented with all of the traditional point-of-purchase advertising, blanket distribution, local bottler under-the-crown promotions, and the numerous other ploys familiar by that time. Nonetheless, Coca-Cola's share of the market slowly eroded in the early 1950s, while the share price tumbled from a high of $200 in 1946 to $109 in 1952. That year, Woodruff fired Bill Hobbs, a sort of Millard Fillmore president who never made much of a mark. Rumor had it that he tried to assert his independence of Woodruff, which was a cardinal sin.[*] In his place, Woodruff placed Burke Nicholson, a dedicated, lifelong Coca-Cola executive who had overseen the Export Corporation. Woodruff never took Nicholson seriously as a president, however, regarding him as an interim caretaker.

KING-SIZE HEADACHES CALL FOR KING-SIZE SOLUTIONS

"Coca-Cola can hardly be said to be foundering," reported one Wall Street analyst in 1955. "Yet it is faltering." It seemed obvious to almost everyone except Robert Woodruff that "the only thing wrong with Coca-Cola is Pepsi-Cola," as a veteran observer pointedly remarked. For the first time, Coca-Cola's primacy as the leading soft drink was challenged, and until Coke matched Pepsi ounce for ounce and penny for penny, the gap between the two

---

[*] One night at dinner in New York, a top executive told Woodruff that the only job that might attract him would be the presidency of The Coca-Cola Company. "You're hired," the Boss said. Later in the evening, Woodruff asked him how he planned to run the Company. "With an iron hand," his friend answered. "I'll take the burden off your shoulders. I'll make the decisions and call all the shots." Deadpan, Woodruff said, "You're fired."

would continue to narrow. Lee Talley, the short, freckle-faced Alabama boy who had joined the Company in 1923 and now ran the Export company, confronted the Boss in the fall of 1954. "Mr Woodruff," he said, "I've never been on the losing side of a business in my life, and I'm not going to start now. Unless you allow me to increase the bottle size, you'll have to accept my resignation." The next day, Woodruff succumbed to the inevitable. While he wouldn't officially grant his permission, he didn't withhold it.

News of Coke's plans to test-market larger sizes in the U.S. rocked the industry. While the soft drink giant had troubles, it still dominated, accounting for 40 percent of domestic soft drink consumption. Digesting the "awesome scope and ramifications" of Coke's decision, a trade journal editor noted, competitors registered "a maximum of interest, anxiety, speculation, and . . . trepidation," and they were not alone. Although many Coke bottlers had been howling for a larger container, others resisted the change, which meant massive capital investment in new equipment. Besides, the emotional attachment to the diminutive standard bottle was overwhelming. "Bringing out another bottle," Ed Forio noted, "was like being unfaithful to your wife."

The plans for test-marketing couldn't come soon enough for Lee Talley, who desperately wanted a bigger bottle overseas, too. At the beginning of 1955, the Export head spelled out his troubles around the world in a long memo to the board of directors. In the Philippines, where Coke bottlers were "very aggressive," sales had still declined by 40 percent over the previous year. The same was true in Thailand, while Egypt was experiencing a "long downward trend." The only real bright spot was Europe. The fault, Talley said, lay in "our dark, scuffed little bottle," which made "a miserably bad showing" alongside the bigger, brighter Pepsi bottles on shelves around the world. Coke needed an applied color label like its competitor, he said. And most important, it must have a twelve-ounce bottle.

In February, Coke test-marketed a twenty-six-ounce Family Size and two nearly identical King Size bottles of ten and twelve ounces, all in the familiar hobbleskirt design. The package suited the times, as Americans reveled in oversized cars and consumption. Coca-Cola executives insisted that research indicated "the majority of the public prefer the standard size bottle"; they were offering alternative sizes only for "group refreshment in the home." Pepsi knew better, jubilantly taking out ads declaring, "It's fun to be followed—to be recognized as the leader." While the 6.5-ounce bottle indeed constituted the majority of sales for a few years, the shift to larger sizes was inexorable. By 1958, King Size Coke was available to 81 percent of the U.S. population, though the traditional small bottle still accounted for 80 percent of Coke sales.

Pepsi responded to Coke's King Size drink by attacking with a 6.5-ounce size, but they had little chance in such familiar Coca-Cola territory. Now on the offensive, Coke men got wind of competitive launches, flooding the markets to prevent the new Pepsi size from gaining cooler space. In the United States as well as in foreign markets, the cola wars became intense by the late fifties. Coca-Cola men obsessively spied on Pepsi and its plans; the Coke archives are filled with reports on the Imitator's conventions, telephone polls, and Nielsen market ratings of the period.

The decision to change the bottle size opened the floodgates of change. In his message to the Export board, Lee Talley recommended a "second line of products" because his bottlers were "finding it difficult to keep their businesses going on Coca-Cola alone." Consequently, he sought permission to resurrect the Fanta trademark, which Max Keith had providentially registered in several Nazi-controlled countries during World War II. In April of 1955, Fanta Orange was introduced in Italy, but Woodruff resisted offering "rainbow flavors" in the U.S. "Competition has successfully used the multi-flavor approach to take exclusive accounts from us," wrote a harried Coke executive to the Boss in 1957, "and the trend is increasing." The next year, Woodruff authorized the test-marketing of a whole new line of Fanta flavors for the U.S., finally providing other Company drinks for vending machines.

At the same time, "pre-mix" Coca-Cola was introduced, precipitating a crisis between the Company and bottlers. In large stainless-steel containers, Coke syrup was mixed with carbonated water. The pre-mix machines were useful at small fountain outlets, baseball games, and other special events, where salesmen with modified backpacks could dispense individual drinks. Recognizing the bottlers' superior distribution system, the Company allowed them to handle pre-mix, but created a special "B-X" syrup and charged 10 cents a gallon more for it than regular bottlers' syrup. Company officials admitted that the B-X cost them exactly the same to produce. The price differential resulted, Lee Talley wrote, because they were "free to negotiate on this" and could finally escape the dead weight of the old contract. Minneapolis bottler Tom Moore sued the Company over the pre-mix issue, claiming with some justice that the original contract applied to all bottled, carbonated Coca-Cola, regardless of its size. The large stainless steel container was, in effect, a huge bottle. Afraid that he would lose his suit, Moore finally settled out of court. Al Steele and his Pepsi men were, of course, delighted with the internecine strife, thankful that they were not saddled with the cumbersome contract which continued to plague Coca-Cola.

The rise of national supermarket chains also caused friction between the Company and bottlers. In order to combat Pepsi, the Company's national sales representatives often offered price incentives to a store without first consulting the local bottler. "Every man that called on national accounts wasn't an angel," one Coke man recalls, "and they did whatever they had to do." As a result, the autonomous franchise owners fumed, chafing under Atlanta's high-handed supervision. At the same time, Coke abolished the antiquated parent bottler organization—at least the portion under Company control. Woodruff had already bought all but the Thomas Company, and now he eliminated the extra layer of bureaucracy, replacing it with the "Bottle Sales" department. Unfortunately, the Thomas Company, which covered 40 percent of the United States population, remained stubbornly independent. When Woodruff encouraged his executive and friend DeSales Harrison to assume control of the parent bottler in 1941, the Boss had expected his troubles to be over. After George Hunter died in 1950, however, Harrison refused to sell; he had come to enjoy his kingdom, and Company representatives who set foot in Thomas territory without permission were in dire trouble.

THE ROBINSON REGIME

During the same February of 1955 that King Size Coke was introduced, Robert Woodruff announced the appointment of Eisenhower's friend Bill Robinson as the new president of The Coca-Cola Company. Loyal Company men were shocked. A rank outsider, a marketing and public relations man, Robinson had very limited experience with Coca-Cola and was—God forbid—a Yankee. Not only that, but Woodruff apparently intended to give Robinson real power. Just turned sixty-five, Woodruff officially retired, assuming the chair of the newly created Finance Committee. Later in the year, Woodruff also brought in Curt Gager from General Foods as first lieutenant. Robinson and Gager, working primarily from Coke's New York offices, made a formidable team. The new president at least conformed to the Coca-Cola mold: a big, bluff, red-faced promoter, he valiantly tried to adjust himself to the prevailing culture, touring the country to meet skeptical bottlers. Gager, on the other hand, was a small ferretlike man who spoke a strange new bottom-line language. Worse, he was rumored to have been a hatchet man at General Foods.

About the same time Gager came on board, Robinson switched ad agencies, curtailing the long-standing D'Arcy relationship in favor of McCann-Erickson, a bigger, more sophisticated New York outfit with worldwide offices—in fact, McCann had already produced Coke's South American programs. The agency switch symbolized the formal end of the gracious golden age of Coca-Cola advertising. Its poet, Archie Lee, had died in 1950, and now the new agency abruptly abandoned the classic oil paintings of Haddon Sundblom and Norman Rockwell in favor of color photography highlighting socialites and glistening King Size Coke bottles. A "devil-ridden" workaholic and fierce devotee of social science research, McCann's Marion Harper, Jr., brought a contemporary "scientific" bent to Coca-Cola commercials. Harper assigned Murray Hillman to work with Curt Gager, jettisoning old dogma in an all-out effort to reverse the Pepsi gains.

The $15 million ad campaign actually bore a noticeable resemblance to Steele's efforts, relying on the same upper-crust appeal to young moderns. Layouts showing sophisticated couples drinking Coke in front on the Taj Mahal and Pyramids flopped with the folks back home, however. "You can sell all the Coke you want in Pakistan," Delony Sledge complained of the McCann efforts, "but we want to sell it in Punkin Center." Even though it took a while for the new ad agency to produce a winning approach, however, Harper's willingness to butt heads with competition stimulated the stodgy soft drink firm. The first campaign slogan, "Almost Everyone Appreciates the Best," marked a clear revolution, since it was a competitive ad, at least implicitly acknowledging Pepsi's existence.

Up until that moment, Coke men had haughtily ignored Pepsi. Inside the Company, the "P-word" was never mentioned. Instead, memos referred to the Competition, the Imitator, or the Enemy. Drinking a Pepsi constituted a capital crime. If a Coca-Cola man and his family pulled into a motel and saw a Competitor's vending machine, they righteously moved on. One Coke bottler, enraged at encountering a Pepsi vending machine in his territory, hauled out his hunting rifle and shot it. In the fifties, a Coke bottler's son hid in the attic with friends on his seventh birthday to smoke cigarettes and clandestinely drink Pepsi. When his father discovered this perfidy, he lectured him sternly, not on the evils of smoking, but on drinking the wrong soda.

Morton Downey, the crooner who appeared everywhere for Coke in the fifties—at druggists' meetings, bottlers' conventions, American Legion affairs—was one of Robert Woodruff's best friends. "Every week the Coke man would drop off six or seven cases," his son remembered, "and whenever we went out we were all required to have a Coca-Cola bottle in front of us for a picture. My father was the best PR they ever had." Such pressure on children could backfire, however. Years later, Morton Downey, Jr., would exact revenge on his father. As "Mortification Mort," he consciously developed an obnoxious, obscene talk-show persona in direct contrast to this father's schmaltz. "My father wanted me to run one of his bottling plants," the son recalled. "The last thing I wanted to do was work for Coke. To this day I only drink Pepsi."

In the fifties, however, there were no such rebels. The immense pride and loyalty to Coca-Cola occasionally stood in the way of necessary business decisions. Gager and Hillman agreed that simply offering a larger bottle wasn't sufficient. There wasn't enough of a difference between Pepsi and Coke to warrant charging more for Coca-Cola. In fact, to their horror, they discovered in blind taste-tests that Pepsi had a slight edge, and they unsuccessfully petitioned Woodruff to increase the syrup throw to produce a sweeter drink. The reaction to the secret taste-tests at Coke headquarters was swift: "Don't *ever* do that again." In general, the Boss resisted *any* change in advertising and marketing.

Setting the price for the King Size was problematical, since bottlers tended to boost it considerably beyond the standard size drink, putting it above the equivalent Pepsi price. McCann man Murray Hillman persuaded bottlers to *cut* the King Size price while *raising* the price of the traditional bottle. "The regular bottle sales were on a steady downhill trend anyway," he said. "People who drank it were loyal regardless of price." The maneuver worked. At the same time, Hillman suggested charging a premium for the twenty-six-ounce Family-Size bottle in the New York City area, where the huge Jewish population accounted for most sales. "Typically, Jewish consumers wanted a big bottle to put on the table and pour at mealtimes," Hillman remembered. "They appreciated quality and demanded a brand name product." Consequently, rather than playing up the savings in price—which would have been difficult, since it cost more per ounce than the smaller sizes—ads for the large bottle bragged: "There's a giant in my house."

Elsewhere, however, King Size purchases fell inexplicably after an initial surge. Sample consumers complained that their Coke didn't taste as good in the big bottle. "You must have diluted it," they reasoned. "How can you afford to offer it at such a low price otherwise?" In response, the McGuire Sisters saturated TV and radio with a lilting jingle in the late fifties: "King Size Coke has more for you, / King Size Coke has more for you, / King Size Coke has more for you: / Flavor, Lift, and Value too."[*]

PROBING THE SUBCONSCIOUS WITH THE DEPTH BOYS

Hillman wasn't alone in discovering that consumer behavior was often irrational, based on subconscious psychological motives. By mid-decade, "the depth boys," as they were known, had brought "motivational research" (MR) into the mainstream. Suddenly, sociologists, psychologists, and anthropologists were jumping out of their ivory towers to tender expert advice to businesses like The Coca-Cola Company. For the first time, the Company attempted to plumb the depths of the subconscious mind. In long tape-recorded interviews, as Delony Sledge explained, the psychologists "probe long enough and deep enough to find out (almost, in some instances, against the will of the interviewee)" what motivated representative consumers to choose either Coke or Pepsi. The unrelenting question, according to Sledge, was "Why? Why? Why?"

While Coca-Cola men may have welcomed the depth boys, many critics were alarmed at this new, manipulative approach, which turned social scientists into "super hucksters" advising on how to write copy with "sell appeal." In *The Hidden Persuaders*, Vance Packard sounded the alarm about this exotic new approach in which people were swayed subconsciously. Typically, he said, the MR men "see us as bundles of daydreams, misty hidden yearnings, guilt complexes." People were "image lovers given to impulsive and compulsive acts." To a large degree, however, the jargon-ridden academics were simply recognizing what Coca-Cola men had known for years. The Color Research Institute discovered that red was "hypnotic," and particularly attractive to female shoppers. Similarly, researchers explained why free samples in supermarkets led to increased sales in other aisles. Without articulating it in the same way, Archie Lee had long ago realized that image was more important than substance. Nonetheless, for the first time

---

[*] Poet James Dickey helped write such glorious lines in the late fifties as a McCann-Erickson employee. "I didn't mind writing for Coke," he recalled. "It was the easiest thing in the world. My wrestling match was with my poetry. I sold my soul to the devil all day and tried to buy it back at night." In 1959, the head of the Atlanta agency introduced Dickey to a bank executive, adding: "And Jim's hobby is writing poetry." Dickey thought, "That ties it. Hobby, my ass! This *job* is my hobby; the poetry is my real work." He quit soon afterward.

Coca-Cola men moved beyond mere "nose-counting" surveys to a more sophisticated positioning of the drink.

In the late 1950s, sensational reports on "subliminal advertising" inflamed public fears of nefarious subconscious manipulation. For six weeks, on alternate nights, a New Jersey movie theater projected "Coca-Cola" and "Eat Popcorn" on the screen every five seconds for three-thousandths of a second—too fast to register on the conscious mind. The directors of the Subliminal Projection Company claimed that Coke sales went up 18.1 percent as a result. At special screenings, journalists then viewed a short film about underwater life in which 169 hidden Coca-Cola messages swam amongst the fish. One *New York Times* reporter wasn't impressed, since he had no urge to drink a Coke after watching the groupers and mackerel. Nor, he reported, did he have any "visions, dreams, drives, images, trances, inclinations or hang-overs that were not directly attributable to conscious guzzling of something else than Coke the night before." While Coca-Cola men may have been initially intrigued by subliminal advertising, it turned out to be a hoax, and the impressive increase in Coke sales in the lobby a fiction.

A BLAND NEW WORLD

The eager motivational researchers were symptomatic of fifties America during the "age of affluence," as John Kenneth Galbraith dubbed it, in which a sales executive exulted that "Capitalism is dead—consumerism is king!" The question was no longer how to produce enough goods to satisfy needs, but rather, how could consumers be induced to absorb the flood of products? By the mid-fifties, the gross national product had increased over 400 percent in just fifteen years. "We must consume more and more," wrote one commentator, "whether we want to or not, for the good of our economy."

On the surface, at least, Americans appeared to be a complacent, conformist lot, nestling into identical little houses in Levittowns across the country, compliantly purchasing ever-increasing cars, TV dinners, and soft drinks. To Mochtar Lubis, a visitor from Indonesia, the United States was a garish hell: "Mass advertisements in newspapers, radio, TV, billboards, for twenty-four hours a day, seven days a week, fifty-two weeks a year, year after year, telling people to go to the same places, buy the same cars, gadgets, dresses, build the same house, read the same pulp literature, to feel the same, think the same." This resulted in a leveling of taste, a uniformity in food and politics. "Everybody liked Eisenhower," Lubis noted, because "he's a nice guy." It was, as Vance Packard wrote, a "bland new world" in which the American per capita soft drink consumption swelled from 177 in 1950 to 235 by decade's end.

"Bland" is the only word to describe McCann-Erickson's early TV spots featuring Johnny, a chunky fourteen-year-old with slickly combed hair and a double chin—a dork even by 1958 standards. "Hi, Mom. Hi, Sis," he exclaimed as he burst through the door with his school books. "Got any ice-cold Coke?" Looking up from her ironing, Mom answered, "Why, Johnny King, you know we have. Only this morning you brought in a whole case of

Coca-Cola," and the charming family scene closed on the bliss of simultaneous Coke consumption, as the announcer affirmed that "everyone likes Coke."

Nowhere was the uniformity of the age more obvious than at "the new jungle called the supermarket," as one critic put it, where housewives, children in tow, dutifully filled their shopping carts. Coca-Cola and Pepsi fought over optimal locations at eye-catching levels with ingeniously designed portable display racks. The battle for supermarket shelf space called for heroic measures from devoted Coca-Cola salesmen like Charlie Bottoms. Wearing his Coke uniform, he entered a store with a big Pepsi display, telling the manager he was compiling a merchandising survey. "The smart-ass said, 'Let me buy you a Pepsi, they've got this new sixteen-ounce size.' I told him I'd like that, since I'd never tasted Pepsi." Bottoms upended the bottle and guzzled it until he gagged. "I threw up all over the damn display and kept saying, 'I didn't know it tasted so *bad.*' The women with their carts all scattered, and the store manager was just mortified. He didn't know what to do. He took the Pepsi out to the dumpster and bought enough product from us to make a beautiful Coca-Cola display." Out in the car, Bottoms' companion turned to him and said, "Can you do that again?"

The housewife, who typically ruled her nuclear household roost with an iron hand while her husband wore his gray flannel suit to the office, busied herself at the heart of American consumption. Ozzie and Harriet Nelson provided role models for millions of fifties' families on their Coke-sponsored television show. Like Eisenhower, Ozzie was a nice guy, but he was endearingly fuzzy-headed and lost without his efficient wife. In a typical commercial, Ozzie got hopelessly confused over which hamburgers were rare or well-done while presiding over the backyard grill. Harriet saved the day by bringing on the Coke.

Advertisers approached this newly powerful woman with some trepidation. As Coca-Cola's adviser Charlotte Montgomery warned, "Mrs 1956" was a new consumer who could be "wooed away by a more convenient package, a big promotion, a slightly more interesting presentation." The insecure young homemaker, anxious for excitement in her circumscribed round of shopping and child-rearing, also yearned to impress the neighbors. Mrs Montgomery advised Coke men to "jump on the bandwagon," depicting the soft drink as an integral part of TV parties and barbecues. When Mrs 1956 went to the supermarket, she might *think* she was "a completely independent agent," but with good promotions, Mrs Montgomery assured the Coke men, "you hold her in the hollow of your hand."

Of course, the housewife was really only a conduit to the fastest-growing market of the decade—children. During the fifties, the total population jumped by almost 30 million, the largest increase in American history. Significantly, 83 percent of that growth occurred in the suburbs, nicknamed "Fertile Acres." As one historian of the period put it, "never in American history had a generation of children been so much the center of attention and so catered to." If children were spoiled anyway, why not spoil them with Coca-Cola?

One new way to reach the kids arrived in the fifties. In 1954, Ray Kroc bought a small chain of California hamburger stands from the McDonald brothers. By the end of the decade, his fast-food golden-arched franchises were sprouting across the country. Kroc offered his customers Coca-Cola, a relationship the Company has jealously guarded ever since. The McDonald's beckoned motorists from nearby interstate highways, the dazzling new arteries where chrome-polishing, car-happy Americans found high-speed travel addictive. Always aware that filling stations provided perfect "use occasions"—McCann-Erickson jargon—Coke revved up promotions for fifties dealers. Murray Hillman's booklet, entitled *Automobilus Americanus*, conveyed a basic message: "Get the guy out of his car, and he'd spend money." Hillman recalls: "It was a great cycle. He'd stop to fill 'er up and go to the bathroom, have a Coke, and drive on. Then he'd have to find a rest room again." Company researchers, spying on over 20,000 gas station customers, concluded that Coca-Cola accounted for 14 percent of all transactions.

Presiding over the materialistic era was a benign consumer-oriented God who blessed the enormous outpouring of American goods, toasting it with a Coke. In the mid-fifties, Congress passed legislation to include the phrase "under God" in the pledge of allegiance. "Religious emphasis weeks" sprang up on college and high school campuses. Billy Graham, Bishop Fulton Sheen, and Norman Vincent Peale prayed their way into American homes through the print media and the TV screen.

By far the most popular religious figure of the period, Peale preached an easy gospel of success based on "the power of positive thinking," the title of his best-selling book. Named one of the "Twelve Best U.S. Salesmen" in 1954, Peale agreed with Billy Graham that "I am selling the greatest product in the world; why shouldn't it be promoted as well as soap?" Peale told his audiences that they could overcome any obstacle and obtain peace of mind, social acceptance, and wealth by simply believing in themselves and avoiding negative, unpleasant thoughts. In the words of one critic, he "turned God into a friend and business partner." Robert Woodruff concurred. Stirred by Peale's comforting message, the Boss provided major funding for the evangelist's *Guideposts* magazine and urged Eisenhower not only to invite him to one of Ike's famous stag dinners for influential men, but to publicly endorse the publication. In the United States, as philosopher Bertrand Russell observed, "God is an adjunct of man."

FLAWS IN THE FABRICS

Still, devils lurked in God's country. Armageddon was only the push of a button away, so that the typical upper-middle-class home not only had two cars, but a bomb shelter. Children routinely drilled for nuclear war by crouching under their school desks. In the 1959 movie *On the Beach*, an American submarine commander, hearing a persistent but random Morse code message, searched for its source in a post-holocaust world. He discovered that a windblown Coke bottle, tangled in a curtain cord, was the sole "survivor," tapping out its feeble message. Under the placid surface of American consumption, then, lay a constant dread so awful it had to be ignored.

Perhaps in part as a sublimated response, other anxieties emerged. While the indulged children gorged themselves on candy, Coke, and frosted flakes, their teeth were riddled with cavities. Coca-Cola, always vulnerable to attack from health faddists, received an inordinate share of the blame. Clive M. McCay, a Cornell professor, led the charge against the soft drink. Testifying before James J. Delaney's Congressional committee on food additives, McCay made headlines with his allegations that Coke would eat away the marble steps of the Capitol Building and soften teeth placed in a glass of the beverage. "The molar teeth of rats were dissolved down to the gum line," McCay told the politicians, when "given nothing to drink except cola beverage for a period of six months."

In response, Coca-Cola's head chemist, Orville May, testified that McCay offered a "distorted picture" intended to frighten unsuspecting consumers. May pointed out that the .055 percent level of phosphoric acid was far below the 1.09 percent acid content of an orange and that McCay's studies ignored the neutralizing effect of saliva. Finally, he noted that orange juice or lemonade would also dissolve ten-penny nails and eat holes in the Capitol steps. Bill Robinson was more forceful. "The only way our product could harm children," he said, "would be for a case of Coke to fall out a window and hit them."

RESTIVE HOUSEWIVES, REBELLIOUS TEENS, UNHAPPY BLACKS

Company officials expected health issues to crop up periodically. Other signs of social unrest were more confusing, however. Women, for instance, were restless and bored in their suburban kitchens. In fact, increasing numbers of them bolted the confines of the home and went to work. By 1960, women constituted a third of the American work force, although they were underpaid and underemployed as secretaries, teachers, nurses, and assembly-line laborers. As in the home, the women often actually ran the office and made executive decisions without receiving credit. At The Coca-Cola Company, this pattern was particularly common, as bright young secretaries like Claire Sims and Mary Gresham ran important sales campaigns.

The docile, spoiled children of the fifties also displayed signs of discontent. Social commentators labeled these inexplicably violent youths "juvenile delinquents." Mystified and alarmed by critical adolescents, Robert Woodruff unsuccessfully sought a solution to a problem that was transforming some of his best consumers into hoodlums. In 1955, Bill Haley and the Comets performed "Rock Around the Clock" in the movie *Blackboard Jungle*, sparking the new reign of rock'n'roll. Parents were appalled by Elvis Presley's suggestively grinding hips and the driving rhythms of their teenagers' music. Even Ozzie and Harriet's cute son, Ricky, grew a ducktail and became a rock star. While Woodruff insisted on the satiny sounds of the McGuire Sisters for his Coca-Cola ads, Chuck Berry and Ray Charles introduced a generation to black soul and funk.

Blacks themselves were causing trouble. On their television screens, they viewed a beckoning middle-class world of white affluence. In the aftermath of the 1954 *Brown* v. *the Board of Education* decision, smoldering racial tensions flared in the South. Several conservative Coca-Cola bottlers served as prominent members of newly formed White Citizens Councils, vowing to close public schools rather than submit to integration. In response, local blacks staged Coca-Cola boycotts. At a black service station in South Carolina, an ominous sign on a Coke cooler read: "This machine has economic pressure. It is dangerous to insert money."

For the first time, The Coca-Cola Company grasped the need to address black consumers. In 1955, before a group of eager black business students, Export chairman James Farley described opportunities in the "15 billion dollar Negro Market," explaining that "American business has of late discovered a vast, unexploited market-within-a-market." By the time of Farley's speech, Coke had initiated advertising efforts aimed at the black market, featuring prominent black athletes such as Jesse Owens, Satchel Paige, Floyd Patterson, Sugar Ray Robinson, and the Harlem Globetrotters. Ads in *Ebony* portrayed wholesome black models in exactly the same poses as their white counterparts. "There's nothing like a Coke", both ads proclaimed. The message was equal, but strictly separate.

The Company also hired Washington, D.C., public relations man Moss Kendrix, a light-skinned, articulate black man, as a kind of roving ambassador who appeared at an incredible number of black functions during the fifties—giving away prizes for guessing the correct number of Coke bottle caps at a National Negro Insurance Association meeting, hosting a career conference at Howard University, applauding the Tuskegee Institute Choir on Eddie Fisher's *Coke Time* show, patting black children on the head at the National Baptist Sunday School Convention and meetings of Negro Scouts. Kendrix attended a hundred or more conventions a year for Coca-Cola. The Company encouraged its Southern bottlers to enlist special black representatives. Reluctantly, older white bottlers like Uncle Jim Pidgeon in Memphis and Dick Freeman in New Orleans hired their first executives of color. Given the explosive racial situation, Company officials had to walk "a very fine line where we're friends with everybody," Delony Sledge told an interviewer, adding that he had taped evidence of Pepsi men spreading rumors that Coke financed White Citizens Councils, while an opposing story claimed that the company had contributed $150,000 to the NAACP.

Everyone kept demanding the adoption of a firm moral stance, Sledge complained. "Sure, we'll stand up and be counted, but we're on both sides of the fence," the advertising man said, noting that blacks constituted 30 percent of the Southern market. "For God's sake, just let us go on selling Coca-Cola to anybody who's got a gullet we can pour it down." With care, the Company managed to avoid any major disasters, its public position determined by the bottom line, as always. Under pressure from Woodruff, Mayor Hartsfield, a staunch segregationist, modified his position, calling Atlanta "a city too busy to hate." Nonetheless, he changed slowly: instead of removing the "white" and "colored" signs from airport rest rooms, the mayor reduced their size.

Woodruff himself had no love for the civil rights movement. In 1956, he betrayed his longtime ally, Senator Walter George, dumping him at the age of seventy-eight in favor of white supremacist Herman Talmadge. At Ichauway, he maintained what aide Joe Jones called "a traditional master–slave relationship." Blacks were valued servants to Woodruff, and he treated them—as he treated most whites—with grace, kindness, and condescension. Ichauway field hands sang moving spirituals so beloved by Eisenhower that he called from the White House to hear them. In an unguarded moment, however, Woodruff revealed his resistance to black equality in a note to Ralph Hayes, sarcastically urging passage of "appropriate civil rights laws" that would protect "the right of a chimpanzee to vote."

Finally, as if the trouble with women, juveniles, and blacks weren't enough, the 1950s brought labor troubles. While no one at the paternalistic headquarters would consider joining a union, many of the Company-owned and independent bottlers faced severe agitation and strikes. In Tennessee, militant Teamsters took out ads in local papers saying "Coca-Cola is being delivered by scab laborers." Union men slashed and shot out Coke truck tires and dynamited local groceries which still dared to stock Coca-Cola. In Houston, on the other hand, the bottler hired union-busting Texas Rangers to ride the delivery trucks with directions to "shoot for the belly" if labor agitators appeared.

BLACK FRIDAY AND BLOODY CHAIRS

Such unrest was unthinkable at the comfortable red-brick building on North Avenue, however, where loyal employees enjoyed a lifelong sinecure, eating 35-cent lunches and drinking all the free Coke they wanted. Jobs at the Company might not yield the highest pay in town, but they did mean prestige and security. Or so everyone thought until the fall of 1957, when Curt Gager, the former hatchet man for General Foods, moved to Atlanta and conducted a series of mysterious meetings with department heads.

On Friday, November 8, one out of ten employees reported to work at 9 A.M. as usual and were summarily fired, given severance pay, and ordered to clean their desks and leave by 9:30 A.M.* Some managers found their offices locked, belongings stacked in the hallway. Black Friday, as the day was quickly labeled, came as a complete shock to almost everyone. Nor did there seem to be any logic to the dismissals. "We had some people that weren't worth a shit, but they stayed," Charlie Bottoms remembered. Others, longtime employees doing "a fantastic job," were dismissed. In the advertising department, Troy

---

*The actual number of people who were fired is unclear, since no one at the Company officially talked about it. Some sources insisted that one out of three were dismissed.

Neighbors, a popular twenty-seven-year veteran, was a victim. The young man reassigned to Neighbors' desk shuddered. "I'm not going to sit in that chair," he said. "The blood's not dry yet."

The event shattered lives. One man drowned himself in nearby Lake Spivey. At the end of the day, after everyone had left the office, a guilt-stricken woman in the personnel office shot herself in the head. Because their identity as a Coca-Cola men or women was so all-important, those suddenly shut out of the soft drink family panicked. "For most people," Bottoms said, "the loss of face in leaving here was so great that they would stay even if they had to wipe the bathroom out."

No trace of Black Friday exists in the Company archives, nor did anything about the layoffs or suicides appear in the Atlanta papers. "At that time, Coca-Cola could have kept anything out of the paper," one employee recalled. "Robert Woodruff could have run naked across the top of the building with flood lights on him without any news reports." It is almost inconceivable that the Boss didn't sanction the mass firings, but he certainly took pains to disassociate himself from the event. A few months later, in the spring of 1958, Bill Robinson found himself kicked upstairs to board chairman, with Curt Gager pushed out of the fold soon after. The two outsiders had done the dirty work, shaking up the tradition-bound Company, and employees were relieved when Lee Talley, an old Coca-Cola man who had come up through the ranks, was named the new president. The son of a Methodist minister, Talley wore red suspenders and spoke with a soft drawl, but underneath his country-boy grin, he was a steel-edged, tough-minded manager.

THE END OF A FRANTIC DECADE

As the noisy, materialistic, conformist Eisenhower era raced toward the turbulent sixties, Coca-Cola and Pepsi were locked into a grim struggle for world domination. Coke's lead had been cut to 2-to-1 and "an era of aloof grandeur had ended," as one commentator noted. The older soft drink would never stand alone again, though Company executives consoled themselves with the knowledge that intense competition spelled increased sales for both colas at other beverages' expense. Coca-Cola stock had resumed its steady upward trend, splitting 3-for-1 in 1960.

The McCann-Erickson men had begun to find more effective themes after the disastrous around-the-world campaign. The McGuire Sisters sang on radio and TV, urging consumers to be "*really* refreshed" with Coke, implying that Pepsi just wouldn't do. For the first time, photographers sought real-life scenes involving Coke for the "America Pauses" series. Coke was the "sign of good taste," a slogan that performed triple duty in reference to the ubiquitous signs, the supposedly refined sensibilities of Coke consumers, and the literal good taste of the product. The "Party From Your Pantry" series depicted Coke as a fitting complement to tempting cold cuts, fruit salads, and barbecued chicken—a direct appeal to supermarket sales. Special displays featured Coke with Ritz crackers and Triscuits, while the Company sent food editors packets of menus, photographs, and party game ideas.

The most innovative program of the late fifties was Coca-Cola's "Hi-Fi Club," aimed at teenagers. Playing on the enormous popularity of local disc jockeys on top-40 radio stations, the Company's public relations agency, Hill & Knowlton, collaborated with McCann men to create instant teen "clubs" built around pop music and the proper soft drink. "The d.j. would run out of things to say," McCann man Neal Gilliatt recalled. "We gave him something to talk about and got good placement. We'd conduct taped interview of hot celebrities and he could put his own voice into them. It worked like gangbusters." By the end of 1959, there were clubs in 325 cities, with over 2 million members. The local Coca-Cola bottler hosted weekly dance parties at which the radio show provided the music and entertainment. The bottler and his wife often chaperoned the affair, ensuring that the lights remained undimmed and that nothing stronger than Coke was served. The $1.5 million invested in the Hi-Fi clubs was well spent, as Coke edged up on Pepsi's lead in the teen market.

Faced with these Coca-Cola tactics, Al Steele redoubled his efforts to fire up his Pepsi bottlers. More than any other man, Steele epitomized the hustling fifties. In 1955, he had married actress Joan Crawford—ironically, a Coca-Cola girl in 1930s ads. Together, the two embarked on a nonstop life of travel, logging over 100,000 miles a year and opening new Pepsi plants in country after country. In 1957, they visited twenty foreign lands, where the actress, always holding a Pepsi bottle, was greeted by ecstatic fans. As Crawford's daughter Christina recalled, "she had bottles of Pepsi next to her at press conferences, cases of Pepsi backstage when she went on talk shows, and she learned to mention the company name whenever she was interviewed for any purpose whatsoever."

In public, Joan Crawford was the perfect wife to her fourth husband, but she did not come cheap, and the Pepsi executive went deeply into debt, which only fueled his frenzied need to boost soft drink sales. In 1959, he conducted a six-week whirlwind tour of the United States he dubbed "Adarama," a $200,000 extravaganza to whip up bottler enthusiasm. On April 18, the night after the grueling tour's end, Steele died suddenly of a heart attack, days short of his fifty-eighth birthday. His widow soon joined the board, where she proved to be, as a Pepsi man said, "one of the company's most treasured and highly valued assets." Ultimately, she logged over 3 million miles for Pepsi.

A few months later, halfway around the world in Moscow, Vice-President Richard Nixon loudly argued with Russian premier Nikita Khrushchev over America's capitalistic virtues, as exemplified by a model kitchen in the U.S. exhibit area. Despite the tension, Nixon fulfilled his pledge to Don Kendall, head of Pepsi's international sales efforts. Leading the belligerent Russian leader to the soft drink stand—Coca-Cola had refused to participate in the Communist fair—he cajoled Khrushchev into sampling Pepsi while the photographers' light bulbs flashed. "KHRUSHCHEV LEARNS TO BE SOCIABLE," declared headlines around the world.

Although Nixon returned home a hero for standing his ground during the kitchen debate, this conniving friend of Pepsi was about to engage in a bitter presidential campaign which he would lose to John F. Kennedy, a Coke drinker. As the sixties ushered in the New Frontier, Coca-Cola led the way.

～ 16 ～

Paul Austin's Turbulent Sixties

Things Go Better With Coca-Cola,
Things Go Better With Coke.

—Advertising slogan, 1963–1968

Do your own thing.

—Unofficial slogan of the Counterculture

IN HIS INAUGURAL ADDRESS, John F. Kennedy, asserting that he represented "a new generation," spoke of renewal, change, energy, faith, devotion, and sacrifice. With his inspirational words, the complacency of the fifties gave way to the adrenal rush of youth, though no one stopped to question exactly what the President's men had in mind. Eisenhower, writing to Robert Woodruff, complained bitterly that Kennedy's cabinet choices lacked experience. One was a "crackpot," the other indecisive, and the third "famous only for his ability to break the treasury of a great state." Why, Ike wanted to know, did Atlanta journalist Ralph McGill praise Kennedy?

Woodruff, however, attracted by the potency of Kennedy's charisma, had already arranged Coca-Cola liaisons with the new President. Boisfeuillet (pronounced BO-full-ay) Jones, an Emory University administrator and Woodruff associate, accepted a top post under Abe Ribicoff at HEW. Ben Oehlert, the perennial Washington insider, befriended Vice-President Johnson, calling him Lyndon and posing with him and a beauty contest winner. Morton Downey, already an intimate of the Kennedy clan, and traditional Democrat James Farley quickly established warm ties to the White House, with Farley offering to be "available at any time" to talk "about anything" with JFK. After a 1961 South American foray, Farley conveyed his lengthy impressions to the President. In 1963, Kennedy scrawled "from a consumer" on an autographed photograph of himself drinking a Coke and dispatched it to Big Jim. "It was kind indeed of you," the Coke ambassador responded, to "publicly give proof of the fact that you find the product—to use the advertising term—'Delicious and Refreshing.'" According to one source, Kennedy offered Robert Woodruff the U.S. ambassadorship to England—a post Kennedy's father held—but the Boss declined.

Kennedy's plans for a manned moon mission, introduced during his first State of the Union address, inspired a number of eager entrepreneurs. "I just heard President Kennedy," one Michigan man wrote to The Coca-Cola Company in May of 1961. "I hereby make formal application for the exclusive

Coca-Cola franchise on the Moon." He also modestly requested sole distributorship for all bodies and planets in space, adding that he could "think of nothing that is more symbolic of our way of life than a Coca-Cola sign." Apparently astronaut Gus Grissom agreed, assuring his son that "when you're my age they'll have Coke machines on the moon."

While requests for Coke franchises in outer space were merely amusing, Coca-Cola jumped aggressively into the sixties under Lee Talley's direction, introducing Fanta flavors nationally and offering Sprite as a lemon/lime alternative to the market leader, 7-Up. The first nonreturnable bottles were implemented to meet the demand for "convenience" packaging. At the same time, Talley delved into Coke's huge cash hoard, buying Minute Maid for $72.5 million. With the orange juice giant, Coke also acquired Tenco, a coffee and tea manufacturer. "THIS IS COCA-COLA?" queried a 1960 *Business Week* headline. The traditionally single-minded Company was in an "expansionist mood" along with the country, the journalist noted. Coca-Cola was even available in cans.

A traditional Coca-Cola loyalist, Talley brought a determinedly objective managerial style to the Company. In 1961, the Company hardly paused to celebrate its silver anniversary, afraid that Pepsi might advance against a self-congratulatory Company. Similarly, Talley had no patience with tension between fountain, bottle, and pre-mix sale of Coca-Cola. No one, he noted sternly in a 1961 memo, "should ever disparage the product Coca-Cola in any of its accepted forms of distribution, or draw unfavorable comparisons of one form against another." As a token of its aggressive new stance, the Company sponsored a Tour of the World Sweepstakes, with $25,000 in traveler's checks as a first prize. The post office complained when a flood of envelopes containing bottle caps jammed their new electronic machines.

STRUGGLING FOR A THEME

Though such promotions temporarily boosted sales, the Company's resolve alone wasn't enough to build and sustain marketing momentum. It sorely needed another Archie Lee. With the baby boomers hitting their teens, the Coke advertising team struggled for a campaign to match the crackling energy of youth in the air. They hired singer Anita Bryant, a fresh-scrubbed born-again Christian who, as a former Miss Oklahoma, combined piety and sex appeal in the traditional Coca-Cola manner. As a fitting farewell to the fifties, Coke canceled its sponsorship of *Ozzie and Harriet* while purchasing TV air time for Bryant to sing the new jingle. "Only Coca-Cola gives you that refreshing new feeling," she chirruped. "Zing! What a feeling with a Coke." The ad men dropped the word "pause" from their copy, since it seemed too staid for the times. Unfortunately, "Zing!" too had an artificial fifties ring to it, while the Imitator's ads were proclaiming "Now its Pepsi for those who think young," lilted by sassy-voiced Joanie Sommers—the debut Pepsi campaign by Batten, Barton, Durstine and Osborn (BBDO). While both Coke and Pepsi ads featured young people disporting themselves with soft drinks, Coca-Cola's direct pitch to any one segment of its vast market was limited by its strategic appeal to every possible consumer—though the Hi-Fi Club still attracted teens to Coke. Pepsi, on the other hand, was better positioned to target one market, since it had less to lose. While Coca-Cola advertising floundered, searching for a unifying theme, Pepsi's efforts to identify with the dynamic youth market appeared more effective.

In 1962, an unhappy Lee Talley called for an "agonizing reappraisal" of Coca-Cola's program. In trying to make commercials "scientifically and mathematically defensible," he observed, the McCann ads had lost direction. In the past year, they had presented Coca-Cola as light refreshment at a ski lift, the contents of a Coke Float with ice cream, or a drink by a swimming pool. "We have been garnishing it with a slice of lemon or lime," Talley complained, or selling Coke as the chief ingredient of a wassail bowl of Lemon Grog. "We are losing sight of WHAT WE ARE," he wrote, "in trying to be all things to all people, and in doing so we are blurring and confusing our image." Talley suggested a new concept for 1963 advertising which would "ELEVATE THE PRODUCT and PUT IT ON A PEDESTAL."

The McCann men had been conducting intensive research for almost three years in search of the right campaign, swimming through "pretty deep motivational research waters," as a *Business Week* writer put it. They discovered that Coke acted primarily as a social catalyst. McCann hired a slim, soft-spoken young copywriter and lyricist named Bill Backer to transpose the research findings into song. Backer, who hailed from a wealthy Charleston family and always wore trademark bow ties, turned out to be the new Archie Lee; he demonstrated an uncanny knack for probing the heart of America during the next two decades. The resulting 1963 campaign, "Things Go Better With Coke," introduced the "one-sight, one-sound, one-sell" approach with a slogan that dominated the sixties. The vaguely promising "things" that went better with the soft drink fit Coke's traditional universal thrust. As the Limelighters, a popular folk group, sang in Backer's upbeat jingle, "Food goes better with, / Fun goes better with, / You go better with Coke." The umbrella ad covered the disparate approaches that had bothered Talley, allowing a Coke Float or ski-slope refreshment. As one McCann man put it, the ad attempted to be "'in' enough to win the young adults without being so 'way out' as to alienate people of other age groups."

The Coke campaign drove Pepsi's advertising men crazy. "'Things Go Better' was killing us," one Pepsi veteran recalls. "No matter what we said, they'd say, 'Yeah, but things go better with Coke.'" In addition, an important subtheme highlighted the product's magical qualities. A Coca-Cola suddenly transformed an unhappy boy in one spot, for instance, while sharing a Coke guaranteed a couple's mutual devotion in another. The McCann ads had indeed succeeded in putting the drink on a pedestal.

Pepsi countered with devastatingly effective advertisements which completely contrasted with their drab old Sociables commercials. In the new TV spots, created by John Bergin of BBDO, a brief, tranquil interlude was broken by the dramatic burst of a motorcycle coming around a bend or a roller coaster cresting a height. After a brass fanfare, Joanie Sommers' insinuating voice beckoned consumers to "Come Alive! Come Alive! You're in the Pepsi Generation." Using innovative techniques—hand-held cameras, "real" California kids instead of actors, spontaneous use of a helicopter flying with a Pepsi vending machine—the new Pepsi commercials effectively identified the drink with the baby boomers and Kennedy's inaugural invocation of a "new generation."

With these two seminal campaigns, the future thrust of both Pepsi and Coke ads was set. Pepsi ads were brash, loud, overtly sexy, centering not on the product but on the consumer. If you drank Pepsi, you could become popular, a part of a new generation. Through life-style advertising, Pepsi sought to woo the 75 million baby boomers. Coca-Cola ads always focused on the product itself. True, they mixed life-style with product attribute themes, but at the heart of the commercial lay a bottle of Coca-Cola. *It* was the star, not the actors.

"Things Go Better" debuted through all of the traditional modes, including point-of-purchase signs, novelties, and radio, but by 1963, television dominated promotions, eating 80 percent of the $53 million ad budget. The nickel gallonage allowance of the bottlers' old contract now amounted to an inadequate pittance. The Company had to persuade bottlers to match TV ad expenditures dollar for dollar, a task complicated by local TV station reception cutting across franchise borders. Cooperative television advertising agreements solved the problem, though they resulted in constant bickering and readjustments.

PAUL AUSTIN'S BEST AND BRIGHTEST

In 1962, Hughes Spalding once again wrote to Robert Woodruff, worried over the grooming of new management. Lee Talley was approaching the mandatory retirement age of sixty-five; the Company needed younger men—"intelligent, sophisticated, cautious, and slightly suspicious. They must know the score." He had penned a perfect description of J. Paul Austin, who became the tenth president of The Coca Cola Company in May of 1962.

Austin, though a native Georgian, formed part of the new breed of Ivy League managers. A graduate of Harvard Law School who spoke Spanish, French, and Japanese, he could easily have served as one of Kennedy's "best and brightest" advisers. In fact, Austin shared several characteristics with the President. Like Kennedy, Austin, forty-seven, had commanded a PT boat during World War II. A tall man with a riveting presence, the new Coca-Cola president had a thick shock of reddish-brown hair that fell on his forehead like JFK's. There the resemblance ended, however. While Kennedy specialized in charm and wit, flashing his ready smile for the cameras, Austin's mouth was usually set in a determine thin line. At Harvard, Austin had rowed for the United States team in the 1936 Berlin Olympics. "If you wanted to beat Paul Austin," his coach once observed, "you'd have to kill him."

Austin's austere managerial style led one journalist to comment on his "seemingly imperious demeanor." Even though he was the youngest president since Woodruff, Austin intentionally terrified his employees. "A certain degree of anxiety and tension has to exist," he insisted, "for people to function at the highest level of their potential," likening this "nervous quickness" to a well-tuned violin string. Normally self-contained, Austin occasionally unleashed a ferocious, quick-flash temper that rendered him still more formidable. Even his metaphors proved alarming. "We really zero in on a problem," he once told a journalist, "pull all the legs off the centipede and see what he's like."

THE COLD WAR TURNS FRIGID

Like Austin, Kennedy relished a sense of tension, and in 1961, the new President faced his first challenge just ninety miles off the coast of Florida. Clearly aligned with the Russians, Fidel Castro had begun nationalizing American companies, including Coca-Cola bottling plants worth over $2 million. A thriving market for Coca-Cola since 1899, the well-developed business disappeared overnight. Austin reacted to Castro with typical Coca-Cola restraint, but Kennedy jumped into the ill-planned Bay of Pigs fiasco, followed the next year by the terrifying Cuban Missile Crisis, when the world teetered on the brink of nuclear war.

Although Coca-Cola men were not engaged in such weighty decisions, they, too, suffered from a Cold War mentality at odds with their usual habit of supplying Coke to every human being on the planet. Stung by the Communist propaganda against the soft drink in the early fifties, Company policy righteously ignored the potentially huge market behind the Iron Curtain. Pepsi had no such compunctions, which accounted for Nixon's 1959 public relations coup with Khrushchev in Moscow. After his 1962 defeat for the California governorship, Nixon joined Pepsi's law firm at a comfortable $250,000 yearly salary. Don Kendall, who had recently assumed the Pepsi presidency, sent the former vice-president globe-hopping as Pepsi's ambassador abroad. While opening doors for Pepsi, Nixon also gained international experience and stature. Kendall, a savvy executive who was to guide Pepsi for over twenty years, was consciously grooming Nixon for a political comeback.

In 1962, Billy Wilder directed *One, Two, Three*, a satire about Coca-Cola's Communist phobia. James Cagney starred as a hard-driving, ambitious Coca-Cola executive in postwar Berlin, where his staff included several ex-Nazis who snapped their Prussian heels whenever the American executive spoke to them. After Cagney opened negotiations with Soviet bureaucrats to sell Coke to Russia, he gloated over "all this virgin territory—300 million thirsty comrades, Volga boatmen and Cossacks, Ukrainians and Outer Mongolians, panting for the Pause That Refreshes." He told his Atlanta superior that "Napoleon blew it, Hitler blew it, but Coca-Cola's gonna pull it off." Cagney was baffled and frustrated when the Boss nixed the deal: "I wouldn't touch the

Russians with a ten-foot pole. And I don't want anything to do with the Poles either."

THE JAPANESE COMPRESS HISTORY

Austin probably agreed with the Cagney character's expansionist attitude. Like many of Woodruff's favorites, he had extensive overseas experience, primarily in South Africa, where he had built the business during the fifties before assuming the presidency of Coca-Cola Export in 1959. Austin's international outlook meant continued growth overseas, particularly in Japan. In 1957, Japanese strict import quotas had been eased, but Coke could still be sold in that country only at selected outlets serving American tourists. There were no such restrictions on Fanta, which sold extremely well, since it lacked carbonated fruit drink competition.

Paul Austin's optimistic 1959 survey of the ripe market was confirmed two years later by Murray Hillman, the McCann-Erickson man, who sensed an "almost fanatical desire to change every fiber of Japanese life." In his 1961 memo to Austin, Hillman described "a set of economic growth forces second to none in the world." Daring teenagers wore blue jeans and danced the Twist. "Today," Hillman wrote, "the Japanese are emulating everything American which they can possibly copy and improve upon. It would appear that they are trying to compress the American experience of the last twenty years into twenty months."

By year's end, thanks to heavy lobbying by Coke executives and Japanese bottler Nisaburo Takanashi, controls were finally lifted, so that Coca-Cola could be sold directly to Japanese consumers. The American soft drink, widely visible in the hands of the occupying forces since World War II, was an immediate sensation. Pacific Export director Hal Roberts (known as "the Emperor" by Japanese bottlers), divided Japan into sixteen bottling territories, larger and more efficient than those in the United States. Coke wisely chose well-connected Japanese business partners as bottlers, including Mitsubishi, Kirin Brewery, Fuji, Sanyo, Kikkoman, and Mitsui. Coca-Cola's direct distribution system, which avoided the traditional Japanese layers of whole-salers, threw the soft drink industry into an uproar, while Coke's insistence on cash upon delivery appalled dealers. This was the American way, though, so it must be good. Soon, other businesses were emulating the revolutionary new methods.[*]

Coke men introduced the Japanese to their first vending machines, placing them in schools, factories, and hospitals. The concept of leisure found its way into Japanese thought, and convenience foods achieved enormous popularity.

---

[*] Much has been written about superior modern Japanese business methods, with their emphasis on utter loyalty, uniform quality, and teamwork. While American consultant W. Edwards Deming deserves much of the credit, Coca-Cola arguably provided an early role model.

Coca-Cola signs sprouted everywhere in lighted plastic and garish neon. The Japanese Coke jingle, even more insipid than the American version, was a hit record. "Let's have some Coca-Cola, cold Coca-Cola, Coca-Cola, Coca-Cola, we are all friends, Coca-Cola, *Skatto sawayaka* Coca-Cola." The phrase *skatto sawayaka*, translated roughly as "bubbly refreshment," became a popular slogan as instantly identifiable as "the pause that refreshes."

At the 1964 Tokyo Olympic Games, Coca-Cola flowed everywhere, while bottlers paid for Japanese TV coverage. The following year, Coke sponsored the Grand Sumo Championship, presenting a gigantic Coke bottle trophy commensurate with the size of the wrestlers. Sales boomed, nearly doubling every year—2.62 million cases in 1962, 6 million in 1963, almost 20 million in 1965. That surge of gallonage, together with some forty new bottling plants opening overseas annually, swelled foreign sales until they accounted for 45 percent of the Company's volume by 1966. Under Austin, Coca-Cola's overseas operations became increasingly standardized and well-managed. In addition to English, German, French, and the like, Coke was now advertised in over sixty languages, including Ashante, Ewe, Ga, Ibo, Lingala, Sindebele, Swahili, Tagalog, Urdu, Xhosa, and Zulu. Regardless of the dialect, advertising was, as Austin commented in 1963, "a world language—the Esperanto of world business," adding: "We used to be an American company with branches abroad. Today we're a multi-national business." To facilitate decision-making, Coke's worldwide Export managers exercised increased autonomy in Austin's decentralized management system.

At the same time, the new Coca-Cola president instituted management courses for his executives and bottlers. Using the "case study" method, Harvard professors taught the latest business concepts to sometimes unwilling Coca-Cola men. "There are an increasing number of management techniques," Austin said, "that are spun off from new and different areas—like organizing to put a man on the moon." A great believer in committees, Austin divided problems into component parts and assigned small teams to work on them.

KEEPING TAB ON BULGING WAISTLINES

One of the first tasks Austin oversaw as president in 1962 was the creation of a new diet drink. Until then, Coke had ignored the diet market, since it threatened its sweet, quick-energy drinks. American women had become increasingly calorie-conscious in the fifties, however, and now they frantically sought to emulate Jackie Kennedy's slim elegance. "The bulging waistline and middle-age spread," wrote one commentator, had taken on "the proportions of a national calamity." In 1961, Royal Crown had taken its Diet-Rite Cola out of the medicine section and promoted it nationally as a soft drink, impacting the traditional cola market. Coke and Pepsi scrambled to catch up with Diet-Rite, particularly after market research revealed that 28 percent of the population were watching their weight.

Austin code-named Coke's diet drink research "Project Alpha," lavishing on it the same manpower and attention more appropriately devoted to a moon shot. Fred Dickson, head of Coke's new marketing division, spearheaded the effort, while Dr Cliff Shillinglaw tinkered with the traditional Coca-Cola formula, trying to discover a saccharin and cyclamate-flavored cola that would have the proper "mouth feel" and wouldn't leave a kerosene aftertaste. Even more effort was spent on finding the proper package and name. Tom Law, head of the subsidiary Fanta Beverage Company that would sell the drink, argued that it should be called Diet Coke. Even for a progressive leader like Paul Austin, however, such a suggestion was heresy. As a flip McCann man put it, "If God had wanted Coca-Cola to have saccharin in it, he would have made it that way in the first place." Instead, Austin sought a suitable name through his huge mainframe computer, which generated over 250,000 random three- and four-letter words, ranging from ABZU, ACHU, and ACK to ZAP, ZORG, and ZUFF. Company personnel also made suggestions. This elephantine labor finally produced TAB—short, easy to remember, and completely different from Coke, it could also suggest keeping *tab* on weight problems.

Coca-Cola introduced TaB in magazine ads asking "How can just one calorie taste so good?" Almost apologetically, the Company explained to bottlers that it had no desire "to injure its existing Coca-Cola bottle business," but it was forced to offer a diet drink to prevent competitors from appropriating "this important segment of the market by default." In addition, the memo asserted that since TaB was *not* Coca-Cola, it wasn't subject to the restrictive bottlers' contract. Because of the Company's ambiguous attitude toward the new diet drink, TaB failed to command a large part of the diet market—which comprised over a tenth of total U.S. soft drink consumption. By 1964, TaB held only a 10 percent share of the weight-watcher market. When Pepsi, less tradition-bound than Coke, debuted diet Pepsi that year, it grabbed even more of the segment.

BLACK WASN'T BEAUTIFUL

John Kennedy and Paul Austin both faced more ominous problems than a newly weight-conscious America, however. Kennedy had wooed blacks during the presidential campaign, but for most of his term, he ignored the pleas of civil rights leaders for federal support, as the aggressive movement, encountering staunch Southern racism, led to confrontation and bloodshed inevitably involving Coca-Cola. The passive bus boycotts of the fifties gave way to a more alarming activism when, on February 1, 1960, four black college freshmen sat down at the Woolworth's lunch counter in Greensboro, North Carolina, where they were refused hamburgers and Cokes. Stoically, they simply sat there, and the next day they returned with twenty-three classmates. The sit-in had been born, and the violence and furor that followed in the next three years jarred America's complacency. By demanding equal rights to Coca-Cola, the civil rights activists were striking at the heart of Southern and American culture. They were also announcing a desire to *join*, not to destroy, middle-class Americans. Coca-Cola men like Delony Sledge who could see through the smoke must have realized that, were it not for the emotionally entrenched racism, the South should have embraced blacks as equal consumers. In fact, the Greensboro sit-in eventually succeeded because of economics. The Woolworth's owner, seeing his business slowly erode, finally capitulated.

The next year, as Freedom Riders were clubbed in Alabama and Mississippi, the atmosphere at the traditional Ichauway Fourth of July barbecue seemed tranquil. Woodruff always threw a huge free party for his black tenants and their families. That year, 3,000 guests enjoyed the Boss's largess, while the Coca-Cola and beer flowed, but racial tensions were lurking there as well. For years, Guy Touchtone, the white Ichauway manager/overseer, had bullied, robbed, and threatened his black workers, sleeping with any black woman he fancied. Woodruff aide Joe Jones, aware that this behavior was demoralizing Ichauway—and angry that Touchtone was stealing timber and beef from the farm—had repeatedly attempted to persuade the Boss to fire him, but to no avail.

During the festivities, Charlie Ware, a black man, made the mistake of flirting with one of Touchtone's mistresses. The overseer complained to his friend "Gator" Johnson, the local sheriff, who had a reputation for brutality. That night, Sheriff Johnson went to Charlie Ware's house, intermittently beating his wife until Ware came home. Then, with the black man handcuffed in the front seat of his car, the sheriff picked up his radio transmitter and said, "This nigger's coming on me with a knife! I'm gonna have to shoot him." Wounding Ware twice in the neck, he said, "He's still coming on!" and shot him a third time.[*] Miraculously, Ware survived, and the incident sparked what became known as the Albany Movement. Charged with felonious assault, the wounded black man languished in jail for over a year because Woodruff didn't come forward to meet his bail bond. In fact, Woodruff apparently ignored the entire incident, though he forcibly "retired" Touchtone the next year by giving him a 300-acre farm adjacent to the plantation and constructing a house for him.

By 1963, neither Kennedy nor Austin could ignore increasingly militant blacks. In August, Martin Luther King, Jr., standing in front of the Lincoln Memorial, declared "I have a dream!" The following month, the Congress of Racial Equality (CORE) demanded that blacks appear in Coca-Cola's television and print advertising. "We are appealing to you on a moral basis," program director Clarence Funnye wrote to Paul Austin, but he added a thinly veiled threat that "selective purchasing committees" would "aid us in our

---

[*] This was by no means the first racial incident at Ichauway. In 1932, Woodruff had hired a Pinkerton agent to investigate a series of lynchings on the plantation. The detective discovered that a white employee was the ringleader, but Woodruff didn't fire him for fear of his possible return to do damage. The blacks didn't blame Woodruff for the lynchings, but they, along with local whites, did resent the rich Atlantan for buying the property and preventing the free range of their hogs and cattle. At least the Boss provided work, however—for 50 cents a day.

bargaining position." In other words, there would be a Coke boycott if the Company failed to respond.

Paul Austin could not afford to antagonize CORE, but at the same time, if he aired integrated commercials in the South, he stood to lose white consumers. In a long memo, Austin bitterly blamed Harvey Russell, Pepsi's black vice-president, for the CORE attack. In addition, he noted, Coca-Cola, "being a Southern institution," provided a satisfactory emotional target. "We are the largest advertiser of a single product; the nature of our product makes it vulnerable to an organized boycott." As a solution, Austin suggested creating a TV commercial at a beach "with a white attendant serving alternatively white and Negro customers." The Company could also agree to produce an integrated print ad, but "we might run it only in a Negro publication, such as EBONY, *if we should decide to run it at all.*" Basically, Austin advocated stall tactics, hoping the furor would die down, and he hoped that others would soon be running integrated ads so that "we will not stand out."

At the same time, Operation Breadbasket, an Atlanta organization of ministers, pushed the Company to hire blacks on the production lines of bottling companies. A local white activist found the Coca-Cola men polite and seemingly cooperative, "doing their best under the circumstances." Black workers were already common in Northern bottling plants. Southerners, however, were still convinced that syphilis was transmitted by drinking fountains and toilets, and they didn't want blacks bottling their Coke. When a boycott loomed, however, the Atlanta bottler promised to hire blacks and remove signs designating "Colored" and "White" bathrooms.

Ivan Allen, Jr., who replaced William Hartsfield as Atlanta's mayor in 1962, bore the brunt of civil rights demands. Coming to power at the same time, Allen and Austin were friends, part of a tight group of white WASPS Allen later described as "business-oriented, nonpolitical, moderate, well-bred, well-educated, pragmatic." It was, he recalled, "not a particularly colorful group," in all of that phrase's meanings. When these complacent young leaders were confronted with angry black men and women, they had no idea how to proceed. In 1963, President Kennedy personally begged Mayor Allen to testify before Congress in favor of his civil rights bill on public accommodations, since the mayor was the only moderate Southern politician who might have the guts to do it. Allen agonized over the decision, finally baring his soul to Robert Woodruff. He told the Boss that he felt compelled to testify in favor of the bill, on both moral and practical grounds. The civil rights movement appeared unstoppable, and Atlanta business would suffer from more violence if some accommodation weren't made.

Woodruff considered what the mayor had said. He hated change of any kind, particularly if it meant upsetting a well-oiled social order. Only three years ago, he had written scathingly about voting rights for chimpanzees. "You are probably right," he told Allen, but suggested that the mayor ask Congress to allow a reasonable delay for rural communities. Similarly, Austin convinced Woodruff to hire Charles Boone, the company's first black bottle sales representative. After all, research demonstrated that while blacks comprised 11 percent of the population, they consumed 17 percent of all soft drinks.

When white Coke veteran Charlie Bottoms learned he would train Boone during a six-month partnership, he resented grooming the black man for a higher-paying position. The odd couple soon closed ranks under duress, however. For the white Bottoms, the experience proved illuminating. "When we pulled into a filling station, they'd see Charles and say their rest rooms were out of order," Bottoms remembers. "When we stayed in a hotel in Greenville, they called my room all night long every fifteen minutes to tell me I was going to be dead by morning." At bottling plants, Boone and Bottoms had to enter through the back door. Willie Barron, the Rome, Georgia, bottler, told Bottoms not to drive his car on a service visit "because it will be full of blood when you leave."

Gradually, however, the bottlers accepted the black Coca-Cola man, who performed his job extraordinarily well. A big man with a deep, booming voice and a startling resemblance to Martin Luther King, Jr., Boone had been a college football star, held a master's degree, and announced radio shows before joining a South Carolina bottler to boost sales to local blacks. A classically dedicated Coca-Cola man, Boone eventually rose to vice-president of Special Markets before dying of a heart attack one Saturday morning, at work in his office.

FROM CAMELOT TO THE GREAT SOCIETY

Just as President Kennedy was maturing in office, taking a strong stand on civil rights and making peace overtures to the Russians, he was assassinated in Dallas. His successor, Lyndon Johnson, strove for the "Great Society," hoping to unite whites and blacks, rich and poor. As the consummate politician and compromiser, Johnson found a friend and kindred spirit in Robert Woodruff. LBJ imagined the same kind of ideal America—founded, as he put it, on "the desire for beauty and hunger for community"—that Coca-Cola advertising portrayed.

Furthermore, Johnson deeply needed a stable father figure. During his White House years, Johnson often sought out Robert Woodruff as a drinking companion and counselor. On the surface, the two men were quite different—Woodruff the quiet, reserved gentleman, Johnson the loud, raw buffoon—but they shared similar philosophies and Southern backgrounds. When Johnson won a landslide victory over Barry Goldwater in 1964, Woodruff wrote to LJB that "I'm sorry the vote was not unanimous." The President scrawled an undated message for Woodruff: "Tell Bob to come see me whenever he's in town." Johnson's motorcade once screeched to a stop when he spotted Ovid Davis, the Coca-Cola lobbyist, on the sidewalk. "Hey, there's Bob's boy!" the President yelled. "You tell Bob I said hey, you heah?"

Only a few years earlier, neither Woodruff nor Johnson had espoused black equality, but they were changing. Whether out of pragmatism or ethics, the two white leaders became significant voices for moderation and the end of racism. When Martin Luther King, Jr., won the Nobel Peace Prize in 1964, Ivan Allen's biracial banquet in his honor nearly foundered, since the Atlanta white establishment at first refused to attend any event featuring "Martin Luther Coon," as they privately called the black leader. Realizing that the national media would embarrass Atlanta and, by extension, Coca-Cola, Woodruff let it be known through Paul Austin that *he* favored the dinner, and the rest of Southern society promptly fell in line.[*]

At the same time, Woodruff finally permitted Coke advertising to showcase blacks. In 1965, Barbara McNair appeared in the first "main thrust" TV commercial for Coca-Cola to use a black celebrity. The cheerful folky sound of the Limelighters gave way to Ray Charles, The Supremes, The Fifth Dimension, Aretha Franklin, Gladys Knight & the Pips, and Marvin Gaye soulfully conveying the message that "Things Go Better With Coke." Each artist created a distinctive version of the song. The Supremes' effort, for instance, sounded almost exactly like their hit, "Baby Love." The Ray Charles blues style featured powerful, emotion-laden visuals of a concert. "In between the sad songs that I sing all night long," Charles wailed, "it's so nice to leave the show / let my throat have a Coke, don't you know."

The new advertising was not simply an accommodation to more militant blacks, though. The entire mood of America was shifting. The docile baby boomers of the fifties had transformed into rebellious teenagers who sought meaning in the revolutionary new music of the Beatles, with their long hair, driving beat, and suggestive lyrics. Coca-Cola couldn't afford to let Pepsi own the new generation. In addition to black performers, Coke hired white pop stars such as Leslie Gore, The Moody Blues, Petula Clark, Neil Diamond, the Everly Brothers, and Jan & Dean to sing upbeat, youthful versions of the jingle. The McCann men even negotiated with the Beatles, who often posed with Coke, but they proved too expensive for Woodruff's taste.

The mid-sixties retained many vestiges of normal middle-class life from the previous decade, however, despite the whiff of change in the air. *Pause for Living*, an extraordinarily popular Coca-Cola publication since 1953, covered "flower arranging, table settings and decorations, food preparation, teen-age entertaining and various handicrafts." The flower arrangements, "enhanced" by bottles of Coca-Cola, continued to mesmerize Garden Clubs and home economics classes across America, pulling some 500 weekly letters to the editor. Similarly, a 1966 television commercial portrayed a "typical" housewife rushing through her day as mother, wife, and student, with no hint that she sought any liberation other than an occasional drink of Coke. Outside each office at The Coca-Cola Company, one journalist wrote, "sits an engaging,

---

[*] It is difficult to know what Robert Woodruff's real feelings about civil rights were by 1964. He remained good friends with J. Edgar Hoover, who had placed Martin Luther King, Jr., at the head of his "enemies list" and delighted in replaying tapes of the black leader's illicit sexual encounters. In August of 1963, the same month in which King made his famous "I Have a Dream" speech, Hoover wrote to Woodruff, assuring him that "all of us at the FBI will strive to continue to merit the support you have given us."

competent secretary who guards her man pleasantly but firmly." Sexism thrived in the America of the mid-sixties. Coca-Cola's "Smile Girl" promotion offered prizes to the most toothsome beauties, while "curvaceous misses" added sex appeal to bottler convention skits.

Unconcerned by sweeping societal changes, Coca-Cola's legal department fussed and fretted over the proper use of the trademark. One should never relegate the product to the status of a "common adjective," for instance, as in "Coke party." Nor should the sacred product ever be pluralized—one drank several bottles of Coke, never several Cokes. Advising disc jockeys in 1965, the Company men gave them a list of appropriate "happy words you may use," such as "Coca-Cola lifts your spirits," or "Any meal goes better with Coke."

Soft drink sales in 1965 were bubbling along, rising to an annual American per capita of 260 drinks. Coca-Cola commanded 41 percent of the market, with Pepsi trailing at 23.5 percent. Nor was the Company resting on its laurels under Paul Austin's management. In 1964, it had acquired a coffee business with Houston-based Duncan Foods in exchange for $30 million worth of Coke stock. Many Company men surmised that Woodruff had pursued the merger primarily in order to bring dynamic young Charles Duncan, Jr., into the Coca-Cola fold. On another front, Coke was offending orange juice competitors by advertising Minute Maid as if it were a soft drink. Ben Oehlert, now the president of the subsidiary, pointed out that traditional ads urged mothers "to see to it the kiddies take a four-ounce dose of the stuff at breakfast." Abandoning such medicinal claims, Coke stressed the "natural sweetness, natural freshness" of orange juice, selling it in vending machines. Along with Hi-C, the Company's diluted fruit drink, Oehlert pushed orange juice as a fine refreshment any time of the day.

Meanwhile, the Company was developing other flavors. In Texas, it introduced Chime, a cherry-flavored cola designed to compete with Dr Pepper. That was a flop, but Fresca, a carbonated grapefruit-lemon diet drink, proved an overnight sensation, surprising even Coca-Cola men. The drink's cool refreshment was emphasized rather than its lack of calories. As an announcer recounted Fresca's virtues, snow drifted down, gradually building to a windblown storm. "It's a blizzard!" he yelled through chattering teeth. Providentially, the worst snowstorm in years hit New York City on February 7, 1967, the day of the local Fresca roll-out. An inspired ad man had his picture taken holding a bottle of Fresca in the white swirls. "New York, We Are Sorry," read the caption.

Pepsi-Cola's Don Kendall matched Coke step-for-step in the creation of other drinks with Teem, Mountain Dew, and others. In 1965, Pepsi joined Frito-Lay to become Pepsico. "Potato chips make you thirsty," Kendall offered as explanation of the merger. "Pepsi satisfies thirst." With the addition of snack foods, Pepsi relied much more heavily than Coke on nondrink income, a trend which would increase with the years. In 1968, Pepsi acquired Trailer Convoy, American Van Lines, and Chandler Leasing.

The Coca-Cola phenomenon garnered most of the attention, though. The Company "gyrates with new products, new packaging, new acquisitions," wrote an awed commentator. Not since Robert Woodruff assumed command in the twenties had the Company been so supercharged. "Growth is essential," Paul Austin said. "We must grow as individuals, as a Company, as a nation." As a sign of change, Austin authorized construction of a multistory edifice on North Avenue to complement the old red-brick building. New marketing head Fred Dickson stressed that "we sell Coca-Cola to a vast, fickle, forgetful public. Right now some new trend may be starting that will change the whole contemporary scene."

Coke was well aware of one clear trend. Fast-food chains were "mush-rooming," a Company publication noted, mentioning McDonald's, Carrols, Burger Chef, Burger King, Henry's, Biff-Burger, Jiffy's, Chip's, and Braziers. While these new outlets dispensed a flood of Coca-Cola, the Company was convinced they could sell more. "Whaddayahave, whaddayahave?" was the impatient query at The Varsity in Atlanta, the world's largest fast-food outlet. In the training film *Walk-Up Hospitality*, Coca-Cola urged counter personnel to smile brightly and suggest a large ice-cold Coke along with that order of fries. McDonald's and Jiffy's were viewed as battlegrounds in a deadly serious contest. Veteran Lee Talley reveled in the challenge, issuing a call to arms in the cola wars, taking "joy in the fray, asking no quarter and giving none." Coca-Cola skits, elaborately staged by Jam Handy Productions with profes-sional actors, whipped Company men into a frenzy. "We'll fight 'em in the streets, in the drive-ins, in the skating rinks," an actor playing a district manager promised in 1965.

THE ARAB BOYCOTT BLUES

That same year, Paul Austin convinced Woodruff that things could go better for Coke behind the Iron Curtain as well as in the drive-ins and skating rinks of America. The Bulgarian government signed on as a Coca-Cola bottler, importing concentrate from the Company, since the local imitation, Bulgar Cola, failed to find a market. Rumania, Czechoslovakia, and Yugoslavia soon followed suit.

Austin initiated contacts with the Soviet government, but he was afraid that selling Coke in the USSR might prompt an American backlash. Testing the waters, he dispatched Boisfeuillet Jones, who now worked for Robert Woodruff's philanthropic endeavors, to meet secretly with Averell Harriman in Washington. When Jones asked whether the State Department would object to the sale of Coca-Cola in Russia, Harriman responded that the venture would be "in the national interest." After a favorable consensus from other advisers—even cold warrior Jim Farley approved, writing that if Coca-Cola didn't "get in there," Pepsi undoubtedly would—Austin sent Alex Makinsky and another Russian-speaking Coke man to the Kremlin to work out the details. Coca-Cola would be bottled in Moscow for sale only to outlets operated by Intourist, the Russian travel bureau, as part of an overall Soviet plan to attract foreign money. When word leaked of the impending deal, however, the Company received negative press. The profits from

Russian Coke, one paper complained, would "help the Kremlin's pals—in Red China and Viet Nam—pals whose troops and Viet Cong puppets are killing, wounding and capturing good U.S. fighting men." Concluding that Americans probably weren't yet prepared for a rapprochement with the Communists, Austin—possibly at Woodruff's behest—postponed the project.

In 1966, despite Austin's best efforts, Coca-Cola became a hot political topic anyway. The Company refused to grant a franchise to an Israeli bottler, and the Anti-Defamation League accused Coca-Cola of compliance with the Arab Boycott of Israel. Within a week, the American Jewish community was calling for a boycott of its own. Manhattan's Mt. Sinai Hospital stopped serving Coke in its cafeteria, and Nathan's Famous Hot Dog emporium on Coney Island threatened to turn off the spigot as well. Offended Jews threw Coke coolers out of second-story windows in Chicago and Los Angeles. Coca-Cola had to act quickly if it didn't want to lose the lucrative American Jewish market. James Farley defended the Company by pointing out that Coca-Cola had attempted to enter Israel back in 1949, but had been denied because of rampant anti-American feeling. Furthermore, market research had revealed that conditions in Israel weren't conducive to profitable sales. No one bought Farley's explanations, and boycott plans progressed.

Swiftly, The Coca-Cola Company moved to find a bottler, announcing within days that New York banker Abraham Feinberg, one of the original applicants back in 1949, was interested in funding an Israeli franchise, and the Company had signed a letter of intent with him. The hubbub in the United States died down, but the war drums began beating in the Arab countries, where Coca-Cola sold 100,000 cases a year through thirty locally owned bottling plants. The hot, dry Middle Eastern countries provided ideal customers for Coke, since Muslims were not allowed to touch alcohol. "From Morocco to Pakistan," one journalist noted, "the modern oasis is the soft-drink stand." Now, the Arabs gave Coca-Cola until August 15 to cancel its commitment to Feinberg. The Company stood to lose some $20 million in profits per year, in addition to handing over the huge territory to Pepsi, which was avoiding Israel without fanfare.

Coke's customary lobbyists shifted into high gear. Ben Oehlert brought a personal plea from President Johnson to Mostafa Kamel, the United Arab Republic's ambassador to the United States. His Excellency Kamel was terribly sympathetic, writing that "nothing is closer to my heart than participating through my modest efforts in promoting cooperation between our two countries," but he was powerless on "this delicate issue." Feinberg, he suggested, should proceed as slowly as possible to gain time. Meanwhile, Alexander Makinsky rushed around the Middle East taking stock of the grim situation. Egypt, whose lead other Arab countries would follow, was looking for an excuse to jettison Coke anyway, since it needed to save on foreign exchange. Makinsky hoped that his friend Angel Sagaz, the Spanish ambassador to Cairo, who had once served as the Coke lobbyist's intermediary with Franco, could help. Since the Spanish were firm friends of the Arabs and refused to do business with Israel, perhaps Sagaz could intercede for the soft drink in Cairo.

Coke's only real hope, Makinsky felt, lay in immediate negotiations to construct a concentrate plant in Egypt, which would result in most of the capital remaining in the country. The Egyptians, he pointed out, were realists; money spoke louder than anti-Semitism. Makinsky also stressed that all of the bottling plants were owned by Arabs and that the boycott would put some 25,000 natives out of work. In addition, Coca-Cola men emphasized that they were not investing one cent inside Israel—like Hilton Hotels and other international companies which had franchises in Israel without actually owning the business there themselves.

Nothing worked. Coca-Cola fell victim to its own symbolism as *the* typical American product, and the Arab demagogues whipped up such an emotional climate that the soft drink company could find no middle road. Refusing to renege on the promise to Feinberg, Coca-Cola watched helplessly as the Arab boycott against the product finally commenced in August of 1968. Coca-Cola men like John Brinton, who watched the Middle Eastern business collapse after nearly twenty years of hard work, insisted that it was ultimately a business rather than a moral decision: "They would have lost a lot more if they hadn't given the franchise to Israel because of the Jewish boycott in the United States."

UNRAVELING AT HOME

By the time the Arab Boycott officially went into effect late in 1968, America itself was coming unglued, primarily because of protest over the escalating conflict in Vietnam. Regarding the civil strife in Vietnam as a fight to the death with Communism, Lyndon Johnson was determined to win at any cost. As the war heated up, Coca-Cola men first saw it as one more patriotic opportunity to sell soft drinks to GIs, as with World War II and Korea. They sent Anita Bryant to Southeast Asia to sing for the boys in 1965, tagging a photo with the caption, "Our Anita Cheers Troops With Bob Hope." The same year, the Company built bottling plants in Danang and Qui-Nhon to supplement the overworked Saigon operation. As American troops poured into Vietnam, where returnable bottles presented quite a problem, the Company also shipped over nearly 400,000 cartons of canned Coca-Cola. In the John Wayne movie *The Green Berets*, an entire pallet of Coca-Cola parachuted to thirsty jungle troops.

Writer Tom Wolfe suggested that rather than saturation bombing, the U.S. should "seduce its way to victory" by showering North Vietnam with Coca-Cola. A Japanese philosopher urged the same tactic for a different reason. "That will destroy them faster than bombs," he said. The war in Vietnam starkly contrasted with World War II, however, and the Company soon realized it. While wartime advertising in the forties highlighted Coca-Cola's vital presence in the foxholes, no ads proclaimed that things went better with Coke in Vietnam. James Farley, the aging Coca-Cola Cold Warrior, couldn't understand the escalating antiwar protests, offering his "unhesitating support" to the President. Similarly, Robert Woodruff wrote to LBJ that the "American people are supporting your position. I am with you."

Johnson's earnest appeals to "my fellow Americans" fell on increasingly deaf ears, however, as television escorted bloody jungle scenes into American living rooms. The Tet Offensive early in 1968 nailed the final peg in the coffin of a presidency devoted to unifying America, eliminating poverty, and promoting peace throughout the world. Instead, Johnson faced race riots, burning inner cities, massive antiwar demonstrations, and a growing counter-culture that rejected all the American virtues of hard work, cleanliness, respect for authority, and restraint. By the end of March, Johnson was completely demoralized and announced that he would not run for another term.

The dismal year of 1968 also heralded personal tragedy for Robert Woodruff. In January, his wife, Nell, suffered a stroke at Ichauway and died soon after. Though Woodruff was often away from his wife, she had provided his emotional anchor. At the age of seventy-eight, with the America he had known in shambles, Woodruff, always a heavy drinker, now increasingly turned to alcohol rather than Coca-Cola. When news of Martin Luther King's assassination reached the White House, President Johnson and Robert Woodruff were there together, drinking away their mutual sorrows. Aware that the country, and particularly the South, could explode with racial violence, the Boss called Atlanta's mayor Ivan Allen. "Ivan," he said, "the minute they bring King's body back tomorrow—between then and the time of the funeral—Atlanta, Georgia, is going to be the center of the universe. I want you to do whatever is right and necessary, and whatever the city can't pay for will be taken care of. Do you understand what I'm saying?" The mayor understood that he could dip into the deep pockets of Woodruff and Coca-Cola, and he promptly dispatched the Windship, Coca-Cola's Lear jet, to bring Coretta Scott King back to Atlanta. As blacks rioted in over a hundred American cities, Atlanta avoided major bloodshed, thanks largely to the collaboration of Allen and Woodruff.

Richard Nixon, resuscitated and scripted by Pepsi men and their ad agency, BBDO, won the presidency at year's end, after a campaign appealing to the "Silent Majority" of Americans who recoiled in horror from the discord tearing the country apart. Nixon's election, however only signaled more trouble ahead for a deeply divided country. Coca-Cola's vintage advertising appeared more and more out of synch with the times. In an attempt to stay hip and cool, the company hired Bruce Brown, creator of the film *Endless Summer*, to narrate a 1968 "Things Go Better" commercial in which California surfers swigged Coke. "Someone's always makin' waves in this world," Brown philosophized on the voice-over. "Maybe that's why Coca-Cola is the world's most popular drink." The implication of this non sequitur was that people who "made waves" drank Coke, but the young people who were shaking up America had advanced beyond the Beach Boy mentality. Johnny the Dork of the fifties Coke commercial had grown into Johnny the Hippie.

By 1968, in other words, things weren't going better anywhere in America, and the six-year-old campaign was showing its age. In an attempt at relevance, the Company ran an ad which was an elaborate takeoff on the Statue of Liberty inscription. "America," it read, "give me your hot, your thirsty, your weary, . . . your sons, your daughters, your surfers, your skiers, your football players, . . . your sun worshipers, your moon worshipers, your potato chip nuts, your pretzel eaters, . . . your vacuum cleaner salesmen, your ushers, your hippies, your high school students yearning to pass math. Things go better with Coke." The message, of course, was that Coca-Cola stood for America and appealed to everyone, but the Coke ad seemed flat, forced, and unbelievable.

Looking toward the seventies, Coke men searched desperately for a new unifying theme. Again, lyricist Bill Backer came through with the perfect vehicle. McCann's psychological researchers reported that young people despised hypocrites and phonies and valued genuine, spontaneous feelings. With these findings, Backer resurrected an old 1942 slogan and created "The Real Thing" campaign. Coca-Cola was "real," not phony. It was part of the authentic, natural goodness that the counterculture was seeking. At the same time, of course, the phrase was a subtle dig at Pepsi, which by implication was a fraud. The new slogan echoed the hippies' catch-all invocation to "do your own thing." Sure, the song implied—but do it with the Real Thing in hand.

The visuals to accompany the sincere new lyric utilized still documentary style photography, with the movie camera performing the action by zooming and tilting to highlight each shot. One of the first "Real Thing" television commercials, launched in October of 1969, opened in Manhattan with a group of white and black teenagers playing basketball—the first real integrated Coke TV spot. It then traveled across America showing peaceful dirt roads, farms with windmills, log cabins, pretty young women, the American flag, and a California beach scene. The ad implied that *this* was the real America, not the violence and dissonance seen on the evening news.

Coca-Cola had miraculously implemented a slogan and campaign which appealed to both hawk and dove, National Guard and hippie, parent and child. While the commercials were innovative, however, they remained firmly grounded in the Coca-Cola tradition. Although the ads were oriented to "life-style" and emotional issues, the drink itself remained the star of the show. Somewhat illogically, Paul Austin observed that the new ads would "reflect Coke's awareness of minority and other social sensitivities by stressing the product rather than people."

Pepsi changed campaigns the same year, returning to the social implications of the earlier Pepsi Generation. "You've got a lot to live," the jingle asserted, "and Pepsi's got a lot to give." The emphasis was on people, however, not Pepsi. Unlike Coke's tranquil, almost elegiac commercials, the Pepsi efforts showcased strenuous group activity. These young cola drinkers were "coming at you, growing strong," bursting with energy and good times. As Coca-Cola men smugly noted, Pepsi people had to try harder in an effort to catch the leader.

As Coke's "Real Thing" commercials flooded the airwaves late in 1969, the

Company performed a simultaneous face-lift. Coca-Cola men concluded that the Company had done its work *too* well with its ubiquitous signs. Ike Herbert, Coke's new advertising chief, enjoyed pointing toward downtown Atlanta from his office window. "There are eleven signs down there," he said, "but most people can find only two or three, and they know what they are looking for." The innumerable Coke signs had vanished into the landscape. Particularly concerned about the battered old red disks and multi-colored signs in the nation's urban ghettos and rural outbacks, the Company hired a New York firm, Lippincott & Margulies, to design a "mod" look for Coke. Code-named Project Arden as a reference to the famed cosmetic line, the assignment, as a Company memo put it, was to "take Coca-Cola, shorten her skirt, lift her face, give her a new hairdo, a whole 'now' style and catapult her back into the awareness of the consumer." The resulting square sign sported a white "Dynamic Ribbon"—echoing the hobbleskirt bottle contour—running under the traditional script logo. At the same time, the simple phrase "Drink Coca-Cola" was altered to "Enjoy Coca-Cola"—a more fitting command from the image-conscious Company.

In a burst of self-important pizzazz, the Company introduced the new look and the Real Thing campaign simultaneously at its national bottlers convention in October of 1969 with a sound-and-light show that was the biggest thing to hit Atlanta since *Gone With the Wind* premiered there in 1939. Some journalists weren't impressed with the hype, comparing it to "a flourish of trumpets and a roll of drums—followed by two Coke bottles clinking weakly together."

The new look and campaign were, however, more than window-dressing: the Company really *had* changed, and many longtime employees didn't like it. In 1965, when the brand manager system commenced, different groups were scattered around Atlanta in satellite locations, pending the completion of a new eleven-story complex on North Avenue. During the remainder of the decade, the separate departments swelled, often duplicating functions. "Whenever you needed something done," Charlie Bottoms recalled, "you just created a new position." Within a few years, a staff below 500 mushroomed to 1,500 people. When the Company moved into its new quarters in 1969, secretary Mary Gresham found her surroundings drab and depressing as she sat behind her coffinlike black desk in the hall, staring at the modern wallpaper which, she thought, resembled aluminum foil. The 35-cent lunch served by waiters had ceased. Instead, employees filed through a cafeteria to buy blander, more expensive food. "For so many years," Gresham lamented, "it had been like living in a small town where everyone knew everyone else and their business. That closeness just wasn't there anymore."

POTENT NUTRITION AND THE GREAT CYCLAMATE SCARE

With a new decade only two months away, Paul Austin had navigated Coca-Cola through the turbulent sixties in remarkably good shape. The stock had split 2-for-1 twice, in 1965 and 1968. In 1969, gross sales for the Company topped $1.3 billion, with its $121 million profit more than doubling that of Pepsi. True, Coke was spending nearly that amount with its $100 million annual advertising campaign, but thinner profit margins were simply a fact of life in a competitive market. Coca-Cola was now sold in 135 countries, and the overseas opportunities appeared limitless.

Nonetheless, the Company could hardly rest easy with its new campaign and logo, particularly in its home market, which still produced 50 percent of its sales volume. The Vietnam War had artificially stimulated the U.S. economy, now tottering from accumulated debt. Meanwhile, the protesters were shifting their attention from the war to pollution, poverty, malnutrition, racism, sexism, poor education, and chemical additives. Sensitive to increasing criticism about Coca-Cola's lack of vitamins or nutritional value, Paul Austin authorized the development of Saci (pronounced "SAH-see"), a protein-rich soft drink—equivalent to a glass of milk—that would also taste good. The previous year, test marketing had begun in Brazil, but kids apparently didn't like the taste. In 1969, Ralph Nader, fresh from his victory over General Motors, attacked Coca-Cola in a hearing before the Select Committee on Nutrition and Human Needs. "While The Coca-Cola Company is distributing a high protein chocolate drink . . . to developing countries," the crusader complained, "it supplies the United States with cola—a massive affliction that someday may be characterized as a disease."

On short notice, Paul Austin rushed to testify before the committee, exercising damage control. "The Coca-Cola Company is keenly mindful of its responsibility as a member of society wherever it does business," he informed the senators. Nonetheless, it couldn't just give away the new drink, but must create a sound business venture, making Saci "equally attractive to the consumer and producer." Austin promised that the Company intended to market Saci to America's undernourished children as soon as the kinks were finessed. The Coca-Cola executive admitted that "we are twisting and turning" and that the taste had been modified twice and was still unsatisfactory. One senator who had brought two Saci bottles home to his Coke-loving children told Austin they hated the protein drink. "I thank you for your candor," Austin replied between gritted teeth.

The beleaguered Coke executive would find plenty of reasons to grind his molars in the years to come. Only a week after the flashy bottlers' convention unveiling the Real Thing and the Dynamic Ribbon, the Food and Drug Administration sounded another theme of the approaching seventies by revealing alarming test results on cyclamates, the sweetener in most diet drinks. The experiments, funded in part by the sugar industry, showed that laboratory rats on a cyclamate diet developed malignant bladder tumors. The FDA had no choice but to remove the chemical from the Generally Recognized As Safe (GRAS) list, and to ban it under the 1958 Delaney Amendment.

It didn't matter that the rats had ingested fifty times the amount a human was likely to absorb. Coke's Fred Dickson pointed out that an adult would have to drink 550 Frescas a day for the equivalent dosage. "You'd drown before you'd get cancer," he told a reporter. Another soft drink executive noted bitterly that "under that law, you can ban sunshine." With sensational coverage in all the media, however, the country panicked. Cyclamates, virtually unheard of the week before, were suddenly the equivalent to poison. Even before the drinks were banned, The Coca-Cola Company started pulling TaB and Fresca from the shelves.

The Company quickly produced alternative versions of the drinks, converting Fresca completely to saccharin, while adding sugar to TaB's saccharin. Trying to mask the new calories, the Company obtained FDA approval to advertise TaB as "six calories per fluid ounce" rather than revealing the total amount per drink as it had before. Coke men worked feverishly around the clock on new formulas and labels. The cyclamate ban didn't hurt the Company too much domestically (a mere $2.5 million loss in the fourth quarter of 1969), since its diet drinks accounted for only 10 percent of sales. Royal Crown, whose Diet-Rite dominated the market, was badly shaken. Oddly enough, Coca-Cola experienced its worst problems in Japan, where the Company didn't even market drinks with cyclamates. Rumors spread that Coca-Cola itself contained the alarming sweetener, and Japanese consumers, even more finicky and quick to panic than their American counterparts, stopped buying the American soft drink. It took a determined public relations campaign to build sales volume again.

Another American problem spilled overseas to South Africa, where Coca-Cola's thirty-seven bottling plants dominated the soft drink industry. Because of America's heightened racial awareness, in 1968 Congress passed sanctions on the apartheid regime for the first time—a particular blow to Paul Austin, who had managed the South African business in the fifties. The newly imposed restrictions would "force us to milk our European business," Austin complained.

As the year drew to a close, Paul Austin outlined his concern over "anti-establishmentarianism" in a detailed memo to Robert Woodruff. The under thirty generation had literally forced LBJ out of office and was now focusing on other concerns. Because of its dominant position, Austin noted, The Coca-Cola Company "epitomizes the Establishment" and needed to implement programs to deflect criticism. "Following withdrawal from Vietnam," he predicted, "the Group's target will become pollution." Austin observed that "we participate in the litter to a significant degree" with throw-away bottles and cans, not to mention billboards. The nutritionally empty drink also lay open for criticism. Its highly visible truck fleet made Coke an "ideal target." Coca-Cola, the star of the show, desperately needed supporting products and programs to appeal to idealistic youth. Austin urged prompt action on several fronts. Perhaps more important than any profit, however, he sought what he called "the halo effect." Coke must appear to be doing good in the world.

Austin's words proved prophetic, if too late to avert trouble. Coca-Cola, the "ideal target," had already caught the eye of politicians and government bureaucrats. Worse, the Company had attracted the ferocious attention of Cesar Chavez, a hero of the baby boomers. For Coca-Cola, the seventies would commence on a sour note.

～ 17 ～

Big Red's Uneasy Slumber

We used to say, "Be careful not to wake up Big Red. Be aggressive, but don't wake up Big Red."

—Deke DeLoach, retired Pepsi lobbyist

IN 1979, a Coca-Cola executive reviewed a dismal decade. "Had we stood in Atlanta in 1969 on the threshold of the seventies," he told assembled bottlers, "and were endowed with some Gypsy ability to see into the future, I think that we would have quailed at the prospect that lay before us." Paul Austin had no such "Gypsy ability" in 1969, but he sensed trouble when Cesar Chavez, fresh from his victory over the California grape growers, toured Florida. "His next target," Austin lamented in a memo to Woodruff, "will be Citrus. He mentioned our Company by name." Austin knew that Chavez couldn't be lightly dismissed. "He has adopted the role and general mien of a Messiah," he wrote gloomily. The situation in Florida's Minute Maid groves was vulnerable, since the Company hired some 6,000 migrant workers during the picking season. Most were black. Pay was minimal. Men, women, and children lived in "barrack-like structures" without bathrooms or recreation facilities. "If we were the subject of a pictorial news report," Austin concluded, "we would come off badly."

In 1960, the same year in which Coke acquired Minute Maid, Edward R. Murrow had first spotlighted the horrendous conditions in Florida's orange groves in the CBS documentary *Harvest of Shame*. No one at the soft drink company had shown much concern. Ten years later, just months after the alarmed Austin memo, Chet Huntley narrated an NBC update called *Migrant*, showing that nothing had changed in a decade. Coca-Cola's groves were highlighted, with an irate Minute Maid overseer caught on camera, belligerently ordering the TV crew to leave. Although Paul Austin and Luke Smith, the president of Coca-Cola Foods, had explained Coke's strategies to improve conditions to Martin Carr, the show's producer, the documentary did not mention them.

Only days before *Migrant* was aired, Smith and Austin sat in on a closed-circuit pre-screening for Houston NBC affiliates. They were not happy with what they saw. Enraged, Austin called NBC president Julian Goodman, screaming that the station was doing "a bitch job on Coke." The television executive listened politely, since Coca-Cola had already purchased over $2 million worth of TV spots on NBC for the 1970 season. In the end, NBC agreed to add one sentence about Coke's "major plan which it claims will correct . . . failings," and to delete a statement that Coke set the standards for the entire industry.

The cosmetic changes failed to deflect bad publicity. When Martin Carr told the press of the "enormous pressure" applied by the Coke men to modify his documentary, the Company came across as a corporate censor. Less than a week after the documentary aired on July 15, Senator Walter Mondale chaired a subcommittee to explore the migrants' plight. "Nothing will change," Mondale chaired in his opening statement, "until this rotten system is exposed and held accountable." Philip Moore, the head of the Project on Corporate Responsibility, told the senators that while the migrants worked for slave wages, Paul Austin earned $150,000 a year and owned 55,000 shares of Coke stock paying annual dividends of $79,200. "I would like to ask Mr Austin," Moore said, "why is it that when it comes to profit, corporations work fast, but when it comes to human conditions, corporations at best plod along?" Moore concluded with a scathing forecast. "I just know that Austin and other Coke officials are going to come breezing into these hearings and they are going to say, 'Boys, we're sorry. We're sorry for raping these people. We're sorry that we don't pay them enough to live a month, much less a year. We're sorry that migrant workers die at the age of forty-nine . . . But now we're going to be better.'"

Several days later, when Austin, accompanied by lawyer Joseph Califano, appeared before Mondale's committee, he fulfilled Moore's expectations.[*] He admitted that conditions for the Minute Maid workers were "deplorable," but the Company now planned to hire many migrants as regular employees with full benefits. Coca-Cola would properly house and feed them, provide adequate child and health care, and offer recreational opportunities. Finally, Austin called for a National Alliance of Agri-Businessmen, modeled on the National Alliance of Businessmen.

Austin's performance was nearly flawless under the senators' hard questioning. He observed that in addition to problems of malnutrition and poor housing, the migrants suffered from "a profound sense of futility." He proposed giving them "human dignity" and a chance "to rise not only in our citrus operations but throughout the whole structure of our organization." The Coca-Cola executive slipped only once, betraying a condescending racism. "These people," he explained, "do not have a philosophy of work discipline."

Combined with tangible results of the subsequent Agriculture Labor Project (ALP), Austin turned the initially adverse media reaction into a public relations bonanza. *Time* headlined Austin's Senate speech as "The Candor That Refreshes." Black orange-picker Willy Reynolds became a star inter-

---

[*] Califano recalled that "it was the most hostile hearing room I've ever walked into, jammed with interns and angry students. A young, dark-haired woman with glasses came up to me and said, 'You shit, you've sold out.' It was Hillary Clinton."

viewee after moving into his own home in Frostproof, Florida. "It's like bein' born again," he said. "I'd been in houses like this but I was always a visitor. I never thought I'd own one." *Business Week* gave Coke its 1970 Award for Business Citizenship. Even Ralph Nader was impressed by Austin's sincerity when Joe Califano arranged a dinner for the two men. After listening politely to the Coca-Cola executive's description of his horror at conditions in the orange groves, Nader asked, "What's a sensitive man like you, with a degree from Harvard Law School, doing pumping syrupy brown drinks into people's stomachs?" Looking the consumer crusader straight in the eye, Austin answered, "I don't think there's anything wrong with selling a refreshing drink."

LITTER, POLLUTION, AND OTHER IRRITANTS

Even as the Company narrowly escaped accusations of cold-hearted neglect of migrant workers, however, it faced angry environmentalists. By the beginning of the seventies, 40 percent of all soft drinks were packaged in "one-way" containers, and the figure was steadily rising. Just after Earth Day during the summer of 1970, protesters dumped mounds of nonreturnable Coke bottles in front of the North Avenue headquarters. At the same time, bottle deposit bills cropped up in state legislatures. One 1971 survey claimed that 5 percent of the country's solid waste litter were containers manufactured by The Coca-Cola Company. Company men explained, with some justification, that if Coke went back to returnable bottles and Pepsi didn't, they would invite disaster in the marketplace. Consumers demanded an end to litter in the abstract, but at home they wanted the convenience of a throw-away container.

Hoping to defuse criticism, Coca-Cola urged recycling, stressing that most of the Company-owned bottling plants were returning glass and paper to vendors for reuse. Company advertising teams introduced billboards with a clever wordplay on the hawkish chant of Vietnam hard-liners to either love America or leave it. "If you love me," exhorted the sign displaying Coke cans and bottles, "don't leave me." To catch the public's attention, the Company willingly broke its rule about overt sexuality in the interest of litter prevention. "Bend a little," one ad teased, showing a pretty girl's behind as she leaned over to pick up a bottle.

While Austin had clearly approached the migrant uproar as a pragmatic business problem, he appeared to be genuinely concerned about environmental issues. In the tropical serenity of the Bahamas, Coca-Cola managers engaged in a series of Harvard-run seminars with high-power academics from across the United States. Unlike the standard management meetings, these humanistic sessions emphasized broad, sweeping visions, self-actualization, and environmental awareness. They had an enormous impact on Austin and his associates. In the world of the future, they learned, clean water would prove more valuable than gold. Austin asked Bob Broadwater, already in charge of subsidiary acquisitions, to hire a cadre of eager young Harvard Business

School graduates and devise practical ways to apply the seminar's lesson. Reporting directly to Austin outside of the run-of-the mill Coke bureaucracy, the group soon earned its nickname as "Austin's Orphans."

Broadwater and his Orphans delighted in their freedom to explore new areas. Their first find was Aqua-Chem, a leading company in the field of desalinization and water purification which might also provide leverage for ending the Arab Boycott, since the arid countries of the Mideast badly needed desalinization plants. The Orphans purchased a natural-water bottler in Massachusetts; raised hydroponic fruits and vegetables under plastic on Kharg Island in Iran; bought a Wisconsin plastics company to experiment with biodegradable garbage bags and bottles; shrimp farmed in Mexico. After an all-day session with Sterling Livingston, a former Harvard professor who had founded his own management-teaching complex in Boston and Washington, D.C., the educator suggested the enterprising Coke men buy his Sterling Institute outright. "Hell, it was only a million dollars," Broadwater recalled. "We spilled that much before breakfast in those days."

With the exception of the natural-water company, none of Broadwater's acquisitions paid handsome returns. Clearly, Paul Austin was willing to forgo immediate profits to pursue his "halo effect." After all, in 1970 the Company sat on $150 million in cash, and the money kept pouring in from soft drink sales, mounting to $300 million by 1974. Why not let the idealistic young managers have a go? Austin took a fatherly interest in them. "It's fascinating," he said. "In three years you watch a boy grow into a businessman."

Not merely a paternalistic executive treating new businesses as toys, Austin was a born-again ecologist, lecturing the Georgia Bankers Association in an apocalyptic 1970 address grandly titled "Environmental Renewal or Oblivion . . . Quo Vadis?" The Coca-Cola president passionately reviewed "the stark evidence of environmental homicide," warning of "an oblivion comprised of undrinkable water and air that can't be breathed." The complacent Southern bankers must have been astonished to hear the head of Coca-Cola sounding like Ralph Nader on amphetamines. "We're firing rockets at the moon—while standing knee deep in our own garbage," he continued. "Unless *all* of us begin *immediately* to reverse the processes of impending self-destruction which *we* have set in motion—this green land of ours will become a *graveyard*!"

Not only that, but Austin was alarmed over the population explosion. "Within the lifetime of a child born *this* year, there will be some *fifteen billion* inhabitants on this incredibly delicate Earth." Austin called these "vast hordes of humanity" a frightening prospect, but his fellow Coke men must have thought he had lost his mind. What had happened to the traditional value system which held that a human being's primary function on earth was to serve as a conduit for Coca-Cola? On one level Paul Austin sincerely believed what he told the bankers; however, he never lost sight of his ultimate goal of selling more soft drinks. As one commentator observed a few years later, The Coca-

Cola Company and its men "seem to function simultaneously on two levels: one lofty, even Platonic, the other unrelentingly practical." After all of Austin's fulminations, his concrete proposals for Coca-Cola were rather tame. As soon as some "efficient device" came along to eliminate hydrocarbon emissions, he promised to convert the enormous fleet of Coke trucks to it. In the meantime, they would continue to go their polluting rounds. He noted that 70 percent of Coke's containers were still returnables, and he hoped to find a one-way plastic bottle which could be incinerated without releasing hydrocarbons.

THE FTC ATTACKS

Sincere or not, Austin's speeches and Coke's ecological efforts failed to avert renewed governmental attention. Any Coca-Cola man with a sense of history must have foreseen it, since the Federal Trade Commission had sued Asa Candler over fifty years before. Now, led by crusading commissioner Robert Pitofsky and encouraged by the strong consumer movement, the FTC again attacked Coca-Cola.

The first brush concerned Big Name Bingo, an under-the-crown promotion. TaB and Coke consumers could win $100 by attaching appropriate bottle-cap liners, on which twenty famous people were portrayed, as answers to ten questions on the Bingo card. The FTC objected to the contest, since the rules didn't clarify that the trick questions demanded multiple answers. Most entrants, for instance, correctly identified Admiral Byrd as having gone on an Arctic expedition. To win a prize, however, they also had to glue Horatio Nelson's bottle-cap liner to that question. Similarly, both Woodrow Wilson and Guglielmo Marconi attended the Paris Peace Conference. Not surprisingly, there were only 831 winners out of 1.5 million entries. Shortly after the FTC lodged its complaint, two class-action suits, totaling $425 million, were lodged against Coca-Cola and the Glendinning Company, which actually administered the contest for the soft drink company.

While the Bingo farce garnered unfavorable headlines, it cost the Company little money. Undaunted, the FTC promptly mounted a second front. In 1971, it brought suit against Coca-Cola for allegedly misleading Hi-C advertisements in which a hapless father allowed his children to consume potato chips, cookies, and other junk food. "Some lunch!" the narrator said. "But Dad knows the only sensible thing about it is ice-cold Hi-C." The drink was, he continued, "made with real fruit and it's high in Vitamin C." FTC prosecutors observed that there was little real fruit juice in Hi-C and that it contained less vitamin C than orange juice, while the ads implied otherwise. The commercials also conveyed the notion that it didn't matter whether kids ate junk food or not, as long as they drank Hi-C. The FTC men were particularly upset by a joint promotion with Kellogg in which a little girl ate a Pop Tart and drank Hi-C for breakfast. The Company defended itself by declaring that the complaint was based on "personal and unscientific dietary notions." Just because the Commission preferred the consumption of natural fruit juices was no reason to penalize Hi-C and "discourage the American public from exercising its free choice of refreshment beverages." In 1972, the Commissioners agreed with Coke's lawyers and dismissed the case.

The same year, however, the FTC struck at the heart of the soft drink industry, alleging that the exclusive franchise system violated the Sherman Anti-Trust Act, since a bottler's monopoly over particular territory prevented fair competition. A mighty howl of protest rose over the United States, while Coke and Pepsi banded together to fight the common enemy. The FTC suit would drag on for years, casting a pall over the entire decade. The Coca-Cola Company and its bottlers pursued two strategies simultaneously, seeking vindication through the courts while lobbying hard for specific legislation to exempt soft drinks from prosecution. The legal twists and turns would profoundly affect the traditional relationship between the bottlers and the Company, but no one could have foreseen that in 1972.

TRICKY DICK WORKS HIS MAGIC

By the time of the third FTC suit, some frustrated Coca-Cola men smelled a rat, feeling that the many-pronged assaults could not be coincidental. President Nixon, deeply indebted to Pepsi's Don Kendall, must have decided a few dirty tricks were in order. "It's just my humble feeling," wrote one longtime fountain man, "but I think someone was sure trying to please the boss." Of course, the FTC case impacted Pepsi too, but the paranoid Coke men reasoned that the destruction of the exclusive franchise system would harm the leader far more. Concerned about the situation, Coke lobbyist Ovid Davis suggested the need for a high-level Washington retainer who would be "wired to the Nixon Administration."

Whether Nixon gave the word to the FTC or not, he clearly facilitated Pepsi's entry into the Soviet Union. Paul Austin had directed Export president John Talley to reopen negotiations with the USSR, and in September of 1972, Talley reported to Robert Woodruff that "it would seem that we have carried our 'holier than thou' attitude towards Russia far beyond the limits of good business judgment." What Talley didn't know was that Don Kendall had already cemented a deal with Soviet Premier Kosygin nearly a year before, during Kendall's Moscow visit as chair of an American delegation on U.S.-Soviet trade. Eager to buy U.S. wheat, Kosygin surmised that working a deal with Nixon's friend from Pepsi would be politically expedient. It took ten more months to iron out the details, but in November of 1972, just after Talley wrote his memo, Pepsi announced a ten-year exclusive contract with the Soviet Union.

Infuriated, Paul Austin berated himself for backing out of his opportunity in the late sixties. Determined to gain a Russian foothold, he assured Coca-Cola executives of his confidence that "Coca-Cola as the world's most popular soft drink in due course will be available in the Soviet Union," delegating the project to Bob Broadwater, who made over twenty trips to Russia during the next few years.

Nixon may have succeeded through back-door diplomacy with the Chinese and Russians, but he failed in many other presidential endeavors. As campus antiwar protests erupted, he sent National Guardsmen to Ohio to suppress dissent at Kent State University, where they opened fire, killing four students. The war had come home to roost. Incredible as it seemed, now Americans were killing their own children.

TEACHING THE WORLD TO SING

In the stunned aftermath, the antiwar movement lost its momentum, as many counterculture baby boomers abandoned the political struggle for a more personal peace. They clustered at love-ins, rock festivals, communes and cults, seeking meaning in a society which seemed bent on destroying itself. Popular music reflected this yearning for serenity and security. In 1970, Simon & Garfunkel's "Bridge Over Troubled Waters" went platinum, while the Beatles' "Let It Be" was a gold record. In the meantime, Coca-Cola's "Real Thing" campaign still clung to the theme song introduced in 1969, together with vignettes of American life. One commercial called "Wheels" focused on the country's obsession with mobility, while another flashed a quirky collection of sixty-three pictures in less than a minute, including the Statue of Liberty and, in a rare moment of self-parody, literally featuring Mom and apple pie. The campaign showed its age, though, and the frenetic style didn't match the shattered country's search for tranquillity.

In response, Bill Backer modified the "Real Thing" song as a quiet folk ballad that spoke of "Friendly feelings, friendly feelings, / Hope they're happenin' to you." The new lyric glided over visuals of happy, clean-cut young hippies—a boy and girl, guitar slung over her shoulder, dancing in a rural field, an outdoor wedding ceremony, a teen couple with white stars on their shirts, along with a suitable mixture of blacks—all laughing and enjoying a Coke. As the song ended, a warm-toned announcer informed audiences that "a bottle of Coke has brought more people together than any other soft drink in the world." In the final shot, one bottle of Coca-Cola leaned for comfort against another.

Backer's timing was, as usual, impeccable. A few months after "Friendly Feelings" aired in February of 1971, James Taylor's version of "You've Got a Friend" debuted with similar sentiments. Meanwhile, Backer was working on another variant of the "Real Thing" which would extend this yearning for friendship and brotherhood beyond the borders of the U.S., uniting the entire world in a fantasy of togetherness. Billy Davis, a black Motown producer and former member of The Four Tops, had joined the ad team, composing the music for one of the most popular commercials ever made.

On a hilltop in Italy, Coca-Cola assembled some 200 fresh-faced young adults from every corner of the world, clad appropriately in their national costumes. Standing in ordered ranks in an inverted pyramid and clutching bottles of Coke, they looked straight ahead as they earnestly sang, "I'd like to buy the world a home and furnish it with love, / Grow apple trees and honey bees and snow white turtle doves." The vision of the idealistic youths crooning to a weary world soothed like a hymn in an outdoor church, and their firmly clasped bottles of Coca-Cola were hopeful peace talismans. Just as Coke was building homes for its migrant workers, it meant to house the world in some ambiguous way. As hippies were retreating to hill farms, Backer's song spoke lyrically of growing apples and tending bees.

"I'd like to teach the world to sing in perfect harmony," the sweet voices continued. "I'd like to buy the world a Coke and keep it company. That's the real thing . . ." Released in July of 1971, the commercial caused a sensation. It didn't strike anyone as preposterous that a soft drink was somehow supposed to save the world, that the lyrics were oozing with stereotypical sentiment, or that the young people in the ad were only lip-synching to the voices of the New Seekers, a British pop group. The Company and bottlers were deluged with over 100,000 letters and requests for sheet music. Coke granted them, along with 45rpm records of the song. When radio stations balked at giving a commercial free air time, Backer rewrote the ballad to eliminate any reference to Coca-Cola, and the New Seekers recorded it. When their record hit the top of the charts, a hastily assembled group called the Hillside Singers issued a country-and-western version. By the beginning of 1972, the two recordings had sold a combined total of a million copies. It was, as *Newsweek* wryly observed, "a sure-fire form of subliminal advertising." Although Coca-Cola wasn't mentioned in the lyrics, everyone automatically thought of the soft drink every time they heard the song.

THE GOOD OLD DAYS AND TRAYS

As Americans struggled to fathom their troubled times, they not only sought the solace of a world singing in harmony, but looked back fondly to a time that now appeared sweetly innocent, when Americans believed in a benevolent God, rebellious kids did nothing worse than wear ducktails, the economy boomed, and America and its products dominated the world. In 1972, with the advent of *Grease* on Broadway, nostalgia for the fifties swept the country. Along with it, somewhat to the Company's surprise, a Coke memorabilia craze boomed.

In that same year, Cecil Munsey wrote the *Illustrated Guide to the Collectibles of Coca-Cola*, complete with early Hilda Clark and Lillian Nordica serving trays, twenties' flappers, Norman Rockwell's freckle-faced boys of the thirties, Haddon Sundblom's Santas, World War II fly-boys sipping their soft drinks, and wholesome fifties' beauties announcing Coke time. Across the country, collectors discovered one another through antiques publications, chance meetings at flea markets, and word of mouth. By 1975, the Cola Clan had been born. Kentucky architect Thom Thompson, still an active collector decades later, was one of the charter members. "When Munsey's book came out, we treated it like the Bible," he recalled. The book was dedicated to Wilbur Kurtz, Jr., the Company archivist, pictured among the trays and old bottles. At the club's first convention in Atlanta, Kurtz escorted the Coke devotees to his sanctum at North Avenue. "Wilbur was like a god to us," Thompson remembered. "We'd seen him in Munsey's book, and here he was in person. He was a great storyteller, even though a lot of his lore was probably fiction."

Suddenly, old calendars and trays swelled in value, selling for tens, then hundreds of dollars. Kurtz was at first startled by the flurry of interest, then delighted to find himself the center of attention, especially since various Company officials had tried to fire him in the past. "They thought I wasn't making any real contribution to the Company," Kurtz reminisced in an interview shortly before his death. "These were businessmen. They didn't think in terms of history and preservation." The nostalgia boom elevated the lowly archivist's status within the Company, as Coke marketing men, eager to cash in on the memorabilia, came to Kurtz for old items. Reproducing them, they resurrected early models like Hilda Clark on trays sold as premiums and given as prizes through the bottler system.

As riots and smog clouded once-vital cities, Coke's ad men mined America's mythic rural past. In 1972, country singer Dottie West wrote and performed another classic Coke commercial. "I was raised on country sunshine," she twanged, "I'm happy with the simple things: / A Saturday night dance, a bottle of Coke, and the joy that the bluebird brings." Shifting away from the quick vignette, this commercial told a sentimental home-coming story. As the young woman's taxi drove down the farm's dirt road, her brother jumped from the hayloft, little sister left the tire swing, Grandma beamed joyfully, and Dad abandoned his tractor. The final scene showed the prodigal daughter rocking on the front porch swing with her handsome hometown boy, talking quietly and drinking Coke as the music concluded that this was the real thing. This and other carefully crafted sixty-second short-short stories were minor gems which consumed thousands of feet of film, multiple takes, and thousands of dollars for each second of finished product. The apparent bliss and spontaneity resulted from monu-mental labor. "You in the striped shirt," yelled a McCann director in 1972, "hold the bottle lower down so we can see the label. Blonde girl in the back, lie on your stomach!" Every gesture in the commercials was scripted to achieve the maximum effect.

CHARLES DUNCAN'S MOMENT IN THE SUN

As McCann's creative geniuses were filming inspired commercials, The Coca-Cola Company itself was slowly changing and evolving. In 1970, Robert Woodruff had recalled Charles Duncan from London, where he had gained valuable international experience as head of Coca-Cola Export's European office. At the end of the following year, the Boss installed Duncan as president of the entire Company, leaving Paul Austin as chair of the board. While Austin's elitist philosophy had steered Coca-Cola throughout the sixties, Duncan supplied much-needed hands-on management. Together, the two men composed a potentially complementary team. The real power, however, continued to reside with Austin.[*]

Duncan still pulled enough weight to change the way Coca-Cola Export was run. As the overseas business exploded during the fifties and sixties, Export men operated independently as rough-and-ready adventurers, ready to improvise and make split-second decisions, displaying a macho disdain for deskbound Atlanta executives. By the early seventies, however, labor unrest, socialist governments, and anti-corporate backlash around the world spelled trouble for the autonomous Export leaders. In Uruguay, when two Coke employees were arrested for their involvement in a liberation movement, their fellow workers revolted and took possession of the bottling plant. Salvador Allende's Marxist government "bought" all the Chilean Coca-Cola operations, installing their own personnel. A series of Argentinian Coke officials were kidnapped and held for ransom. In Italy, when a Company-owned bottling plant declared bankruptcy rather than submit to a strong union, the workers promptly occupied the facility. Back in Atlanta, just before Charles Duncan's arrival as president, a Company spokesman shrugged off the Italian situation. "It may be serious; it may not," he said. "These things have a tendency to lose something in the translation."

That kind of attitude, coupled with worldwide unrest, persuaded Duncan to bring the Coca-Cola Export offices from New York City to Atlanta in 1972. Also, by that time foreign earnings far exceeded domestic income. "There was a real danger that the tail would start wagging the dog," one Export man remembered. The move to the still-parochial heart of the South provoked tremendous resentment among the overseas Coke men. They opted for crosstown offices, as far away from North Avenue as possible. Nonetheless, Austin's decentralized system had begun to pull back toward Atlanta.

Taking advantage of Duncan's day-to-day attention to operations, Austin traveled more extensively, spending over half his time globe-hopping. To his dismay, he often encountered hostile attitudes toward his Company. As colonialism dwindled, nationalism grew, along with a tendency to vilify powerful multinational corporations. Coca-Cola, as the most ubiquitous product on earth, provided a tempting target. The authors of *Global Reach*, a book published in 1974, blamed Coke for "commerciogenic malnutrition," claiming that Mexican families commonly sold their eggs and chickens to buy Coke for the father, "while the children waste[d] away for lack of protein." African health officials called a local form of malnutrition "the Fanta syndrome" because they thought it was related to overconsumption of sugary soft drinks. The following year, in *Sugar Blues*, William Dufty blamed most of man's ills on overindulgence in white sugar, Coke's primary ingredient. "The

---

[*] At Coca-Cola, power was where you found it. Robert Woodruff, "retired" since 1955, continued to rule from his perch on the Finance Committee. When Paul Austin was appointed president of the company, he maintained real control, although Lee Talley chaired the board. Austin retained that ultimate authority when he became chairman.

sugar pushers are our predators," he wrote, "leading us into temptation, peddling a kind of sweet, sweet human pesticide." Only the strongest would survive, the sensationalistic author claimed, "while the rest go down in another biblical flood—not water this time, but Coke."

While coping with such allegations, Austin and Duncan also strove to accommodate themselves to the women's liberation movement. Throughout the early seventies, women gradually struggled into lower and middle level positions previously occupied only by men at The Coca-Cola Company. In 1973, the *Refresher* profiled Carol Hinkey, the first female field representative. While she "lives and works in a man's world," the article assured any threatened males that she was "amply feminine." In the same year, the Company conducted an internal "social audit" to determine how well it was coping with affirmative action and women's issues. The consultant's report specified that "considerable progress" had been made but there was "still some distance to go."

For the first time, Coca-Cola employees convened in small groups to discuss something beside the wonders of the soft drink. In "normative sessions," they spoke freely in a kind of business-sponsored encounter group. Mary Gresham, who had started working in the mail room in 1943 and had slowly wended her way up to a managerial position in the advertising department, found herself in an all-women's seminar. The young secretaries complained that men addressed them by their first names, while expecting a "Mister" in return. Gresham finally broke in: "They can call me anything they want, if they would only pay me the same salary as the man whose job I took." The meetings resulted only in men cracking jokes. "I hear you'll be calling me by my first name now," one told Gresham with an edge in his voice. Diane McKaig, hired away from HEW to advise Coca-Cola on how to deflect threats from the consumer movement, was one of the few women who commanded a decent salary.

Even powerful men weren't always safe, however. With Austin in Africa on an extended 1974 trip, Robert Woodruff decided that the time was ripe for a power shift. He prompted an independent consultant to suggest that the president of the Company needed to receive more authority—i.e., Duncan should really guide Coke. Woodruff had acted prematurely, however, before Duncan had sufficient support at the board level. When Austin returned from overseas and found what had happened, he angrily went straight to the board, demanding Duncan's resignation. In a thunderous session, he won his point, the first man ever to stand up to Woodruff and survive.

The relationship between Paul Austin and Robert Woodruff had always been a peculiar love-hate affair. "One minute they were as close as son and father," an associate recalled. "The next, they were spitting at each other like two cats." Now the younger man had seemingly asserted his independence of the aging company patriarch once and for all. Woodruff recovered from two successive strokes early in 1972, but his health gradually declined throughout the decade. In the ousted Duncan's place, Austin promoted J. Lucian "Luke" Smith, a popular traditional Coca-Cola man who had joined the Company in

1940. Although a bright man, Smith was no dynamic leader, looking to Austin for ultimate guidance. Most important, from Austin's viewpoint, Luke Smith had a fine relationship with the all-powerful bottlers—a relationship soon to become crucial.

THE THOMAS COMPANY AND THE FTC TANGO

By the beginning of the seventies, Coca-Cola clearly had too many bottlers. From a peak of 1,200 in the twenties, the number of American Coke franchises had dwindled to 800 by 1970, but almost two-thirds of them carbonated their syrup in cities with populations of 50,000 or fewer. While the small-town bottler remained a Company tradition, he simply wasn't terribly efficient in the modern marketplace. The Company facilitated mergers and sales with a new Bottler Consolidation Department. In the century's early decades, the independent franchise system had effectively disseminated the soft drink throughout the United States. Now, however, the fifty-mile-radius territories, appropriate for the horse and buggy, proved minuscule to tractor trailers thundering down American superhighways with full loads. High-speed bottling and canning lines could spurt enough product to cover whole states. Supermarket chains such as Winn-Dixie or Safeway didn't want to negotiate with multiple local bottlers offering different services and prices. Coca-Cola faced stiff competition not only from Pepsi, but generic colas mass-produced for private-label sale in the chains.

Because of the perpetual bottling contract, however, the Company had limited power to enforce change—unlike Pepsi, where Walter Mack had commenced with larger territories, fewer bottlers, and more flexibility. Consequently, Pepsi could easily offer lower prices to large national outlets. When Coca-Cola Company national sales representatives negotiated cut-rate deals with supermarkets, bottlers who hadn't been consulted resented the intrusion, since they were forced to sell for a narrow profit margin. An intolerable tension built inside the Thomas Company territories, where silver-haired DeSales Harrison still held absolute sway, collecting a 12.5-cent tithe on each gallon of Coca-Cola syrup sold to his bottlers, making it almost impossible to match Pepsi's prices.

In 1973, Harrison finally died, and Company men immediately negotiated to acquire the Thomas Company, whose territory contained over a third of the U.S. population. Even though past offers had failed, Paul Austin was more optimistic this time around, for several reasons. First, the inflation of the early seventies was gnawing away at the 12.5-cent fixed income of the Thomas Company. Second, "allied brands" such as Sprite, Fanta, Fresca, and TaB were steadily eroding Thomas Company profits, since the perpetual contract applied only to Coca-Cola with an added pittance for TaB. As more products came on line—such as Mr. Pibb, a 1973 creation designed to challenge Dr Pepper—the Thomas bargaining position would weaken.

The real pressure, however, stemmed from the pending FTC case against the exclusive franchise system. While ostensibly The Coca-Cola Company

Sculpture with inscription by E. BOISSEAU, Artiste sculpteur.

"Here's the best feeding bottle!"

Painting with inscription by G. HAQUETTE, Artiste peintre.

"It's good, my boy; it's Vin Mariani!"

Vin Mariani, the popular coca-laced Bordeaux wine (and forerunner of Coca-Cola), was unabashedly touted as a beneficial drink for everyone, from babies to the elderly.

Sketch with inscription by A. ROBIDA, Artiste illustrator.

"Vin Mariani unites all nations."

Long before Coca-Cola, Vin Mariani spanned the globe, providing a nerve tonic for people in every clime.

John Pemberton, Coca-Cola's inventor, has usually been portrayed as the scraggly-bearded inventor seen in this oil portrait (right). In his younger years (left), however, his beard was well kept, and his eyes appeared at once sorrowful and reflective.

Asa Candler in 1888, the year of Pemberton's death, when Candler solidified his claim to Coca-Cola. (*Candler Papers, Special Collections, Emory University.*)

Three little boys proudly announce their preference for Coca-Cola in 1894, when it still contained cocaine.

As controversy swirled around the drink, the Company explicitly declared it "the Great National Drink," here served by Uncle Sam himself from a Capitol tap.

Here, a gruff old tycoon examines the ticker tape along with his rising colleague. The 1907 text clarifies the lingering medicinal claims that Coca-Cola eases "nerve racking and physically exhausting terrors."

"SATISFIED"

The Chicago Coca-Cola bottler found that overt sexual appeals sold in his drink. Here, a 1907 beauty (above) is obviously "satisfied" in several ways. The same bottler portrayed the bare-breasted young woman holding her Coca-Cola bottle (left). The straight-laced Asa Candler was infuriated, not only by the sexual content, but also by the reference to Coca-Cola "high balls" and "gin rickies."

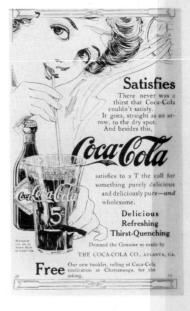

Satisfies

There never was a thirst that Coca-Cola couldn't satisfy. It goes, straight as an arrow, to the dry spot. And besides this,

Coca-Cola

satisfies to a T the call for something purely delicious and deliciously pure—*and* wholesome.

Delicious Refreshing Thirst-Quenching

Demand the Genuine as made by

THE COCA-COLA CO., ATLANTA, GA.

Free Our new booklet, telling of Coca-Cola vindication at Chattanooga, for the asking.

Even though Asa Candler professed horror at Western Coca-Cola's risqué advertising, this 1913 Company effort echoed the double-entendre prostitute portrayed five years earlier. Here, the "satisfied" female isn't quite so overtly sexual, although "it goes, straight as an arrow, to the dry spot" could be read several ways.

In a contemplative pool of light, this 1905 student enjoys a prescription to keep "the brain clear and mind active."

Three Coca-Cola salesmen proudly pose before one of the ubiquitous wall signs. By 1914, the Company had painted over five million square feet.

Any powerful drug, such as caffein is acknowledged to be, should not be offered indiscriminately to the public in other than its natural condition, and certainly not without the knowledge of the consumer

In this 1912 *Good Housekeeping* cartoon, Harvey Wiley warns a gullible public against the gremlins of indigestion, nervousness, and addiction lurking in Coca-Cola.

In D. W. Griffith's short 1912 film, *For His Son*, desperate heroine Blanche Sweet shoves aside a newsboy to get at her Dopokoke. Griffith's moralistic tale capitalized on anti–Coca-Cola feeling following the 1911 Barrels and Kegs trial, though the drink had contained no cocaine since 1903.

The 1915 prototype of the classic hobbleskirt bottle was a buxom affair, which may have inspired the nickname "Mae West bottle." It proved too bulky for bottling machines, however.

Here are a chronological procession of six-and-a-half-ounce Coca-Cola bottles, beginning with the unsatisfactory Hutchinson stopper, then the straight-sided bottle with diamond-shaped labels, and finally the classic hobbleskirt bottle, adopted in 1916.

Benjamin Thomas (left) and Joseph Whitehead (right), the two portly lawyers who finally convinced Asa Candler to let them bottle Coca-Cola, made a fortune while democratizing the soft drink, though both died relatively young.

Even at the age of two and a half, Robert Woodruff observed the world from a calm, adult face—contemplative, serious, calculating, and melancholy. (*Woodruff Papers, Special Collections, Emory University*)

Robert Woodruff jauntily steps onto a running board in 1923, the year he assumed the helm at Coca-Cola.

In 1929, Archie Lee introduced "the pause that refreshes" as the appropriate social role for Coca-Cola. He also coined a phrase to take advantage of its huge sales volume: "It had to be good to get where it is."

Coca-Cola advertising always matched the times. In the 1920s, this flirtatious flapper espoused the drink. Note the line on the special Coca-Cola glass, indicating the proper syrup level before mixing with carbonated water.

During the thirties and forties, Coca-Cola commissioned artists like Norman Rockwell and N. C. Wyeth to paint bucolic ads, such as this country boy with his dog, fishing pole, and Coke.

For years, Haddon Sundbloom's Christmas ads depicted a jolly, red-clad Santa Claus who paused for a Coca-Cola while making his rounds. As a result, Sundbloom shaped the American version of St. Nick.

Actress Joan Crawford smiled for Coca-Cola in 1933, but when she married Pepsi president Al Steele in the fifties, she became a roving ambassador for the rival soft drink.

Indomitable Ma Candler and her boys in 1891. The diminutive Martha Candler, a "hardshell Baptist," ruled her brood, passing on a grim, down-turning mouth. Asa is standing, third from left. John, the lawyer and judge, is the youngest, standing far left. Pugnacious Bishop Warren sits at the left on a stool. (*Candler Papers, Special Collections, Emory University.*)

Asa Candler with his family in 1899, the year Howard (standing at left) took to the road selling Coca-Cola. Asa put enormous pressure on his children to excel, but none of them ever lived up to their father's expectations.

Frank Robinson, the unassuming "unsung hero" of Coca-Cola, who named the drink, wrote out the graceful script logo, and manufactured the soda fountain favorite.

The Coca-Cola staff in 1899, on the cusp of a new century. Frank Robinson (first row, far left) was even shorter than Asa Candler, who stands next to him here. Candler nephew Sam Dobbs, sporting a mustache, stands in the middle of the second row. Baby-faced Howard Candler, Asa's oldest son, stands to the right of Dobbs, next to Mrs. Dobbs. In front of her, Walter Candler poses with his hands on his younger brother William's shoulders. Looking ill at ease and separate, the two black workers to the right are labeled: "Jim Reed, Porter (col.); Will Cartright, Drayman (col.)."

During World War II, Coca-Cola "Technical Observers" flew overseas to bottle the drink behind the lines for homesick GIs such as these, for whom the drink assumed an almost mystical significance.

"Congratulations. You're the 100th soldier who has posed with that bottle of Coca-Cola. You can drink it."

Cartoonist Bill Mauldin took a somewhat jaundiced (but probably realistic) view of Coca-Cola's superhuman efforts to reach soldiers during World War II.

Max Keith, who developed a thriving German business during the Nazi era against great odds, bore a physical resemblance to Adolf Hitler and led chants of "Sieg Heil!" during Coca-Cola conventions.

In 1939, Coca-Cola trucks massed in Essen's Adolf-Hitler-Platz in a show of strength.

Max Schmeling, former heavyweight champion and the symbol of Aryan supremacy during Hitler's reign, is now a born-again Coke bottler in Hamburg, Germany.

When Robert Woodruff refused to allow his portrait on this May 15, 1950, *Time* cover, the magazine commissioned a classic painting depicting the worldwide flood of the soft drink. (*Copyright 1950 Time Warner Inc. Reprinted by permission.*)

TIME

THE WEEKLY NEWSMAGAZINE

WORLD & FRIEND
Love that poster, that lira, that tickey, and that American way of life.

In 1950, the French Communists led the fight against Coca-Cola, depicted here as a seductress luring France away from his legitimate Beaujolais wife. (*Cartoonists & Writers Syndicate*)

Coca-Cola welcomed the post-war world with the 1946 "Yes" girl. Before the Freudian "depth boys" discovered phallic symbols in advertising, the Coke men were using them.

That Great Taste of Coke makes life more fun!

You taste the difference . . . Even the bubbles taste better.   You feel the difference . . . There's life, there's lift in Coke.   Guests notice the difference . . . serving Coca-Cola says you do things right.

In the mid-fifties, Coca-Cola targeted the burgeoning black middle class for the first time in publications like *Ebony*. It would be years, however, before minorities appeared in mainstream ads designed for general audiences.

"Big Jim" Farley served as a roving ambassador for Coca-Cola for three decades, routinely consorting with government heads, religious leaders, and welcoming committees, such as these Japanese geishas. Japan would grow to become the Company's largest profit centre.

On a 1945 radio set, crooner Morton Downey shares his favourite drink with young Margaret O'Brien. One of Robert Woodruff's closest friends, Downey served as a Coke goodwill ambassador and acheived fabulous wealth from his Coca-Cola stock and bottling plants. Despite his smooth public appearance, however, he regularly beat his children and had his daughter lobotomized.

From the Depression on, Coca-Cola men received rousing messages at Company conventions. By the sixties, the Jam Handy Corporation produced the skits using professional actors and singers.

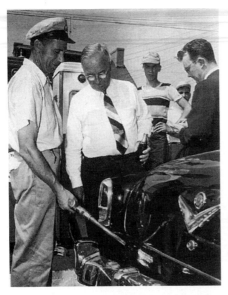

Coca-Cola photographers loved to snap pictures of presidents and other rulers with the proper soft drink. Here Truman, Eisenhower, Kennedy and Johnson were caught imbibing, and even Fidel Castro enjoyed the fizzy beverage.

The Beatles didn't mind posing with Cokes, and they nearly signed a deal to sing commercials, but the proposed fee was too stiff for Robert Woodruff.

Before promoting diet Pepsi with the "Uh-huh" girls, Ray Charles sang for Coke in the late sixties. Here he pretends to enjoy the Real Thing with Aretha Franklin, though Charles didn't drink colas at all, preferring milk.

Clasping their Cokes like talismans of peace, world youth taught the world to sing in perfect harmony while encouraging consumption of the right soft drink in the 1971 "Hilltop" commercial.

It's the real thing. Coke.

Real life calls for real taste.
For the taste of your life—Coca-Cola.
Here and now.

By 1973, the company finally appealed to hippies and blacks in this relaxed, integrated magazine spot.

"Mean" Joe Green chugged eighteen 16-ounce bottles of Coke for his famous 1979 commercial, vomiting after the sixth. After all that, the producers used the first take.

Coke CEO Paul Austin, looking depressed, worried, and lost in his 1979 executive suite, suffered from undiagnosed Alzheimer's disease. (*The Atlanta Journal-Constitution/Louis Favorite*)

John Bergin, (below) father of the "Pepsi generation," switched allegiances to help create the breakthrough "Coke Is It" campaign in 1981. (*The Atlanta Journal-Constitution*)

The implacable, inscrutable Boss at his desk. (Above)

CEO Roberto Goizueta (right) and president Don Keough stand outside Atlanta's World of Coca-Cola Museum, opened in 1990. During the eighties and early nineties, the two executives complemented one another perfectly – at least in public.

Doug Ivester, who took over as CEO after Robert Goizueta's death in 1997, looked mild-mannered, but he liked to think of himself as a predatory wolf. After a brief reign, he announced his resignation late in 1999, to be replaced by Australian Coke executive Doug Daft. (*The Atlanta Journal-Constitution /Renee Hannans*)

Bill Clinton – shown here chugging Coke with wife Hillary at the Moscow bottling plant – joined a long line of U.S. presidents who appreciated Coca-Cola (AP WIDE WORLD PHOTOS)

In the late 1990's Coke and Pepsi offered millions of dollars to American school districts for exclusive vending privileges. (©Jerry Dolezal)

The 1996 Olympics were known as the Coca-Cola Olympics because of the soft drink's pervasive presence (AP WIDE WORLD PHOTOS)

fought valiantly against the FTC, there were strong hints that it *wanted* to lose the case in order to weasel out of the perpetual bottling contract. When a Taft, California, bottler sued the Company for permission to sell product in an adjoining territory, Coca-Cola responded with an ingenious argument. If the Taft businessman or the FTC won, Luke Smith served notice, the Company intended to use the ruling as an excuse to abrogate the sacred perpetual contract. Without the exclusive territory clause, the Coke lawyers argued, the entire contract could be declared null and void.

Smith's threat panicked the Thomas Company managers. Through the grapevine, they learned that Paul Austin felt further negotiations were unnecessary, since he thought that, given time, the contract would be worthless anyway. Soon thereafter, Thomas Company representatives agreed to a price of $35 million, and in 1975 the sale was consummated. Viewed by most standards, the price seemed absurdly high for rights which had been given away by Asa Candler in 1899. By the seventies, the parent bottling company performed no major useful function. From the Company's point of view, however, it was a bargain, since it was paying over $8.5 million annually under the old Thomas contract, and the price rose each year. Within four years, the sale would pay for itself.

A FORCED LOOK UPWARD

The shorter duration of ad campaigns provided another indication of the Company's concern over its bottlers. As soon as they launched a slogan and song, the McCann men began brainstorming a new one, since the bottlers and their wives tired of whatever they saw on TV long before anyone else. And the bottlers had to be appeased, since they were paying for half of the enormous television budget. Consequently, in the summer of 1974, the Company introduced a new twist on the "Real Thing" theme, even though the McCann men had been generating incredibly powerful commercials. Ike Herbert, the normally placid Coke director of marketing, grabbed Bill Backer by his bow tie. "Give me a campaign that'll make the bottlers come to their feet," he told him, "or I'll have your balls."

By that time, the country's gloom had deepened. Nixon remained in the White House under a state of siege as the Watergate hearings revealed the underside of American politics. The OPEC countries, in retaliation against U.S. support of Israel, imposed an oil embargo, and the energy crisis worsened. With the dollar devalued, inflation hit double digits. The unemployment figures swelled. The Vietnam War was clearly lost. Since Coca-Cola symbolized America more than any other product, Company executives perceived the country's faltering self-image as a direct threat. Pulling back from messages of worldwide brotherhood, they directed the McCann men to implement an ad campaign that would renew American pride.

In response, Bill Backer created "Look Up, America" in march time, orchestrated with plenty of brass. Unabashedly patriotic, the first commercial portrayed the Liberty Bell, Niagara Falls, the Empire State Building, cowboys, pounding surf, a farm family dining on roast beef, amusement parks, the Rocky Mountains, a bald eagle, a county fair, buffalo stampeding, a square dance, a corn harvest, a softball game, a football player, and a marching band—all in sixty seconds. "We've got more of the *good* things in this country than anywhere else in the world," a narrator informed viewers. "Have a Coke and start looking up!" The soft drink men actually felt that they could swing the nation from despair to joy. "It's up to people like us," an executive told employees, "to dispel the nation's mood of gloom." A month after the campaign debuted, word circulated that Nixon would announce his resignation in a televised speech on August 8, so Coca-Cola bought prime-time slots on all three stations just prior to the speech, repeating the maneuver the next day before Gerald Ford was sworn in as President. "Let in the sunny side of living," Backer's lyrics entreated. Regardless of who was in the White House, Americans should remember their priorities and keep on drinking Coke.

The ads weren't nearly as effective as their predecessors. They seemed forced. The march tempo and voice-over announcer weren't as memorable or singable as Backer's best efforts. "Look Up, America" did, however, match the country's frantic desire to deny its faltering economy and loss of world power. As the Bicentennial of 1976 approached, Americans whipped up an artificial patriotic fervor, and the company announced that it was sinking $800,000 into sponsoring *1600 Pennsylvania Avenue*, a Broadway show written by Alan Jay Lerner and Leonard Bernstein, intended as an upbeat American history lesson.

THE INITIATION OF A CUBAN REFUGEE

Worldwide sales for the first quarter of 1975 reached all-time highs, but the figures hid an alarming trend. In the United States, gross sales had actually fallen below those of the previous year. Despite the bravura of Coke's ads, Pepsi was slowly gaining in the domestic market, causing Paul Austin to value the international business even more. To keep tabs on the far-flung Coke empire, Austin went outside the normal Export hierarchy, relying instead on high-level technical men such as Cliff Shillinglaw, mixer of the top-secret 7X formula, who traveled the globe to monitor ingredients. Since only two or three men in the Company knew the formula at any one time, they never flew on the same airplane. In 1974, Shillinglaw, in the Far East to retrieve some cassia leaves, felt chest pains as he boarded his plane for London, where he intended to replenish the European 7X supply. Once in England, he suffered a serious heart attack.

In Atlanta, news of Shillinglaw's critical condition provoked a frantic transfer of power and knowledge. Asa Candler had passed the secret to his son Howard, who in turn had taught the company's first chemist, W. C. Heath. In 1948, Dr. Heath had given the 7X formula to his successor, Orville May, who had initiated Cliff Shillinglaw in 1966. Now, in February of 1974, Dr. May came out of retirement to instruct a young Cuban chemist named Roberto Goizueta (pronounced Goh-SWET-a), who had fled his native land in

October 1960 when Castro was poised to nationalize the business. Aide Joe Jones informed Robert Woodruff that Dr. May had also shown Goizueta "the system for purchasing the highly sensitive ingredients. Roberto is now our full-fledged No. 2 man in this area." On March 15, May and Goizueta, on separate planes, flew to London to rebuild the 7X inventory.

In the meantime, Bob Broadwater, returning from a negotiation session in Moscow, picked up Shillinglaw's cassia leaves in order to smuggle them to Atlanta. "I was afraid I'd get caught," Broadwater recalled, "so I stuffed them into the Russian fur hat I was wearing." Despite the anxiety at the top echelon, the situation was soon resolved. Broadwater arrived at headquarters with the cassia. Mild-mannered Roberto Goizueta, who had been brought to Atlanta and groomed by Cliff Shillinglaw, quietly assumed much of his ailing boss's authority. Although Shillinglaw recovered in due time, he never regained his former power, and he died in 1979. Most significantly for the Company's future, Roberto Goizueta had entered the inner circles of power.

PURPLE PROBLEMS IN JAPAN

By the early seventies, the Japanese business had blossomed into the largest Coke market outside the United States. In 1973, Japan contributed 18 percent of Coca-Cola's entire corporate profit, despite an increasingly militant consumer movement and administrative mishandling. When "Emperor" Hal Roberts, the head of Coca-Cola there, died of cancer in 1971, Paul Austin named Masaomi Iwamura as president of the Japanese Export business, making him the first native manager of an American company in Japan. A brilliant chemist, Iwamura turned out to be a miserable administrator. "He had a complex mind that saw 27 alternative plans of action," a colleague remembered, "but he couldn't get himself to take any of them." Iwamura, a member of the prestigious Samurai class, also refused to speak to Nisaburo Takanashi, the Tokyo bottler descended from lowly merchant stock.

To make matters worse, the huge twenty-six-ounce Home-Size bottles received an inordinate amount of attention from the Japanese media when a few of them exploded and the American area manager failed to offer the traditional Japanese apology. "The Coca-Cola Company wasn't about to say, 'Oh, we're sorry this lady got her eye put out,'" a Coke veteran explained. "We were afraid she was going to sue." Even as Paul Austin directed that the big bottles be encased in protective plastic, regardless of the extra cost, an even greater disaster struck in Japan. An active consumer movement spurred a crisis by objecting to the artificial coal-tar coloring in Fanta Grape. Protesters smashed vending machines, and sales plummeted. In response, the Company developed a new version tinted with real grape skins. It tested well in the winter, but by the summer of 1974, Fanta Grape on shelves all over the country fermented, leaving an unpleasant though harmless precipitate in the drink. "It looked like a snowstorm in the bottle," a Coke man recalled. Millions of recalled cases, poured into the ocean, literally turned Tokyo Bay purple for several days.

In 1975, a desperate Paul Austin placed a telephone call to Morton Hodgson, enjoying his poolside retirement in the Virgin Islands. "I'm in big trouble out in Japan," Austin told him. "We've lost half of our net profit in less than eighteen months, and that's big enough to jolt the entire Company's balance sheet." At first, Hodgson demurred when Austin asked for help. "Why don't you send out some of your young tigers?" Austin explained that he needed someone with plenty of experience in converting bottling plants from mismanaged jokes into money-making outfits. "The real reason I want you to go," Austin admitted, "is that the Japanese revere ancient things, and you are an old bastard." Knowing Hodgson's sensitivity to accusations of nepotism, Austin didn't mention one other crucial element in his scheme—Hodgson was Robert Woodruff's nephew.

When the impressive Coca-Cola veteran, then sixty-six, emerged from retirement to head the Japanese business, the bottlers were suitably humble. The legendary Old Man was sending his own beloved kin to save them. Unlike Iwamura, who was kicked upstairs to supervise a worldwide technical project, Hodgson immediately established cordial relations with the Japanese bottlers. He apologized profusely to the media for the Fanta fiasco, promising to restore goodwill and harmony. With a battle cry of "Back to the Basics," Hodgson applied time-honored marketing techniques, concentrating on better service to dealers and consumers. He arranged "Sawayaka Tours"—week-long sightseeing tours to Paris and other European cities—for Coca-Cola bottlers and prominent *sake* store owners. A "Big Sky and Big Sound" sweepstakes attracted 20 million entries. A new ad campaign, "Come On In, Coke," featured American, Italian, and British youth joyously imbibing. The Company introduced Georgia Coffee, a canned sweetened coffee product, with a commercial spoof on *Gone With the Wind* in which the Rhett Butler character chose the drink over Scarlett O'Hara. When Hodgson left Japan three years later, sales for Coca-Cola products had surged to record highs.

A MASTER AT FAKING IT

By the time Hodgson retired for the second time in 1978, it was clear to everyone close to Paul Austin that something was wrong. He kept inexplicably forgetting things. Bob Broadwater first noticed trouble late in 1975: "I knew Paul was drinking a little, and I just put it down to that. We all did." At the age of fifty-nine, Paul Austin had begun the slow, terrifying descent into Alzheimer's Disease. Throughout the latter part of the decade, as his condition gradually worsened, Austin reacted defensively. "He was a master at faking it," Broadwater remembered. Always an austere, aloof figure, Austin now withdrew from all but his closest associates.

His charade was effective, in large measure because his memory lapses were temporary. Despite his persistent drinking and increased irritability, Paul Austin remained a commanding presence who functioned not just as a figurehead, but as a real leader. In 1975, he unveiled plans for a new multimillion-dollar tower, to soar twenty-six stories above the dwarfish old brick building next to it. The next year, reacting to the complexity of the worldwide industry, he reorganized the Company into three operating groups, nominally reporting to President Luke Smith. At that time, Coca-Cola Export finally transferred to North Avenue, firmly tucked under the corporate wing.

Based in Atlanta, all three group leaders were strong managers, any of whom might reasonably replace Austin instead of Smith. German Claus Halle, president of the Export Corporation until 1976, had survived the autocratic rule of Max Keith and brought an urbane, meticulous approach to his sector. South African Ian Wilson, who had learned under Austin during the fifties, emerged as an aggressive, cultured, hardheaded manager who had recently turned the ailing Canadian business around. Don Keough, an Iowa native, had arrived as part of the Duncan Foods purchase in 1964. A masterful speaker and marketer, Keough quickly sounded more like a traditional Coke man than anyone else.

THE CARTER CONNECTION

Austin's control of the Company was highlighted by his much-publicized friendship with Democratic presidential nominee Jimmy Carter. When the peanut farmer had run for governor of Georgia in 1970 against Carl Sanders, a longtime friend of Coke, Austin had naturally supported Sanders, particularly since Carter publicly castigated "big business." When it became clear that the man from Plains would win, however, Austin and his forces contributed $6,200 to his campaign. As it routinely did for Georgia governors, Coca-Cola flew the Company plane for Carter trips to conferences and paid for limousine service to and from airports. Like his predecessors, Carter reciprocated with almost obsequious gratitude, frequently requesting Austin's council. Normally, businesses seek to influence local politicians, but in Georgia, that scenario was reversed. As one commentator noted, public officials received with an ice-cold Coke at North Avenue felt "honored, like the commoner invited to take tea with the Queen."

In 1972, Carter revealed that he had ambitions beyond Georgia, asking Austin for Coca-Cola's support if he ran for President. Austin laughed and said, "Sure," never dreaming that the nationally unknown Carter would actually pull it off. Nonetheless, when the Georgia governor groomed himself by traveling overseas to Tokyo and Brussels—ostensibly to boost the state's trade, but also garnering international experience and exposure—local Coca-Cola men squired him around the country, providing background information on the local politics, culture, and economy. With Austin's sponsorship, Carter joined the prestigious Trilateral Commission as a fellow member.

In 1974, Carter bragged, "We have our own built-in State Department in The Coca-Cola Company. They provide me ahead of time with . . . penetrating analyses of what the country is, what its problems are, who its leaders are, and when I arrive there, provide me with an introduction to the leaders of that country." Two years later, during the 1976 presidential campaign, Paul Austin hosted a luncheon at New York's swanky "21" restaurant, where Carter reassured nervous businessmen that his speeches about the "unholy, self-perpetuating alliances" between money and politics was just talk. "I will be a friend of business," Carter told the assembled economic elite. "I would not do anything to subvert or minimize foreign investment." When the Federal Election Commission ruled that the $500-a-plate dinner constituted an illegal campaign contribution, Austin, embarrassed, began to downplay his friendship with the Democratic candidate.

Nonetheless, in the closing days of the campaign, when Carter's ambiguous position on issues was pulling down his popularity ratings, he hired Tony Schwartz, a New York media consultant who had developed hundreds of Coca-Cola commercials. "Whether it's Coca-Cola or Jimmy Carter," Schwartz explained, "we don't try to convey a point of view, but a montage of images and sounds that leaves the viewer with a positive attitude." The commercial puffery worked. Carter assumed the mantle of leadership as a humble born-again Christian peanut farmer, an outsider who stood for justice and righteousness. He tapped quite an array of Coca-Cola figures—Charles Duncan became the Deputy Secretary of Defense (before graduating to Secretary of Energy), Joseph Califano snagged HEW, Griffin Bell of King & Spalding served as Attorney General, as law partners Charles Kirbo and Jack Watson remained close advisers. The "Georgia Mafia" was securely in power. Unfortunately, Carter and his cronies brought none of Coca-Cola's good-old-boy political savoir faire with them to Washington. The hype had apparently gone to the new President's head, and he really behaved as an outsider, disdaining normal protocol and alienating important Democratic figures such as Tip O'Neill and, almost as important, the press.

As a consequence, the media pounced on any morsel suggesting Carter's favoritism, such as the President's banishment of Pepsi from the White House and its replacement by Coke vending machines. When Bert Lance caught a secretary drinking Pepsi, a journalist overheard him ribbing her and reported it verbatim: "You know, ma'am, our crowd drinks a good old Democratic drink, Coke." The President couldn't even attend a National Gallery of Art exhibit of antique masks without newspapers noting that it was cosponsored by Coca-Cola and its Japanese bottlers. And when Jimmy and Rosalynn journeyed down the Mississippi on the *Delta Queen*, syndicated reporter Jack Anderson pointed out that the free publicity was a lifesaver for the failing tourist boat—which happened to be owned by the New York Coca-Cola Bottling Company.

Some reports had more substance, though. In 1977, when sugar prices dropped, a U.S. Trade Commission study recommended a 2-cent duty on imported sugar to help protect domestic growers. Coca-Cola used a million tons annually, making it the world's largest consumer. Lobbying through the Sugar Users Group (run by Coke man John Mount), the Company prevailed on Carter to approve a plan *paying* 2 cents a pound to the domestic industry, effectively keeping prices down. Indirectly, then, the taxpayers were subsidizing Coca-Cola. When Mount maladroitly commented that Coke would have to "call in a few chits" to ensure that things went their way, some congressmen labeled the piece of legislation the Coca-Cola bill.

In 1977, Paul Austin quietly flew to Cuba, where he held secret meetings with Fidel Castro—presumably to negotiate the Company's return to the country, even though Coca-Cola officially held a $27.5 million claim against Cuba for confiscating its plants in 1961. His mission failed, except for some Havana cigars which Castro sent to Robert Woodruff by way of Austin. Having promised President Carter that he would report on his trip, Austin met with him briefly in the White House. When acid-penned William Safire learned of the episode, he concluded that it was a nefarious scheme to obtain Cuban cane. "The Carter-Coke-Castro sugar diplomacy is not merely a potential conflict of interest," wrote Safire. "It's the real thing."

OPENING DOORS AROUND THE WORLD

Austin was more successful in negotiating for Coca-Cola's entry into Portugal, Egypt, Yemen, Sudan, the Soviet Union, and China. Though none of these coups could be attributed directly to Carter's intervention, the American President's well-publicized bias toward the soft drink undoubtedly provided essential leverage. It just happened, for instance, that the long-awaited Portuguese permission coincided with the U.S. Treasury Department's approval of a badly needed $300 million loan. Likewise, when Austin met with Anwar Sadat, delicately preparing to ease back into Egypt despite the Arab Boycott, the Coke executive asked Sadat whether he should keep their wide-ranging discussion confidential or report it to his government. "I'd like very much if you would report it," the unruffled Egyptian answered. "That's the reason for our conversation."

With the implicit Carter clout behind them, the Coca-Cola men triumphed in country after country—with the exception of India, where Coke departed in 1977 rather than reveal its formula to the government. Their achievements, however, came only after years of patient negotiations that predated any presidential aid, as with Bob Broadwater's Moscow efforts. Although Pepsi's exclusive Soviet cola contract ran through 1984, Kosygin's men decided Coca-Cola could be served at special events. In 1978, Broadwater signed a contract to supply Coca-Cola to the Spartakiada, the Eastern Bloc sports festival, the following year. But that would only serve as a warm-up for the 1980 Moscow Olympics, where Coke paid $10 million for exclusive rights. Fanta Orange would fizz not only during the sporting events, but on a long-term basis throughout the Soviet Union. The real Austin plum, however, fell into his lap late in 1978, when Coke executive Ian Wilson, holed up in a Beijing suite, hammered out an arrangement with the Chinese Communists only days before the U.S. State Department normalized relations. Now, despite Mao Tse-tung's pronouncement in his *Little Red Book* that Coca-Cola was "the opiate of the running dogs of revanchist capitalism," the symbolic beverage found a home on the Chinese mainland.

PEPSI'S UNGENTLEMANLY CHALLENGE

While Coca-Cola grabbed headlines around the world, however, the business back home was stagnating, as Pepsi made inroads on the valuable take-home market, scooping Coke with one-and-a-half- and two-liter plastic bottles. As a symbol of Coke's loss of direction, *1600 Pennsylvania Avenue*, the Broadway production which had cost the company $800,000, folded after seven performances, as *New York Times* critic Clive Barnes pronounced it "tedious and simplistic." While Coca-Cola switched to the lackluster "Coke Adds Life" campaign in 1976, Pepsi bounced back with its new invocation to "Have a Pepsi Day." As usual, Coca-Cola maintained a product focus while its rival concentrated on life-styles.

Almost by accident, however, Pepsi launched a simultaneous strategy in direct contrast to its traditional approach. Pepsi man Dick Alven had been sent to Dallas with the seemingly hopeless mission of injecting life into the business there, where Pepsi claimed a miserable 4 percent of the soft drink market. Alven convinced his boss that they needed drastic measures, so they petitioned Pepsi headquarters to allow them to use the local Stanford Agency instead of BBDO. Bob Stanford, who had discovered that Pepsi beat Coke in taste-tests while promoting a 7-Eleven generic cola, suggested a daring assault on Coca-Cola. In 1975, Dallas TV stations aired commercials urging viewers to "Take the Pepsi Challenge," showing candid shots of die-hard Coke consumers astonished to discover that they preferred Pepsi in blind taste-tests. Only Pepsi would have stooped to such an outrageous, virtually taboo approach, since comparative ads were considered unsportsmanlike. Nonetheless, the results were indisputable: within two years, Pepsi's Dallas market share jumped 14 percent.

At first, the local Coca-Cola franchise ignored the scurrilous new ads, pretending that their effect was temporary and unworthy of response. Then, however, Coke slashed prices, initiating a price war. In "Project Mordecai," named after the Biblical figure who saved the Chosen People from a plot to destroy them, Coke purchased huge chunks of air time on all three networks to block Pepsi commercials. "One sip is not enough," Coke spots asserted. Another featured a grizzled Texan complaining about the New York Pepsi types with their "little bitty sips, . . . skinny britches and pointy lizard shoes." Echoing a racist line, he ended, "You've got to watch what you do down heah, boy," and swigged a Coke. Other commercials tried to reduce the Challenge to absurdity, showing chimpanzees taking the taste-test, or actors deciding which of two tennis balls was fuzzier. By mocking the Challenge, though, the Coke ads backfired. Pepsi men and viewers sensed their panic. Back in Atlanta, Coke's technical men conducted their own secret tests, and, to their horror, they discovered that consumers actually did prefer Pepsi by a 58–42 split. Encouraged by the results, other Pepsi bottlers in the Southern Coke heartland adopted the Challenge, along with the aggressive Los Angeles franchise. By decade's end, the Challenge commercials were airing in a quarter of the U.S. markets.

While Coca-Cola's domestic market share remained relatively flat, Pepsi's steadily rose throughout the latter seventies. In 1977, Pepsi's advertising budget actually surpassed Coca-Cola's for the first time, with each firm spending just over $24 million a year on their main brands. By the following summer, Nielsen market figures demonstrated that Pepsi had finally overtaken Coke in supermarket sales, which Pepsi dubbed the "free choice" arena. Defensive Coke men asserted that their drink still held an edge in the total retail outlets. "They must use some strange numbers," speculated John Sculley, the combative young Pepsi-Cola president.

Because Coca-Cola still dominated the vending machine and fountain outlets, it maintained a considerable overall lead, but corporate pride and self-confidence suffered. The trends, too, were disheartening. In 1978, Coke products' U.S. market share fell from 26.6 percent to 26.3 percent while Pepsi's rose from 17.2 percent to 17.6 percent. At a time when every fraction of a percent amounted to millions of dollars, such shifts would have alarmed any company. For Coca-Cola, steeped in a corporate culture which rendered its primary product a religious artifact, the numbers were horrifying.

MULTIPLE HEADACHES

Coca-Cola men were equally paranoid about issues affecting the entire industry. The FDA ruled that saccharin, like cyclamates, caused cancer in laboratory rats and must therefore be prohibited under the Delaney Amendment. Responding to heavy lobbying from the diet industry, Congress voted a "moratorium" on the saccharin ban, but that had expired in May of 1978, and no one knew what lay ahead for all-saccharin TaB. Zero population growth represented a more ominous, long-range threat, however. Ever since a 1977 *Business Week* cover article had warned of "The Graying of the Soft-Drink Industry," demographers had forecast a gloomy future. The baby boom was over, the domestic market seemed saturated, price wars raged, and future advances would be carved inch by inch.

In addition, colas, while still comprising over 60 percent of U.S. soft drink consumption, were challenged by a welter of new beverages aimed at more specific audiences. The segmentation of the soft drink market, gaining momentum during the 1960s, was a well-researched and financed war by the end of the seventies. Pepsi's Mountain Dew, only a regional phenomenon as a hillbilly drink, surged ahead by "going into John Denver country," as one wry analyst put it, with an ad campaign of "Hello sunshine, hello Mountain Dew." Coke quickly responded with Mello Yello.

Rather than setting the pace within the industry, The Coca-Cola Company had become reactive and fragmented. Although still a massive money machine, it seemed to meander aimlessly, without any particular sense of purpose. By the late seventies, only 70 percent of Coke's business stemmed from soft drinks, as the increasingly confused Austin insisted on his shrimp farming, water projects, and the like, despite their slim or negative profit margins. Bottler consolidation had shrunk the number of U.S. franchises to 550, but that was still far too many. In 1977, Coke diversified into the wine business, but viniculture, unlike Coke syrup, required major capital expenditure and time for proper aging. Coke's Wine Spectrum (created by combining several labels) never earned much money, while angry Southern Baptist stockholders complained that their pure Company should not promote alcohol.* Coca-Cola responded to its multiple problems by pouring unprecedented amounts of money into ad campaigns.

COKE AND THE DEATH SQUADS

Meanwhile, smoldering foreign crises exploded, as Coca-Cola's cozy relationship with dictators blew up one after the other. In 1978, after the Shah of Iran was deposed, the Ayatollah Khomeini handed over the nation's Coca-Cola plants to the Association of the Oppressed, but the formerly down-trodden did not make good bottlers, and the business soon died. The following year, the Sandinistas threw Somoza out of Nicaragua. Adolfo Calero, the Coke bottler there, had opposed Somoza, who had jailed him (Jimmy Carter, friend of Coke, secured his release). Although Calero continued bottling as the eighties loomed, his strident criticism of the Sandinistra leadership jeopardized the business.

The worst problem, however, loomed in neighboring Guatemala, where the Guatemala City Coke workers had unionized in 1975, sparking a chain of intimidations and violence which became very public news at The Coca-Cola Company's annual Delaware meeting in May of 1979. The Company had always prided itself on its brief, untroubled yearly business affair, which usually lasted only fifteen minutes. In 1979, however, Sister Dorothy Gartland, a diminutive but strong-willed nun representing the 200 shares of Coca-Cola stock owned by the Sisters of Providence, submitted a resolution calling for the development of minimal labor-relations standards in its worldwide franchises. Sister Gartland lamented a South African Coke franchise that employed black prisoners on work-release, paying them only 25 cents a day. In Laredo, Texas, she continued, the Coca-Cola manager paid a $2.40 hourly wage to Mexicans, informing them that they were disposable. But the nun was most urgently concerned over the Guatemalan situation. To explain why, she introduced Israel Marquez, former general secretary of the Guatemalan Coca-Cola union, who had traveled from Central America to tell his story in person.

As the uneasy Coke executives listened to a translator, the Guatemalan delivered an emotional speech. A cooler repairman at the Guatemala City Coke plant, Marquez spoke scathingly of John Clayton Trotter, Sr., the Houston lawyer who managed the franchise for Texas widow Mary Fleming.

---

* In the meantime, Pepsi had become much more diversified than Coke, with its Frito-Lay division performing well. In 1978, Pepsi purchased Pizza Hut and Taco Bell, which of course guaranteed exclusive national soft drink outlets. Coke men consoled themselves: PepsiCo had become more of a conglomerate than a soft drink company, with over half of its sales coming from nonbeverage enterprises after 1975.

Trotter, a tall, lanky right-winger with a fondness for polyester suits, perceived his workers' unionization as a conspiracy fomented on the one hand by Communists and on the other by the competitive Pepsi franchise. According to Marquez, Trotter had at first unsuccessfully resorted to bribes, bullying, and legal maneuvers to quell the nascent union.

In 1978, when repressive General Romeo Lucas Garcia stormed to power in Guatemala, sporadic violence escalated into a bloodbath, as the notorious Secret Anti-Communist Army (ESA) and its Death Squad terrorized the country. A few days after Marquez narrowly avoided death from gunfire at his Jeep, union leader Pedro Quevedo was murdered, shot twelve times while delivering Coca-Cola. Soon afterward, Marquez' tenant, mistaken for the union man, fell in a machine gun barrage. After a third attempt on his life, Israel Marquez reluctantly fled Guatemala, seeking refuge in nearby Costa Rica. Although he could not prove it, Marquez was absolutely certain that Trotter had collaborated with the Death Squads in plotting the violence directed at the union, although there was no evidence linking him with any specific incident.

As the flood of Spanish was haltingly translated into stories of atrocities in some faraway banana republic, the executives in the Delaware boardroom stirred uneasily. Marquez told them that after he left Guatemala, Manuel Lopez Balam replaced him as union secretary. Just a month before the board meeting, Balam's throat was slit as he retrieved a case of empty Coke bottles from a grocery store. "Besides being inhuman," Marquez concluded, "the situation is also one of poor economics. Coca-Cola's image in Guatemala could not be worse. There, *murder is called 'Coca-Cola.'*"

For a moment, there was a stunned silence. Then Paul Austin swiftly concluded the meeting. The nun's labor resolution, he said, would mean an "unnecessary intrusion into the internal activities of . . . affiliates" and would be difficult to foist upon independent bottlers. "While lamenting the problems in Guatemala," he said, "we also must respect the laws and processes of other nations." The board meeting ended in a chaos of loud protests from the minority stockholders, while Austin slammed his gavel.

Austin's performance was uncharacteristic of the man who had displayed such concern for migrant workers when testifying before the Senate nine years before; that spring he was often confused and belligerent, as he entered the serious second stage of Alzheimer's. Nonetheless, his statement accurately reflected the Company policy of denying responsibility for independent bottling franchises. Since Coke affiliates now bottled in 135 countries, the implications of the proposed resolution were mind-boggling. If the Company really assumed responsibility for the welfare of workers in every plant, it could easily devolve into a nightmare for the personnel department—not to mention the public relations team.

The Guatemalan situation refused to go away, however, and Marquez' dramatic recitation caused headlines across the country, including *The Wall Street Journal*. During the summer of 1979, as the killings, kidnappings, and beatings proliferated, Amnesty International and the Swiss-based

International Union of Food and Allied Workers' Associations (IUF) joined the chorus of voices demanding that The Coca-Cola Company replace Trotter and his management. Although the Company dispatched security chief Leo Conroy to Guatemala for a week-long investigation, the ex-FBI man failed to uncover evidence directly linking Trotter to the killings, which was hardly surprising, since Conroy spoke no Spanish, didn't meet Trotter, and never even entered the bottling plant. Confidentially, Conroy told another Company man that he wouldn't return to Guatemala. "It's not safe there," he said. "I value my life!"

Brandishing Conroy's report, Coke executive Don Keough told critics that the Company couldn't proceed without proof. "We have revulsion and are embarrassed by the kind of shenanigans Mr. Trotter is doing," Keough said, "but we haven't got the luxury to operate in any environment but the legal one." In fact, the Company would have loved to dump Trotter, but they didn't want to look as if they were yielding to external pressure. Under Trotter's mismanagement, Coke's market share in Guatemala City had dwindled to 30 percent. He also bottled Dr Pepper, 7-Up, and other flavors, despite Coca-Cola's protests, and there were allegations that he had charged the Company for import taxes he never had to pay.

Unfortunately, the wily Texan knew that he could now charge an outrageous amount for his troubled bottling plant, since the Company yearned so desperately for him to disappear. Consequently, Company men decided to wait until 1981, when the franchise contract was due to expire. With more blood than syrup flowing at the Guatemalan bottling plant, however, Coca-Cola's critics grew more shrill. Congressman Donald Pease escalated pressure on the Company by writing a letter to President Carter about Coke's "callous disregard" of the "wave of murder, torture, kidnapping, and intimidation." Citing Carter's close ties to the soft drink concern, Pease demanded action. The "confidential" letter was leaked to the press and widely publicized.

AMENDING THE SACRED CONTRACT

While Don Keough realized that the situation in Guatemala was spiraling out of control, a battle much closer to home diverted his attention. Company executives had decided that many of their domestic troubles were attributable to the ancient bottling contract, which did not allow for increased labor costs, advertising, overhead, or ingredients besides sugar. In late 1977, with inflation raging, Paul Austin directed President Luke Smith to secure a contract amendment at all costs, now that the Thomas Company no longer stood in the way.

If anyone could pull off such a seemingly impossible task, it was Smith, a traditional, warm Southerner whom the bottlers loved and trusted. Although a nucleus of faithful franchises agreed that the Company needed some relief in order to advertise more effectively, Smith's proposed contract amendment, allowing the Company unlimited flexibility in pricing syrup, proved a hard sell. In May of 1978, Smith and Keough took what derisive bottlers called their "dog-and-pony show" to six meetings around the country to persuade hesitant bottlers to sign.

Bill Schmidt, whose grandfather first bottled Coke in 1901, exemplified the devout Coca-Cola man, having just opened a museum full of memorabilia and artifacts inside his Elizabethtown, Kentucky, bottling plant. At first, he listened with an open mind to the Company presentation, but he was disgusted by the Company's high-handed amendment. Finally, as he recalled later, "it just boiled up in me," and he penned a series of protests sent to a growing list of fellow bottlers. Unintentionally, Schmidt found himself the unofficial leader of the opposition. The most divisive issue to hit Coca-Cola since its great internecine battle of the early twenties, the amendment split men whose forebears had pioneered the business.

Both sides argued that the still-pending FTC assault on the exclusive territorial provision supported their position. Schmidt's contingent, the "unamended bottlers," argued that it was unwise to tamper with the contract until the FTC matter was settled, since it might rouse the bureaucrats to greater efforts. Luke Smith wielded the potential dissolution of territories as a club, as he had with the Thomas Company—just in case the FTC case went against them, the bottlers should sign the amendment to ensure they had a contract.

Into this maelstrom stepped Brian Dyson, an Argentinean brought in to assume control of the U.S. Company division. When his friend Don Keough begged him to leave his position as head of the South Latin America Division, Dyson initially demurred. "Why don't you get an American?" He knew that the American system was in chaos, and if he failed to turn it around, it could signal the end of his career. Keough remained convinced, however, that Dyson could salvage the situation. After all, the Argentinean had cut his teeth on the business in Venezuela, one of the few places where Pepsi utterly dominated the market. As a consequence, Dyson was accustomed to scrapping for every sale. In addition, the Argentinean, a grandson of British immigrants, was tall, lean, athletic, and urbane. Moving to Atlanta in August of 1978, he immediately tangled with the amendment dispute.

The next month, the Company finally yielded to criticism, modifying the amendment to put a ceiling on the amount the syrup price could be raised. Now there would be two sliding scales—one for sugar and one for the "base element" of all other ingredients, tied to the Consumer Price Index. As a bonus, the Company agreed to eliminate the awkward BX premix syrup, with its artificially inflated price, and to allow amended bottlers to purchase concentrate instead of bulky syrup. Schmidt still objected, since the CPI rose more quickly than inexpensive ingredients. Nonetheless, after hard lobbying, the Company finally succeeded in signing more than half the bottlers by April of 1979, when two huge outfits, New York and United, capitulated.

THE GREAT GET-TOGETHER

The agreement arrived just in time for Brian Dyson's June "Great Get-Together," a gigantic San Francisco convention—the first bottlers' assemblage since the Real Thing campaign, launched in Atlanta ten years before. Still battered and divided over the amendment issue and discouraged by Pepsi's advances, the bottlers warily gathered to see what this South American would say. Hardly any of them had seen him in person, much less heard him speak. After the customary Broadway-style song-and-dance number, the tall, angular Dyson somewhat nervously approached the podium, clutching the traditional six-and-a-half-ounce bottle. As he spoke, his image was projected onto a huge video screen.

"In recent times," Dyson told the bottlers, "we have all been through a period of self-appraisal." Ears pricked up. Perhaps he would actually acknowledge some of their problems instead of making the expected rah-rah speech. After mentioning the amendment debate, he ticked off the decade's disasters—the FTC, energy crunch, sugar crisis, saccharin attack, refund legislation, consumer movement, inflation, wage and price controls. He admitted that Coke's corporate share had grown a mere three-tenths of one percent in ten years. "In the same period, Pepsi's [Cola] corporate share has grown from 21.4% to 24.2%." The bottlers collectively gasped. Dyson had broken all precedent and uttered the "P" word in front of most of America's Coca-Cola men. Pepsi, Dyson continued, had labeled Coca-Cola "the nostalgia company, an enterprise that is wholly preoccupied with its past glories." If so, the Company was doomed. But, Dyson promised, "we are willing to do *whatever is necessary* for as long as is necessary to turn this business around . . . Together, we must *fix the problem*, however long it may take."

Dyson clearly meant business, but could Big Coke really deliver? As a first step, the bottlers knew they needed a spectacular ad campaign. Could McCann pull it off? On the big video screen, the new commercials took over. "Have a Coke and a smile," sang effervescent young people. "It makes me feel goo-oo-ood, / it makes me feel *nice*, have a Coke and a smile." They danced energetically about. Coke fizzed and gurgled. In the audience, feet tapped. This was all right. It sounded like something Bill Backer might have written, though he had recently left McCann to form his own agency. "That's the way it should be, / and I'd like to see / the whole world smiling with me."

In between screenings of the new ads, deadly serious marketing man Bill Van Loan explained that just as the macho cowboy was associated with Marlboro cigarettes, "the world of smiling Americans can be literally owned by Coca-Cola." But it couldn't be just any smile. "It must always come out of the product itself." Unlike Pepsi's ads, which urged people to join some mythical group, the new Coke commercials featured the product as hero. "*Coke* causes the smile."

In most of the ads, though, the rehearsed smiles were too obviously forced, with one extraordinary exception. While others flashed vignettes, this one conveyed a heartwarming story. As wounded black Pittsburgh Steeler "Mean"

Joe Greene limped down a stadium tunnel toward the locker rooms, a shy, moonfaced boy holding a sixteen-ounce Coke timidly called after him: "Mr. Greene, Mr. Greene." The defeated football player half turned. "Yeah?" he snarled. The kid stammered, "I just want you to know I think, I think you're the best ever." Unmoved by this praise, Greene grunted "Yeah, sure," and started to leave. In desperation, unable to think of anything else, the boy offered his Coke, but was rebuffed. "Really," he persisted, "you can have it." With resignation, Greene relented, upending the bottle and draining it in one long, glorious chug. The music swelled while joyful voices harmonized, "Have a Coke and a Smile." As the boy turned away dejectedly, the player, now thoroughly refreshed, shouted "Hey, kid!" and threw him his jersey. Flashing an incredible smile that made all right with the world, he headed for the lockers.

The Mean Joe Greene drama created an instant sensation. Though it wasn't planned for airing until a year after the campaign's introduction, bottlers mobbed Bill Van Loan after the presentation, demanding its immediate release. Thousands of viewers wrote to thank the Company for the greatest commercial they had ever seen. The media liked it just as much, running articles on Mean Joe's performance in *Newsweek*, *People*, *Sports Illustrated*, and *The New York Times*, while the Steelers' lineman/actor appeared on *Good Morning America* and the *Today* television shows. The ad even inspired a made-for-TV movie. Greene revealed that the effort had consumed three grueling days, in part because Tommy Oken, the ten-year-old actor, kept muffing his lines on account of his genuine awe for Greene. The final day, the football player guzzled eighteen 16-ounce bottles of Coca-Cola, and still managed to smile.[*] "When Joe turns around at the end," one literate Coke executive said, "he looks like he's playing Othello." It was, former Pepsi ad-maker John Bergin noted ruefully, "the perfect commercial."

A STAB IN THE BACK

The Coke bottlers felt encouraged as they left the great convention hall that June of 1979. Shortly afterward, however, they received a mailgram from Paul Austin that radiated shock waves throughout the system. The beloved Luke Smith, only sixty years old, was "retiring for personal reasons," Austin announced. "The board has not named a successor. I will assume the additional duties of the presidency." Rumors flew within the Coca-Cola family as to what had really happened. Everyone in the Company understood that Luke Smith had almost single-handedly secured the amendment signatures of the majority of the bottlers. He had cajoled, charmed, threatened,

---

[*] Greene threw up after the sixth Coke, but he manfully continued to chug drink after drink—all for nothing, since the directors eventually used the first take. One bootleg clip became a famous TV blooper in which Greene was supposed to say "Hey, kid! Catch!" Instead, he said "Hey, kid!" and emitted a gigantic belch.

pled; had crisscrossed the country, spent hours on the telephone. To relax, he took two weeks in August to putter around Lake Lanier, just north of Atlanta, on his houseboat. On a Friday, he got a call over the radiophone from Fil Eisenberg, Coca-Cola's Chief Financial Officer. "Paul wants you out," Eisenberg told Smith.

No one ever knew exactly why Austin had suddenly fired Smith, though Austin's rapidly progressing Alzheimer's certainly contributed. At the Great Get-Together in June, Austin had fumbled through brief comments, refusing to allow the video cameras to project him onto the big screen, which would have shown his quivering facial expression. Later that year, he flew to New Orleans to deliver a speech and forgot why he was there. Even without a diagnosis, Austin realized that something was terribly wrong with him, and his reaction was to cling desperately to power.

A *Business Week* headline blared, "SUCCESSION AT COKE IS A HORSE RACE AGAIN." Austin created the new position of vice-chairman and named six men to the post, any of whom might assume control. Within the Company, the arrangement was soon dubbed the "vice squad," or "beauty contest," with bets on the winner. *Business Week* picked Don Keough, though insiders thought South African Ian Wilson a more likely candidate. In fact, Wilson himself was quite sure he would be chosen, since both Woodruff and Austin had privately told him he was the one. At any rate, as one journalist noted, "Austin does not look like a man thinking of retirement." Though he was approaching his sixty-fifth birthday, the board could extend his mandatory retirement year by year.

As Austin failed, his wife grabbled power within the Company. The former Jeane Weed, a Mississippi native, was a secretary at the Chicago bottling company when Austin met her in 1950. Now, as her husband grew more confused, she tried to help, taking particular interest in plans for the nearly completed Tower. Mrs Austin raised the hackles of traditional employees with her haughty approach to interior decorating, replacing classic Norman Rockwell Coca-Cola paintings with avant-garde artists. Disaffected employees called her Mrs. Vice-Chairman, while others placed grades such as D-plus or F on her paintings.

STUMBLING INTO THE EIGHTIES

Late in 1979, when the huge old Coca-Cola Spectacular, which had blinked the time and temperature in Atlanta's Margaret Mitchell Square for thirty years, crumbled to make way for a park, the demolition was emblematic of Company morale, which had never dipped so low. The approaching eighties found Coca-Cola in disarray, except for one brilliant new commercial.

The bottlers remained divided and angry. The courts had ruled against the Company in the FTC case, with overriding legislation still pending. Market share was slipping, and the Company had severed communication with the financial press. Nuns and labor leaders protested death squad killings in Guatemala. Anita Bryant, "the voice that refreshes," shrilly crusaded against homosexuals. In 1979, Coca-Cola stock was worth less than its value at the beginning of the decade, despite a 2-for-1 split in 1977 that was supposed to encourage the small investor. While reported annual growth for the decade registered 12.5 percent, the 7.1 percent inflation rate reduced that to an unimpressive 5.4 percent.

Even Coke's much-publicized friendship with Jimmy Carter didn't prevent the President from declaring a U.S. boycott on the 1980 Moscow Olympics to protest the invasion of Afghanistan, rendering Coke's exclusive contract with the Soviets meaningless. Besides, association with Carter was becoming a liability, with the peanut farmer appearing powerless and indecisive in the face of spiraling inflation and the Iranian hostage crisis. Paul Austin, wandering the top floors of the North Avenue Tower, screamed "Get out of my office!" in the wrong executive suite, while his wife antagonized everyone. The six vice-chairmen jockeyed for position, and Robert Woodruff, nearing his ninetieth birthday, was reportedly near death from pneumonia.

No one would have guessed that a hopeful new era was about to commence, sparked by a frustrated secretary's letter.

Part V

~

*The Corporate Era
(1980–1999)*

If any father had a right to feel proud of his son, it was Crispulo Goizueta. When Roberto graduated from Yale, his father had wanted him to settle down in the family's Cuban sugar empire. After a year, however, the young man became restless, eager to strike out on his own. In 1954, thirty-one years ago, Roberto answered a blind ad and went to work as a chemical engineer for Coca-Cola.

So much had happened since then, Crispulo reflected. Castro had stolen his land, his heritage, and most of his wealth, and now he lived in Mexico City as an expatriate. In the meantime, Roberto had risen within the Company, achieving more than he or his father could ever have dreamed. As CEO, he had galvanized the staid old soft drink company in just a few years, transforming it into an aggressive dynamo.

Yet Crispulo's pride was tempered with anxiety. Mexicans were saying that his son had committed a grave error: he had changed the formula of Coca-Cola, and the entire world seemed in tumult over it. The change hadn't even come to Mexico yet, but it seemed that people spoke of little else. The troubled former plantation owner looked at Roberto now and saw a handsome man in his mid-fifties, a slight bulge beginning around the belt. Roberto, attending his own son's marriage on this hot May day in Florida, appeared typically unruffled and in command, yet Crispulo sensed a hesitancy he had never noticed before.

When the two men were alone, they spoke in Spanish, making polite conversation about the weather, the joyful occasion, and other small talk. Finally, Crispulo could bear it no longer. He had to know why his son had alienated so many people. "Roberto," he burst out, "this is awful, terrible! People are calling you names. What have you done?"

~ 18 ~

Roberto Goizueta's Bottom Line

*Two vultures [are] sitting on a branch of a dead tree in the middle of the
desert where, frustrated, they have been waiting for days on end for
something to eat. One vulture finally turns to the other and says,
"Patience, hell. Let's go kill something!"*

—Roberto Goizueta

HER JAW CLINCHED, Dianne Smith stormed back to her office. The
blonde secretary had worked at The Coca-Cola Company for ten years and,
like most employees, she was fiercely loyal, proud to work for Atlanta's best
company. In 1972, she had won the Miss Refreshing contest. On this particular
May morning in 1980, however, with the dogwood in bloom, something inside
the secretary snapped. The Company used to feel like one big gracious
Southern family, but in the last two years, ridiculous corporate strictures had
descended from on high. And today, when Smith had walked across North
Avenue to the little park for her lunch, security guards informed her that no
one was allowed to eat there anymore. Mrs. Austin didn't want anyone to
attract pigeons and their droppings, which would sully the manicured
grounds. The frustrated secretary defied the guards and grimly, determinedly
ate her sandwich on a bench anyway.

Back in her office, Dianne Smith rolled a fresh sheet into her typewriter,
banging the keys with a letter of complaint to Paul Austin. "I am speaking for
'the little people,'" she wrote, "who do not have releases from the daily
pressures, and the park affords us the opportunity of a wonderful outlet." It
had always been "a major source of pride for me to say that I am employed
with this fine company," she typed, "but as of late, I have reason to doubt my
source of pride." Smith wrote that she had never seen morale lower. With a
flourish, she ended the letter with her full name, Constance Dianne Smith.
"That ought to get some attention," she said to herself. Just to make sure,
though, she sent a blind copy to Robert Woodruff. After all, the pigeon-
plagued park was named after him.

The secretary's letter galvanized the Boss. Just the week before, Woodruff's
chauffeur had returned empty-handed from an errand to North Avenue, when
a security guard had told him he couldn't park in front of the building—sorry,
no exceptions, orders of Mrs. Austin. Shortly afterward, Grumman Aircraft
had called Woodruff's office to iron out some details on the new jet which Mrs.
Austin had just ordered to facilitate her search for works of art. Then came the
crowning blow. On May 28, the Company announced a $100 million debt

offering to pay for the new tower. Woodruff, who prided himself on steering the Company out of debt in the twenties, was livid. The ninety-year-old patriarch now summoned Paul Austin to his office and demanded his resignation, effective the following year, and he insisted that Austin appoint his successor immediately as the Company president.* A shaken, confused Austin drafted a letter nominating his friend Ian Wilson, who was traveling in Asia on a month-long business trip. When word of the recommendation spread through the North Avenue Tower, concerned executives—none ever willing to admit their role—convinced the Old Man that Ian Wilson, an autocratic Austin acolyte, would simply be more of the same. The Company needed a new direction. Besides, the appointment of a white South African would be foolhardy and might alienate black consumers.

THE RISE OF ROBERTO

At a special meeting of the board on May 30, Roberto Goizueta was appointed president of The Coca-Cola Company. Virtually everyone was surprised, since Don Keough seemed the obvious choice after Wilson. A skillful politician, tough marketer, and the best speaker and motivator since Harrison Jones, Keough could "read from the phone book and make you cry," as one admirer put it. Goizueta, on the other hand, a technical man with no operating experience, spoke in a halting accent, a curious amalgam of Cuba and Dixie. It seemed strange that a Latin chemical engineer should run the Company that produced the most American of products. Insiders like Joe Jones weren't so surprised, however. Only forty-eight, Goizueta, the consummate corporate politician, had risen quickly within the Company since his arrival in Atlanta in 1964. Most important, he had grown very close to Woodruff in the last year, joining him every day in his private dining room for lunch. Goizueta flattered Woodruff's vanity, seeking his opinion, deferring to his wisdom. The Boss in turn called Goizueta his "partner," perceiving something in the Cuban which reminded him of himself when he first took over the Company.

Like Woodruff, Goizueta, the son of a very wealthy man, had established his own career outside the family business. Raised in his grandfather's baronial mansion, paid for by sugarcane, he grew up in a culture which valued tradition and older people. Goizueta enjoyed the attention of his grandfather, and his conversation was still sprinkled with the Cuban proverbs he learned from him. In Woodruff, Goizueta found another wise old man. While his devotion to the Boss was politically expedient, it was also probably genuine. Woodruff's simplistic aphorisms reminded him of his grandfather's, and Southern culture resonated with the same social graces Goizueta had acquired in Cuba.

---

* In the meantime, word of the defiant secretary's letter spread through the efficient Company grapevine, and Dianne Smith won folk hero status. One clever employee posted a sign in the foyer. "Why worry about pigeons in the park," read the query, "when there are turkeys in the tower?"

As journalists dug into Goizueta's past, trying to assess the dark-horse winner, they discovered a remarkably intelligent man. In 1948, when eighteen-year-old Roberto Goizueta attended the prestigious Cheshire Academy in Connecticut for his senior year, he knew little English. He learned the new language by going to the same movies over and over again, absorbing American values along with the lingo. His discipline, combined with a photographic memory, helped him to excel. "My professor said that my sentence structure was textbook-perfect," Goizueta recalled. "It should have been; it came right out of the textbook! The only way I could accurately convey a thought was to memorize, word by word, entire passages." Incredibly, by the end of the year he delivered the valedictory address. Later, he graduated tenth in his class at Yale.

Coca-Cola associates knew Goizueta as a dedicated, impeccably dressed employee who left a bare desk every night. Never a brilliant researcher, he was an able administrator, a notorious perfectionist with an eye for detail. "He knew where every grain of sand was in the office," a fellow worker recalled. Goizueta's courtly, affable manner and Latin good looks hid what some called ruthlessness, but he rewarded results, and he never assumed an absolute position, quoting one of his grandfather's proverbs: "The quality of one's compromises is much more important than the correctness of one's position." Intensely pragmatic and somewhat cynical, he once observed, "It's a pretty good bet that human beings will act in their own self-interest most of the time." Although Goizueta kept his emotions under a steely, logical con-trol—"his mind is like a piece of crystal," an associate said—the surface tranquillity was belied by his chain-smoking and slight hand tremor. Outside of work and family, he had few interests aside from swimming laps and reading everything in sight. Somewhat incongruously, the Cuban blue-blood also developed a fondness for downhome country music.

Asked what he would do if he weren't the head of Coca-Cola, Goizueta gave a wholly unexpected answer: "I'd probably be a good teacher in a business school." What would he assign? Not *In Search of Excellence* or other popular management tomes, but *The Brothers Karamazov* and the *Gospel of St Luke*. His answer revealed not only his eclectic reading, but deep philosophical and religious concerns. Nonetheless, the Coca-Cola executive's brand of religion did not call for turning the other cheek. When asked for his best characteristic, Goizueta did not speak of his devotion to God, incisive mind, intuitive grasp, or managerial expertise. "I'm very persistent." His greatest fault, he said, was impatience. These two traits together produced a man who, like the vultures in his parable, favored well-planned aggression over passivity.

SETTING THE SLEEPY GIANT IN MOTION

Before assuming the chairmanship from Paul Austin in March of 1981, Goizueta spent an uneasy year as a president without full powers. He used the time well, making alliances with key executives and solidifying his power base. Recognizing that Don Keough's interpersonal skills would complement his more private analytical bent, Goizueta told the Iowan that he wanted him as his Chief Operating Officer. Goizueta and Keough began to appear everywhere together. In their speeches, each talked about what Don or Roberto had said about this or that. In a sense, Keough acted as Goizueta's master of ceremonies, a kind of Ed McMahon of Coca-Cola.

In the meantime, Goizueta made certain that Ian Wilson's star did not rise again within the Company. "There was never any doubt that it was Keough or me," he informed journalists. "I do not think Wilson had a chance." He noted that Wilson's territory of Canada and the Far East only contributed 15 percent of the Company's sales and hadn't maintained a high profit margin. And when Wilson's name came up in a scandal, Goizueta did nothing to clear it. The South African couldn't secure his U.S. citizenship, since a black Atlanta immigration official took pleasure in blocking his application. Anxious to obtain his Green Card before his anointment as CEO, Wilson had contacted Washington "fixer" Irving Davidson. Now, when word leaked of Davidson's imminent indictment in conjunction with an alleged Mafia don, Wilson splashed onto the papers and national TV for his involvement with the shady character, and the official Coke spokesman left the South African twisting in the wind with a "no comment" response.

Similarly, Wilson suddenly found himself implicated within the Company for illegal shipments of concentrate to Rhodesia in the late sixties, in violation of U.S. sanctions. Although in charge of the southern African territory at the time, Wilson denied any knowledge of the shipments, claiming he was framed. One anonymous source hypothesized that for Goizueta, "the stakes were enormous. What would you do if you were a displaced Cuban whose only recognized expertise was engineering and quality control for soft drinks, and you were confronted with someone who might do you in? On one side, there was the power and glory; on the other, the absolute abyss." Symbolically, after Wilson's departure, Goizueta appropriated his locker at the Peachtree Golf Club, where Woodruff had long controlled the sought-after membership.

At the same time, Goizueta worked on a major strategy statement which would, he hoped, revolutionize the way the Company did business. Grasping that an eighties' CEO would have to become a financial wizard, the new president determinedly taught himself about accounting, currency fluctuation, and economics, applying the same persistent curiosity and spongelike memory to the task as he had to acquiring English. "He used to come into my office fifteen or twenty times a day," Sam Ayoub, who was then the assistant financial officer, remembered. "He didn't know a word about accounting or finance, but he just asked questions and questions and questions."

The more Goizueta learned, the more uneasy he felt about management decisions within the Company. The fountain business, for instance, which Coke had always dominated, was considered the financial backbone of the Company, since the syrup price was flexible, unlike the bottler contract, which hamstrung the Company. Goizueta noted, however, that capital expenditures on fountain had gone up substantially since the introduction of the five-gallon (known as figal) aluminum fountain dispenser in the late sixties. The figures showed that while the fountain business returned 12.5 percent, the cost of capital was 16 percent. In theory, at least, the business was liquidating itself. Goizueta's technical men quickly solved the problem for their old boss by inventing inexpensive disposable bag-in-a-box containers.

Similarly, Goizueta concluded that the corporate obsession with market-share figures meant neglect of the bottom line. The Pepsi paranoia had blinded everyone to the ultimate goal of a good return on investment. Goizueta had, in fact, already demonstrated his ability to merge his technical background with concern for a cost-effective business when, in January of 1980, he persuaded Robert Woodruff to let him use high-fructose corn syrup (HFCS) in Coca-Cola in lieu of cane sugar.

CORN SYRUP AND ANGRY NON-AMENDERS

Luke Smith and Paul Austin had insisted that corn syrup lent an "off-taste" to Coca-Cola, but now a taste panel found no discernible difference. Although cane sugar would have been cheaper in a free market, HFCS offered a 20 percent savings over prices imposed by the traditional U.S. protective tariffs on sugar. At first, Goizueta had a difficult time convincing Woodruff to substitute HFCS, since it would, after all, change the sacred formula. Before the Finance Committee, the Cuban chemist elaborately explained the technical aspects, muddling Woodruff. John Sibley, even older than Woodruff but just as sharp, intervened, giving Goizueta his cue. "Remember when we approved of beet sugar back in the thirties, Bob? Well, this is just another kind of sugar, that's all." Once the decision was couched in such fundamental, simple terms, Woodruff quickly agreed.

In his war against Pepsi, Coca-Cola USA head Brian Dyson locked up almost the entire fructose supply with long-term contracts, then boosted the Company's share of advertising. While holding out such carrots to most bottlers, though, Dyson used HFCS as a stick to beat the non-amended renegades. The 1978 amendment specified that any savings in the cost of sweetener would flow through to the amended bottlers. But for the minority who had refused to sign, the Company held firmly to the old syrup price.

Bill Schmidt, already angry at Big Coke's cavalier attitude, became apoplectic at this financial blackmail. Didn't his perpetual contract call for 5.32 pounds of cane sugar per gallon of Coca-Cola syrup? They couldn't just foist off this corn syrup without permission. Schmidt ventured forth from tiny Elizabethtown, Kentucky, in search of an Atlanta lawyer to pursue his case, though he had little hope of finding anyone willing to risk collision with the monolithic Coke/King & Spalding business establishment.

Providentially, the disaffected bottler located Emmet Bondurant, who had already established a reputation for championing unpopular causes. Representing the ACLU, for instance, Bondurant had decimated Georgia's loyalty oath. In February of 1980, only months before Schmidt appeared, Bondurant had gone beyond the bounds of Atlanta propriety, however, when he took on King & Spalding in a sex discrimination suit. "You've lost your damn mind!"

a fellow lawyer told him. "Suing King & Spalding—Good God Almighty—in Atlanta!" Now, Bondurant agreed that Schmidt did indeed have a case, and in 1981, he brought a class-action suit for Schmidt and seventy other disgruntled bottlers. Bondurant, who professed admiration for Atticus Finch, the courageous Southern lawyer in Harper Lee's *To Kill a Mockingbird*, saw himself as a moral crusader, the underdog's last hope. With implacable diligence, he amassed material for the case.

THE SPARKLE OF DEATH

As a new Coca-Cola civil war brewed, however, Goizueta was relieved to resolve two other menaces he had inherited from the seventies. The International Union of Food and Allied Workers (IUF) had ushered in the new year with a Coke boycott because of the Guatemalan atrocities. On January 2, 1980, the IUF mailed a gory picture of Pedro Quevedo, a slain Coca-Cola union organizer, to its affiliates. The international union flexed its muscles as Coca-Cola bottling lines clattered to a halt in Finland, New Zealand, and Sweden, with threatened stoppages in six other countries. The relatively brief pause in Coca-Cola's production delivered its intended message to the Company. Hastily, Latin American Coke chief Ted Circuit assured the union, the nuns, and other critics that John Trotter's contract would be canceled in September of 1981.

Unfortunately, the assurance failed to prevent more bloodshed. In May of 1980, four more Coke union members were killed, including Marion Mendizabal, the third murdered union secretary. Letters from Amnesty International members poured into Guatemala. Throughout Latin America, angry protesters ripped down point-of-purchase signs and, by changing one word, converted them to placards with the chilling legend, "Coca-Cola: La Chispa de la Muerte"—"Coca-Cola: The Sparkle of Death." IUF head Dan Gallin insisted that The Coca-Cola Company act immediately to get rid of Trotter. In July, as the situation deteriorated, Goizueta, now president, directed Ted Circuit and Company lawyers to fly to Geneva to confer with Gallin. As a result, Circuit arranged for Antonio Zash, a Mexican McCann-Erickson executive with operating experience, and Roberto Mendez, a Mexican Coke plant manager, to buy out Trotter. The Company, however, supplied most of the purchase price and retained some managerial control over the franchise. In December, Zash and Mendez signed a union contract, and the Guatemalan crisis was over for the time being.[*]

The quick, bold action to halt the boycott was characteristic of Goizueta, who understood that Coke men couldn't simply sit in Atlanta and wait for the

---

[*] Four years later, Zash and Mendez declared bankruptcy, but the union workers occupied the plant, claiming that the owners had milked the franchise before closing its doors to defeat the union. Again, the IUF called for a boycott and Coca-Cola once more forced a solution, locating Carlos Porras Gonzalez, a Salvadoran economist, to restart the bottling plant.

world to come to their door. By flying directly to Geneva, they had signaled their willingness to compromise. Goizueta was also ready to risk criticism from hard-line industrialists who would never negotiate with an international union. While Coke men denied that they had done any such thing, they were clearly playing with semantics. "If this isn't a negotiating situation," Gallin crowed, "I don't know what is. Our objectives were exactly what we got."

GETTING AGGRESSIVE WITH BOTTLERS

The month before Circuit flew to Switzerland, another seventies headache was laid to rest. In June of 1980, the Soft Drink Interbrand Competition Act passed both houses of Congress. Finally assured of exclusive territorial rights, bottlers could thumb their collective noses at the FTC. Without the grass-roots clout of the small-town bottler, the bill would never have become law. Ironically, though, the law's passage cleared the way for Brian Dyson and his aggressive team to hasten the demise of the small bottler.

Free of the FTC threat, which had discouraged potential franchise buyers, a flurry of mergers and acquisitions commenced, and the price of bottling territories, held down artificially for many years, spiraled dizzily. Many long-time family names sold out, retiring on the proceeds. Big Coke not only encouraged sales of weak bottlers, it actively promoted consolidation, some-times buying an interim equity position while looking for a new owner. Still, Dyson, Keough, and Goizueta repeatedly vowed that they had no intention of assuming permanent ownership. In fact, the Company jettisoned its Baltimore plant and Dyson promised to unload other Company-owned bottlers unless they performed well.

In 1980, Pepsi's John Sculley, who sensed a worthy opponent in Dyson, decided to push the Pepsi Challenge nationally, hoping to maintain the momentum of the late seventies and retain leadership in the supermarkets. Sculley faced unexpectedly violent opposition from within his own ranks; terrified Pepsi bottlers begged him "stop this madness," convinced that in *their* territory, Pepsi would lose the Challenge, or that Coke would initiate vicious price wars. Their apprehension was justified. Dyson reacted by funneling Company money into areas where the taste tests ran. At one Challenge campaign kickoff, Coca-Cola trucks surrounded the Pepsi plant in an attempt at pure intimidation. The Company hired Mean Joe Greene to wield a sledgehammer against Pepsi vending machines at Coke rallies. Dyson's blunt message to Pepsi bottlers, as Sculley interpreted it, stated: "If you're in the Challenge program, we're going to go out and kill you." Nonetheless, the taste test continued to plague Coca-Cola.

FINDING A BETTER DIET DRINK

As early as 1979, Goizueta had directed Mauricio Gianturco and his technical people to launch work on Project David, an ultimately unsuccessful attempt at a cola formula to trounce Pepsi in taste tests. Frustrated in the sugar cola arena, he now focused on a drink that would outperform *diet* Pepsi, since the fast-growing diet segment would soon account for 20 percent of the entire soft drink market. Goizueta and Dyson agreed that Sergio Zyman should head the diet project. The brilliant, aggressive, multilingual young Mexican had been lured from Pepsi along with a raft of other key employees active in the Challenge campaign—a reversal of the Coke defections led by Al Steele thirty years earlier. In February of 1980, Zyman initiated Project Harvard. Zyman fashioned a number of code names for the new product he was working on—Fresca Plus, Lucy, Shrimp, and BPS, which stood alternatively for "Bottler Productivity Study," "Best Product Under the Sun," or "Beat Pepsi Soundly." If the Mexican had really proposed any of these silly names, Austin and other Coke executives wouldn't have been disturbed. The whole point of the project, however, was to utilize the "brand equity" of the Coca-Cola name. The new product, Diet Coke, would constitute a "line extension."

To lend the magical Coke name to any other soft drink was heretical. When a few daring Company men suggested the idea in 1963 when TaB was invented, Austin had condemned them for it. Now, TaB held a commanding lead over all other diet drinks. Why would the Company want to cannibalize its venerable drink with another diet entry? Furthermore, wouldn't another product with the Coke name simply dilute the brand, confuse consumers, and contribute to already poor bottler morale?

Zyman, Dyson, Keough, and Goizueta were convinced, however, that the introduction of Diet Coke would energize the business. As Zyman put it in a February 1980 memo to Brian Dyson: "Over the last few years, the Company has drifted . . . to a perceived image of a traditional, sedentary, conservative company." The bold introduction of Diet Coke would have a "tremendous impact" on this image, revitalize the bottlers, and capitalize on the Coca-Cola name. It would also be profitable, since a saccharin-sweetened drink wouldn't cost as much to produce. The timing was demographically perfect as well: the aging baby boomers weren't drinking fewer cola drinks, as doomsayers had warned, but were switching to diet drinks as part of the emerging fitness craze. Zyman concluded that "*competition cannot duplicate this effort*," simply because there already *was* a diet Pepsi. Because Coke had held back so long, this late bloomer would have an enormous catalytic effect, motivating bottlers to "go out and *really* get aggressive." In short, concluded the Mexican marketer, "this could be the silver bullet."

Then Paul Austin abruptly and inexplicably pulled the plug on Project Harvard in a cryptic April telegram to Don Keough, who was plotting strategy with Zyman and Dyson in Buenos Aires. Convinced of the project's wisdom and urgency, Goizueta sought Woodruff's support. He had learned his lesson from the corn syrup presentation—to win approval from the Old Man, it was necessary to argue the case in its starkest, most simple terms. Besides, Woodruff displayed limited patience and attention span. Goizueta explained that the market share for sugar colas had been declining for years, while diet drinks were steadily growing. "In a few years, Mr Woodruff, we might have to rename this operation The TaB Company if we don't do something." When his trusted "partner" described it that way, Robert Woodruff readily agreed to Diet Coke, but Austin still stood in the way. The Boss took care of that, too. When the board convened on August 6, Goizueta was elected Chairman of the Board and Chief Executive Officer to replace Paul Austin upon his retirement, which would occur on March 1, 1981. Posing for pictures after the board meeting, Goizueta looked like a movie star, while Austin, looming beside him like a great disheveled bear, grimaced a thin-lipped imitation of a smile. Immediately afterward, Goizueta gave Zyman the go-ahead.

THE AUSTIN LEGACY

Following his retirement, Austin was finally diagnosed with Alzheimer's disease, and, after a swift decline, he died in 1985 at seventy. Although his troubled final years tend to obscure his achievements at Coca-Cola, his overall record reveals the astonishing growth he fostered. In 1962, when he assumed the presidency, the Company was still essentially a one-drink outfit with bland, old-fashioned advertising and deep-seated corporate racism. Profits amounted to $46.7 million on sales of $567.5 million, with the overseas branches accounting for 30 percent. Austin provided visionary, professional management, deftly guiding the Company through the difficult sixties and seventies. Under his supervision, the Company introduced a rainbow of drinks for a segmented market, developed a social conscience—albeit under considerable pressure—and aired some of the most powerful commercials ever made.

Austin's greatest legacy, however, was his globe-girdling zeal in spreading the business to country after country. By the end of 1980, Coke earned $422 million on revenues of nearly $6 billion—a tenfold increase over 1962—and 65 percent of the profit flowed from outside the United States. Even Austin's pet projects—his ill-fated shrimp farming, desalinization plants, and whey-based nutritional drinks—reflected a curiosity and daring that the Company had never seen. "Paul was too big for Coca-Cola," mused his friend Ian Wilson, who quit the same day Austin retired. "His vision was too broad to be satisfied selling colored carbonated sugar-water."

UPENDING SACRED COWS

Soon after the Coca-Cola board announced that Goizueta would succeed Austin, Company managers from around the world convened in Atlanta for their annual October meeting, where they usually presented a five-year plan for their sectors. Goizueta, assuming that no one could see ahead that far, requested three-year plans instead. Once again, Goizueta asked "questions and questions and questions" of his ill-prepared executives, who dubbed the collective two-week grilling the "Spanish Inquisition." Frustrated that Coke men were simply reacting to competition in setting their goals—with some going after increased sales, some market share, and only a few concerned over return on capital—Goizueta felt that something had to be done.

Determined to shake up the staid, stuffy Company, Goizueta labored over an aggressive strategy statement. Within a month of his official investiture as CEO in March of 1981, he summoned the top fifty Coca-Cola managers from around the world to a five-day conference in Palm Springs. "A company starts to worry about holding on to success when it's decided it has more to lose than it has to gain," he told them. "At that point, it gets timid and overly concerned with appearances." Goizueta promised that the days of Coca-Cola's passivity were over. "Those who don't adapt will be left behind or out—no matter what level they are." He flatly stated that "there are no sacred cows." To prevent competition from winning, Goizueta stressed, he would consider "the reformulation of any or all of our products."

Goizueta's carefully crafted "Strategy for the 1980s" was passed out at Palm Springs and reprinted for widespread distribution to financial analysts, the media, and Coca-Cola employees. At the heart of the innocuously worded statement lay the profit target—"a rate substantially in excess of inflation, in order to give our shareholders an above average total return on their investment." In order to accomplish that, the document warned that the Company would probably diversify. Ruling out heavy industry, Goizueta promised to search instead for "services that complement our product lines and that are compatible with our consumer image."

Although few people, including the media, took Goizueta terribly seriously, his managers soon discovered that he followed through. Those who bucked Goizueta's authority or failed to address the bottom line effectively were ruthlessly weeded. "Roberto was a tyrant," Sam Ayoub recalled: "Fire him!" was often the peremptory order, but Ayoub usually arranged for a gentler exit with an early retirement package. On the surface, though, it was business as usual at Coca-Cola for the rest of 1981. Brian Dyson strove for further bottler consolidation and rejuvenation of the domestic system, producing a motivational film in which Coca-Cola men shot it out in a Western-style gunfight against Pepsi's "Big Blue Gang." As a climax, a tank clanked over a hill and blew a Pepsi vending machine to bits. Dyson also attempted to placate disaffected bottlers by allowing them to choose from alternative seasonal commercials and by responding more promptly to local problems. Most bottlers were pleased when Goizueta announced his intention of boosting the Company's domestic earnings, since they felt that their importance had diminished with increasing income from abroad. Goizueta wanted to achieve a 50–50 balance by the end of the decade. With the dollar strengthening against most other currencies, it made sense to look for more profits at home. In addition, foreign sales had flattened in 1980, due partially to record rainfall in Japan.

IN THE PHILIPPINES: #/&$ PEPSI!

The dismal performance of Coke's business in the Philippines also contributed to the poor showing overseas. Where Coca-Cola had once ruled the market, Pepsi now dominated with a 70 percent share. Andres Soriano, Jr., the heir of an enormously influential, wealthy family, had neglected his Coke franchise in order to push his beer business. In the meantime, Pepsi dumped huge amounts of money into its company-owned Philippines plant. The haughty Soriano refused to listen to the bright young men Coca-Cola sent to him, dismissing them as "pipsqueaks."

Clearly, drastic measures were necessary. Breaking precedent, the Company bought a $13 million 30 percent equity position in the business in return for managerial control. Neville Isdell, an impressive 6'5" Irishman summoned from a Coke post in Australia, quickly assessed the situation in June of 1981. Although a basic infrastructure—over 1,000 delivery trucks and 7,500 employees—was already in place, dispirited workers perfunctorily bottled in filthy plants. Isdell set out to instill pride and aggression into the employees. While the Sorianos had worn a traditional upper-class *barong tagalog*, Isdell deliberately fostered an informal, gutsy image, sporting a T-shirt with the Coca-Cola logo. He inspected every toilet, not only to promote cleaner hands on the bottling line, but to deliver the message that he cared about plant conditions.

With twelve-ounce and liter packages, as well as new flavors such as Mello Yello, Isdell sought to rejuvenate the market, holding a spirited rally for each product introduction. For Mello Yello, advertised as "the world's fastest soft drink," he wore running shorts and led the workers in push-ups and a sprint around the bottling plant. To dramatize the liter, Isdell proved he was *literally* willing to work in the trenches with his employees. Wearing Army fatigues, he led a military-style rally, hurling a Pepsi bottle against a wall.[*]

The new approach galvanized the workers. Within a year, Coke's Philippine share grew by 30 percent even as the local economy took a 4 percent dive, and within two years, Coke had overtaken Pepsi. By decade's end, Coca-Cola would command 71 percent of the business, neatly reversing the market-share figures at the beginning of 1981. Lauded as a hero, Isdell rose quickly in the Company. More important, a long-standing taboo had been broken. Big Coke clearly could take an equity position in its own bottlers with impressive results. The lesson was not lost on Goizueta, who would soon lead the Company into many such ventures.

JESSE JACKSON PUSHES COKE

In 1981, Goizueta and Keough, while searching for ways to show the world that Coke had revived, encountered the exact type of publicity they did not need. Reverend Jesse Jackson, the outspoken, politically ambitious black activist, turned his attention to Coca-Cola. To some degree, his call for more jobs for blacks repeated CORE demands twenty years previously, but neither Coca-Cola nor the South were overtly racist anymore. In fact, the soft drink

---

[*] As he threw the bottle, the Coke commando screamed an epithet in Filipino. Relating this incident, Isdell paused. "I won't say what I said." When urged to supply a paraphrase, he responded, "Beat Pepsi," and laughed.

company supported local black colleges, the NAACP, and other civil rights groups; 24 percent of the Company's work force was black. Like others before him, Jackson chose Coke not so much because of any glaring corporate abuse, but because the firm was so temptingly vulnerable due to its cherished image. In July, he and his Chicago-based People United to Save Humanity (PUSH) threatened to launch a boycott—euphemistically termed a "withdrawal of enthusiasm"—if Coke did not bow to their demands. Jackson complained that there were no black-owned bottling plants or syrup wholesalers; nor was there a black on the board of directors. While Coke spent over $500,000 on ethnic ad agencies, that wasn't enough, considering the $169 million budget for annual advertising.

Don Keough and Carl Ware, an impressive black Coke executive who had once headed the Atlanta City Council, were negotiating with Jackson when he abruptly escalated publicity. Declaring an impasse, he called for a boycott and told the press that Atlanta's black ministers would denounce Coca-Cola from the pulpit that Sunday. Though nothing of the sort occurred, Keough and Ware didn't want to tangle with PUSH, and on August 11, with a triumphant Jesse Jackson standing at his side, Don Keough held a press conference heralding Coca-Cola's new "moral covenant," promising blacks a package worth $34 million. In the audience were Atlanta mayor Maynard Jackson, Coretta Scott King, Andrew Young, and other prominent black leaders. Coca-Cola gave Jackson everything he had asked for, promising to spend more on minority advertising, increase the number of black managers, and find suitable ethnic owners for a bottling franchise. Fooling no one, Keough insisted that the new program had nothing to do with the PUSH boycott, but rather represented Coca-Cola's sincere effort to obey President Ronald Reagan's recent summons for private industry to intervene as government affirmative-action programs were trimmed.

Neither Keough nor Goizueta anticipated the reaction to their well-intended plans, though the election of the archconservative Reagan should have given them a hint. Many white Americans were sick of civil rights agitation. Even the name of Jackson's organization was offensive—they were tired of being PUSHed around by loud-mouthed blacks. A severe white backlash whipped the soft drink firm. Lewis Grizzard, the *Atlanta Constitution*'s syndicated professional redneck, complained of Coca-Cola's "show of spinelessness," comparing PUSH activists to Chicago mobsters and suggesting that Jesse Jackson be granted the bottling franchise on the moon. Even *Barron's*, the well-respected financial weekly, chided Coca-Cola for agreeing to find black entrepreneurs to bottle or wholesale the drink, since it would "injure meritorious whites." Similar letters of protest deluged the Company, such as one Tennessee businessman who wrote to protest "blackmail pressures of one minority organization." Keough painstakingly responded to these concerned white Southerners, tactfully refuting the presumed "cave-in." Finally, the Coca-Cola president was forced to admit publicly that he had made a mistake—he should never have called a press conference with Jackson at his side.

COKE IS IT

Soon, however, Goizueta and Keough forgot all about the uproar over Jackson, when a new advertising campaign, "Coke Is It," was unveiled in February of 1982, after over a year of unprecedented research and consumer testing. The man behind the commercials was John Bergin, who had created the Pepsi Generation and "You've Got a Lot to Live, and Pepsi's Got a Lot to Give" at BBDO. Now at McCann-Erickson, the advertiser inherited "Have a Coke and a Smile," with its pretty tune and feel-good approach, which he considered "limp-wristed," without real punch. Bergin yearned for a feistier battle cry to reassert the leading cola's confidence. He discovered it in a Canadian campaign that Ken Schulman, another McCann man, had cobbled together with New York songwriter Ginny Redington. Bergin was immediately taken by the compelling music: after a gradual buildup, it punched a brassy climax with three quick blasts in succession: "Coke is it!"

Bergin modified the lyrics to eliminate references to Canada, and Goizueta and Keough loved it. Just before the launch, however, Ginny Redington made a startling admission. She had originally written the music for a network news show promotion. The three beats were initially intended for "N-B-C!" The studio heads had rejected the music, however, judging that it was too flashy for a simple station identification theme. Bergin, aware of the touchy Coca-Cola pride, was outraged. "We had egg all over us, not just our faces," he recalled. Fortunately, Coke executives were understanding, since they sensed a winner.

On February 4, Coca-Cola unveiled the commercials on all three TV networks at 9:15 P.M. in a "roadblock." Simultaneously, 2,000 bottlers gathered at the Atlanta Civic Center to watch the same ads. By midnight, more than 150 million Americans had heard "Coke Is It," which Don Keough dubbed the Company's new marching song. On screen, as the song's momentum developed, students, parents, and toddlers threw crates and scrap wood onto a large pile. "The most refreshing way / To make the most of every day," sang eager voices. "And wherever you go and whatever you do, / There's something big waiting for me and you." Then, just as the pile was torched into a huge bonfire, the message slammed through: "Coke is it! / The biggest taste you've ever found. / Coke is it! / The one that never lets you down." The fire turned out to be the centerpiece for an all-American pep rally before a football game. Of course, it wasn't altogether clear whether the cheerleaders, appropriately garbed in Coca-Cola red, were leading the crowd in joyous celebration of the home team or Coca-Cola, which was displayed in fifteen separate scenes of the sixty-second commercial. In all the "Coke Is It!" spots—whether a farmer's surprise birthday party or a break for energetic young dancers—consumers pulled glistening Coke bottles from ice chests. After gulping, they conveyed their overwhelming joy, holding the bottle up to admire and sighing with relief.

Roberto Goizueta hailed the new campaign as a fitting introduction to his reign. "This strong, assertive message," he told his bottlers, "mirrors the nature of Americans today. We say what we mean and we tell it like it is."

Actually, the lyrics intentionally *didn't* say exactly what "it" was. As Brian Dyson admonished, "We should not be too precise, too descriptive or too literal." That way, each consumer could fantasize appropriately. "Whatever the feeling, whatever the need," Dyson concluded, "Coke is it. *Period.*"

At the same time, Coke unveiled its secret weapon against the Pepsi Challenge: Bill Cosby. The black comic's love affair with Coke dated to his childhood, when he sometimes drank fifteen Cokes by 2 P.M. during his "periods of addiction," as he put it. "It helped me to burp very good and clear the area." In the late sixties, the Company had sponsored Cosby's radio show. More recently, he had made commercials for the "Coke and a Smile" campaign, appearing in person at the Great Get-Together in 1979. John Bergin now directed Cosby in "Coke Is It" commercials which mocked the Pepsi Challenge. Directly addressing the audience, mugging with his well-rehearsed charm, Cosby simply drank a Coke and talked. "This is real refreshment, real big taste," he said. "Now see, if you were another cola, number 2 or number 29, you'd do taste tests and challenges and stuff and try to compare yourself to this, wouldn't you? Sure, don't shake your head, you would too, you sneaky devil." Other Cosby commercials did the previously unthinkable, showing a Pepsi vending machine, but only in order to knock it. "If you're number two," he said, "you know what you want to be when you grow up. Yes, Coke is it. You're nodding, yes?" In one ad, Cosby spied on a Pepsi taste test with binoculars, pointing out that the Challenge commercials never depicted *anyone* choosing Coke, which was misleading.

Bergin credited Cosby with killing the Challenge, which halted in 1983. "He was brilliantly entertaining in his ridicule." As the comedian immodestly informed bottlers at the Great Get-Together, "I don't think there is anyone who, when they believe in the product, can sell it as well as I as a projectionist." Bergin found Cosby "inconceivably arrogant," but he had to admit that "magic happens when the camera starts. That man is the greatest thing I've seen in terms of making his face work." Despite blow-ups on the set, the ad man acknowledged that "our greatest weapon has been Bill Cosby when we have used him." In 1983, Cosby invested more personally in Coke's future when he bought part ownership of the Philadelphia bottling plant along with black entrepreneur James Bruce Llewellyn. The sale fulfilled Coke's promise to PUSH to give blacks management of a bottling plant, though Cosby was hardly an underprivileged minority member.

THE IMAGE MASTERS DIVERSIFY

Although pleased with the universal acclaim given "Coke Is It," Goizueta was smarting from the adverse reaction to his acquisition of Columbia Pictures only two weeks earlier. The field of entertainment was alluring, particularly to Goizueta, who had been seduced by Hollywood in his schoolboy days. Coca-Cola commercials were, after all, mini-movies. Furthermore, the eighties were transforming into a decade of glitz, image, and instant replay. The "Gimme Generation," as some journalists dubbed eighties consumers, was obsessed with video, so Columbia's library of 1,800 classic films promised to be a gold mine. Consequently, Coca-Cola surprised even Columbia's management team of Herb Allen and Fay Vincent by paying $750 million for the studio, the equivalent of nearly twice its stock market value at the time.

Financial analysts dumped on the deal. Coke had paid too much, they said, and besides, what did a soft drink company know about making movies? Coca-Cola stock lost 10 percent of its value within a few days. Goizueta was angry and puzzled, since he had served notice that he wanted to diversify and to increase the Company's U.S. profits until they contributed half of the revenue, and, with domestic soft drink growth slowing, Columbia offered a solution. "We're doing absolutely the only thing we could have done to maintain our growth into the future," Goizueta told reporters.

During the rest of the year, the critics had to admit that Coke hadn't been so stupid after all. Columbia churned out three smash hits in a row with *Tootsie*, *Gandhi*, and *The Toy*. More important, the Company signed an unbelievably sweet deal with Home Box Office, Time Inc.'s pay-cable movie channel. HBO agreed to pay for a quarter of the production cost for all Columbia movies, as well as forking over whopping rental fees. At the same time, Columbia, HBO, and CBS formed a new studio called Tri-Star. Goizueta and Keough had no direct hand in the deals, but they soon befriended Allen and Vincent, who had pulled off a real coup. Soon thereafter, Herb Allen joined the Coca-Cola board.

Although Goizueta and Keough repeatedly denied meddling with Columbia's creative output, they did install Peter Sealey, one of Coke's top marketers, as the studio's new researcher. Sealey started asking questions never before addressed, using the jargon of the soft drink industry. Who were the movies' "heavy users," and what did they really want? How effective was Columbia's advertising campaign? How badly did home video "cannibalize" movie attendance? Sealey even discussed "pre-testing" script concepts. By combining ad budgets with its new owner, Columbia immediately benefited from the Coke tie-in, getting discounts on bulk advertising.

While Goizueta and Keough did not overtly fiddle with the creative content at Columbia, they made sure that certain products never appeared in their films, sending a memo to studio executives forbidding the use of any PepsiCo or Philip Morris (owner of 7-Up) items. As expected, under its new ownership Columbia's celluloid featured a goodly amount of Coca-Cola, particularly in feel-good, happy-ending efforts such as *Murphy's Romance*, a James Garner/ Sally Field film that premiered three years later. Pepsi appeared, too, but only in a negative context, as Field's son was denied a job in an inhuman supermarket where, as film critic Mark Crispin Miller wrote, "two blue Pepsi signs loom[ed] coldly on the wall like a couple of swastikas."

Of course, it wasn't necessary for Coke to buy a studio to ensure product placement. In 1982, the movie *E.T.* galvanized marketers' attention when Reese's Pieces experienced a 70 percent sales jump the month after the cute alien munched them on screen. The message was not lost on Coke, also plugged in *E.T.* Soon, all manner of consumer goods prominently paraded on movie screens. Ken Manson, Coke's full-time film agent, suddenly found his job more difficult and competitive. While other firms paid thousands of dollars for product placement, Manson offered vintage Coca-Cola soda fountains or trucks as "authentic" period props. Almost unbelievably, he continued to place Coke in films without paying for the privilege.

DIET COKE ROCKETTES AWAY

In July of 1982, when Brian Dyson held a press conference to trumpet the pending debut of diet Coke—the cutesy lower-case "d" presumably indicating that its dietary qualities were secondary to its Coke-ness—Goizueta quickly discovered that the Columbia deal wasn't the *only* thing he could do to boost domestic growth. News of the project hadn't leaked, despite a widening circle of people aware of it. The can alone had gone through 150 possible designs. Over 10,000 consumers had participated in extended home-use and purchase-simulation tests. It was, in Dyson's words, "the most carefully developed and researched product in the history of The Coca-Cola Company." As a show of the Company's confidence, diet Coke would roll out in the tough New York territory, which accounted for 10 percent of the country's volume. In August, Charles Millard of the New York Coca-Cola Bottling Company, with support from Big Coke, rented Radio City Music Hall, complete with the dancing Rockettes, to launch the drink. Then SSC&B/Lintas (hereafter called Lintas), McCann's sister organization responsible for the diet Coke account, rented an auditorium in Los Angeles for a day, filled the theater with extras, and hired scores of stars to appear as if they had been at the New York premiere. Altogether, the resulting sixty-second commercial cost some $2.5 million, making it the most expensive spot ever.

The gamble was worth it, though. An instant phenomenon, diet Coke surpassed all Company expectations. Much of the drink's impact undoubtedly stemmed from its clever positioning as the drink for the eighties' life-style. In contrast to TaB, using "perfumy and lacy imagery" to appeal exclusively to women, diet Coke's theme song proclaimed that "you're gonna drink it just for the taste of it." Men, increasingly worried about their weight, health, and appearance, already bought 30 percent of diet beverages. Coca-Cola research indicated that diet Coke could grab the majority of the newly named Yuppies—those young urban professionals who did aerobics and worked out on their Nautilus machines. As Roy Stout's research had shown, however, many of the new consumers were attracted simply because of the magical brand name—Coke. In labeled taste-tests, consumers preferred TaB to Pepsi by a slim margin, but when Stout dispensed TaB from a can marked "Diet Coke," the name alone swung the results twelve more points in Coca-Cola's favor. In essence, the consumers were tasting the world's best-known trademark, with goodwill built over a ninety-six-year history. Whatever the reason, diet Coke took off. By the end of 1983, it had captured 17 percent of the diet soda market, making it the fourth-best-selling American soft drink, and it was already available in twenty-eight overseas markets.

Not all Coke men delighted in diet Coke's unprecedented surge, however, since the Company charged more for the new syrup than it did for Coca-Cola, even though the saccharin-sweetened drink cost considerably less to produce. Big Coke's proposed bottling contract for diet Coke awarded the parent company total control of pricing, in addition to numerous other restrictions. When many bottlers balked, the Company dragged out negotiations while the roll-out and national advertising sparked an intense public clamor for diet Coke, forcing reluctant franchisees to sign a temporary contract. At that point, renegade bottler Bill Schmidt, and thirty cohorts, already suing the Company over the HFCS issue, instructed lawyer Emmet Bondurant to file suit over diet Coke for the non-amended bottlers. A few weeks later, Bondurant also filed a separate case for selected amended bottlers.

Though legally complex, the basic Diet Coke Case issues boiled down to an existential question: What was Coca-Cola? Bondurant and the disaffected bottlers argued that diet Coke constituted an alternatively sweetened form of the old soft drink. After all, the Company called it Coke, and the advertising claimed similarity to the "real thing." If so, the Company had to abide by its original contract with the non-amended bottlers, rendering diet Coke technically illegal, since it didn't contain 5.32 pounds of sugar. For amended bottlers, the case seemed clear-cut, since their 1978 contract called for the Company to pass through any savings on alternative sweeteners.

All of the cases—E-Town, the nickname for the argument over corn syrup, and the diet Coke suits—would be decided by Murray Schwartz, a district court judge in Wilmington, Delaware. Over the course of the decade, Schwartz, an unusually meticulous and attentive jurist, would develop an unwanted expertise in the history and nuances of the soft drink industry. Publicly, Big Coke pooh-poohed the lawsuits, dismissing the angry bottlers as a disgruntled minority with little effect on the Company's bottom line. Coke's lawyers regarded the cases as simple contract disputes over incremental profits. Nonetheless, the outcomes remained crucial, since they tested the Company's right to bend bottlers to its will. For Schmidt and Bondurant, the battle assumed the dimensions of a moral crusade. With neither side interested in an out-of-court settlement, a bitter legal war commenced.

GLORY DAYS

By the end of 1983, Goizueta felt vindicated in the eyes of the world. Columbia, a money machine, earned $91 million in its first full year as a Coca-Cola subsidiary. In 1983, following hard on the heels of diet Coke's unparalleled achievement, the company introduced caffeine-free versions of Coca-Cola, diet Coke, and TaB. As usual, Big Coke lagged behind the rest of the market in terms of innovation. Philip Morris was already trumpeting that 7-Up "never had it, never will," while Royal Crown had pioneered the previous year with the first cola to lack a stimulant. The day before the diet Coke announcement, Pepsi unveiled Pepsi Free. At first, Coca-Cola resisted any movement that implied that caffeine constituted a health hazard, since the ingredient provided the drink's famous "lift." Goizueta proved that Coke could adapt, however, and once the giant finally stirred, it usually dominated a market segment.

Later in the year, Brian Dyson revealed that diet Coke's taste would be improved with NutraSweet, the brand name for aspartame, a revolutionary new alternative sweetener just approved by the FDA. The only drawback to aspartame—aside from serious unanswered questions about its effects on the human body—was its instability, which would limit shelf life. Consequently, diet Coke initially derived its sweetness from a half-and-half blend of saccharin and NutraSweet. Soon afterward, the Company opted for 100 percent of the better-tasting sweetener, despite its limits and exorbitant expense. The diet drink market share, 24 percent and still climbing, convinced Coke to guarantee that its new drink measured up to the boasts about taste.

As if to symbolize the dramatic changes, the wrecking ball smashed into the sixty-three-year-old red-brick building on North Avenue to make way for a fancy new entrance rotunda. The squat, solidly built veteran of the cola wars resisted demolition as nostalgic older employees looked on, but the job was completed by the fall. Memorial bricks, distributed to every Coke employee as souvenirs, served as the only link to the past. Goizueta, suddenly the media's darling, dominated a spring 1983 issue of *Business Week* in a cover story on "Coke's Big Market Blitz." At a press conference for 100 market analysts late in 1983, the confident CEO declared that the Company intended to double its size by the end of the eighties. To emphasize his determination, he held the meeting in a Boston bottling plant with a backdrop of 3 million cans stacked twenty-five feet high which would, he told the audience, land in vending machines and on grocery shelves within forty-eight hours. Emanuel Goldman, a longtime follower of the Company, proclaimed that "the giant has awakened." *Adweek* named Goizueta the "marketer of the year," while *Dun's Business Month* praised him for running one of America's five best-managed companies.

1984

The next year only intensified Goizueta's triumph. The Cuban had established a dynamic eighties management style while capitalizing on the nearly century-old asset of Coca-Cola's identification with American culture. Naturally, Coke became the official soft drink of the 1984 Summer Olympics in Los Angeles, where everything coalesced for the soft drink concern—projecting an active, healthy, athletic worldwide image, with competitors drinking gallons of Coca-Cola and diet Coke right there next to Hollywood, where Columbia slaked the country's thirst for entertainment. Even the nation's "Teflon" president, a former movie star, signaled the triumph of image over substance, the apotheosis of the soft drink mentality. As a conservative Republican, Reagan was primarily a Pepsi man, but what did it matter?

Increasingly, the two cola giants were squeezing competition out of vending machines, fountain spigots, and grocery shelves. The much-publicized "cola wars," while real enough on one level, actually benefited both brands. There was no more essential difference between Coke and Pepsi than the line separating most Democrats and Republicans. When Reagan hired Pepsi advertising guru Phil Dusenberry to produce his 1984 campaign commercials, it was not so much an endorsement of a particular brand of soft drink as an indication that, in America, politics had been reduced to the art of master image manipulators. Even Walter Mondale's most cutting criticism of Reagan during the campaign—"Where's the beef?"—derived from a fast-food commercial.

"I'm always going to be searching for emotion," Phil Dusenberry told reporters. "In an age when most products aren't very different, the difference is often in the way people feel about [them]." In his Reagan spots, Dusenberry highlighted elderly couples smiling and holding hands, children playing, and important officials meeting in the Oval Office. What they were discussing seemed immaterial—the fact that they conveyed a serious, competent atmosphere sufficed.

It was so evident that Reagan would win by a landslide that the Coke PAC contributed no money at all to Walter Mondale, even though the Southern soft drink company traditionally supported Democrats. Instead, $5,000 went to Reagan, while Jesse Jackson got $1,500, since Coke wanted to avoid accusations of racism. At the same time, the Company contributed $1,000 to archconservative Jesse Helms for balance.

Researchers of the eighties, whether working for political campaigns or soft drinks, honed sophisticated techniques for identifying target groups to an extent that would have alarmed cola drinkers had they been privy to insider documents. At the end of 1984, the depth researchers at Lintas developed a profile of the "typical" Coca-Cola and diet Coke user. According to the study, Coca-Cola drinkers possessed rigid personalities; a drink should taste a particular way. They lived in a "traditional reality based on early experiences, stereotypes and cultural generalizations." To a Coke drinker, the world should remain immutable, ruled by "certain self-evident truths." The researchers also identified a feeling of resignation and "lack of personal control." Consequently, Coca-Cola drinkers demanded immediate gratification and didn't really worry about putting on weight.

Diet Coke consumers, on the other hand, felt that "the world is changeable" and that they could exercise personal control and a degree of choice. Capable of long-range planning, they could delay gratification. While diet Coke drinkers, like their Coca-Cola counterparts, often valued family relations, they sometimes assumed alternative family roles with greater flexibility. "Both the husband and wife could work, the husband can go shopping and prepare a dinner while the wife comes home late from the office." More critical, diet Coke drinkers cared deeply about personal appearance.

Though the Lintas researchers didn't mention it, 1984 diet Coke consumers might snort a line of cocaine or two while seeking self-fulfillment. The Peruvian drug, popular with the upper crust in 1885 and 1925, once more enjoyed a vogue with hedonistic Yuppies. T-shirts with "Cocaine" written in

Coca-Cola script caused consternation at North Avenue, where no one discussed the soft drink's coca leaf content, decocainized or not. As a defensive measure, the legal department reversed its long-standing taboo against the logo's use on anything except the soft drink. Now, the Company licensed script Coca-Cola for clothes, furniture, toys, clocks, art objects, and innumerable other items. By selling the rights to quality manufacturers, the lawyers hoped to ensure easy prosecution of violators.

Aside from the embarrassing cocaine connection, the Goizueta regime seemed charmed, an energized juggernaut that couldn't fail. By then, Coca-Cola had jettisoned low-margined Aqua-Chem, Wine Spectrum, and shrimp farming. *Ghostbusters*, the highest-grossing Columbia film ever produced, provided ideal tie-in opportunities for local bottlers. A new Coca-Cola USA tower rose steadily over North Avenue. A toll-free 800 line allowed instant feedback from consumers, while the just-established Coca-Cola Foundation provided a high profile for corporate donations. Diet Coke leapfrogged past 7-Up to become the third-best-selling soft drink in America. The Company signed Julio Iglesias, the popular Spanish crooner whose records trailed only Elvis Presley and the Beatles in global popularity, to woo swooning older women, foreign consumers, and 30 million Hispanics in the United States.

By the time Brian Dyson summoned his bottlers for another "Get-Together" in Atlanta five years after his promise to shake things up in 1979, he was bursting with self-confidence, having overseen the refranchisement of over 50 percent of Coca-Cola's bottling territory. Coke commanded a 37 percent share of the U.S. market. Despite Burger King's defection to Pepsi in 1983, the Atlanta firm controlled a whopping 63 percent of the fountain business. "We believe in two eyes for an eye and two teeth for a tooth," Dyson boasted, "and if our competitor swats us in the face, we will turn around and knock the hell out of him." He promised the assembled bottlers: "We will go for it. Ready, Fire! Aim."

Roberto Goizueta had every reason for self-congratulation. Since he had assumed the presidency in the spring of 1981, Coca-Cola stock had appreciated 95 percent, including dividends, more than doubling the performance of the S&P 500 index. The Company had recently demonstrated confidence in its own future by repurchasing 6 million shares of common stock. Still, Goizueta felt uneasy. When someone told him that he looked nervous, the Cuban replied, "We live nervous." Now he uttered a prophetic warning: "There is a danger when a company is doing as well as we are. And that is, to think that we can do no wrong. I keep telling the organization: We can do wrong and we can do wrong big." In April of 1985, a shocked nation learned just how right he was.

The Marketing Blunder of the Century

To the Master Dodo this concerns: What ignoramus decide to change the formula of Coke?!?! The new formula is gross, disgusting, unexciting, and WORSE THAN PEPSI!!

—Coke Consumer, Anniston, Alabama, May 12, 1985

AS THE COMPANY coasted triumphantly into mid-decade, one nagging problem refused to go away. For twenty years, the market share of the world's most famous drink had steadily declined. In 1984, Coca-Cola lost one percent of its market share, while Pepsi-Cola gained one and a half points. The Company had tried everything—massive, effective advertising; aggressive marketing; price promotions; almost universal distribution—and nothing had halted the slide. It was difficult to avoid the conclusion that, just as the Pepsi Challenge had asserted, the real problem was the product's taste. People no longer appreciated the Coca-Cola bite. They wanted a sweeter drink.

Late in 1983, Goizueta had authorized the Mexican wunderkind Sergio Zyman to spearhead a supersecret new project, and ordered Mauricio Gianturco to speed up his search for a cola flavor that would trounce Pepsi in taste tests. The ultra-suspicious Zyman wrote his own reports and shredded all memos. As with the diet Coke project, he kept changing the code name from Zeus to Tampa, then Eton, and finally Project Kansas, in honor of Kansas editor William Allen White, who would have hated the idea of changing Coca-Cola if he'd still been alive. After all, White had called the drink "the sublimated essence of all that America stands for." While the technical department rushed to concoct a winning formula, Roy Stout's market researchers asked sample consumers a long list of questions, based on the supposition that the Company had "added a new ingredient" that rendered Coca-Cola "smoother." The results indicated that 11 percent of the exclusive Coke drinkers would be upset, but Stout figured half of them would get over it. The remaining 5 percent probably would remain angry.

No one dared to say explicitly that Coke was planning to alter its formula. Even John Bergin of McCann-Erickson remained unaware of the Company's plans, though he might have guessed. In 1982 and 1983, he and Zyman toured the country for "focus groups" composed of local consumers, primarily to test potential commercials. At the end of each session, however, the moderator presented an unrelated scenario. Pretend, he told them, that a great new formula for Product X had already been introduced in a nearby city, where everyone loved it. Now it was coming to *this* town. Would you be in favor of it?

No one objected to a new, improved Budweiser or Hershey Bar, but Bergin was astonished at the outburst over Coca-Cola. "Goddam it, don't tell *me* you're taking my fucking Coke away!" The focus groups also revealed another disturbing fact. Although many interviewees forcefully asserted that Coca-Cola was their favorite drink, when asked what cola they actually drank, they wavered—Coke, sure, but sometimes Pepsi or even the generic store brand if it was on sale. Stout thus discovered that while Coca-Cola had a place in the heart, it wasn't necessarily in the refrigerator.

In the fall of 1984, Gianturco finally devised a new cola which, he assured Zyman and Stout, would beat Pepsi. Sure enough, Stout's blind taste tests showed that consumers preferred the new formula by a six-point margin. Enormously excited, Zyman convinced Dyson that the time for action had arrived. The "ready, fire! aim" philosophy had worked so far, and this audacious, bold move would prove Coca-Cola's flexibility and leadership to any doubters. At almost the same moment, Scott Ellsworth was interviewing Pepsi's Dick Alven for a Smithsonian Institution oral history of Pepsi. Alven told Ellsworth that the Pepsi Challenge had been completely halted, but that "it's a nice thing to have in your arsenal. See, for them to put that thing to rest totally, they would have to do something to their formula—I mean *dramatically*—and I don't think they're going to do that. It's too risky." Alven noted that Coca-Cola was, after all, a good product that sold a lot of drinks. "It's kind of dangerous for them to play with it."

Goizueta, who had promised in 1981 that he was willing to reformulate "any or all of our products," didn't question the new recipe, but he wasn't sure it should replace the standard drink. Why not call it Coke Two or some other name? There were multiple objections to that idea, though. The product called "Coca-Cola" had to be the best, number one. It just wasn't conceivable to market a better-tasting drink as a competitor. Such a move would also probably split Coke drinkers into two smaller shares of the market, allowing Pepsi to emerge as the undisputed leader. Nor could the Coke men alter the formula quietly. Consumers would notice an entirely different flavor complex, and then the Company would have to lie to the public or admit tampering with the world's most famous secret. Clearly, they must introduce the new flavor with great fanfare.

Aside from these considerations, the Company never publicly acknowledged another underlying motivation to replace the old formula. New Coke would contain no decocainized coca leaf, and the never-ending rumors about the drink's supposed drug content could finally be put to rest. Furthermore, Reagan's announced determination to eradicate the South American coca plantations made Company officials nervous, even though their supply grew in fields owned by the Peruvian government. As head of the technical division in the late seventies, Roberto Goizueta had encouraged Dr. Andrew Weil, who planned to market a coca-based medicinal chewing gum, because a legitimized coca leaf might "take the heat off of Coca-Cola," as Weil put it. Weil even persuaded Goizueta to pay $10,000 for an Ecuadoran conference on coca, but nothing ever came of the project.

ROBERT WOODRUFF'S WILL

Over the Christmas holidays of 1984, Roberto Goizueta, Don Keough, Brian Dyson, and Ike Herbert decided unanimously to change the world's best-known product just short of its hundredth anniversary. First, however, they needed the Boss's blessing. Robert Woodruff had celebrated his ninety-fifth birthday a few weeks earlier. Despite his failing hearing and sight, he had lost none of his mental acuity. On New Year's Day, Goizueta made the pilgrimage down to Ichauway. Alone with the old man, the Cuban CEO kept his story short and simple, reviewing the rationale for the formula modification—dwindling market share coupled with a superior new taste. In the end, Woodruff agreed, convinced that Goizueta was right and that tastes had shifted.[*] It was more important that Coca-Cola be the best-tasting drink in the world than to cling to an outmoded formula. Strangely, though, the Boss couldn't eat his dinner that night. The next morning, he refused his customary huge breakfast. An era was ending, and Robert Woodruff would end his life with it. The Boss demonstrated the remarkable power of his will one last time. He simply stopped eating.

As Woodruff literally shrank from life, Edith Honeycutt, his father's old nurse, cared for him. Connected to intravenous tubes in his private suite at Emory Hospital, Woodruff held her hand and asked, "Honey, where am I?" When she told him, he whispered, "Don't you ever leave me." She recited his favorite poem, Rudyard Kipling's "If," as she had many times before, and, as always, he cried at the last line: "And—which is more—you'll be a man, my son!"

Honeycutt knew why he cried. No matter what Robert Woodruff did, it had never been enough for his father. When Ernest Woodruff visited Ichauway in his final years, for instance, he had been horrified by the number of servants and guests and had predicted his son's imminent bankruptcy. Now, as Robert Woodruff lay dying, the man everyone called Boss, one of the world's most brilliant entrepreneurs, reverted once more to his unhappy childhood. Despite a lifetime of achievement, he would never be a real man in his father's eyes.

In a rare moment of public introspection, Woodruff once recalled his youth, when he sought answers not from his disapproving father, but from Samuel Jones, a neighboring parent who understood his "boyish and immature searching after the realities of life." As they were talking one day, Jones asked the boy to jot down the greatest things life had to offer. Woodruff wrote "wealth, power, influence, genius." The older man nodded and said those were fine goals, but that he had left out the greatest of all—peace of mind. "I'm

---

[*] Since Goizueta and Woodruff were alone during this crucial meeting, we have only Goizueta's word for what took place. While no one has accused Goizueta of telling an untruth, many old-time Coca-Cola men adamantly refuse to believe that Woodruff would *ever* have sanctioned a changed formula. Others question whether he could hear well enough to understand what Goizueta was saying, or speak clearly enough to give a clear assent.

not sure I have [ever] achieved what he suggested," Woodruff said. "Some drive has always impelled me to keep reaching—struggling."

On March 7, 1985, at the age of ninety-five, Robert Woodruff finally stopped struggling, a little over a month before the world learned that The Coca-Cola Company was transforming the flavor of its most famous soft drink. While making Coca-Cola a global drink, he had dismissed those who praised him as a visionary. "I was just curious," he would say, "to see if people in other countries would like it, too." Though he lived almost a century, he remained an enigma even to his closest associates. "I'm not sure anyone really knew him," Joe Jones reflected. Woodruff left Jones, his long-suffering secretary, a million dollars in his will. "And he earned *every penny of it*," Wilbur Kurtz emphasized.[*]

To the end, Woodruff embodied contradictions. A sentimental, loyal, gentle man who gave his friends a single rose on their birthdays, he could also be harsh, vindictive, autocratic—a real bastard who sometimes barked obscenities. He had donated untold anonymous millions to worthy causes, including $230 million to Emory University, but he failed to provide bail for Charlie Ware, the black man shot as a result of conflict with the white Ichauway overseer. Woodruff could be a gruff, manly hunter, lord of the plantation, a huge cigar clamped between his teeth. Beneath his macho image, however, lay a fundamental insecurity and a phobia about being alone, leading to 3 A.M. vigils with his doctor or friends when he couldn't sleep.

Whatever the truth may be, the inscrutable tycoon carried his secrets to the grave, leaving his "partner," Roberto Goizueta, to face an incensed American public. Perhaps, having granted his permission to change the formula, Woodruff viewed his successor's summer of agony with a wry smile from his vantage point in heaven, toasting Goizueta's future health with a six-and-a-half-ounce bottle of good old-fashioned Coca-Cola.

THE BUNKER MENTALITY

Only days after Goizueta's fateful January meeting with Woodruff, five McCann employees filed into an isolated fourth-floor room. With a paper shredder and Pinkerton guard posted at the door, Ike Herbert and Sergio Zyman informed them that they must produce an exciting set of introductory commercials in less than four months while maintaining strict secrecy. Although John Bergin and the other creative talent were flabbergasted, the decision appeared irrevocable. At first, Herbert forbade the word "new," an indication of drastic alteration, but focus groups showed that a "new" product provoked the most immediate response, and Goizueta, afraid the introduction would be greeted with a gigantic American yawn, authorized the use of the

---

[*] Liberated by Woodruff's death, Jones soon became absorbed in administering Ichauway, which he converted to an environmental preserve, where biologist identified over 900 species of plants among the longleaf pines—the largest single tract still in existence anywhere in the world.

word in bold black type on the label. The harried, claustrophobic McCann men quickly dubbed the tiny New York City U-shaped office "the Bunker." Any new footage had to be shot with actors unaware they were pitching a new formula.

The meetings in the Bunker were disastrous. Gradually, more McCann men joined the secret team, but no one could brainstorm a campaign that would really resonate. Partly, they were handicapped by Sergio Zyman's insistence on eschewing "reason why" advertising which described the new flavor or explained its replacement of the old formula. In desperation, they amended the recently modified "Coke Is It" campaign, which proclaimed the drink a "kick" and a "hit." In London's "Bunker II," Marcio Moreira, the Brazilian who headed McCann's international ad efforts, oversaw high-tech product shots featuring the new can. Later, these would be incorporated into commercial footage filmed in the United States. To the British production crews, a transformed Coca-Cola formula didn't mean much. When the film director asked why "new" appeared on the Coke can, Moreira answered, "It's a new tin," eliciting a disinterested shrug. "We shot the whole fucking thing without anyone saying anything," Moreira recalled. By this time, with barely a month left before the scheduled public introduction, an impatient Sergio Zyman assumed direct creative control, reducing McCann men to flunky status. In this nerve-racking atmosphere, the premier commercials lurched into final edit.

A DISASTROUS PRESS CONFERENCE

As the feverish ad men labored in their bunkers on both sides of the Atlantic, the media love-feast with Coke persisted in the early months of 1985. In January, Don Keough revealed a contract to bring Coca-Cola to Soviet citizens for the first time. Then, in March, the Company rolled out cherry Coke, violating yet another old commandment never to add other flavors to the drink. Consequently, on Friday, April 19, 1985, when Goizueta invited the media to a press conference the following Tuesday for news on "the most significant soft-drink marketing development in the company's nearly 100-year history," he was confident of a friendly reception. The three-day lag virtually guaranteed a leak, allowing stunned Pepsi executives time to prepare their rebuttal. On Tuesday, the day of the big announcement, readers of the nation's major newspapers saw a full-page ad in which Pepsi president Roger Enrico's open letter to his employees crowed that "the other guy just blinked" and was "reformulating brand Coke to be more like Pepsi," obviously because "Pepsi tastes better than Coke." He concluded by declaring a companywide holiday that Friday.

In New York City on Tuesday morning, Keough and Goizueta were exhausted, not fully recovered from the previous day's bottler convention in Atlanta. They walked onto a stage at Lincoln Center for a press conference before 700 journalists and film crews, along with satellite hookups to media in Los Angeles, Atlanta, and Houston. The lights dimmed, leaving only three huge red screens with the logo. "We are, we always will be . . ." swelled a chorus. "Coca-Cola, All-American history." The screens filled with shots of the Grand Canyon, wheatfields, cowboys, athletes, the Statue of Liberty, and old Coke commercials. Even for a gullible public, this effort would have been too much. For a jaded press, it was insulting. No one saluted or dabbed away a tear.

Then Goizueta declared that "the best soft drink, Coca-Cola, is now going to be even better." He explained that the new flavor had been discovered as a result of experimentation on diet Coke and that the Company would now "buy the world a new Coke." It was, he asserted, "the boldest single marketing move in the history of the packaged consumer goods business," adding that it was also the "surest move ever made." Keough emphasized that while the new formula beat old Coke 55–45 in 190,000 blind taste-tests, it *increased* the margin by 61–39 when both drinks were identified. Coke had always provided a "mirror of the times," Keough explained, sometimes even shaping them, and now the new formula would "propel Coca-Cola into this second century." He promised that the superior taste would flow globally by the centennial celebration in May of 1986.

As soon as the floor was thrown open, however, the media lobbed unfriendly questions. "Are you one-hundred-percent certain that this won't bomb?" a St. Louis reporter inquired. Another journalist asked Goizueta to describe the new taste. At first, he demurred, saying that "it's a matter better left to poets or copywriters." When pressed, he stumbled through a chemist's reply: "I would say it is smoother, uh, uh, rounder yet, uh, yet bolder . . . a more harmonious flavor." Keough added that "the taste kind of surrounds you."

Even though Keough and Goizueta had carefully rehearsed every answer, their attempts at humorous deflection fell flat. Had they changed the product in response to the Pepsi Challenge? "Oh, gosh, no," Goizueta answered. "The Pepsi Challenge? When did that happen?" Would the old formula remain in the Trust Company vault? High-strung and miserable without his cigarettes, Goizueta slowly lost his composure. "It stays there," he snapped. A hostile reporter, phoning from the traditional Coca-Cola heartland of Houston, began to ask a question but turned it into a protest: "Are you tell—I mean, if we wanted Pepsi, we'd buy Pepsi," prompting a big laugh from her fellow journalists. "Well, honey," Keough replied partronizingly before correcting himself and calling her Ma'am, "this new product is Coca-Cola, even better." Goizueta interjected: "It's not even close to Pepsi. Not at all. Not at all." Unaccountably, when asked if they had tested the new Coke against Pepsi in taste tests, the executives refused to divulge that in fact it *did* beat Pepsi by a small margin. Instead, Goizueta arrogantly responded: "Surely, we did. But we don't have to show them and we don't want to."

In response to the final question, asking whether diet Coke might be reformulated "assuming that this is a success," Goizueta answered testily. "No. And I didn't *assume* that this is a success. It *is* a success." Moderator Carlton Curtis, the Company's top public spokesman, quickly cut off further questions, and the ordeal was over. It had not been a shining moment for the executives. Even the normally unflappable Keough admitted at one point during the grilling, "There's a lot of things I'd rather be doing than being here right now."

COKE WAS IT

Despite the ordeal, Goizueta and Keough remained certain that their bold move would succeed. They had told the simple truth—New Coke, as it was inevitably called, tasted better than the old version. It was only a matter of time before Coca-Cola would sweep past Pepsi and reclaim the coveted Nielsen rating lead in supermarket sales. With great pageantry, the Company launched its sampling campaign, literally transforming downtown Atlanta into a three-ring circus. "Step right up to the greatest taste on earth," the barker cried. In New York, the first cans off the line were ceremoniously delivered to workers renovating the Statue of Liberty. Red and white balloons, fireworks, and banner-waving airplanes filled the skies. "We're using every glitzy thing you can imagine," one spokesman confided to the press.

No amount of hoopla could mask the shocked misery of loyal Coke drinkers, however. All of the taste tests had missed one crucial point. Roy Stout's researchers had never informed their respondents that the hypothetical new formula would *replace* the old. Incredibly, no one had examined the psychological ramifications of withdrawing the old formula. In the rush to unveil the great new flavor, a kind of corporate hypnosis had occurred. "No one would have listened if someone had said we were going to catch unholy hell," Sergio Zyman admitted later. "Everybody just said, 'This can't go wrong.'"

For Coke loyalists such as Dan Lauck, a San Antonio television news reporter, New Coke couldn't go right, however, and taste tests were irrelevant. Lauck drank nothing but six-and-a-half-ounce bottles of ice-cold Coca-Cola at the rate of fifteen a day. The thirty-six-year-old was so fond of Coke that he skipped breakfast and lunch to keep his weight down so he could drink more. When he heard about the flavor change, Lauck rushed out and bought 110 cases. He had no intention of conducting taste tests; he would never switch.

If Sergio Zyman had taken the 1984 Lintas report on the personality of Coca-Cola drinkers more seriously, he wouldn't have been so surprised at the reaction of devoted consumers like Lauck. "The world is immutable, it doesn't change, there are certain self-evident truths," the report had stated. Bill Backer had crawled directly into their minds back in 1969 when he had written, "That's the way it is, / And the way it will stay, / What the world wants today / Is the real thing."

That truth was quickly and forcibly brought to the Company's attention. Within a week, over a thousand calls a day were jamming the company's 800 line, almost all of them expressing shock and outrage at New Coke. The media loved the hot story, which pierced the American heart. "Next week, they'll be chiseling Teddy Roosevelt off the side of Mount Rushmore," a *Washington Post* columnist groaned. The *Detroit Free Press* mocked Goizueta's "smoother, rounder, bolder" taste, wondering in print if that made the old drink "lumpy, square, and bashful." Bob Greene of the *Chicago Tribune* mourned the passing of his old friend. "Every part of my life is associated with Coke," he wrote, chiding the Company for "a sort of smugness—that if you don't like New Coke, you will." *Newsweek*'s headline declared, "Coke Tampers With Success," identifying the old soft drink as "the American character in a can." At the press conference, Keough had promised that "you're just flat going to enjoy it," but many consumers modified his remark, complaining that it was difficult to enjoy a drink that was so flat. One elderly woman, interviewed at an Atlanta supermarket, sipped New Coke and gave her verdict: "To use the vernacular of the teenagers, it sucks." George Pickard, a Nashville novelty song writer, quickly cashed in on the publicity with a recording entitled "Coke *Was* It."

At first, Goizueta and Keough revelled in the avalanche of free publicity, negative or otherwise. Within days, 96 percent of all Americans knew about the flavor change. The Company proceeded with the national roll-out, along with a new Cosby campaign and modified "Coke Is It" spots. Even granting the rushed and secretive conditions under which the commercials were spawned, they seemed inexplicably clumsy, all too literally interpreting the singsong lyrics, often with negative or violent implications. As the singer bragged of "a style, a groove," a little girl watched her wobbly bowling ball drift toward the gutter. "It is Saturday night" showed an ugly professional wrestler twirling an opponent before a body slam, the spinning feet catching the referee in the head. A teen shook up her New Coke and sprayed it in her boyfriend's face; a master sergeant screamed at a private; a Brahma bull rider ended a commercial rolling helplessly on the ground with his legs splayed in front of a huge Coke sign. Coca-Cola had always promoted romance. In *these* commercials, a girl jumped up, threw her napkin in the boy's face, and stormed off. As a fitting capper for the stumbling campaign, several commercials ended with the line "it's more than a taste, it's the smile on your face," as a hockey goalie lifted his face mask to reveal a smiling teenager—only he was missing four or five teeth.

The Cosby ads weren't much better, even though the comedian's new television show achieved enormous popularity. In the TVQ (Television Quotient) ratings of celebrity endorsers, Cosby dominated the number one spot for "most persuasive" and "most familiar." It didn't help, however, that the overexposed Coke sponsor had stressed the tart taste of old Coke just before the sweeter version replaced it. Now, he switched gears. Dressed in a silly-looking toga, Cosby intoned: "The words I'm about to say will change the course of history. Here they are. Coca-Cola has a new taste." His words weren't terribly convincing. "Now, more than ever, Coke is it!" he finished, but his fatuous smile looked pasted on.

A LONG, DRY JUNE

At first, Roy Stout's weekly surveys indicated a positive response to the new flavor; as delivery trucks roared into U.S. cities throughout May, millions of curious consumers tried the notorious taste. But the furor refused to die. By the middle of the month, 5,000 calls a day were assaulting the ears of the poor employees manning the consumer hot line. Roberto Goizueta was shaken when his father, who lived in Mexico City, told him that everyone there was in an uproar, even though New Coke hadn't arrived yet. Even Goizueta's nemesis, Fidel Castro, took potshots at Coke, directing Radio Havana to pronounce that the death of the Real Thing was symptomatic of American decay.

By the beginning of June, 8,000 calls a day were coming in. The media still hyped the story, particularly when a fifty-seven-year-old Seattle opportunist named Gay Mullins saw New Coke as his ticket to fame and fortune, founding the Old Cola Drinkers of America. The chubby, white-bearded Mullins, wearing a protest T-shirt, publicly dumped bottles of New Coke into the city sewers. The self-appointed spokesman became the media's favorite gadfly, even though he repeatedly failed to identify Coke in blind taste-tests. After one suit was thrown out of court, Mullins filed a second class-action attempt to force the Company to return to the old formula. New Coke became, according to one journalist, "a universal conversation topic, like the weather or money or love." Houston Astrodome crowds vehemently booed New Coke commercials on the stadium's giant video screen. One Beverly Hills wineshop owner obtained a limited supply of the rare old formula, selling bottles for three times their list price. As Roberto Goizueta noted with annoyance, it was chic to dump on New Coke. "We could have introduced the elixir of the gods," one bitter Coke man said, "and it wouldn't have made any difference."

In addition to phone calls, the Company fielded over 40,000 letters of protest. Each unhappy consumer received a form letter from Lynn Henkel, an assistant manager at Coca-Cola USA, assuring them that "our latest research shows that . . . consumers overwhelmingly like our great new taste." This official response was cold comfort to most consumers, who either mailed back the enclosed coupon or tore it up. The letters, like the phone calls, were cries from the heart, making it clear that much more than a soft drink was involved. A bewildered consulting psychologist told Company officials that the emotions he heard were similar to those of grief-stricken parents mourning the death of a favorite child. Most letters came from people who had never written to a company—young and old; upper, middle, and lower class; literate and unlettered. The message, however, was essentially the same—The Coca-Cola Company had betrayed them:

> I'm 61 and have been a confirmed "Coke" drinker since that memorable day my Dad took me on a little excursion up Mill Mountain in Roanoke, Va., and bought me my first Coke with a package of Planter's Salted Peanuts . . . I was five years old . . . "Old" Coke is sensual, it has pizzazz. God! On a hot day you wish you could jump into a tub of it and gulp down a 16 oz. bottle all at the same time.

> My littele sisther is cring because coke changed and she sayed that shed is not

going to stop cring every day unitl you chang back . . . I am geting tryer of hearing her now if you don't chang I'll sue evne if I'm just 11.

I am a very heavy coke drinker. I do not drink coffee, tea, milk, water, nothing but coke. I drink coke all day long. I always have a glass or can of coke. Always. I have now to try and find something to drink that I can tolerate. It will not be new coke. Never.

Changing Coke is just like breaking the American dream, like not selling hot dogs at a ball game.

We want the old and wonderful Coke back *PLEASE*. Keep the "New" Coke if you want and call it Cokesi if you like . . .

For years, I have been what every company strives for: a brand-loyal consumer. I have purchased at least two cartons of Coke a week for as long as I can remember . . . My "reward" for this loyalty is having the rug pulled out from under me. New Coke is absolutely AWFUL . . . Don't send me any coupons or any other inducements. You guys really blew it.

Millions of dollars worth of advertising cannot overcome years of conditioning. Or in my case, generations. The old Coke is in the blood. Until you bring the old Coke back, I'm going to drink RC.

Where's the Fizz-zz-zz? What happened to the fizz? *I MISS THE FIZZ*!!!

I do not drink alcholic beverages, I don't smoke, and I don't chase other women, my only vice has been Coke. Now you have taken that pleasure from me.

Who is this Roberto Goizueta and where did he come from that is Chairman? Who is Sergio? They don't sound mainstream American . . . *OLD COKE IS IT AND THERE WILL NEVER BE ANYTHING TO TAKE ITS PLACE.*

Your bright marketing people will figure out that instead of converting Pepsi drinkers, you're losing us Cokaholics to indifference if not suicide . . . You're just kidding, right? You did this as a stunt, to teach us all a lesson in humility and gratitude . . . Well, OK, I get the point. You can stop any time now.

Would it be right to rewrite the Constitution? The Bible? To me, changing the Coke formula is of such a serious nature.

There are only two things in my life: God and Coca Cola. Now you have taken one of those things away from me.

You Fucked Up! What you inherited *WAS* the real thing.

Can you imagine anyone ordering Rum and Pepsi? I've been hearing such blasphemy.

My dearest Coke: You have betrayed me. We went out just last week, as we had so often, and when we kissed I knew our love affair was over . . . I remember walks across campus with you discussing life and love and all that matters . . . I remember the southern summer nights we shared with breezes leaving beads of water hanging delicately from your body . . . But, last week, I tasted betrayal on your lips: you had the smooth, seductive sweet taste of a lie . . . You have become a prostitute, corrupted by money, denying your ideals.

One retired Air Force officer, explaining how much Coca-Cola had meant to him, revealed that his will called for his cremated ashes to be sealed in a Coke can for interment in Arlington National Cemetery, but he was rethinking the matter. A more pragmatic writer said that Coca-Cola used to make an excellent douche. "Does the 'New Formula' Coke pack the same wallop?"[*] One enterprising correspondent included a blank, signed check for up to $10 million, with a note: "Since you are no longer making Coca-Cola, perhaps you would like to sell me the recipe?"

All along, the standard Coke response remained that New Coke, the better-tasting soft drink, had replaced the old formula. Period. The self-confident assertions masked anxiety bordering on panic by the end of June. Bottlers begged for the old drink back, since they were becoming social pariahs. In rural Alabama, a minister led his congregation in prayer for the local bottler's soul, which was undoubtedly destined for hell. In Marietta, Georgia, a woman assaulted a Coke delivery man with her umbrella as he tried to stock a supermarket shelf with New Coke. "You bastard," she screamed, "you ruined it, it tastes like shit!" When a nearby Pepsi driver laughed, she spun around. "You stay out of it! This is family business. Yours is *worse* than shit." Clearly, something had to be done. "I'm sleeping like a baby," Roberto Goizueta told his friends. "I wake up crying every hour." Sergio Zyman, already quite thin, lost ten pounds during the month. Monitoring the consumer hot line, he staggered away in disbelief, muttering, "They talk as if Coca-Cola had just killed God." In desperation, the chemists increased the acidity level in New Coke it give it more "bite," but nothing helped. June's sales plummeted, and Roy Stout's surveys underscored that Coke's image was slipping badly.

THE SECOND COMING

On Friday, July 5, the MacNeil-Lehrer Newshour devoted twenty minutes to the New Coke disaster, showing Mullins and his cronies pouring the drink out on the street. The protests were not subsiding, nor was the media's negative coverage. Over the next week, the only real argument involved what to call the old formula when it returned. Dyson favored "original," but the Company lawyers objected, since they suddenly saw a way to benefit from the situation. If they called it "classic," as Goizueta ultimately determined, they could argue that it was an entirely new drink, not covered by the original contract. Schmidt and Bondurant would be outfoxed.

As usual, plans for Coca-Cola Classic leaked, and the Company had to issue a terse acknowledgment on July 10, a day before the scheduled press conference. Peter Jennings interrupted an ABC soap opera to bring America the news, while Arkansas senator David Pryor, in a speech sandwiched between debate over South African disinvestment and action on the Safe

---

[*] Although the Company did not respond to the New Coke douche query, the answer was "No," according to a scientific study conducted by a group of Harvard Medical School researchers who found that Coca-Cola Classic killed five times as many sperm as New Coke. The researchers didn't recommend any form of postcoital douche, however, since "sperm can make it into the fallopian tubes in minutes."

Drinking Water Act, solemnly declared that the return of the original formula was "a meaningful moment in American history." Within the Company, employees rejoiced over what they termed the Second Coming. Thursday morning, virtually every newspaper in the country carried a front-page story on Classic Coke, bumping reports on President Reagan's cancer operation out of the spotlight.

The same day, the chastened Goizueta, Keough, and Dyson faced the press in Atlanta, less than three months after the glitzy New Coke debut at Lincoln Center. While Goizueta curtly told Americans, "We have heard you," Keough stole the show by eloquently confessing just how badly the Company had miscalculated, speaking of the "passion" that had taken them by surprise and calling it "a lovely American enigma" which was no more measurable than "love, pride or patriotism." Some, Keough said, portrayed this moment as a Company retreat, a victory of the little man over a giant corporation. "How I love that!" he said. "We love any retreat which has us rushing toward our best customers with the product they love most." He concluded with an accurate prediction. "Some critics will say Coca-Cola made a marketing mistake. Some cynics will say that we planned the whole thing. The truth is we are not that dumb and we are not that smart." At the close of the press conference, a reporter asked Goizueta, "If you knew in April what you know now, would you have gone ahead with the reformulation?" The CEO deflected the question with a Spanish proverb from his grandfather: "*Si mi abuela tuviera ruedas seria bicicleta*," which translated, "If my grandmother had wheels, she would be a bicycle."

The euphoria following the return of old Coke surpassed the despair of the past three months. Supporters deluged Gay Mullins with celebratory bottles of Coke as he sprawled in a bathtub. A small airplane circled North Avenue headquarters with a banner reading, "THANK YOU, ROBERTO!" Dan Lauck heaved a sigh of relief, since he was down to a mere sixty-five cases. Eighteen thousand calls of gratitude jammed the toll-free line on the day of the announcement. Now the mail inundating the Company read like love letters. "Thank you for bringing old Coke back," wrote one sixty-eight-year-old woman. "The only thing better is sex!" Astonished Coke marketer Ike Herbert remarked, "You would have thought we had invented a cure for cancer."

> We love you for caring! You have given us back our dream! We are grateful . . . You have made our hard lives easier to bear and have given us confidence in ourselves to change things for the better.

> I drank Coke the morning of my wedding to calm me . . . My first request after the births of my two children was for a Coke on ice. I drank a Coke on the way to my father's funeral . . . You've made my day and I appreciate that.

> With the return of "Coca-Cola Classic," you might say that the old coke has been "reincarbonated."

> I feel like a lost friend is returning home.

> Thank God for Coca-Cola! We DO Have It GREAT in America!

God does work in mysterious ways and I thank him for answering my prayers to bring back the "real" Coke.

The old Coke recipe reflects the love of every good American today. There is only one Holy Bible, one Elvis Presley, others have tried to copie them, but never quit make it.

How can you say the old Coke is only liked by the older generation? I'm 13, the now generation. I happen to like old Coke the best!

I am most pleased that you announced today that I will again be able to obtain the Coca-Cola I have been drinking since 1909. I am now 91½ years of age.

Keough's brilliant one-liner, asserting that the Company was neither that dumb nor that smart, was only half true. While a few analysts and consumers were certain that the Company had staged the entire fiasco simply to grab publicity and remind their loyal consumers how much Coca-Cola meant to them, the Company clearly did no such thing. Goizueta and colleagues *had* been "that dumb," however, naively committing what *Business Week* termed "the marketing blunder of the decade." Oddly enough, pride still blinded the executives. Despite the return of Coca-Cola Classic, they steadfastly maintained that New Coke would surge ahead.

In his letter to shareholders confirming the original formula's return, Goizueta insisted that New Coke (a term he despised) was "the best-tasting Coca-Cola we have ever made," condescendingly referring to a group of older consumers who demanded "a taste of nostalgia." Consequently, Coca-Cola Classic would appear "alongside our flagship brand, [New] Coca-Cola." In an obvious attempt to minimize embarrassment, Goizueta illogically called the reintroduced Classic "the newest addition to the lineup of Coca-Cola branded products," which he termed "the most formidable megabrand in the soft drink industry." The Coke executives were so certain that New Coke would flourish that they cooperated with Thomas Oliver, the *Atlanta Constitution* business reporter who planned to knock out a quick book on the flavor change. Now, in the fall of 1985, he conducted lengthy interviews with Stout, Herbert, Zyman, Dyson, Keough, and Goizueta.

A DRAMATIC COURTROOM TWIST AND OTHER DISASTERS

Meanwhile, the legal battle between Bill Schmidt's group of disaffected bottlers and the Company heated up. Under oath, Roberto Goizueta insisted that Coca-Cola was whatever he and the Company *said* it was. On April 22, 1985, it had been one formula, and the next day, it was something completely different. Now, the Company insisted that Coke Classic constituted a completely "new" drink with a different name, reserving the right for flexible pricing in the future. Emmet Bondurant dubbed this mentality "Alice in Wonderland thinking," and quoted Lewis Carroll's officious Humpty Dumpty, much to the amusement of Judge Murray Schwartz:

"When *I* use a word," Humpty Dumpty said, in rather a scornful tone, "it means just what I choose it to mean—neither more nor less."

"The question is," said Alice, "whether you *can* make words means so many different things."

"The question is," said Humpty Dumpty, "which is to be master—that's all."

An August ruling from the bench stunned Goizueta and his lawyers. Judge Schwartz ordered the Company to reveal the secret formula for virtually every cola drink it made, including Coca-Cola Classic, New Coke, diet Coke, and all the decaffeinated versions. He could thus determine whether diet Coke was, in fact, similar to Classic or New Coke, which would help legitimize the litigious bottlers' claims. To no one's surprise, Big Coke categorically refused. "The Company has never disclosed its formulae even to its own General Counsel," wrote a Company lawyer, and it was not about to let a bunch of bottlers see them now. The media loved the drama. *U.S. News & World Report* printed a story about the Company's "brazen defiance" along with a picture of a Trust Company guard inside the vault containing the famous formula. For the next eight months, the matter lay unresolved, since Judge Schwartz was reportedly incapacitated by a mysterious illness.

At the same time, the embattled Company found itself mired in more controversy from an unexpected quarter—the result of the recent licensing program. The new line of Coca-Cola clothes, manufactured by Hong Kong's Murjani International, caused a fashion sensation with their July debut. "Suddenly," a Company trademark lawyer mused, "people are like walking billboards for the product." Not only that, Murjani was *paying* Coca-Cola for the privilege. There was, however, a downside to Coca-Cola's magical, symbolic name. Even as Americans proudly donned their hip clothing, Southern textile plants cried foul. How could the Company have allowed a foreign company to make these sweatshirts and pullovers, advertised as "All-American"? Coca-Cola officials quickly admitted their mistake and promised that Murjani would find domestic sources for its garments soon.

Even a supposed coup turned sour. Coca-Cola had arranged for its new taste to travel aboard the space shuttle in a special can which permitted carbonation under zero-gravity conditions. It would be the first soft drink in space. NASA reneged on the promise, however, allowing Pepsi to go along for the ride as well. Furthermore, the astronauts complained that lukewarm cola wasn't terribly satisfying.

Roberto Goizueta smarted under the glee with which journalists jumped upon any negative news about Coca-Cola. At the *Atlanta Constitution* offices, the CEO had earned a reputation for thin skin, since he often sent reporters handwritten, pedantic corrections for the most minor inaccuracies. Company men recognized this trait as perfectionism, not petulance. Thin-skinned or not, Goizueta's precise engineering mind did not understand feature writers and their penchant for human interest hooks. In October of 1985, addressing a national group of editors, he vented some of his frustration, beginning with a sarcastic reference to the publicity over New Coke. "How boring this past summer would have been for you," he said, without the tumult over the changed formula. "Just picture those reporters on your staffs with little to do all summer long!" He proceeded to chide the media for "pandering to what is provocative," preferring stylistic cuteness to objective investigation. "Journalists need to remember," Goizueta lectured, that "they are entering quickly into other persons' minds. They must understand this power they possess." It didn't seem to occur to the Coke executive that Coca-Cola commercials were subject to precisely the same criticism and had given the cue to newsmen by emphasizing image and the quick gloss.

COKE ARE IT

The return of the original formula as Coca-Cola Classic posed a major conundrum for Coke advertising. The New Coke disaster effectively killed the "Coke Is It" campaign, since it wasn't quite clear *which* Coke was it. *Newsweek*'s headline declared, "Hey America, Coke Are It!" Nor could the Company rely on Cosby again. "May we now expect to see a commercial featuring Bill Cosby speaking from both sides of his mouth simultaneously?" a snide consumer inquired. During the fall of 1985, the ad men floundered with two weak "megabrand" slogans—"We've Got a Taste for You" and "Coke Belongs to You." The commercials tried to push *both* colas at once, displaying New Coke and Classic together. Sergio Zyman lamely explained that both drinks shared "the same affection for and identification with the brand." Ed Mellett, recently hired away from Pepsi as Coke's new marketing chief, admitted that "we don't know the relative role and importance of each sugared cola."

By year's end, however, Classic was clearly surging while New Coke's market share shrank. Worse, Pepsi-Cola had snagged the lead as the best-selling single sugar cola in America. The combined sales of Classic and New Coke still fell slightly *below* Coca-Cola's comparable 1984 figures. As he hurried to finish his book, Thomas Oliver suddenly sensed a distinct chill at the Company. His calls weren't returned, and several appointments were broken. "The Coca-Cola executives had been giving me a lot of information about why they had changed the formula," Oliver recalls, "and I think they realized that they were supplying me with ammunition which could shoot their number one brand in the foot again." In February of 1986, the McCann men abandoned their attempt to promote both colas at once. For New Coke, they exhorted consumers to "Catch the Wave," a reference to the logo's dynamic ribbon. The curvy line was supposed to lead to New Coke, the "wave" of the future. "The advertising addresses the visionary," Brian Dyson insisted, "those consumers who are peering into tomorrow." To position New Coke as the "in" taste, he promoted commercials which united "high-tech promotion with highly contemporary imagery."

The new ads couldn't find a center. Some showed people doodling or globbing catsup in the shape of the curve. In "Horizontal Pour," an enormously expensive, slick production, a rugged hunk served a bikini-clad woman basking in a recliner—only he poured the Coke *sideways* through the house, and she caught the liquid in her empty glass. While the ad was a technical masterpiece, accomplished by turning a house on its side, it was practically devoid of content, a perfect New Wave product. Other ads for the new formula broke every rule, overtly comparing Coca-Cola with Pepsi. In one, a castaway on an island found a bottle of the rival soft drink. While Italian opera inexplicably blared in the background, the desperate man opened the bottle, dumped the drink onto the sand, and tossed the bottle with an SOS note into the surf. The tide, of course, returned a six-pack of Coke.

As a final assault on viewers' intelligence and sanity, the Company launched a series of New Coke commercials aimed primarily at teenagers, who were depicted as mindless zombies playing video games. On the screen, Max Headroom would suddenly appear—a smiling, simpering, narcissistic, computer fad with a dazzling smile, dark glasses, airbrushed hair, and an annoying stutter. The ads proved enormously popular with adoring teens, who imitated Headroom's admonition to "C-C-Catch the Wave," followed by a sigh or growl. At a mass meeting of "Cokeologists," Headroom asked, "So what I want to know is, if you're drinking Coke, who's drinking Pepsi?" The commercials debuted on MTV, the all-music video channel, and on David Letterman's hip late-night show, testing extraordinarily well with high recall and brand association.

In the meantime, Lintas's Coca-Cola Classic advertising remained closer to traditional Coca-Cola values, overplaying the all-American nature of the drink with the slogan "Red, White & You." Instead of celebrating Coca-Cola Classic as an integral part of everyday life, these ads, aired during soap operas and the Cosby Show, harkened back to the overpatriotic "Look Up, America" campaign of 1974, replete with the Statue of Liberty, the Grand Canyon, rural folk, and celebrities sprinkled throughout for good measure. Although the Company spent far more on New Coke ads than on efforts for Classic, the new formula's share continued to slip as Classic climbed. The kids loved Max Headroom, but they failed to translate their affection to the vending machines, or they misunderstood which Coke he was touting. By the end of April, two weeks before the Centennial bash, New Coke had fallen below a 3 percent market share, while Classic had fizzed past Pepsi to regain the overall sugar cola lead. The final blow came when McDonald's switched its huge account to Classic. Since one out of every twelve Americans passed through the Golden Arches daily, that amounted to a gigantic vote against New Coke.

AN EXPENSIVE HISTORY LESSON

It cost The Coca-Cola Company $4 million to research and develop New Coke. The masses of data, the taste tests, the well-honed strategy had failed to reveal just how well Asa Candler and Robert Woodruff had done their jobs. Coca-Cola, as much icon as soft drink, stood for traditional values. In the shifting kaleidoscope of the late twentieth century, Americans felt rootless and ill-at-ease. Computers seemed to know more than people. Avuncular Walter

Cronkite had retired and no longer calmed the national psyche every night. The Latin mass no longer soothed with its sonorities. The full-service filling station was a rarity, and the old-fashioned soda fountain lingered only in a few anachronistic small Southern towns.

Only Coca-Cola stayed the same—the perky, fizzy, social drink that made instant friends of strangers, gave a little jolt of energy, rewarded hot work on a summer day. In the stampede to assign blame for the New Coke debacle, many American consumers and veteran bottlers sneered at the "Latin mafia" of Goizueta, Zyman, and Dyson. Since they weren't "real" Americans, how could they comprehend the nation's passion for good old Coke? This racist scenario didn't factor in Keough, who jokingly referred to himself as the "token American" at the Company, and who was just as sure as Goizueta about New Coke's ultimate triumph. The corporate blindness stemmed not so much from geography or cultural background as from the eighties mentality. Aggressive, ruthless, and cocky, the new team wanted to repeat the blockbuster breakthrough of diet Coke. In the process, they overlooked the most vital emotion of all—love.

The American public loudly and clearly taught the corporate strategists a history lesson. Like William Allen White, they revered a drink that symbolized America, that was associated with almost every aspect of their lives—first dates, moments of victory and defeat, joyous group celebrations, pensive solitude. As a poetic Texas consumer had written in his June 1985 love letter to the drink, "Whenever things began to look too bleak, I'd come over and pick you up, we'd share a few minutes together, and I would be comforted. And do you remember the times I and our friends shared concerns when you were around? It seems as if the richest hours of my life have been shared with you." As a result of the New Coke disaster, original Coca-Cola garnered much more than $4 million worth of publicity, rendering the Company's horrendous advertising irrelevant. The venerable cola roared back to claim its lead as the premier American soft drink. Unintentionally, Goizueta and Keough had converted the gigantic marketing blunder into a commercial coup.

20

The Big Red Machine

Can Big Red make its soda as ubiquitous as water? . . . One gets the feeling there's a recurring nightmare in the marketing department of Coca-Cola USA. A plane goes down in the desert. Everyone is safe, everyone is sound. They make their way to an oasis. Plenty of food. Plenty of water. Plenty of shelter. But no Coke machines.
—Jeffrey Scott, *Adweek*, Dec. 12, 1988

FOR FOUR DAYS, Coca-Cola literally painted Atlanta red for its $23 million centennial bash. John Pemberton would have retreated hastily to his laboratory if he had stumbled into the Omni on the evening of May 7, 1986, where laser beams blazed, miniature Coke trucks zipped up and down the aisles, a Coca-Cola blimp floated overhead, and scantily clad dancers twirled to loud music—all to honor the moment when the kindly pharmacist and morphine addict perfected the formula.

The Company outdid itself to impress the 12,500 bottlers who came from all over the world. First, 650,000 dominoes toppled across six continents, brought live by satellite to the audience. The Nairobi segment nearly stopped the chain reaction, since gigantic African moths kept knocking over the carefully stacked pieces ahead of time. It wasn't terribly clear what the point of the topple was—perhaps it was a play on "Catch the Wave" or a demonstration of the Company's global connections—but it was great fun, particularly since the final domino in London triggered a bomb that blew a huge Pepsi bottle to smithereens. Celebrities galore studded the festivities. Dick Cavett hosted the domino topple, for instance, wryly inquiring of a Swahili-speaking spokesman via satellite, "So, do you have any hobbies?" Merv Griffin was there, since Coca-Cola had just purchased his television production interests, including *Jeopardy!* and *Wheel of Fortune*. Chuck Berry twanged his guitar and one-footed it across the stage, Kool and the Gang electrified, Marilyn McCoo crooned, Lionel Hampton and his orchestra swung.

The multimedia show, narrated by Ike Herbert, covered all of Coca-Cola's history in typical Company fashion, presenting it as a seamless success saga, the rise of a humble drink to deserved greatness. Herbert, the quintessential marketing man, noted that "people in remote corners of the world who don't even know the names of their own capital cities know the name Coca-Cola," because "we've been able to infiltrate Coca-Cola into the minds and hearts and lives of everyone everywhere." Throughout the audience, bottlers cheered and stomped as singers chanted the refrain, "Take it to the people."

The assembled throng was, as Herbert said, "one family with one mighty voice raised in bold self-congratulation." Just before midnight, a seven-and-a-half-ton birthday cake was wheeled onto center stage, where, instead of a gigantic party girl, a fourteen-foot Coke bottle rose from the middle of the cake as loyalists sang "Happy Birthday." On Saturday, almost everyone in Atlanta turned out for a parade down Peachtree Street with over a hundred floats and 500,000 balloons wafting the Coca-Cola logo skyward. Two members of the Coca-Cola Collectors Club (who had met and fallen in love amidst the memorabilia) exchanged marriage vows on a float. Mickey Mouse and Goofy cavorted for Coke, along with Uncle Sam and a tinsel-haired Statue of Liberty, also celebrating her hundredth anniversary. Thirty marching bands blared, while Miss Universe and America's Junior Miss waved to the crowd. Cobot, the Coca-Cola robot, jerked along the pavement while a baby elephant from the Atlanta Zoo lumbered nearby. Cruising in his convertible, *Miami Vice* star Michael Talbott held a Coke can aloft and asked, "Is this a great country or what?" Although the colossal event, well-choreographed down to the last hostess dressed as a cocktail glass, went without a hitch, some demonstrators carried anti-apartheid placards admonishing the Company to "Get Coke Out of South Africa."

Underlying the celebration was an uneasy, unspoken awareness of the recent New Coke debacle. While Company officials had promised that the new formula would be available around the world by the centennial, it had never traveled beyond Canada and the United States. The formula change's failure in America shook the confidence of Coke men around the world, however. In private interviews, Goizueta continued to describe New Coke as "the product of the future," but its highest market share was already receding into the past. In one of the few minor crises during the big parade, a walking can of New Coke symbolically deflated in midstride.

ASSESSMENT AT MID-DECADE

Well aware of their awkward situation, Roberto Goizueta and Don Keough emphasized to the assembled bottlers that the Company was in excellent shape. In fact, it really was. Despite—or because of—the New Coke fiasco, the Company's soft drink market share in the United States had swelled to 39 percent versus 28 percent for Pepsi. Between them, the two giants were squeezing out other players. "Coke and Pepsi Stomp on the Little Guys," a 1985 *Fortune* headline had bluntly stated. Just before the centennial, Pepsi announced it was buying 7-Up, and Coke countered by attempting to gobble Dr Pepper. The FTC intervened to prevent both deals, which was pretty much what Coke had anticipated, but the Company didn't really care. Not only had Coke Classic surpassed other sugar colas, Sprite had surged past 7-Up in the lemon/lime category.

The Company's entertainment sector also raked in money from video-cassette sales and TV show syndication, but Columbia's creative endeavors proved embarrassing flops—and there were a great many of them, since Coke pushed the movie company to disgorge a glut of films such as *Perfect*, *Crossroads*, and *The Slugger's Wife*. One forgettable effort, *Fast Forward*, cost $17 million, netting only $500,000 at the box office. Nor did Columbia's television shows fare any better, despite Peter Sealey's focus groups and surveys. All five of the Company's productions that season were canceled, killing any future syndication possibilities. To Goizueta's chagrin, the media paid no attention to the overall health of the bottom line, instead gloating over the box office failures. "Coke: Flat in Hollywood," *Newsweek*'s headline read, while *Business Week* asked, "Columbia Pictures: Are Things Really Better with Coke?" Stung by the criticism, Goizueta hoped that the forthcoming *Ishtar*, the expensive comedy starring Dustin Hoffman and Warren Beatty, would reverse the studio's public fortunes.

By that spring of 1986, Goizueta had accomplished his every goal. Earnings per share averaged 10 percent per year, and the stock had shot up from $35 in 1980 to $120, which spelled a compounded annual return of 24 percent compared to 13 percent for the S&P 500. As he had predicted, the domestic operations were now accounting for about half of the Company's profits. What difference did it make whether New Coke and Columbia were causing bad publicity? "My job is not to be right," Goizueta philosophized. "It is to produce results."

IVESTER THE FINANCIAL WIZARD

Goizueta owed many of those results to a bright young Georgian named Doug Ivester, who was promoted to chief financial officer when Sam Ayoub retired at the end of 1984. Despite his folksy manner, Ivester, a shrewd businessman, perceived that strategic debt could boost the bottom line, particularly if he recycled the borrowed money for a sizable return. By the time of the centennial celebration, Coke maintained a 20 percent debt-to-equity ratio, up from virtually nothing five years before. Besides, the new debt load reduced the corporate tax rate from 45 percent to 39 percent because of deductible interest payments. Ivester also brought financial innovation to the film industry when he sold Columbia's accounts receivable for cash. This process, known as "factoring" in the garment industry, had never been applied to Hollywood. TV stations didn't have to pay for syndication rights until shows aired, which could entail a delay of several years. By selling the receivables, Ivester gained immediate access to the money.

By increased debt offerings, lowered percentages of dividend payouts, and inventive financing, Coca-Cola found itself sitting on enormous piles of cash, amounting to some $1.5 billion by its centennial year. Goizueta, Keough, and Ivester faced the pleasant though difficult task of allocating the funds. In the past, excess cash had been used for more subsidiary acquisitions and repurchase of the Company's stock. Now, Goizueta clearly wanted to refocus the Company on its primary mission of worldwide soft drink saturation.

LOOKING OVERSEAS

He had good reason. Late in February of 1985, the dollar peaked. Concentrating on U.S. investments during the decade's first half made sense because of the muscular dollar. During the latter part of the eighties, however, the massive U.S. trade and budget deficits drove the dollar to 70 percent of its top value by the end of 1990. Against specific currencies, such as the Japanese yen, it lost nearly half of its buying power. Although the dollar's demise spelled disaster for most American firms, it furnished a wonderful opportunity for the multinational Coca-Cola. Sales in Germany or Japan yielded fatter profits due to favorable exchange rates. As Goizueta and Keough hastened to point out, Americans accounted for less than 5 percent of the world's population. The other 95 percent remained a largely untapped market. Goizueta thus decided to pursue the same hard-driving strategies in countries around the world as he had already in the United States.

The possibilities were tantalizing. If the rest of the world's human beings drank anywhere *near* the same amount of Coca-Cola as the typical American, the Company would experience more than exponential growth. By 1986, every man, woman, and child in the United States drank an average of 660 eight-ounce soft drinks every year. The steady growth of American soft drink per capita had overtaken beer in the early sixties and swept past coffee and milk in the late seventies. By 1986, it had surged beyond imagination. "Right now," Roberto Goizueta informed the assembled bottlers at the centennial, "in the United States, people consume more soft drinks than any other liquid—including ordinary tap water." The Coke CEO then painted a glorious scenario. "If we take full advantage of our opportunities," he said, "someday, not too many years into our second century, we will see the same wave catching on in market after market, until, eventually, the number one beverage on earth will not be tea or coffee or wine or beer. It will be soft drinks—*our* soft drinks."

Internationally, Coke led Pepsi 3-to-1, and the gap between American and foreign consumption beckoned the eager Coca-Cola men. In Africa, per capita amounted to only 4 percent of the U.S., while the economically surging Pacific Rim stood at 8 percent. In Western Europe, where Coca-Cola dominated competition, the per capita remained 23 percent of that in America, while Latin America held at 29 percent.[*] The future for soft drinks, as Don Keough told *Beverage Digest*, appeared rosy. "As population centers become more complex, potable tap water is very difficult to find, and there is an anti-alcohol phenomenon here and abroad." Fizzy, enjoyable, tasty soft drinks could jump into the thirst gap.

Keough, the Company motivator, concluded the centennial celebration with a magnificent proof of the Coke system's power and unity, asking everyone

---

[*] Brand Coca-Cola accounted for nearly 70 percent of the Company's overseas volume, followed by 14 percent for Fanta Orange, making Fanta, a virtually ignored name in America, the world's third most popular soft drink.

present—over 12,000 people—to stand and hold hands. "This is the world of Coca-Cola," he told them. "What other international group in the world could do this right now? From every continent, from every culture, over 125 countries in this room. The United Nations can't do it. We're not mad at anybody. We love each other. Can you feel the energy—can you feel the love—can you feel the affection?" The bottlers left Atlanta with Keough's words ringing in their ears, returning to their corners of the world with renewed inspiration. "You are the Michelangelo of Coca-Cola in your territory," Keough had told them. "And tomorrow the canvas for Coca-Cola as we begin that second century is blank, is bare. You are the artist."

THE TRIPLE A'S

While the bottlers may have been the "artists," Keough and Goizueta, exceedingly aggressive tutors, often grabbed the paintbrush right out of the bottlers' hands. By the time of the centennial, the Company had already taken a 49 percent equity position in the ailing Taiwanese bottler and had divulged a partnership with Cadbury-Schweppes in Great Britain, to take effect in 1987. Inspired by the results in the Philippines, Coca-Cola went on to form joint ventures in country after country throughout the remainder of the decade. In the past, the Company had assiduously avoided the "vertical integration" which buying bottlers implied. Consequently, the quality of the market depended on how motivated or competent the bottlers were. In addition, a certain cultural fatalism had hampered growth in selected countries. In Great Britain, for instance, Coke men always blamed their lackluster showing on the drizzly weather, along with the British penchant for quaffing warm beer; they simply weren't used to ice-cold drinks. Similarly, the reasoning went, the French would never accept Coca-Cola because they loved their wine too much and objected to the Americanization of their culture.

Goizueta refused to accept these excuses. While cultural deterrents existed, they were not insurmountable. The same traditional methods that had prevailed in the United States would work anywhere in the world, with appropriate modifications. The Cuban CEO coined an alliterative slogan— *availability, affordability, acceptability*. Before the drink could be sold, it must be *available*, or, as Woodruff always put it, "within arm's reach of desire." Coca-Cola should elbow its way into every conceivable retail outlet, while vending machines dotted roadsides and invaded sports arenas, factories, offices, shopping malls. Because soda fountains had always remained a strictly American phenomenon, convincing small cafés and bistros to dispense "post-mix" Coke posed problems, though as McDonald's franchises spread throughout the world, fountain Coke tagged along.

Second, Coca-Cola must be *affordable* even to those living below the poverty line. While maintaining a hefty profit margin, the soft drink shouldn't ascend to luxury status. Increasingly, the Company pushed larger containers of two and three liters, resulting in bulk sales at lower cost. Keeping Coke cheap enough for cash-poor African consumers proved particularly challenging. In

Latin America, where governmental controls checked price and packaging, the Company had little choice but to offer the drink at low cost.

Third, and perhaps most important, Coca-Cola had to be *accepted* by consumers as a refreshing, healthy, sparkling beverage associated with good times, friends, achievement, athletics, and patriotism. Massive advertising and promotion were essential to that acceptance. Attractive, smiling girls must carry trays with free samples at Company-sponsored sporting events, overwhelming any negative rumors with a wave of good feeling.

In each country, Keough and Goizueta understood, implementation would vary somewhat, depending on the culture, economy, and stage of industrial development. They coined another Company slogan: "Think globally, but act locally." In China and Indonesia, for instance, the first task involved building a strong infrastructure—concentrate factories, glass manufacturers, bottling plants, trucks, point-of-purchase signs, and the like—in American terms, time-warping back to 1905. In Germany, on the other hand, the Company already had a well-established business, but, as in the United States, too many bottlers vied in small territories. In 1985, Neville Isdell left a thriving Philippine business to supervise Germany, where he undertook the delicate task of consolidating the country's ninety-six bottlers.

THE 49 PERCENT SOLUTION

Shortly after the centennial celebration, The Coca-Cola Company fortuitously found itself in possession of two gigantic bottling concerns. Jack Lupton, the grandson of the original Whitehead partner, elected to sell the JTL Corporation for $1.4 billion just before the California bottling concerns owned by Beatrice Foods went on the block for $1 billion. Coke snapped them up and, together with the bottling plants it already owned, wound up controlling a third of American Coke production. The purchases matched Company strategy, but they added unwieldy debt to the bottom line. In addition, they threatened the Company's profit margins, since selling syrup and concentrate was far more profitable than bottling, and less capital-intensive.

Doug Ivester solved the problem by creating an entirely new corporate entity called Coca-Cola Enterprises. As with other joint ventures, The Coca-Cola Company would retain a minority interest—in this case, 49 percent, guaranteeing control while shoving the huge bottling operation's debts off of Big Coke's balance sheet. Goizueta tapped Brian Dyson, a fine guerrilla fighter in the cola wars, as the new head of CCE, removing him from the main Company, where he was too closely linked to the New Coke disaster. The week before Dyson's appointment, Sergio Zyman resigned, providing another convenient fall guy for New Coke in the public mind, though Zyman continued to serve as a well-paid consultant for the Company.

In the next two years, Big Coke gobbled stray bottling concerns and added them to CCE, consolidating the world's largest single bottler. Despite its mammoth size and Dyson's best efforts, the new corporation stumbled from the start. First, CCE was embarrassed when reluctant capitalists twice forced its initial stock offering—the largest in history—down from $24 a share. By the time it finally hit Wall Street, CCE stock sold for $16.50 and promptly lost another $2 a share within a few days of going public. Investors remained unimpressed by the much-touted cash flow, which would supposedly boost the stock price. While huge amounts of money did wash in and out of the bottling concern, its profits remained razor thin because of price wars with Pepsi.

For Big Coke, however, CCE fulfilled its purpose. Because the parent company could call the shots, it sold concentrate to CCE at relatively high prices, leaving the bottler to scrape out narrow margins. Emmet Bondurant scornfully called CCE "a syrup pump for Big Coke, pure and simple." Doug Ivester didn't care what it was called. The "49 percent solution," as insiders dubbed the arrangement, made financial sense. Quickly, he employed the same trick with Company-owned Canadian bottling plants, spinning them off as TCC Beverages Ltd, with the Company maintaining a 49 percent interest.

Shortly afterward, Ivester again performed his "financial alchemy," as a *Fortune* writer put it. He packaged all of the Company's entertainment holdings as publicly held Columbia Pictures Entertainment Inc., merging with Tri-Star in a stock swap leaving Coke with an 80 percent stake. He avoided an awkward initial stock offering by issuing 31 percent of the stock as a "dividend" to Coke shareholders. When the smoke cleared, The Coca-Cola Company owned just less than half of the new movie conglomerate, while netting $1.5 billion—about the same amount it had paid for everything in the sector. Goizueta was delighted with the new arrangements, which swept $3 billion in debt off the Company books, reducing the debt-to-equity level to a modest 12 percent and disassociating Big Coke somewhat from Columbia flops. Finally, it constituted what *The Wall Street Journal* termed "a potent takeover defense," with "layer upon layer of poison pills." Goizueta declared that Coca-Cola led the vanguard of "the emerging post-conglomerate era," comparing unwieldy traditional corporations to fifties cars with gratuitous tail fins.

PLACATING THE DO-GOODERS

Only months after the anti-apartheid activists picketed the centennial celebration, The Coca-Cola Company revealed that it planned to disinvest in South Africa, following a boycott threat from the Reverend Joseph Lowery and his Atlanta-based Southern Christian Leadership Conference. Furthermore, it would try to sell its bottling plants to qualified black owners. The Company set up an Equal Opportunity Fund (EOF) with a $10 million endowment, to be administered by Nobel Peace Prize winner Desmond Tutu and the Reverend Allan Boesak, among others. Finally, the Company's concentrate plant relocated from Durban to black-controlled Swaziland, instantly doubling the tax revenue of that tiny country.

Most apartheid critics lavished praise on Coca-Cola for "making a strong moral statement," as the Reverend Lowery said, while Mayor Andrew Young proclaimed it "a bold and significant step in the battle against apartheid." In fact, Coca-Cola had reduced its actual ownership of bottling plants in South Africa since 1976 because of the politically unstable situation, and its divestment involved less than $50 million in assets. The Company had no intention of relinquishing its domination of the South African soft drink market, continuing to supply its independent bottlers with syrup and marketing advice.

A few hard-line anti-apartheid activists challenged Coke's "disinvestment." Tandi Gcabashe, the daughter of former African National Congress leader Albert Luthuli, lived in Atlanta and persistently agitated for a boycott, while privately admitting that "Coca-Cola is in the forefront of good companies." She argued that for every 80-cent bottle of Coke sold in South Africa, 10 cents went as tax revenue to the government, and that Coke therefore still supported the racist regime. She dismissed the $10 million EOF as "an insult, a drop in the bucket." When critics pointed out that other American companies offered more logical targets, Gcabashe shrugged them off, pragmatically asserting that Coke was the ideal scapegoat because of its worldwide presence and image. "They are so visible and so *good* with their advertisements," she explained, "that it works to our advantage. We can say, 'What company profits from apartheid? Coke is it!'" College students, ever eager for noble causes, fervently responded to Gcabashe's anti-Coca-Cola pamphlets, forcing the Company to counter with its own literature. Suave Carl Ware, Coke's highest-ranking black executive, traveled to reassure students personally of the Company's exemplary position. Desmond Tutu, visiting Atlanta to deliver the commencement speech at Emory, posed with Keough, Goizueta, and the Atlanta archbishop for a photograph in which all four smiled broadly. The boycott sputtered, though Gcabashe refused to let it die completely.

In the meantime, Coca-Cola Foods provoked an international uproar as well. Late in 1985, frustrated by repeated freezes which had decimated Florida orange groves, the Houston-based subsidiary purchased 196,000 acres of Belizean forest and grasslands, intending to clear 25,000 acres to guarantee a supply for Minute Maid. Paying only $6 million, Coca-Cola suddenly owned an eighth of the entire land mass of tiny Belize, formerly British Honduras. The deal, helped along by a new pro-business Belizean regime, quickly translated into a cause célèbre for environmentalists, nationalists, and angry native fruit growers.

Unfounded rumors flew that Coca-Cola had bought the land for use as a resupply base for Nicaraguan Contra rebels, since Contra chief Adolfo Calero was, after all, a Coca-Cola bottler.* When other growers discovered that Prime Minister Manuel Esquivel had sweetened the deal by granting Coke a fifteen-year tax holiday, they were livid. Nor were the U.S. grove owners pleased with the situation, since the Coke move directly threatened their profits. The

---

* Calero's Coke plant had been seized by the Sandinista government in 1983 when he was out of the country. He soon became the kingpin of the Contra movement.

American citrus lobby blocked the issuance of essential "political-risk insurance." Without it, the Company couldn't reasonably proceed.

The greatest agitation, however, developed from environmental groups such as the International Audubon Society, Rainforest Action Network, and Friends of the Earth, which screamed that the contested forest nurtured unique wildlife such as ocelots, pumas, howler monkeys, harpy eagles, and the world's largest jaguar population. By 1987, the protests were garnering international headlines, with demonstrations in Stockholm and the occupation of a German bottling plant by Green Party activists. In September, Coke finally relented, placing the Belize citrus project on "indefinite hold." In addition, the Company donated 40,000 acres as a nature preserve and declared its intention of selling most of the balance. As usual, the Company managed to transform a public relations disaster into a bonanza. Coca-Cola, a Sierra Club publication declared, had "joined the rainforest generation."

THE APRIL MASSACRE

Meanwhile, Judge Murray Schwartz had recovered from his mysterious ailment and delivered two 1986 interim judgments, apparently decisive victories for the upstart bottlers led by Bill Schmidt. First, Schwartz issued a "preclusion order" in the Diet Coke Case because of the Company's refusal to divulge its secret formulae. In doing so, he allowed Emmet Bondurant to assert that the difference between diet Coke and Coca-Cola was "as narrow as the width of a piece of paper," varying only in type of sweetener used. Unfortunately for Bondurant, Schwartz stopped short of saying that diet Coke was *exactly* equivalent to Coca-Cola and therefore covered by the same contract.

Later in the year, Schwartz ruled in the E-Town Case that high-fructose corn syrup did *not* equal cane sugar according to the wording in the original bottling contract. The Company did not, therefore, have the right to switch to HFCS without the bottlers' permission. In his summary, the judge wrote that "this case was a pleasure to try because of the outstanding ability of both teams of lawyers," but suggested that their talents were misdirected. What was the use of the protracted, bitter dispute, since it was clearly in the best interests of both parties to compromise? Surely, these superb lawyers could convince their clients to negotiate a more reasonable contract with the object of "increasing the bottom line rather than incurring horrendous litigation expenses."

The judge's gentle admonition fell on deaf ears. Bondurant and Schmidt, jubilant over their apparent victories, were not about to relent. Nor, it soon appeared, would Big Coke. In an unexpected move the following March, the Company reacted to Schwartz's sugar judgment by *insisting* on supplying the non-amended bottlers with cane-sweetened syrup, even though that would cost the Company a projected $7 million annually. At the same time, the Company cut off all cooperative funds to non-amended bottlers. "We underestimated the vindictiveness of The Coca-Cola Company," Bondurant lamented, switching tactics to insist that the corn syrup had become the standard and must therefore be supplied under the contract. "The Company," he wrote, "is attempting to win through unfair and coercive tactics a victory it has lost to the bottlers in court." The Company responded by declaring that non-amended bottlers had until May 1 to sign the 1978 amendment. After that, the window of opportunity would stay closed forever.

Many of the non-amended bottlers panicked, particularly the smaller outfits who relied on other bottlers for cans and large plastic containers. They knew that the bigger amended supplier would cut them off rather than arrange for a separate cane syrup flow through their lines. Bill Schmidt, a medium-sized bottler who supplied nearby plants with canned Coke, wasn't in such dire straits, though he would now have to run two separate lines—one for amended, another for non-amended bottlers. He assured his fellow plaintiffs that he would ship them canned goods, but that failed to stem a flood of defections which Schmidt lamented as the "April Massacre." Many bottlers called in tears to apologize. "I believe in what you're doing," they said, "but I'm scared. This could ruin my whole business." Within a month and a half, the number of non-amended bottlers fell from sixty-four to twenty-nine. As the lawyers jockeyed, however, the final outcome of both trials remained uncertain.

NOT FUN ANYMORE

The dwindling renegades were the last holdouts against the dramatic changes the entire Coca-Cola system had undergone in the prior ten years. The small-town bottler, king of his countywide domain, had been replaced by a warehouse. In 1937, for example, Bill Carson built his gorgeous plant in Paducah, Kentucky, with select maple, stained glass, and a thirty-foot round dome. Its gilded splendor now held only a few offices; no one actually bottled Coke in Paducah anymore. Instead, in an impersonal process known as "double-bottoming," two loaded semitrailers pulled into the parking lot. In the old days, the bottler called each of his customers by first name, and each route driver developed a personal relationship with even the smallest account. For forty years, for instance, Charlie Schifilliti serviced Vermont. Because his name was difficult to pronounce, customers often called asking for "the Coca-Cola man," and the operator would give out Schifilliti's home phone number. If Pepsi dared to place a cooler, the typical Coke bottler would simply express disappointment in his old friend, who would remove the interloping machine. Now, the gigantic modern bottler shipped product hundreds of miles away, primarily to chain accounts: K mart, 7-Eleven, Piggly-Wiggly. Because of mergers and consolidations in almost every industry, including supermarkets, convenience stores, and service stations, the most important customers were bigger and bigger chains which expected commensurately large, efficient service.

By 1988, the top ten U.S. Coke bottlers accounted for 78 percent of the brand's volume, and Big Coke owned equity positions in half of them. The raging price wars between Coke and Pepsi steadily narrowed profit margins.

As industry commentator Jesse Meyers put it, discounting had become "not just a way of life, but . . . life itself," resulting in prices which were actually lower per ounce than in 1970, when adjusted for inflation. Inevitably, the squeeze on profits prompted a private cease-fire among some competing Coke and Pepsi bottlers—an illegal practice known as price-fixing.

Even though the Reagan administration's trustbusters had been notably lenient, Tony Nanni, the litigation chief appointed by Carter, was relentless once he smelled soft-drink blood. In a speech before bottlers, he spoke of his job as a "mission," and the shudder running through the room testified to his sincerity and power. After filing his first price-fixing case in 1986, he rapidly uncovered other cases of collusion. In 1987, CBS's *60 Minutes*, in a report called "Cola Payola," revealed that Coke and Pepsi bottlers had conspired in hotel bathrooms, parking lots, fast-food booths, and airport coffee shops to forge price agreements. By the end of 1988, Nanni had filed twenty-nine separate legal actions against bottlers and was investigating many others. Jim Harford, president of a major Coke bottling plant, was jailed in 1987 for collusion in price-fixing, and admitted that he had created "an environment where people got hurt. Frankly, we were street-fighters. We were cocky, really cocky, competitively boastful that we could do anything because we were winning the war."

In this cutthroat world, only bullies won. Royal Crown and other smaller competitors were slowly being crushed between Coke and Pepsi, who literally left them no room through "calendar marketing agreements" (CMAs) in which the bigger bottlers paid supermarkets huge fees for the rights to exclusive end-of-aisle promotion space, dividing the year between them. Complaining that these CMAs were more properly termed "lock-out agreements," Royal Crown unsuccessfully sued.

The frantic effort to reap profits in such a volatile market forced most Coca-Cola bottlers to apply severe pressure on their employees. Traditionally, the Coke delivery man took immense pride in his work, since he represented a worthy, gracious product and company. Now, for a driver at Coke Consolidated (in which Big Coke held a 20 percent equity position), the job became "psychologically devastating," to quote former route salesman Allen Peacock. During his fifty-four weeks with the Company, he routinely worked from 5:30 A.M. until 11 P.M. "They threatened termination if you didn't finish your route," he recalled. If the product didn't sell before its ninety-day shelf life expired, the salesman had to buy it out of his salary. That sort of pressure led to a 260 percent annual turnover rate at Consolidated in Nashville, where Peacock worked. Working strictly on commission, he pulled down $35,000 a year, but the stress and abuse weren't worth it. When his car broke down, he was told to appear anyway or face dismissal. The following day, his boss told him he could have one more chance. "I told him to kiss my ass," Peacock said. "I had never been written up or missed a day of work. I walked out, and I'll never go back."

Life at The Coca-Cola Company didn't become that vicious or harried, but the eighties brought unwanted change there as well. Coca-Cola men had always worked like hell, but in the corporate, computerized, buttoned-down world of the North Avenue Tower, there was less room for creative flair. Particularly under Ed Mellett, the former Pepsi manager, Coca-Cola USA men chafed under increased bureaucratization, paperwork, and a top-down system of orders. The new, impersonal world at headquarters disheartened Company veterans. "At one time," Charlie Bottoms recalled, "I could have walked through the building and I would have been glad to give you a million dollars for anybody we passed that didn't know who I was and I couldn't at least call their first name. I can't call their names anymore." Bottoms complained of a "different breed" of employee who had never known the passionate loyalty to the Boss or the Company and regarded his or her job merely a rung on a career ladder. "Some of them don't even drink our products. That's a sin. They work for money. They don't work for Coca-Cola." One day in 1988, Charlie Bottoms discovered one of his co-workers cleaning his desk in preparation for early retirement. "Why?" Bottoms asked him. "You've still got so much left in you." The man sighed. "Charlie," he answered, "I always promised myself that when it wasn't fun anymore, I would go. Well, it isn't fun anymore." Bottoms, who chose early retirement himself a few years later, could not find a rebuttal.

WITHIN WRIST'S LENGTH OF DESIRE

The same sort of centralization also destroyed the fun in the Fountain Division, Woodruff's old "Marine Corps," though Coke continued to dominate Pepsi in the post-mix wars. Income from fountain constituted a third of the Company's domestic profits. The most important accounts by far were fast-food outlets—all 122,000 of them. Dual-income families, too hassled to cook, grabbed more and more quick meals at the franchises, along with recently divorced singles. McDonald's, of course, topped the list. Although the Golden Arches had always served only Coca-Cola beverages, there was no written contract, and nervous Coke men knew that McDonald's could walk away without notice, taking the firm's largest single account with them. By the late eighties, McDonald's sold 3 billion drinks annually. To keep the big fountain accounts happy, Coke had to be satisfied with nearly invisible profit margins and offer superb, quick service.

In 1986, PepsiCo acquired Kentucky Fried Chicken, making the soft drink concern the world's second-largest restaurateur and providing one more exclusive outlet for Pepsi-Cola. Clever Coke salesmen exploited the KFC purchase to woo Wendy's, however, noting that Pepsi now competed for the fast-food dollar at Pizza Hut, Taco Bell, and Kentucky Fried Chicken. Wendy's switched to Coke. "Pepsi was subsidizing its expansion with *our* soft drink dollars," a Wendy's spokesman complained. "We were supporting a competitor." Similar thinking caused Domino's Pizza to dump Pepsi soon afterward. To Coca-Cola's delight, Pepsi was metamorphosing into a fast-food conglomerate more than a beverage company, and Coke men fervently hoped that Pepsi's attention would be diverted from the cola wars.

Determined to fill every niche of American society, in 1988 the Coca-Cola fountain men introduced the BreakMate, a miniature dispenser that could fit on a countertop in any office.* "Now we're targeting one of the last remaining dry channels in the United States—the workplace," a Coke executive exulted, though industry observer Jesse Meyers opined that the unit was really the prototype for a home soft-drink dispenser. Whatever the ultimate goal of the newest dispensing gadget, Coke was attempting to place its soft drinks not just within *arm's* length of desire, but within *wrist's* length, as Meyers put it. People could even buy a Coke on some intercity buses. "Perhaps coming years will see a time," Goizueta mused dreamily, "when consumers will have Coca-Cola taps in their homes."

BEATING THE FEELING TO DEATH

By the beginning of 1987, it was clear that the "Red, White & You" campaign was more black and blue than effective and that New Coke had fizzled, despite Max Headroom's popularity. Consequently, McCann-Erickson compromised on a "megabrand umbrella" approach intended to advertise all products with the Coca-Cola name. "When Coca-Cola is a part of your life," the new song promised, "you can't beat the feeling." This rather vague concept was supposed to claim consumers with a "special relationship" to Coke. At the end of each spot, a tagline for Classic, New Coke, diet Coke, and cherry Coke materialized, but the ads emphasized the "flagship brand," Classic. Roberto Goizueta stubbornly refused to abandon New Coke, however, and during 1987 the Company spent over $21 million on commercials for the controversial cola while allocating only $36 million to Classic—slightly more than half of Pepsi's main-thrust budget.

In the meantime, Pepsi was lavishing big money on celebrity campaigns, once again turning to Michael Jackson, whose *Bad* album reaffirmed his hold on young consumers. Michael J. Fox performed in funny, innovative Diet Pepsi ads created by Roger Mosconi (director of the Mean Joe Greene spot), who had quarreled with John Bergin and shifted from McCann-Erickson to BBDO. Phil Dusenberry continued to mastermind Pepsi attack spots, such as one in which an archeologist of the future could not identify a Coke bottle. Finally, Pepsi resuscitated a modified Challenge, once again airing taste tests touting Pepsi as "America's Choice" over Classic by a wide margin.

No one cared anymore. American consumers were sick of taste tests, and they kept drinking more Classic despite "evidence" of their ignorance. Throughout 1987 and 1988, Pepsi regained a slight edge in the take-home market, however, while most analysts agreed that Pepsi ads were more effective than Coke's diffuse efforts. As head of Coca-Cola USA, Ed Mellett had antagonized almost everyone, and when he fired 200 people because of the

---

* The BreakMate failed to find a major market, primarily due to technical malfunctions and cost.

reorganized bottling system, morale bottomed. At the end of 1988, Ike Herbert replaced Mellett, promising to revitalize the ad campaigns and restore good feeling to the American division.

Herbert's first change was, as Jesse Meyers noted, an "elegant marketing maneuver." Since third-place diet Coke gained market share faster than any other soft drink, Herbert decided to position *diet* Coke against sugar Pepsi-Cola, asserting that the aspartame-sweetened drink would eventually surpass the Imitator to become number two—a doubtful claim in the short term, since diet Coke claimed 8.5 percent of the soft drink market compared to Pepsi's 17.7 percent. Still, the diet Coke attack ads, featuring black singer Whitney Houston, hunk actor Pierce Brosnan, and sexy actress Demi Moore, helped to reposition the rivalry in Coke's favor. Don Johnson of *Miami Vice*, a previous shill for Pepsi, now confessed the error of his ways in diet Coke spots. The surprise assault was called Project Manhattan—an obvious reference to the development of the atomic bomb. Making the military analogy explicit, Ike Herbert explained that he had carefully defined a battlefield of his own choosing.

Simultaneously, Herbert virtually abandoned New Coke advertising. Within a year, McCann men improved "Can't Beat the Feeling" by a simple inversion of the lyrics. Research indicated that no one remembered or cared about the ethereal "feeling." As a Pepsi man queried, "What is the feeling? Why can't you beat it? It just doesn't express anything." Now, instead of mentioning the "real thing" in the penultimate position, the song crooned: "Can't Beat the Feeling, Can't Beat the Real Thing." With the minor change, warmth and effectiveness flowed back into the commercials, and the recall rate jumped.

Meanwhile, Pepsi embroiled itself in an unwanted controversy precisely because of its chosen image—hip, wild, creative, and slightly risqué. The pop superstar Madonna agreed to shoot a Pepsi spot in the spring of 1989, a video to her new song, "Like a Prayer." Roger Mosconi loved working with Madonna, who was professional, savvy, and took direction beautifully. The $5 million ad campaign, in which the singer touchingly encountered her eight-year-old self, debuted in the U.S. and forty other countries. Without telling Mosconi, however, Madonna had filmed a rock video of the same song to premier simultaneously on MTV. In the sacrilegious video, Madonna cavorted in front of burning crosses, displayed Christ's stigmata on her hands, and made love with a black saint on a church pew, instantly provoking a public furor. Pepsi had to pull its ads.

THE POWER OF PRESENCE

Despite an improved campaign, by the late eighties Coke men appreciated that traditional television, radio, and print ads were not the only effective forms of advertising. Coke's sheer presence in public venues, or "prestige" locations, provided enormous exposure. Don Keough emphasized "the power of presence" in a 1987 internal memo. "It is at the play, at the game, at the sorority and at the drugstore," Keough wrote. "The name, Coca-Cola, is in front of every pair of eyes, every day, everywhere." That, he pointed out, was what separated Coke from Pepsi. Through its exclusive presence at the Houston Astrodome, the San Diego Zoo, Madison Square Garden, Yankee Stadium, Disney World, and 400 other prestige U.S. locations, Coca-Cola encountered over 280 million patrons a year. "We reach into the soul of America through these accounts," a Coke man observed.

The Disney account was by far the most important avenue into America's soul, and not just because of presence at the entertainment parks in California, Florida, and Japan. Coke's association with the beloved animated characters dated back to the fifties and sponsorship of *The Mickey Mouse Club*. In 1985, Coke signed an exclusive global marketing agreement. As a Company publication observed, "even a fairy godmother or sorcerer would be hard-pressed to match the wizardry of Mickey Mouse and Coca-Cola," since they were both "family-oriented" and "stand for good things." In 1987, to help celebrate Disney World's fifteenth birthday, Coke sponsored a tie-in contest with the April Disney Sunday Movie. "We've always wanted to lock up Easter as a major sales period," a Coke executive glowed. Forget celebrating the resurrection—a "Watch & Win" sweepstakes with free vacations to Disney World provided infinitely better advertising.

By the late eighties, advancing beyond mere product placement in movies, Coke paid for advertisements on rental videos. In addition, at thousands of theaters around the country, Coke ads introduced the main feature. Theater managers were delighted, since the ads boosted Coke sales at the concession stand, with its standard 80 percent markup. And more than ever, Coke relied on the films themselves for product placement and co-promotions. To offset *Ishtar*'s dismal performance earlier in the year, Coca-Cola turned to Bill Cosby, hoping for a blockbuster comedy for the 1987 Christmas season with his *Leonard Part 6*, a spy spoof which Cosby himself had written. Coke men could hardly contain their joy over the co-promotional opportunities. "The synergies between soft drinks and entertainment are endless and growing," a Coke marketer crowed. "We want to capitalize on these opportunities to the fullest."

He wasn't kidding. Coca-Cola soft drink divisions were prepared to spend over $12 million for *Leonard*, including tiny promotional spy cameras, supermarket displays with Cosby's smug smile presiding over stacked six-packs, Porsches as sweepstake prizes, and a deluge of cups, posters, pullover shirts, and buttons featuring Cosby and Coke. The movie seemed a surefire winner, with the comedian's TV show at the top of the charts and his book on parenting the world's fastest-selling hardback thus far. Cosby himself assured everyone that his film was "flat-out comedy, with punch lines that people will be able to laugh at over and over. I've been in this business for a long time, and I know this is really funny stuff." Unfortunately, he was wrong. "The audience *hated* it," the film's editor noted. "Jesus Christ, a rainbow trout got a bigger laugh than the great God Cosby!" The film failed utterly, pulling in only $5 million at the box office and incurring a net loss of $33 million.

Undeterred, Coca-Cola cut a deal for the ultimate product-placement film the following year. *MAC and Me*, an unabashed *ET* rip-off, made Coca-Cola the alien's only source of sustenance. "This must be like what they drink on their own planet," young Eric informed his brother as MAC slurped his Coke. Near the movie's end, sips of magical Coke revived the alien's nearly dead family members. In the final scene, the visitors from another planet drove into the sunset in a Chevy convertible, chewing bubble gum and drinking Coke. Though the movie was predictable, with a pedestrian script and poor acting, it undoubtedly helped to sell a lot of Coke and grossed over $34 million at the box office in just over a month.

WE'LL BUILD A BETTER WORLD FOR YOU

While Coke was engaged in a bitter struggle for supremacy in the U.S.—often looking somewhat silly in the process—the real action had shifted overseas, where Coke totally dominated Pepsi. Embarrassed by the New Coke debacle, Coca-Cola ordered Marcio Moreira to make a new commercial to restore worldwide Company pride. Once more, free-lancer Ginny Redington devised a winner in which over a thousand eager, fresh-faced youngsters of every ethnic and geographical origin intoned an uplifting message reminiscent of the Hilltop commercial.

"I am the future of the world," sang a fifteen-year-old blonde girl with sweet sincerity, sitting alone at a table. "I am the hope of my nation. / I am tomorrow's people, I am the new inspiration," she continued, rising as hordes of other teenagers streamed into the imposing assembly hall and joined the song. "Please let there be for you and for me a tomorrow," they begged, each clutching a bottle of Coke. "If we all can agree, there'll be sweet harmony tomorrow." A girl laid her head on her boyfriend's shoulder. "Promise us tomorrow, and we'll build a better world for you." After panning the throng, the camera once more focused on the original soloist, while across the bottom scrolled, "A message of hope from the people who make Coca-Cola."

The song was beautiful, touching, stirring, and, as always with Coke's best efforts, not terribly specific. The emotional rush sufficed, particularly if all these young people kept drinking Coca-Cola. McCann men filmed "General Assembly," the perfect pattern commercial, in St George's Hall in Liverpool, a harbor town where they could easily gather kids from around the world. The creative team shot the mob scene for the first two days, then filmed various soloists in nineteen different languages for as many versions of the commercial.

First released early in 1987, "General Assembly" effectively reasserted Coca-Cola's global image of peace, brotherhood, and all-encompassing good-will. Over the next few years, it was broadcast again for appropriate events such as a Gorbachev–Reagan summit and the 1992 Olympics. In the Philippines, it served as the entire campaign for two years, with new versions filmed locally. In Peru, an entirely new Spanish cast assembled at Machu Picchu for a dramatic restaging. Where the Inca had once grown terraced fields of coca atop the world, singers now claimed the future for Coca-Cola. The wheel had come full circle.

Outside the United States, the Company maintained "Coke Is It" well beyond the introduction of "Can't Beat the Feeling" domestically—a normal procedure to see how well the American campaign was progressing and to allow time for testing it in foreign venues. Finally approved for overseas ads late in 1988, it didn't translate well in several markets, where "beating a feeling" meant something nonsensical or obscene. In Chile, the new slogan was transmogrified into "The Feeling of Life," in Italy "Unique Sensation," and in Japan, with its fractured English, "I Feel Coke."

Marcio Moreira, constantly frustrated by Coca-Cola's prudish standards, traveled the world in the early eighties policing women's nipples, which were taped over for swimsuit ads. "Sexiness and sensuality are a more acceptable part of many foreign life-styles," the Brazilian ad man knew. By late in the decade, Moreira's international ads, extremely racy by American standards, featured lingering shots of swaying behinds, suggestive kissing and embracing, and commercials such as "First Time," which implicitly associated the excitement of an initial sexual encounter with drinking Coke. Re-recorded without reference to Coke, the song dominated the top rock spot in England for several weeks.

Under Moreira's direction, Coke's pattern advertising became more "universal," as he put it. In previous years, international commercials featured a careful blend of blacks, Orientals, and whites. Now, research revealed that actors with dark Latin looks—a kind of middle ground—played well everywhere except Japan and a few other countries. "Anything that is too topical or local or ethnic won't work," Moreira explained. Likewise, wardrobe, locations, and props were carefully screened to avoid "contravening any major cultural streams."

ROCKIN' AND SOCKIN' WITH COKE

Around the world, ads and promotions strengthened Coke's ties with two universals—music and sports. Any singers used for international ads—such as George Michael, Cyndi Lauper, Whitney Houston, or Sting—had to appeal worldwide, particularly to teens. While America was graying, the world population as a whole grew younger, and satellites and cable TV rendered rock videos universal fare. In Brazil (average age: seventeen), Coke sponsored "Rock in Rio," a gigantic nine-day concert attended by over a million people. Lulu Santos, a Brazilian pop star, indicated his appreciation for Company support by mentioning Coke frequently in his song lyrics. In the Philippines, Coca-Cola actually recruited and groomed local rock groups, carefully fostering their popularity through concerts, tours, and TV commercials. Thailand's fans started wearing Coca-Cola clothes to Carabao concerts, due to the singers' close identification with the soft drink, while in France, the Company sponsored a daily radio/TV show, the "Coca-Cola Top 50."

Similarly, Company athletic sponsorship spanned the globe. Taking advantage of the Japanese fascination with American football, the Company flew two U.S. college teams to Tokyo for the "Coca-Cola Bowl," in which Oklahoma

State beat Texas Tech 45–42. Since 1982, the Company had sponsored Sawayaka (Refreshing) Baseball Clinics in Japan. When the Brazilian soccer league nearly went bankrupt in 1987, Coke stepped in to sponsor it—but only if every player on every team sported a gigantic bright-red Coca-Cola logo. "The visual effect is stunning," a Company publication crowed. "Next year, even the game ball will bear the red and white trademark." Because of Coke's midfield signs at all World Cup venues it reached 25 *billion* viewers during the 1990 playoffs. During the Tour de France, the famed bicycle race, all cyclists carried a water bottle with the Company logo as they whizzed past giant Coke cans and signboards along the route before crossing a Coca-Cola finish line—quite a change from 1950, when French spectators had violently protested Coke support of a bicycle race. Regardless of the sport—field hockey, basketball, volleyball, gymnastics, sumo wrestling, motorcycle races—Coca-Cola sponsored it in almost every country in the world.

The Olympics, of course, furnished the world's most outstanding sports tie-in opportunity. In 1988, the Company paid for the Coca-Cola World Chorus, a 100-voice choir selected from participating countries. For the opening ceremonies at Calgary and Seoul, the chorus debuted the official song of the event, "Can't You Feel It?" While the lyrics didn't mention Coca-Cola, their resemblance to "Can't Beat the Feeling" conveyed the appropriate message anyway. As a Company publication observed, the Olympics represented "a hot marketing opportunity," and Coke was determined to leverage Olympic symbols to promote sales—through special promotions, contests, and jackets emblazoned with the Coke trademark and the Olympic rings. At the events, the Coke logo was scrawled gaudily in neon, on murals and banners, on huge inflated cans atop buildings, on umbrellas and blimps, while the Company hosted a popular pin-trading center. Altogether, Coke invested about $80 million on its 1988 Olympic promotions.

CREATING SOFT DRINK HEAVEN

By the end of 1988, Coke's international vision had resulted in new joint ventures in Taiwan, China, Indonesia, Belgium, and Holland, while the triple-A program functioned smoothly. For the first time, the Company's after-tax net income topped a billion dollars, with 76 percent of that amount deriving from outside the United States—a dramatic increase of 15 percent in just three years. Highlighting the global business, the 1988 annual report featured Keough and Goizueta smiling in front of a vast world map; breaking precedent, the report touted the international performance before mentioning the U.S.

Indeed, the ontlook around the world made Coke executives drool. In Norway (annual per capita for Company products: 176), the top three soft drinks were Coca-Cola, Coke light, and TaB, with a combined market share of 87 percent. Halfway around the world in China, customers lined up each morning outside the local bottling plant, where supply couldn't keep up with demand. Though the per capita remained minuscule—only 0.4—a new concentrate plant in Shanghai had just opened and three more bottlers would follow within a year. In the Soviet Union, Coke had barely begun. Under Gorbachev, however, the future of free enterprise appeared favorable, and Coke yearned to overtake Pepsi's early lead there. So far, the Company had garnered only an abortive U.S. grand jury investigation into charges that it had bribed its way into the USSR. Neither the bribery accusations nor the lack of hard currency disturbed Coca-Cola particularly. Someday, the Soviet market would bear fruit.

As the chief operating officer of the Company, Don Keough, so charming in public, was proving himself a tough operator who sometimes lost his Coca-Cola patience. Although Keough was immensely likable, immediately establishing contact and rapport—"it is hard not to be knocked over," wrote a *Fortune* reporter, "by his cocked smile, his jet-engine voice, and his touchy-feely nature"—that hands-on management style could turn rough if you didn't produce results. Goizueta found complaints from shell-shocked area managers amusing. "In 1981," he laughed, "everyone thought I was the bad cop and Don the good cop. Now I'm the nice guy and he's the SOB." In planning sessions with Coke men, Keough could be ruthless. When a manager complained of Pepsi's recent inroads, Keough snapped back, "You'll never spend cheaper money than stopping them in their tracks."

In the long run, Keough and Goizueta viewed the Pacific Rim—with 2 billion people, roughly 40 percent of the world's population—as the ultimate promised land for Coke. Keough's eyes glazed when he talked about Indonesia, a country which, he was quick to point out, sweated squarely on the equator and consisted primarily of Moslems (median age: eighteen) who didn't touch alcohol. "Now you tell me," Keough beamed, "where else would heaven be for a soft drink?"

BRINGING GRITS TO FRANCE

A better prospect for the early nineties, however, lay in Western Europe, where Coca-Cola already predominated. By the end of 1992, the Company knew, the European Community (EC) planned to remove most of the economic barriers between the nations, effectively unifying a market whose population, one-third larger than the United States, was compressed into a relatively small, accessible area. While other U.S. companies worried about a "Fortress Europe" mentality, Coca-Cola already held the keys to the citadel.

Nonetheless, Keough and Goizueta were dissatisfied with European per capita, just eighty-one drinks a year. To focus on the area, the Company reorganized its three world divisions in the fall of 1988, carving out a fourth EC Group. The central troublemaker of the sector—geographically as well as culturally—was France, with its miserable per capita of thirty-one, despite Coke's presence there since 1920. The Company blamed longtime franchisee Pernod Ricard, too busy selling its Orangina to push Coke properly, and after a protracted legal battle, Coke finally wrenched the concession away from Pernod early in 1989. In Dunkirk, construction was already under way on a gigantic canning plant to serve all of Europe, while Coke's third-largest concentrate factory opened at Signes. The Winter Olympics would arrive at Albertville in 1992, the same year that EuroDisney was slated to debut just outside Paris, and the Company wanted to prime the French palate. William Hoffman, they decided, was just the man for the job.

Although Hoffman spoke no French—he had never even visited France, having spent most of the eighties developing vigorous Atlanta supermarket promotions—he confidently spearheaded the French renaissance, initiating a program called "Let's Think Big," exhorting his newly hired merchandisers to build Europe's largest displays. Hoffman launched his textbook Coca-Cola marketing blitz in Bordeaux, the heart of French wine country, where vending machines and massive soft drink displays were considered gauche. Hoffman and his gang quickly convinced skeptical hypermarket managers that their profits from Coke would spiral if they showcased a solid wall of reduced-price Coke. Beautiful women dressed in red-and-white outfits distributed coupons for free drinks, while Coke men slapped up 35,000 logo stickers, along with 550 illuminated outdoor signs. By the spring of 1989, 500 vending machines lined Bordeaux sidewalks, where a Company publication proclaimed them "an accepted and welcome part of the landscape."

The Company journalist had mistaken immobilized shock for acceptance, however. Hoffman exerted a bizarre fascination for the natives. "He's so *American!*" they exclaimed, not knowing whether to be charmed or horrified. Stunned by Coca-Cola's "Georgia Week," which included American football, a screening of *Gone With the Wind*, and imported grits, the local café owners watched helplessly as their young consumers abandoned the overpriced $2.50-per-drink Cokes served at their establishments in favor of the 90-cent variety now available from the streetside vending machines. As the café operators mobilized for a boycott of Coke products, the Company hastily agreed to remove the offending Bordeaux vending machines. Elsewhere in France, however, the flood of coin-operated dispensers only increased. When a right-wing politician accused Coke of subverting French culture and luring youth away from wine, others responded by raising a glass of the bubbly American vintage, proclaiming it "our anti-fascist drink."

The American tactics eventually prevailed, even in France, where volume swelled by 23 percent in 1989.[*] Meanwhile, in Great Britain, the alliance with Cadbury Schweppes doubled sales in three years, with a huge new bottle/can plant at Wakefield in northern England to supply the increased demand. Throughout Europe, the same dynamic yielded a 10 percent annual volume growth. By the end of 1989, the EC Group contributed 29 percent of the Company's operating profits.

---

[*] In 1991, Coke pulled William Hoffman out of France and back to the corporate womb in Atlanta. He had served his purpose by shaking up the French industry but was considered too abrasive for the long haul. French per capita continued to rise, however.

LAPPING UP THE SWEAT AND MUCOS

Unlike the French, the on-the-go Japanese loved vending machines—first introduced by Coke in the early sixties—which now supplied them with ice cream, eggs, beer, whiskey, pornography, toothbrushes, or dating services in addition to beverages, cold or hot—a necessary trait for dispensing Georgia Coffee, Coke's popular noncarbonated, sweetened coffee drink. Because of ferocious competition in the Japanese beverage market, 5,000 different flavors vied at any one time. Of the thousand new drinks annually introduced to consumers, only 10 percent survived. To stay in contention, Coca-Cola offered a bewildering array of carbonated, fruit, and coffee beverages, averaging one new flavor per month. The vending manufacturers adapted by proffering up to thirty different choices. Out of the 2 million machines in Japan selling soft drinks, over 700,000 dispensed Coca-Cola products.

As one Coca-Cola manager observed in 1987, "It's hard to overstate the significance of our business in Japan." That year, the island reaped more profits than any other country, including the United States. By the end of the decade, however, the crucial Japanese trade flashed warning signals. Coke's soft drink market share remained high at 84 percent, but per capita stalled and then slipped, as rumors about illness caused by the bubbly beverages rippled through the entire industry. Japanese health drinks with fiber, calcium, vitamins, and other nutrients gained market share, while carbonated sodas suffered.

As usual, Japanese marketers scoured dictionaries for English names, often with disgusting results by American standards. "If you feel your body and skin become dry," one ad suggested, "try to drink Pokka's Mucos please." An isotonic drink similar to Gatorade received the label Pocari Sweat. Coke responded with less nauseous-sounding drinks such as Aquarius (isotonic), FiBi (soluble fiber), and Mone (honey-lemon), but product Coca-Cola's sales still dwindled. Company marketers were frustrated even more when Regain, a noncarbonated caffeine-and-vitamin tonic billed as a pick-me-up, premiered in Japan. The Regain jingle, issued as a CD, hit the top of the pop charts. "Can you fight twenty-four hours, Japanese businessman?" the lyrics inquired, as lightning bolts sizzled from a dark-suited figure clutching a briefcase.

Regain effectively utilized an approach familiar to John Pemberton and Asa Candler, while Coke commercials depicted mindless Japanese teenagers imbibing on sunny summer afternoons—conveying the implicit message that Coke was a drink for indolent youth, not necessarily for industrious students or hardworking adults. Typical Japanese employees commuted up to four hours a day, labored long hours, and returned to cramped apartments in a gray city. They were likely to dismiss the commercials as irresponsible propaganda. Furthermore, Coca-Cola's American image, previously a boon in Japan, had transmuted into a questionable asset. The Japanese no longer looked up to America, with its ailing economy, crime, poverty, and AIDS epidemic. To the Japanese, American workers appeared lazy and self-satisfied, and the "I Feel Coke" commercials only reinforced that view. Despite Coke's frantic marketing efforts—splashing the logo on an entire train and wheeling a "MOBO-TRON" van complete with sixteen-foot video monitor through Tokyo's streets—sales remained flat. As a new decade loomed, frustrated researchers commissioned a sociological study to address the Japanese problem, while dispatching veteran ad man John Bergin to assess the situation.[*]

BACK TO THE BASICS

As Toyotas and Hondas cruised U.S. highways and Japanese corporations snapped up American real estate and banks, a backlash mentality escalated. Just days after the stock market crash in 1987, Sony Corporation had outraged Japan-bashers by purchasing CBS Records, along with its cache of classic American song rights. Now, as 1989 drew to a close, Goizueta revealed that Coke was selling Columbia Pictures to Sony for $3.4 billion, by far the largest Japanese buy-out of an American enterprise. Suddenly, *Mr. Smith Goes to Washington* belonged to the Nipponese. According to one commentator, the Japanese had "bought a piece of America's soul."

Goizueta ignored the uproar following the sale, which netted $1.2 billion for the Company's 49 percent of the stock. The Japanese paid almost four times the value of CPE stock upon its creation the previous year. As far as the Coke CEO was concerned, the sale perfectly capped the Hollywood venture, which had been a financial bonanza but a public relations failure. He was still smarting over the David Puttnam affair, in which the outspoken new British head of Columbia, director of *Chariots of Fire* and *The Killing Fields* before coming to work for Coke, had alienated the American movie establishment without making a single smash movie. Consequently, Goizueta was delighted to unload Columbia for a healthy profit. As an immense money machine, the entertainment sector had boosted the bottom line while the Company put its beverage house in order. Now, Goizueta intended to pump the cash from the sale into the international business. Just as he had sought diversification when he took over the Company, he now cheerfully refocused on soft drinks. "There's a perception in this country that you're better off if you're in two lousy businesses than if you're in one good one—that you're spreading your risk," he complained. He challenged anyone to "tell me something that gives me the return or the growth potential of soft drinks."

Investment guru Warren Buffett agreed with Goizueta. The "Sage of Omaha," Buffett, chairman of Berkshire Hathaway Inc., was an old friend and neighbor of Don Keough, who had converted the financier to cherry Coke back in 1986. Long known as a "white knight" for his long-term equity positions in companies without attempting takeovers, Buffett plunked down a

---

[*] As a result, the Company launched "The Moment That Refreshes" ("Sawayaka Ni Naru Hitotoki"), a variant on the old "Pause That Refreshes" theme. These ads were aimed at hard-working, stressed adults rather than indolent teens. Coke used the word "moment" because Japanese presumably would resent the idea of "pausing." Nevertheless, the Japanese market would suffer as Japan entered a period of economic decline in the 1990s.

billion dollars for a 6.3 percent stake in The Coca-Cola Company in 1989—an unusual move for the Midwestern investor noted for picking undervalued stocks. With its price-to-earnings ratio hovering around thirty, Coke was not cheap, but Buffett shrewdly spotted its limitless potential. Not surprisingly, he joined the board of directors soon afterward.

MURRAY SCHWARTZ: SICK OF COKE?

As the corporate Coca-Cola juggernaut plunged ahead, Emmet Bondurant and Bill Schmidt awaited final decisions from Judge Murry Schwartz. After eight years of bitter litigation, the two trials, which took five months to hear, ended in January of 1989, generating 13,000 pages of transcripts. As both sides prepared for possible closing arguments, Schwartz developed another undisclosed illness and could not render judgment on the cases. Bondurant and Schmidt couldn't believe it, since the fifty-eight-year-old Schwartz knew every nuance and angle of the case, for which he had already issued twelve interim opinions. How could he abandon it now?

No one knew the exact nature of the judge's illness, though it was perhaps related to a long history of heart trouble. Nonetheless, rumors also circulated that he had suffered a nervous breakdown, and the Coke cases may have been a contributing factor. Schwartz had lived and breathed the bitter battle for nearly a decade, the theory went, and now that the decision loomed, he apparently couldn't face it.

The case was reassigned to Judge Joseph J. Farnan, Jr., a Reagan appointee who signaled his hostility to both sides at the outset, commenting, "Counsel in this case couldn't agree on which door to take to the courtroom." As they prepared their arguments once again, both sides learned that Murray Schwartz had miraculously recovered and climbed back into his judicial seat—but he would not resume the Coke cases. As the retrial commenced, Judge Farnan signaled his complete disdain for the proceedings by openly perusing the L. L. Bean catalog during testimony.[*]

REVISITING THE HILLTOP

Meanwhile, as the retrial bored Judge Farnan, Coca-Cola decided to reclaim its heritage along with the high ground in cola-ad battles, which had degenerated into a rather confusing star wars. That year, Coke and diet Coke commercials had showcased twenty-seven different celebrities, along with thirty-one football players, while Pepsi starred Billy Crystal, Robert Palmer, and Magic Johnson, among others. "I think there can be a real sense of

---

[*] Eventually, the cases ended in a whimper, with The Coca-Cola Company assessed a dollar in damages to each bottler in the suits. The Schmidts sold their bottling company but planned to raise $15 million to build a new museum to house their spectacular Coca-Cola memorabilia collection.

confusion ultimately as to who stands for what," an outside creative director commented. It didn't help when Don Johnson crossed over from Pepsi to diet Coke, or Ray Charles, a Georgia musician who had sung powerful Coca-Cola odes in the past and presided at New Coke's unveiling, extolled diet Pepsi in "blind" taste-tests. By the end of the eighties, advertising was expensive, imitative, and corporate, with the glorious days of innovation apparently receding into the past. Technically, the gorgeously filmed spots excelled, crammed with special effects, dancing, and music, but they were dead inside. The few genuinely moving commercials often harkened back to classic ads of another era.

In September of 1989, McCann-Erickson temporarily escaped the celebrity onslaught by remaking the 1970 commercial, "I'd Like to Teach the World to Sing." Scheduled to premier during the Super Bowl in January as a twenty-year anniversary of the beloved ad, this time the peaceful celebrants would share Cokes with their children, singing "Can't Beat the Real Thing" in counterpoint to their parents' more traditional tune. A detective hunt turned up only 25 of the 200 original cast members, so actors from different countries filled in the balance.

The four-day shoot did indeed cover the original Italian hillside, but fashioning commercials required more elaborate preparations than twenty years before. "We had to wake the kids up at 4:30 A.M.," producer Scott Seltzer recalled, "to get there in time for wardrobe, breakfast, make-up, and trundling up the hill. We had tents, food service—it was like a small army on maneuvers." By 9:30 A.M., the hot, tired children were crying for their parents, and production assistants, makeup artists, and wardrobe specialists dropped everything to comfort them. "When I did it last time, it was only half a day. I mean, it was nothing," Linda Neary, the blonde who mouthed the Hilltop introduction, wearily observed. As in the original commercial, it was not Neary's voice which actually sang the song, but Eve Graham, the soloist from the New Seekers. Even in the opening shot of "Reunion," when Neary told her daughter, "You know, it happened right here, twenty years ago," her voice was dubbed to give her an American accent.

A behind-the-scenes video revealed the laborious process behind the seemingly spontaneous final product, as the director drilled the children to enunciate properly, sounding painfully like a first-grade reading lesson: "feeee-ling . . . you . . . get . . . from . . . a . . . Co . . . Ca . . . Co . . . La." Nevertheless, when the children scampered into their parents' arms, the scene elicited a collective gasp, even from the hardened McCann crew. It had an even bigger impact on a forty-year-old American vacationing in Italy. Trudging up the opposite hillside to see what the commotion meant, he heard the faint strains of a song from his youth: " . . . and furnish it with love, grow apple trees and honey bees . . ." He couldn't believe it. Was he in the Twilight Zone? Just as he crested the top, the children dashed up the hill. Caught by the magical moment, the tourist burst into tears.

THE INESCAPABLE PRODUCT

What other product could call forth such strong, spontaneous emotions? None, according to repeated worldwide polls conducted by Landor & Associates. "Coca-Cola is so powerful it's practically off the charts," one journalist marveled. Goizueta loved to cite the soft drink's impressive figures. The Company sold over 45 percent of all the world's carbonated soft drinks, more than double Pepsi's record. Coca-Cola stock had appreciated more than 735 percent during the eighties, creating some $30 billion in additional stockholder wealth and more than doubling the performance of the S&P 500 index. In 1989, Goizueta submitted a revised strategy statement, looking toward the millennium. The goal for the 1990s, he wrote, was to "expand our global business system, reaching increasing numbers of consumers who will enjoy our brands and products more and more often."

At the turn of the decade, the Company appeared poised for ten more years of extraordinary expansion. All over the world, Coca-Cola's devoted field force sought every possible niche. In the Amazonian swamps of Brazil, thirteen-year-old Shirley Batista da Silva peddled Coke from a battered canoe. Every day in the Philippines, Valentin Lachica, a proud seventy-three-year-old, refused to leave his stand until he had sold fifty cases of Coke, one bottle at a time. In South Africa, where the Company had "disinvested," increasing numbers of lower-class blacks earned their living by hawking the soft drink from tiny outlets called "*spazas*." Around the world, Coca-Cola men—some-times father/son teams—delivered their product to the most remote locations by burro, gondola, helicopter, and ski lift. The more remote the destination, the more consumers seemed to appreciate Coke. Residents of Ushuaia, Argentina, the world's southernmost city, drank an average of 420 servings per year.

With world momentum going Coke's way, it seemed only a matter of time before the drink was available in every country in the world. The Arab Boycott steadily eroded, with Kuwait, Saudi Arabia, and the United Arab Emirates lifting the ban on Coke. In Latin America, rebounding economies followed the Mexican lead by opening up to free enterprise, loosening price controls, and finally permitting Coke's profits to match its volume. A gigantic new neon Spectacular lit up Moscow, opposite the huge McDonald's that would serve its first Russian hamburger in January.

One final 1989 event perfectly symbolized Coca-Cola's opportunity and impact. In November, before the world's astonished eyes, the Berlin Wall fell, and as it did, Coca-Cola men filled the gap, handing out free drinks. Cars lined up for miles to receive cases as they drove through the West Berlin bottling plant. When a young East German soldier stationed on a watchtower yelled down from his lonely perch, a quick-witted Coca-Cola man tossed him a twelve-pack. Western civilization and its favorite fizzy beverage poured through crumbling walls. The East Germans had watched tantalizing Coke commercials on their TV sets for years; now they could sample the essence of capitalism.

"The Coca-Cola Company is in a stronger position today than it has ever been in its history," Roberto Goizueta observed, and no one could gainsay him. "Frankly," Don Keough added, "we have become the benchmark for companies with global aspirations." If Pemberton and Candler could have seen the worldwide spread of their bubbly pick-me-up, they might have been flabbergasted. On the other hand, Goizueta's monomaniacal vision would have seemed comfortingly familiar. "Our success," the Cuban wrote, unconsciously echoing a statement Harrison Jones made nearly seventy years before, "will largely depend on the degree to which we make it impossible for the consumer around the globe to escape Coca-Cola."

21

Global Fizz

Coke may have created the closest thing we know of to a perpetual motion machine.

—Financial analyst David Goldman, 1996

If you look in your kitchen sink, there's one spigot that has a C and another spigot that has an H. That spigot that has a C should be used for what God intended.

—Roberto C. Goizueta, CEO, The Coca-Cola Company

Entering the last decade of the twentieth century, the efficient Coca-Cola juggernaut prepared to flood the world, setting the stage for a millennial celebration of unquestioned global dominance. During the penultimate decade of the 1980s, CEO Roberto Goizueta had revamped and refocused the Company. Now, he saw with perfect clarity that the fall of the Berlin Wall signalled the crowning opportunity of his career. "Every day, every single one of the world's 5.6 billion people will get thirsty," he observed early in 1994. "Only in the last few years have world events allowed us true access to more than half of those people."

Late in 1989, Doug Ivester, the bright accountant who had invented the "49 percent solution" that created CCE and allowed Big Coke to invest in bottlers around the world, had been handed his first operational Coke role in Europe, a kind of testing ground for the up-and-coming executive. During the evening of January 8, 1990, Ivester and Heinz Wiezorek, the head of the Company's West German subsidiary, strolled through Alexanderplatz, the main square in East Berlin. Construction cranes towered over them, while newly energized citizens socialized. "We looked around us and said, 'Let's do it,'" Wiezorek recalled. "We decided to start selling Coke for East German marks." When Ivester talked it over with Goizueta, he warned the CEO that he wasn't sure how they would get paid. "I don't care," Goizueta said. "Just ship the product." The gamble paid off nine months later, when East and West Germany united, and the two currencies were given equal weight.

The move into East Germany, with its 17 million new customers, exemplified Goizueta's new mantra that the soft drink behemoth had to be fast, focused, and flexible. "You need to shorten your reaction time by using your instincts and your experience," Goizueta emphasized. "We are relying more on our gut feelings." It also showed that the Company was determined to continue to strengthen its worldwide bottler system on a country-by-country basis, forming joint ventures with big, aggressive bottlers. In the early 1990s, for instance, Coca-Cola Amatil, the huge Australian bottler half owned by Big Coke, would move into Austria, Hungary, Czechoslovakia, as well as Indonesia, Papua New Guinea and New Zealand.

East Germans gulped Coca-Cola as though they had never had a decent soft drink before—mostly because they hadn't. The foamy, foul-smelling Hit Cola, the socialist beverage, sometimes contained bugs and other surprises. Everyone was delighted when Coca-Cola red replaced KBG red, as in Leipzig, where a huge Coke flag hung from the side of the town's once-dreaded secret police headquarters, while hundreds of people lined up at the city's first Coke kiosks. "I get at least 50 letters every day asking how to get Coca-Cola," an amazed East German Coke official told a reporter.

In February 1991, the Company upped the ante, promising to sink $450 million into East Germany alone, to upgrade outmoded government plants and transform 1,500 ex-Communists into devout Coca-Cola men and women. "Coca-Cola is a lucky break for Weimar," one city official observed of the new bottling plant there. "We'll get three to four hundred recession-proof jobs, a steady corporate taxpayer and a major purchaser of goods and services from area companies." Within two years of the fall of the Berlin Wall, sales soared from zero to 1.7 billion drinks. It was, as one industry analyst noted, "the soft drink equivalent of the Marshall Plan."

A GLOBAL BLITZKRIEG

Few marketing gurus were surprised by Coke's swift surge in East Germany, whose citizens had watched Western advertising on their televisions for years while yearning for consumer goods they couldn't get. Eastern Europe and Russia were another matter, however. There, Pepsi had long dominated. Determined to come from behind there, too, Goizueta and his board committed an even $1 billion, to be spent by mid-decade on what they called Project Jumpstart. Previously, Coke products were sold in small amounts for "countertrade," barter for shoddy products. Now, the Company invested directly in Poland and Romania. "Coca-Cola," said a senior Romanian official, "is the symbol of our new life. It brings jobs and color to our streets." Crowds gathered to cheer the arrival of the first Coca-Cola truck in Warsaw, reminiscent of the welcome given the liberating U.S. tanks of World War II. By the end of 1993, Coca-Cola had taken the lead from Pepsi in all of the former Eastern Bloc countries. In Albania, which had no regulatory code for foreign investment, Coke lawyers obligingly helped write laws to ease entry for the soft drink.

As the Soviet Union disintegrated, Coke formed a Ukrainian joint venture, as well as a partnership in Moscow to fund a syrup plant and 2,000 kiosks throughout the city. Symbolically, in a kind of modern swords-into-plowshares, the round metal kiosks were produced by the same factory that had made Soviet missiles. The Company announced that it would build another huge bottling plant in St. Petersburg. "We are committed to building a modern

soft drink system throughout Russia and to having Coca-Cola produced for
Russian consumers and sold for rubles," Don Keough emphasized. Because of
desperate economic conditions, Coke could hire overeducated new employees.
One former physicist, now a soft drink salesman, gratefully pledged all of his
energy towards growing the Coca-Cola worldwide business.*

Undeterred by the 1989 massacre in Tiananmen Square, Coke continued to
expand quickly, establishing joint ventures with the Chinese government as
well as Hong Kong's Swire Group and the Kerry Group, run by savvy
Chinese businessman Robert Kuok. By 1993, there were thirteen bottling
plants already in place near the more populous coast, and the Company had
received approval to build ten new facilities in the interior, capping a $500
million investment there. "The government now sees Coca-Cola as a symbol
of China's 'socialist market' economy," a Coke executive exulted.

The young revolutionaries who once faced tanks in Tiananmen Square
eagerly embraced Western culture, including Coca-Cola and disco dancing.
They wanted to make money and spend it on consumer goods. In crowded
Hong Kong, Swire built the world's tallest bottling plant, 57 stories high,
indicating its faith that when Hong Kong joined China in 1997, nothing would
deter the fizzy onslaught. Despite persistent rumors that the soft drink was
laced with addictive drugs and caused impotence—familiar historical problems—its market grew swiftly, up 38 percent in 1993, bringing the annual
Chinese per capita consumption to two Company drinks a year, and offering
an enticing vision of potential future growth in a country with a billion people.

After a 16-year enforced absence because it refused to divulge its formula to
Indian officials in 1977, Coca-Cola returned to India in late 1993, forming a
strategic alliance with Parle Exports, the nation's largest soft drink company,
and moving quickly to upgrade existing plants. Goizueta salivated over a
virtually untapped market of 840 million people. As in China, the Company
paid new entrepreneurs to wheel tricycle Coke carts down alleyways to bring
the bubbly drink to new customers. "I used to drink Coke 20 years ago," one
50-year-old Indian spectator recalled as he hugged a Coke official during the
opening ceremonies for the first Coke bottling plant in India. "I will drink it
again."

"Just as nature abhors a vacuum," observed one Coke executive in 1992, "so
the Coca-Cola system abhors an untapped opportunity." Coke returned to any
country where conditions looked a bit more stable. When the war in
Afghanistan eased, the soft drink came back. When the repressive Marxist
regime in Ethiopia was overthrown, Coca-Cola men turned up in Addis Ababa
to do business with the victorious rebels, as they did with the old government.
Soon afterwards, the soft drink was available in the newly created splinter
nation of Eritrea. After a hiatus caused by civil wars, Coke reappeared in

---

* There were a few glitches as Coke flooded the former Soviet Union. In Tbilisi, Georgia,
Eduard Shevardnaze celebrated the opening of a new Coke plan by taking a big sip and
declaring, "It's just like Pepsi-Cola!"

Angola and Sudan. As the U.S. trade embargo on Vietnam looked like it might be lifted, Coke formed a joint venture with a Saigon bottler, ready to jump back in.

Although the Arab boycott officially had ended, bottling rights in Saudi Arabia bogged down in a bitter inter-familial lawsuit, and re-entry into the market there was temporarily delayed, just as Saddam Hussein invaded Kuwait and Operation Desert Storm commenced. Frustrated by Pepsi's Saudi Arabian inside track, Coke dispatched refrigerated semi-trailers across the desert from Al-Ain in the United Arab Emirates with 20,000 cases of free drinks, accompanied by a military escort. Coke hired photographers to snap candid pictures of soldiers enjoying the all-American drink as well as sponsoring USO programs. Unfortunately, Stormin' Norman Schwarzkopf signed the cease-fire with a Diet Pepsi can prominently on display—but Coke countered by sponsoring Schwarzkopf's homecoming celebration in Tampa Stadium.[*]

Meanwhile, with falling trade barriers and government deregulation to permit higher prices and larger package sizes, Latin America opened wide for more Coke. In 1993, the average Mexican drank 306 servings of a Coca-Cola Company soft drink—three more per year than Americans. The same year, Chile's consumption rate climbed 16 percent. As the Sandinista regime ended in Nicaragua, Coke moved in again. In Guatemala, there was relative peace at the troubled bottling plant whose union employees had been killed by death squads a decade before, though several Coca-Cola union workers involved in political theater were threatened, beaten and murdered.

In South Africa, in February 1990, Nelson Mandela, 71, was finally released from his 27-year incarceration, emerging a heroic symbol of freedom and justice. While on his triumphant 1990 American tour, Mandela snubbed Coke's offers of help, raising the hopes of Tandi Gcabashe and her boycott. "They [Coke representatives] are not the kind of people we do business with," an African National Congress member said. "They are making money off us. Apartheid is good business for Coke." Still, South African black activist Desmond Tutu and Coretta Scott King, widow of the slain civil rights leader, praised Coke, but to no avail. The soft drink was banned from hotels at which Mandela stayed, and he pointedly drank Pepsi during his Atlanta visit.

Soon, however, Carl Ware, Coke's persuasive black executive, befriended Mandela, who pressured the African National Congress to call off the boycott. Behind the scenes, Coca-Cola worked feverishly to help ease what they perceived to be the inevitable end of apartheid.[†] Ware assured Mandela of the

---

[*] Pepsico CEO D. Wayne Calloway told a gathering that he'd had a wonderful dream in which Schwarzkopf held a bag of Doritos in one hand and a Diet Pepsi in another. Then Saddam Hussein strolled into the dream drinking a Coca-Cola.

[†] One of Nelson Mandela's oldest friends and supporters was Richard Maponya, an elder statesman of the anti-apartheid movement, and one of the wealthiest black men in South Africa. Maponya owned a Coca-Cola bottling plant as well as the Soweto BMW dealership, a chain of supermarkets, gas stations, liquor stores, and a bus company. Undoubtedly, Maponya helped persuade Mandela to befriend Coca-Cola. "I think Nelson [Mandela] is coming to see that what is holding us back now is not apartheid but money," Maponya observed in 1990.

Company's support in a new black-run regime. When Mandela again arrived in Atlanta three years later, in July 1993, he stepped off of a Coca-Cola corporate jet along with Carl Ware, and Coke squired Mandela about the city and hosted a luncheon for him at the Ritz-Carlton. When Mandela received an honorary degree from Clark Atlanta University, Carl Ware—the head of the college's board of trustees—gave a raised fist salute as the choir sang, "Lord Bless Africa." At a fund-raising dinner, Mandela explicitly acknowledged his debt to the Coke executive: "Mr Carl Ware has shown a quiet commitment to the problems that bear on our country," he said. "He has quietly helped the ANC stand on its feet. I want to acknowledge publicly that he has done this."

Despite the global recession of the early 1990s, the soft drink giant grew inexorably around the globe. There were always trouble spots somewhere, of course—Japan and Europe had cold, rainy summers in 1993—but all the factors for continued expansion were in place. It had taken over a hundred years for the Company to make $1 billion in annual net income in 1988, but it took only another five years to break $2 billion a year in 1993.

In 1990, after its shares gained 20 percent (while the S&P 500 declined 7 percent), Coke stock split two-for-one, then jumped an astonishing 73 percent in 1991, allowing *another* stock split early in 1992. For the banner year of 1991, Roberto Goizueta was awarded over $86 million in compensation, much of it quietly buried in a proxy statement in the form of a one-time bonus of one million shares of Coke stock. With excessive salaries of American CEOs under attack during the recession, Goizueta's reward made front-page national headlines, but admirers retorted that he had earned it—if the stock had not gone up, he wouldn't get so much money.

As the recession deepened, however, Coke shares languished for the next two years, even though the soft drink company's steady global growth continued. True, it slowed to a total case volume rise of only three percent in 1992, but in 1993 it climbed five percent. The thin-skinned Goizueta grew increasingly irritated, eager to convince skeptics that Coca-Cola's fundamentals were sound and that the stock should resume its extraordinary growth.

TROUBLE ON THE HOME FRONT

Although Coke's world-wide momentum appeared unstoppable, the flagship U.S. market was flashing warning lights—one of the primary reasons for Wall Street's nervousness. Seeking to capitalize on Coke Classic's historic image, in 1990 the Company opened a glitzy $15 million museum in downtown Atlanta, followed by a store to sell products emblazoned with the Coke logo on New York's Fifth Avenue. A gigantic new spectacular in Times Square, lit just before midnight on New Year's Eve, December 31, 1991, featured a 42-foot Coke bottle which, aided by 60 miles of fiber-optic tubing, a mile of neon, and 13,000 incandescent light bulbs, uncapped itself, offered a straw to a huge invisible mouth—perhaps God's?—and emptied itself in each cycle.

Despite such hoopla over the core brand, however, in 1991 and 1992 the Company's domestic case volume sales grew barely two percent. Refusing to admit defeat, Goizueta repositioned the moribund New Coke—its unfortunate nickname aging quickly—as Coke II. Atlanta consumers suggested tongue-in-cheek slogans such as: "Coke II: The Embarrassment Continues." The renamed drink again failed to garner significant sales. A Coke "MagiCan" promotion garnered piles of negative publicity when, instead of cash popping out of "prize" cans, a foul-smelling and tasting liquid—sealed into the bottom to add weight—leaked out and hit some consumer tongues. The $100,000 promotion was scrapped.

On top of such temporary glitches, beverage analysts feared that the market for old-fashioned colas may have reached saturation point. After more than a century of deluging North America with Coke and Pepsi ads, could the marketers hope to squeeze out any more substantial gains? The diet segment, which had grown at 20 percent annual rates during the 1980s, had now slowed to three percent yearly growth, as consumers switched from obsession with weight to health. Upstart "New Age" drinks such as Snapple and Clearly Canadian were stealing market share. Some experts felt that a decade of Coke/Pepsi domestic price wars may have eroded brand loyalty, turning the drinks from image-rich elixirs into mere commodities bought on sale. Roberto Goizueta sniffed at such suggestions, pointing out that Mello Yello—Coke's minor-league response to Pepsi's popular Mountain Dew—sold more than Snapple.

Meanwhile, private-label colas, spurred by aggressive Dave Nichol, the CEO of Canada's Cott, were making inroads into brand-name sales.[*] Cott's high-quality private-label beverage sold as President's Choice Cola in Canada and as Sam's American Choice in U.S. Wal-Marts. In Great Britain, Cott supplied supermarket giant Sainsbury's cola, as well as entrepreneur Richard Branson's upstart Virgin Cola. "Coke and Pepsi are passé," Nichol boasted. "Cott," Goizueta snarled in response. "We sell more Coke in Nigeria than they sell worldwide." In blind taste-tests, *Consumer Reports* noted in an August 1991 cover story, private colas were indistinguishable from Coke or Pepsi. In a funny, nasty commercial, RC Cola depicted Coke and Pepsi men baiting fish-hooks with their respective soda cans, then pulling humans from the ocean, a can bulging their cheeks. "For years you've been fed the same old line—that there are only two great-tasting colas to choose from," intoned the narrator. "Hey, you don't have to swallow that."

COKE CALLING HOLLYWOOD

But the real problem, as Roberto Goizueta saw it, was his main brand's lackluster advertising. The Interpublic Group, which included McCann-Erickson, Lintas, and others, had produced all Coke product ads for decades. Since the 1985 New Coke debacle, however, the ads had lost fizz and focus. In

---

[*] Simultaneously, old-fashioned but quirky non-cola soft drinks such as Barq's Root Beer and Dr Pepper suddenly took off.

the fall of 1990, Goizueta complained that "Can't Beat the Real Thing" wasn't working. A Coke marketing executive noted that Pepsi's spots were "hipper" than Coke's. "Then go to a hipper source," Goizueta snapped.

Soon afterwards, Ike Herbert, Coke's veteran head of marketing, called Peter Sealey, who had fallen in love with Hollywood and the relaxed California lifestyle when he oversaw Columbia Pictures. Sealey had left Coke in 1989, staying in California when the Company sold Columbia to Sony. "I had a beautiful place on the ocean, a hot tub, Chardonnay. I was blissing out," Sealey recalled later. "I totally believed I would never return to Coke." But now Coke wanted him back, along with his Hollywood connections. Sealey agreed, though he had to move back to Atlanta and shave his beard because of Goizueta's Castro phobia.

Sealey took over as Coke's first director of global marketing just as Coke stumbled again. During the Superbowl in January 1991, Coke pulled its planned advertising to run a serious rolling text, explaining that frivolous ads were inappropriate because the Gulf War had just begun. Football fans were simply annoyed. One critic called the Coke ads "cheap, phony, patronizing and holier-than-thou." Meanwhile, Diet Pepsi introduced Ray Charles singing, "You've got the right one, baby, uh-huh," surrounded by a chorus of slinky young black women. The Pepsi spots were enormously popular—a particularly bitter blow, since Georgia-born Ray Charles had once sung for Coke. Even Bill Cosby, Coke's former pitchman, included the slogan in a gag on his TV show. People in offices and schools across the country began to say "Uh-huh"—except in the corporate halls of Coca-Cola, where the expression was forbidden.

Pepsi gleefully mocked Coca-Cola's stodgy image. In one ad, after taking a sip of Coke, rap singer M. C. Hammer burst into a smarmy rendition of "Feelings." In another spot, when Pepsi accidentally arrived at a nursing home, the elderly imbibers boogied about and said "Awesome," while frat house boys who received Coke played a sedate game of bingo.

In this tense atmosphere, something had to give. Don Keough, who would retire in two years, didn't want his departing legacy to be a lame campaign. In the summer of 1991, he flew to Manhattan to plead with McCann-Erickson executives to come up with something spectacular. "If you don't pull this off, folks, you are staring at a loss of the business," he told them. In the meantime, Peter Sealey was talking to superagent Mike Ovitz, the founder of Creative Artists Agency (CAA), who was eager to do a deal with Coke. In the fall of 1991, Ovitz flew to Atlanta to make his pitch to Goizueta. "Here we've got the greatest star in the world, Coca-Cola," Ovitz told the CEO. "It's instantly recognizable, the most bankable star in the world." Ovitz proposed that CAA use Hollywood actors, directors, and writers to create innovative Coke commercials.

The Coke executives weren't yet willing to go quite that far. Instead, they wanted CAA to work with McCann to create a sure-fire new theme for Coca-Cola. The news of the Coke/CAA partnership terrified the ad industry late in 1991, though no one knew exactly what CAA would do for Coke. Ovitz babbled about bringing "macrovision" to the task, while Peter Sealey said that CAA's job was "to be in tune with culture. They know what is going to pop a year from now."

With the CAA threat looming, the soft drink ad blitz continued. In a frantic effort to counter the Diet Pepsi "Uh huh" campaign, Interpublic's Lintas agency went one step further in the celebrity ad wars by exhuming Humphrey Bogart, James Cagney and Louis Armstrong to appear in diet Coke commercials. Not only were the dead stars colorized, but they interacted with live actors, while Elton John sang a twist on the long-standing "Just For the Taste of It" theme. Ad critic Bob Garfield was not impressed. "Coca-Cola is obsessed with Pepsi-Cola's youthful image in the U.S., and has been trying desperately, pathetically to approximate it," he wrote. "It speaks to Coca-Cola's notion of the pop-culture vanguard that its lead presenter, in order to seem contemporary, must be surrounded by dead people."

When the Super Bowl rolled around in January 1992, Coke shocked the ad world by opting out of the $1.7 million-per-minute commercials. Instead, Peter Sealey orchestrated "Hellos," the first truly global ad for Coca-Cola, in which McCann-Erickson demonstrated its worldwide capacity. Airing on the same day as the Super Bowl, happy Coke drinkers greeted viewers in twelve languages. The ad, which ran at 6 A.M. Eastern Standard Time on CNN, appeared simultaneously in some 130 countries to kick off the Company's 1992 Olympic coverage.

Meanwhile, Pepsi's much-hyped Super Bowl ads were an inexplicable departure from the venerable "Choice of a New Generation" theme, switching to a blander "Gotta Have It" slogan that was intended to appeal to *all* generations. Instead, as the ever-acerbic Bob Garfield noted, "out of nowhere, Pepsi has decided to be like Coke: to embrace everybody, to be all colas to all people." He objected to the new slogan's "licentious overtones," concluding that "it's the wrong message, to the wrong audience, at the wrong time."

With the traditional feel-good global campaign under way, it appeared that McCann may have found its footing again, at least internationally. But behind the scenes, the infighting continued. From the beginning, the enforced relationship between McCann and CAA was plagued by "suspicion, jealousy, resentment, and one-upsmanship," as Goizueta biographer David Greising observed. McCann had recently recruited Gordon Bowen from Ogilvy & Mather to save the domestic Coke account. But when Bowen suggested "A Spark of Life" as the new theme, Shelly Hochron of CAA blasted him. "That is the worst advertising idea I've ever heard of," she said, and Peter Sealey agreed with her.

Things only got worse for Bowen at a crucial July 1992 presentation in Atlanta. The CAA storyboards weren't particularly impressive, featuring a dog digging up a Coke bottle. Gordon Bowen stuck to his "Spark of Life." But veteran McCann ad man John Bergin, an old friend of Keough's, stole the show with a presentation that took Bowen completely by surprise. They were all missing the essence, the majesty of Coca-Cola, Bergin said. "Let the brand be itself." In his talk, he built up to the lyrics of a song he had written: "Always there, Always new, Always real, Always you—Always Coca-Cola." In secret, Bergin had even created a "steal-a-matic," working over an old McDonald's commercial showing a Taiwanese little league team visiting the United States, which he now showed. Bergin staged a coup. Peter Sealey ordered both CAA and McCann to create their own ads, using the "Always" theme.

On October 15, 1992, both teams came to Atlanta for the final shoot-out. This time, Roberto Goizueta would join Don Keough to view sample ads. It was clear from the outset that CAA would win. Peter Sealey had flown to California in order to escort the CAA team back to Atlanta. Ovitz tantalized Goizueta by promising that famous directors like Francis Ford Coppola and Rob Reiner would create Coke spots. Then they rolled the sample CAA spots. As John Bergin watched, he was dismayed by their uneven quality and scatter-shot approach. There was the dog digging up the Coke bottle. In another one, space men identified an alien by asking him trivia questions about Coke. The only appealing ad, Bergin thought, was one in which computer-animated polar bears admired the northern lights and drank Coke.

Bergin was even more dismayed by the reaction of the Coca-Cola executives. Already programmed to like the CAA efforts, they roared with laughter, nudged one another appreciatively, and acted "absolutely giddy," as another McCann man recalled later. Don Keough bounced happily to the lilting "Always Coca-Cola" tagline sung at the end of each spot. Bergin scribbled a note and passed it to a colleague: "We are dead." CAA had co-opted Bergin's two-word theme, but there was nothing left of his lyrics or core Coke concepts. When the new Coke ads debuted in February 1993, McCann made only two, while CAA produced 24 in what Peter Sealey dubbed a "new paradigm" approach to advertising.

The ads signalled the end of the traditional "one sight, one sound, one sell" approach. Instead, each of the disparate spots was supposed to represent a "rifle-shot" directed at one particular market segment. To some critics, they simply appeared uncoordinated. At least, however, they represented new energy and change. Though he called the two dozen commercials "flawed," critic Bob Garfield was basically impressed, calling them "the best Coca-Cola advertising campaign in at least a decade." He loved the polar bears watching the aurora borealis, calling the spots "sweet, unexpected, visually arresting and very nearly majestic." The other efforts were all over the place, but they were at least united by the brilliant new "Always Coca-Cola" theme, along with the red Coca-Cola disk, resurrected from the 1950s.

Most members of the traditional advertising community were under-whelmed by the CAA efforts. "Coke is willing to try anything in its effort to stumble across what made it great," sniffed one ad man. The much-vaunted commercials made by famous movie directors weren't particularly impressive. Indeed, Francis Ford Coppola's was scrapped. "Directing commercials is a whole different world than directing movies," one veteran ad man noted. "You have to think a lot faster on your feet and improvise a lot more." Another advertising executive called the CAA efforts "a creative gang bang with no strategic centrality and not enough gate-keeping to keep the good stuff away from the bad stuff."

Peter Sealey didn't care what the critics said. He was ebullient, pointing out that the 24 CAA ads cost less than the seven elaborate commercials McCann made the year before. At the press launch for the commercials, he watched the audience stir and murmur, not sure what to think until the polar bear ad came on. "From then on," he recalls, "it was a love fest. This was an audience on a ride." It appeared that Sealey's California psycho-babble would work in Atlanta. "God, you're ringing all the emotional bells there," he burbled about a new ad. "You're talking social facilitation, self-actualization." Sealey glowed. "This has been one of the more rewarding experiences of my career," he said. Years later, he observed, "I have never been more happy in my life than I was in early 1993." Just as he seemed to be on top of the Coca-Cola world, however, Sealey was about to be dethroned.

THE RETURN OF THE AYA-COLA

Although he didn't know it, Sealey's fate was sealed the day Don Keough retired in April 1993. Keough, whom one long-time admirer described as "the heart and soul and probably most of the vascular system of Coca-Cola," would be sorely missed. A master communicator and motivator, Keough could fire up the bottlers, wax poetic about his favorite soft drink, or turn tough task-master when needed. Instead of replacing him, CEO Roberto Goizueta allowed people to speculate whether Doug Ivester or John Hunter would eventually succeed him. Ivester, who had shone in his brief stint in Europe, came back to head the North American Coca-Cola business in July 1990, while gruff Australian John Hunter was made head of international operations.

Most insiders bet on the aggressive Ivester, who, at 44, was ten years younger than Hunter. In addition, Goizueta clearly favored him, regarding him as a kind of junior version of himself. Both men were detail-oriented, demanding of themselves and others, and came from the technical rather than marketing side of the business. In order to complete his grooming for the top Coke position, for more than a year Ivester met on Saturday mornings with Sergio Zyman—the *enfant terrible* widely perceived as the "fall guy" for New Coke—for lessons in marketing theory. During these sessions, Zyman took the opportunity to criticize Sealey's advertising and marketing programs. Im-pressed with his tutor's acumen, Ivester briefly tried to get Zyman and Bowen to come up with alternative advertising to CAA.

Now that Ivester was the *de facto* number two man in the Company, he convinced Goizueta that Sealey was too slow and cautious. Worse, Sealey had failed to rejuvenate diet Coke advertising or sales. Abandoning the back-from-the-dead colorized-celebrity approach and the ten-year-old "Just For the Taste of It," in January 1993 he had approved a new slogan, "Taste It All," with frenetic life-style spots featuring active consumers of all ages. The ads misfired, in part because the product wasn't emphasized enough. "I saw diet Coke on the screen for maybe one second," a bottler groused. At the end of May, Coke cut diet Coke's ad budget to the bone, then announced in mid-July that the campaign would be modified or scrapped.

A week later, Doug Ivester marched into Sealey's office at 3 P.M. and told him, "This just isn't working out." Afterward, Coke's personnel director told a stunned Sealey, "You're going to be radioactive now. You'd better leave quickly." Sealey cleaned out his desk. In public, however, Ivester praised Sealey for "taking our advertising to a new level of excellence." The next business day, Sergio Zyman arrived to take his place. Perhaps with some relief, Sealey moved back to California.

The resurrection of Sergio Zyman caused a shudder to run through Coca-Cola and Madison Avenue offices. Known as the "Aya-Cola," the mercurial, arrogant Zyman had antagonized almost everyone with whom he had worked back in the 1980s. "Why him?" one secretary asked, bursting into tears. "They used to say they needed one office for [Zyman] and one for his ego," a long-time Coke watcher said. "If you take a vote, there wouldn't be a lot of people who would like Sergio," an Atlanta ad man added. "I have no desire to work for or with Sergio Zyman ever again," a former Coke brand manager stated bluntly. "Sergio was very much a 'for me' or 'against me' sort of leader. There was no middle ground. He was not subject to logic or numbers or reason." Goizueta defended his new marketing guru, explaining that time had mellowed him. He apparently hadn't changed all that much, however, since Ivester and Goizueta later passed out T-shirts proclaiming "GUTS—Get Used to Sergio." One woman forced to work closely with Zyman couldn't do it, though, and quit within a few months.

COKE GOES NEW AGE

Zyman's immediate mission was to create hip products to compete with New Age challengers like Snapple and Clearly Canadian and to meet the private-label cola challenge. Until then, Coke had mounted feeble efforts to reposition Fresca and to introduce Nordic Mist, a Clearly Canadian rip-off, but neither had been given much marketing muscle. In January 1993, Roberto Goizueta called his two top lieutenants, Doug Ivester and John Hunter, into his office to announce a new initiative. Coke wouldn't just sit back and let these products nibble away at market share. Instead, he planned to introduce a flurry of new products, developed and launched in a hurry. The Company already did it in Japan, where new products were continually surfacing, selling, and disappearing. Why not in the United States? "I want it all," Goizueta said. "I don't want them [competitive New Age drinks] to have even these niche products." Nor did it matter, the CEO said, whether they all survived. He envisioned "new products going in, making money, and then you take them out."

It was easy to see why Goizueta was alarmed. In 1984, colas had accounted for nearly 64 percent of the U.S. non-alcoholic beverage market. By 1993, colas slipped below 59 percent, while alternative drinks had grabbed 10 percent of the market. Even before Sealey's ouster, Goizueta hired Sergio Zyman to spearhead the swift creation of Tab Clear, Coke's answer to Crystal Pepsi, a colorless cola intended to appeal to the New Age crowd.* While Zyman created the ad campaign in England, Sealey remained unconcerned. "I thought it was a stupid product," he recalled later. "I wanted no responsibility for it." The introductory commercial, cast as a *faux* news program using a real CNN anchor, brought a flood of complaints from viewers who felt it was deceptive. Neither Tab Clear nor Crystal Pepsi dented the market, and they were withdrawn a year later.†

Goizueta and Ivester didn't care. They wanted brash new products, they wanted them quickly, and they agreed on the man who could deliver them—Sergio Zyman. When he took over as global marketing director in July 1993, Zyman arrived like a whirlwind. Goizueta also gave Zyman a bigger ad budget to boost Coca-Cola Classic, diet Coke, and its other brands. He was determined to squash the upstart private-label colas in the wake of April 2, 1993, the day Philip Morris had slashed its cigarette prices to halt inroads from generic cigarettes. That day, which came to be known as "Marlboro Friday," supposedly signalled the deathknell of brand-name dominance, according to many doomsayers. Goizueta protested angrily when Coke stock took a hit, complaining of "irrational market behavior" and claiming, "We are getting a bum rap."

Goizueta was even more incensed in January 1994, when *Barron's* quoted mutual fund guru John Neff's negative comments on Coke. Neff advised shorting the Company's stock. He called it "the Philip Morris of this year," and observed that Coke managers "tout their stock almost outrageously." Goizueta was incredibly frustrated. Despite a healthy 5 percent worldwide case volume growth in 1993, Coke stock had advanced only $4.50 per share in the last two years, not even breaking $45 as 1994 arrived. Goizueta gave orders on all fronts to move aggressively to increase market share in every conceivable way.

Sergio Zyman immediately initiated work on two new drinks, to be called Fruitopia and OK Soda, and stepped up promotions for the newly introduced PowerAde, Coke's counter to Gatorade, the dominant isotonic beverage. In March 1994, Zyman launched non-carbonated Fruitopia in eight fruit flavors with self-consciously hip, New Age names—Citrus Consciousness, Grape

---

* While Pepsi could introduce a clear version of its flagship cola without any flack, Coca-Cola knew better than to mess around with a colorless Coke, which would have caused an uproar. Hence, Goizueta opted for Tab Clear, altering the lowly old diet drink.

† Sergio Zyman would claim later that Tab Clear was never intended to succeed, but to "kill the whole clear cola category by muddying it up" and recasting it as a diet segment. Such a revisionist rationale is quite unlikely. Zyman also boasted that New Coke was a great success because of the way it turned out—true enough, but completely unforeseen by Zyman at the time.

Beyond, Cranberry Lemonade Vision, Lemonade Love & Hope, Pink Lemonade Euphoria, Raspberry Psychic Lemonade, Strawberry Passion Awareness,
and—perhaps labeling the reaction of many consumers who thought the
names were overly cute—Total Fruit Integration. The bottles were covered
with psychedelic, funky icons depicting body, mind, and planet, and offered
aphorisms suitable for Fruitopian Life, such as "If you can't judge a fruit by
the color of its skin, how can you judge a person that way?" Coca-Cola
announced that Fruitopia would go national immediately, supported by a $30
million marketing budget, with plans to go international soon afterwards.
Zyman boasted that it was "the first truly global launching of an alternative
product."

The quick launch of Fruitopia, without local test marketing, startled
beverage veterans, but Zyman claimed that he had invented *Presearch*, "the
study of assumptions and hypotheses developed from current worldwide
market information." He was only following the dictates and desires of the
marketplace. Consumers, he said, were the real directors of marketing. And
what did they order? "We found that consumers want the yin of the new
mixed with the yang of the traditional," Zyman explained. Some commentators were not impressed with the Fruitopia strategy, which one called "mind-
bogglingly cheesy," asking "What's the next Fruitopia flavor going to be,
Coke? Putrid Peach Paranoia?" There was a chance, he granted, that the
Company would succeed. "They've got the ad bucks, the distribution, and
probably the same view of 'consumer democracy' as that held by many a
prominent politician—that is that the American public is capable of buying
anything if you ram it down their throats hard enough."

Though Zyman asserted that Fruitopia would compete with "all alternative
beverages," it was clearly positioned to counter Snapple. Even its widemouth
embossed glass bottles imitated Snapple. Aside from its ultra-hip retro-sixties
image, however, the Fruitopia line seemed an odd choice. Snapple's biggest
sellers were teas, and Fruitopia didn't offer any tea products. Those were left
to a newly formed partnership Coke had formed with Nestlé, established in
Tampa, Florida. In addition Fruitopia's shelf-stable flavors had to be "hot-
filled," which meant expensive bottler line alterations. "Bottlers hate this
stuff," observed one industry analyst. Zyman merely shrugged. "We will be
launching more and more new brands," he said. "We're going to hit home
runs, then we're also going to have to hit some profitable singles and even
endure some sacrifice bunts."

The month after Fruitopia's debut, Coke introduced another new product.
While "Coca-Cola" was the second best-known word on earth, "OK" was the
first, so Zyman wanted to co-opt it, too. A typically edgy Zyman enterprise,
OK Soda was a brash effort, utterly uncharacteristic of anything The Coca-
Cola Company had ever done. Intended to appeal to disaffected Generation
Xers, the cynical, disenfranchised 12-to-25-year-old MTV crowd, OK Soda's
can was the antithesis of Coca-Cola's bright, up-beat image. Instead, the cans
featured the black-grey-and-white, bleak post-modern face of a young man
who looked utterly blank, with a square saying "OK" slapped part-way over

his forehead. The can had no discernible front or back. "There is no point to OK," one observer noted. The odd flavor didn't seem to have much point, either. Mildly carbonated, it was similar to the old "suicide" drink, a mixture of every flavor available at the soda fountain, with a touch of spicy orange. Zyman predicted that OK Soda would be one of his home runs, eventually snaring $1 billion dollars of the market and grabbing 4 percent of the entire U.S. soft drink share.

That seemed an odd prediction for a drink whose bland motto was "Things are going to be OK." The drink was deliberately positioned to be blasé. It wasn't exciting, delicious, or sexy. It was just OK. Nonetheless, beverage analyst Tom Pirko thought it might succeed by appealing directly to seen-it-all teenagers. National Public Radio host Noah Adams was skeptical. "Wouldn't you, if you were 19 years old, . . . feel a bit manipulated that they were coming after you so blatantly?" No. The only problem, Pirko observed, might be that "they're already sort of already truly wasted. I mean, their lethargy probably can't be penetrated by any commercial message." Thus, even though OK was designed to appeal to "their concerns and their angst and their anxiety," it might not be enough.

Teenagers weren't quite as disaffected or stupid as Sergio Zyman and Tom Pirko thought. "The better you understand something, the more OK it turns out to be," one can proclaimed. Teenagers surveyed by the Atlanta newspaper simply found it confusing. None of the teens liked the taste. The most positive comment one could summon was: "It's better than water." They didn't like the name, either, which made it sound as if the soda weren't worth drinking. Consumers were supposed to call 1–800-I-FEEL-OK to report "coinci-dences" of OKness. Though millions of kids did call, just to see what happened, the calls didn't substantially increase sales. A little more than a year later, OK Soda was quietly pulled from the market.

Supported by a massive ad campaign, Fruitopia did somewhat better than OK Soda, but even with new flavors—Tangerine Wavelength, Apple Raspberry Embrace, and Tropical Consideration—it never really contributed to Coke's bottom line. When Coke decided to imitate Ken Kesey and send psychedelically painted "Magic Buses" across the country to promote Fruitopia, a 20-year-old sniffed. "It's sort of like they were really looking too hard for something to sell us," she said. "Them pitching it as an out-of-body, out-of-mind experience seems kind of trite to me." The Coke–Nestlé partnership never worked, either. In 1994, the two companies closed the corporate office in Tampa but agreed to continue joint beverage ventures.

BOOSTING THE CORE BRANDS

While Sergio Zyman was chasing New Age chimeras, he also tried to recharge the Company's major brands—Coca-Cola, diet Coke, and Sprite. Here, his efforts were apparently more successful. Zyman continued to use CAA as the creator of many ads, including "Hypnosis," which played on the old fears of subliminal messages, with the announcer intoning: "You are getting thirsty, very thirsty . . . Disregard all other soft drink advertising and drink only Coca-Cola." Others featured the popular polar bears flying off a ski jump and sliding bare-backed down a luge run, to promote Coke's sponsorship of the 1994 Lillehammer Winter Olympics.* Critic Bob Garfield, usually a hard sell, loved the new ads, hailing them as the best Coke advertising in decades. Since most of them had been under development when Sealey left, however, Zyman couldn't legitimately take much credit.

In fact, Zyman had considered dumping CAA entirely, but Mike Ovitz intervened with Goizueta, who loved the polar bears. Nonetheless, Zyman began to farm out work to other boutique agencies such as Fallon McElligot, Weiden & Kennedy, and Bartle Bogle Hegarty. Eventually, he would hire some 25 different agencies to do ads for various company beverages. Zyman, who clearly enjoyed the exercise of power, played one agency off against another. He also hired his own marketing people—most of them without soft drink experience—and placed them around the world, reporting directly to him. "It's very exciting to have all these creative agencies around," one anonymous ad man observed, "but holding them to the same brand values can prove almost impossible." Another critic called the Coke approach "profoundly flawed."

Flawed it may have been, but 1994 produced positive results for Coca-Cola Classic, whose sales drove an impressive 7 percent annual increase in case unit volume in the United States. The increased sales probably had less to do with advertising than with the return of the "contour" bottle in a plastic container with a fatter waist than the old hobbleskirt bottle. Chemist, engineer, and marketer Ray Morgan, who had joined Coke in 1969 right out of college, had already proven that proprietary packaging could make a huge difference—first with Fresca, then with the dimpled green Sprite bottle. In 1990, when Doug Ivester took over the North American sector, Morgan pitched him with the idea of a 20-ounce contour bottle for Coca-Cola Classic. Ivester enthusiastically approved the project. In March 1994, when the bottles hit Chicago test markets, they outperformed anyone's wildest expectations, boosting sales by 224 percent in a matter of weeks. By the end of the year, the contour bottle was available across three-quarters of the United States, and it went international the following year. Even though Zyman had little to do with the contour bottle, he called it "the best-known package in the world, with the possible exception of the egg."

Zyman could, however, take more credit for the resurgence of Sprite, which had traditionally been sold for its intrinsic qualities as a bubbly lemon-lime drink like 7-Up. Zyman repositioned Sprite as a youth drink with an attitude. While his "anti-hype" approach had flopped with OK Soda, it worked for

---

* At the end of 1994, tiny Polar Corporation aired an ad in which its mascot polar bear tossed a can of Coke in a trash bin next to a sign saying "Keep the Arctic Pure," then drank a Polar Seltzer. Even though the Worcester, Massachusetts, soda firm had used a polar bear as its trademark for over 70 years, Coca-Cola sued, and a judge ordered the humorous ad yanked.

Sprite. "Image Is Nothing," ads proclaimed. "Thirst Is Everything. Obey Your Thirst." Funky ads showed camels sipping Sprite, and the Company linked the drink to its National Basketball Association sponsorship.

Diet Coke remained a problem child, however. Zyman dumped Lintas, the old agency, in favor of Lowe & Partners, which debuted new ads in 1994 with the bland slogan, "This Is Refreshment." Most of the new diet Coke spots were aimed at "liberated" women, some of whom simply seemed angry and self-absorbed. In one ad, a young women threw all of her boyfriend's belongings at him, including his cowboy hat, which she stomped on. Then she swigged her diet Coke. In another spot, the camera panned over a trail of shed clothing, down to the underwear, but instead of leading to a bedroom scene, it ended with a woman enjoying a solitary hot bath with her diet Coke. While the spots had plenty of attitude, they apparently didn't sell many soft drinks.

The only successful ad relied on good old-fashioned sexism, although of the reverse variety. Women office workers gathered at the window to ogle a sweaty construction worker, a hunk who stripped off his shirt, downed his diet Coke and smiled at them, as Etta James sang, "I Just Wanna Make Love to You." "They drink in his every ripple," one critic wrote. "When it's over, you almost feel the need for a cigarette ad." The hunk, 33-year-old model Lucky Vanous, quickly became a celebrity, appearing in *People* magazine, doing the talk circuit, and appearing on TV shows. A Lucky Vanous calendar and workout video appeared. Taking advantage of their newly created star, Coke sponsored a radio contest in which 30 women won a lunch with Lucky Vanous by writing the best "Diet Coke fantasy." When he showed up in Atlanta to lunch with the two winners there, Vanous attracted a crowd of 300 drooling women. Even more converged on him at the New York City lunch. "I mean, look at that!" one woman swooned. "With a body like that, a hunk like that . . . He's making me hot." Apparently a guileless if not terribly brainy man, Vanous told an interviewer that he didn't indulge in soft drinks. "But if I were to drink one," he added, "I'd drink a diet Coke."

Despite the hunk phenomenon and other innovative commercials (in one spot, a swimming elephant stole the soft drink from a raft, paying for it with a few peanuts), diet Coke sales stagnated, along with the rest of the diet drink segment. The baby boomers were no longer quite so obsessed with their weight, it appeared. During the 1980s, diet Coke had surged to claim a 10 percent share of the total U.S. soft drink market, but now it slipped to 9.7 percent. "Eventually, any category—no matter how hot—will hit its peak," a bottler observed philosophically. Had that happened to diet drinks? He hoped not, but he doubted any advertising would help much.

IVESTER THE WOLF

In July 1994, Roberto Goizueta finally recommended Doug Ivester to the board as president and chief operating officer, officially anointing him as his heir apparent. Outwardly, the round-faced Ivester, 47, appeared to be a quiet, almost introverted accountant. Unlike the aristocratic Cuban-born Goizueta, Ivester was a Georgia boy. A textile factory mechanic's son, Ivester was raised in New Holland, Georgia as a good, hard-working Southern Baptist. If he got an A, his father commented, "They give A-pluses, don't they?" Ivester worked as a Kroger bag boy to pay his way through the University of Georgia. After auditing Coke's books for an accounting firm, Ivester joined the Company in 1979. He still enjoyed eating collard greens at Mary Mac's restaurant, near the Coca-Cola tower. Inside the Company, he was known as a reclusive workaholic. Like Robert Woodruff, he was childless, and some felt that he treated Coca-Cola as his love-child. "His hobby is work," observed one acquaintance. After a celebratory dinner with Ivester and the board, Goizueta called him at home at 9 P.M. and got his answering machine. Ivester had gone back to work until 11 P.M.

But Ivester soon proved that he was not such a nerdy introvert. Indeed, his quiet manner hid a fierce competitive spirit, a driving ambition, and a demanding aggression. On October 25, 1994, Ivester gave his first speech to "InterBev94" in Atlanta, where the beverage industry held its annual convention that year. As Ivester took the stage, the lights dimmed and the baaaing of sheep bleated over the loudspeakers. Videos showed sheep running in panic back and forth, intercut with commercials from Pepsi, Gatorade, and other Coke competitors. In his speech, Ivester lambasted other soft drink firms. "Sheep are only comfortable right up against each other," he said. "They are only capable of looking a few inches past their noses. When troubled, they cry loudly and back into each other." Worst of all, he observed, they panic and engage in price wars that hurt everyone.

But Ivester saved his utter contempt for the private-label soft drinks, which he called "parasites" who relied on the major brands to advertise for them. "The parasites in the soft drink world latch onto normal organisms," he said. "They have never helped build the business, never created new products or packages, and have given nothing back to the community." Their only positive attribute was that, in a Darwinian sense, they helped weed out the weaker sheep. Private-label parasites, Ivester observed, were losing ground in 1994, and he intended to make sure that trend continued, by being neither a sheep nor a parasite, but a wolf—noble, independent yet loyal, turf-oriented, and fond of mutton. "Are there any soft drink wolves?" Ivester asked rhetorically. "I hope you are looking at one now."

The new Coke president told his audience that it would be nice if he could earn their friendship, but that wasn't really his priority. "This is what I really want," he said, leaning forward. "I want your customers, I want your shelf space across the country, your share of customers' stomachs, and I want every single bit of beverage growth potential that exists out there." Ivester ended his dramatic speech with another question. "Will I act like a sheep, parasite, or a wolf? At the Coca-Cola Company, we answer it something like this." Immediately, the auditorium resonated to the eery sound of howling wolves.

In his first speech inside the Company, Ivester quoted McDonald's founder Ray Kroc. "What do you do when your competitor is drowning? Get a live hose and stick it in his mouth." He pulled a garden hose from beneath his podium. "I've got the hose. I think you know what to do with it." Goizueta observed admiringly, "Doug has the nerve of a night prowler."

True to his word, Ivester instituted a take-no-prisoners marketing blitz that did not rely solely on advertising to drive the business. Coke introduced new packaging for most of its products to complement the return of the contour bottle. Going back to its roots, the Company initiated sampling campaigns in markets worldwide, giving away drinks to get consumers hooked. It also took advantage of its high-profile sponsorships of sporting events as never before. To combat the private-label threat, Coke salesmen offered a detailed analysis of a store's profitability on each beverage and its returns on shelf-space allocation, demonstrating that Coke products added more to their bottom line. The Company concomitantly sponsored the Coca-Cola Foodservice Research Forum to prove its worth for fast food purveyors. Small, independent bottlers struggled to stay in business, while the largest ten bottlers, led by behemoth Coca-Cola Enterprises, accounted for 90 percent of U.S. soft drink sales.

Meanwhile, the New Age threat receded. Snapple sold out to Quaker Oats, which changed the drink's distribution while sales floundered. Coke pounded away at private labels with a commercial showing a man trying to photocopy a Coke. "No matter how hard they try," the announcer intoned, "it always comes out a little flat." By the end of 1994, Coca-Cola had regained its momentum and was named "Marketer of the Year" by *Brandweek* magazine. World-wide case volume grew an impressive 10 percent. Coke's stock resumed its upward march, growing 15 percent and reaching $51.50 by year's end, while the S&P 500 *declined* by two percent. In a passage in the annual report clearly directed at John Neff and other nay-sayers, Roberto Goizueta sniffed, "We will never allow ourselves to waste our time listening to those skeptics who claim we can't maintain our historical growth rates, recycling the same cynical reasoning we've heard for several decades now."

INFINITE OPPORTUNITY

The Company was on a roll and appeared unstoppable. In April 1995, Goizueta, Ivester, and Zyman felt comfortable enough to poke fun at themselves as they marked the tenth anniversary of the New Coke fiasco. Imitating television comic David Letterman's lists, Goizueta ticked off his "Top Ten Favorite Blunders" that yielded positive results, such as buying Columbia Pictures or bringing out New Coke. He could afford the levity, pointing out, "Today, we're in the best shape we have been in many decades." Sergio Zyman, widely considered the fall guy for New Coke, basked in the attention. "Anybody who thinks New Coke hurt his career hasn't seen his new house," Doug Ivester quipped.

In the first six months of 1995, Coke captured 85 percent of the growth in the U.S. soft drink business, as the stock jumped past $60. Goizueta wanted increased volume everywhere, including neglected markets in the United

States, pointing out that Southern Californians drank less Coke per capita than Hungarians. The Company pushed vending machines into nontraditional outlets such as casinos, churches, nail salons, and post offices. No longer content with mere "availability," Goizueta now talked about "pervasive penetration," a project spearheaded by Doug Ivester. On a trip to Rome, Georgia, which boasted the highest Coke per capita consumption on earth, Ivester still found plenty of places without Coke—a national park, a Ford dealership, a video store, and a karate studio. The videotaped record of the trip, "The Road to Rome," became an internal company hit.

"The ruthless push to sell Coke absolutely everywhere made Mr. Ivester a star at Coca-Cola," noted the *Wall Street Journal*, and the obsession spread throughout the Coke universe. In South Africa, trademarked taxis served chilled Cokes out of coolers, while a Dutch railroad offered cold Coca-Cola from specially designed vending machines. In Moscow, the Company opened "Coca-Cola University" to indoctrinate former communists in the pursuit of stomach share. To show their support, Bill and Hillary Clinton visited the Moscow bottling plant in May 1995, posing for photographers as they chugged Coke. In Japan's Ginza shopping district, the Company installed a 93-foot wide, 49-foot high neon sign. At U.S. theme parks, the Company installed "Coca-Cola Cool Zones," climate-controlled pavilions with cooling fog and rows of vending machines.

Coke had always tried to entice children without overtly advertising to them, but now the campaign to infiltrate schools intensified. "Based on the awareness that it's easier to establish brand preference at a younger age than it is to change consumers habits later in life," wrote a Coke spokesman in an internal 1995 newsletter, "The Coca-Cola Company is focusing upon the education market with revitalized efforts around the world." With educational funding from governments in decline, Coke recognized an opportunity to offer money in return for access to young consumers. Carlton Curtis, director of the global effort to penetrate schools, said, "This is an investment channel—investing to build brand and consumption preferences for a lifetime." In Uruguay, where 40,000 children a year trooped through the Montevideo Coke bottling plant, the Company even put out a book in Braille to explain the wonders of Coke to blind children. In the United States, Coke paid schools for the exclusive right to install vending machines and signed a licensing agreement to market back-to-school items featuring the cute Coke polar bears.

Alarmed, Vermont Senator Patrick Leahy proposed tougher nutritional requirements for federally funded school lunch programs. Coca-Cola not only lobbied against the bill in Congress but sent a mass mailing to school officials claiming that soft drinks were "USDA-approved." A spokesman for the National Soft Drink Association protested: "Students drink water during the day and water doesn't contain any nutritional value." Testifying at the committee hearing, Leahy lambasted Coke for what he called its "major misinformation campaign," complaining that company officials refused to testify before his committee. "It seems that Coca-Cola would rather work behind the scenes to try and kill my bill than confront me and the public face to face." Eventually, a much-diluted version of the bill passed, obliging the federal government to provide state agencies with "model language" to ban soft drinks in elementary schools. It had little effect, much to the relief of many school superintendents badly in need of soft drink dollars. University administrators also raked in money, as Pepsi paid $15 million for a ten-year exclusive beverage deal at Pennsylvania State, with Coke paying even more to the University of Minnesota, soon to be followed by Rutgers, Texas A&M, and others.

Around the world, Coke pumped money into newly designated "anchor bottlers"—Coca-Cola Enterprises in the United States, Australia's Coca-Cola Amatil, Mexico's FEMSA, Mexico's PANAMCO, South Africa's SABCO, and Malaysia's Fraser & Neave—that executed Coke strategy across geographical borders. They had little choice, since Big Coke owned a substantial chunk of all of them. Doug Ivester proved that he was indeed aggressive, pushing the remaining independent bottlers to carry only Coke products on their trucks. When Ivester visited Vietnam, managers there told him that they couldn't keep up with consumer demand. He immediately got on the phone, found a bottling line sitting on a ship in Singapore harbor, and diverted it to Hanoi. Ivester got the reputation for being hard-nosed but fair. "He follows up on absolutely everything," an associate observed. "He is probably the most competent beverage executive that I have ever met," added a beverage analyst.

In a September 1995 issue, *Fortune* magazine named Coke the "New Champ of Wealth Creation," according to a *market value added* formula (market value of all equity and debt minus total capital investments). "The most valuable product on this planet," the *Fortune* reporter concluded, "is sugar water, or at least a particular type of it known as Coca-Cola." To help it stay that way, the Company offered $55 million in prizes during its second "Red Hot Summer" under-the-cap promotion and another $1.5 billion in potential retail discounts. The Discovery space shuttle took a special portable soda fountain—dubbed a "fluids generic bioprocessing apparatus"—into space for "research into fountain dispensers in weightless environments," according to NASA.[*] Adding to its arsenal of drinks, Coke bought Barq's, a popular root beer with a hip, offbeat image. In a fit of hubris, Coke USA president Jack Stahl announced that the Company planned to capture 50 percent of the U.S. beverage market by the end of the year 2000—a tall order, since company products held only 42 percent at the time.

By the end of 1995, Roberto Goizueta was euphoric. Coca-Cola stock had jumped to $74.25, an annual hike of 44 percent. Worldwide unit case volume

---

[*] The dispenser, which cost Coke $750,000 to build and NASA $1.75 million to fly into space, malfunctioned. After astronauts rewired it for nearly two hours, it finally spewed foam that slowly settled down to an almost-recognizable drink. Meanwhile, Pepsi paid Russian cosmonauts to appear in a filmed-in-space Pepsi commercial.

had grown another eight percent. In the United States, per capita consumption of company beverages reached 343 drinks—nearly one a day for every man, woman, and child. In the annual report, an infinity symbol signified "our virtually *infinite* opportunity for growth," as Goizueta observed. All of this had been achieved despite economic problems in major markets such as Mexico, Japan, and Argentina. In a new Coke mantra, Goizueta observed that the human body requires at least 64 ounces of liquid every day. "Our beverages currently account for not even 2 of those ounces," he lamented. His goal, of course, was to make sure that every human being on earth drank 64 ounces of Coca-Cola—or some other company product.

With 80 percent of Coke's profits coming from sales outside the United States, Goizueta officially recognized the global nature of the business by reorganizing the Company's management structure. Previously, there had been two primary units—"North America" and "International." Now, he simply divided the world into five groups, North America being one of those partitions. "We not only *see* our business as global," he wrote, "but we *manage* it that way . . . We understand that, as a practical matter, our universe is *infinite*, and that we, ourselves, are the key variable in just how much of it we can capture."

THE COCA-COLA OLYMPICS

For Goizueta and Coca-Cola, 1996 was to be the year of ultimate triumph, as the world media descended on Atlanta for the centennial celebration of the modern Olympics. Back in 1987, an Atlanta real estate lawyer named Billy Payne had decided that his city deserved to host the summer Olympics and, although he was initially skeptical, Goizueta eventually threw his support behind the effort. He made sure that the money came from Coca-Cola USA and giant bottler Coca-Cola Enterprises rather than Big Coke itself, however, and the Company also gave money to Olympic Committees for Toronto and Melbourne. Still, Coke donated $350,000 to the Atlanta bid, far more than it gave any other city. It made its corporate jets available free of charge, hosted luncheons for the International Olympic Committee (IOC) members, and fielded hundreds of volunteers.

In 1990, when IOC head Juan Antonio Samaranch announced that Atlanta had won the 1996 Olympic bid, the Athens, Greece, officials cried foul. It seemed obvious that the event should have gone to Greece, where the games began originally and where they were re-started in 1896. "Morally, the Games belong to us," complained Greek bid organizer Spyros Metaxa. "The Olympics deserve Atlanta, the capital of Coca-Cola and of American crime," observed another bitter Greek commentator, referring to the city's high homicide rate. "In the long run, it will perhaps prove better that we did not get them."

It is quite unlikely that Coca-Cola officials overtly bribed anyone, although it is now widely acknowledged that IOC officials have accepted all manner of special favors. Peter Ueberroth, who had presided over the first corporate-sponsored Los Angeles Olympics in 1984, and who served on Coca-Cola's board of directors, candidly advised: "Remember there are ninety votes and those people are not all of the highest integrity."[*] There is no question that Coca-Cola, the largest Olympic sponsor, wielded enormous power. "The ones who decide where the Olympics shall take place," wrote one insider in the 1980s, "are big companies like Coca-Cola, ABC-TV, Adidas." Two IOC members, Kenya's Charles Mukora and France's Jean-Claude Killy, were directors of Coca-Cola companies.

In addition, Roberto Goizueta and Juan Antonio Samaranch had become personal friends since they met at the 1984 Sarajevo winter games. They shared Spanish descent, though Goizueta came from a long line of blue-blooded aristocrats, while Samaranch, the son of a textile mill owner, was designated a noble "Marques" in 1991. Apparently it did not bother Goizueta that Samaranch had served dictator Francisco Franco faithfully for many years, routinely giving him the stiff one-armed fascist salute. When Samaranch arrived in Atlanta during the bidding process, he went straight to meet Goizueta at Coke headquarters, then flew to Washington aboard the Coke jet. When Billy Payne offered Samaranch a set of mint julep glasses, he smiled and asked, "Can you drink Coca-Cola out of these?"

Regardless of how the Olympics came to Atlanta in 1996, Goizueta and his executive team were determined to milk the opportunity for all it was worth. "As a marketing property and a volume-driving opportunity, the Games in Atlanta will be like nothing this Company has ever seen," gloated an internal publication. "Really, it's a soft drink marketer's dream: During one of the hottest periods of the entire year, millions of scorched, thirsty visitors from all over the entire world will be packed into a circle 3 miles in diameter [and] the Company's products will be within an arm's reach."

Coke had already established sports as the ideal way to connect with consumers. Doug Ivester continually urged, "We need to activate our sponsorships," while Sergio Zyman, a running enthusiast, wanted to paint the Coke logo on every possible sporting event. Zyman realized that mere advertising was insufficient. Experiential event marketing to "bring the brand alive"—a concept pioneered by former ski racer Mark "Dill" Driscoll in the 1980s—could touch individual consumers most effectively.[†] Driscoll had

---

[*] In *The New Lords of the Rings*, investigative journalist Andrew Jennings wrote: "In the spring of 1990 another wave of Olympic committee freeloaders arrived [in Atlanta] and were met by a motorcade of Cadillacs. Then it was off to the seaside in a fleet of corporate jets to inspect Savannah's Olympic yachting facilities. Lest they got peckish there was caviar and mint julep, and to save on washing up, they kept their silver julep cups." Later, a German newspaper accused the Atlanta committee of offering cash bribes, free gold credit cards, free hospital care, and college scholarships for IOC members' children. Though Billy Payne stoutly denied the charges, similar allegations have proven to be true for Salt Lake City Olympic bidders.

[†] Thus, when the Super Bowl came to Atlanta in 1994, the Company had sponsored "Coca-Cola Big TV," a pre-game show that cost less than one minute of advertising during the game. There were also interactive sports exhibits there and at soccer's World Cup, also held in the United States in 1994.

already promoted an NBA tie-in for inner-city kids, featuring basketball shooting contests and wildly painted Cherry Coke vans. He repainted VW bugs to resemble basketballs, with backboards stuck onto the back and coolers full of Sprite in the front. With special springs, they bounced as they rolled along. His Coca-Cola Road Trip featured every sports tie-in imaginable—and a chance for consumers to play—for Coke Classic. Now, the Company called on Driscoll to choreograph the Olympic Torch Relay.

Although the idea of a torch relay ostensibly hearkened back to ancient Greece, it actually came from the Nazis, who invented the dramatic prelude to the Berlin Games in 1936. At the 1984 Los Angeles Olympics, AT&T sponsored an American torch run, but it made participants pony up $3,000 for the privilege. In 1996, Coke paid $12 million for the right to sponsor the torch as it crossed America on an 84-day, 15,000-mile journey during which 10,000 runners—none of whom had to pay anything—would carry the flame. Over half of the participants were "Community Heroes" chosen for their good works by local United Way agencies. Coca-Cola chose another 2,500 winners of a contest called "Share the Spirit: Who Would You Choose?" in which consumers could nominate either themselves or a friend—500 of them coming from 60 foreign countries. The remainder of the slots were reserved for former Olympic athletes and corporate sponsors.

The event was masterfully planned and executed down to the minute. In addition to foot-power, the torch traveled by bicycle, train, horse, canoe, steamboat, sailboat, and airplane. The circuitous route brought the Olympic flame within two hours of 90 percent of the U.S. population. NBC-TV covered the event every day, while internet junkies could keep abreast of its progress on America Online and the Atlanta Committee on the Olympic Games (ACOG) website. Although the runners did not wear Coke logos, just about everything else did, including the "escorts" who ran alongside. "The torch relay will be one long commercial," lamented Michael Jacobson of the Center for Science in the Public Interest, and Sergio Zyman was delighted to agree. "Three things have been constant at the Olympic since 1928—the athletes, the fans and Coca-Cola."

Dill Driscoll hired enthusiastic, fresh-faced young promoters to stage what he called a "15,000-mile rolling street party."* Ahead of the torch runner, his crew arrived with five flatbed trucks, accompanied by motorcycles with Coke-bottle-shaped sidecars. The "Red Army" set up a mobile stage for the welcoming ceremony, with a big screen depicting stirring Olympic moments intercut with stirring Coca-Cola commercials. "I wonder if Coca-Cola has anything to do with this," one onlooker pondered sarcastically. "A few high-spirited spectators have even run with a Coke held high," observed a contemporary reporter, "as if it were the sacred flame from Greece." The crew sold pins, jackets, pennants, mugs, gold Coke bottles, license plates,

---

* One observer called the Coke kids "relentlessly cheerful."

baseball hats, and key chains with the Coke logo on them, as well as ice-cold Coke, with the proceeds going to a local charity.

"It's almost like hosting the Olympics for one day," Wisconsin Governor Tommy Thompson said at a ceremony en route. Thompson asked high school band members, "Did you all get a bottle of Coke? Next to milk, it's a good drink." They shouted back, "Better!" The feel-good Coke reps had a harder edge, however, towards any Pepsi that dared to appear during the relay. In a small town in Ohio, they refused to allow high school students to escort the torch because the school district sold Pepsi products, and they knocked a Pepsi carton off the wall when a spectator refused to trade it for Coca-Cola. In Senoia, Georgia, Coke officials suggested draping the Pepsi vending machine next to the town hall with a black cloth but eventually settled for putting a Coke machine next to it.[*]

It was indeed a "sea-to-shining-sea Coca-Cola carnival," as a cynical foreign journalist observed. Yet it also provided overwhelmingly heart-warming moments. A boy with Down's Syndrome carried the flame while his mother ran alongside shouting to the crowd, "This is my son! This is my son!" Children with recorders played "America the Beautiful" along the roadside. War veterans from a hospital lined the roadside and waved tiny American flags from their wheelchairs. Parents took their children out of school for this one-time event. In Selma, Alabama, blacks and whites walked together over the Edmund Pettus Bridge where civil rights marchers once were beaten back. "My God, the relay is the biggest thing to happen [here] since the illegals starting coming across," exclaimed a resident of a tiny town near the Mexican border. Even in big cities, even in the ghettos, the torch relay worked. "This is the first time I have seen New York City as a small town," a resident said. As one reporter observed, the torch relay was "crassly commercial and touchingly open-hearted—all at the same time."

Everywhere, people were moved by genuine emotion – including the Coke employees traveling with the torch. One handicapped young man took more than an hour to carry the flame a half-mile. "He barely made it," staffer Susan McWhorter remembered, "but the accomplishment on his face was phenomenal." The torch runners themselves were transformed. "The whole thing was like a mountain-top experience," one participant recalled. "I equate it to the birth of my children, graduation, or getting married." Another runner was initially skeptical. "I was cynical because of all the Coke hype, but I was so moved by the reaction of everyday people, crying and waving flags. It was a real revelation. Though I never thought I would do it, I ended up buying the torch."[†] Coca-Cola bussed some 40 million people to the relay, where they cheered, cried, and drank Coke. The memory of the

---

[*] Big Coke distributed a 91-page guidebook to its local bottlers along the route, instructing them to hang Coke signs everywhere and police for any Pepsi banners that might appear.

[†] Each runner received a torch, so that it was the flame that was passed rather than the torch. When it was all over, runners could purchase their torch for $275.

event, as one Coke executive observed, was indelibly burned into their brains. On Day 84 in Atlanta, riding one of the Harleys with a Coke sidecar, Dill Driscoll led the torch parade into the courtyard at Coke headquarters on North Avenue, where a literal red carpet was rolled out as Company employees cheered.

Muhammad Ali, the former boxing great, shambled up to the great Olympic saucer in Atlanta on July 19, 1996, and finally lit the giant caldron for the 17-day Olympics. The rolling street party was at an end, but the Coca-Cola Games, as many journalists dubbed them, were just beginning. "Coke Here, There, Everywhere," observed the *Atlanta Journal-Constitution*. "Within the Ring, the Coca-Cola trademark was so omnipresent it seemed an atmospheric condition." Hawkers with Coke-bottled-shaped backpacks dispensed the drink. The red logo flashed on the floors and ceilings of Atlanta rapid transit stations. Collectors traded various Coke-embossed Olympic pins. Visitors crowded the World of Coca-Cola museum.

The centerpiece, however, was Coca-Cola Olympic City, a 12-acre theme park where Coca-Cola charged adults $13 for the privilege of gazing at a 65-foot high Coke bottle and buying company soft drinks from bottle-shaped vending machines that attracted children with a cool spray from underneath giant bottlecaps.* The real attractions, however, were ingenious interactive games in which consumers could "compete" against Olympic athletes, simulating a sprint against Jackie Joyner-Kersey, batting against a video of pitcher John Smoltz, taking part in a wheelchair race, or mountain biking down a virtual reality trail. On the way out, screaming fans on a video screen begged visitors for their autographs. Meanwhile, for those who couldn't make it to Atlanta, Coke developed "Olympic Celebration Zone" merchandising areas in supermarkets around the country as part of its Coca-Cola Red Hot Olympic Summer promotional campaign, with $1.6 billion in discounts and prizes.

Determined to prevent Pepsi from horning in on the action or "ambushing" the Olympics, Coke successfully pressured Atlanta organizers to keep Frito-Lay, a Pepsico subsidiary, out of the Games. Coke's designation as the official Atlanta soft drink prevented other brands from being served at city-sponsored events or on city property during the Olympics. "The odds of finding a cold (or a lukewarm, or a hot) Pepsi in Olympic Atlanta were akin to discovering the Holy Grail inside the George Dome," one reporter observed. Pepsi was reduced to offering "Pepsi Stuff"—ranging from T-shirts to mountain

---

*Coca-Cola Olympic City and the Olympic Park displaced subsidized Techwood housing for lower-income people, who were promised that they could eventually return to a much nicer mixed-use site after the Games were over. Since there were fewer places, however, many were permanently dispossessed. Critics pointed out that Woodruff Park, across the street from Coke headquarters, had been redesigned with a fountain, waterfall, and new benches at a price of $5 million. The benches discouraged the homeless, featuring arm rests making it impossible to lie down. "The Olympic people [want] the world to believe a big lie—that Atlanta has no poor people," one Atlanta activist said. "They're hiding the homeless, chasing them away, and locking them up because they're afraid people are going to see."

bikes—in return for massive numbers of Pepsi purchases. A denim jacket required drinking 960 cans.

In pre-Olympic spots, Coke aired ads with the tag-line, "For the Fans," trying to connect with audience-as-consumer. In one commercial, a camera strapped to a swimmer's body allowed an athlete's view of screaming fans. "What makes a swimmer carry on is lung capacity—yours," the announcer said. And Coke quenched the thirst of the hoarse fans, of course.[*] During the games, the Company switched gears to feature Coke as the star in 100 commercials, each airing only once, in 135 countries, tailoring the approach so that Coke supported appropriate patriotic fervor. In Ukraine, for instance, Coke ads featured pole vaulter Sergey Bubka. Many of the ads were reruns from the previous few years, including the familiar polar bears, but to lend an international flair, some were imported from other countries, such as a spot showing boys from India playing cricket, using a Coca-Cola crate as a wicket. These were augmented by "just-in-time" ads created from the previous day's Olympic events.[†]

While Coke's Olympic efforts were often heart-warming, they were clearly focused on the bottom line. "It's a good investment," Doug Ivester told a group of securities analysts. Given the international implications, "it becomes a very economic buy for us." Roberto Goizueta put it more poetically: "We have gone from simply teaching the world to sing, to teaching the world to drink Coca-Cola." Goizueta and Ivester greeted powerful customers and bottlers from all over the world, each executive shaking at least 2,000 hands during the course of the Games. There seems little question that Coke's Olympic efforts, which cost some $250 million, paid off, although the Games themselves were marred by disorganization, a bombing, and complaints about commercial tackiness. "Atlanta's Olympic Games," wrote French newspaper *Le Monde*, "touched on some classic themes of the American myth—immodest ambition, an obsession with gold, the powerful reign of the dollar." Groused another reporter: "Atlanta was every bit as ready for the Olympics as America was for New Coke."

1996: YEAR OF TRIUMPH

Goizueta and Ivester were too busy celebrating to worry about such carping. Ten days after the Olympics ended, Goizueta greeted Oswaldo and Gustavo Cisneros to Coke headquarters in Atlanta, where they signed a contract to

---

[*] The Olympic ads were created by ad agency Wieden & Kennedy. A few months before, Mike Ovitz had left CAA to join Disney as an executive, and Shelly Hochron had also left to form Edge Creative, a kind of independent yet in-house ad agency for Coca-Cola. Edge Creative continued to make non-Olympic Coke advertisements.

[†] The Company also included a smattering of ads for PowerAde, Sprite, diet Coke, and Fruitopia. While the Coca-Cola commercials did not focus on athletic performance, the PowerAde ads did. Coke executives hoped to boost PowerAde as the official sports drink of the Olympics, but Gatorade still held a huge share of that market.

form a joint venture with the huge Venezuelan bottling family. For $500 million, Coke grabbed 50 percent ownership in the only country in the free world where Pepsi had always predominated. It was a remarkable coup, administering a stunning blow to Pepsi's pride, particularly since new Pepsico CEO Roger Enrico had been personal friends with Oswaldo Cisneros. "Ozzie took his 30 pieces of silver and ran," Enrico observed bitterly. The purchase followed years in which Pepsi management had ignored the Venezuelan bottlers. Doug Ivester negotiated the top-secret deal, meeting the Cisneros team in hotels and airplane hangars. Once the bargain was made, a 727 jet carrying thousands of Coke bottles flew from Mexico to Caracas, and crews worked overtime repainting 2,500 delivery trucks with the Coca-Cola logo. Overnight, Pepsi virtually disappeared from Venezuela.*

Less than two weeks later, Goizueta declared victory in Russia, another long-time Pepsi stronghold. In 1994, Pepsi still held 60 percent of the Russian market, but now Coke had pulled ahead. After the 1985 New Coke debacle, Roger Enrico had penned *The Other Guy Blinked: How Pepsi Won the Cola Wars*. "If he thinks we blinked," Goizueta said testily a few years later, "we will respond by giving Pepsi two black eyes." Now, he had done just that. *Fortune* crowned the Coke CEO the monarch of soft drinks. A March 1996 *Fortune* cover showed Goizueta, arms folded, sitting atop a giant Coke bottle, as Coca-Cola grabbed top ranking as America's most admired company. "Pepsi's Enrico: Bottled Up By Coke," an October 1996 cover announced, featuring a somber Enrico trapped inside yet another oversized Coke bottle.†

Indeed, Roger Enrico had plenty to worry about. The 51-year-old Enrico had rejuvenated the three Pepsico divisions he had led—first soft drinks, then snack foods, and finally fast-food restaurants—but now he faced his greatest challenge. Reluctantly, he took over as CEO when lackluster chief Wayne Calloway stepped down, suffering with prostate cancer. Enrico inherited an international soft drink business in crisis. Under hard-charging Pepsi executive Chris Sinclair, Pepsi had poured $3 billion in three years into ambitious expansion projects, mostly in Latin America. "If Coke starts growing 8 percent," Sinclair boasted in 1994, "we'll do 10 percent or 12 percent." In Mexico, attempts to introduce a non-returnable bottle flopped as the peso crashed. But Sinclair pinned his brightest hopes on Buenos Aires Embotelladora, commonly known as Baesa, the Argentinean superbottler headed by

---

* Eventually, Pepsi found a new bottler, and Coke had to pay a $2 million anti-monopoly fine, but Venezuela belonged to Coca-Cola. The following year, Coke sold the Venezuelan bottler to the anchor bottler Panamco, getting its $50 million investment back along with a larger ownership in the anchor bottler.

† The only part of the Coke behemoth that perennially faltered was Coca-Cola Foods, which Goizueta renamed the Minute Maid Company in 1996, since that's essentially what it was, having jettisoned pasta and coffee long ago. Despite efforts to counter Tropicana's not-from-concentrate orange juice, a new taste formula, a bigger ad budget, and innovative distribution through dairies, Minute Maid results were disappointing. Rumors that Coke would sell its troubled subsidiary were inaccurate, however.

former Coke man Charles Beach.[*] With borrowed money, Baesa expanded into Brazil, Chile, and Uruguay.

Coca-Cola counterattacked by spending heavily on marketing and cold drink equipment, essentially locking Pepsi out of lucrative small retail accounts. Goizueta successfully lobbied Argentine President Carlos Menem to reduce the 24 percent tax on colas to 4 percent. With Baesa earning most of its money from non-cola beverages, it amounted to a tax break for Coke. Running at one-third capacity, Baesa lost $300 million during the first half of 1996, Beach and Sinclair departed, and Enrico installed staid Craig Weatherup as the new Pepsi president. Weatherup essentially abandoned Coke strongholds such as Germany, Japan, and South Africa, announcing that he would target emerging markets such as India, China, and Eastern Europe. "We need to be a hell of a lot more pragmatic," he said. In 1996, Pepsi-Cola International lost $264 million. A jubilant Goizueta declared victory in the cola wars, explaining that he had thrown away his papers on Pepsico. "As they've become less relevant," he sniffed, "I don't need to look at them very much anymore."

By year's end, Coca-Cola Company sales accounted for over half of non-U.S. soft drink consumption. The stock, which had split two-for-one in May, climbed to $53 for a 43 percent total return for the year.[†] "If you invested in our Company just two years ago," Goizueta wrote in the annual report, "your investment has more than *doubled*." Worldwide unit case volume for the year was up 8 percent, with 6 percent growth in the United States. Earnings per share grew 19 percent, boosted by company share repurchases and the sale of French, Belgian, and British bottlers to Coca-Cola Enterprises, the huge American anchor bottler that moved into Western Europe during the year.

"It may sound incongruous from one of the world's most valuable companies, about to celebrate its 111th birthday," Goizueta said, "but, truly, *we are just getting started*." Just turned 65, Goizueta clearly felt that he himself was just getting started, too. "As long as I'm having fun and adding value," he said, he planned to remain CEO. At the annual company meeting, one shareholder rushed up to Goizueta and gushed, "You should be like the pope and never retire." Delighted, Goizueta repeated the anecdote over the next few months. He intended to be another Robert Woodruff, the grand old man of Coca-Cola, pulling the company strings for years to come. And, like Woodruff, Goizueta was so obsessed with Coca-Cola that he regarded its sales record as the pinnacle of human progress. "A billion hours ago, human life appeared on Earth," Goizueta intoned. "A billion minutes ago, Christianity appeared. A billion seconds ago, the Beatles changed music forever. *A billion Coca-Colas ago was yesterday morning*." The overwhelmingly important question remained: "What must we do to make a billion Coca-Colas ago be

---

[*] In the 1980s, Beach had been convicted of price fixing as a Virginia Coke bottler.

[†] Giant anchor bottler Coca-Cola Enterprises, whose stock had languished for years, did even better in 1996, up over 80 percent.

this morning?" As Goizueta himself observed, "Working for The Coca-Cola Company is a calling. It's not a way to make a living. It's a religion."

DEATH AT THE PINNACLE

The following year, the Coke juggernaut rolled on, with a January 1997 "Get Caught Red Handed" promotion offering 200,000 instant prizes, including T-shirts, cameras, coupons, and Club Med vacations, to Coca-Cola Classic drinkers "caught" imbibing by a roving Red Crew, deployed by Dill Driscoll's experiential marketing outfit, that made flash visits to stores, movie theaters, and residential neighborhoods. The promotion signalled Coke's intention to expand Coke Classic marketing year-round rather than focusing only on summertime. Come summer, the Company offered more than 500,000 MasterCard ATM money cards worth $20 to $100 inside selected 12-packs and cases of Coke Classic and Cherry Coke.

At the Super Bowl, Coke introduced a Coca-Cola Red Zone where fans could play interactive simulated football games, while Harleys with Coke sidecars passed out drinks for "tailgate parties." One lucky fan won Coke-sponsored Super Bowl tickets for life. Like Coca-Cola Olympic City, such interactive marketing was intended to involve fans, going beyond the mere presence of ubiquitous Coke signs. The Company allowed Pepsi to pay exorbitant amounts for exclusive pouring rights for teams such as the Seattle Mariners and Los Angeles Lakers (leaving Coke with 24 of 28 major-league baseball teams and similar domination of other sports). Meanwhile, Coke opened Coca-Cola Sky Field, an entertainment park at Turner Field, the home of the Atlanta Braves, and Monster Refreshment, a similar effort featuring three 25-foot Coke bottles, at Fenway Park in Boston. "Five years ago, we were just there," said Steve Koonin, in charge of sports marketing for Coke. "Now, we're a friend of the fan, and we're fun. And we're winning."

In the same spirit, Coke opened a new store and museum in Las Vegas, featuring a 100-foot glass elevator in the shape of a Coke bottle. In the Everything Coca-Cola store, cash registers sat inside giant bottle caps, T-shirts were stacked in huge six-packs, and the fitting rooms were shaped like old fountain glasses. An 8-foot fiberglass Coke polar bear loomed over customers. Coke hired Chris Lanning, a former Gap executive, to oversee its new retail division. "We'll find out what shop concepts best connect with consumers," he said, "with their special Coca-Cola memories." In the Las Vegas World of Coca-Cola, digital artist Dana Atchley created instant interactive stories based on such memories in his Storytelling Theater, illustrating sentimental or funny experiences with Coke. Incredibly, when visitors were asked to contribute their own Coke stories, more than 1,800 responded within the first three weeks.

Coke also forged ahead with new products. With no formal test marketing, Coke introduced Surge, its highly caffeinated citrus counter to Pepsi's Mountain Dew. The first ads—launched during the Super Bowl—featured a teenager placing a can atop a pedestal, then screaming "Surge!" A group of crazed adolescents then swarmed up a muddy hill to claim the green-tinted carbohydrate-loaded beverage. The slogan for the "fully loaded" drink was "Feed the Rush."[*] Coke clearly meant business, giving away millions of free drinks to high schoolers and slotting $50 million for marketing. The positioning for Surge aped Pepsi's "Dew Dudes," the hip, dare-devil teens who engaged in sky surfing and street luging while fueled by Mountain Dew. Surge's name and positioning were precisely the opposite of Mello Yello, Coke's weak previous effort in the category. Soon afterward, Coke introduced Citra, a yellow non-caffeinated grapefruit drink targeted against Squirt, a similar product from Cadbury Schweppes.

In the meantime, Sprite, with its "Obey Your Thirst" campaign and interactive "Sprite Playgrounds" at state and county fairs, pushed past Mountain Dew, Dr Pepper and Diet Pepsi to claim the No. 4 U.S. soft drink spot behind Coke Classic, Pepsi, and diet Coke. And Coke pushed its Cool Nestea brand past Snapple (sold by Quaker Oats for a loss) to claim second place in the iced tea category behind Pepsi's Lipton. The Company finally test-marketed its long-delayed contour can, a ribbed, bulging aluminum container with a top-secret manufacturing process. Not only did consumers like the way the can looked and felt—they perceived that the Coke inside *tasted* better. Overseas, Coke sales bounced back in Latin America and Europe after a slow period. In Russia, Coke now outsold Pepsi two-to-one, and the Company revealed that it would sink another $100 million there by the end of 1997. The Company announced a $360 million capital investment program in South Africa, Zimbabwe and Tanzania.[†] Big Coke continued to buy and sell bottlers at a furious pace—$7 billion worth announced or completed in the first six months of 1997—building an ever-stronger anchor bottler system over which the Company exerted ever-growing control.

For the second year in a row, *Fortune* named The Coca-Cola Company the most admired American company. When Coke stock surged to $60 in March, some financial analysts once more irritated Roberto Goizueta by declaring the price hyperinflated, with a high price-to-earnings ratio of 37. "Nowhere is it written," sniped Alan Abelson in *Barron's*, "that Coke will continue to grow even at 18 percent a year appreciably into the future," and famed analyst John Bogle agreed. Nonetheless, the stock continued to climb, nudging over $72 in June. Mutual fund manager John Neff, who had slighted Coke stock (incorrectly, as it transpired) back in 1994, again warned that a correction could come at any moment. Always testy towards the financial media, Goizueta became even more suspicious of reporters. Nonetheless, he

---

[*] R. J. Corr Naturals, a New Age drink purveyor that sold Dr. Rush, among others, sued Coca-Cola over the "Feed the Rush" slogan, complaining that its "Feel the Rush" came first and that Coke's ads featured "risky and unhealthy activities" that would ruin the Dr. Rush image.

[†] In 1997, Hillary Rodham Clinton praised Coca-Cola for its African investments as she gave a "corporate citizenship" award to Doug Ivester at a celebration sponsored by the Corporate Council on Africa.

hesitantly agreed to cooperate with David Greising, the Atlanta *Business Week* bureau chief, who wanted to write his biography. When the business writer refused to give Goizueta control over the book's contents, however, the CEO slammed shut the door, and no one at Coke would return Greising's phone calls.

Still, Goizueta was clearly thinking about his legacy. At the pinnacle of success, he began to sound even more philosophical than usual. "What's it like to be you?" one young admirer asked. "Sometimes I wish I was like you," Goizueta answered. "It isn't easy. You work 24 hours a day. You don't take much vacation." Then he brightened. "But I'm having a great deal of fun, and I'm blessed to be in a position to be paid handsomely to have a lot of fun." Though still absorbed in the Company, he began to reach out more into the community and the world. Fretting over Atlanta's downtown area, he warned that the city should not lapse into a "giant, collective nap" in the wake of the Olympics. "A great city cannot have a hollow center." He seeded a newly formed Goizueta Foundation with $38 million, preparing to become a philanthropist in the Woodruff tradition. He expressed admiration for the late Cardinal Bernardin, a strong voice for social justice.

Yet Goizueta insisted on a fundamental, bottom-line credo: "The mission of any business is to create value for its owners." Churches could minister to spiritual needs, governments to civic needs, and charities to social needs. "While performing its role, business distributes the lifeblood that flows through our economic system, not only in the form of goods and services, but also in the form of taxes, salaries, philanthropy." He said that he got his "psychic income" from the impact he had, not only on his company, but on society as a whole. "When I was in Eastern Europe," Goizueta explained, "I saw people who for the first time had a real job and were getting paid real money. They thanked me for that, but they really were thanking The Coca-Cola Company." He espoused a strict *laissez faire* philosophy. "It puzzles me that many Americans want our government to 'fix' our economy or even protect our jobs when much of the rest of the world is thrilled to have government finally playing its appropriate role." He explained that he knew the perils of a socialist system first-hand. "It's the reason I came to this country from Cuba."

Goizueta argued that by boosting the share price, he had done more good than any number of charities, in just one year creating nearly $3 billion dollars in additional wealth for nonprofit organizations holding Coke stock. He emphasized, however, that such gains should not come at the expense of employees. He lamented the "downsizing" trend in which corporations laid off thousands of loyal employees. "I am against a scorched earth adherence to profits at all costs." Such short-sighted policies would inevitably harm the consuming public upon which businesses relied. "We cannot for the long term exist as a healthy company in a sick society," Goizueta stressed. He praised a recent book by theologian Michael Novak entitled *Business as a Calling*.

As part of that calling, Goizueta was unrepentant about forming alliances with nonprofit organizations that helped promote company products. In a 1997 speech to the annual meeting of the Boys & Girls Clubs of America, the CEO laid out his vision of "strategic philanthropy," a program through which bottlers would place vending machines and help with retail programs and special events at Boys Clubs throughout the country. Coke would help the organization raise $60 million over the next decade, he promised. "It's a new world of giving," he said. Of course, while Coke gave nonprofit organizations a piece of the profits, the Company made money, too, while gaining exclusive access to young consumers. In the coming years, Coke would extend such "strategic philanthropy" to financially strapped high schools, installing vending machines in educational institutions that took a percentage of the proceeds.

Goizueta's enthusiasm and dedication to his job were clearly undiminished by time or age. By 1997, he had been CEO for 16 years, compiling an incredible record. "Hell, considering what he's done for the shareholders," one analyst said, "you should make him CEO of the Century." Yet Goizueta wasn't satisfied. "Success is a journey, not a destination," he said, translating one of his grandfather's aphorisms. Obviously, he wasn't ready for that journey to end, as he jetted around the world on Coca-Cola business. When asked about his successor, Goizueta made a point of *not* naming Doug Ivester. "He or she must have energy, intellectual character, integrity, an inquisitive, innovative mind, determination, a sense of purpose, and an engaging personality," he answered, naming his own qualities—other than the last, a trait he always envied in Don Keough. Over after-dinner drinks in the spring of 1997, Bernard Marcus, chairman of Atlanta-based Home Depot, confided to Goizueta that the two of them were the soul of their companies, and that souls lived on forever. The comment pleased Goizueta, who nonetheless pointed out later that evening that he was two years younger than Marcus.

In August 1997, Goizueta flew to Monte Carlo for a meeting with fifty of Coke's biggest international bottlers, adding a day trip to Spain, his ancestral home. When he returned to Atlanta, he never quite recovered from the jet lag. Lunching with Morgan Stanley analyst Andrew Conway on September 2, Goizueta assured him that case volume growth worldwide would continue at around 7 percent for the next few years. Then, chatting about his recent travels, the CEO admitted, "Andrew, I'm a little fatigued. I haven't quite recouped from the trip." Four days later, Goizueta checked himself into Emory University Hospital, where doctors detected a growth on his lungs. Goizueta, a heavy smoker since his teenage years in Cuba, had lung cancer.

During his two-week stay in the penthouse Woodruff Suite in the hospital—where Robert Woodruff spent his last days—Goizueta frequently checked Coke's stock price, which had declined from its June high, while reviewing financial plans and global strategy with his top executives. Two fax machines in an adjoining room brought reports from around the world.

By the time they detected the cancer, however, it was too late for anything but desperate measures. Doctors administered massive radiation doses in combination with chemotherapy and sent the Coke chief home, where he got a get-well card signed by 2,000 employees. "Please let my talented doctors and my terrific family worry about me," he dictated in reply. "You, my Coca-Cola family, just worry about the Company." With characteristic determination, Goizueta faced death calmly. When doctors or nurses asked how he was feeling, he said, "Fantastic."

Goizueta's wife of 44 years, Olguita, kept vigil by his side, and his three living children visited frequently.* Olga lived in Atlanta, but Roberto ("Robby"), a theology professor at Loyola, arrived from Chicago, while Javier, a Procter & Gamble employee, flew from Brazil. Goizueta's attention to detail never wavered. Reading aloud a letter to him, Olguita tried to skip over the pleasantries at the end. "Don't et cetera me," her husband said sternly. "Now start over, from the top."

On October 7, Goizueta returned to the hospital, suffering from a throat infection and fever, probably due to damage to his immune system caused by the aggressive radiation and chemotherapy. On October 16, the board of directors met without Goizueta for the first time in seventeen years. The next night, Goizueta asked to take a final communion with Olguita. Just after midnight, on Saturday, October 18, 1997, Roberto Goizueta died, his head cradled in his wife's arms. He was 65 years old, one month shy of his birthday.

At the funeral ceremony, attended by over a thousand mourners—including Jimmy and Rosalyn Carter, Warren Buffett, and other luminaries—former Atlanta mayor and United Nations ambassador Andrew Young delivered the eulogy. "For him," Young said, "business was not a job, it was a mission ordained by God." The black leader praised Coca-Cola as the fourth largest employer in South Africa, asserting, "This is certainly a better community, and indeed this is a better world, because of the love, the dedication and the devotion that he shared through business as his calling." Goizueta was marketing, not just a product, Young said, but "a way of life." Eldest son Roberto S. Goizueta also spoke at the funeral. "He died as he had lived," he said, "fully engaged in the Company's affairs." As the service ended, the organ began a solemn recessional. As mourners filed out of the church, they recognized the tune and began to hum along as it swelled and quickened, hearing the familiar words in their heads: "I'd like to teach the world to sing in perfect harmony." Goizueta would have loved it.

The outpouring of tributes and grief was remarkable, similar in many respects to the death of a head of state. Coke offices around the globe closed for the day of his funeral. Flags flew at half-mast not only at Coca-Cola plants around the world, but at 22,000 McDonald's restaurants. The *Atlanta Journal-Constitution* devoted page after page to Goizueta testimonials, including a huge pen-and-ink cartoon of a polar bear gripping a Coke in its paw, a giant tear falling from its eye. "He Was the Real Thing," a typical headline read.

Roberto Goizueta left an astonishing legacy. When he became CEO in 1981, The Coca-Cola Company was a stumbling giant, diversified into a hodgepodge of businesses, many of which weren't terribly profitable. Many of the bottlers

---

* Goizueta's youngest child died of leukemia in 1970 at the age of four.

were bitter at the Company for forcing them to give up their birthright to cheap syrup. Paul Austin, the former leader, had Alzheimer's. The stock was languishing, and Pepsi was gaining. Under Goizueta's long reign, Coke got rid of ancillary businesses but diversified into the world of entertainment by buying Columbia Pictures, then selling it a few years later for a huge profit. During the 1990s, he had narrowed his vision only to soft drinks. "He was the most focused human being I ever met," Don Keough recalled now, after his death. Goizueta applied his laser-beam intelligence to the marketing of Coca-Cola. "He didn't play golf or tennis," Keough continued. "All of his hobbies were linked to The Coca-Cola Company. It was his passion." Goizueta made a few blunders—notably New Coke—but no one could argue with the results. Under his direction, the Company's market value exploded from $4.3 billion to $145 billion and Coke increased its U.S. market share by nearly 10 points, up to nearly 44 percent. Worldwide, Coke's soft drink share had grown from 35 percent to 50 percent.

Yet as a human being, Roberto Goizueta remained an enigma. When David Greising published his biography, *I'd Like the World to Buy a Coke*, a few months after Goizueta's death, it proved to be a workmanlike business narrative. "His unique gift as an executive," Greising wrote, "was his ability to change his own formula, to quickly understand his mistakes, adapt, and ultimately triumph." But readers learned little of the leader's inner life. Perhaps, when you knew his devotion to his family and product, you knew Goizueta. For all his aloof grandeur, however, the business giant sometimes showed a softer side. Pictures of the CEO with children at the Varsity showed him grinning as he delighted in passing out Coca-Cola pins. He also loved the Coke polar bears, giving away ties emblazoned with them.

Goizueta rarely spoke about his past, insisting that he preferred to look forward. But he never forgot the day he fled Castro's Cuba in 1960 with $40 and 100 shares of Coke stock. On July 4, 1995, Goizueta addressed a group of immigrants who had just taken the oath of American citizenship. "For me, looking into your eyes this morning is like looking into a mirror," he said, then wondered aloud at his own good fortune, "that a young immigrant could come to this country, be given a chance to work hard and apply his skills, and ultimately earn the opportunity to lead not only a large corporation, but an institution that actually symbolizes the very essence of America and American ideals." He also revealed how he got there. "You must sense the opportunity in your nostrils with every breath, and you must see it in your dreams when you are asleep." Perhaps, as he was laid to his eternal rest, Roberto Goizueta still dreamed of Coca-Cola.

Ivester Inherits a World of Trouble

"One of the virtues of a 113-year-old company is that we've traveled over bumpy roads before. We have seen the movie before."
—M. Douglas Ivester, CEO, The Coca-Cola Company, 1999

Although Goizueta had never specifically anointed Doug Ivester, his ascension to become chairman and CEO of The Coca-Cola Company was a foregone conclusion. "Now that Ivester will be calling the shots," a reporter wrote the day after Goizueta's death, "the only real mystery is whom he will pick as his No 2." The top contenders were Neville Isdell, 55, the Irish "Indiana Jones" who had turned around the Philippines, then led the charge into Eastern Europe and Russia, Jack Stahl, 45, former chief financial officer and head of domestic operations, and Sergio Zyman, 52, the volatile marketing head. As the months rolled by, the mystery cleared: Ivester did not intend to appoint a second banana at all. At the age of 50, he had reached the apex of power, and he had no intention of sharing it. The ambitious, disappointed Zyman soon departed.[*] Neville Isdell, arguably the most competent and charismatic choice for second-in-command, was removed from Big Coke ranks, heading up the new Western European anchor bottler Coca-Cola Beverages, split off from Coca-Cola Amatil.

When an interviewer asked the new Coke CEO point-blank what it would take for him to appoint a president, Ivester coyly replied, "I'm very fortunate right now in that I've got six [presidents]," referring to the heads of his six operating groups. "If I put someone between them and me right now, would there be great advantage to that?" He wanted "short lines of communication." Indeed, Ivester encouraged frequent direct calls and e-mails from his executives, and he deluged them with messages and questions in return. Ivester neither smoked nor drank and, at least on the surface, he was always calm and polite, if demanding. Watching a TV show on animals and stress one night at home, he commented to his wife Kay, "You know, I don't feel stress." She answered, "Of course you don't. You're a carrier."

The transition between Goizueta and Ivester was seamless, but even as

---

[*] Zyman and Ivester had always been an odd couple, despite their bonding during Ivester's Saturday morning marketing lessons. Zyman was notorious for his roving eye, while Ivester was a straight arrow. Zyman shot from the hip; Ivester studied every aspect of a situation before taking action.

Ivester took command, there were signs of trouble. The stock was down, not because of Goizueta's death, but because a stronger dollar hurt Coke, which took 80 percent of its profits overseas. In addition, analysts carped at Coke's bottling transactions, complaining that the Company artificially boosted its earnings figures by manipulating the price and timing of sales to captive anchor bottlers. "We question the manner in which these inter-company transactions are reported," wrote two accountants, calling them "nothing more than an exercise in self-dealing" and objecting to the one-sidedness of Big Coke's power. "What is clear is that these affiliates are part of Coke's business model to subsidize Coke's earnings in every way possible."

Just before Ivester took over, *Financial World* put a smashed Coke can on its cover, with the headline, "Why Coke Could Get Crushed." The investment magazine complained that Big Coke took profits from its bottlers and their new stock issues while loading them with debt. "How much longer will Coke be able to use the bottler as a whipping boy?" If gains from bottling sales and stock issuance were excluded, Coke's operating earnings had improved only 11 percent annually over the past five years, nowhere near its lofty goal of 17 to 20 percent.

Nonetheless, Ivester could look back at 1997 with some satisfaction. Just before Christmas, he made his first big move as CEO, announcing the $840 million purchase of Orangina, the fizzy French drink with real orange pulp. Since CCE now owned the Coke bottling system in France, it stood to gain substantially if regulators allowed the deal. Although the "Asian Miracle" was turning into the "Asian Flu"—with the sudden July 1997 devaluation in Thailand spreading across the continent—Ivester and chief financial officer James Chestnut reassured analysts that Coke saw the turmoil as an opportunity to buy Asian bottlers at bargain prices. Ivester compared the situation to the Mexican peso crisis of 1994, during which his company continued to invest, resulting in a 10 percent rise in its Mexican market share.

Coke stock finished strong at $67, up 27 percent for 1997. Worldwide case unit volume grew by 9 percent, and earnings per share 19 percent, just as Coke executives had promised for the past decade. In the annual report, Ivester admitted that 1998 might present "a significant challenge" because of the stronger dollar, but "over time, we manage our currency exposures to mitigate any negative impact from currency fluctuation." He reaffirmed the Company's goals and stated unequivocally, "Never before has this Company been more perfectly poised for pioneering."

He was right, but the world's most far-flung corporate empire was also poised for a world of trouble, rippling out from Asia. In Indonesia, the rupiah went into free fall in January 1998, unemployment soared, and Coke sales plummeted. Doug Ivester urged managers to fight back rather than "to simply hunker down and ride out the storm." He reminded them, "We're investing for the long term and building new capabilities to deal with *any* type of uncertainty." Asian Coke managers tossed out their carefully articulated annual marketing plans and adjusted to new conditions, creating "market impact teams" to work at the street level, getting product to vendors as quickly and cheaply as possible. With more strenuous marketing efforts, promotions, and new cooler placements, sales in the first half of the year steadied. Coke stock rose to $89 a share in mid-July.

Then the bottom dropped out as economic woes hit nearly every country outside the United States in what pundits began to call a global economic crisis. "What started out as a blip on the radar screen in Thailand," said financial guru Paul Volcker, "has somehow turned into something of a financial contagion, particularly in Russia and Brazil." Hedge fund king George Soros spoke darkly of "the disintegration of the global capitalist system." Coke's net income for the third quarter dropped 12 percent. Until then, even with currency exchange problems, Coke had been able to use its expert hedging to minimize the impact, and the volume growth had continued unabated. Now effective hedging became impossible, with most foreign currencies falling, and overall case sales grew only 3 percent for the quarter rather than the usual 7 percent. Indonesia was devastated, with the economy in ruins, riots in Jakarta, and Suharto stepping down.

News of Russian instability caused Merrill Lynch to downgrade Coke stock, but as the ruble collapsed in August, a Coke executive said, "We are advanced with our [Russian] plans and there is no turning back for us." Indeed, the Company had spent $750 million in Russia since April 1994 to build 12 plants, some of which were running at half-capacity or less. Before the devaluation, a British-owned bottler agreed to sell its Russian bottling business to Coke for $187 million, but two months later, it was happy to take $87 million and run.

As the world economy deteriorated, Coke projections kept changing. "The numbers keep getting ratcheted down and ratcheted down," complained one analyst. "It's like water torture." In Latin America, Brazilian volume rose only one percent for the third quarter. Japan was flat, and in Germany, where poor weather and bottler reorganization plagued Coke, volume fell 9 percent. Coke had always been considered a safe bet because it was diversified in nearly 200 countries, but the global malaise of 1998 descended everywhere. Ivester had reassured analysts that, even in bad times, everyone got thirsty. Yet as a *Wall Street Journal* reporter observed, "The economic condition in some countries is so dire that people don't have money to buy bread, let alone sugar water." Coke stock dropped severely, then rallied briefly.

Doug Ivester remained outwardly unflappable, just as he had once on the Amazon, when a guide accidentally flipped a crocodile into his narrow boat. Ivester now counseled despondent Coke executives around the world, advising them not to cancel Christmas parties, which would send the wrong message. "Let's capitalize on this," he said, urging managers to look for opportunities in the ruins of the economy. Ivester, whose posture and stride reminded one reporter of the lumbering Coke polar bears, exuded "an almost surreal confidence," she observed. He espoused a mindset in which Coke managers set specific goals as inevitable destinations. "It's not a matter of *if* we're going to get there. It's a matter of *when*."

As 1998 ended, such destinations appeared to be a mirage on the horizon, however. When Ivester abruptly summoned securities analysts for a meeting on December 11, with only a few hours' notice, they wondered whether it was to announce a new disaster. Indeed, Ivester disclosed that the Company's fourth-quarter performance would be even more dismal than he had estimated a few weeks before, due to currency devaluations, higher marketing expenses, and continuing economic turmoil. Yet Ivester underscored his determination to continue Coke's world domination by announcing, at the same meeting, that Coca-Cola would purchase most of Cadbury Schweppes' overseas soft drinks—Dr Pepper, Crush, Schweppes, Canada Dry, and a range of juice drinks and bottled water—for $1.85 billion. The deal excluded Cadbury products in the United States, France, and South Africa. Despite this news, Coke stock immediately tumbled 5 percent to become the day's worst performing Dow stock. Even the unflappable Ivester admitted during the meeting that Russia was "just a mess." The Cadbury deal was not earth-shattering, and besides, there was no guarantee that regulatory agencies in various countries would allow the sale. French authorities were, after all, still holding up the Orangina purchase of the previous year.

After some wild ups and downs during the year, Coke's share price ended 1998 precisely where it had started, at $67. Operating income for the year had dropped a percentage point, but net income was off 14 percent. With most of the bottling consolidations completed in 1997, Coke could no longer rely on reselling bottlers to boost earnings per share, which fell 13 percent. Nonetheless, even with an atrocious fourth quarter, Coke grew its case volume by 6 percent worldwide—just slightly below its goal of 7 percent.

PEPSI BOUNCES BACK

To make matters worse for Coke, Roger Enrico was leading a recharged Pepsico. In October 1997, Enrico spun off Pepsi's restaurants, including Taco Bell, Kentucky Fried Chicken, and Pizza Hut, as Tricon Global Restaurants, allowing Pepsi to focus only on soft drinks and snack foods. Until then, Coke fountain salesmen could stymie Pepsi sales by asking fast food chains, "Why would you want to buy from a competitor?" Pepsi soon struck deals with Pizza Inn, Hard Rock Cafe, Planet Hollywood, and Warner Brothers theaters. Nonetheless, Coke owned 65 percent of the U.S. fountain business, compared with Pepsi's 22 percent. Coke countered by cementing a multi-year contract with Burger King and Wendy's and adding other outlets.

In frustration, Pepsi sued Coke in 1998, alleging that Coca-Cola violated the Sherman Anti-Trust Act by threatening to cut off supplies to food-service distributors if they carried Pepsi, too.[*] Coke freely admitted dumping distributors that carried Pepsi. Indeed, its contracts specified that offering

---

[*] The lawsuit was symptomatic of Enrico's new litigious strategy. Pepsi had already sued Coke in India, accusing its rival of unfairly hiring away Pepsi employees, and in France Pepsi had filed a motion to block Coke's proposed purchase of Orangina. In Italy, Pepsi was delighted when the government began an anti-trust probe against Coke.

Pepsi was a "conflict of interest." But Coke asserted that its arch-enemy could always sell its soda directly to customers and that its distributors were "an extension of Coca-Cola." The complex lawsuit would probably remain unresolved for years to come.

In 1998, as it celebrated its centennial, Pepsi also moved aggressively to offer or acquire new drinks. When acesulfame potassium, trade-named Sunett, a new sugar-free sweetener with a longer shelf-life than aspartame, was approved by the FDA, Pepsi came out with Pepsi One, a new one-calorie diet drink. Pepsi's Mountain Dew continued to grab chunks of market share with teenagers, hardly disturbed by Coke's Surge, which wasn't surging.[*] To counter Coke's highly successful Sprite, Pepsi now introduced Storm, its own caffeinated lemon-lime effort. Finally, Pepsi bought Tropicana for $3.3 billion, giving it the market-leading premium orange juice to counter Coke's Minute Maid.

The Pepsi Stuff campaign proved to be much more successful than anyone thought, fueling a 6 percent sales hike in supermarkets. Still, Pepsi was playing catch-up ball. In 1997, Pepsi paid $50 million to become the official sponsor of Major League Baseball for five years, even though Coke was sold exclusively in most ball parks. At Shea Stadium, the Pepsi Party Patrol used a shoulder-mounted air cannon to launch Pepsi T-shirts into the upper decks.

Overseas, Pepsi sharpened its focus to markets where it had a chance, forming an alliance with Brahma, Brazil's largest brewer, and signing a franchise bottling agreement in Norway. Pepsi built new bottling plants in Venezuela, Russia, Greece, India, China, and elsewhere. From a huge international deficit in 1996, Pepsi International came back the following year with a modest $17 million in positive operating income. As Coke stumbled in its return to India, Pepsi made inroads there. In Venezuela, in the wake of the Cisneros switch to Coca-Cola, Pepsi came roaring back, teaming up with Polar, a local bottler, and offering deep discounts, heavy advertising, and numerous vending machines. Coke's Venezuelan market share dropped from 81 percent to 70 percent.

On the domestic front, marketing chief Brian Swette resigned amidst complaints from bottlers about ineffective ads and declining Pepsi share. During the 1990s, Pepsi's ad campaigns and slogans had been uncharacteristically lame. "Gotta Have It" implied that people bought the caffeinated beverage only because it was addictive. "Be Young, Have Fun, Drink Pepsi" sounded like a bland fifties' throwback, while "Nothing Else Is a Pepsi" lacked fire. "Generation Next," introduced in 1997, was a word-play on Generation X, and the ads targeting that young cohort—one featured a teen with multiple piercings in ears, nose, and eyelids—alienated older consumers. In 1999, new

---

[*] In 1999, Coke changed its Surge slogan to "Life's a Scream," abandoning the dark, edgy "Feed the Rush" spots. Now the ads featured less grungy, more upbeat interracial teens. Regardless, Mountain Dew continued to command two-thirds of the heavily caffeinated citrus category.

marketing chief Dawn Hudson (with input from Pepsi veteran Alan Pottasch) introduced the "Joy of Cola" campaign, in which a cherubic little girl turned nasty when given a Coke instead of a Pepsi, her voice suddenly deepening to a man's. The ads were funny and appealed to a broader audience.

After ignoring the high-margin vending machine market for years, Pepsi threw itself into cooler placement, increasing the number by 240 percent in two years. In the marketplace, Roger Enrico stressed the synergies of Pepsi-Cola, Frito-Lay and Tropicana, which accounted for $11 billion in annual supermarket sales. Following Coke's lead, Pepsi spun off its company-owned bottlers as the publicly-owned Pepsi Bottling Group, while also arranging other bottler consolidations. The cover of the 1998 Pepsico annual report featured a line of its products headed by a duckling. "You get your ducks in a row," Enrico wrote in his message to shareholders, "then put some real money behind them." That appeared to be exactly what Pepsi was doing.

HARD EDGE TO A SOFT DRINK

Despite Pepsi's new feistiness, Coke continued to dominate Pepsi outside the United States by a 3.6-to-1 margin. Although it would take a miracle for Coke to reach its goal of 50 percent of the U.S. market share by the year 2001, it had snared 45 percent by 1999, versus Pepsi's 31 percent. The Big Red Machine may have been slowed by global economic woes, but it still appeared unstoppable in the long run. And under Doug Ivester, it was indeed more of a machine. As *Fortune* reporter Betsy Morris put it, Ivester was the model CEO for the twenty-first century. "He marshals data and manages people in a way no pre-Information Age executive ever did or could." Ivester was the driving force behind Project Infinity, a superlative Coke information network, and he had hired a "chief learning officer" to institutionalize the Coke mantra.

Like Robert Woodruff, who used to root in the trash to ascertain the proportion of Coke bottle caps, Doug Ivester liked to prowl the back alleys of the world to see where Coke was or was not. He spent a third of his time on the road. In a 1998 visit to Shanghai, he was annoyed to find no ice-cold Coke on an impromptu foray. "Why wouldn't you put Coke in here?" he asked a manager as they popped into a tiny cosmetics store. As chief Coke invester Warren Buffett put it, "He looks at anytime anyone swigs any beverage other than a Coke as a personal insult."

Like his predecessors, the straight-laced Doug Ivester stressed the need to "do the right thing." Coke employees should always obey the law while helping communities where the Company sold drinks. Even in philanthropy, however, everything had to contribute to the bottom line. "It's the right thing to do, and it's very right for business, too," he stressed. "Use your imagination to leverage community-relations activities against marketing activities," a Coke memo urged. "Make sure the project is measurable." Also, Coke should be assured that it was the "signature" partner that would get public credit for do-gooding.

But many Coke veterans wondered whether a warm heart really beat deep inside Ivester's well-oiled machine. "It is not that Ivester is a brute," wrote

Fortune's admiring Betsy Morris, "so much as a relentless force." Tell that to long-time Coke employees such as Ray Morgan, who was forced out of the Company at Christmas 1998 after a thirty-year career that included spearheading innovative vending machines and the return of the Coke contour bottle. While still based in Atlanta, Morgan had been assigned to the Greater European Group and spent most of his time jet-lagged, trying to care for his 87-year-old mother and 7-year-old daughter. When he asked for a reassignment, he was refused. His story was not unique. "A lot of people have left Coke in the last few years," he said in a 1999 interview.

One former CCE manager commented "Doug is a very calculating, brilliant guy. He's quietly aggressive. He'll cut your legs off and you won't know it." To his credit, however, Ivester initiated an internal audit of Coke, asking employees to answer the question, "Is The Coca-Cola Company arrogant?" Few people dared to respond, but one anonymous contract worker answered with an emphatic *Yes*. "There is grave cause for concern in a company that has high turnover in any given department and no one bothers to understand why, cause for concern when people are fired because they did not say what others wanted to hear."

Even during Goizueta's last few years as CEO, Doug Ivester's imprint was on company policy, particularly at giant bottler CCE, where he was chairman. Although Ivester was unfailingly soft-spoken and polite in person, he demanded a no-holds-barred business style, and in such a fierce competitive environment, unpleasant allegations began to surface. A former CCE driver claimed that two managers tried to bribe him in August 1994 in order to defeat a union. U.S. Attorney James Deichert portrayed the CCE corporate culture as a "pressure cooker." The government eventually lost the 1997 federal bribery trial, however, despite compelling evidence and testimony. In another case, Coke allegedly advertised a Minute Maid apple juice as containing 100 percent apple juice, when in fact it had added sweeteners from non-apple sources. Coke settled out of court for $1.5 million.

Even as Coke was claiming in the Pepsi lawsuit that its distributors were an extension of the Company, CCE aggressively competed against its own distributors for lucrative vending machine profits. One morning when a California distributor stopped to inspect his coolers on a college campus, he found a CCE machine right next to it, undercutting his price by 10 cents a can. "There's just no way I can compete," he complained. Across the country, traditional soft drink distributors found themselves in the same situation. They could buy product cheaper from a Walmart Sam's Club than they could from CCE, but the Coke bottler asked Walmart to limit the amounts it would sell to distributors. Because of the 1980 Soft Drink Interbrand Competition Act, distributors were forbidden to "transship" cheaper product from outside their territories. Ironically, the law had been passed to protect small bottlers, an endangered species twenty years later.[*] When desperate Maryland

---

[*] In 1980, there were 353 Coke bottlers in the United States. By 1999, there were 96, and analysts predicted that the number would dwindle to fewer than 50 within the next five years.

distributor B. K. Miller Company sued CCE, accusing it of fraud, wiretapping, and charging discriminatory prices in an effort to drive the distributor out of business, the big bottler countersued, accusing the distributor of transshipment. The case was settled out of court.

Meanwhile, two issues from Coke's past reappeared to haunt Ivester. Coca-Cola had sold its Florida orange groves in 1996, and protesters outside Atlanta's World of Coca-Cola complained that the new Brazilian owners were using child labour.

The orange juice protest fizzled, but in April 1999, four African-Americans brought a class action suit against The Coca-Cola Company for discrimination in pay, promotions, and performance evaluations. Cyrus Mehri, the lawyer representing the plaintiffs, had made his name as part of the legal team that won a $176 million discrimination settlement against Texaco in 1998. The complaint alleged that there were "dramatic differences in pay" at Coke's corporate headquarters, such that the average black employee was paid nearly $27,000 less than the average white employee. A "glass ceiling" was supposed to prevent most African-Americans from advancing upwards, and "glass walls" kept them out of powerful areas such as marketing and finance. If the suit were granted class action status, it would be open to any black employee who had worked at Coca-Cola since April 22, 1995.

The complaint included juicy hearsay anecdotes, including the allegation that the marketing director for an Alabama Coke bottler introduced himself in 1996 or 1997 as the "Grand Cyclops," a clear reference to the racist Ku Klux Klan. It also quoted Doug Ivester as saying a few years earlier that it would take 15 or 20 years before African-American employees were well represented at senior management levels. The Company emphatically denied that it practiced any form of racial discrimination, while it hastily created a council on racial diversity. If U.S. District Judge Richard Story were to grant class action status to the suit—a decision pending as this book goes to press—it is likely that Coke would settle the case quickly rather than endure an embarrassing and extended public trial. At least, this is the advice that most legal experts rendered. Knowing Ivester's combative nature, however, the outcome is uncertain.[*]

MASS HYSTERIA IN BELGIUM

Even as Coke struggled to recover from the global recession, it suffered a catastrophic health scare in Europe. On June 8, 1999, thirty-nine students in

---

[*] Coca-Cola was further embarrassed when an internal report from December 1995 surfaced, recommending that Coke enhance diversity and address "why there are so few African-Americans in certain areas and levels of the business." The project leading to the report was apparently led by Carl Ware, president of Coke's African unit. To his credit, Doug Ivester had asked Ware to do so. Since Coke was a major supporter of African-American education and civil rights issues, groups such as Concerned Black Clergy were inclined to give Coke the benefit of the doubt.

Bornem, Belgium, collecting bottle caps for a contest, complained of nausea and headaches and attributed it to their Cokes. They were sent to a health clinic. The media reported it. Two days later, Belgian students in another city reported dizziness and stomach-aches after drinking canned Cokes from a vending machine. The media reported it.

Coca-Cola Enterprises, the U.S.-based mega-bottler partially owned by the Coca-Cola Company, supplied the questionable Coke, although the bottles came from an Antwerp plant and the cans from the mammoth Dunkirk facility. Scrambling to determine the possible cause, company investigators found that some of the bottled drinks had a faint rotten egg smell because a batch of carbon dioxide had been contaminated with hydrogen sulfide. At the canning plant, some wooden pallets had been disinfected with phenol, another chemical with an unpleasant odor. The media reported it. Although neither problem should have caused any illness, taken together they were embarrassment enough for Coke, which has always prided itself on stringent quality standards.

As fears mounted, Coke officials explained what they had discovered. The company voluntarily recalled affected bottles and began to seal off its vending machines. Then, on June 14, more students fell ill after buying vended Cokes, and the panicked Belgian government ordered a complete recall while banning all of the company's products. The media reported it. Word of the purportedly poisoned soft drinks spread rapidly, along with consumers claiming to have imbibed company products that made them ill, too. Eventually, some 250 European imbibers came down with the mysterious Coca-Cola bug. France, the Netherlands, and Luxembourg banned Coke products, too.

Clearly, the Coke brass were caught off-guard by how rapidly the crisis escalated. On June 16, two days after the ban, Doug Ivester issued his first public statement, a bland bit of bureaucratese saying that the company was "taking all necessary steps" to ensure its beverages' quality. But the next day, Ivester flew to Europe to exercise personal damage control. He penned an apology that ran in full-page ads in European newspapers, he appeared in a 90-second TV spot, and he offered to buy every Belgian—all 10 million of them—a free Coke.

Finally, by June 24, both Belgium and France had rescinded their bans, though Coke still had to destroy its surviving stock before it could gear up again. The massive recall cost the company and its major bottler over $100 million, not to mention a severely tarnished image.[*]

---

[*] Just as the Belgian crisis finally wound down, the French publicized rumors that rat poison had somehow contaminated Coke. Then a Polish consumer found some mold in BonAqa, Coke's European bottled water. The mold was not a health problem, but it resulted from inadequate cleaning of reusable bottles. As a result, Coke spent $1.8 million to withdraw and destroy bottles. Meanwhile, egged on by Pepsi, the European Union raided Coca-Cola offices in four countries, seizing documents it hoped would prove that Coke illegally tried to force competitors out of the market. Jumping on the Coke-bashing bandwagon, Australian regulators announced an investigation of Coca-Cola Amatil for possible marketing abuses.

Yet Coke probably didn't make anyone sick, as every scientist who studied the matter concluded. Perhaps there was an off odor (even that much was unclear), but nothing to account for the panic, the nausea, the dizziness. Those are the classic, vague symptoms of psychosomatic illness. Coke found itself embroiled in a case of mass hysteria, or what the psychiatrists call mass sociogenic illness.[*] Belgians were already spooked by the recent revelation of dioxin in their meat and poultry, which itself had come in the wake of "mad cow disease". They were ready for another food scare, and what better victim than a gigantic American company that corporation-bashers love to vilify? It was because of Coke's size, ubiquity, power, and popularity, that the rumors spread so quickly. The media reported it, with insufficient explanations and a great deal of sensationalism and credulity. Caught in a Catch-22 bind, Coke had no choice but to apologize for something it probably didn't do. Nonetheless, the Company's slow, ambiguous response troubled analysts, and some observers questioned whether Ivester should try to manage such problems single-handed—wasn't it time to appoint a second in command?

GLOBAL IS THE WHOLE POINT, STUPID

As Coke prepared to enter the twenty-first century, then, it was beset with worries. During the first two quarters of 1999, the Company's world-wide volume declined for the first time in a decade, while net income dropped 13 percent in the first quarter, then 21 percent in the second, in the wake of the Belgian health scare. At the Company's annual meeting in Wilmington, Delaware, Ivester admitted that every major market outside the United States was "stagnant or slumping," which had a "gravitational pull on earnings and volume." Even the domestic volume fell one percent in the second quarter because of retail price hikes.

The vaunted anchor bottler program appeared to backfire as well. The huge bottlers, in which Big Coke held substantial shares, were struggling in the difficult economic climate. In Brazil, for instance, cheaper, inferior local soft drinks called "Tubainas" were cutting into Coke's dominant market share. As a result, anchor bottler Panamco—saddled with debt from purchasing the Cisneros bottlers in Venezuela—reported its first loss. Meanwhile, Australian anchor bottler Coca-Cola Amatil suffered in the troubled Asian economy. Former chief executive Norbert Cole, ousted during a restructuring, sued Coke, claiming that it had hurt Amatil by forcing it to give up its European holdings. Big Coke's equity income from its ownership in bottlers dropped from $155 million in 1997 to $32 million in

---

[*] As this history documents, Coca-Cola and other soft drinks have always been subject to slander and rumor. In 1950, in Belgium, the health ministry declared the drink a harmful laxative. In 1993, it was Pepsi that suffered from what folklorists call an "urban legend"—that the company was somehow putting syringes into its cans. Sure enough, people around the United States came forward to claim that they had found needles in their drinks—all a hoax.

1998, and it promised to dwindle further in 1999. The anchor bottlers, which were supposed to be Coke's growth engine, now needed cash infusions in the form of increased marketing funds or improved infrastructure. In 1998, for instance, Coke pumped $1.84 billion into its bottlers, of which $1.2 billion went to Coca-Cola Enterprises.

With many bottlers working at partial capacity, Coke hoped to fill the bottling lines with Orangina and Cadbury products, but both deals ran into regulatory roadblocks early in 1999. A French appeals court ruled against the Orangina deal. Australian and Mexican regulators vetoed the Cadbury sale, and the European Union asserted its authority to stop it as well.

While such problems might have given other CEOs sleepless nights, Doug Ivester appeared unfazed, as did his stockholders, who lined up for his autograph at the 1999 annual meeting. "Our long-term growth potential remains unchanged," Ivester said. "Our system has never been better equipped to convert that potential into long-term value."

There is little question that the CEO was correct. Even as the global economy appeared to have reached bottom in early 1999, Coca-Cola continued its implac-able world conquest, fueled by a product that cost almost nothing to produce, with one of the highest profit margins on earth. While it promised to pump close to $1 billion into Brazil over the next three years, Coke bought a 20 percent stake in Peru's Inca Kola, a popular yellow bubblegum-flavored drink invented in 1935. Coke announced plans to market and distribute Inca Kola internationally.

The patient Company revised its Orangina and Cadbury proposals to meet regulatory objections. In France, Coke agreed to relinquish Orangina distribution rights for ten years in return for a slightly reduced purchase price of $758 million. To placate the European Union, Coke modified its Cadbury deal to exclude all of Europe except the United Kingdom, Ireland, and Greece and slashed the purchase price to $1.1 billion.

With Big Coke as the midwife, two major Japanese bottlers merged to form Coca-Cola West Japan Company, Coke's eleventh anchor bottler, in which the Company held a 5 percent interest. In Europe, a huge Greek bottler merged with Coca-Cola Beverages PLC to form Hellenic Bottling (Big Coke owning about a quarter share), second-largest world bottler after CCE. In its Middle East and North African division, Coke forged ahead of Pepsi with a 41 percent market share, opening new bottling plants in Saudi Arabia, Eritrea, and Algeria. In Shanghai, Coke turned a 26-story skyscraper into a gigantic advertisement, wrapping it on all four sides with signs of mammoth Coke bottles, illuminated by 120 spotlights at night. Located near the People's Square, the sign would "add fun to everyone's life," according to Steve Chan, a Chinese Coke executive.

The Company continued its relentless marketing initiative around the world, offering larger sizes and multi-packs in Germany, lowering prices in South Africa, promoting a "Win Millions" contest in Thailand where consumers could win a million baht in gold, and enticing Venezuelan consumers with free product and prizes such as houses, salaries for a year, and a free shopping spree. To help restore the faith of Belgian consumers, the Company offered Coke-embossed cell phones for half the going rate, if they would only drink 100 Cokes. In India, the Company sponsored a 30-city concert tour by singing sensation Daler Mehndi and launched Sprite as "refreshingly honest." In troubled Indonesia, Coke's new ad slogan urged: *Teguk Lagi, Semangat Lagi!*—"Drink Again, Be Spirited Again!"

Even in the disastrous Russian economy, the Company persevered with a "Drink the Legend" campaign, based on an old Russian folktale to appeal to resurgent Russian nationalism. Early in 1999, Doug Ivester flew to Ukraine to open a new $100 million bottling plant, emphasizing that Coke's belief in the future of the former Soviet Union was unshaken. Although its most popular drinks worldwide were Coca-Cola, Fanta, Sprite, and Coca-Cola Light (the inter-national name for diet Coke), the Company owned more than 160 brands worldwide.

For those not blessed with a Coca-Cola museum/store such as those in New York, Atlanta, and Las Vegas, the Company took portions of its memorabilia on the road as the Traveling World of Coca-Cola. In Paris, the Louvre even hosted a popular exhibit of 60 original Coke and oil paintings. The Company launched a range of international fashion and sports clothing, signing up partners for its Coca-Cola Wear label. "The clothes will reflect Coca-Cola's values of authenticity, genuineness and [being] part of people's lives," a company spokesman said.

Back in the United States, third-generation Coke-bottling man Charles Frenette took over as global marketing director when Sergio Zyman left, with a mandate from Ivester to stress local marketing initiatives around the world. While advertising might be high-profile, it had not been the driving force behind Coke's recent market growth. It was the execution on the ground, with the proliferation of vending machines, promotions, and interactive consumer experiences, such as the new NASCAR "Wall of Speed," in which fans could drive their own cars in a "virtual reality" race. Roberto Goizueta himself had observed, "You let me have the bottling plants and the trucks and the highly efficient systems, and I'll let you have the TV commercials. I'll beat you to a pulp over time." Even with ads, the content wasn't as important as the ubiquity in places such as pre-movie spots or the Internet.

Frenette, who had proven his ability to grow the business in South Africa, was friendly, customer-oriented, and maintained a low public profile—the opposite of Zyman. Frenette orchestrated a co-promotion with AT&T, affixing free calling cards to millions of fountain-beverage cups to appeal to teens. The promotion was designed not only to sell more soft drinks, but to garner important marketing information as the cards were used. The new marketing head didn't rush to change the agency-du-jour smorgasbord he inherited from Zyman, but he apparently did ask the agencies to modify the quick-cut, disco-beat, techo-hip Coke ads—which old-style Coke adman Bill Backer called "mean-spirited and self-absorbed," and John Bergin termed "bizarre and uncommunicative"—and refocus on the traditional Coke heart-tug.* In one spot, a solemn little boy, watching a heart-rending rendition of *Pagliacci* from the wings, walked onstage to give the suffering opera clown a Coke. It was a subtle tribute to the old Mean Joe Greene ad. Sprite, the fastest-growing U.S. soft drink, continued to thrive with its anti-hype "Image Is Nothing" campaign.

Frenette initially floundered when it came to long-troubled diet Coke advertising. In 1998, his advertising head, Ian Rowden, ran two-year-old ads while trying to come up with something new. Frenette was never billed as an advertising man, but he excelled as a marketing pro. In 1999, he offered excerpts of six bestselling novels in diet Coke 12-packs. It was a brilliant, innovative move, spurred by research indicating that diet soft drink consumers tended to be affluent, well-educated, voracious readers. The romance novels—including an excerpt from best-selling Nora Roberts, who admitted to being a diet Coke addict herself—appealed to diet Coke's primarily female constituency, though there was also an excerpt from an Elmore Leonard thriller for the men.

Finally, Frenette settled on "Live Your Life" as the diet drink's slogan. Featuring liberated, self-assured, svelte young women, the Wieden & Kennedy ads had a clever edge. In one, a beautiful young woman stopped in the middle of a desert for a diet Coke. When a good-looking man pulled up, she watched his car roll over a cliff without stopping it, then casually asked, "Do you need a ride?" In another spot, after interviewing a cute young blond, the head of a video dating service observed, "Sounds like you have a pretty good life." Taking a long, ruminative sip from her diet Coke, the young woman said, "Thank you," in a tone of sudden revelation, and left without completing the interview, as the slogan "Live Your Life" appeared. The message? To be fulfilled, you don't need a man: you just need diet Coke.

Meanwhile, Coca-Cola intensified its drive to penetrate schools to snare youthful consumers early. "Whether it's a morning pick-me-up, a lunchtime refresher or for after class with friends," a Coke internal organ advised, "students want their drinks easily accessible." School officials, eager for soft drink money to supplement their meager budgets, agreed. The Colorado Springs School District signed a 10-year exclusive contract with Coke that guaranteed to bring in $7.5 million—provided, that is, that its 32,500 students bought a sufficient number of soft drinks from the schools' vending machines. A school district official wrote a letter to each of the principals. "We must sell 70,000 cases of product," he wrote, "at least once during the first three years of the contract." To do so, he urged schools to "allow students to purchase and consume vended products through-out the day" and to add more coolers. "The Coke people surveyed the middle

---

* Typical of the techno-wizardry in the Zyman era was "Loft Party," a 1997 diet Coke spot with special effects executed by a California firm called Digital Domain, using its own proprietary software aptly named Elastic Reality. The ad's director sought a "disorienting sort of feeling," which Digital Domain achieved through a process called "single-camera morphs."

and high schools this summer and have suggestions on where to place additional machines." The school official signed off as "The Coke Dude."

In 1998 and 1999, hundreds of schools became active participants in marketing soft drinks, signing up for exclusive Coke or Pepsi deals in a veritable feeding frenzy.[*] "This contract is a godsend," a procurement director for a Washington, D.C., public school said as he signed on with Coke, allowing the schools to pay for bus tokens for needy students and to replace textbooks. In yet another Colorado contract, a school district planned to build a new stadium with the Coke cash windfall, as well as to improve computer and video technology and boost literacy programs. "Kids and teachers who spend hour after hour after hour in school get thirsty," Coke spokesman Scott Jacobson observed. "Every time they consume a beverage from home, it's a lost revenue opportunity for the school [and Coke]. So it's kind of a 'win win win.' It's good for us, good for people who are thirsty who want our products, good for schools."

Coke soon received an unexpected bonus. Although it was illegal to sell soda as part of the school lunch program, many schools began to give away soft drinks in order to lure students on open campuses into staying for lunch. When Senator Patrick Leahy and several other politicians from milk-producing states proposed legislation to close this loophole, the American School Food Service Association objected, defending the give-away soft drinks as the only way to keep some school lunch programs alive. Ever since John Pemberton, Coca-Cola purveyors had known that "sampling" programs were an excellent way to build business. Now, the schools were doing it for them!

Several new Coke ads made an unabashed appeal to high school students. In one spot, a teenage boy taking an exam reached up and grabbed a Coke that magically appeared overhead. He and a beautiful classmate were lifted up into a fantasy sky of blue. In another ad, a teenager went on and on about philosophical matters until his bored girlfriend suggested, "Do you wanna have a Coke and make out?" In a third, a young girl tried on different outfits while drinking her Coke. In a surreal ad called "Machine Teen Central," active teens swarmed around a Coke vending machine. Fueled by soft drinks, they rode bikes up buildings, glided above the earth on skateboards, and finally tossed schoolbooks into the air to form a stairway to heaven, the book covers changing to a Coke logo.

Unlike Pepsi, with its lip-synching six-year-old consumer, Coke stuck to its seldom-breached rule that it should not show human children under 12 drinking the beverage. But that didn't stop Coke from conveying the appropriate message. In a feel-good polar bear ad, Momma Bear lured a

---

[*] Schools were not the only ones to grab Coke money in return for exclusive deals. In 1999, the first *city* in the United States signed a ten-year deal with Coke. Huntington Beach, California, agreed to allow the local bottler to put up Coke signs and to sell beverages on all city property for $300,000 a year in cash and an additional $300,000 in community programs.

wayward baby cub into swimming to safety by offering a Coke. In another spot, baby robins in a nest fought amongst themselves until Mom flew up with a Coke. "Hey, Mom, you rock," one of her chicks said as he sucked down a Coke.

Roberto Goizueta had always said that Coke products should be more popular than water. Now Doug Ivester went his old mentor one better, introducing a new Coke-bottled water called Dasani—an invented word with an African/Italian ring that supposedly connoted crisp purity. Coke had considered a bottled water product for a long time but could never figure out how to make its customary profits. It hit upon a plan to sell its bottlers a patented mix of minerals, which they would add to regular municipal water and bottle in light blue bottles. "All water is basically the same," admitted Ira Bachrach, the president of NameLab, a think-tank that created the names Acura and Slice. "It's the packaging [that differentiates it]. It's an idea. The name [for a water product] is even more important than it is for colas." He praised Dasani for its "smooth rolling sounds."[*]

With all of this activity, Doug Ivester didn't appear to be worried. "I have to chuckle sometimes," he said, "when I read that some analyst is fretting about our 'global exposure.' I hate to tell them, but that's the idea."

IVESTER'S SUDDEN DEPARTURE

But time was running out for the unflappable Ivester. He may have been supremely competent, ruthlessly aggressive, and thoroughly imbued with the Coca-Cola spirit, but he had presided over a disastrous end to the 20th century, during which Coke's share price fell to a heart-stopping low of $47 in October 1999 before staggering back to drift in the $60s. Coca-Cola shareholders were howling. They wanted someone's blood. Something had to be done.

On Sunday, Dec. 5, 1999, the Coca-Cola board met, and the 52-year-old Ivester announced the following day that he would retire in April 2000. Starting immediately, Australian Coke executive Douglas N. Daft, 56, would step in as president and chief operating officer. He would become the CEO when Ivester departed.

Leaders in the business world, even other Coca-Cola executives, were stunned by the news, since board luminaries such as Warren Buffett had repeatedly reaffirmed their faith in Ivester.

In a way, the departing CEO was a scapegoat. Had Goizueta lived, he would have faced the same disasters – a global economic downturn flowing out of Asia, a stronger dollar hurting overseas profits, a mass food hysteria over supposedly defective Belgian Coke, and the rest. Conceivably, however, the astute, aristocratic Goizueta would have moved more guickly to counter each

---

[*] Ironically, some dentists warned that the popularity of bottled water, which contained no fluoride, might result in more cavities.

threat to his beloved company. And Goizueta would have sought help from his chief operating officer.

Ivester's refusal to appoint a second-in-command may have sealed his fate. Under pressure, he had finally designated two second lieutenants – Jack Stahl in charge of the Western Hemisphere and Doug Daft overseeing the Middle and Far East as well as Africa – but he could not bring himself to appoint a COO. Worse, that realignment apparently prompted a frustrated Carl Ware to resign, since Daft was installed over his head in Africa. Ware, the Company's highest-ranking black executive, announced his imminent departure just as the racial discrimination suit was heating up, which could not have made the board happy.

Meanwhile, the French government had issued a final rejection of the revised Coke bid to buy Orangina from Pernod Ricard. The European Union, Italy, and Austria were investigating Coke and its bottlers over charges of heavy-handed marketing and anti-trust violations. And, in an attempt to boost profits, Ivester had sharply increased the price of soft-drink concentrate, which antagonized the bottlers. Some stockholders faulted him for failing to repurchase huge chunks of stock to stem the share price tumble. All in all, Ivester probably fell, like Caesar, from a "thousand cuts," as one observer put it. And certainly, Ivester's lukewarm personality did not win him many close friends in the company. Now, of course, the big question was what would happen to Coke. Doug Daft, a former math teacher, had thirty years of experience with Coca-Cola, primarily in the Middle and Far East. Soft-spoken, affable, and direct, he was untested at the top level, but he had the marketing background that Ivester lacked, and he had overseen the building of the Chinese business from scratch. Would Daft, the Australian Coke veteran, be able to turn the company around and restore morale? Or would Coke slowly go flat?

Given Coca-Cola's history, the question almost answers itself. Consider that Coca-Cola is the most widely distributed product on our planet, and that it is the second best-known word on earth (after "OK"). Even if a Coke CEO tried to kill the brand, he or she probably couldn't do it.

Recall what happened in 1985 with the misguided New Coke episode. All it did was re-invigorate the traditional brand as Coke Classic.

Given the company's enormous marketing clout, its sheer persistence, and the developing world's almost universal hunger for Western symbols, it was difficult to imagine Coke failing over the long haul. As the Coke machine rolled towards the 21st century, it may have encountered a few bumps, but it appeared unstoppable.

~ 23 ~

World Without End?

You can run from it, but you can't hide. Sooner or later, no matter how far you think you've ventured from the comforts and conveniences of the modern world, Coke will find you. Go to the foothills of the Himalayas, the hurricane pounded fishing islands off the coast of Nicaragua—go to the birthplace of civilization, if you like. Coca-Cola will be waiting for you.

—*New York Times* editorial, 1991

Traditionally called "Mecca" by devout employees, the North Avenue complex, where I spent five months researching this book, throbs with the worldwide Coca-Cola heartbeat. But the headquarters represent less than the tip of an ever-expanding iceberg. One way or another, something like a million people around the world work for Coca-Cola—either directly for the Company or as a bottler or wholesaler. And that doesn't count the drink's 8 million retailers or the countless people who indirectly earn their livelihood from Coke by producing containers, trucks, water purifiers, pallets, computers, and the innumerable give-away promotional items.

A personal anecdote illustrates the astonishing range of the soft drink. On May 21, 1991, I was interviewing Doug Ivester—who would succeed Goizueta as CEO a few years later—when we were interrupted by the news that Rajiv Ghandi had been assassinated hours after casting a ballot for himself in the Indian elections. We adjourned to a TV monitor and watched CNN in sorrowful silence. As we walked back, another pragmatic Coke executive said, "Well, that's not too good for us." And it occurred to me that any major world event would have an impact on Coca-Cola, but that none would really impede the drink's inexorable advance for long. Though company men had been working closely with Ghandi, they soon enough struck a deal with the new government, and Coke is now available in India again.

At the outset of this book, I asserted that Coca-Cola both affected and was affected by its times. Clearly, company officials have reacted to events more than they have caused them. Coca-Cola didn't plot the passage of the Pure Food and Drug Act, for instance, or the Depression or World War II—all moments in which Coca-Cola played an important part. Coke men themselves have always insisted that the soft drink is just a "small pleasure," one that people could certainly live without if absolutely necessary. "No one thinks the world will shift on its axis if Coca-Cola ceased to exist," one executive told me. And yet. And yet . . .

There is no question that this fizzy, syrupy beverage means much more than the Coca-Cola men would have us believe. Certainly, it means more to them—it is a way of life, an obsession. In the lobby at North Avenue headquarters, there is a large medallion with an image of a Coke bottle superscribed on top of the globe, with visions of other galaxies yet to conquer spinning wildly above it. These guys really are missionaries. In their homes, many of them maintain what I privately termed Coca-Cola shrines—autographed photos of Robert Woodruff, gold replicas of the hobbleskirt bottle, and other personal memorabilia. These Coca-Cola "grads," as they are called, assemble regularly to relive old times.

Members of the Coca-Cola Collectors Club International and the newer Cola Club are, if anything, more obsessed with their shrines. Germinating in a basement room or garage, their collections often literally push them out of their bedrooms and homes. "It's kind of like a drug addiction," one collector told me at a gathering which filled an entire Atlanta hotel. At the silent auction, where bids were placed on items and might be topped by someone else, the tension crackled. "It makes you sick, you're so worried," a Delaware woman moaned. Late into the night at these affairs, club members swap and dicker, invading one another's room.

While these fanatical collectors may simply appear ludicrous, they are not the only ones to take Coca-Cola seriously. Social commentators, political activists, nutritionists and anthropologists have all attacked Coca-Cola as if it were the distillation of Evil on earth. One angry observer called Coca-Cola's history "the most incredible mobilization of human energy for trivial purposes since the construction of the pyramids." It was, he said, "what went wrong with the American dream." Much of the criticism focuses on advertising, which, according to one distressed clinical psychologist, conveys the notion that "life will never be boring, that you will be sexually popular beyond your wildest dreams, and that you'll always be able to dance well if you drink colas."

Coke men wouldn't argue with that statement. In fact, it seems rather restrained. Beginning with John Pemberton, Frank Robinson, and Asa Candler, its manufacturers have touted the soft drink/patent medicine as a magical potion, though the message has been modified over time, abandoning overt medicinal claims in favor of uplift, joy, and other image-intense attributes. Nonetheless, it still bears a startling resemblance to the fabled Elixir of Life sought by the alchemists. An "elixir" was defined by an eighteenth century reference book as a "dark-coloured medicine composed of many ingredients and dissolved in a strong solvent"—a pretty good description of the acidic, caramel-colored soft drink. The Fountain of Youth, which lured Ponce de Leon to the New World, was a variant of the potion, reputed to extend life to a Methuselah-like length. Coca-Cola sprang from this New American World to spread its revivifying promise of eternal youth and energy to the rest of the world.

A NEW RELIGION

Throughout this book, Coca-Cola has been treated as a tongue-in-cheek religion of sorts, but the notion actually isn't so far-fetched. After all, the world's first coin-operated vending machine, invented in the first century A.D., dispensed holy water. The metaphor continually crept into the interviews I conducted. "Coca-Cola is the holy grail, it's magic," one Coke man told me. "Wherever I go, when people find out I work for Coke, it's like being a representative from the Vatican, like you've touched God. I'm always amazed. There's such a reverence towards the product." Shortly before his death, Roberto Goizueta even made it explicit: "Working for The Coca-Cola Company is a calling. It's not a way to make a living. It's a religion."

What else but a religious impulse could account for the idolatry with which corporate worshipers treat the outsized Coca-Cola bottles the Company produced for its 1986 centennial celebration, Coca-Cola Olympic City in 1996, or its huge iconic bottle signs, such as the one wrapped around a 26-story Chinese skyscraper? Or the insane statistics it dispenses to the press? "If all the Coke ever produced were in traditional six-and-a-half ounce bottles and placed end to end, they would reach all the way through outer space from earth beyond Mars to Jupiter." Or, "If all the Coke ever produced were to erupt from Old Faithful at its normal rate of 15,000 gallons per hour, the geyser would flow continually for 1,685 years." Similarly, "if all the Coca-Cola ever produced were poured into one tremendous swimming pool . . ." But enough. Unless you, too, are a Believer, the idea of a breaststroke through 20 miles of dark, sweet, fizzy waters probably doesn't appeal.

Anthropologist Clifford Geertz defines religion as "a system of symbols which acts to establish powerful, pervasive, and long-lasting moods and motivations in men by formulating conceptions of a general order of existence and clothing these conceptions with such an aura of factuality that the moods and motivations seem uniquely realistic." That's quite a mouthful, but it's a fairly accurate description of the world according to Coca-Cola. The "pause that refreshes" surfaced just when organized religion was suffering from the writings of Charles Darwin, Albert Einstein, and other scientists. Coke has achieved the status of a substitute modern religion which promotes a particular, satisfying, all-inclusive world view espousing perennial values such as love, peace, and universal brotherhood. It provides a panacea whenever daily life seems too difficult, harried, fragmented, or confused. As a sacred symbol, Coca-Cola induces varying "worshipful" moods, ranging from exaltation to pensive solitude, from near-orgasmic togetherness to playful games of chase.

Most religions have relied on a drug-laced drink of one sort or another. Christianity reveres its communion wine, which Coca-Cola has literally replaced at various times. The Greek gods drank nectar, while Dionysus sported as the lord of wine. Teutonic deities quaffed their mead. Arab Sufi monks drank coffee to keep them awake for midnight prayers. In India, the juice of the soma plant placated the gods. Throughout history, shamans have relied on coca, tobacco, caffeine, and other mind-altering drugs to induce trance and contact God. "The widespread use of drugs around the world," asserts a contributer to *Man, Myth & Magic*, "makes it plain that man is a discontented animal beset by psychological and physical troubles, by boredom and spiritual ambitions." As Robert Woodruff observed, the world belongs to the discontented.

The most powerful Coca-Cola appeal has not, ultimately, been sexual or physiological, but communal: if you drink Coke, the ads suggest, you will belong to a warm, loving, accepting family, singing in perfect harmony. If we can't quite succeed in finding that stress-free society today, never mind—we'll find it tomorrow. We'll build a better world for you, and me, and everyone. Always. Always Coca-Cola. It's a beautifully seductive message, because it's what we all want. A harsh critic of Coca-Cola once admitted that she found the Hilltop commercial "almost irresistible," even though it disturbed her.

For some moralists, this manipulation of basic human desires is evil. In *The Brothers Karamazov*, one of Roberto Goizueta's favorite books, the terrifyingly hypocritical Grand Inquisitor mocks all of us "pitiful creatures" who must find "something that all would believe in and worship; what is essential is that all may be *together* in it. This craving for *community* of worship is the chief misery of every man individually and of all humanity from the beginning of time." For the Grand Inquisitor, we are all pathetic, insecure souls desperately seeking any sort of meaning. We must, therefore, find mystery and miracle—a secret formula for living, a 7X of the soul.

In February of 1992, ten Tibetan monks visited the World of Coca-Cola Museum in Atlanta. Standing in front of an endless conveyor belt simulating a bottling operation, the maroon-robed monks smiled and nodded, chattering in their own tongue. A translator explained that they enjoyed finding "modern discoveries," and Coke was one of the great ones. Taking turns, the Buddhists stuck their heads through a cardboard cut-out scene depicting a waiter pouring a glass of Coca-Cola. In the gift shop, one monk found a voice-activated dancing Coke can with sun-glasses and gave it jittery exercise with a traditional otherworldly chant. The Buddhists seemed delighted with this temple to the great American soft drink—"this church of consumption," as one snide commentator put it. Perhaps instinctively, they saw the museum as a religious manifestation, a necessary ordering of the universe. According to Buddha, all such order is, of course, illusory, part of the world of *maya*, but that rendered it no less important. "Like all great love affairs," Ike Herbert told an group of fountain salesmen shortly before he retired, "ours depends to a large extent on creating a set of illusions, feelings that we are special. We are who we are because we are all things to all people all the time everywhere." Paul Foley, the long-time head of McCann-Erickson's umbrella agency, summarized it best. "We're selling smoke," he always reminded his creative staff. "They're drinking the image, not the product."

SHADES OF HARVEY WILEY

No wonder my mother wouldn't let me drink Coca-Cola, the opiate of the people. She thought it was bad for me: it would rot my teeth, keep me awake, and spread chemicals throughout my body. There was something mysterious and enticing about the dark, bubbly liquid, though. In high school, when I read the witches' incantation in *Macbeth*, I naturally assumed that they were brewing Coca-Cola in their caldron. Like generations before me, I longed for the forbidden drink. Sometimes, after we finished playing football, Billy Krenson and I would go to his house, where his mother served up Coke with cracked ice. Nothing has ever tasted so sinfully good. As another surreptitious Coke drinker described it, "the effervescence was boldly astringent and as clean as a knife; the flavor suggested the corrupt spices of Araby and a hint, perhaps, of brimstone."

Ever since Harvey Wiley, reformers have identified Coca-Cola as the temptation of the Devil, particularly for innocent children. Today, Michael Jacobson, founder and executive director of the Center For Science in the Public Interest, has taken up the crusade, lamenting that a twelve-ounce Coke can contains the equivalent of ten teaspoons of sugar, supplying "empty" calories—and the now-popular 20-ounce bottle delivers 17 teaspoons. In his 1998 publication, *Liquid Candy*, Jacobson observed, "Twenty years ago, boys consumed more than twice as much milk as soft drinks." Today, those figures are reversed. Jacobson was particularly concerned about girls, who also consume twice as much soda as milk, and who build 92 percent of their bone mass by age 18. Americans drank an average of 576 twelve-ounce servings of soft drinks per year in 1997—or 1.6 cans a day for every man, woman, and child.

For then-CEO Doug Ivester, of course, that is cause for jubilation rather than concern. "Actually," he observed in 1998, "our product is quite healthy. Fluid replenishment is a key to health . . . Coca-Cola does a great service because it encourages people to take in more and more liquids." Indeed, a fifth of American toddlers of one or two drink soft drinks at an average of seven ounces a day.

So what? Why all the concern? By relying primarily on the instant energy of glucose, people forego vitamins, minerals, fiber, and other necessary nutrients. While it is possible to get those vital nutrients elsewhere, Jacobson argues that the more Coke you drink, the less room you find for healthy food in a typical 2,500-calorie daily "budget." It is more likely that Coca-Cola fiends, particularly those who use it to wash down fatty junk foods, will ingest too many calories—one of the reasons that 12 percent of teenagers and 35 percent of adults in the United States are overweight. Worse, poor and black American children are three times more likely to become obese while suffering from malnutrition. Even the conservative *Wall Street Journal* ran a front-page series on the inner-city "deadly diet" of high-fat, salty, sugary food and drink sold in popular fast food outlets, which offer a refuge from the ghetto. "Ain't no hip-hop [music], ain't no profanity," a black visitor to a Harlem McDonald's explained. "The picture, the plants, the way people keep things neat here, it makes you feel like you're in civilization."

As the world shrinks to a global village, the appeal of Coke and Big Macs as "luxury" items are increasing, and some nutritionists express concern that these will displace cheaper, traditional, healthier fare. "When advertised in a culturally appropriate way with appealing symbols," writes an anthropologist, "the public consumption of such foods and soft drinks turns out to be a principal form of identification with Western lifestyles and power . . . Their long-term negative consequences are not fully assessed, but it is highly probable that they will progressively undermine the older [core diet] of poor agrarian societies." In the United States, the "core diet" now consists of fast food and soft drinks for so many teenagers that, as I observed in the previous chapter, many schools are giving away Coke and Pepsi in an attempt to keep students in school lunchrooms.

The other major villain in Coke, according to Jacobson, is caffeine, even though a twelve-ounce can contains only a third the stimulant in a strong cup of coffee. Like Wiley, Jacobson objects to children ingesting any caffeine, though there are no conclusive studies which show the drug's deleterious effects. Scientists tell us that caffeine promotes stomach-acid secretion, temporarily raises blood pressure, and dilates some blood vessels while constricting others. Caffeine is mildly addictive, and when used excessively, it can lead to "caffeinism" and its attendant shaky nerves and insomnia. In the past two decades, various contradictory caffeine studies have highlighted our ignorance more than anything else. In 1980 and 1981, caffeine was blamed for everything from pancreatic cancer to miscarriages and birth defects, but none of these findings has stood the test of time. In general, unless a woman drinks ten or more cans of Coke a day, Jacobson doesn't think there's any danger, though pregnant women should cut down or eliminate caffeine intake, since the drug is transmitted to the fetus, as it is through the breast milk of a nursing mother. Surprisingly, caffeine has not been proven to harm children. Jacobson is concerned, however, about withdrawal symptoms. In some studies, children deprived of caffeine display impaired performance and attention.

Besides caffeine and sugar, critics have traditionally complained about the phosphoric acid that gives Coca-Cola much of its fabled bite. Science teachers still routinely drop extracted teeth into Coke to show how it softens and blackens them, and the soft drink does indeed clean windshields, chrome, and battery terminals quite nicely. Nonetheless, Coke's acidity—equivalent to orange juice—does not harm the digestive tract, already an acidic environment anyway. As a matter of fact, many doctors still prescribe Coke to sooth upset stomachs. Some studies appear to link soft drinks containing phosphoric acid (but not citric acid) with kidney stones, however. Nor does the acid normally do much damage in the mouth, where saliva tends to neutralize it. Still, according to Dr. William H. Bowen, professor of dentistry in the Center for Oral Biology at the University of Rochester, it is Coke's phosphoric acid rather than sugar which poses problems for teeth. The few available studies indicate, surprisingly enough, that Coca-Cola does not contribute to cavities. Rather, the acid eats away at tooth enamel, particularly if a consumer habitually sips through the front teeth. Consequently, Bowen suggests drinking through a straw, taking the beverage deep into the mouth.

Ever since Pemberton invented Coca-Cola, people have attacked it because of its purportedly bad health effects. Company officials usually just dismiss such critics. Don't you think maybe, they inquire, after a hundred-plus years of massive Coca-Cola consumption, we'd notice toothless, neurotic, cancerous heavy users falling over dead on every street corner? Roberto Goizueta used to joke about the "immutable law of the cynical elite," which holds that "nothing so available, so inexpensive, so much enjoyed by so many . . . can be good for you." As for those who lump Coke with junk food and blame it for the poor nutrition of immigrants, inner-city blacks, and Third World people abandoning their traditional diet, the Coca-Cola executives reply that they advocate drinking the beverage only as part of a balanced diet. It isn't their fault if people don't eat well.[*]

Certainly, if individual cases prove anything, Coca-Cola is not only harmless, but may even be the life-extender Pemberton claimed. Look at Robert Woodruff, who died at 95 and presumably drank his fair share of Coke. On her 97th birthday in 1959, an Alabama woman attributed her longevity to drinking a Coke at precisely 10 A.M. every day since 1886. But she was nothing compared with legendary figure Luke Kingsley, a Memphis car salesman who told a reporter in 1954 that he had routinely drunk over 25 Cokes a day for the past fifty years. "I have been to the funerals of five or six doctors who predicted it would kill me," the 65-year-old chortled. At the end of the interview, the parched journalist asked for a drink of water. "Water!" barked Kingsley. "That's something you wash your face in. Have a Coke!"

THE TEA/COKE CONSPIRACY

One of the most compelling (and fascinating) criticisms of Coca-Cola, however, comes from anthropologist Sidney Mintz, whose book, *Sweetness and Power*, traces how sugar and tea were initially considered exotic luxuries available only to the wealthy nobility in Great Britain. In addition to their use as rare spices, they were supposedly potent medicines for almost any ailment. In the 1500s, one writer claimed that "nice white sugar . . . cleans the blood, strengthens body and mind." As a result, a German traveler who met Queen Elizabeth in Shakespearean times described her black teeth—"a defect the English seem subject to, from their too great use of sugar." By 1700, a bad British poet penned "Panacea: A Poem Upon Tea," praising the brew as "the Drink of Health, the Drink of Souls!" Soon, however, a kind of trickle-down

---

[*] In 1959, one Coke director told E. J. Kahn, Jr.: "I sometimes shudder at the thought of all those poor people paying a nickel for a Coke when they probably ought to be spending it on a loaf of bread." If any company men harbor those reservations today, none of them have shared them with me.

cultural phenomenon occurred, with the British middle and lower classes emulating the elite, as tea and sugar, now staples in the English diet, lost their medicinal patina. Poverty-stricken factory workers learned to grab a quick meal away from home, using hot sweetened tea as a pick-me-up. Teatime, a new British social ritual, was gradually assimilated into all aspects of daily life.

This should all sound familiar. Like tea and sugar, Coca-Cola started life primarily as a medicine, though not strictly for the upper crust. Like sweetened tea, Coke contained caffeine and sugar, along with a tiny amount of cocaine for fifteen years or so. A Coke break quickly became the American equivalent of the British teatime, while advertising stressed the role of the "pause that refreshes" as an aid to industry. In Mintz's view, then, Coca-Cola fits right into an insidious modern trend and is in part responsible for it. "The experience of time in modern society is often one of insoluble shortage," he writes, "and this perception may be essential to the smooth functioning of an economic system based on the principle of ever-expanded consumption." In essence, he argues that Coke has helped to transform the American attitude towards time. Like Asa Candler, we never feel we have enough of it, and so we attempt to cram life full of pre-packaged pleasures. As an example, Mintz conjures an exaggerated but disturbingly familiar scene: "Watching the Cowboys play the Steelers while eating Fritos and drinking Coca-Cola, while smoking a joint, while one's girl sits on one's lap" becomes a way of "maximizing enjoyment."

Mintz blames advertising for turning us into such all-consuming monsters. "We are what we eat; in the modern western world, we are *made* more and more into what we eat, whenever forces we have no control over persuade us that our consumption and our identity are linked." As a result, the anthropologist argues, we allow television images of happy Coca-Cola drinkers to determine not only what we imbibe, but who we are. Surely, however, this criticism is a bit overblown. Most of us *do* in fact exert control over our choice of beverage, food, and lifestyle. I admit that I find many Coca-Cola commercials appealing, and I enjoy drinking the product every now and then. But it doesn't rule my life, and (although I hesitate to admit this to all the kind souls who plied me with Coke during interviews) I usually drink a lot more coffee, tea, wine, fruit juice and water. I am left cold by frenetic Coke commercials aimed at teens. Finally, while it is unfortunate that our presidents are now sold to us like soft drinks, it may be an oversimplification to blame that American penchant exclusively on Coca-Cola.

It will be interesting, however, to see how Mintz interprets a current British trend. In 1970, when Brits took a beverage break, they drank tea 61 percent of the time. By 1990, that percentage had dropped to 43 percent, and it kept dropping for the next decade. "Many young people cannot be bothered with all the ceremony involved with fixing a 'proper' cup of tea," one commentator has noted, adding that the traditional process involves ten minutes or so of heating, pouring, and steeping. "You had time in the old Britain," a 25-year-old financier commented as he gulped his Coca-Cola.

GLOBAL COCA-COLA CULTURE

Even if Coke can't necessarily be held accountable for all the ills of modern life, most intellectuals express revulsion at its on-going world-wide conquest. To many commentators, Coca-Cola typifies the worst of Western culture. "Coke is the American's fuel, just as television is his soul," a German sneered in the late seventies. Twenty years earlier, Adlai Stevenson asked, "With the supermarket as our temple, and the singing commercial as our litany, are we likely to fill the world with an irresistible vision of America's purpose and inspiring way of life?" The current answer appears to be a resounding "YES!" Coca-Cola has indeed taught the world to sing to its harmonics, or it is doing so as quickly as possible.

The movie industry has always loved Coke as a convenient symbol of Western civilization—witness *Dr. Strangelove* and *On the Beach*, both films in which a Coke bottle serves as a wry commentary on our shallow values in the midst of Armageddon. At the beginning of *The Gods Must Be Crazy*, the totemic bottle falls out of the sky onto the sands of the Kalahari Desert, where it completely transforms the lives of the innocent Bushmen as surely as Eve's apple in Eden. In *The Coca-Cola Kid*, a similar invasion takes place in Australia. In all of these films, the soft drink is presented as a sinister force, a harbinger of unhealthy values.

Whether Coke deserves such criticism or not, no one doubts that it is invasive. Many years ago, a Coca-Cola executive told his followers, "You have entered the lives of more people . . . than any other product or ideology, including the Christian religion," and that truth has only grown more profound with the passage of time. "The number of truly global brands," writes a columnist for the *Economist*, "are few indeed: the only indisputable mass-market one is Coca-Cola." Today, at North Avenue, Doug Daft and other senior Coke managers can punch their computers and call up the history of per capita consumption growth for any country as easily as *Star Trek*'s commander can summon details of obscure planets.

It is certainly unnerving when Coke marketers talk about the battle for "stomach shelf space" or the drink's advertisers discuss its "share of mind," which keeps swelling, crowding out other perhaps more worthy uses of our brain cells. The soft drink seems to be on everyone's mind lately, from disgruntled journalists who renamed the over-hyped 1996 Atlanta sports event the "Coca-Cola Olympics," to liberated East Europeans and Chinese with a craving for American symbols such as blue jeans and Coke. Freed communists aren't alone in coveting Coke and other symbols of Western culture. Satellite and cable are bringing the Real Thing into homes all over the world. It is Always Coca-Cola in all ways. As Harvard Business School professor Ted Levitt has written, "Everywhere people learn from the same communal messenger," leading to "people who've become increasingly alike and indistinct from one another." Or, as Roberto Goizueta once put it, "People around the world are today connected to each other by brand-name consumer products as much as by anything else."

"From infancy to adulthood," historian Barbara Tuchman wrote in 1980, "advertising is the air Americans breathe, the information we absorb, almost without knowing it. It floods our minds with pictures of perfection and goals of happiness easy to attain." Now, decades later, advertising permeates the air that *everyone* breathes. Even the purportedly neutral *International Encyclopedia of Communications* observes that television has made "this opulent, imaginary world" of advertising universally familiar, leading to unrealistic expectations, frustrations, and unhealthy attitudes among poor Third World inhabitants for whom the price of a Coke may constitute a substantial part of the daily wage. Whether harmful or not, the messages bounced from satellites certainly connect. One researcher attempted to define the "global teenager" by surveying a representative sampling of young people from Argentina, Brazil, China, Egypt, Britain, Guatemala, India, Israel, Kenya, the Soviet Union, and Thailand. He discovered that while only 40 percent could correctly identify the United Nations logo, 82 percent knew Coke's symbol.

Such trends alarm many observers, who fear that the variety and spice of human culture will be destroyed by the Coca-Colonization of the world. In his book, *Jihad vs. McWorld*, political science professor Benjamin Barber argued that Coke insidiously infiltrates and distorts cultures. "In the new McWorld of global sales," he wrote, "the trademark has surpassed the sales item and the image has overtaken the product." Even when multinationals focus only on consumption figures, Barber observed, "increasingly they can maximize those figures only by intervening actively in the very social, cultural, and political domains about which they affect agnosticism." During the Vietnamese War, the U.S. propaganda spoke of winning the hearts and souls of men. "The Cola Wars are *only* about the hearts and souls of men," Barber said. "By persuading people they must have the products you sell, you win a war much more permanently . . . than if you simply occupy a town." He dismissed the supposed freedom of choice between Coke and Pepsi as illusory. "What these new cola wars do is to diminish our fundamental choices by the extension of invisible monopolies, new sets of needs, new sets of goods for those needs."

Yet Barber's alarmist views are ultimately unconvincing. In his book, he attempts to link "Jihad"—the fragmentation of countries into warring ethnic groups—with its seeming opposite, the globalization of culture. "Ironically, a world that is coming together pop culturally and commercially is a world whose discreet subnational ethnic and religious and racial parts are also far more in evidence, in no small part as a reaction to McWorld." Still, as even Barber admits, multinationals such as Coke hate wars, which are bad for business. "The market imperative," he wrote, "has in fact reinforced the quest for international peace and stability," even though that doesn't guarantee democracy.

Although Coke unquestionably exerts an influence on cultures and does change drinking habits—witness the virtual disappearance of *kvass*, the traditional Russian drinks—local habits (and ethnic groups) are far stronger than many critics recognize. They are horrified, for instance, that in regions such as Chiapas in Mexico, Coke and Pepsi are used in Mayan religious services in lieu of *poch*, the traditional alcoholic drink. The scene certainly is startling, as Indians in traditional Mayan dress pour Coca-Cola as a ritual offering. But the fact remains, they still *are* in traditional dress, and there still *are* rituals.*

In a chapter entitled, "The Future of Humanity," an anthropology textbook portrayed a black-robed, grey-bearded patriarch reading the paper below a Hebraic Coca-Cola sign. "The worldwide spread of such products as Coca-Cola and Wrangler jeans," the caption read, "is taken by some as a sign that a single, homogeneous world culture is developing." Others refuse to panic, however. Already an accepted part of the landscape and lifestyle in an enormous array of cultures, Coca-Cola doesn't appear to be destroying them. In the picture in the anthropology book, the Jewish patriarch is still wearing his black robes and reading his paper, not boogying in his blue jeans.

Similarly, although French critics initially called Euro Disneyland "a terrifying giant step toward world homogenization" and "a cultural Cherno-byl," another Frenchman pointed out: "If French culture can be squashed by Mickey Mouse . . . it would have to be disturbingly fragile." Yes, Coke is now widely available in French cafés, but it is served almost as if it were an aperitif rather than a soft drink. "One might want to consider the 'Frenchification' of America," wrote Richard Kuisel in *Seducing the French*, "as well as the Americanization of France . . . If anything, we have learned that modern culture is eclectic and porous." In other words, we might regard the current cross-pollination of cultures as a kind of evolution rather than homogenization. "The differences among races, nations, cultures and their various histories are at least as profound and as durable as the similarities," wrote Australian essayist Robert Hughes, who predicted that the future belongs to "people who can think and act with informed grace across ethnic, cultural, linguistic lines"—a perfect description of today's top Coca-Cola managers.

What Coca-Cola does—with remarkable success—is identify the commonal-ities of human experience without necessarily altering cultures fundamentally. "You'll find plenty of social scientists who'll point up the differences," Don Keough once told me, "but wherever I go, boys and girls meet, walk in parks, fall in love, get married, have children, have family gatherings. They celebrate the joys of life just the way you and I do." Consequently, Coca-Cola is able to make its pattern advertising appeal to virtually all human beings. In America, this process has been unbelievably thorough, so that when a junior high boy bought a Coke for a girl—whether in 1920 or 2000—it would conjure romance.

One American essayist, writing about Coke's global availability, has com-mented: "Somehow that is very, very comforting. It means we can go into much of the world and find our security blanket waiting." While that may sound like the statement of an Ugly American, other travelers who leave their native lands

---

* There are more insidious aspects to the Mexican situation, however. The town leaders tend to be Pepsi or Coke distributors who profit not only from the rituals, but who have allegedly administered local justice by forcing people to purchase soft drinks. It is also common for a young man to ask for a woman's hand in marriage by offering her parents a case of Coke.

routinely experience the same feeling. For the German, Greek, Japanese, Argentine, or Nigerian, the sight of a familiar Coca-Cola sign is often reassuring. Coca-Cola is unlikely, however, to homogenize world culture completely, with religious sects, nationalistic fervor, and proud ethnic groups reasserting themselves. As change quickens, Ted Levitt has observed, people around the world desperately seek "roots, remembrance, attachments, fantasy, and transcendence, while wanting simultaneously everything else that beckons within palpable reach." Naturally, Coca-Cola fits right in, attempting to assuage that need for fantasy and transcendence with its advertising. Roberto Goizueta was correct when he told a group of bright-eyed high school seniors: "Corporations are not as pious as I might be tempted to tell you they are. Nor are they evil as some portray them to be. The truth is somewhere in the middle."

COCA-COLA POLITICS

Just as missionaries feel that any human soul is ripe for the True Gospel, Coca-Cola men rarely distinguish among nations. "We believe in the future of [all] countries," Don Keough once wrote. "We'll ride through whatever political or economic conditions exist." Consequently, Coke never pulled out of Chile when Pinochet was in power. Indeed, the Company appreciated the booming, stable economy under the South American dictator. Nor did the Company leave Indonesia because of atrocities committed by the Suharto regime. "We *do* have a social conscience," one Coke manager told me, "but we don't enter politics. We've never lost an election, because we never run. Our job is simply to provide a moment of pleasure to consumers around the world without concern for the form or type of government under which they live." He paused and smiled broadly. "We make life a little brighter. We serve humanity." Asa Candler would have applauded.

It seems disingenuous, however, for the manager to assert that Coca-Cola does not enter politics. At least since World War II, the soft drink, as highly charged with symbolism as with CO_2, has *been* politics. If, instead of courting the Chinese, Roberto Goizueta had tried to persuade his friend George Bush to withdraw China's most-favored-nation status, perhaps that country's leaders would have reconsidered Tiananmen Square or the prolonged Chinese rape of Tibet. After all, those sweet-faced Tibetan monks who visited the World of Coca-Cola Museum cried when asked about their country's plight, and with good reason. Even though Bill Clinton spoke out strongly on Chinese human rights abuses, he proved to be a strong supporter of business relations with China—and a friend of Coke's in general, as he demonstrated when he visited Coke's Moscow bottling plant and guzzled Coke for photographers.[*] In

---

[*] Clinton's mentor, former Arkansas Senator J. W. Fulbright, was also devoted to Coca-Cola, since his father bought the Fayetteville bottling plant in 1910. "I worked there in the summer of 1915, washing bottles by hand," Fulbright recalled. "We were always proud of Coca-Cola; it was the main thing my father left us."

China, where annual per capita consumption of Coke products grew to seven drinks in 1998, Coke has built over two dozen bottling plants, many of them jointly owned with the Chinese government.

In their own defense, Coca-Cola men argue that the only way to ensure their power is to maintain their ubiquitous presence. Besides, if Coke pulled out, Pepsi would simply move in unimpeded, a thought much worse than any human rights violations. The world's largest McDonald's—taking that record away from Moscow—opened near Tiananmen Square, and the Coke, of course, flows profusely there. Given time, the argument goes, the influx of Coca-Cola and Big Macs will create goodwill towards the West and may eventually soften China's dictatorial, repressive policies more effectively than sanctions.

Indeed, that argument is fairly convincing. When documentary filmmakers interviewed young Chinese adults in 1997, they were unconcerned about the influx of Coke and Pepsi. "Yes, they bring something other than the drink itself to China," said one student. "So if you like it, you will say, 'Hey, they bring something new.' But if you don't like it, 'Oh, it's a cultural invasion.'" He laughed. His dream, he said, was to "make money to the degree that I don't have to worry about money." James Watson, a Harvard professor specializing in China, must have heard similar sentiments. "Asian economies are entering a 'new consumerism' phase," he has written. "The 'meaning of life' is now expressed in consumer products; people's sense of being is verified by how much they can consume." As shallow as that may be, it could lead to a more open society with a middle class, social climbing, and the like. Already, there are new words for Chinese yuppies (*dushi yapishi*), though the vast majority of the Chinese population still belong to the working poor (*qionglaogong*).

Coca-Cola's official South African divestiture represents an exception to ignoring political considerations, but public opinion obviously dictated that decision. South Africa is one place where Coke officials clearly do serve humanity. Aside from establishing the well-regarded Equal Opportunity Fund there, Coca-Cola executives practiced a kind of corporate shuttle diplomacy, meeting with Nelson Mandela and other black leaders to assure them of the Company's support in the struggle against apartheid and to ensure The Coca-Cola Company a presence in the new order. In a bloodbath, Coke sales would have gone down. Coke remained a steadfast friend of Mandela throughout his South African presidency and has moved its concentrate plant back into the country.

And therein lies the true beauty of capitalism. The Coca-Cola religion has no real morality, no commandment other than increased consumption of its drink. Consequently, it has been perfectly willing to co-exist with Hitler, bejeweled Maharajas, impoverished migrant workers, malnourished Africans, Guatemalan death squads, clear-cut Belizean rainforests, or repressive Chinese. Unlike most world governments, however, The Coca-Cola Company eventually acts out of enlightened self-interest. Because it values its squeaky-clean image above all else, it reacts far more quickly to bad publicity than any potentate. Consequently, it is arguably up to us, the public, to monitor its corporate behavior. Faced with boycotts of sufficient size, documentaries of appropriate proportion, or shareholder resolutions representing large chunks of stock, the Company will act. Sometimes, it will even act pre-emptively to avoid such trouble. For its own selfish ends, then, Coca-Cola does indeed try to promote the peace and harmony it promises in its commercials.

In the perfect world of a Coke executive's dreams, the biggest conflict will be similar to the fight between Miss World and Miss Universe of 1995—the latter signed up to advertise Coke, while her rival shilled for Pepsi. Global politics will be run, not by small-minded, war-prone, ethnocentric nation-states, but by benign multinationals who want only for you to swallow their soft drinks. Their local bottlers—Serbs, Albanians, Hutus, Tutsis, Indians, Pakestanis, Chinese, Tibetans, Germans, French, Russians, Americans, Arabs, Jews—will discourage strife in order to boost per capita consumption. All you need to restore tranquillity is a good burp. As Roberto Goizueta used to say in a different context, "The world is first a cola world, then an orange world, then a lemon-lime world. The rest just come and go."*

Unfortunately for Coca-Cola (and perhaps for the rest of us), the world doesn't work that way all the time. In the post-Cold War euphoria of the mid-1990s, it appeared that a global economy based on freewheeling international free enterprise would lead automatically to the greater good for all. But the global economic crisis that began in 1997 made everyone realize that capitalism can have a grim face, and that interconnected economies can prove perilous. "For much of the world," wrote one commentator in 1999, "the magic of the marketplace extolled by the West in the afterglow of victory in the Cold War has been supplanted by the cruelty of markets." Over such matters, Coca-Cola has little control. Nor can it promise a fizzy utopia, other than in advertise-ments. "It would be nice to think that the next century could be better, that a certain stability would take hold now that the world is rid of the Cold War," wrote another rueful observer in 1999. "But as the century ends the way it began, there is every indication that in the next millennium, dogs will still be eating the dead along the roadsides as endless columns of the dispossessed pass by."

Keeping such harsh realities in mind, it is difficult to take critics such as Benjamin Barber too seriously when they rant against Coca-Cola as the monstrous corporation that is ruining the world. Given the choice between Jihad and McWorld, in other words, I'll take McWorld any day.

BORN AGAIN

When I started researching this book, I was surprised to find that officials of an American soft drink company had such ready access to powerful world figures.

---

* "More and more multinational companies don't have a 'home' market," observed a financial advisor in 1999. "They're based in a particular country as an accident of history, but their business is done around the world."

Now, nothing would startle me. After all, Coca-Cola's annual sales surpass the entire economies of many countries in which the drink is bottled and sold. As the colorful Harrison Jones once put it, "The Coca-Cola Company is like an elephant's ass. You throw a rock in any direction and you're likely to hit it." Or, as another more recent commentator has written, "Coca-Cola is more durable, less vulnerable, more self-correcting than the Roman Empire. This product is destined to outlast the USA." And, aside from controversies over nutrition, culture, advertising, and politics, The Coca-Cola Company has been a force for good in the world.

Even though Coke's motivations stem primarily from concerns over its image, the firm and its bottlers always supply fresh, clean water (or soft drinks) when natural disasters—earthquake, flood, fire, famine—strike. When Hurricane Georges struck Puerto Rico, for instance, Coke was there to help homeless victims. "They particularly enjoyed and appreciated the Coca-Cola, Sprite and water we gave them," wrote a Coke employee. "It was a great feeling to help, even in a small way." Similarly, when a terrible tsunami (tidal flood) devastated Papua New Guinea, Coke donated relief supplies.

Unfortunately, Coke lobbies strenuously against bottle-bill legislation and has even set up a Civic Action Network, a "non-partisan grassroots" organization to protest such bills. Comparing the litter along Georgia roadsides to states with a redeemable nickel deposit such as Vermont certainly indicates that container bills work. But Coke can legitimately point out that its cans and plastic bottles are recyclable and account for less than one percent of the solid-waste stream in the United States. People end up wearing many of the recycled bottles in the form of soft fur-like apparel.

The Company supports innovative educational programs in the U.S. and elsewhere, and no one could calculate the amount of philanthropical largess directly or indirectly attributable to Coca-Cola. Aside from the Company's foundation, gigantic funds devoted to the public good contain Woodruff, Whitehead, Lupton, Thomas and Bradley money, not to mention innumerable local charities of American and foreign bottlers. Robert Woodruff correctly observed that everyone who touched the magical drink would make money— and, fortunately, a great deal of it has been spent wisely, particularly in the city of Atlanta.

Even in normal times, Coca-Cola has certainly proved a boon to local economies around the world, regardless of what one may think of its impact on local culture and dietary habits. University of South Carolina researchers studied what happened as Coke entered Poland and Romania during the 1991–1994 period. They concluded that for every job in the Coca-Cola bottling system, ten jobs were created in the retail sector. In essence, Coke helped to create an entrepreneurial class where there had been none. This "multiplier effect" was documented in China as well. The researchers also concluded that Coke's presence meant improved productivity and higher quality standards.

One of my best friends from high school days now works for The Coca-Cola Company. Call him David. He looks and seems the same as ever, aside from touches of gray, and we've kept in touch over the years. David once showed me family pictures taken during a beach vacation. Smiling into the camera, he wore a Coca-Cola T-shirt. "God," I laughed, "you can't even get away from it on vacation, can you?" He laughed, too, then said simply, "I don't want to." I realized at that moment that a subtle transformation had taken place within my friend. Some would call it a transfusion in which his blood flowed a caramel shade. He had been born again, and though he has never tried to convert me, I knew he believed in a religion which I continue to find somewhat amusing, somewhat alarming, and ultimately mystifying. He had become a Coca-Cola man.

Appendix 1: The Sacred Formula

When I set out to write a comprehensive history of Coca-Cola, I had no idea I would stumble across the original formula, particularly not in the bowels of the Company itself. After all, this was the world's best-kept trade secret, one which the Company had already refused to reveal under two judges' orders. In 1977, the Company departed from India rather than hand the sacred formula to the insistent government. Yet I appear to have accomplished the impossible. One day an archivist brought out a file with individual yellowing, tattered papers that had been lovingly restored and laminated inside plastic. He explained that this constituted the remains of John Pemberton's formula book, donated to the Company in the 1940s.

I already knew the story behind this formula book. As a young man, John P. Turner had traveled from his home town of Columbus, Georgia, to apprentice with John Pemberton in his final few years. After Pemberton's death, Turner took the formula book back to Columbus, where he served as a pharmacist for many years. In 1943, Turner's son showed the book to a member of the Coca-Cola board, opening it to a page containing *the* formula. The board member persuaded the Turner heir to let him have the book. "My God!" Harrison Jones, the board chairman, exclaimed when he saw the formula. "Where did you get that?" And that was the last anyone ever saw of it.

The file I received in the Coca-Cola archives stated that this was the "account and formula book belonging to Dr. J. S. Pemberton while a druggist in Columbus," but that is almost certainly incorrect, since one of the recipes for a celery cola includes Coca-Cola by name as an ingredient, undoubtedly placing it in 1888, since that is the drink Pemberton was working on at the time of his death. My heart raced as I carefully leafed through the preserved pages, but of course I assumed that the Company had hidden one crucial item deep in a vault somewhere. Consequently, I was astonished to find what appeared to be a Coca-Cola recipe, unlabeled except for an "X" at the top of the page:

Citrate Caffein	1 oz.
Ext. Vanilla	1 oz.
Flavoring	2 ½ oz.
F.E. Coco	4 oz.
Citric Acid	3 oz.
Lime Juice	1 Qt.

Sugar	30 lbs.
Water	2 ½ Gal.
Caramel sufficient	

Mix Caffeine Acid and Lime Juice in 1 Qt Boiling water add vanilla and flavoring when cool.

Flavoring

Oil Orange	80
Oil Lemon	120
Oil Nutmeg	40
Oil Cinnamon	40
Oil Coriander	20
Oil Neroli	40
Alcohol 1 Qt.	
let stand 24 hours.	

The "flavoring" section is obviously the "7X" portion of the formula, though there are only six ingredients (unless you count the alcohol). Perhaps he later added the vanilla to the flavoring section as the seventh component. "F. E. Coco" means fluid extract of coca, but kola nuts are not mentioned, only "Citrate Caffein." Pemberton almost certainly received his caffeine from Merck in Darmstadt, Germany, because he praised that firm as producing a superior form of the stimulant from kola nuts.

I photocopied the document, but I simply couldn't believe that anyone in the Company would hand over the original formula to me. Surely, it must only be a forerunner of the real thing. Then I received an unexpected confirmation that I had stumbled onto something far more valuable than I knew. While interviewing Mladin Zarubica, the Technical Observer who made "white Coke" for Russian General Zhukov, I mentioned that I had a formula. "Oh, really?" he said. "So do I. The Company gave me one when I had to take the color out for Zhukov. Want to see it?" I did indeed. When the photocopy of his January 4, 1947, correspondence arrived, it contained *exactly the same formula* that I had found in the archives—same amounts, same format, even the same misspelling of "F. E. Coco." The only difference was that Zarubica's formula was incomplete, leaving off the final two ingredients in 7X (coriander and neroli). It appeared that they hadn't wanted to release the complete formula and had taken the precaution of altering it in this fashion.

I was astounded. Not only had I come into possession of Pemberton's original formula, deep in the bowels of the Company itself, but it had ostensibly survived unchanged for at least sixty years after the inventor wrote it out on that acidified paper. This was truly a mystery, however. It contradicted Howard Candler's assertion that his father, Asa, had substantially altered the way Coca-Cola was made. And why didn't the Zarubica formula mention *decocainized* coca leaf, or the fact that the Company no longer used citric acid, but phosphoric? Or that the amount of caffeine had been reduced? And that wasn't the only formula change. Old Asa supposedly fiddled around with 7X as well. Through the years, the amount and type of sweetener has also varied.

It appears that even when the original ingredients and proportions are revealed, the mystique around the formula continues. My final conclusion: the Company did not, in fact, give Mladin Zarubica the *current* working formula for Coca-Cola in 1947—not even a partial version of it. Instead, Zarubica received a truncated version of the *original* formula, enough for his chemist to figure out how to turn brown Coke to white. The mystery of why the Company handed the formula to me in its own archives remains. I can only assume that there had been another clearly labeled Coca-Cola recipe in the Turner book, which had been hidden away, but no one had examined the rest of the formula closely and the "X" variety had slipped through.[*]

In his 1983 book *Big Secrets*, William Poundstone printed *his* version of the formula, a reasonably accurate guestimate of the current mixture. It makes one gallon:

Sugar:	2400 grams, in just enough water to dissolve
Caramel:	37 grams
Caffeine:	3.1 grams
Phosphoric Acid:	11 grams
Decocainized coca leaf:	1.1 grams
Kola nuts:	0.37 grams

Soak coca leaf & kola nuts in 22 grams of 20% alcohol, then strain and add liquid to the syrup.

Lime juice:	30 grams
Glycerine:	19 grams
Vanilla extract:	1.5 grams
7X Flavoring:	
Orange oil:	0.47 grams
Lemon oil:	0.08 grams
Nutmeg oil:	0.07 grams
Cassia (chinese cinnamon) oil:	0.20 grams
Coriander oil:	trace
Neroli oil:	trace
Lime oil:	0.27 grams

Mix in 4.9 grams of 95% alcohol, add 2.7 grams water, let stand for 24 hours at 60 degrees F. A cloudy layer will separate. Take off the clear part of the liquid and add to the syrup.

Add enough water to make 1 gallon of syrup. Mix one ounce of syrup with carbonated water to make a 6.5 ounce serving.

Poundstone and various other sources claim that oil of lavender may also belong in the formula, and one young specialist from the technical department with whom I shared an elevator agreed. She had just returned from Grasse,

---

[*] Although I have repeatedly asked archivists and Coke spokesmen to comment on this formula, they have not done so. Apparently they did speak to Frederick Allen, who noted in his book, *Secret Formula*, that the formula "is thought to date from the 1940s." No one can know for sure, but for the reasons stated above, I believe it to be the original formula.

where for centuries French experts have extracted various oil essences—including neroli (rendered from a variety of orange blossom) and lavender.

While the *Big Secrets* formula may be close, it doesn't jibe with the sworn testimony given by Coca-Cola chemist Dr Anton Amon in a recent court case. According to him, it takes 13.2 grams of phosphoric acid to make a gallon of syrup, not 11, and 1.86 grams of vanilla extract, not 1.5. Anton said the Company adds 91.99 grams of "single-strength commercial caramel," considerably more than Poundstone's 37 grams. Nonetheless, the formula's ingredients are probably accurate.

Beginning with Asa Candler, no one at the Company referred to the ingredients by name. Instead, sugar was Merchandise #1; caramel, Merchandise #2; caffeine, Merchandise #3; phosphoric acid, Merchandise #4; coca leaf and kola nut extract, Merchandise #5; 7X flavoring mixture, Merchandise #7; vanilla, Merchandise #8. This nomenclature stuck, although since the Candler era, numbers 6 and 9—perhaps lime juice and glycerine—fell by the wayside, probably subsumed into 7X or some other ingredient.

I cover the effects of the coca leaf and kola nut at length in the body of the text, but the herbal lore surrounding the other ingredients is fascinating, if inconclusive, considering the minuscule amounts of each ingredient and the questionable veracity of ancient sources. Cassia, for instance, has been used as a cure for arthritis, cancer, chills, diabetes, dizziness, goiter, headache, and stomachache. Nutmeg fought infection during the Black Plague, has served as a psychotropic and narcotic, and is prescribed in India for dysentery, flatulence, malaria, leprosy, rheumatism, sciatica, and stomachache. Vanilla is variously an aphrodisiac, stimulant, or antispasmodic, cures hysteria, inhibits cavities, and reduces flatulence. And so it goes for the other ingredients.

Since astonishing amounts of money have flowed from the secret formula, it didn't surprise me when no one at the Company wanted to talk about the drink's ingredients. Allowed to interview almost anyone else, I was denied access to Mauricio Gianturco, the head of the technical division. Finally, they did let me interview Harry Waldrop, a "senior psychometrician" (no kidding, that's his title) who once served as one of the elite corps of taste testers who sample batches of Coca-Cola Classic.

The panel members know 7X by smell as much as by taste, and can discern the minute differences that aging causes. Just as some wine tasters can roll a 1945 Mouton-Rothschild around their palate and differentiate it from a 1946, Waldrop can spot a two-month-old batch of Coke syrup. "We all know the taste and aroma of the right stuff," Waldrop said, "but it's hard to put it into words. It's when it's off that we attempt a description." The panel members might break up into small groups, for instance, to discuss a slight bitter note they don't like. Although all of the ingredients are carefully measured and tested by gas chromatography and other scientific gauges, Waldrop doesn't think a computer can replace human beings. "An electronic nose couldn't pick up the subtleties, the hedonics," he assured me.

Although scientists can probably detect the different ingredients in Coca-

Cola, even estimating the approximate amounts, they cannot, according to Company officials, duplicate the precise mixture. Incredible as it may seem, only two people active with the Company supposedly know how to mix 7X. That would necessitate their flying frequently to Cidra, Puerto Rico, and Drogheda, Ireland, to replenish the supply at those two huge concentrate factories, which supply the building blocks for most of the world's Coke. There are other, smaller concentrate plants around the world, too. No one, of course, would talk about such logistics.

Despite all the mystique and paranoia built around the famous formula, one day a Company spokesmen let down his guard when I asked what would happen if I published the bona fide formula with explicit directions in this book. He grinned. "Mark," he said, "let's say this is your lucky day. I happen to have a copy of that formula right here in my desk." He opened his drawer and handed me a phantom document. "There you go. Now what are you going to do with it?"

"Well, I'd put it in my book."

"And?"

"Somebody might decide to go into business in competition with The Coca-Cola Company."

"And what are they going to call their product?"

"Well, they couldn't call it Coca-Cola, because you'd sue them. Let's say they call it Yum-Yum, and they strongly imply, without being liable for a lawsuit, that Yum-Yum is actually the original Coca-Cola formula."

"Fine. Now what? What are they going to charge for it? How are they going to distribute it? How are they going to advertise? See what I'm driving at? We've spent over a hundred years and untold amounts of money building the equity of that brand name. Without our economies of scale and our incredible marketing system, whoever tried to duplicate our product would get nowhere, and they'd have to charge too much. Why would anyone go out of their way to buy Yum-Yum, which is really just like Coca-Cola but costs more, when they can buy the Real Thing anywhere in the world?"

I couldn't think of a thing to say.

Appendix 2: Coca-Cola Magic: Thirty Business Lessons

As I researched The Coca-Cola Company's long history, I was struck by the remarkably consistent vision which has permeated it since Coca-Cola was first invented by that gentle morphine-addicted genius, John Pemberton. He considered his drink an elixir of life, a nerve tonic to cure the ills of man. After Pemberton's death in 1888, Asa Candler carried on that tradition of fanatical belief in his product, as did Robert W. Woodruff, the Boss, and aristocratic Roberto Goizueta. Current CEO Doug Ivester has shown himself to be of the same missionary stripe.

What, then, can readers glean from my lengthy romp through Coke history, aside from the original formula in the previous appendix? Are there messages for the modern entrepreneur? I have distilled the convoluted history's essential parables into thirty commandments. Most are simple and seemingly obvious dicta such as those dispensed by the Boss, but Coke illustrates them dramatically. They are, unfortunately, not quite so simple to put into practice. Other points were learned less willingly in agonized accidents such as the New Coke debacle. Here, then, are time-tested management lessons from the image-masters at Coke:

1) **Sell a good product.** And if it contains a small dose of an addictive drug or two, all the better. The product doesn't have to talk or fly, but it does have to perform some useful, universally appreciated function. Coca-Cola tastes pretty good, once you get used to it (as the international managers know, Coke is an acquired taste); it tickles the nostrils; it quenches thirst; it produces a little caffeine lift. Some people think (following inventor John Pemberton) that it cures headaches, hangovers, and stomach aches, and teenagers can still achieve a cheap, if illusory, high by glugging it with a couple of aspirin. Alas, it no longer contains a smidgeon of cocaine, but it's still a good product. In its early days, Coca-Cola was bottled under less than ideal conditions, resulting in a variable product spiced upon occasion with blowflies, worms, and shards of glass. Now, however, it is standardized and sanitary, providing a safe drink in parts of the world where sampling the water can be fatal.

2) **Believe in your product.** And I don't just mean an intellectual exercise here. Make your product an icon and your job a religious vocation. Instill in employees the notion that *this* is the finest product on earth, and that they are

working for the best company around. Your salesmen should be missionaries, not mere paid hacks. In the 1920s, Robert Woodruff summoned his entire sales staff and stunned them by announcing that they were all fired. The following day, he rehired them for a "new" service department. He informed them that they were no longer salesmen, because no one needed to be sold on the virtues of Coca-Cola any more. No, they were only *servicemen* who were there to help assure that the soda fountain sold a perfectly mixed ice-cold Coke. There is a standing joke among Coke employees that when you go to work for the company, you receive a transfusion of Coca-Cola syrup rather than blood.

3) **Develop a mystique.** An air of mystery, with a touch of sin, sells. As a company official admitted to me, the secret formula really doesn't make much difference to them. The real formula for success is in the product's "brand equity," developed over the last century. So what if somebody took the formula from this book and made a fake Coke? "Why would anyone go out of their way to buy this fake cola," he asked me, "when they can buy the Real Thing anywhere in the world?" True enough, but the formula's mystique, its famed "7X" flavoring, has always been an important part of its appeal. Who knows what's *really* in that dark, fizzy potion?

4) **Sell a cheaply produced item.** Coca-Cola has always cost only a fraction of a cent per drink to produce, the sweetener (cane sugar in most places outside the U.S., now high-fructose corn syrup domestically) constituting most of the expense. Like most patent medicines of its time (1886), Coca-Cola wasn't capital-intensive; its manufacture, while highly secretive, was neither difficult nor laborious.

5) **Everyone who touches your product before it reaches the consumer should make substantial amounts of money.** This rule follows naturally. If your product is cheaply produced, it allows for a gigantic mark-up at the retail end. Coca-Cola achieved a kind of Midas quality. For many years, everyone who touched it became wealthy, including bottlers, stockholders, wholesaling jobbers, and those who provided the trucks, bottles, pallets, dispensers, etc. Of course, such success fostered gratitude and devotion.

6) **Make your product affordable to everyone.** For an unprecedented time, from 1886 until the 1950s, Coca-Cola sold for a nickel a drink, and it remains relatively inexpensive around the world, so that a Third World denizen can purchase the beverage without going broke. Consequently, Coke has usually survived and even thrived during hard economic times.

7) **Make your product widely available.** Robert Woodruff always strove to place his drink "within arm's reach of desire," a lovely phrase which translated into an obsession to provide outlets virtually everywhere—the ballpark, barbershop, office, trains, overseas. As old-time Coke evangelist Harrison Jones put it in 1923, "Let's make it impossible ever to escape Coca-Cola."

8) **Market your product wisely.** That sounds simple, but how, when, and where you market and advertise your product will ultimately determine its success. By 1911, Asa Candler spent over $1 million in creating public demand

for his drink, making Coca-Cola the best-advertised single product in the world. He hired itinerant sign painters to spread the distinctive logo, white on red, on almost every blank wall in America, covering over 5 million square feet. In 1913, the company issued over 100 million novelty items with the logo prominently displayed, all on items which required repeated visual use—thermometers, calendars, matchbooks, blotters, baseball cards, Japanese fans, and signs. It is no surprise that a Coke salesman of that early period reported that one new consumer, "hounded almost to a state of imbecility with Coca-Cola signs," suffered recurring nightmares in which big white devils with red mantels chased him, screeching "Coca-Cola! Coca-Cola!" It would be even less of a surprise today, when the company spends over \$4 billion to market its product worldwide.

9) **Advertise an image, not a product.** As one Coke advertiser liked to remind his creative staff, "We're selling smoke. They're drinking the image, not the product." In its earliest years, Coca-Cola ads made much of the drink's medicinal qualities, touting the beverage as a nerve tonic which would perk up "brain workers," provide solace for hangovers and headaches, and generally prove a "boon to mankind." Frank Robinson, the man who named the drink, provided the distinctive script, and wrote most of the ads, soon realized that he could appeal to more people—and avoid more lawsuits and attacks—by marketing Coca-Cola simply as a refreshing beverage rather than a patent medicine. It was Archie Lee, however, who established a golden age of Coke advertising in the 1920s and 1930s, after watching his four-year-old daughter and her friends fighting over her old stuffed Pooh bear. "It isn't what a product is," Lee concluded, "but what it does." While most other products relied on negative advertising, trying to frighten consumers into buying handcreams to avoid unsightly wrinkles, Lee positions Coca-Cola as a gracious product, "the pause that refreshes," providing a social binder. People who drank Coke were always happy, energetic, wholesome, and friendly. With variations, other advertising greats such as Bill Backer and John Bergin later embellished that message in TV spots for the soft drink, and Shelly Hochron continues the tradition.

10) **Welcome an arch-rival.** Although some Coke employees might not like to admit it, Pepsi has been good for Coca-Cola. "If Pepsi-Cola didn't exist, I would try to invent it," Roberto Goizueta once said. "It keeps us, and them, on our toes and keeps us lean. We're magnificent competitors." People love stories from the "cola wars," and wise marketers from both companies recognize that the publicity fostered by fierce competition is good for sales, regardless of which company appears to be winning an individual battle. Unlike many other products, the big colas have yet to feel any major pressure from generic imitators, largely because no one even thinks of an alternative besides Coke or Pepsi.

11) **Use celebrity endorsements wisely—but sparingly.** From its earliest years, Coca-Cola hired celebrity sponsors, hoping that consumers would identify with baseball great Ty Cobb or actress Hilda Clark. By the 1930s, movie stars from Clark Gable and Cary Grant to Jean Harlow and Joan

Crawford were pushing Coke, and in the late 1960s, singers ranging from Neil Diamond and Leslie Gore to Ray Charles and Aretha Franklin crooned that things went better with the soft drink. There are dangers, however, in relying too heavily on celebrity endorsements. For one thing, viewers may remember more about the star than the product. Coca-Cola has always remained the *real* star of its commercials. Pepsi's headaches with its overpriced celebrity campaigns illustrate another hazard in relying too much on a single spokesperson. Both Madonna and Michael Jackson garnered a great deal of publicity, but not always the kind Pepsi wanted. Coke solved this dilemma by resurrecting dead stars like Louis Armstrong, Groucho Marx, and Humphrey Bogart for cameo appearances. It was unlikely that anyone would accuse them of child molestation or screen a video in which they made love to a black saint in a church pew.

12) **Appeal to universal human desires.** Ever since the 1950s, Coke has created "pattern advertising" which, with little or no modification, can appeal to any culture in the world. The Coke message has universal appeal—by drinking this product, you will be self-assured, happy, popular, sexy, youthful, and well coordinated. To reinforce the message, Coke sponsors every sporting event imaginable, from sumo to soccer, as well as musical extravaganzas around the globe.

13) **Get 'em young.** Of course, the sports and music promotions are meant to engage teenagers, among others. Obviously, if you can achieve loyalty among youthful consumers, you've possibly fostered lifelong consumption. In 1894, Coca-Cola postcards depicted three five-year-old boys in sailor suits proclaiming, "We drink Coca-Cola." After the U.S. government sued the company in 1911—partly because it provided caffeine, an addictive drug, to children—the company halted all overt advertising to anyone under twelve. This did not stop bottlers from giving away free tablets and rulers with engraved logo, nor did it prevent Coca-Cola from co-opting the image of Santa Claus in the 1930s, firmly establishing him as a fat, jolly gentleman clad in Coca-Cola red, with a decided preference for the proper soft drink. Nowadays, Coke is signing up school systems for exclusive vending placements.

14) **Develop cultural sensitivity.** If you intend to sell your product around the world, do not trap yourself in an "Ugly American" image. In the 1920s, when Robert Woodruff authorized the drink's global spread, he attempted to make the drink a German drink in Germany, a French drink in France. The company signed bottling contracts with prominent natives and encouraged the development of a soft drink infrastructure so that the trucks, bottles, pallets, and signs were all produced by local firms. The only thing the company typically sold, and the only thing that had to be imported, was the Coca-Cola concentrate. Thus, the company could proudly and accurately point out how much it contributed to local economies. Through the years, Coca-Cola has developed a group of savvy, culturally sensitive managers from all parts of the world, transferring them frequently in an attempt to transfuse universal Coke values, at the same time providing a broader background for the managers.

15) **Hire aggressive lawyers.** If you succeed, you will undoubtedly need lawyers to protect your trademark, defend your good name, and scare off potential competitors. Coca-Cola lawyer Harold Hirsch practically invented modern trademark-patent law. Before and after World War II, Coca-Cola hired local attorneys throughout the world in an attempt to stifle imitators and competitors and to defend the company against widespread rumors about its ill effects on health. Coke remains one of the more litigious companies.

16) **Don't break the law.** Although Coca-Cola officials or bottlers have indeed resorted to bribery and kick-backs in the past—and, according to some allegations, a bottler hired hit men in Guatemala to eliminate undesirables —the company does, by and large, live up to its squeaky-clean image. There is no percentage in illegal activities which could besmirch the company's good name. It simply isn't worth it to risk the reputation of a huge multinational concern.

17) **Become masters of influence.** Just because you don't break the law doesn't mean you must sit back and act like an angel. Robert Woodruff was a master at backroom influence. He practically owned Georgia senator Walter George and Atlanta mayor William B. Hartsfield. Woodruff befriended presidents. In fact, he and his cronies arguably *created* President Dwight D. Eisenhower, even helping him decide whether to run as a Republican or Democrat. Similarly, Coke CEO Paul Austin gave Jimmy Carter a crucial boost into the White House. Do not, however, abuse your influence by asking too much of politicians. Just clarify that your product's spread serves the national interest. You don't even need to ask for specific help. The mere *impression* that Coca-Cola chummed with Carter was, for instance, enough to open doors.

18) **Be patient but implacable. Plan for the long haul.** Coca-Cola managers know that they will ultimately sell their fizzy product in every country in the world. It is only a matter of time. There will be temporary set-backs due to war, famine, or politics, but they will always maintain contacts, always remain civil, always be prepared to take advantage of any situation. Thus, when the Arabs boycotted the company in the 1960s because Coke allowed an Israeli franchise, Coca-Cola immediately began a campaign of re-entry which paid off in Egypt during the Carter administration. Similarly, they are back in India following their 1977 expulsion. Ditto China, the former USSR, Nicaragua and Vietnam. Some day, Cuba. Do not be seduced into pursuing short-term gains at the expense of long-term vision. As Doug Ivester has stressed, there will be bumps along the road, but set your goals on the horizon.

19) **Adhere to simple commandments.** None of Robert Woodruff's guiding principles—many enumerated here—were terribly complicated. Woodruff himself was practically illiterate; according to associates, he never finished a book in his life. His genius lay in looking at the big picture and in concentrating on a few elemental truths.

20) **Be flexible enough to change.** Nonetheless, you must strike a balance between tradition and change. If Coca-Cola has ever displayed an Achilles'

heel, its reluctance to adjust to current conditions is it. Asa Candler almost delayed too long before removing the last trace of cocaine from the drink in 1903. Woodruff fought hard against the King Size Coke of the 1950s, against bringing out other flavors, against using rock music in ads, against lifting the nickel price barrier—all necessary changes. Roberto Goizueta, determined to shake up the staid company in the 1980s, believed in the necessity of change and was proved correct when he authorized the introduction of Diet Coke, a heretical product because it assumed the sacred Coke name. When he tampered with the original formula in the 1985 New Coke debacle, however, Goizueta was flexible enough to change back in time to avert disaster. To maintain this valuable flexibility, a certain amount of neurosis helps. "The world belongs to the discontented," Woodruff liked to intone. Goizueta simply said, "We live nervous."

21) **Don't use defensive, negative advertising**. Maybe for an Avis or a Pepsi, comparative ads make sense. Maybe. You're still giving your opponent free publicity, however. Every time Coke has stooped to such tactics, it has looked silly, including Asa Candler's attempts to justify caffeine's presence in the drink. When Coke mocked the Pepsi Challenge taste tests by showing chimpanzees trying to decide which tennis balls were fuzzier, the Atlanta firm looked like the choice chump, not the chimps.

22) **Diversify only when necessary**. When Roberto Goizueta took over as CEO in 1981, he promptly diversified by purchasing Columbia Pictures, a move which made sense at the time. Before the decade was out, however, he unloaded it on Sony for a healthy profit and refocussed solely on beverages. Coca-Cola, whose stock performance has been historically extraordinary, is one of the *least* diversified companies in the world. "There's a perception in this country that you're better off if you're in two lousy businesses than if you're in one good one, that you're spreading your risk," Goizueta used to say. But that's silly, when soft drinks offer a better profit margin than any alternatives.

23) **Pay attention to the bottom line**. This seems such an obvious point, yet until Goizueta arrived, it wasn't something anybody at Coke thought much about. In the paranoid anti-Pepsi culture, Coke men were more concerned with share-of-market figures than with profits. Goizueta discovered, among other things, that the highly regarded soda fountain sector was actually losing money because of costly capital expenditures on metal five-gallon drums.

24) **Terrify your employees**. Perhaps that's putting it a bit strong, but traditional Coca-Cola CEOs from Asa Candler to the present have encouraged a climate of respect and awe. Austere Paul Austin put it well: "A certain degree of anxiety and tension has to exist for people to function at the highest level of their potential." Certainly, Woodruff the Boss inspired terror and adoration. Today, Doug Ivester, a demanding perfectionist, is the man before whom all tremble.

25) **Promote from within**. The best Coca-Cola managers, almost without exception, have come up through the ranks, inculcated with the company mission. They have received the transfusion of Coke syrup. Grooming for

management traditionally included a form of Coca-Cola boot camp, inductees emerging from a day on the bottling line with bloody knuckles and aching back. Only Coca-Cola Export's long-time chair James Farley, FDR's former postmaster general, achieved lasting fame as a Coca-Cola man without much soft drink experience, and Farley served mostly as a diplomatic figurehead and door-opener. Bill Robinson, a New York ad man, proved a brief, unpopular leader in the 1950s. Don Keough arrived at Coke in the 1960s along with Duncan Foods, but it was twenty years before he achieved high status at the company, by which time he sounded more like a traditional soft drink man than anyone.

26) **All publicity is good publicity,** at least after a certain point. Because Coca-Cola already meant so much to so many, the 1985 flavor change actually helped the company, even though it blew $4 million in the process. When management bowed to public pressure and brought back Coca-Cola Classic, the encore beverage scored heavily against Pepsi. This was the same drink which had been steadily losing market share for twenty years prior to New Coke. Clearly, the experience of nearly losing their old friend caused many consumers to renew their loyalty to Coke—so that many observers thought that Goizueta and company had stage-managed the whole affair. As Don Keough admitted, they weren't that smart, but they did learn that even negative publicity can ultimately help a well-entrenched product.

27) **Use cash wisely.** Robert Woodruff, scared by the debt he inherited in 1923 when he took over the company, took great pride in accumulating a cash hoard. Consequently, the conservatively run company was never in danger of being overleveraged during the go-go Reagan years. Under Goizueta, however, the company finally took on a reasonable debt load. With bottom-line logic, Goizueta and financial wizard Doug Ivester realized that it made sense to borrow money if you could then re-invest it at a substantially higher rate of return. One simple method: repurchase your own stock, thereby driving the price further up.

28) **Form joint ventures.** Another wise use of cash involved breaking a long-standing company commandment: thou shalt not own bottling plants. Ever since Asa Candler gave away the bottling rights in 1899, the company had viewed itself primarily as a syrup spigot. The bottlers, whose profit margin was narrower than the company, prospered on their own. The company *did* own selected plants, but only to serve as training grounds for rotating managers, and they never did very well. The conventional wisdom held that bottlers performed better as independent entrepreneurs. In 1981, Goizueta was forced to break this taboo in the Philippines, where the Soriano family, which owned the franchise, had allowed Pepsi to chew off 70 percent of the cola market. By purchasing 30 percent of the franchise, the company negotiated the right to manage the bottling. Within a few years, Irish executive Neville Isdell, using traditional, aggressive motivation and marketing tactics—including a military-style rally during which he hurled a Pepsi bottle against a wall—turned the market share numbers on their head. Taking the Philippines as a precedent, Goizueta and his heir Doug Ivester pursued successful joint ventures around

the world, taking a proactive stand with ailing bottlers, pumping money into a more vertically integrated soft drink system. The company never purchases more than a 49 percent interest, however, which keeps the bottlers off the company balance sheet.

29) **Think globally, but act locally.** This catch-phrase probably originated with Goizueta, though other CEOs snapped it up in the trendy 1980s and used it as their own. Regardless of its provenance, though, Coca-Cola has demonstrated its wisdom, dipping into its own history for guidance. In China and Indonesia, for instance, the first task involves building a strong infrastructure—concentrate factories, glass manufacturers, bottling plants, trucks, point-of-purchase signage—in American terms, time-warping back to 1905. In the former West Germany and Japan, on the other hand, the company already has a well-established business, but, as in the United States of the 1970s, too many bottlers vying in small territories. The task there is to consolidate.

30) **Pursue the halo effect.** In the troubled early 1970s, Coke CEO Paul Austin tried to create what he termed "the halo effect" for Coca-Cola. By that, he meant that the firm should appear to be in the vanguard of the environmental movement, progressive in race relations, setting up model programs for its Minute Maid migrant workers, creating nutritional soft drinks, and the like. None of Austin's ancillary do-good businesses ever amounted to much, but the company continues to promote the halo effect, which makes sense. It also really *does* promote good causes, through philanthropy, support of minority programs, educational innovation, and relief aid in troubled countries. As Doug Ivester has said, "It's the right thing to do, and it's very right for business, too."

Notes:

ABBREVIATIONS

AC	*Atlanta Constitution*
AGC Papers	Asa G. Candler Papers
AJ	*Atlanta Journal*
AJ/C	*Atlanta Journal/Constitution*
Bateman & Schaeffer	William E. Bateman and Randy S. Schaeffer Private Collection
BD	*Beverage Digest*
CC Archives	The Coca-Cola Company Archives
CC *Bottler*	*Coca-Cola Bottler*
CC Legal Library	The Coca-Cola Company Legal Library
CC *Overseas*	*Coca-Cola Overseas*
CHC, *AGC*	Charles Howard Candler, *Asa Griggs Candler* (Atlanta, 1950)
CHC Papers	Charles Howard Candler Papers
Dept. of Justice	U.S. Department of Justice Files, Anti-Trust Division, Legal Procedures Unit
Dun	R. G. Dun & Company Collection
FDA Files	U.S. Food and Drug Administration
Hartsfield Papers	William B. Hartsfield Papers
Hunter Papers	Floyd Hunter Papers
NA CC Army File	National Archives, Washington, D.C., AGO Document File #1239224
NBG	*National Bottlers Gazette*
NYT	*New York Times*
Pepsi Collection	Pepsi-Cola Advertising History Collection
RB	*Red Barrel*
Robinson II	Frank Robinson II Collection
RWW Papers	Robert W. Woodruff Papers
Sizer File	J. B. Sizer Correspondence
WC Papers	Warren Candler Papers
WSJ	*Wall Street Journal*

FRONTISPIECE

v First two items from CC Archives; letter to Kahn courtesy of E. J. Kahn, Jr.; *Beverage Digest*, July 10, 1985, Special Issue.

NOTES ON THE TEXT

xi Lee Talley, "*men*": "What makes a Business Great," Oct. 1957, Box 83, RWW Papers.

PROLOGUE: A PARABLE

2 "old man stopped eating": The scenario depicted here is based on interviews with Roberto Goizueta, Edith Honeycutt, and Joe Jones. All three stated that while Woodruff was in terrible physical shape, his brain was as sound as ever. He could hear and understand, and, with effort, could express himself. Just after Goizueta's visit, Woodruff simply stopped eating.
"grass purple": Oliver, *The Real Coke*, pp. 155–156.

PART I: IN THE BEGINNING

5 "Whiskey Ring": The items referred to all come from the *Atlanta Constitution* between Aug. 15 and 19, 1885.

CHAPTER 1: TIME CAPSULE

7 "kind of decoction": Mark Twain, *The Gilded Age*, pp. 97–100.
"He leaned over the pot": Wilbur Kurtz, Jr., "Papers and Speeches," pp. 172–173. (CC Archives)
8 "industrial and competitive age": Richardson Evans, "Advertising as a Trespass on the Public," *Living Age*, July 1895, vol. ccvi, p. 131.
"modern civilization": George M. Beard, "Causes of American Nervousness" from *American Nervousness, Its Causes and Consequences*, as quoted in *Popular Culture*, p. 57. The following quotes come from the same article, pp. 57–70.
"sign of good breeding": See Beard and Tom Lutz, *American Nervousness*, 1903.
9 "patent medicines": The definitive work on patent medicines is *The Toadstool Millionaires* by James Harvey Young. Other background sources are Adelaide Hecthlinger's *The Great Patent Medicine Era* and Gerald Carson's *One for a Man, Two for a Horse*.
10 "immigrants": Frank Presbrey, *The History and Development of Advertising*, p. 341.
"stunning proportions": "50 Years, 1888–1938," special retrospective issue of *Printer's Ink*, July 18, 1938, p. 11.
"*Scientific American* announced": "Advertising in the Drug Business," *Scientific American*, Oct. 5, 1895, vol. 73, p. 214.
11 "flagrantly disreputable": "50 Years," *PI*, p. 18.
"Enormous signs are erected": "An Intolerable Nuisance," *New York Tribune*, May 13, 1886, p. 4.

12 **"William James . . . reacted"**: William James, "The Medical Advertisement Abomination," *The Nation*, Feb. 1, 1894, vol. 58, no. 1492, p. 84.
"4000 American millionaires": W. A. Swanberg, "1890," in *The Nineties*, p. 10.
"Acres of Diamonds": Bernard A. Weisberger, *Steel and Steam*, vol. 7 of *The Life History of the United States*, p. 37, and Swanberg, p. 9.
"palace of the millionaire": Carnegie, "Wealth," *The Gilded Age*, p. 45.
"Mark Twain noted": Mark Twain, quoted in *Steel and Steam*, p. 104, vol. 7 of *The Life History of the United States*.
13 **"Henry Grady . . . informed"**: Henry Grady as quoted in C. Vann Woodward, *Tom Watson: Agrarian Rebel*, p. 115.
"Let the young south arise": AC, Aug. 16, 1883, quoted in Woodward, *Tom Watson*, pp. 118–119.
"Religious zeal is perpetually warmed": Alexis de Tocqueville, *Democracy in America*, vol. 1, p. 317.
"churning about the high seas": "50 Years," *PI*, p. 23.
"Joseph Priestly learned": Joseph L. Morrison, "The Soda Fountain," *American Heritage*, Aug. 1962, pp. 10–19. Unless otherwise noted, most of the information on the history of soda fountains comes from this article.
14 **"Mary Gay Humphreys, an 1891 commentator"**: Mary Gay Humphreys, "The Evolution of the Soda Fountain," *Harper's Weekly*, Nov. 21, 1891, p. 924.
"Hires Herb Tea": Fucini, *Entrepreneurs*, p. 150.
"Charles Alderton created": For more information on Hires, Moxie, and Dr Pepper, see "Charles E. Hires: Hires Root Beer," pp. 150–152, in Fucini, *Entrepreneurs*,; Bowers, *The Moxie Encyclopedia*; Ellis, *Dr Pepper: King of Beverages*.
15 **"time is everything"**: "Some Soda Water Fountain Statistics," *Scientific American*, Aug. 12, 1899, p. 99.
"the following 1886 Atlanta ad": "A Card from Beermann," AC, June 8, 1886.
"Soda-water is an American drink": Humphreys, p. 924.
"ingredients usually cost less": Price of ingredients based on cost of producing Coca-Cola, 1895 CC annual report.
"summer trade in soft drinks": "Some Soda Water Fountain Statistics," *Scientific American*, p. 99.

CHAPTER 2: WHAT SIGMUND FREUD, POPE LEO AND JOHN PEMBERTON HAD IN COMMON

17 **"use of the coca plant"**: "Wonderful Coca," AC, June 21, 1885.
"average life expectancy": *Historical Statistics of the United States*, Part 1, p. 56.
"Born in 1831": Monroe King, "Dr. John S. Pemberton: Originator of Coca-Cola," *Pharmacy in History*, vol. 29 (1987), no. 2, pp. 85–89; Allen, *Secret Formula* pp. 18–22.
"the wisdom of Samuel Thomson": For an excellent overview, see Young, "The Old Wizard," in *Toadstool Millionaires*, pp. 44–57.
"screw auger": Spencer Klaw, "Belly-My-Grizzle," *American Heritage*, June 1977, vol. 28, no. 4, p. 98.
18 **"their instruments of death"**: Samuel Thomson, as quoted in *The Reform Medical Practice*, p. 118. (Pemberton Archives, File 145)
"a second American revolution": John Uri Lloyd, "Concerning the American Materia Medica," *American Journal of Pharmacy*, Feb. 1910, p. 83.

"the eyes of the world": Smith, *The History of Education in Monroe County*, p. 52.

"modified their reliance on lobelia": John Uri Lloyd, p. 87.

"he went to Philadelphia": An R. G. Dun credit man specified that Pemberton was "a graduate of School of Pharmacy, Philadelphia." The Philadelphia College of Pharmacy, the only school he could have attended, has no records that Pemberton went there, however. (Georgia Vol. 13, p. 394, Dun; Michael Ermilio, Archivist, Philadelphia College of Pharmacy and Science, to Mark Pendergrast, Oct. 7, 1991)

"a prominent local plantation owner": 1850 Census, Summerville, Georgia, a town near Rome, Pemberton Archives; Georgia Vol. 20, p. 69, Dun; Ernestine Walker Sherman, "Elbert Lewis Family," in *History of Stewart County Georgia*, vol. 2, p. 909.

"he was spoiled": Mary Elberta Lewis Newman, Cliff Pemberton's sister, was the grandmother of Mrs. Ernestine Sherman, a resident of Albany, Georgia. Most of the personal memories about Pemberton come from Mrs. Sherman's collection.

"two slaves": "Elbert Lewis to John S. Pemberton," Office of the Clerk of the Superior Court, Muscogee County, Georgia, Deed Book G, Folio 327. (Sherman Collection)

"eye surgery": *Columbus Enquirer*, Feb. 1856. (Pemberton Archives)

"Dr. Sanford's Great Invigorator": *Columbus Enquirer* ads, Feb. 16, March 25, May 6, July 13, 1856, Dec. 3, 1857; *Albany Patriot*, Dec. 1, 1857. (Sherman Collection and Pemberton Archives)

"Pemberton wrote Cliff's mother": Pemberton to Mrs. Lewis, handwritten letter, March 24, 1861. (Sherman Collection; copy also in CC Archives)

19 **"Pemberton was shot and cut"**: Pemberton Archives and Sherman Collection have extensive material on Pemberton's war record. Widow's Indigent Pension 1901, C. L. Pemberton, Approved April 22, 1901. (Pemberton Archives, File 131)

"buying spree in New York City": Nov. 23, 1865, notice from Pemberton, quoted in "The Legend of John Pemberton" by E. D. Murphy, 1967. (Sherman Collection and CC Archives)

"forget all about the war": Long letter from Clifford Lewis Newman to his mother, Mary Elberta Lewis Newman, dated 1929. (Sherman Collection)

"Globe Flower Cough Syrup": CC Archives; Feb. 4, 1875, ad in *Albany News*. (Sherman Collection)

"regaled my olfactories": Murphy, p. 5, from June 23, 1867, *Columbus Enquirer*, letter from "A Lady Traveler."

"Free and Rowdy Party": Norman Shavin, *Atlanta: Triumph of a People*, p. 31.

20 **"sole idea . . . make money"**: Robert Sombers, *The Southern States Since the War, 1870–1871*, quoted in James Michael Russell's *Atlanta: 1847–1890*, p. 153.

"devil of a place": *Atlanta Daily New Era*, Oct. 30, 1866, as quoted by Russell, p. 126.

"the elegant Kimball House": Georgia Vol. 13, p. 224, Dun; James Michael Russell, pp. 121–122.

"lack good management": Georgia Vol. 13, p. 223, Dun.

"suffered through two major fires": Georgia Vol. 13, p. 394, Dun, Jan. 29, 1874, report of first fire. Georgia Vol. 14, p. 194, Dun, March 20, 1878, report of second fire; also page 194, Nov. 18, 1878, "broken down merchant."

"varying success": "Incorruptible Man," AC, April 18, 1886, p. 14.

"recalled his niece": Mary Newman Walker, handwritten in the 1950s. (Sherman Collection) "forget meal times": Newman letter, 1929.

"more energy than anybody": "Columbus Career," *Industrial Index*, 1942, p. 22.

21 "he showed his work-in-progress": "Worthy of Special Notice," *AJ*, Dec. 11, 1886.

"an article by Sir Robert Christison": We know that Pemberton read this 1876 article, or a later reprint, since he showed it to a reporter for the *Atlanta Constitution* in 1885. ("Wonderful Coca, A Plant That Ponce de Leon Should Have Found," AC, June 21, 1885)

"the elderly doctor reported": Robert Christison, "Observations on the effects of Cuca, Or Coca, the Leaves of Erythroxylon Coca," *The British Medical Journal*, April 29, 1876, p. 530.

"in an 1880 Detroit drug journal": "Erythroxylon Coca as an antidote to the Opium Habit," *Detroit Therapeutic Gazette*, Sept. 15, 1880.

"Woe to you, my Princess": Sigmund Freud to Martha Bernays, June 2, 1884, as quoted in Freud's *Cocaine Papers*, p. 10.

"made Koller famous": "Wonderful Coca," AC. 1885.

22 "veritable *coca-mania*": *American Druggist*, Nov. 1886, p. 214.

"Coca-Bola": Coca-Bola ad in *American Druggist*, Dec. 1885, p. 36. For other coca products, see David Musto, *The American Disease*, p. 7.

"an enterprising Corsican": William H. Helfand, "Vin Mariani," *Pharmacy in History*, vol. 22 (1980) no. 1, pp. 11–19. Other sources on Mariani include "Contemporary Celebrities and Vin Mariani," *Harper's Weekly*, Oct. 28, 1893, vol. 37, p. 1040; *Collective Testimony of the Benefit and Virtue of the Famous French Tonic Vin Mariani; Album Mariani* (14 volumes, 1886–1910), property of William Helfand; William Helfand, "An Assay of Coca Wine: An Eyewitness Account," *Pharmacy in History*, vol. 30 (1988) no. 3, pp. 155–156; "The Effrontery of Proprietary Medicine Advertisers," pamphlet in Toner Collection, Library of Congress (R112.M458, no. 9); W. Golden Mortimer, *Peru: History of Coca*, pp. 177–180; Allen, *Secret Formula*, pp. 22–24.

"Pemberton's French Wine Coca": In his application for a trademark patent, Pemberton claimed to have been making French Wine Coca since 1882. Trade-Mark No. 12,257, "J. S. Pemberton, A Nerve Tonic," registered May 19, 1885. (Sherman Collection)

"Mariani specialized in testimonials": *Collective Testimony*, p. 11.

"an 1887 biography of Pope Leo": O'Reilly, *Life of Leo XIII*, pp. 566–575.

"kings, princes, pontentates": *Collective Testimony*, unpaged preface.

"a testimonial from God": "Angelo Mariani," *La Nouvelle Revue*, 1914, Series 4, Tome XIII, pp. 218–219. Translation by Meda Stamper.

"two major production laboratories": *Collective Testimony*, verso of title page.

"a chemist studying various wine cocas": "Coca Wines of the Market," *The Druggists Circular and Chemical Gazette*, Feb. 1886, p. 32.

"claret-glass full": Helfand, p. 12.

23 "2.16 grains of cocaine per day": Actually, Vin Mariani may have contained considerably more cocaine than the chemist found. Mariani claimed that he put two ounces of leaf into each bottle—the proper daily "dosage"—the same amount chewed by the average Peruvian, amounting to just over 7 grains per day, or 460 milligrams (1 gr = 65 mgs). (Taylor, *Plant Drugs*, p. 16)

"Mariani traveled to New York City": *American Druggist*, July 1885, p. 39.

"advertised the general's use of his product": *Journal of Cutaneous and Venereal Diseases*, Oct. 1885.

"twenty *ersatz* wines": ibid.

"discredit a really useful drug": Mariani, p. 52.

"one cynical writer": K. Eller, "Pill-Purveying Doctors and Prescribing Apothecaries," *Druggists Circular and Chemical Gazette*, Aug. 1887, p. 171.

"a March 1885 interview": "A Wonderful Medicine," *AJ*, March 10, 1885, p. 4.

"new disease, neurasthenia": For a full treatment, see Tom Lutz, *American Nervousness, 1903.*

24 "Pemberton advertised . . . his wine": undated French Wine Coca ad from CC Archives.

"taken as an aphrodisiac": "West India Kola," a folder from the Toner Collection.

"Two drugs, so closely related": "Further Notes on the Utility of Coca and Kola," *A New Idea*, June/July 1884, p. 327.

"same page in parallel columns": 1883–1884 catalog, Frederick Stearns & Company, page 38, Dixi-Cola Case, p. 2154, CC Legal Library.

"defined by a vintage Webster's": *Webster's New International Dictionary*, p. 665.

"Mormon Elder's Damiana Wafers": *American Druggist*, Feb. 1885, p. 6.

"Enthusiastic and wordy": *AJ*, March 14 and 18, 1885.

25 "he was a drug fiend": J. C. Mayfield, Sr., Koke Case Testimony, p. 776.

"addicted to the morphine habit": "Mrs. Diva Brown's Story of Coca-Cola," *The Southern Carbonator and Bottler*, Sept. 1907, p. 49. Found in E. J. Kahn's papers. Also quoted in pamphlet in CC Collection, Emory.

"distasteful": A. O. Murphy, Koke Case, p. 392.

"Morphinism . . . prevalent": J. B. Mattison, "Opium Addiction Among Medical Men," *Medical Record*, June 9, 1883, vol. 23, as reprinted in Morgan, *Yesterday's Addicts*, pp. 62–65.

"importation . . . increased dramatically": W. S. Watson, "On the Evils of Opium Eating," *JAMA*, May 10, 1890, vol. 14, p. 671.

"Army disease": H. Wayne Morgan, *Yesterday's Addicts*, p. 37; Garrison, A *Treasury of Civil War Tales*, p. 195; "Medical Purveying for the U.S. Army During the Late War," *American Journal of Pharmacy*, Jan. 1866, p. 273.

"His formula book": Pemberton formula book from John Turner. (CC Archives)

"renewed energy for the time being": W. S. Watson, p. 672.

"Pemberton . . . told a reporter in 1885": *AJ*, March 10, 1885.

26 "A German doctor": A. Erlenmeyer, "The Cocaine Habit," translated and reprinted in *American Druggist*, Aug. 1886, p. 154; "The Cocaine Habit," *The Druggists Circular and Chemical Gazette*, July 1886, p. 1.

"injudicious use of cocaine": AC, June 17, 1885.

"a rambling interview": "Wonderful Coca," AC, June 21, 1885.

"888 BOTTLES": AC, June 28, 1885, p. 9.

27 "red-nosed whisky devils": Quotes and information on Sam Jones from Kathleen Minnix, "The Atlanta Revivals of Sam Jones, Evangelist of the New South," *Atlanta History*, Spring 1989, pp. 5–34.

"raked us fore and aft": Tom Watson, quoted in *The Life and Sayings of Sam P. Jones*, p. 79.

"ban on liquor": Franklin Garrett, *Atlanta and Environs*, vol. 2, p. 95.

"Methodist minister . . . murdered": W. J. Rorabaugh, "Beer, Lemonade, and Propriety," *Dining in America 1850–1900*, pp. 30–34.

28 "equal partners": Most of this scenario is derived from Frank Robinson's 1914 testimony. (Koke Case, pp. 347–366)

"wonder of the world": April 7, 1887, document. (Frank Robinson II) "**last visit to Auntie's**": Newman letter and scribbled Newman note. (Sherman Collection)

"**sent down to the drug store**": *Industrial Index*, 1942, p. 26. (Sherman Collection)

"**accidentally mixed with soda water**": Charles Howard Candler, "The True Origin of Coca-Cola," p. 6, CHC Papers.

"**his uncle's 1886 laboratory**": Newman letter.

29 "**a major speech**": Pemberton Speech from Minutes of the Eleventh Annual Meeting held in Savannah, GA, April 1886, pp. 17–21. (Sherman Collection)

30 "**Swift's Sure Specific**": S.S.S., formerly known as Swift's Syphilitic Specific and still manufactured in Atlanta, is the world's oldest surviving patent medicine—though nowadays it is a Geritol clone with a 12 percent alcohol content. (SSS label)

"**because it was euphonious**": Frank Robinson, undated handwritten note. (Frank Robinson II)

"**meaningless but fanciful**": Lee Talley, "When I Think of the Future," CC *Bottler*, April 1959, p. 43.

"**script logo**": Bateman & Schaeffer, "Script Coca-Cola: The First Hundred Years," *Cola Call*, Feb. 1986, pp. 6–7, 11–12.

"**COCA-COLA SYRUP AND EXTRACT**": Coca-Cola label patented June 28, 1887. (CC Archives)

31 "**total advertising expense**": When Pemberton sold his inventory in July of 1887, he listed advertising materials worth $69.25. Assuming that he and Robinson had already distributed many of these signs, and adding the cost of sporadic newspaper ads leads to a guestimate of $150. ("Chain of Title," CC Archives. These documents are also reprinted in the back of *Coca-Cola: Opinions, Orders, Injunctions*.)

"**streetcar signs**": Bateman & Schaeffer, "Street Car Signs for Coca-Cola," *Cola Call*, Nov. 1984, pp. 7–10.

"**thousand coupons**": These figures can be deduced from the inventory in Chain of Title documents.

"**Within a year**": Pemberton's 1887 sales inventory included fourteen oilcloth signs already at fountains, 1,600 posters, 500 streetcar signs, and 5,000 Coca-Cola cards. Collector Thom Thompson argued persuasively these cards, with a pretty girl on one side and a poem entitled "Parody" on the other, were printed in September 1886, making them the earliest known piece of Coca-Cola memorabilia. The poem tells the story of a lawyer, "overcome with heat," whose lips "could only just repeat, Coco-Cola." Once he had a drink, of course, he won his case. If Pemberton had that many posters, signs, and cards on hand, it is likely that many more had already been distributed. (Thompson, Thom, "Earliest Known Piece of Coca-Cola Memorabilia Identified," *Coca-Cola Collectors News*, March 1998, p. 5–8, Chain of Title, CC Archives)

"**an arch note to Jacobs' Pharmacy**": Pemberton to Jacobs' Pharmacy, May 10, 1887. (CC Archives)

"**advertising French Wine Coca**": AC, Nov. 17, 1886.

32 "**On May 1, 1887, an article**": "Pemberton Chemical Co.: An Increase of $10,000 in the Stock of the Company," AC, May 1, 1887, p. 12.

"**sold twenty-five or thirty gallons:**" Frank Robinson, Koke Case, p. 353.

"**M. P. Alexander**": AC, May 1, 1887.

"**pronounced limp**": Sam Dobbs, Bottler Case, p. 2266; "Muster Roll of Captain J. S. Pemberton Cavalry, July 2nd, 1864." (Sherman Collection)

"**Charley Pemberton . . . payroll**": Frank Robinson, July 22, 1887, balance sheet (Frank Robinson II Collection); D. B. Candler, "A Brief History of Coca Cola." (CC Archives)

"champion catcher": Garrett, *Atlanta & Environs*, vol. 1, pp. 883–884.

"failed romance": Charley Pemberton's first cousin, Lewis Newman, wrote a thinly veiled fictional account of his early years in which Charley Pemberton had such a romance. (Sherman Collection)

33 **"local saloon"**: June 14, 1951, letter from Wilson Newman to Ernestine Sherman. (Sherman Collection)

"Phospho Lemonade": AC, May 1, 1887.

"high road to fortune": "An Incorruptible Man," AC, April 18, 1886.

CHAPTER 3: THE TANGLED CHAIN OF TITLE

34 **"Pemberton sold two-thirds"**: "Chain of Title" folder at Coca-Cola Archives. This contract was amended five days later, specifying that Pemberton would receive the first $1,200 from *all* Coca-Cola sales, not just his third of the profits.

"According to Lowndes": George Lowndes, Koke Case, pp. 514–521. Most of the information on Mr. Lowndes is from these pages.

"Lowndes, I am sick": Lowndes interview as quoted in Franklin Garrett manuscript, CC Archives.

"If I could get $25,000": Newman notes. (Sherman Collection)

35 **"small item"**: "The County Courts," AC July 10, 1887, p. 11. Unfortunately, this is apparently the only record available on the case.

"calmly informed": Frank Robinson, Koke Case, pp. 347–366. Information for the rest of this section comes primarily from Robinson's testimony.

"reconstructed a financial statement": July 22, 1887, inventory, Robinson II Collection.

36 **"Candler . . . paid a visit"**: John S. Candler, Koke Case, p. 388.

38 **"first man to sell . . . Coca-Cola"**: Willis Venable, Koke Case, p. 390.

"resolved to sell it": Lowndes in Garrett manuscript, CC Archives.

"ownership . . . yet more fractured": The contract specified that Mrs. Dozier was to get a third and Walker the balance. Since they were buying 2/3 of the entire formula, that works out to the odd fractions in the text.

"Joseph Jacobs": Information on Jacobs comes from the Jacobs Papers and James Harvey Young, "Three Atlanta Pharmacists," *Pharmacy in History*, vol. 31 (1989), no. 1, pp. 17–18.

"druggist later recalled": Jacobs placed this transaction in 1886, though it clearly must have been 1887. (Jacobs quote from undated article, AC, in Sherman Collection, and Joseph Jacobs, "How I Won and Lost an Interest in Coca Cola," *Drug Topics*, July 1929, reprint in Jacobs Papers.)

"He later testified": Joseph Jacobs, Rucker Case, p. 99.

"a royalty of 5 cents": If the 5-cent royalty is correct, it means that we are missing yet another document in which Pemberton sold the rights to Coca-Cola.

"pressed for money": Joseph Jacobs, "How I Won and Lost," p. 1. The rest of the quotes in this section are from this document.

39 **"blind ad did not . . . address"**: Mayfield, Koke Case, p. 1604.

"After much correspondence": Most of this information comes from A. O. Murphey, Koke Case, pp. 384–402.

"Robinson had found": While working for Pemberton, Robinson had served as part-time bookkeeper for Asa Candler. (Cecil Stockard interview)

"a difficult time convincing": Information from Frank Robinson's only

daughter, Goldie Robinson Stockard, quoted in "Soft Drinks," *Saturday Evening Post*, Sept. 28, 1957. Typed out and found in CC Archives.
"See that wagon": Asa Candler as quoted in Watters, p. 22.
"I had the whole control": Asa Candler, Koke Case, pp. 375–376. To make matters even more confusing, in 1921 testimony Candler identified Dr. Joe Dick—unknown except the mention here—as a previous owner of the formula. (Asa Candler, Bottler Case, p. 2139)

40 **"Frank Robinson had given . . . formula"**: Asa G. Candler deposition, Sept. 2, 1924, My-Coca Case.
"Joe Jacobs complained": Jacobs, "How I Won and Lost," p. 2. The dating is problematical, since Jacobs gives none. He says that "Dr. Pemberton died about this time," which would place the event in 1888. Yet he also says this transaction occurred as Candler was selling his wholesale drug business (1890).
"Diva Mayfield often helped": Mayfield denied that his wife ever worked with him in the laboratory, but Bloodworth later wrote that she "spent considerable time in our laboratory and took quite an interest in the business." (Quoted in "The Original Coca-Cola Woman, Mrs. Diva Brown," CC Collection, Box 11, Emory)
"bomb in our camps": J. C. Mayfield, Koke Case, p. 777.

41 **"incorporation of the Coca-Cola Company"**: Aside from Asa Candler, Charley Pemberton, Woolfolk Walker, and Mrs. Dozier, two of the incorporators of the Coca-Cola Company were simply the lawyers handling the papers, while A. B. Bostwick, a sixth name, remains a mystery.
"The purposes of this Company": Fulton County Superior Court Writ Book R, p. 267.
"mysterious endorsement letters": Reprinted in "Asa G. Candler & Co.," AJ, May 1, 1889, p. 22. One of the letters is actually dated Jan. 25, 1887, but that is probably a misprint. There are three other letters with 1888 dates.
"an 1898 pamphlet": "Dedication of Home Office." (AGC Papers, Box 7, Emory)

42 **"Asa Candler wrote to . . . Warren"**: Asa Candler to Warren Candler, April 10, 1888. (AGC Papers, Box 1)
"why . . . camouflage": J. S. Pemberton vs. J. S. Iverson et al. No. 46, Atlanta Circuit Supreme Court of Georgia, September Term, 1883. Transcript of record: File No. 212, Pemberton Archives; AC, August 12, 1883.

43 **"stomach cancer"**: Mary Newman Walker, "I Remember Dr. Pemberton," Sherman Collection. The death certificate listed "enteritis" as the cause of death. (Pemberton Archives)
"offering a very poor article": Asa to Warren, June 2, 1888. (AGC Papers, Box 1.)
"He wanted something new": J. C. Mayfield, Koke Case, p. 2775.
"newspaper notice . . . death": "Dr. Pemberton's Death," AC, Aug. 18, 1888, p. 5.

44 **"one of his best friends"**: Asa Candler, Koke Case, p. 373.
"drink's sole proprietor": Full-page ad, AJ, May 1, 1889.
"Behind these bare facts": CHC, *AGC*, p. 101.
"I did not sign any paper": Mrs. M. C. Dozier, Koke Case, pp. 1829–33.
"Woolfolk Walker . . . forged": Frank Robinson, who witnessed the document, insisted in court testimony that Mrs. Dozier had indeed signed it in his presence. In her last testimony, Mrs. Dozier noted that "the formation of our letters were obliged to be somewhat alike," since her brother taught her to write (Robinson, p. 351; Dozier, p. 1842, Koke Case)
"without even saying goodbye": Dozier, p. 1833.

45 **"handwriting expert George Pearl"**: George Pearl to Mark Pendergrast, Aug. 11, 1991.

"Both forgeries . . . control of Coca-Cola": Candler later filed a copy of the April 14 document (signed by the Pembertons) as part of his official chain of title with the U.S. Patent Office. In doing so, he submitted a completely new document, all written in a single anonymous hand. Whoever copied it over mistook Charley Pemberton's middle initial, writing it as an "M" rather than an "N." Candler may have deliberately had the document recopied to avoid submitting the forged signature. (Sherman Collection)

"Your Auntie sold the Formula": Elberta Newman to Lewis Newman, Aug. 12, 1919. (Sherman Collection)

"My aunt . . . Methodist": Mary Newman letter (Sherman Collection). Pemberton left a confused estate embroiled in litigation, possibly involving Asa Candler. The estate administrator wrote early in 1889 that Mrs. Pemberton needed "proper representation in pending suits"—though no record of them has been found. ("In Re estate of J. S. Pemberton, Application of C. L. Anderson for Temporary and Permanent Letters of Administration," no. 36, Fulton Court of Ordinary, March 22, 1889, Pemberton Archives)

"Other versions of the family story": All Sherman Collection.

46 **"sensation-loving Atlanta newspapers"**: "With Crude Opium," AC, June 24, 1894.

"notice of his death": "Charley Pemberton Is Dead," AC, July 4, 1894.

"something mysterious": Wilson Newman to Mrs. Sherman, April 18, 1951. (Sherman Collection)

"suicide was unlikely": Monroe King interview.

"verified by Price Gilbert": Gilbert's conversation with Dean William Tate, quoted in John W. English and Rob Williams, *When Men Were Boys*, p. 263. There is no record, however, of Price Gilbert ever having served as a lawyer for The Coca-Cola Company or the Candlers.

"earliest records . . . burned": According to "The Beginning of Bottled Coca-Cola as Told by S. C. Dobbs," in the Coca-Cola Archives, "Mr. Candler ordered all the old books and official records burned over Mr. Dobbs' protest."

"Coca-Cola became a go": Rob Stephens to Mrs. Sherman, undated. (Sherman Collection)

CHAPTER 4: ASA CANDLER: HIS TRIUMPHS AND HEADACHES

47 **"If people knew"**: CHC, *AGC*, pp. 108–109.

"I don't know a single day": Asa Candler, "Confidence in Your Product," *1916 Bottlers Convention Booklet*, p. 76. (CC Archives)

"high, squeaky voice": Julian Harris, "Asa G. Candler: Georgia Cracker," *Uncle Remus's Home Magazine*, Nov. 1909, reprinted in *Emory University Quarterly*, vol. 7, Dec. 1951.

"people selling mink skins": Asa Candler, quoted in CHC, *AGC*, p. 45. Unless otherwise noted, biographical material on Candler comes from this book.

"speculation in pins": CHC, *AGC*, p. 46.

48 **"She tried to boss everybody"**: Pierce, *Giant Against the Sky*, p. 26.

"imaginary potions": CHC, *AGC*, p. 47.

"$25 a month": Julian Harris, "Asa G. Candler: Georgia Cracker," p. 199.

"more money . . . as a druggist": Asa Candler to Asa Griggs, Sept. 11, 1872. (AGC Papers, Box 1) "he told a reporter in 1909": Julian Harris, "Asa G. Candler, Georgia Cracker," p. 199.

"the clerk led him": ibid.

"first pay check": Asa Candler to C. H. & A. G. Candler, Jr., Oct. 16, 1897. (AGC Papers, Box 1)

49 "clever young men": Georgia Vol. 14, p. 160, Dun, March 31, 1877.

"reliable young men": Georgia Vol. 14, p. 160, Dun, Oct. 15, 1879.

"bury the hatchet": George Howard to Asa Candler, Nov. 1878. (*AGC* Papers).

"my Mother's patience": Charles Howard Candler, "Thirty-Three Years with Coca-Cola 1890–1923," p. 2. (CC Archives)

"well-nigh slave": CHC, *AGC*, p. 78.

"her every need": ibid., pp. 238–239.

50 "Atlanta exceeded all cities": James Harvey Young, "Patent Medicines: An Element in Southern Distinctiveness?" in *Disease and Distinctiveness in the American South*, p. 181.

"thriving metropolis": Clarke, *Atlanta Illustrated*, pp. 71, 134, 209.

"a Massachusetts visitor": "Atlanta: A New Engineer's Description of Our Famous Gate City," *AJ*, July 7, 1886.

"electric doorbell": "Atlanta Enterprise," *AJ*, March 19, 1885.

"Celebrated Voltaic Belt": "Nervous Debilitated Men," AC, Aug. 18, 1885.

"a few electric men": "Electric Men," *AJ*, Feb. 28, 1885.

"Candler described himself": "Active, Pushing and Reliable," *AJ*, Oct. 14, 1886.

"You are feeling depressed": "Brace Up," *AJ*, Aug. 5, 1886.

51 "he was miserable and exhausted": CHC, *AGC*, p. 211.

"periodically morose": Manic depression ran in the family. Candler's grand-father had killed himself, while his father fought debilitating depression during the Civil War. Asa's brother Charlie (Samuel Charles Candler) died in a mental institution in 1911 after several unsuccessful suicide attempts. (Graham, *Real Ones*, pp. 75–76, 115)

"Do not allow yourself to get billious": Asa Candler to Howard Candler, Sept. 9, 1899. (AGC Papers, Box 1)

"fraught with some danger": CHC, *AGC*, p. 211.

"positively cures piles": "Bucklen's Arnica Salve," *AJ*, Oct. 5, 1886.

"for consumption, colds": "Active, Pushing and Reliable," *AJ*, Oct. 14, 1886.

"will whiten the teeth": 1891 calendar in *AGC* Papers, Box 7.

"venerable Botanic Blood Balm": The 1890 purchase date of BBB is an intelligent guess. Candler's 1890 almanac featured Blood Balm, but he may not have owned it outright. He must have purchased it by Jan. 25, 1891, when an article in the *Atlanta Constitution* listed BBB as one of Candler's proprietaries, along with De-Lec-Ta-Lave and Coca-Cola.

"Dromgoole": "Atlanta Ahead," *AJ*, Jan. 1, 1885.

"landmark . . . case": Blood Balm Case, p. 458.

52 "in bad health": Julian Harris, "Asa G. Candler: Georgia Cracker," p. 200.

"impress . . . reporter": "Asa G. Candler & Co.," *AJ*, May 1, 1889, p. 22.

"Dobbs got his position": Letter from Thomas E. Basham to Martin Schmidt, Aug. 19, 1932. (CC Archives)

"drummers . . . swarm": Clarke, *Illustrated Atlanta*, p. 211.

"only 40% of Coca-Cola sales": Thom Thompson to Mark Pendergrast, Oct. 18, 1991.

53 "Foster Howell": "Soda Water Drinkers," AC, Aug. 18, 1889. Howell placed the drink's introduction "four years ago" in 1885, but he must have meant the spring of 1886.

"actual amount of cocaine": Frank Robinson II interview; Andrew Keegan, "Caffeine May Increase Cocaine's Effects," *NIDA Notes*, Winter 1990/1991, pp. 23–24; Dr. John Flynn to Mark Pendergrast, Jan. 27, 1992.

"Total sales for 1889": Frank Robinson, Coca-Cola annual report, Dec. 4, 1895. (CC Archives)

"personal balance sheet": *AGC* Papers; also cited in "Thirty-Three Years with Coca-Cola" by C. H. Candler, p. 3.

54 "he wrote a form letter": Letter on letterhead, "Office of Asa G. Candler, sole proprietor of Coca-Cola." The form letter date read "189–," but the letter's contents indicate it was written in Feb. 1890. (CC Archives)

"In almanacs distributed": *Grier's Almanac*, 1890. (CC Archives)

"Going Out of Business": "Going Out of Business," AC, Jan. 25, 1891, p. 17.

55 "ooze . . . floor-boards": CHC, *AGC*, p. 111.

"One photograph of the period": Photograph in CC Archives.

"1917 biographical sketch": "Frank M. Robinson," Knight, *A Standard History of Georgia and Georgians*, Vol. VI, p. 3205.

"Maine Volunteers": After two rejections because of his size, Robinson enlisted by wearing shoe lifts. (Cecil Stockard interview)

"greatest sources of pride": Frank Robinson II interview.

"I challenge the world": Undated ad in Schmidt Coca-Cola Museum, Elizabethtown, Kentucky.

56 "the headline": "What's in Coca Cola?" AC, June 12, 1891, p. 10.

"If I thought . . . hurt anybody": From Coca-Cola advertising scrapbook, 50ARS. (CC Archives)

"the Pemberton formula . . . ten times": From Frank Robinson II's copy of his great-grandfather's formula, kept in a safe deposit box.

"legitimate distinction": For a modern discussion of the difference between coca and cocaine, see Weil, *The Mariage of the Sun and Moon*, pp. 139–165.

57 "contained too many things": C. H. Candler, "The True History of Coca-Cola," p. 10. CC Collection, Emory, Box 2.

"At least ten people": Those with access to the formula were: Willis Venable, George Lowndes, Woolfolk Walker, Charley Pemberton, Cliff Pemberton, Joe Jacobs, J. C. Mayfield, Diva Mayfield, A. O. Murphey, E. H. Bloodworth.

"from $1,000 down": Jacobs, "How I Won and Lost," p. 2.

"proudest moments of my life": CHC, *AGC*, pp. 122–123.

58 "Prescott, an entrepreneur": Prescott article in advertising scrapbook. (CC Archives)

"contacted stock brokers": CHC, *AGC*, p. 107.

"as an added incentive": ibid., p. 108.

"Fowle brothers urged": Copies of *Coca-Cola News* in CC Archives.

"To my good friend, Coca Koller": Freud, *Cocaine Papers, p. 291.*

59 "panacea for all those tired": Kent's Coca-Cola trademark, application registered Jan. 22, 1889, Trademark No. 16,209. (Sherman Collection)

"spirits of frumenty": William R. Cobb testifying in Chero-Cola Case, pp. 529–536.

"John Kerr, a Paterson lawyer": John F. Kerr, testifying in Feb. 1917, Chero-Cola Case, pp. 502–524.

"Atlanta's version . . . given precedence": John Candler testimony, Rucker Case, p. 78.

"Candler quietly bought out Kent": Kerr testimony; Frank Troutman, "Report on Pepsi-Cola," 1939, p. 92. (CC Archives)

"$22,500 on ingredients": All figures and quotes from annual reports are from CC Archives.

"early ads . . . medicinal": All 1892 ads, from CC Ad Scrapbook, 14ARS. (CC Archives)

"ladies . . . right along": 44ARS. (CC Archives)

"attract smokers": 13ARS. (CC Archives)

"small boys in sailor suits": Hoy, p. 26.

"free tickets were mailed": CHC, *AGC*, p. 161.

"ingenious, effective way": Bateman & Schaeffer, "Complimentary Tickets for Glasses of Coca-Cola," *Coca-Cola Collectors News*, March 1988, pp. 4–9.

60 "Candler refused . . . open mail": CHC, *AGC*, p. 223.

61 "*should* have that much money": Asa Candler to Howard Candler, Nov. 5, 1894. (AGC Papers, Box 1)

"I expect you to be first": Asa to Howard, Sept. 24, 1894. (*AGC* Papers)

"exhibit Christ": CHC, *AGC*, p. 236.

"empty bottle troubles": Asa to Howard, Feb. 28, 1895; Sept. 26, 1895. (*AGC* Papers)

"great American Eagle": *Coca-Cola News*, June 15, 1897. (CC Archives)

"salaries . . . moderate": CHC, "33 Years," p. 14.

62 "Stronger! stronger!": *Coca-Cola News*, 1896.

"cut most seriously": CHC, "33 Years," p. 14.

"she threatened to kill him": Mayfield, Koke Case, p. 2769.

63 "She sniffed righteously": "The Original Coca-Cola Woman, Mrs. Diva Brown." (CC Collection, Box 11, Emory)

"as long as sin abounds": Asa Candler, Rucker Case, p. 52.

"I do not know the formula": From *The Spatula*, quoted in *Coca-Cola News*, June 1899, p. 3. (CC Archives)

"feel guilty": Asa Candler, Rucker Case, p. 125.

"advertise to the masses": Frank Robinson, Rucker Case, p. 86.

"over a million items": Robinson, Rucker Case, p. 84.

"Mr. Asa will like this one": CHC, *AGC*, p. 162.

"actress Hilda Clark": Bateman & Schaeffer, "Madame Lillian Nordica," *Cola Call*, March 1986, pp. 6–11; "Hilda Clark: The Queen of Coca-Cola Advertising," *Coca-Cola Collectors News*, Jan. 1988, pp. 4–11.

64 "About ten percent": John Candler, Rucker Case, p. 72.

"as large as the Mississippi": *Coca-Cola News*, Aug. 1899. (CC Archives)

"greatly enthuses a dealer": Eighth annual report, Jan. 11, 1900. (CC Archives)

65 "His eyes would shine": CHC, *AGC*, p. 353.

"this kind of fervor": Not everyone was impressed with Candler's religious devotion. Pemberton's niece, Mary Newman Sherman, called Candler a "sanctimonious pipsqueak"; she and other members of his Sunday school class ridiculed him behind his back, imitating his high-pitched voice. Another Sunday school pupil made national headlines by sending Candler a series of fake blackmail threats promptly dubbed the Black Hand Letters. (Sherman Collection; CHC, *AGC*, p. 224)

"an almost mystical faith": CHC, *AGC*, p. 170.

"*sprees* to the detriment": July 11, 1902, quoted in CHC, *AGC*, p. 167.

"gentlemen in every respect": Sixth Annual Report, Jan. 13, 1898. (CC Archives)

"greatest company on . . . earth": CHC, *AGC*, p. 170.

66 "Asa wrote frequently to his son on the road": All letters from Asa Candler to Howard Candler, AGC Papers, Box 1.

67 "Howard quit medical school": Though Howard Candler joined the company full-time, he would never be a charismatic public figure. Shy and rather uncertain, he wrote to his father: "I really enjoy the office part of the

work, but I don't like to distribute tickets and sell goods. More, I don't like to have to be sociable with the trade." (Allen, *Secret Formula*, p. 54)

"Dobbs . . . sales force": Howard Candler wrote that Dobbs was assigned this position at the Dec. 28, 1899, meeting. (CHC, *AGC*, p. 139)

CHAPTER 5: BOTTLE IT: THE WORLD'S STUPIDEST, SMARTEST CONTRACT

69 **"hardy . . . determined lot"**: Lee Talley, CC *Bottler*, April 1959, p. 43.

"all the dumb sonsuvbitches": Campbell, *Big Beverage*, p. 37. Campbell's thinly disguised version of Ben Thomas was named Bert Simpson. For clarity, "Ben" is used in this quote rather than "Bert."

"drive to make money": Ned L. Irwin, "Bottling Gold: Chattanooga's Coca-Cola Fortunes," unpublished manuscript, Sept. 1991, p. 3 (courtesy Ned Irwin, Chattanooga).

"a new scheme to make a million dollars": Fred Hixson, "Fear of Investing Years Ago Cost Him Millions, Sam Erwin Reveals," *Chattanooga Times*, July 17, 1941, p. 2.

"Piña Fria": Franklin Garrett, "Benjamin Franklin Thomas," *CC Bottler*, April 1959, p. 86 (where the drink is spelled "Pina Frio").

"he arranged an introduction": Fred Hixson, "Fear of Investing," *Chattanooga Times*, July 27, 1941, p. 2.

70 **"Wouldn't it be great"**: The quote (as well as the general scenario) stems from J. J. Willard, who had it directly from Thomas. "Some Early History of Coca-Cola Bottling," J. J. Willard, *CC Bottler*, Aug. 1944, p. 10.

"samples of bottled Coca-Cola": Sidney M. Shalett, "Nation's Thirst Made Fortunes," *Chattanooga Times*, July 7, 1937.

"two men met with . . . Candler": In Franklin Garrett's version of the story, Thomas and Whitehead visited Candler together in 1899 and were quickly granted the contract. First, however, Thomas almost certainly made several trips alone to see Candler, as he told J. J. Willard. Candler testified that the first conversation took place almost a year before the contract was signed and couldn't recall how many "conferences" they had. (Franklin Garrett, *CC Bottler*, April 1959; J. J. Willard, *CC Bottler*, Aug. 1944, p. 10; Asa Candler, Bottler Case, p. 2144)

"fugitive nigger": Asa Candler, "Confidence in Your Product," 1916 Bottlers Convention Booklet, *Equip Yourselves With Knowledge*, p. 74. (CC Archives)

"florid, sweaty face . . . pronounced waddle": Franklin Garrett, "Founders of the Business of Coca-Cola in Bottles," *CC Bottler*, April 1959, pp. 89, 189.

"putrid": Sam C. Dobbs, "The Beginning of Bottled Coca-Cola," Oct. 13, 1933. (CC Archives)

"we can't handle it ourselves": Asa Candler, "Confidence in Your Product," p. 74.

"born salesmen, friendly and jovial": Garrett, "Founders of the Business," pp. 89, 189.

71 **"Whitehead's father"**: Dimond, *The Reverend William W. Whitehead*, pp. 43–44.

"specialized in tax law": Irwin, p. 5.

"contract they had prepared": Asa Candler, Bottler Case, p. 1696.

"If you boys fail": Whitehead related this quote to Charles Veazey Rainwater, "Observations and Comments," *CC Bottler*, April 1959, p. 121.

"dynamic franchising systems": It was also among the *first* franchises in the world. (Vaughn, *Franchising*, pp. 19–21) "laws of Georgia would not permit": Asa Candler to Seth A. Fowle, March 6, 1899. (CC Archives)

72 "Bottle it": Kahn, *Big Drink*, p. 69.

"same day . . . wrote a letter": Asa Candler to Howard Candler, July 21, 1899. (AGC Papers, Box 1)

"special fountain glasses": From the turn-of-the-century on, Coca-Cola salesmen sold logo-embossed fountain glasses at low cost, serving not only to advertise the beverage, but to encourage soda jerks to mix the drink properly, a horizontal line towards the bottom indicating a one-ounce syrup level. The delicately fluted "flare" glasses broke too easily and were replaced by the well-known "bell" glass in 1929. (Batemen & Schaeffer, "Classic Fountain Glasses for Coca-Cola," CC Collectors News, Oct. 1987, pp. 3–13)

"one bottler was interviewed": "Popular Mixed Drinks," *American Druggist*, Dec. 1885, pp. 7, 9.

"amazing array of . . . designs": Riley, *A History of the American Soft Drink Industry*, p. 94.

73 "Hutchinson bottles": ibid., p. 97; Bateman & Schaeffer, "Diamond-Shaped Paper Labels for Coca-Cola," *Cola Call*, Oct. 1984, p. 4.

"Sam Dobbs remembered": Sam Dobbs, Bottler Case, pp. 2266–68; Dobbs, "The Beginning of Bottled Coca-Cola." (CC Archives)

"it was 'fine'": J. A. Biedenharn to Harrison Jones, Sept. 11, 1939, as quoted in *CC Bottler*, April 1959, p. 94.

"not-too-wholesome odor": E. R. Barber to W. H. Warwick, Aug. 26, 1954. (C-C Collection, Box 8, Emory)

"change was well under way": Riley, p. 102.

"hose often came loose": Irwin, pp. 11–12.

74 "article running adjacent": DeSales Harrison, "Footprints on the Sands of Time," NY: Newcomen Society, 1969, p. 15.

"paying him $2,500": J. T. Lupton, Bottler Case, p. 1052.

"incorporated The Coca-Cola Bottling Company": Actually, Whitehead's concern was first incorporated as Dixie Coca-Cola Bottling Company in Tennessee, then changed in 1901 to The Coca-Cola Bottling Company.

"cost a bit over $2,000": Thomas to Myron J. Browning, June 27, 1903, Benwood.

75 "induce the 'right man'": J. T. Lupton, Bottler Case, pp. 1052–53.

"His entire business life": Dobbs to W. C. D'Arcy, April 20, 1920. (CC Archives)

"Lupton installed . . . innumerable relations": John T. Lupton's half brother Cornelius had fourteen children, almost all of whom made fortunes from Coca-Cola. By the 1950s, there were dozens of scattered relatives sporting Lupton as a first, middle, or last name. A later executive of The Coca-Cola Company offered advice: "It doesn't matter a damn what you do as long as you never say a word against a Lupton." (Raymond Witt interview; Kahn, *Big Drink*, pp. 73–74)

"depopulated Chattanooga": J. J. Willard, *CC Bottler*, Aug. 1944, p. 11.

76 "Describing Butts and his kind": Campbell, *Big Beverage*, p. 218. The book's "Solo Soda" has been replaced here with "Coca-Cola."

"sober, honest, hard-working": Thomas to CC Co., Sept. 17, 1900, Benwood.

"nothing but a cheap rubbish": Thomas to Heck, Nov. 7, 1900, Benwood.

"absolutely certain": Thomas to Heck, April 13, 1901, Benwood.

"want some profit": Ewing to Heck, May 24, 1901, Benwood.

77 "Heck's demise": 1903 annual report, Dec. 31, 1903, Thomas letterbook, Benwood.

"Thomas wrote . . . Evansville": Thomas to John F. Carson, Aug. 26, 1904, Benwood.

"Pratt began . . . imitator": All of the direct quotes and information for this section come from Arthur Pratt, "My Life with Coca-Cola," *CC Bottler*, April 1959, pp. 168–180.

"Thomas wrote . . . congratulate": Thomas to Whitehead, April 1, 1901, Benwood.

78 "street car placards, calendars": Willard, *CC Bottler*, Aug. 1944, p. 10.

"Pleading with Frank Robinson": Thomas to Robinson, April 13, 1901, Benwood.

"infiltrate elementary schools": Thomas to J. J. Bornschein, Sept. 15, 1903, Benwood.

"local paper . . . highest circulation": Thomas to bottler in Helenwood, TN, Sept. 11, 1900, Benwood.

"solicited testimonials": Thomas to James A. Muncie, Sept. 3, 1900, Benwood.

"testy letter": Ewing to CC Co., June 23, 1901, Benwood.

79 "special employee was a slob": Ewing to Louis F. Smith, July 4, 1901, Benwood.

"an undated amendment": Previous histories have assumed that this amendment was signed soon after the original contract in 1899, but a letter from Ben Thomas to W. D. Boyce of Nov. 15, 1901, clearly refers to this "new arrangement" with The Coca-Cola Company, specifying "$10 worth of advertising matter for each 100 gallons"—i.e., 10 cents per gallon. (Benwood)

"negro boy": Thomas to W. D. Boyle, Jan. 29, 1902, Benwood.

"rush-ordered . . . saccharin": Thomas to Merck & Co., Sept. 2, 1901, Benwood.

"a coded recipe": Thomas to W. D. Boyle, Jan. 16, 1902, Benwood.

"tastes vary": Thomas to W. E. Birchmore, May 21, 1902, Benwood.

80 "essential job": Sebert Brewer, Jr., interview.

"great surprise to every one": Thomas to B. A. Stockard, May 22, 1902, Benwood.

"*death* of your specialty": Buntin Drug Co. to CC Co., June 23, 1904, Bottler Case, pp. 1309–10.

"Company . . . reassured": CC Co. to Buntin Drug Co., June 24, 1904, Bottler Case, pp. 1310–11.

81 "Company published a booklet": quoted by C. V. Rainwater, Bottler Case, p. 197.

"THERE IS MONEY IN IT": Hoy, p. 43.

"into the Oconee River?": as quoted by Charles Veazey Rainwater, *CC Bottler*, April 1959, p. 123.

"an enormous field": C. V. Rainwater, Bottler Case, p. 198.

PART II: HERETICS AND TRUE BELIEVERS (1900–1922)

85 "little man walked away": This scenario is based on fact. Candler wrote letters to his son Howard from Atlanta until March 30, 1911, when he stated, "I can't avoid wanting to be with you all, but Uncle John advises staying away. I am ready to go on a moment's notice." (AGC Papers, Box 1) He then briefly attended the trial in Chattanooga sometime in April.

CHAPTER 6: SUCCESS UNDER SIEGE

87 **"since the rising tide"**: John Candler, "Every Knock Is a Boost," *CC Bottler*, Aug. 1909, p. 5.

"vend a poison": Asa Candler to Rev. Lindsay, Aug. 18, 1898; Asa Candler to Rev. J. W. Quillian, Aug. 20, 1898. (CC Archives)

"inflammatory newspaper accounts": Garrett, *Atlanta and Environs*, vol. 2, pp. 500–504. "Every ingredient in Coca-Cola is a poison," one North Carolina newspaper editor wrote. "Brother, what ailed thee, to seek such a cure?" he asked. (Allen, *Secret Formula*, p. 47)

"crazed Negroes": Morgan, *Drugs in America*, pp. 92–93.

88 **"white Georgian complained"**: "Cocaine: Use of the Drug Increasing Among Negroes of the South," June 21, 1903, *New York Daily Tribune*, p. 11.

"soft drinks . . . contain cocaine": "Cocaine Is Sold Illegally," AC, Nov. 20, 1901, p. 5.

"in a very nervous . . . condition": Dr. M. A. Purse, Rucker Case, pp. 146–147.

"can't find his way home": Dr. W. P. Nicholson, Rucker Case, p. 218.

"according to one witness": Dr. Charles A. Crampton, Rucker Case, p. 159.

"a hung jury": 1901 annual report. (CC Archives)

"four-hundredths of a grain": Dr. George F. Payne, Rucker Case, p. 59.

"severe headaches": Rucker Case, pp. 49, 52.

"in August of 1903": Sam Willard and Sam Dobbs, Affidavits, July 13, 1907. (NA CC Army file)

"removed by the following year": In a later court brief, a Coca-Cola lawyer placed the date somewhat earlier, stating that "about 1899 or 1900 [The Coca-Cola Company] decocainized the coca leaves used and thus eliminated the cocaine entirely from the beverage." (Harold Hirsch, "Reply Brief and Argument for Petitioner," Koke Case, p. 6) John Candler and Sam Dobbs also admitted that the cocaine had been removed during the IRS trial. (1907 clipping scrapbook CC Archives; "The WCTU and Coca Cola," *The Druggists Circular*, Dec. 1907, p. 784)

89 **"Georgia legislature"**: "Cocaine, How Sold," No. 61, Approved Dec. 5, 1902, *Acts and Resolutions of the General Assembly of the State of Georgia, 1902*, p. 100.

"anything they *don't*": John Candler, Rucker Case, p. 71.

"a million pieces": Frank Robinson, Rucker Case, p. 122.

"single best-advertised product": Sam Dobbs, "Aggressiveness Necessary in the Selling of Coca-Cola," *CC Bottler*, April 1909, p. 5.

"During 1913, the company advertised": Lawrence Dietz, *Soda Pop*, pp. 54–55

"every man, woman and child": Louis & Yazijian, p. 94.

"love of the animal kingdom": Kahn, *Big Drink*, pp. 110–111, 164; Hoy, p. 67.

"Oh! mother": Howard Johnson, Harry Pease & Eddie Nelson, "Oh! Mother, I'm Wild" (NY: Leo Feist, 1920), courtesy Thom Thompson; song on *Fountain Favorites* cassette tape, CC Company.

"composer dedicated": Erle Threlkeld, "Follow Me, Girls, to the Fountain, and Be My Coca-Cola Girl" (Charleston: Erle and Leo Publishing, 1915). Courtesy Thom Thompson.

"a moving picture cannot": Asa Candler, "Confidence in Your Product," 1916 Bottler Convention Booklet, p. 78.

"silent film stars": Bateman & Schaeffer, "Coca-Cola and Stars of the Silent Films 1916–1919," *Coca-Cola Collectors News*, Oct. 1986, pp. 4–9.

"Hollywood sex scandal": Yallop, *Day the Laughter Stopped*, p. 158.

"we are working along lines": S. L. Whitten to Asa Candler, Jan. 7, 1907, Bottler Case, p. 1518.

"bare-breasted young woman": Petretti, p. 22; Bateman & Schaeffer, "Those Naughty Collectibles," *Cola Call*, Jan. 1984, pp. 4–5.

"Satisfied": Schmidt Museum; Dietz, *Soda Pop*, p. 40.

90 "Coca-Cola chewing gum": Thom Thompson, "Coca-Cola Chewing Gum," in Petretti, p. 35; Martie Michael interview; Bill Schmidt interview.

91 "bewitching sirens": Mrs. Bessie Linn Smith, "Save the Cyclorama," *Atlanta Civics*, Oct. 1917, p. 2. (AGC Papers, Box 7)

"pictures of Betty": Petretti, pp. 9–10, 43–45.

"thirty-two-foot-high effort": *CC Bottler*, Aug. 1909, p. 7.

"first wall": Bateman & Schaeffer, "Coca-Cola Painted Wall Signs," *Coca-Cola Collectors News*, Feb. 1988, pp. 3–15.

"Hounded almost to . . . imbecility": *The Coca-Cola Institute*, 2d session, Oct. 1–5, 1906, pp. 22–23. (CC Archives)

"greatly enthused": 1903 annual report. (CC Archives)

"Never be ashamed": This and subsequent quotes are from *Proceedings of The Coca-Cola Institute*, 1st session, Dec. 15–18, 1903. (CC Archives)

92 "to avoid counterfeits": In 1906, the free ticket budget was drastically cut, resulting in an equivalent loss in sales. The experience convinced Frank Robinson of sampling's value, and the budget was increased. Nonetheless, when Robinson retired in 1913, the firm abandoned the program (Bateman & Schaeffer, "Complimentary Tickets for Glasses of Coca-Cola," *Coca-Cola Collectors News*, March 1988, pp. 8–9)

"a rousing rendition": Asa Candler routinely closed meetings by singing "Onward Christian Soldiers." (Treseder, *As I Remember*, p. 13)

"short, barrel-shaped man": CHC, *AGC*, pp. 354–355.

"bulldog": Charles Candler, "Bishop's Young Son," *AC*, March 21, 1911, p. 5.

"Tom Watson . . . called Bishop Candler": Quotes from two sources: C. Vann Woodward, *Tom Watson: Agrarian Rebel*, p. 433; Thomas Watson, *Jeffersonian Weekly*, Aug. 15, 1907.

93 "Romanism has made": Warren Candler, *Great Revivals and the Great Republic*, p. 12. Following quotes: pp. 275–277.

"missionary enterprise": Warren Candler, *Wit and Wisdom*, p. 30.

"war was scarcely over": The Spanish-American War sparked military support of American businesses in Latin America—most affiliated with Coca-Cola. As Major General Smedley Butler of the U.S. Marine Corps reminisced: "I helped make Haiti and Cuba a decent place for the National City Bank boys to collect revenue in. I helped purify Nicaragua for the international banking house of Brown Brothers from 1909 to 1912. I brought light to the Dominican Republic for American sugar interests in 1916. I helped make Honduras 'right' for American fruit companies in 1903." The Coca-Cola Company was to form lasting alliances with every business listed by Butler. (Louis & Yazijian, p. 168)

"ripest missionary field": Pierce, *Giant Against the Sky*, p. 99.

"duty and . . . interest coincide": Asa Candler Speech, "Southern Business Power," ca. 1914. (AGC Papers, Box 2)

"John Ralphs": CHC, *AGC*, p. 158.

94 "great conquests": Asa to Howard, July 20, 1900. (AGC Papers, Box 1)

"Candler bragged to a reporter": Smith Clayton, "The Story of Coca-Cola," *AC*, Nov. 20, 1901, p. 4.

"distributed through New York": CHC, *AGC*, pp. 159–160.

"crushing disappointment": Asa to Howard, Sept. 12, 1901. (AGC Papers, Box 1) "**wait for the *Reaper***": Asa to Howard, March 22, 1902. (AGC Papers, Box 1)

"**in great torrents**": Asa to Howard, Jan. 12, 1901. (AGC Papers, Box 1)

"**surplus of nearly $200,000**": CC 1900 annual report.

"**cater to *dives***": Asa to Howard, March 28, 1902. (AGC Papers, Box 1)

"**a fad only**": Asa to Howard, May 29, 1902. (AGC Papers, Box 1)

"**exemplification of . . . unrest**": "The Automobile as an Index," part of "Sunny South" Supplement, *AC*, Nov. 16, 1901, p. 2.

"**habituated to hurry**": Asa to Warren, Oct. 10, 1911. (AGC Papers, Box 1)

95 "**never at leisure**": Charles F. Wilkinson, "Asa G. Candler: Pioneer Capitalist," *Building and Buildings Management*, Pre-Convention Number, Sept. 1915, p. 69. (AGC Papers, Box 7)

"**rushing and striving**": J. J. Willard, *CC Bottler*, July 1909, p. 6.

"*hustle* **that will *tell***": Burgess Smith, "Get Busy." (AGC Papers, Box 21)

"**The world owes**": Nathaniel Hawthorne quoted in AGC Papers, Box 21.

"**building's cornerstone**": CHC, *AGC*, p. 257.

"**heavy wind storm**": Candler Building booklet. (AGC Papers, Box 7)

"*my enemies*": Asa to Warren, June 16, 1908. (WC Papers, Box 1)

"**I do not trust Him**": Asa to Howard, May 7, 1909. (AGC Papers, Box 1)

"**Candler coat of arms**": CHC, *AGC*, pp. 262–263.

"**wattage of light bulbs**": ibid., p. 281.

"**literally be impossible**": ibid., p. 302.

"**built a huge warehouse**": ibid., pp. 308–316.

96 "**panic of 1907**": ibid., pp. 269–270.

"**Nothin Doin**": 1908 cartoon in *AGC* Papers.

"**not talking friendship**": William A. Landers, "My 38 Years with Coca-Cola." p. 5. (CC Archives)

"**Candler sent him $10**": Rev. Ellison Cook to Asa Candler, April 10, 1899; Candler to Cook, April 12, 1899. (AGC Papers, Box 4)

"**women approached Candler**": Mrs. Bessie L. Smith, *Atlanta Civics*, Oct. and Nov. 1917. (AGC Papers, Box 7) Mrs. Smith's attacks on Candler were clearly libelous, so these stories may be somewhat embroidered.

"**present her case properly**": Mary Walker to Ernest Walker, July 29, 1909. (Sherman Collection)

"**child labor legislation**": For a comprehensive history, see Davidson, *Child Labor Legislation in the Southern Textile States*.

"**beautiful sight . . . child at labor**": Asa Candler, "Proceedings of the Fourth Annual Meeting of the National Child Labor Committee," reprinted in *The Annals of the American Academy of Political Science*, 1908, pp. 159–160.

"**altogether optimistic**": June 15, 1913, Hearst's *Sunday American* clipping. (AGC Papers, Box 21)

97 "**recover my nerve steadiness**": Asa to Warren, June 29, 1913. (WC Papers)

"**tough it through**": Asa to Mrs. F. C. Harris, June 22, 1913. (*AGC* Papers)

"**embarrassed and angered**": Asa to Warren, May 1914. (WC Papers)

"**a crumbling castle**": Asa to Warren, June 29, 1913. (WC Papers)

"**I do not possess by a vast deal**": Asa to Warren, July 16, 1914. (WC Papers)

"**see an Arrow**": 1910 Coca-Cola ad. (CC Archives)

"**a powerful influence**": Frank Robinson in 1905 annual CC report.

98 "**Cut to the quick**": Charles Howard Candler, *Asa Griggs Candler: Coca-Cola & Emory College*, p. 18.

"**Uncle Sam himself**": July 1906, *Everybody's Magazine*. (CC Archives)

"**All Classes**": 140ARS, 1907. (CC Archives)

"**businessman in the foreground**": May 20, 1905, *Saturday Evening Post*. (CC Archives)

"**Mrs. Blue exclaims**": *New Idea Woman's Magazine*, 1907.

"**enjoyable as the play**": Sept. 1906, *American Theater*, 103ARS (CC Archives); Hoy, p. 31.

"**Rattled Nerves**": *Scientific American*, Sept. 1, 1906, 104ARS. (CC Archives)

"**Sun is Red Hot**": Hoy, p. 16.

"**many other baseball players**": Dave Lindsay, "Coca-Cola Ads Featuring Baseball Players (1906–1916), *Cola Call*, July 1983, p. 14.

"**playing a double-header**": 1906, 124ARS. (CC Archives)

99 "**metropolitan beverage**": July 1907, 139ARS. (CC Archives)

"**drinks in their automobile**": *McClure's*, 1905. (CC Archives)

"**variety of outlets**": 1907 bottle sampling ticket, Bottler Case, p. 1343.

"**motorlaunch *Josephine***": *CC Bottler*, July 1909, pp. 8–9.

"**Automated bottling, soaking**": Although the first coin vending machine was marketed in 1909, the concept failed to catch on for three decades. (*CC Bottler*, May 1909, p. 6; *CC Bottler*, March 1910, p. 14; "An Automatic Vendor," *CC Bottler*, June 1909, p. 6)

"**instant enthusiastic friend**": H. F. Bray, "Our Cuban Letter," *CC Bottler*, 1911, p. 11.

"**like a big balloon**": Lettie P. Evans, Bottler Case, p. 1116.

"**Other women took direct**": Arthur P. Pratt, "My Life with Coca-Cola," *CC Bottler*, April 1959, p. 174.

100 "**grocer named Hudgins**": Hudgins Case, p. 974.

"**Mrs. Mattie Allen**": Dec. 10, 1916, "$1500 Suit Filed Against Coca-Cola Bottling Company." (AGC Papers, Box 21)

"**first liability insurance**": Ralph B. Beach, "History of The Coca-Cola Bottlers' Association," *CC Bottler*, April 1959, p. 99.

"**deaf mute**": "Bottlers Successfully Defend Bottle Suit," *CC Bottler*, April 1913, p. 18.

"**wave of sanitary ideas**": "The Sanitary Drink," *CC Bottler*, April 1909, p. 10.

"**cut out the milk diet**": "A Safer Drink," *CC Bottler*, 1911, p. 13.

101 "**little mushroom beverages**": J. J. Willard, *CC Bottler*, June 1909.

"**sued John B. Daniel**": Daniel Case.

"**Grenelle and Schanck**": see "Complaint and Answer," Queens Case, pp. 14–16.

"**Suppose I am substituting**": R. M. Wiley testimony, Chero-Cola Case, pp. 1260–86.

"**Afri-Kola, Cafe-Coca . . .**": Names are taken from these sources: *Coca-Cola: Opinions, Orders, Injunctions and Decrees*, 1923,; J. C. Mayfield testimony in Koke Case, p. 1640; *Nostrums and Quackery*, pp. 416–418; CHC, *AGC*, p. 172; *Reports of the President's Homes Commission*, 1909 (in Wiley Papers), pp. 372–373.

"**Fake-Colas**": *CC Bottler*, March 1910, p. 14.

102 "**Trademark Law of 1905**": McCarthy, *Trademarks and Unfair Competition*, pp. 116–117.

"**dogged courtroom pursuit**": For an excellent overview of Coca-Cola court cases, see James K. Boudreau, "Protecting the Trademark 'Coca-Cola' in the Courts," *Georgia State Bar Journal*, Aug. 1991, vol. 28, no. 1, pp. 42–49; Allen, *Secret Formula*, p. 78.

"**within the last twelve months**": John Candler to J. T. Lupton, Jan. 8, 1913, Bottler Case, p. 1426.

"**known every human emotion**": Harold Hirsch, "The Product Coca-Cola . . .," March 7, 1923, address to CC Bottlers Convention, p. 21. (CC Archives)

"**Coca-Cola becomes sacred**": Harold Hirsch, Bottler Case, p. 253.

"**demand the genuine**": July 1914, 419ARS, 474ARS (CC Archives); 1915, Hoy, p. 33.

"**It is not dope!**": "Is Coca-Cola a Menace," *Town Topics* Nov. 20, 1913, Wiley Papers; Watters, p. 43; Kahn, p. 103.

"**other four-letter . . . words**": Treseder, *As I Remember*, pp. 3–4.

"**Pinkerton detectives**": See reference to Pinkerton bills by Coca-Cola cashier W. O. Mashburn, July 24, 1913, and Nov. 1, 1913, Bottler Case, pp. 950, 966.

"**mausoleum**": Roy W. Johnson, "Why 7,000 Imitations of Coca-Cola Are in the Copy Cat's Graveyard," *Sales Management*, Jan. 9, 1926, p. 28.

103 "**one case per week**": Jerome H. Spingarn, "Of Coca, Cola, and the Courts," *The Nation*, June 7, 1941, p. 666.

"**no paper label at all**": Bateman & Schaeffer, "Diamond-Shaped Paper Labels for Coca-Cola," *Cola Call*, Oct. 1984, pp. 4–9.

"**our own child**": Harold Hirsch, Bottler Case, p. 257.

"**recognize it by feel**": Thomas as quoted by George Hunter, "Golden Anniversary Dinner," Oct. 4, 1949. (CC Archives) For a detailed summary of the bottle's creation, see Bateman & Schaeffer, "The Story of the Hobbleskirt Bottle," *Cola Call*, March 1985, pp. 4–8.

"**company auditor failed**": "Interview with Mr. T. Clyde Edwards," Aug. 15, 1949. (CC Archives)

"**a few sample bottles**": Betty Mussell Lundy, "The Bottle," *American Heritage*, 1986, vol. 37, no. 4, pp. 99–101.

104 "**Raymond Loewy waxed**": Lundy, "The Bottle," pp. 98–99.

"**brains and beauty**": Bessie Linn Smith, "A Correction," *Atlanta Civics*, Oct. 1917, p. 4. (*AGC* Papers) For more on conflict between Dobbs and Robinson, see Allen, *Secret Formula*, p. 74–77.

"**one great machine**": Dobbs, "Report of the Sales Department," 1907 annual report.

105 "**hired his personal friend**": The shift to D'Arcy was gradual, but by 1910, D'Arcy placed $225,000 in annual ads, while Massengale was reduced to $50,000. (Charles Bottoms interview; Wilbur Kurtz, Jr., to Delony Sledge; J. J. Willard to Frank Rowsey, April 10, 1956, CC Archives; "A Radio Greeting," *CC Bottler*, Jan. 1923, p. 20)

"**calm, deliberate**": Frank Robinson undated memo. Robinson's recommendations begin with Dec. 1906, placing the likely date of the memo in Nov. 1906. (Frank Robinson II)

"**Truth in Advertising**": Fox, *The Mirror Makers*, p. 68.

"**advertising man . . . a schoolmaster**": Sam Dobbs, "Address to the Coca-Cola Bottlers," *CC Bottler*, 1911, pp. 8–10.

"**singularly limited vision**": Dobbs to W. C. Bucher, April 15, 1908, and May 4, 1911; Dobbs to *The Chemist & Druggist*, June 20, 1910; J. D. Hampton to Dobbs, Oct. 24, 1911; Dobbs to Hampton, Nov. 16, 1911; Dobbs to C. Mitchell & Co., June 10, 1915. (Duckworth Case Box, CC Archives)

"**objections of parent bottler**": Ben Thomas to Sam Dobbs, March 30, 1907, Bottler Case, Exhibit 19-H, p. 1306.

106 "**Dobbs reacted defensively**": Sam Dobbs to Ben Thomas, April 2, 1907, Exhibit 19-1, Bottler Case, pp. 1307–8.

CHAPTER 7: DR. WILEY WEIGHS IN

107 **"Wiley is now made"**: "A Real Investigation of Wiley," *American Food Journal*, Feb. 15, 1912, p. 25. (Wiley Papers)

"Harvey Washington Wiley": For information on Wiley and the Progressive Era, see the following publications: Crunden, *Ministers of Reform*; Wiley, *Harvey W. Wiley: An Autobiography*; Anderson, *The Health of a Nation*; Young, *The Toadstool Millionaires*; Young, *Pure Food*; Sullivan, *Our Times*.

"We're on the hunt": ibid., p. 217.

"understanding . . . two Houses": ibid., p. 202.

108 **"William Allen White"**: For information on White, see Griffith, *Home Town News*; White; *Autobiography of William Allen White*.

"refusing to bow": Adams, *The Great American Fraud*, p. 5.

"conscience of America's heartland": While White refused what he considered bogus patent medicine ads, he actively solicited business from Coca-Cola in 1910, assuring the Company that "your display . . . would not have to compete with trash." At least in Kansas, Coca-Cola had shed its patent medicine image. (William Allen White to CC Co., Sept. 27, 1910, Letterbook 17, White Papers)

"aimed at the public's heart": Crunden, *Ministers of Reform*, pp. 173–174.

"cyclonic wave of reform": J. J. Willard, "When Doctors Disagree," CC *Bottler*, April 1909, p. 12.

"providing secret funds": *CC Bottler*, Aug. 1909, p. 13.

"Wiley's Law": Young, *Toadstool*, pp. 226–244.

"misguided fanatics": John Candler, CC *Bottler*, Aug. 1909.

"adverse legislation": George Hunter, Bottler Case, p. 1257.

"clear to Judge": John Candler, Koke Case, p. 386; John Candler, Rucker Case, p. 80.

"resigned from the bench": John Candler, Bottler Case, p. 1426.

"imitators with cocaine": The new law *did* spell the end of cocaine-laced cola drinks. Celery-Cola, one of J. C. Mayfield's drinks, was seized under the Pure Food and Drugs Act and given a "black eye," as Mayfield put it. Others, such as French Wine Coca and Vin Mariani, survived by removing the cocaine, but their popularity and sales soon faded.

"traveled to Washington": 1907 Scrapbook, newspaper article, "Coca-Cola Is Defended by Candler." (CC Archives)

"salesmen used the new law": *The Coca-Cola Institute*, 2d session, Oct. 1–5, 1906, p. 16. (CC Archives)

"object to saccharin": Wiley, *Autobiography*, p. 241.

109 **"special state taxes"**: Kahn, *Big Drink*, p. 141.

110 **"William Allen White reported"**: *Emporia Gazette*, Jan. 14, 1908, p. 5.

"work vast detriment": Candler to Wiley, Feb. 25, 1907, Bureau of Chemistry General Correspondence, Record Group 97, National Archives, file 2719 for 1907 (notes courtesy James Harvey Young).

"heinous sin": Wiley, *Autobiography*, p. 27.

"then go ahead": ibid., p. 236.

"tall and massive": Edwin Bjorkman, "Our Debt to Dr. Wiley," *The World's Work*, Jan. 1910, p. 12, 443. (Wiley Papers)

111 **"nickname Father Wiley"**: Wiley, *Autobiography*, p. 255.

"admirers called him": "A Preacher of Purity," *The Nation*, July 27, 1916, p. 79.

"zealot": "Dr. Wiley, A Zealot," *The Medical Herald*, April 1912, p. 1. (Wiley Papers)

"chemical fundamentalist": Crunden, *Ministers of Reform*, p. 186.

"injury to public health": Anderson, *Health of a Nation*, p. 165.

"substances illegal": Cocaine was not made illegal until the passage of the Harrison Narcotics Act of 1914. After intensive lobbying, Coca-Cola succeeded in having a loophole written into that law, allowing the importation of coca leaves if they were decocainized under government supervision.

"heard many complaints": Wiley to Candler, Feb. 28, 1907, National Archives (notes courtesy James Harvey Young).

"book about hidden alcohol": Unidentified Syracuse, NY, paper, Oct. 9, 1911, "Mrs. Allen Honored by Association of Science," from Onondaga Historical Society files.

112 "who wrote in May": Army Circular No. 14, from Wiley Papers.

"besieged the Army": Coca-Cola Army file, National Archives.

"South Has the Habit": Newark, NJ, *Evening News*, July 9, 1907, quoted in Bowers, *Moxie Encyclopedia*, p. 191.

"letters . . . from alarmed organizations": Coca-Cola Army File, National Archives.

"competitors considered us dead": H. F. Bray, "Cuba—Early History." (CC Archives)

113 "gives largely to missions": This quote and following (including the letter from Samuel Hopkins Adams) are from Martha M. Allen, "The WCTU and Coca-Cola," *The Druggists Circular*, Dec. 1907, pp. 783–784.

"Rats in the vats": Wolfe, *Look Homeward*, Angel, p. 271.

114 "stranger in an alien . . . land": James Harvey Young, "Three Southern Food and Drug Cases," *The Journal of Southern History*, Feb. 1983, p. 11.

"drug deputy characterized": Lyman F. Kebler report, undated, Seizure No. 352 file, FDA records, 19 pages.

"confirming Wiley's worst fears": When Asa Candler learned of the Kebler tour, he exploded: "The idea of his [Wiley] sending a man over the country picking up such rumors as he refers to . . . is enough to stagger the patriotism of a better man than myself." Allen, *Secret Formula*, p. 51.)

"Poison Squad . . . for soft drinks": 1907 scrapbook, Oct. 30, 1907, "Herald." (CC Archives)

115 "combating prejudice": 1907 annual report. (CC Archives)

"3 million gallons": 1908 annual report. (CC Archives)

"bureaucratic interference": Atkinson, "The Drink That Made Atlanta Famous," *The Devil's Candle*, p. 145, courtesy Suzanne White, FDA Historian.

"George McCabe . . . repeatedly refused": McCabe Memorandum, March 12, 1909. (Wiley Papers)

"stay by the ship": Wiley to Adams, Feb. 8, 1909. (Wiley Papers)

"Dunlap pointed out": F. L. Dunlap to Board of Food & Drug Inspection, March 27, 1909. (Wiley Papers)

"merit discussion": Wiley memo, March 18, 1909. (Wiley Papers)

"If their parents knew": Wiley memo, May 12, 1909. (Wiley Papers)

"surprised and grieved": Wiley, *Autobiography*, p. 261.

"nominated . . . Nobel Prize": Box 71 note. (Wiley Papers)

"cook's dirty undershirt": J. L. Lynch, Barrels Case, p. 79. That same month, just after Kebler's visit to the Coca-Cola factory, Martha Allen published "Coca-Cola, A Drug Drink" in Tom Watson's *Weekly Jeffersonian* on August 12, 1909.

"hired a dirigible": *CC Bottler*, Dec. 1909, pp. 6–7.

"defensive tract": *The Truth About Coca-Cola*, 1910. (CC Archives)

116 "Ben Thomas's objections": Thomas to Dobbs, Aug. 25, 1909, Bottler Case, p. 1450.

"not once . . . Federal prosecution": John Candler, "Every Knock Is a Boost," CC *Bottler*, Aug. 1909, p. 5.

"Seely, a New Jersey native": Franklin Garrett, *Atlanta and Environs*, vol. 2, p. 498.

"Seely had threatened": Candler memo, May 19, 1990, (AGC Papers, Box 3); Allen, *Secret Formula*, p. 57.

"fear of publicity": Wiley, *Autobiography*, p. 262.

"God-damned carpenter": Lynch, Barrels Case, p. 119.

117 "dig up dirt": Kebler handwritten note attached to note from W. G. Campbell, Feb. 8. 1911. FDA seizure 352 file; C. T. Smith to Chief Inspector, Bureau of Chemistry, Feb. 27, 1911, (FDA Seizure File 352).

"equivalent . . . Atlanta": Wiley, *History of a Crime*, p. 378. Actually, Wiley may only have been searching for excuses, since another source indicates the Chattanooga seizure was plotted because Judge Sanford, a Wiley acquaintance, had ruled in favor of other pure food cases. (Atkinson, *Devil's Candle*, p. 149)

"very low class men": Daniel M. Walsh, Inspector, to Chief Inspector, April 13, 1911. (FDA files)

"almost useless now": A. R. Sudler to Chief, March 24, 1911. AF. (FDA files)

"married Anna Kelton": Wiley, *Autobiography*, pp. 281–282.

"Coca-Cola was misbranded": In the trial, Harold Hirsch made much of Coca-Cola's *hyphen*, which, he argued, rendered the trademark a single word unrelated to the two substances, coca and cola. Unfortunately, the name frequently appeared on bottle caps and correspondence without a hyphen, which the government lawyers pointed out.

"impossible to cut": "Fight on Coca-Cola Is Waxing Warm," *Atlanta Georgian*, March 16, 1911. For other coverage of the trial see Allen, *Secret Formula*, p. 51.

118 "other insect fragments": H. C. Fuller, Barrels Case, p. 130.

"wild nocturnal freaks": Inspector Lynch to W. G. Campbell, April 28, 1910, FDA files; George R. Stuart, "Is Coca-Cola a Menace to the Public Health?" *Town Topics*, Dec. 7, 1913. (Wiley Papers)

"three co-editors": *The National Dispensatory*, ed. by Hare, Caspari, and Rusby.

"often amusing conflict": Harry Hollingworth, "Years at Columbia," unpublished autobiography written in 1940, pp. 64–72, Hollingworth Papers; Hollingworth, "The Influence of Caffein Alkaloid on the Quality and Amount of Sleep, *American Journal of Psychology*, Jan. 1912, vol. 23, p. 100; "Harry Levi Hollingworth: 1880–1956," *American Journal of Psychology*, 1957, vol. 70, pp. 136–140; for an excellent overview, see Ludy T. Benjamin, Jr., et al., "Coca-Cola, Caffeine, and Mental Deficiency: Harry Hollingworth and the Chattanooga Trial of 1911," *Journal of the History of the Behavioral Sciences*, Jan. 1991, pp. 42–55.

"dyspeptic letters": Asa to Howard, March 15, 1911; Asa to Howard, March 16, 1911. (AGC Papers, Box 1)

"EIGHT COCA-COLAS": *Atlanta Georgian*, March 18, 1911.

"on various animals": The Bureau's scientist testified that rabbits on a Coca-Cola diet had died—little wonder, since he had run the feeding tube into the rabbits' lungs instead of their stomachs and had drowned them all. ("The Bureau of Chemistry and Its Work," *Scientific American*, Nov. 23, 1912, p. 439)

119 "feed a frog": "Caffeine's Effect Bad, Say Experts," *Atlanta Georgian*, March 17, 1911.

"rat rabbit & frog evidence": Asa Candler to Sam and Joe Willard, March 21, 1911. (AGC Papers, Box 1)

"not qualify as an expert": *Southern Carbonator and Bottler*, Oct. 1911.

"Wiley would have testified": Harold Hirsch later made much of Wiley's admission that he did not qualify as an expert. Even the impartial *Scientific*

American complained of Wiley's pseudo-science. ("Dr. Wiley's Resignation," *Scientific American*, March 30, 1912, p. 282)

"Father likes it": 1907, 141ARS. (CC Archives)

"an unwritten law": The trial also had another immediate effect. The decorative border of coca leaves and kola nuts gracing Coca-Cola trays and syrup barrels now disappeared. In general, advertising in the post-Barrels and Kegs era stressed the wholesome, refreshing qualities of the drink, while tonic claims were nearly abandoned. The Company simultaneously stepped up defensive efforts, offering a series of booklets praising caffeine and quoting scientists in its favor. (*The Truth About Coca-Cola*, 1910; *Truth, Justice and Coca-Cola*, 1914; *The Truth, the Whole Truth and Nothing But the Truth About Coca-Cola*, 1915; *The Romance of Coca-Cola*, 1916; Bateman & Schaeffer, "Trays: An Overview," *Cola Call*, June 1985, pp. 7–8; "Truth, Justice, Romance," *Coca-Cola Collectors News*, May 1988, pp. 10–14)

"two bills were introduced": Ludy Benjamin, "Coca-Cola, Caffeine, and Mental Deficiency," *Journal of the History of the Behavioral Sciences*, Jan. 1991, p. 54, footnote 36.

120 **"president of Dr Pepper"**: R. S. Lazenby to Wiley, July 12, 1912. (Wiley Papers)

"Advantages of Coffee": Edwin J. Gillies to Wiley, Nov. 9, 1912. (Wiley Papers). *See also* Pendergrast, *Uncommon Grounds*, pp. 108–110.

"Wiley joined *Good Housekeeping*": From 1907 through 1911, Coca-Cola advertised steadily in *Good Housekeeping*. Not surprisingly, the ads ceased in 1912 after Wiley's articles appeared there. (CC Archives)

"opinions . . . purchased": Several of Coca-Cola's expert witnesses had indeed written books or articles critical of caffeine before accepting money to testify that it was harmless.

"crawling inside a giant glass": Harold Hirsch contacted Wiley and the editor of *Good Housekeeping* seeking rebuttal space, but was refused. Instead, Hirsch published his lengthy answer to Wiley in serial form in *The Coca-Cola Bottler*, where he reached a limited but vastly sympathetic audience.

"moralistic young filmmaker": Barry & Bowser, *D. W. Griffith*, p. 11. For the filmmaker's first experience with Coca-Cola, see Griffith, *The Man Who Invented Hollywood*, p. 51.

"anti-Coca-Cola epic": D. W. Griffith, *For His Son*, Biograph, 1912, 12 minutes. Film at Emory University.

"played by . . . Blanche Sweet": Prof. Martin S. Pernick to Mark Pendergrast, June 9, 1991.

"corporation is becoming": Reuben D. Silliman, "Government Regulation of Wealth," *Outlook*, Dec. 25, 1909, p. 990.

"a penalty tax": "Accumulated Earnings Tax," *BNA Tax Management Portfolios*, vol. 35, p. 49, A1–A5.

121 **"double taxation"**: Thanks to accountant Tom Scanlon for this interpretation.

"thinly defined": CHC, *AGC*, p. 266.

"in Biblical times": ibid., p. 146.

"whopping dividends": 1914 and 1915 CC annual reports; CHC, *AGC*, p. 266.

"leaving the bench to run for president": Hughes—vociferously supported by Harvey Wiley—lost by an extremely slim margin. ("One More Reason," newspaper clip, *AGC* Papers, Box 21)

"puritanical attitude": "Charles Evans Hughes," *The Justices of the United States Supreme Court*, pp. 1893–94.

"Hirsch commenced negotiations": W. P. Jones to Dr. Alsberg, July 28, 1916, FDA files.

"Alsberg asked for more time": Secretary of Agriculture to Attorney General, March 28, 1917. (FDA files)

"Company agreed to reduce": Hirsch to Attorney General, Feb. 16, 1917. (FDA files)

122 "tacit agreement": Harvey Wiley, disgusted by the settlement, continued to agitate for action against Coca-Cola right up until his death in 1930. (Wiley, *History of a Crime*; Ludy Benjamin, p. 55, footnote 41)

"accepted a bribe": Brad Ansley interview.

"over $250,000": Harold Hirsch, Bottler Case, p. 1553.

"entire destruction": ibid.

CHAPTER 8: THE SINISTER SYNDICATE

123 "Complainant now shows": Bottler Case, p. 22.

"selling both drinks": J. C. Mayfield, Sr., Koke Case, p. 1592–1604; for an excellent review of the use of "Koke," "Coke," and "Dope," see Bateman & Schaeffer, "The Story of How and Why Coca-Cola Is Coke," *Coca-Cola Collectors News*, Dec. 1988, pp. 6–13.

124 "A-Shot-in-the-Arm": For many years, the sign used by the deaf for Coca-Cola was a mimicked hypodermic needle to the arm. (Betty Molnar interview)

"amusing array of nicknames": J. B. Pendergrast, Koke Case, pp. 496–498.

"Koke Case was pending": The Koke Case was decided in Coca-Cola's favor on Sept. 16, 1916, on the Arizona District Court level. Mayfield immediately appealed to the Ninth Circuit Court of Appeals.

"illegitimate business practices": Francis M. Phelps to Harold Hirsch, March 27, 1916, FTC correspondence. (CC Legal Library)

"special agent": E. Y. Chapin to Harold Hirsch, Nov. 27, 1915, FTC booklet. (CC Legal Library)

"Asa Candler received . . . FTC": Joseph E. Davies to Asa G. Candler, July 15, 1916, FTC booklet. (CC Legal Library)

125 "poor financial shape": CHC, *AGC*, p. 321.

"amounting almost to anxiety": ibid., p. 147.

"intending to remain": ibid., p. 322.

"I do want it": Garrett, *Atlanta and Environs*, vol. 2, p. 698.

"the people's candidate": "Asa G. Candler's Race for Mayor," Sept. 27, 1916, clipping. (AGC Papers, Box 21)

"some ordinary gink": All quotes from newspaper clippings. (AGC Papers, Box 21)

"union was disbanded": Garrett, *Atlanta and Environs*, vol. 2, pp. 688–689.

"demagogue whose radical measures": Asa Candler speeches. (AGC Papers, Box 2)

126 "Asa boomers": AGC Papers, Box 21.

"exclusively to Candler-bashing": "Why does a 'victim' rush for a glass before he can eat breakfast?" Bessie Smith asked. "No man save Mr. Candler alone, really knows the actual amount of cocaine in Coca-Cola, and we do not expect him to give away the secret of his wealth." ("Will Restitution Ever Be Made?" *Atlanta Civics*, Nov. 1917, p. 3, AGC Papers, Box 7)

"souls would be purged": Mrs. Bessie L. Smith, *Atlanta Civics*, Oct. 1917, p. 2. (AGC Papers, Box 7)

"paper from a newsboy": ibid., p. 1.

"Soft Drink Ordinance": Feb. 18, 1918. (CC Archives)

"a more alarming peril": Feb. 2, 1918, Asa Candler to WCTU woman. (AGC Papers, Box 4) "what about the soda jerker": Jan. 18, 1917, Dalton, GA, *Citizen*. (AGC Papers, Box 21)

"Two New York lawyers": Colby, who was to serve as Woodrow Wilson's Secretary of State in 1920, was a well-connected politician and lawyer. Ed Brown, a native of Albany, Georgia, was Harold Hirsch's brother-in-law, father Samuel Brown, a wealthy cotton broker and banker from Albany, Georgia, was the real mover behind the deal. Brown had been negotiating with Asa Candler since 1908 to purchase the company, but something always went wrong. Candler said he wanted to sell, but in fact he was reluctant to follow through. (Allen, *Secret Formula*, p. 55–56, 64–65, 85–88; Harold Hirsch, Bottler Case, p. 2432).

"the deal fell through": "Says Colby Firm Got $1,000,000 in Stock," *NYT*, April 28, 1920, p. 7; Hirsch, Bottler Case, p. 2431.

127 "I, Asa G. Candler": William A. Landers, "My 38 Years with the Coca-Cola Company," CC Archives, p. 6; Harris, "Asa G. Candler: Georgia Cracker," p. 205; Ovid Davis interview.

"received a million dollars": *NYT*, April 28, 1920, p. 7.

"Candler had turned over": CHC, *AGC*, pp. 127, 267. According to family legend, Lucy Candler pressured her husband into giving the children the Coca-Cola stock. (Graham, *Real Ones*, pp. 87–88)

"Statue of Liberty": June 1918, 568ARS. (CC Archives)

"Hirsch disagreed": Hirsch, Bottler Case, p. 2443.

"abnormal conditions": Bottler Case, p. 32.

128 "we can't get the sugar": "Coca-Cola Drink Supply Curtailed," *National Bottlers' Gazette*, Jan. 5, 1918, p. 121.

"serving AFRI-KOLA": "Coca-Cola Substitution," *NBG*, July 5, 1918, p. 85.

"business would be decimated": John Candler, *Revenue to Defray War Expenses*, 1917, pp. 122–131.

"I *must* make a profit": P. H. Russell to J. F. Johnston, March 6, 1919, files of Coca-Cola Bottling Company, Paris, TN, in possession of Bill Schmidt.

"use of sugar substitutes": "Sugar Substitutes," *CC Bottler*, June 1918, p. 22; "The Use of Saccharin," Sept. 1918, p. 16; "Sugar and Its Substitutes," Dec. 1918, p. 16.

"nothing changed, cheapened": March 1919, 588ARS. (CC Archives)

"bent the truth": One positive outcome of the war was Howard Candler's discovery that Coca-Cola syrup did not need to be heated. Coal having been rationed as well as sugar, Candler tried dissolving sugar in cold syrup, just as he did with his iced tea. Using what amounted to a giant butter churn, he eliminated the expensive, time-consuming boiling process (CHC, *AGC*, pp. 124–126)

"returning soldiers": *CC Bottler*, Dec. 1918, p. 19.

"huge new manufacturing plant": CHC, "33 Years," pp. 61–62; Feb. 12, 1919, minutes. (CC Archives)

129 "unconscionable conduct": Koke Case, Opinion, Feb. 24, 1919, pp. 2602–3; Iver P. Cooper, "Unclean Hands" and "Unlawful Use in Commerce," *Trademark Reporter*, vol. 71, pp. 38–40.

"utterly helpless": Elton J. Buckley, "A Bottling Trade as Well as a Trade Mark Decision of Great Importance," *National Bottlers' Gazette*, July 5, 1919, p. 83.

"probably behind the original attempt": W. C. Wardlaw, Bottler Case, p. 2349.

"powerful tax incentives": Sam Dobbs, Bottler Case, p. 2246; Dobbs to Dennis A. Reeser, Oct. 27, 1919. (CC Archives)

"Dobbs agreed": Sam Dobbs, Bottler Case, p. 2206.

"**Woodruff sought**": Martin, *Three Strong Pillars*, pp. 24–41; Allen, *Secret Formula*, p. 92–100; *'Where Peachtree'*: Pomerantz, p. 101–103.

"**petty frugality**": Kahn, *RWW*, p. 43.

"**Nobody knows**": "Woodruff Wins 'Wizard' Title in Financial Deals Here," *Atlanta Georgian*, Aug. 28, 1919.

130 "**Eugene Stetson**": Before moving to New York, Stetson was a Macon, Georgia, banker. (A. B. Simms III interview)

"**Be it resolved**": Aug. 13, 1919, Trust Co. minutes, (CC Archives)

"**only $1.8 million**": *Atlanta Georgian*, Aug, 24, 1919.

131 "**$40 a share**": Underwriters across the country offered the stock for $40, but $5 of that was taken as profit; the "actual" sales price was $35.

"**By 3:45 P.M.**": W. C. Wardlaw, Bottler Case, p. 2335.

"**their mansions would spring up**": The Candler mansions survive. Howard built Callanwolde, now an arts center. Asa Jr. created Briarcliff, which became (ironically enough, since "Buddie" was a drinker) an alcohol rehabilitation center. Walter's Lullwater House is now the home of Emory's president. William owned Rest Haven, complete with lake and swans. Lucy built Rainbow Terrace, renovated as condominiums. Asa Sr.'s 1903 home, Callan Castle, was bought and refurbished in the 1980s by Charles LeChasney, a wealthy French aristocrat who turned out to be a Cuban con artist named Herriberto Figueroa, subsequently jailed for laundering drug money. Asa's final Ponce de Leon monstrosity, built for $210,000 in 1916, has been converted into the St John Melkite Catholic Church. (Michael Booth, "The Classic Style of the Coca-Cola Homes," *Southern Homes*, Spring 1986, pp. 86–99; Tracy Thompson, "Confessed Money-Launderer Chased Wealth and Friendships," *Atlanta Journal/Constitution*, Oct. 24, 1988, p. 6)

"**immediate profit**": Harold Martin gives a figure of $2,085,000 in *Three Strong Pillars*. The bottlers' lawyers claimed the figure was $5 million; see also Allen, *Secret Formula*, p. 103.

"**manipulations**": Bottler Case, p. 23.

"**lingering IRS suit**": The matter was finally settled out of court in 1929 for $1 million, though the Trust Company then spent years trying to pry money out of the original sellers. (William A. Landers, "My 38 Years with the Coca-Cola Company 1910–1948," CC Archives, pp. 12–13; *New York Times*, May 28, 1924, p. 36; Harold Hirsch to W. D. Thomson, Aug. 23, 1929, property of Frank Robinson II; John Sibley to RWW, Nov. 22, 1930, Sibley Papers, Box 1)

"**beginning balance sheet**": Howard Candler, Bottler Case, pp. 2472–73.

"**good will**": McCarthy, *Trademarks and Unfair Competition*, p. 60.

"**tangible financial results**": "A New Yardstick for Sales and Advertising Policies," *Sales Management*, Nov. 17, 1928, p. 419.

"**worth nearly $7 million dollars**": Cynthia Mitchell, "Coke Stock: Formula for Fortunes," AC, April 15, 1992; Kahn, *Big Drink*, p. 62; CC Co. Public Relations. In small-town Quincy, Florida, almost every citizen can still attest to the stock's phenomenal growth, since a local banker cajoled townspeople into buying 1919 Coca-Cola shares. Today, despite the exodus of various kin over the years, Quincy residents still hold about $300 million worth of Coca-Cola stock.

132 "**profoundly shocked**": CHC, *AGC*, pp. 184–185.

"**I can't bring myself**": Asa to Howard, April 12, 1921. (AGC Papers, Box 2)

"**ashes, just ashes**" Graham, *Real Ones*, p. 115

"**lost my way**": Asa Candler speech to Rural Sunday School Celebration. (AGC Papers, Box 2)

"**I was once counted**": Asa to Howard, April 12, 1921. (AGC Papers, Box 2)

"Catholic divorcee": Graham, *Real Ones*, pp. 117–22; AC, Oct. 13, 1922; Feb 5–6, 1924; Allen, *Secret Formula*, pp 151–152)

"mutual acquaintance": James E. Dickey to Asa Candler, Sept. 2, 1922. (WC Papers)

"Jesuit plot": J. E. Harrison to Bishop Warren Candler, Nov. 24, 1922. (WC Papers, Box 47)

"life companion": Asa to Howard, June 19, 1923. (AGC Papers, Box 2)

"a little party": Graham, *Real Ones*, p. 123.

"Candler filed for divorce": Asa G. Candler vs. Mrs. Mae L. Candler, Fulton County Superior Court, filed on June 17, 1924.

"killed a five-year-old": Elizabeth Lawrence Lunsford vs. Mrs. Mae Little Candler et al., Oct. 8, 1924, Fulton County Superior Court. Settled upon payment of costs, March 23, 1926. The Candler divorce was never finalized. Mae Little Candler continued to live in the mansion on Ponce de Leon until Candler's death in 1929. Candler languished during his last years in a private suite at Emory Hospital. (Graham, *Real Ones*, pp. 123–24)

"Everybody is dead": Asa G. Candler deposition, Sept. 2, 1924, My-Coca Case (courtesy Bob Hester).

133 "dislike to go out": Asa to Howard and Asa Jr., Dec. 25, 1924. (AGC Papers, Box 2)

"his baboons climbed": Kahn, *Big Drink*, p. 59; Graham, pp. 169–235.

"rape another man's wife": Candler vs. Byfield, Byfield vs. Candler, Nos. 4478, 4496, Supreme Court of Georgia, July 16, 1925; Graham, pp. 273–83.

"rumors persisted": Nan Pendergrast to Mark Pendergrast, Oct. 1, 1991; Graham, pp. 262–73; 283–89. The third generation also suffered from the ravages of easy wealth. Of the twenty surviving grandchildren, half became hopeless alcoholics. (Graham, pp. 312–23).

"Howard who wrote the curious book": Though Charles Howard Candler's name is on the title page, the book was actually ghostwritten in 1950 by Brad Ansley, a young Emory public relations man. "I never made any attempt to exercise judgment. I just took what the old man [Howard] said and wrote it." (Brad Ansley interview)

"story of Frank the pony": CHC, *AGC*, p. 217.

134 "Powerful interests": Bottler Case, pp. 1474–75. Hirsch wrote the letter from New York on Colby & Brown stationery, indicating that those two lawyers were actively involved in their second "syndicate."

CHAPTER 9: COCA-COLA'S CIVIL WAR

135 "Family quarrels": F. Scott Fitzgerald, as quoted in *Crown Treasury*, p. 272.

"hate each other": Sebert Brewer interview.

"Sam Dobbs wrote": Sam Dobbs to C. V. Rainwater and George Hunter, Nov. 18, 1919, Bottler Case, pp. 929–931.

"truly grateful": Howard Candler to George Hunter, Dec. 5, 1919, Bottler Case, p. 935.

"plan of readjustment": Bottler Case, p. 2215.

"New Year's greetings": Charles Howard Candler, "New Years Greetings," Charles V. Rainwater, "Have Faith," Harold Hirsch, "Greetings from the General Counsel," *CC Bottler*, Jan. 1920, pp. 1, 16–17.

136 "change our whole method": Charles Veazey Rainwater, Bottler Case, p. 2556. His testimony covers the following section as well.

"Hirsch owned a bottling plant": Harold Hirsch bought the troubled Nashville plant several owners after the notorious William Heck.

"unheard-of $37,500": Hirsch, Bottler Case, p. 2376.

"little shops": Sam Dobbs, Bottler Case, p. 2230.

"refused to attend": Bottler Case, p. 2214.

137 **"complicated sliding scale"**: Bottler Case, p. 66.

"Dobbs vehemently rejected": Sam Dobbs letter, Bottler Case, pp. 1579–82.

"contracts would be terminated": Howard Candler, March 2, 1920, Bottler Case, p. 74.

"losing $20,000 a day": Howard Candler, Bottler Case, pp. 1608–9.

"stinging denial": Jack J. Spalding to Coca-Cola Company, March 6, 1920, Bottler Case, p. 75.

"The fight is on": Dobbs to D'Arcy, April 16, 1920. (CC Archives)

"your welfare . . . affected": Sam Dobbs to Actual Bottlers, April 17, 1920. (Sizer File)

"The Chattanooga crowd": Dobbs to D'Arcy, April 20, 1920. (CC Archives)

"spirit of cooperation": Harold Hirsch to Arthur Montgomery, April 20, 1920. (Sizer File)

"If I go down": Bottler Case, p. 2517; See also Allen, *Secret Formula* pp. 114–121, 127.

138 **"8 cents a glass"**: "Coca-Cola Price Uniform 8 Cents at Founts Monday," AC April 18, 1920.

"Hirsch physically wrenched": "Violence Near When Counsel in Coca-Cola Case Objects to Reading of the Records," *Atlanta Georgian*, April 27, 1920.

"Give me my book back": Harold Hirsch, Bottler Case, p. 2217.

"serve no useful purpose": Bottler Case, p. 100.

"Hunter and Rainwater chronicled": Rainwater, Bottler Case, p. 2521.

"city of Atlanta . . . suing": "City Asks Names of Stockholders in Big Companies," *AC*, April 29, 1920.

139 **"BOTTLERS SUE"**: "Bottlers Sue for Coca-Cola Recipe," *AC*, May 15, 1920.

"came as a thunderbolt": Dobbs to D'Arcy, May 31, 1920. (CC Archives)

"federal questions": "Bottlers to Take Case to U.S. Courts," *Atlanta Georgian*, May 31, 1920.

"he fainted": "Chattanoogan Faints at Coca-Cola Hearing," *AJ*, June 26, 1920.

"contract is perpetual": Hirsch to T. C. Parker, Oct. 28, 1916, Bottler Case, pp. 1570–72. Lawyer John Candler also clearly felt the contracts were perpetual, as he had informed a Senate committee in 1917. (John Candler, *Revenue to Defray War Expenses*, pp. 125, 128)

"re-examined": Hirsch, Bottler Case, pp. 1552–53.

"greatest incentive": Rainwater, Bottler Case, p. 195.

140 **"price had fallen"**: "Sugar Situation" articles, *National Bottlers' Gazette*, Sept. 5, Oct. 5, 1920, Jan. 5, 1921.

"case of diabetes": Treseder, *As I Remember*, p. 20; "Big Sugar Cargo for Coca Cola Company Arrives in Brunswick," *AJ*, Dec. 15, 1920.

"we are NOT manufacturers": Crawford Johnson to J. B. Sizer, Oct. 16, 1920. (Sizer File)

"company actually *boosted*": "Price of Syrup," Oct. 30, 1920. (Sizer File)

"outraged letter": Rainwater to Howard Candler, Oct. 30, 1920. (Sizer File)

"Discouraged shareholders": "Bears Hammer Coca-Cola, But Dobbs Buying," *Sunday American*, Aug. 22, 1920. (CC Scrapbook)

"Lupton and his bunch": Dobbs to D'Arcy, May 18, 1920. (CC Archives)

"no more than $1.2 million": Pre-war Coca-Cola advertising for 1916 was $1.7 million, while it had reached $1.9 million in 1919.

"I asked him pointedly": Dobbs to D'Arcy, July 29, 1920. (CC Archives)

141 **"confidential conversations"**: Dobbs to D'Arcy, Oct. 5, 1920. (CC Archives)

"plummeted the stock": "Violent Break in Coca-Cola on Exchange," *Atlanta Georgian*, Oct. 11, 1920.

"Howard Candler was installed": "Dobbs Quits Presidency," *AC*, Oct. 26, 1920.

"forceful and conclusive opinion": Sizer to Messrs. Ward, Gray & Neary, Nov. 15, 1920. (Sizer File)

"Oliver Wendell Holmes . . . opinion": It was only by a quirk of fate that Holmes delivered this opinion rather than Charles Evans Hughes. If the puritanical Hughes had not run for president in 1916, the Koke Case might have had a different outcome. Holmes, however, was a pragmatist. "The life of the law has not been logic," he once wrote, "it has been experience." Consequently, his Coca-Cola ruling looked at the commonsense situation as it existed in 1920. ("Oliver Wendell Holmes," *The Justices of the United States Supreme Court*, pp. 1755–59)

"a single thing": Koke Case, Dec. 6, 1920, opinion by Holmes.

"utmost importance": "Coca-Cola Co. of Delaware Wins Koke Case," *AJ*, Dec. 6, 1920.

"Johnson moaned": Crawford Johnson to J. B. Sizer, Dec. 15, 1920. (Sizer File)

142 **"yet another suit"**: "Fraud Charged in Coca-Cola Suit," *Atlanta Georgian*, Feb. 16, 1921.

"hiding something": "Coca-Cola Co. Shows Big Gain in Loans," *WSJ*, Feb. 22, 1921.

"hurriedly filed . . . statement": "Coca-Cola Co. Amplifies Its '20 Statement," *Atlanta Georgian*, Feb. 24, 1921.

"Company threw a bash": *Friendly Hand*, May 2, 1921, p. 1. (CC Archives)

"court-appointed official": Sizer to Crawford Johnson, May 6, 1921. (Sizer File)

"war . . . resolved": "Coca-Cola Fight Has Been Settled," *AC*, June 27, 1921.

"A jobber explained": Carl F. G. Meyer, *Friendly Hand*, June 6, 1921. (CC Archives)

"dominated its home territory": Rainwater, Bottler Case, p. 2522.

"came down in favor": Chero-Cola Case; Murphy, "The Legend of John Pemberton," pp. 9–12.

"a very large gentleman": "To Pause and Be Refreshed," *Fortune*, July 1931, pp. 110–111.

143 **"thirty brand-new cars"**: *Friendly Hand*, Aug. 1, 1921, p. 3. (CC Archives)

"all steamed up": Treseder, *As I Remember*, p. 29.

"Give 'em hell": Rowland, p. 18.

"leaped up in church": Treseder, pp. 31–34.

"Brass Tacks Lane": W. B. Edwards, "How Coca-Cola Teaches Distributors Best Use of Dealer Helps," *Printer's Ink Monthly*, Aug. 1923, pp. 50–52.

144 **"This is a great day!"**: *Friendly Hand*, April 2, 1923; Harrison Jones, "Blazing the Trail," *Report of Sales and Advertising Conference*, March 7, 8, 1923. (CC Archives)

"best speaker": Treseder, p. 36.

"talking nonstop": Even in his final hospital stay, Jones regaled doctors with continuous anecdotes. (Dr. William R. Fisher to Mark Pendergrast, Sept. 25, 1991)

"He could sell anything": Thomas Wolfe, *Look Homeward, Angel* p. 253.

"bottled horse-piss": Sebert Brewer, Jr., interview; J. B. Pendergrast, Jr., interview.

"franchise for the North Pole": *Friendly Hand*, Nov. 7, 1921. (CC Archives)

"snowball in Alaska": Tom Law interview.

"introspective, quiet sort": Archie Lee began writing for Fred Seely's *Atlanta*

Georgian in 1908, perhaps covering the Barrels and Kegs trial. It is certainly ironic that Archie Lee, soon to be Coca-Cola's most formidable advertising man, commenced his career with Asa Candler's archenemy.

145   **"something really worth while"**: Archie Lee to Mama, April 5, 1917. (CC Archives)

"It is hard work": Lee to Papa, March 13, 1920. (CC Archives)

"I feel confident": Lee to Parents, March 8, 1921. (CC Archives)

"over fifty pieces": Lee to Papa, Oct. 29, 1921. (CC Archives)

"featured two women": 492ARS, 1916. (CC Archives)

"a favorite friend": June 30, 1917, *Collier's Weekly*, 541ARS. (CC Archives)

"A *Life* ad": 1920, 608ARS. (CC Archives)

"clean-cut young soda jerk": July 1921, *Modern Priscilla*, 646ARS. (CC Archives)

146   **"direct mail letters"**: "Let's go!" packet, April 27, 1923, D'Arcy Advertising Company. (CC Archives)

"Thirst Knows No Season": 652ARS, 653ARS. (CC Archives)

"fountain salesmen . . . delighted": *Friendly Hand*, Feb. 6, 1922, p. 3. (CC Archives)

"winter campaign": Despite its claims as an all-weather drink, Coca-Cola has never quite escaped a seasonal winter dip in sales. (Rowland, pp. 33–34)

"A fellow about my age": Lee to Mama, July 7, [1923]. (CC Archives)

PART III: THE GOLDEN AGE (1923–1949)

147   **"Zhukov was exhausted"**: Scenario based on Mladin Zarubica interview. Background material on Zhukov in Khrushchev, *Khrushchev Remembers*, pp. 218–219, 556–557; Donovan, *Eisenhower: The Inside Story*, pp. 347, 396.

CHAPTER 10: ROBERT W. WOODRUFF: THE BOSS TAKES THE HELM

151   **"Great things are done"**: John Henry Cardinal Newman, *Historical Sketches*, vol. III, quoted in *Crown Treasury*, p. 322.

"initial objections": One historian calls it "an elaborate fable" that Ernest Woodruff initially objected to his son Robert's appointment as president, though his evidence is circumstantial. At any rate, there is no doubt that the father eventually agreed, however reluctantly, to placing his son at the head of the Company. (Allen, *Secret Formula*, p. 130, 151–156.)

"a never-ending pattern": Elliott, *Mr. Anonymous*, p. 21.

"much harder on me": ibid., p. 22.

"rough-house": Della Wager Wells, *George Waldo Woodruff*, p. 105.

"befriended the groom": Elliott, p. 80.

152   **"With her encouragement"**: ibid., p. 81.

"Raising money": ibid., p. 83.

"visited James S. Floyd": ibid., p. 84–85.

"math homework": Martha Ellis interview.

"widely quoted dictums": E. J. Kahn, Jr., *RWW*, p. 93.

"devastatingly direct letter": Elliott, p. 87–88.

153   **"Coca Cola School"**: Kahn, *Big Drink*, p. 89.

"Buffalo Bill Cody . . . met": Elliott, p. 86.

"general laborer": ibid., pp. 89–90; "From Sand Shoveler to Coca Cola's President," *The City Builder*, May 1923, pp. 1–2.

"lesson in hard knocks": Morton Hodgson interview.

"mighty important men": Elliott, p. 91.

"advised his nephew": Morton Hodgson interview.

154 "hunting buddy, Ty Cobb": When they weren't feuding, Woodruff and the volatile Cobb remained lifelong friends, which does not speak particularly well for Woodruff's taste. Ty Cobb sharpened the spikes on his shoes to intimidate other players when he slid into a base. Even his teammates despised him. At Cobb's death, his Coca-Cola shares were worth $1.7 million. (Alexander, *Ty Cobb*, pp. 3–5, 38–40, 57, 77, 155, 173–174, 213; Leonard Ray Teel, "A Ballplayer and His Money," *Georgia Trend*, Aug. 1987, pp. 95–98; "Ty Cobb, Baseball and Coca-Cola," *Cola Call*, Sept. 1985, p. 3; Joe Jones interview)

"his falling Coca-Cola stock": Elliott, p. 101.

"Teagle had tendered": Morton Hodgson interview.

"price of stock back": Robert Woodruff actually was never in any danger of taking a loss on his stock, having bought it at $5 per share.

155 "Woodruff assumed the presidency": Howard Candler was kicked upstairs as a board member. (*Friendly Hand*, May 7, 1923, p. 1)

"never finished a book": It is possible that Woodruff was dyslexic, like many other notables such as George Patton, Nelson Rockefeller, Woodrow Wilson, and Thomas Edison. (Landmark College correspondence)

"stuck in traffic": Joe Jones interview.

"simple pronouncements": Kahn, *Big Drink*, p. 82.

"There is no limit": "Boss Emeritus," Coca-Cola Company, March 1985.

"What's so good": Rowland, pp. 30, 212; Mary Thomas interview.

156 "moth near a flame": Wilbur Kurtz, Jr., interview.

"Boss in definite command": Woodruff proscribed a rigid Ichauway itinerary for each guest. "When you are with Bob Woodruff," remarked Freeman Gosden, the white actor who played Amos in *Amos & Andy*, "you are going to have a good time all right, but you are going to have it his way." One visitor wrote Woodruff a note after his Ichauway sojourn thanking the Boss for his "dogmatic hospitality," from which he was just recovering. (Elliott, *Mr. Anonymous*, p. 55; Cliff Roberts file, RWW Papers)

"count . . . bottle caps": Morton Hodgson, Sr., to Woodruff, Jan. 19, 1942. (RWW Papers, Box 41); Jack Tarver interview; Kahn, *RWW*, p. 72.

"fly in a holding pattern": Martha Ellis interview.

"angry and not revealing": Hughes Spalding to RWW, Aug. 18, 1961. (RWW Papers, Box 80)

157 "but he will": Elliott, p. 30.

"assuring a nickel drink": For decades, the same price structure prevailed. Coca-Cola sold syrup for $1.40 a gallon to bottlers, who then delivered a case of twenty-four bottles for 80 cents. At a nickel a drink, the retailer could sell the same case for $1.20. All along the line, there was a healthy profit margin.

"first professional managers": Ingham, *Biographical Dictionary of American Business Leaders*, vol. 1, p. xv.

"procedure manuals": Frank Troutman, April 27, 1928, memo, "Office Routine Memorandum No. 303," *Clearing Desks at Night*, in Administrative Notebooks, CC Archives.

"initially balked": "Coca-Cola International," *National Bottlers' Gazette*, Feb. 15, 1923, p. 74; "Lists Securities of 14 Corporations: New York Stock Exchange Announcement Makes No Reference to Coca-Cola Shares," *NYT*, Feb. 15, 1923, p. 31. The International stock was finally listed in 1926. Because the IRS ruled that exchanges of International stock for Coca-Cola common would trigger capital gains taxes, the stock was rarely traded through the years. Finally, as International shares dwindled, the Company was "merged" in 1980 with The

Coca-Cola Company with no tax consequences. (Joe Jones interview; Jimmy Sibley interview; "Coca-Cola in Open Market," *NYT*, April 16, 1926, p. 36)

158 **"his last hurrah"**: Thomas E. Watson, Oct. 12, 1921, *Congressional Record*, quoted in *National Bottlers' Gazette*, Nov. 15, 1921, p. 170.

"White wrote sarcastically": William Allen White, *Emporia Gazette*, quoted in Huntington, W. Va., *Advertiser*, March 27, 1929. This and associated quotes from clippings in Coca-Cola Collection, Box 12, Emory.

"gently took its place": "Coca-Cola in History," *NYT*, March 14, 1929, p. 26.

"take a man's measure": John Love biography of RWW, 1930, p. 6. (RWW Papers, Box 34)

"'Pig Iron' Brownlee": Rowland, pp. 7, 46–49.

159 **"John Sibley"**: Spalding, *The Spalding Family*, vol. 2, pp. 170–171; Wells, *The First Hundred Years*, pp. 145–148.

"In directing a sizable business": John Sibley to RWW, Jan. 14, 1938. (Sibley Papers, Box 1, Emory)

"address Woodruff as Bob": Delony Sledge to RWW, April 28, 1978. (RWW Papers, Sledge File)

"most period advertising": Marchand, *Advertising the American Dream*, pp. 102, 151, 152, 216.

160 **"always delightful"**: 740ARS, 731ARS, 704ARS. (CC Archives)

"idea in an illustration": "Barclay Talks in His Studio," *Red Barrel*, Feb. 1924, pp. 12–13. This quote comes from *The Red Barrel*, a much more dignified publication than the gossipy *Friendly Hand*, which it replaced in 1924.

"at all soda fountains": 781ARS, May 1924, *Ladies' Home Journal*. (CC Archives)

"nothing like it": 720ARS, Aug. 1923, *LHJ*. (CC Archives)

"Atlanta Virgins": Dick Halpern interview.

"Pause and Refresh Yourself": 766ARS, 1923. (CC Archives)

"Talk about the tempo": quoted in Marchand, *Advertising the American Dream*, pp. 3–4.

"Pause that Refreshes": By 1942, the word "pause" had become so well associated with Coca-Cola that the U.S. Patent Office refused to register a new soft drink called "Pause," calling it an infringement on Coca-Cola. ("The Coca-Cola Company Fights 'Pause' as Soft Drink Name; Wins," *Red Barrel*, April 1942, p. 36)

161 **"speedier, jazzier"**: Charles W. Stokes, "The Simple Life—and How!" *New Republic*, July 10, 1929, p. 203.

"fresh-scrubbed rural beauty": 710ARS, June 1923, *Ladies' Home Journal*. (CC Archives)

"Norman Rockwell's ads": Hoy, pp. 68–71.

"6,000,000 a Day": Hoy, pp. 44–49.

"million pairs of eyes": Turner, *The Shocking History of Advertising!*, p. 261.

"mammoth parade ground": "The Coca-Cola Spectacular in the Middle of Broadway's Mammoth Parade," *RB*, Oct. 1929, pp. 9–11.

"Mabel Millspaugh": Jim Jordan, p. 42; Glen Watson, "The Advertising of Coca-Cola 1927–1933," no date, p. 4. (CC Collection, Box 5)

"pioneering market research": In 1922, young Arthur Nielsen invented the concept of share-of-market, and industries have been measuring themselves religiously ever since. (Jack J. Honomichl, "Since First Straw Vote in 1824, Research Grows," in *How It Was in Advertising*, p. 62)

162 **"posed the question"**: Robert W. Woodruff, "After National Distribution— What?" *Nation's Business*, Aug. 1929, pp. 125–126.

"field workers . . . outlets": Roy Dickinson, "Finding the Profitable Outlets," *Printer's Ink*, May 1, 1930, pp. 3–6, 154–158.

"soft-sell movies": "Selling Merchandising Ideas to the Chain Stores," *Printer's Ink*, March 13, 1930, pp. 57–58; Frank W. Harrold, "Fifty Calls an Hour—And a Better Job with Each," *Printer's Ink Monthly*, May 1931, pp. 43, 99–100.

"GOES TO BED": "Coca-Cola Gets Up and Goes to Bed with the Consumer," *Advertising Age*, April 12, 1930, reprinted in *RB*, May 1930, p. 14; "Meet the New Coca-Cola Serviceman: He Is Busy Following the Crowd," *RB*, May 1930, p. 12.

163 "oases for the motorist": "The Filling Station—What an Outlet for Bottled Coca-Cola!," *RB*, June 1929, pp. 12–13.

"alphabetical list": *RB*, March 1924, p. 12.

"inexpensive, standard cooler": "Merchandising Magic," *RB*, pp. 133–136; Rowland, pp. 43–44.

"handle of invitation": "Merchandising Magic," p. 130; *CC Bottler*, April 1959, "Closing Session," *CC Bottler*, March 1923, p. 22.

164 "My Six Appeal": *RB*, Oct. 1928, p. 7.

"hired Ralph Beach": Ralph B. Beach, "History of the Coca-Cola Bottler's Association," *CC Bottler*, April 1959, pp. 99–106; John Beach interview.

"Fattig's culinary habits": P. W. Fattig, "Experiments with Foreign Substances in Beverages," *National Carbonator and Bottler*, Jan. 1933; Kahn, *Big Drink*, p. 94; Matthews & Shallcross, *Partners in Plunder*, p. 110.

"refused to attend": Mae Beach interview.

165 "Standardization Committee": Frampton King, "The Standardization Committee of Bottlers of Coca-Cola," *CC Bottler*, April 1959, pp. 144–146.

"You wipe your ass": Gordon Bynum interview.

166 "official press release": "Big Deal Closed as Journal Forecast," *AJ*, Aug. 1919, Scrapbook. (CC Archives)

"started all over Europe": Hodgson interview.

"poisonous brew": Morton Hodgson told the story of the nauseating European Coca-Cola, having heard it from several industry veterans when he arrived in France in 1935. In the properly acidic environment of standard Coca-Cola, bacteria could not thrive, but fermentation due to alkaline water was common in the early foreign markets. Nonetheless, Hodgson's vomit story appears to contradict other evidence, since the soft drink had been bottled in France (presumably without incident) since 1919, though the café proprietors admired the Coca-Cola calendar girl more than the beverage. (Al Staton, "Miscellaneous Recommendations," April 29, 1937, pp. 5, 31, 51–56, Case 5, RWW Papers; "Coca-Cola in France," *CC Bottler*, Feb. 1920, pp. 15–18)

"Georges Delcroix": "Coca-Cola in France," *CC Bottler*, Feb. 1920, pp. 15–18; 1921 correspondence, CC Archives; Roy Stubbs, *Compilation on France*, 1951, (pp. 316–317, 396, CC Legal Library)

167 "whether only Americans": Hodgson interview.

"Long-term prospects . . . good": Hamilton Horsey, "Preliminary Report" and "Final Report," Dec. 1924, CC Archives. All following quotes and figures are from these reports.

"three-month trip": "Itinerary, Travel" file. (RWW Papers)

"roofs were designed": Claus Halle interview.

"throughout the world": Coca-Cola's overseas thrust set the pace for the Roaring Twenties. Until then, U.S. foreign investment had been relatively limited, but the decade witnessed a sharp increase. During the following two decades, however, as other U.S. firms sold foreign subsidiaries because of the Depression and World War II, Coca-Cola's expansion continued unabated. (Aliber, *The International Money Game*, pp. 250–251)

168 **"In Amsterdam"**: Roy Stubbs, *Labeling (Foreign)*, no date, pp. 250–257. (CC Legal Library)
"Duckworth syrup": The Coca-Cola Company v. Duckworth & Co., In the High Court of Justice, Chancery Division, March 28, 1928; John Sibley to Arthur Acklin, Dec. 27, 1939, March 18, 1940; Roy Stubbs. *Compilation on England*, pp. 76–77. (All in CC Legal Library)
"Toni-Kola in Holland": Roy Stubbs, *Compilation on Peru*, 1946, p. 32.
"complete disaster": The *real* Coca-Cola had been turned down in Mexico in 1902 and legally registered in 1904, then allowed to lapse in 1924.
"without accomplishing anything": Roy Stubbs, *Compilation on Mexico*, 1947, pp. 5–6.
"man in a tuxedo": "Coca-Cola as Sold Throughout the World," *RB*, Feb. 1929, pp. 1–32. Much of the information in the following section is from this article.
169 **"bite the wax tadpole"**: N. F. Allman, "Transliteration of Coca-Cola Trademark to Chinese Characters," *CC Overseas*, June 1957, p. 11.
"Teme Coca-Cola": Treseder, *As I Remember*, p. 42.
"bullfight": ibid.
"few Americans realize": "Coca-Cola as Sold Throughout the World," *Red Barrel*, Feb. 1929, pp. 1–32.
"ancestors back from the dead": Eric Clark, *The Want Makers*, p. 43.
170 **"lost nearly $400,000"**: John E. McClure to Commissioner of Internal Revenue, May 10, 1937. (Sibley Papers, Box 1, Emory); Allen, *Secret Formula*, p. 179–188.
"dreaded the negative publicity": ibid.
"an unheard-of feat": "Heads White Motor Co.," *NYT*, Oct. 3, 1929, p. 41.
"a secret memo": McClure to Commissioner of Internal Revenue, May 10, 1937, p. 7. (Sibley Papers, Box 1)

CHAPTER 11: A EUPHORIC DEPRESSION AND PEPSI'S PUSH

172 **"That merry symphony"**: Joseph D. Kelly, "The Outlook for Coca-Cola," *Barron's*, Nov. 7, 1938, p. 13.
"By what magic": Henry Richmond, Jr, "A Soft Drink That Has Resisted Hard Times," *Magazine of Wall Street*, April 16, 1932, p. 802.
"Regardless of depression": "Coca-Cola Co.," *Magazine of Wall Street*, July 23, 1932, p. 414.
"specialty product": "Companies That Are Profiting," *Magazine of Wall Street*, Oct. 17, 1931, p. 852.
"fitting cap": Goldman, *The Empire State Building*, p. 47.
"bottling ring": "Huge Plant Faking Coca-Cola Raided," *NYT*, April 18, 1931, p. 15.
173 **"The repeal of Prohibition"**: Ward Gates, "A Soft Drink Unaffected by Hard Liquor," *Magazine of Wall Street*, Sept. 15, 1934, p. 562.
"added to the Dow": Phyllis S. Pierce, ed., *The Dow Jones Averages 1885–1980*, unpaged. Even as Coca-Cola prospered during the Depression, however, a nervous Harrison Jones suggested to Robert Woodruff that the Company produce Coca-Cola Beer when "near beer" became legal. The Boss nixed the idea. (Allen, *Secret Formula*, p. 204–205)
"highest-priced industrial": "Coca-Cola, the Highest Priced Industrial," *Barron's*, June 17, 1935, p. 16.
"sack of Vigero": J. C. Cooper to John Sibley, Oct. 29, 1935. (Sibley Papers, Box 1)

"**family quarrel**": Charles Veazey Rainwater, "Yesterday," copy from Bill Bateman and Randy Schaeffer. See also Bateman & Schaeffer, "The 50th Anniversary," *Cola Call*, June 1986, pp. 4–7. Much of the information in this section is taken from their article.

"**miniature Taj Mahal**": Tom Law interview; Bernice L. Thomas to Mark Pendergrast, Feb. 27, 1992. Six Coke bottling plants are listed on the National Register of Historic Places.

"**technological training**": Mickey Walker, "Selecting and Training a Sales Force," 1936 Convention, from Bateman & Schaeffer.

"**not blood, but syrup**": The syrup-in-the-veins metaphor cropped up in almost every interview conducted with Coca-Cola men for this book.

174 "**We are still pioneers**": RWW to 50th Anniv. Dinner, CC Fountain Sales Corp., March 25, 1936. (RWW Papers, Personal File 2) The religious overtones of Woodruff's "beacon" reference probably came from Dick Gresham, a Baptist minister known as "the Coca-Cola Bishop" because he wrote customized sermons for the Boss. In the mid-thirties, Gresham urged Woodruff to "banish forever a narrow nationalism or a smug parochialism," since Coca-Cola's saturation point was "the last man in earth's last country!" (Kahn, *RWW*, pp. 51–52; R. C. Gresham to RWW, Sept. 26, 1934, RWW Papers, Box 36)

"**There will be trials**": Harrison Jones, "Tomorrow," 1936, collection of Bateman & Schaeffer. Shortly after this speech, with the world on the brink of war, the Company created an elaborate film entitled *Always Tomorrow*. After flashing back to the industry's beginnings and its various problems, the heroic bottler admonished: "When you think of tomorrow, you think of more and more people to drink Coca-Cola. That's our job." (*Always Tomorrow*, 1939, CC Archives)

"**far-flung capillaries**": "Coca-Cola Industry," *Fortune*, Dec. 1938, p. 115.

"**Sam Dobbs had remarked**": Sam Dobbs, quoted in "Asa Candler's First Job Was Here in Cartersville," 1947 newspaper clipping. (AGC Papers, Box 21)

"**breakfasting on Coca-Cola**": Richmond, "A Soft Drink That Has Resisted," p. 803.

"**heavenly dew**": Rosemary Redding, "Something's Cookin' on Front Burner," Sept. 12, 1942, Indianapolis newspaper clipping. (CC Archives)

"**neighborhood women congregated**": Oldenburg, *The Great Good Place*, p. 113.

"**Play up the soda fountain**": Turner Jones to Archie Lee, July 18, 1934. (CC Archives)

175 "**her Pooh bear**": Archie Lee to RWW, Aug. 25, 1931. (RWW Papers, Box 57)

"**Depression-era advertising**": When Coca-Cola sales dipped in 1931 and 1932, the Company reacted by substantially *increasing* the advertising budget, which climbed over $5 million in 1932.

"**bounce back to normal**": Gates, "A Soft Drink Unaffected," p. 562.

"**movie stars appearing**": Bateman & Schaeffer, "History of Coca-Cola, Part 2: 1930–1949," p. 10; Hoy, pp. 74–77.

"**Movies have a wider appeal**": Archie Lee to Turner Jones, Jan. 19, 1935. (CC Archives)

"**they subconsciously buy it**": Archie Lee to RWW, Aug. 25, 1931. (RWW Papers, Box 57) Though the Company didn't pay for product placement in movies, there were rumors in 1934 that Coca-Cola had forged a million-dollar deal with Warner Brothers to plug the soft drink in films. The film company's spokesman denied the allegations but admitted to an "arrangement" with Coca-Cola to allow its stars to appear in the soft drink's ads. ("Coca-Cola Film Tie-Up," *Printer's Ink*, March 8, 1934, p. 52)

"**Stanley and Al Barbee**": Randy Barbee interview.

"hired J. Parker Read": Barbee interview.

176 "subtle suggestion": "Firms Get Free Ads in Movies," *Business Week*, Sept. 2, 1939, p. 26.

"some good sexy poses": Turner Jones to Archie Lee, April 7, 1934. (CC Archives)

"lolled on the sand": "Bathing Girls Pose on Coca-Cola Beach," RB, Sept. 1930, pp. 16–17.

"wonder of the refrigerator": Tedlow, *New and Improved*, pp. 304–328.

"new carton": "How a New Package Opened Up a New Market for Coca-Cola," *Printer's Ink*, reprinted in *Red Barrel*, July 1929, pp. 16–17.

"bands of women": "Coca-Cola Industry," *Fortune*, 1938, p. 110; Bateman & Schaeffer, "When You Entertain," *Cola Call*, Nov. 1985, p. 6; Hoy, pp. 47, 53.

"Ida Bailey Allen": Bateman & Schaeffer, "When You Entertain," *Cola Call*, Nov. 1985, pp. 4–6.

177 "Grape Fruit Sections in Coca-Cola": Ida Bailey Allen, *When You Entertain* (Atlanta: The Coca-Cola Company, 1932). (AGC Papers, Box 7) Long before Ida Bailey Allen's efforts, of course, Southerners had been using Coca-Cola to baste ham, make date-nut bread, produce a distinctive barbecue sauce, or cook the family pot roast. Free recipes are still available from the Company.

"natural partner": *The Coca-Cola Company: An Illustrated Profile*, p. 59.

"hard-drinking Swede": Marshall Lane interview; Al Scully in *Cola Conquest*.

"Santa . . . Coca-Cola red": Gwendolyn Davis, "The Story of the Spirit of Christmas," *Sky Magazine*, Dec. 1979; Nancy Cornell, "Collecting Christmas," *Sky*, Dec. 1990; "The Image of Santa Claus," *Cola Call*, Dec. 1985, pp. 4–6; Hoy, pp. 68–70.

"house-to-house sampling campaign": M. F. Hollister, "One Hundred Million Opportunities," 1936 Convention (courtesy Bateman & Schaeffer).

"Nature Study Cards": "The Answer," RB, Sept. 1929, pp. 3-6; J. C. Harrell, "Kansas City Nature Study Bus Hauls Thousands of Children," RB, June 1931, pp. 24–25.

"kids play basketball": "That He Who Shoots May Read," RB, Oct. 1931, p. 21.

"opening wedge": "The Augusta Open House," RB, Oct. 1931, pp. 23–24.

"Toast your own health": N. A. Lapsley, "Use of Birthday Cards," RB, July 1930, pp. 19–21.

"I have a baby boy": "Like Father, Like Son," RB, Oct. 1930, p. 17.

"captured the imagination": Marquis, *Hopes and Ashes*, pp. 21, 41, 48.

178 "Uncle Remus display": Bateman & Schaeffer, "Uncle Remus & The Coca-Cola Company, *Cola Call*, April 1984, pp. 4–9.

179 "committed itself to radio": Five years after radio's debut in 1920, Coca-Cola bought its first air time during a Chicago Cubs baseball game, but radio didn't become a major component of Coca-Cola's advertising strategy until the thirties. (Hoy, pp. 76–79; Jim Jordan, *The Coca-Cola Company*, p. 40; Treseder, *As I Remember*, p. 43)

"sports program": "Coca-Cola Goes on the Air," RB, March 1930, pp. 20–21; "The Coca-Cola Radio Program," RB, April 1930, pp. 8–9.

"special Coca-Cola anthem": Jordan, p. 45; "The Story Behind the Theme Song," *The Refresher*, June 1954. In 1931, radio allowed the reclusive Woodruff to deliver his disembodied message—"Know your stuff, and work"—to servicemen at regional meetings. ("Mr. Woodruff's Message to Regional Conventions," RB, Jan. 1931, p. 5)

"sirens, gongs, and pistol shots": Marquis, *Hopes and Ashes*, p. 25.

"no controversy": Archie Lee to Turner Jones, Oct. 12, 1936. (CC Archives)

"homey hoosier": Hoy, p. 78.

"who crooned": Jordan, p. 52.

"shrieks and howls": Lee to RWW, Oct. 18, 1940, Dec. 6, 1940, Nov. 12, 1941 (RWW Papers, Box 57); Bateman & Schaeffer, "Ray Noble & Refreshment Time," *Coca-Cola Collectors News*, March 1987, pp. 7–9.

"Red Devils": Frank Harrold, "Our Friend the Cooler," 1936 Convention; Raymond Witt interview. At the same time the red Dole dispenser, introduced at the 1933 Chicago World's Fair, guaranteed a uniform fountain drink by automatically mixing syrup and carbonated water in the correct ratio.

"manager, salesman, clerk": "The Bottle Comes Out of the Tub," *RB*, Dec. 1929, pp. 3–7; "The Coca-Cola Cooler, A Star Salesman," *RB*, July 1930, pp. 6–9.

"I am the bottler's friend": Frank Harrold, "Our Friend the Cooler," 1936 Convention, from Bateman & Schaeffer.

180 "8,000 coin-operated coolers": "Merchandising Magic," CC *Bottler*, April 1959, pp. 134–136; "The Coca-Cola Industry," *Fortune*, 1938, p. 110.

"eighteen-passenger Condors": "On Skyways, as on Highways—Coca-Cola Refreshes Thousands," *RB*, Nov. 1931, pp. 4–5.

"expand Delta Airlines": Kahn, *Big Drink*, p. 75; Charles Bottoms interview; Lewis & Newton, *Delta*, pp. 32–48, 74, 98, 142, 247, 301, 307, 349–353, 360, 395. The Delta-Coca-Cola connection has remained strong. Delta CEO Ron Allen joined The Coca-Cola Company board of directors in 1991.

"strange music": "The Voice of the Sky Suggests the Pause That Refreshes," *RB*, Oct. 1931, p. 20.

"a hundred-foot logo": "A Reminder to the Air-Minded," *RB*, Oct. 1931, p. 19.

"hit Donnelly": Turner Jones to Archie Lee, March 6, 1934. (CC Archives)

"organize crown cap counts": Jack Drescher to Turner Jones, Jan. 21, 1937. (CC Archives)

"Even morons": Treseder, p. 39.

"hopelessly confusing": Turner Jones to Archie Lee, Aug. 27, 1934. (CC Archives)

"offend in any way": "Glad to meet you anywhere at any time you wish," Archie Lee assured Robert Woodruff in 1942. (RWW Paper, Archie Lee file)

"Jack Drescher, a fellow": Jack Drescher to Archie Lee, Oct. 24, 1936. (CC Archives)

"nasty practical joke": Charles Bottoms interview.

181 "freshen the viewpoint": Robert Woodruff to William D'Arcy, Dec. 15, 1934. (CC Archives)

"thirty-five different commandments": Jack Drescher, D'Arcy office memorandum, Jan. 19, 1938. (CC Archives)

"Never split": This commandment is still very much in force at the Company, whose computers are universally programmed to disallow a line split at the hyphen.

"circular sign": The red disc, or "bull's-eye," was introduced as a standard sign in 1934, quickly coming to symbolize the drink.

"aspirin, cellophane, and the escalator": Haden-Guest, *The Paradise Program*, p. 69.

182 "Dope with cherry": Jasper Yeomans interview.

"closest thing to the FBI": Tom Law interview.

"derelict behavior cease": Haden-Guest, pp. 75–76; Julius Lunsford interview; Ovid Davis interview; Jasper Yeomans interview.

"bought back the parent bottling": No cash was exchanged in these buybacks. The parent bottlers traded their stock for an equivalent amount of Coca-Cola shares, which left Whitehead's widow, Lettie Pate Evans, with so much

Coca-Cola stock that Woodruff named her to the board, making her one of the few women in the 1930s to have such a seat of power.

"Hunter backed out": Arthur Pratt, CC *Bottler*, April 1959, pp. 178–179.

183 **"holding company"**: In a game of corporate smoke-and-mirrors, Woodruff created a subsidiary, named Coca-Cola Company (note the missing capitalized *The*), which was to be the operating concern. There was already a Coca-Cola Company (a sales organization), but *its* name was changed to Coca-Cola Corporation. ("Coca-Cola's Set-Up to Change Jan. 1," *NYT*, Dec. 28, 1933, p. 30)

"just before midnight": Harold Martin Papers, quoted by Thomas P. Stamps, "A History of Coca-Cola," unpublished thesis, ©1976, p. 79. Stamps gained access to the Harold Martin biography of Robert Woodruff before the Boss bought it and hid it from public view. The state of Georgia and The Coca-Cola Company had actually been playing cat-and-mouse since 1931, but this time the move would be of long duration. ("Coca-Cola to Return to Georgia," *NYT*, Nov. 18, 1931, p. 38)

"John Sibley replaced": Sibley to John E. McClure, Sept. 1935; Sibley to Robert N. Miller, Sept. 23, 1935. (Sibley Papers, Box 1); Allen, *Secret Formula*, pp 219–223.

"lawyer Hughes Spalding": Hughes Spalding, the founder's son, was a partner at King & Spalding. From the time John Sibley and Spalding began working for the Company in the 1930s, a tight Atlanta business network evolved in which King & Spalding, the Trust Company of Georgia, Emory University, and The Coca-Cola Company were really part of one vast concern. Sibley, for instance, jumped from Coca-Cola back to the law firm, only to be drafted later as the president of the bank. (Wells, *King & Spalding*, p. 148)

"What's good for Coke": Ellis Arnall quote, as well as story of editorial persuasion, from Wells, *King & Spalding*, pp. 156–158.

"Acklin wasn't eager": Harrison Jones would have been the obvious choice for president, but he and Woodruff clashed behind the scenes repeatedly. Nonetheless, Woodruff recognized that Jones had "a certain evangelical quality" that was "a determining factor in making Coca-Cola a religion as well as a business." (RWW quoted in *CC Bottler*, April 1959, p. 104)

184 **"200,000 pounds of coca leaf"**: Harrison Jones to Robert Woodruff, July 28, 1930. (RWW Papers, Box 17)

"Senator Walter George": Stamps, p. 73. Like many subsequent Georgia politicians, Walter George considered Woodruff his "best friend" from his election in 1922 until his defeat in 1956. When the Treasury Department later proposed a war tax on soft drinks, Walter George, chair of the Senate Finance Committee, quietly killed it. (Hughes Spalding to John Sibley, Aug. 16, 1938, Box 80; also see Walter George file, RWW Papers; Kahn, p. 142; Louis & Yazijian, p. 61; Alex McLennan interview; Allen, *Secret Formula*, p. 229)

"secretly flew to Peru": Stamps, p. 73; Ralph Hayes to Robert Woodruff, April 2, 1937, Box 17; Hayes to RWW, Jan. 21, 1958, Box 40, RWW Papers.

"overseas outposts . . . grew": "Chronological Listing." (CC Collection, Box 20, Emory)

"illegal to *export* No. 5": Hayes to RWW, July 9, 1936; Hayes to RWW, March 16, 1937. (RWW Papers, Box 17)

185 **"spokesperson and speechwriter"**: "Ralph A. Hayes," undated, Box 39, RWW Papers; "Ralph Hayes, Noted Fund-Raiser, Led New York Community Trust," *NYT*, June 22, 1977.

"Coca-Soda people": Stubbs, *Compilation on Peru*, 1946, p. 154.

"foreign woes": Al Staton, "Miscellaneous Recommendations," April 29, 1937. (RWW Papers, Case 5)

"legal journeyman": Roy Stubbs, *The Confessions of a Country Lawyer.*
"taught himself Spanish": ibid., p. 284.
"lethargic pace of Latin": Stubbs, *Letters from Latin America*, 1941–1942, unpaged.
"Interminable red tape": Stubbs to Robert Troutman, Oct. 12, 1941, *Compilation on Argentina*, p. 6.
186 "rears back on his hind legs": Stubbs, *Letters*, Nov. 29, 1941.
"protocol of amenities": Stubbs, *Confessions*, p. 291.
"daily itinerary": "Farley Quits Chile for Argentina," *NYT*, Feb. 8, 1941, p. 9.
"The tide has turned": Stephen Fox, *Mirror Makers*, p. 126.
"business dictatorship": Matthews & Shallcross, *Partners in Plunder*, p. 111.
"Hypersensitive Nervous system": Letters from consumers to FDA, July 24, 1944, 475.11-.32; July 15, 1939; Sept. 23, 1938, Administrative File, FDA.
"Word of Wisdom": Letter to FDA, June 18, 1938. (AF Files)
"made with guano": Letter to FDA, April 20, 1938, AF; Report of the President's Homes Commission, 1909, p. 372. (Wiley Papers)
"Coca-Cola with aspirin": Letter to FDA, June 1, 1938; Letter, Feb. 13, 1942, 475.11-.20. (FDA Files)
187 "Poison Stomach": Letter to FDA, Jan. 13, 1938, 475.4-.22.
"I like it": Letter to FDA, Jan. 13, 1941, AF, FDA.
"ecgonine": J. W. Sale, "Alkaloids in Coca-Cola," June 24, 1935, AF, FDA; Jan. 25, 1940, FDA Memo, 475.2-.40, FDA; Allen, *Secret Formula* pp. 192–194.
"friendly visit": P. B. Dunbar, "Memorandum of Interview," Feb. 3, 1939, AF, FDA.
"met with FDA officials": "Memorandum of conference on petition of American Bottlers of Carbonated Beverages for exemption from labeling," Nov. 29, 1939, AF, FDA.
188 "failed . . . satisfactory response": FDA to consumer, May 8, 1943.
"remained unlabeled": "Soft Drink Labels Now Speak—Softly," *Consumer Reports*, May 1966, pp. 218–219.
"Pepsi's roots": Milward W. Martin, *Twelve Full Ounces*, pp. 5–36; Stoddard, *Pepsi*, pp. 13–18.
"tried to sell Pepsi": Jim Jordan, p. 37.
"two bottlers remained": Michael Gershman, *Getting It Right the Second Time*, p. 150.
"refused to buy": Jordan, p. 46.
"stormy petrel": Edwin N. Lewis, "Charles C. Guth Biography," unpublished manuscript for The Coca-Cola Co., 1941, pp. i–vi, 1. (CC Legal Library); Allen, *Secret Formula*, pp. 211–216; Stoddard, *Pepsi*, pp. 63–80
"it will stay out": From Coca-Cola Co. vs. Loft, Inc., and CC Co. vs. Happiness Candy Stores, Inc., Appeal from Court of Chancery, Jan. Term, 1934, vol. 2. (CC Archives)
"new Pepsi-Cola . . . born": "The Strange Case of Loft vs. Guth" (NY: Coming Events, Inc., 1939), p. 2. (CC Archives)
189 "Under no circumstances": CC Co. vs. Loft Case, vol. 2.
"barrage of seven countersuits": Nothing ever came of any of the lawsuits. Though Coca-Cola did prove isolated instances of substitution, it was not enough for the judge to rule an intentional fraud. (The lawsuits are covered in Edwin Lewis, "Charles Guth Biography," pp. 249–252, and in *NYT* articles: May 5, 1932, p. 30; May 6, 1932, p. 6; May 13, 1932, p. 28; May 19, 1932, p. 17; July 15, 1932, p. 28; Oct. 22, 1932, p. 6; June 7, 1933, p. 39; Sept. 22, 1933, p. 5.)
"mailed a cartoon": Frank Troutman, "Report on Pepsi-Cola," 1939, p. 48. (CC Archives)

"refused for the third": Jim Jordan, p. 48. Jordan's amateur Coca-Cola chronology is the only printed source for the attempted Pepsi sales, though Company folklore confirms them.

"used beer bottles": Troutman, pp. 47–48.

190 "the men's room": Walter Mack, *No Time Lost*, p. 120.

"knee-deep in litigation": E. J. Kahn, Jr., "More Bounce to the Ounce," Pt. I, *New Yorker*, July 1, 1950, p. 36.

"year-long study": Sibley to RWW, Dec. 22, 1937. (Sibley Papers, Box 1)

191 "sued in Queens": "Coca-Cola Replies to Suit by Rival," *NYT*, Sept. 20, 1938, p. 2; "Complaint and Answer," Queens Case, 1938, p. 26. (CC Legal Library)

"critical year to date": Wilson Corder to John Sibley, Dec. 30, 1938. (Sibley Papers, Box 1)

"resemblance to a bloodhound": E. J. Kahn, Jr., "More Bounce to the Ounce," Pt. II, *New Yorker*, July 8, 1950, p. 28; Stoddard, *Pepsi*, pp. 81–103.

"It seemed overwhelming": Mack, *No Time Lost*, pp. 126–129, covers the rest of this case.

"from Mrs. Herman Smith": Walter Mack incorrectly identified Mrs. Herman Smith as the *Cleo-Cola* owner—impossible, since that case was settled a year later. Ralph Kalish, not Herman Smith, was the actual owner, and Mack probably misremembered the name. (Roy Stubbs, *Compilation on the Trademark "Coca-Cola,"* 1949, pp. 253–256; Cleo-Cola Case, April 10, 1943)

"At the end of 1941": By late 1941, the tide had already turned against Coca-Cola's claim to ownership of "Cola," when, in the Dixi-Cola case, the Court of Appeals struck down Coca-Cola's right to monopolize the last half of its name. (Jerome H. Spingarn, "Of Coca, Cola, and the Courts," *The Nation*, June 7, 1941, pp. 666–668)

"on a temporary basis": Sibley to RWW, Dec. 15, 1941. (Sibley Papers, Box 1)

191–2 "Pope Brock": Sibley bitterly disagreed with Brock's pragmatic decision to abandon the defense of "Cola." (Sibley to Brock, Nov. 16, Nov. 17, Nov. 18, 1943. Sibley Papers)

192 "settled *all* litigation": "Suits Over Use of 'Cola' In Trade-Marks Are Ended," *NYT*, May 26, 1942, p. 32; Robert Troutman to RWW, "Pending Litigation," July 25, 1942. (RWW Papers, Box 78)

"right to 'cola'": As a result of the settlement, Coca-Cola cases around the world were reassessed, and only those with a definite "phonetic similarity" to Coca-Cola were continued. (Robert Troutman to RWW, "Pending Litigation," July 25, 1942. RWW Papers, Box 78)

"nickname 'Coke'": The new trademark was registered in 1945. By recognizing "Coke" as an official nickname, the Company was finally able to leave calls for "dope" in the past as a piece of pre-war nostalgia. ("Coke Is Now a Trademark," *RB*, Oct. 1945, p. 35)

"blue the distinctive color": Mack, *No Time Lost*, pp. 132–133; Louis & Yazijian, p. 69.

"Pepsi logo over city skies": Mack, p. 133; Turner, *Shocking History*, p. 272.

193 "jingle played": Turner, p. 280.

"started a trend": Mack, pp. 134–137.

"Every day's delay": Harrison Jones to RWW, Aug. 15, 1941. (Sibley Papers, Box 1)

"bribe Walter Mack": Mack, p. 137.

"American struggle": Kahn, "More Bounce," Pt. I, p. 34.

"may prove . . . good thing": "Coca-Cola Industry," *Fortune*, p. 115.

"Pepsi and Pete": Kahn, "More Bounce," Pt. I, p. 40.

194 "view a real bottling operation": "World's Fair Lets First Concession," *NYT*, Jan. 17, 1938, p. 21; "Fair Marvelous, Otto Says on Visit," *NYT*, April 17, 1940, p. 18. Over a two-year period, the World's Fair attracted 60 million visitors, who drank a commensurate amount of Coca-Cola. (*Official Guide Book*, New York World's Fair 1939, p. 110, courtesy Queens Museum; Marquis, pp. 193, 199)

"crypt of civilization": "Bottle of Coca-Cola Placed in Crypt at Oglethorpe University," *RB*, July 1940, p. 35.

"synonimous with a 'Date'": Letter to FDA, June 27, 1940, AF, FDA; Dietz, pp. 110–111.

"in Emporia, Kansas": "William Allen White of Emporia: An American Institution is 70," *Life*, Feb. 28, 1938, pp. 9–13.

"sublimated essence": W. A. White to Ralph Hayes, March 9, 1938. (CC Archives)

"Whom the gods": RWW, "Where Does Coca-Cola Go from Here?" 1941 Speech. (RWW Papers, Personal File 2)

CHAPTER 12: THE $4,000 BOTTLE: COCA-COLA GOES TO WAR

195 "Today was such a big day": *CC Bottler*, May 1944, p. 31.

"ad for the U.S. Rubber Company": "What Are We Fighting For?" U.S. Rubber Co. ad, *Newsweek*, Sept. 7, 1942.

"barely had a toehold": At the time, Coca-Cola maintained a minor presence in England. Faced with their own sugar shortage, the British naively suggested that Coke and Pepsi consolidate for the war's duration and sell "American Cola." As a result, Coca-Cola withdrew from the English civilian market until 1948. (Robert Troutman to A. A. Acklin, July 15, 1942, CC Archives; Joe Jones interview; Al Staton, "Miscellaneous Recommendations," April 29, 1937, p. 10, RWW Papers, Case 5)

"four Hawaiian Coke coolers": "Importance of the Rest-Pause in Maximum War Effort," 1942. (CC Archives)

"every man in uniform": *The Coca-Cola Co.: An Illustrated Profile*, p. 77.

195–6 "One military unit": George Downing interview.

196 "I cannot conceive": Major to Aubrey C. Boyce, Sept. 29, 1941. (CC Archives)

"Very few people": Capt. to Andrew K. Kingery, Jan. 17, 1942. (CC Archives)

"Ben Oehlert shifted": Harrison Jones to Robert Woodruff, Dec. 30, 1942. (RWW Papers, Box 54)

"stock-piled sugar": Oehlert to A. A. Acklin, Feb. 5, 1942. (CC Archives)

"aid the policy-making": Oehlert to Sibley, Jan. 16, 1942. (CC Archives)

"thoughtless tendency": Oehlert to A. E. Bowman Feb. 9, 1942. (RWW Papers, Oehlert File)

"masterpiece of pseudo-science": "Importance of the Rest-Pause in Maximum War Effort," 1942. (CC Archives)

197 "docile, receptive": Ralph Hayes to O. Max Gardner, Nov. 12, 1940. (RWW Papers, Gardner File)

"exempted from sugar rationing": Oehlert to P. B. Bacon, March 16, 1942. (CC Archives) Wrigley's Chewing Gum and Hershey's Chocolate for GIs were also exempted from sugar rationing. (Blum, *V Was for Victory*, p. 108; "A Glance at the Past—Hershey's History of Military Ration Bars," *Avenues* [Hershey internal publication], Dec. 1990, pp. 2, 12)

"Army's quartermaster general": Brehon Somervell to Mr. Nelson, June 14, 1942, National Archives. The fear of disclosing cozy deals with the government may be why Coke's official World War II historian suggested in a 1946 memo that it would be "undesirable" to discuss "the workings of company officials with the military heads in Washington." (James Kahn, 1946 memo, CC Archives)

"creative obscenities": Wilbur Kurtz, Jr., interview.

"At its worst": Wartime did bring changes to the drink, however. The sugar content was reduced from 10 percent to 9.3 percent and caffeine from 0.61 to 0.25 grains. ("Cola Drinks," *Consumer Reports*, Aug. 1944, p. 200; H. Wales to Pvt. Boris Breiger, July 21, 1945, AF, FDA Files; P. B. Dunbar, "Memorandum of Interview with B. H. Oehlert," June 23, 1943, AF, FDA)

"Agronsky criticized": James Kahn, Unpublished History of Coca-Cola in World War II, p. 7. (CC Archives)

"Using sign language": Hunter Bell, Unpublished History of Coca-Cola, "From Iceland . . . to Iran." (CC Archives)

"Price Gilbert joined": Henry F. Pringle, "The War Agencies," *While You Were Gone*, p. 175; Blum, *V Was for Victory*, p. 39; Kahn, *Big Drink*, p. 16.

198 "*Heilnaemt og Hressandi*": Red Davis notes. (CC Archives)

"Iceland's annual per capita": 1998 CC Co Annual Report, p.10. The 446 figure is for eight-ounce servings of all Company products.

"ten billion Cokes": Ron Antonio, "Coca-Cola and the War Years," *Cola Call*, July 1983, p. 5.

"on every continent except": During the war, bottling plants were established on Adak in the Aleutian Islands; in Cairo, Accra, Tripoli, Oman, Algiers, and Casablanca in Africa; in Australia; throughout France, Italy, Germany, and Austria; in Calcutta, Chabua, Delhi, and Ledo in India; on Okinawa, Kobe, and Yokahama in the Japanese Islands; throughout the South Pacific in the Admiralty Islands, the Marianas, New Guinea, and the Philippines; in the Persian Gulf; and in Natal and Recife in Brazil. (From Hunter Bell compilations and lists, CC Archives)

"technical observer": Walton, *Miracle of World War II*, p. 451.

"nickname . . . 'Coca-Cola Colonels'": Kahn, *Big Drink*, p. 17. The term appears to have been uncommon, however, since few T.O.s interviewed ever heard it used.

"An anecdote": James Kahn, speech written for James Curtis, ca. 1946, pp. 10–11.

"Hell, we ought": Patton quote from Mladin Zarubica interview.

"MacArthur autographed": Hunter Bell, "Coke Returns to the Philippines with MacArthur." (CC Archives)

"hero of Bataan": "General Wainwright, Symbol of Everyday America," *RB*, Oct. 1945.

199 "Omar Bradley": *NYT Magazine*, May 7, 1944. (CC Archives)

"men blown to shreds": General Carlos Romulo, *I Saw the Fall of the Philippines*, quoted in Hunter Bell, "Affectionately Yours—to the Tune of $5,000." (CC Archives)

"After feasting copiously": "Millions Cheer Ike at Parade Here," *Times Herald*, June 19, 1945. (CC Archives)

"an urgent cablegram": Bell, "Send 10 Coca-Cola Bottling Plants." (CC Archives)

"military-industrial complex": Cook, *The Declassified Eisenhower*, p. viii.

"Marshall quickly validated": July 5, 1943, George C. Marshall, War Department Circular 153, quoted by Oehlert to Marvin Jones, Aug. 9, 1943. (CC Archives)

200 "Circular No. 51": G. C. Marshall, War Department Circular No. 51, from Center of Military History, U.S. Dept. of the Army.

"by Christmas": Bell, "Send 10 Coca-Cola Bottling Plants."

"red ball express": Paul Bacon interview with Hunter Bell. (CC Archives)

"bottling . . . not nearly as feasible": The island of Manus held the sole bottling plant in the Pacific.

"jungle fountain units": Though billed as portable, the jungle unit—developed on special orders from General Douglas MacArthur—was in fact unwieldy, consisting of a dispenser, hand-operated pump, water tank, filter, carbonator, and ice-maker. (Bell, "The South Pacific Pauses Too," "Jungle Fountains for Jungle Fighters," "Island-Hopping Toward Tokyo")

"temporarily integrated": E. D. Hartman, "Refreshment at Camp Croft," *RB*, Feb. 1942, p. 41.

"Talley's retrieval": Talley bribed an Army underwater outfit with a case of Coke, convincing them to dive for the filler, buried in ten feet of mud when a crane cable snapped. A tank evacuator, tires deflated to pass under low bridges with the heavy bottling equipment, finally delivered it to Paris. (Paul Bacon interview with Hunter Bell, March 16, 1966, pp. 7–9, CC Archives)

"Coke didn't actually hit": Mike Barry, "First Things Should Come First," *RB*, Sept. 1944, p. 36.

"over the Hump": Cooke's trip to China in an Army convoy was enlivened when two of the trucks carrying bottling equipment plunged 150 feet down a cliff and had to be winched up. "Death stares you in the face on every turn," Cooke wrote. After all that, Cooke never got to make any Chinese Coke because of an unsympathetic commanding officer who refused to allow air-lifted supplies for adequate operation. (Bell, "India . . . And Over the Hump to China")

"long be a mystery": Gene Braendle, New Guinea, Aug. 1944, *T.O. Digest*, vol. 1, no. 1, p. 6. (CC Archives)

"one most important thing": ibid., p. 7.

"forge a new piece": Paul Madden interview with Hunter Bell, March 2, 1966, p. 12. (CC Archives)

"very cooperative": Jim Parham, Marianas Islands, May 6, 1945, *T.O. Digest*, vol. 1, no. 5, p. 5. (CC Archives)

"You don't fuck with Coca-Cola": Howard Fast, *Being Red*, pp. 109–112. Fast related the same story with minor variations in "Coca-Cola," *The Howard Fast Reader*, pp. 362–369.

"make very good labor": Maurice Duttera, "Duttera's Travelogue," vol. III, June 8, 1945, p. 2. Possession of Maurice Duttera.

202 **"never returned"**: James Kahn, pp. 12–13. In Kahn's account, two T.O.s were killed, but there were actually three, none combat-related.

"game hunting . . . Red Cross nurses": Sydney W. McCabe, India, Oct. 30, 1944; Cy Phillips, Belgium, Dec. 12, 1944; R. J. Cook, Admiralty Islands, Jan. 29, 1945; Cy Phillips, Lille, April 21, 1945 (all from *T.O. Digest*); George Downing interview.

"ashamed to report": Ed McGlade, Tripolitania, Jan. 1945, *T.O. Digest*, vol. 1, no. 3, p. 3. (CC Archives)

"one poor devil": Herb Myers, England, Feb. 18, 1945, *T.O. Digest*, vol. 1, no. 3, p. 8. (CC Archives)

"Men on crutches": Gene Braendle, New Guinea, Oct. 1944, *T.O. Digest*, vol. 1, no. 1, p. 10. (CC Archives)

"T.O. Theme Song": Watt Lovett, North Africa, Feb. 8, 1945, *T.O. Digest*, vol. 1, no. 3, p. 2. (CC Archives)

"avoid . . . excess profits taxes": "Senator on Advertising," *Business Week*, Nov. 20, 1943, p. 111; Raymond Rubicam, "Advertising," *While You Were Gone*, p. 442.

"sailors bellying up": "Have a Coca-Cola=As You Were," *CC Bottler*, April 1944, p. 19.

203 **"The Russians"**: "Have a Coke = Eto Zdorovo," *CC Bottler*, May 1944.

"Yes, around the globe": "Have a Coca-Cola = Howdy, Neighbor," *RB*, Sept. 1944, back cover.

"scenes from the home front": "Have a Coke = You're Home Again," *CC Bottler*, June 1944.

"Feminine readership": "War Ads That Pay," *Business Week*, June 5, 1943, pp. 92–96.

"publicly waving a flag": Sergeant Frederick Ebright, "Memorial to the Great Big Beautiful Self-Sacrificing Advertisers," *Nation*, Jan. 8, 1944, pp. 38–39.

"The Kid in Upper 4": Rubicam, *While You Were Gone*, pp. 438–439.

"Know Your War Planes": "Youngsters Rush in Dimes for New Plane Booklet," *RB*, Jan. 1944, p. 29.

"Our America": Bateman & Schaeffer, "Our America," *Cola Call*, Sept. 1984, pp. 4–6.

"cribbage boards": Jean Gibbs, "Collectibles Featuring the War," *Cola Call*, July 1983. In rural Alabama, the Company constructed and ran the Brecon Loading Company at the request of the War Department, creating a self-sustaining community with some 300 buildings. (Cards & Cribbage Board, collection of Jeff Ehrlich, Palo Alto, CA; C. W. Nimitz memo, July 22, 1941, from Naval Historical Center; "Successful Wartime Job Completed by a Coca-Cola Subsidiary," *RB*, Oct. 1945, p. 33)

"Spotlight Bands": "Facts About Spotlight Bands," *RB*, Sept. 1944, p. 42; Rowland, pp. 113–116; Hoy, p. 81.

"tenor Morton Downey": "Extra Jingles on Downey Program," *RB*, Sept. 1944, p. 41. "Morton Downey Show," *RB*, April 1944, pp. 14–15. When Downey was considering the $3,500-a-week offer from Coca-Cola, his friend Joe Kennedy advised him to take $500 in cash and $3,000 in Coca-Cola stock options. As a result, when Downey stopped singing for Coke ten years later, he was a major shareholder and held bottling interests in Australia, Chile, Uruguay, Argentina, Brazil, and Connecticut. (Morton Downey, Jr., interview; "Morton Downey, Popular Singer," *Atlanta Journal/Constitution*, Oct. 25, 1985; Kahn, *Big Drink*, p. 163)

"Texas Coca-Cola addicts": "There's Nothing Like a Shortage," *Topeka State Journal*, March 7, 1942; *"Deep in the Heart of Texas," American Cyanamid & Chemical Corporation's Monthly News Bulletin*, March 1942, quoted in *RB*, July 1942.

204 "can't shut me off": "Ration Items," *RB*, Jan. 1943, p 44.

"he begged Woodruff": RWW to Ralph Hayes, Nov. 12, 1934, Acklin file, RWW Papers; Ambrose Pendergrast interview.

"temperament that takes": Arthur Acklin to W. E. Robinson, Oct. 23, 1956. (RWW Papers, Acklin File)

"25,000 gallons of vanilla": Hartung to Hayes, June 21, 1940, Acklin files; Administrative Files, General, RWW Papers

"working policy committee": Acklin to RWW, July 23, 1943. (RWW Papers)

"rather heavy toll": Acklin to RWW, Oct. 10, 1944; April 19, 1945; May 23, 1945. (RWW Papers)

"inordinate . . . political influence": Mack, *No Time Lost*, pp. 149–150. Walter Mack tried to exert his own political influence by persuading the President's son, Jimmy Roosevelt, to become a bottler. In the meantime, Joseph Kennedy negotiated with Woodruff to spend $5 million on Coke bottling plants. "He has a number of sons," Archie Lee explained. The elder Kennedy wanted to lay the "foundation for jobs for them." The deal fell through, however, and the boys had to go into politics instead. ("Col. Jimmy Hooks Drink Franchise at $100,000 Per," *Chicago Tribune*, Nov. 29, 1942; Archie Lee to RWW, Nov. 30, 1942, RWW Papers, Box 57)

"Pepsi was in trouble": The initial quotas were based on 80 percent of 1941 sales. While that might dent a huge company like Coca-Cola, it was disastrous for smaller enterprises. (Mack, p. 148)

"Cuban regulations": Kahn, "More Bounce to the Ounce," Pt. II, *New Yorker*, July 8, 1950, p. 44.

205 "New Jersey condiment": "Pepsi-Cola's Walter Mack," *Fortune*, Nov. 1947, pp. 182–184.

"virtual monopoly": ibid., p. 184; "Cola Climax," *Business Week*, Nov. 27, 1943, p. 90.

"Servicemen's Centers": "Pepsi-Cola's Walter Mack," *Fortune*, p. 181.

"ghostwritten messages": Kahn, "More Bounce to the Ounce," Pt. 1, *New Yorker*, July 1, 1950, pp. 43–44.

"ten-ounce fountain drink": "Pepsi-Cola Beat," *Business Week*, Sept. 11, 1943, p. 86.

"Merman loudly announced": Kahn, "More Bounce," Pt. I, p. 41.

205–6 "The syrup is old": Captain Hal Gibson, "Ingenuity in New Guinea Jungles," *RB*, July 1944, p. 42.

206 "It's the little things" and other block quotes: quoted in Hunter Bell, "Affectionately Yours—To the Tune of $5,000"; Cpl. Jack D. Thompson to his mother, *RB*, Jan. 1944, p. 42; Pvt. Clyde Rosenthal, "Italy Pauses to Refresh," *RB*, July 1944, p. 39; Pvt. M. J. Flatauer, "Some More of the Same," *RB*, Dec. 1944, p. 41.

"If anyone were to ask": James Kahn, Speech, p. 5.

"America, Democracy, Coca-Colas": Robert L. Scott, *God Is My Co-Pilot*, quoted in James Kahn, p. 2.

"In civilian life": Cpl. George J. Brennan, "Things That Count," *RB*, Aug. 1945, p. 45.

207 "four high-ranking officers": "Coca-Cola Has New Value to Men Overseas," *RB*, July 1944, p. 38.

"The pop, as you open it": Pvt. George Kavkewitz, "The Saga of a Bottle of Coke," *RB*, May 1944, p. 44.

"auction in Iran": "Truth Is Stranger Than Fiction," *RB*, April 1944, pp. 43–44; Kahn, p. 18.

"famous (and expensive)": The affair at which this bottle was raffled off—to start a fund for children of men killed in action—was reported by war correspondent Ernie Pyle. The actual amount this particular bottle brought is unclear, having been variously reported as $2,000, $3,000, $4,000, $5,007.73, and $6,000. (Hunter Bell, "Affectionately Yours—To the Tune of $5,000")

"Winston's daughter": "Mary Churchill Christens Flying Fortress with Coca-Cola," *RB*, July 1944, p. 33.

"But the wise converted": Cpl. Frank Hardie, "Parable of the Ten Corporals," undated clipping in CC Archives.

"supply a priest": Maurice Duttera interview.

208 "other uses": Ernest Schefer, "Coca-Cola Bottles: Here's How They Did the Job," *CC Bottler*, May 1944, pp. 16–17; "Coke Bottles Harass Japs," *RB*, March 1944, p. 39; "Signal Man John Brooks," *RB*, Jan. 1944, p. 34.

"brushed his teeth": Ed McGlade, Tripoli, Oct. 2, 1945, *T.O. Digest*, vol. 1, no. 8, p. 4; "No Water, Soldier Washes Teeth with Coca-Cola at Camp," *Caruthersville* [Missouri] *Republic*, Sept. 24, 1942, clipping. (CC Archives)

"battle password": Hunter Bell, "Coke Returns to the Philippines"; George Downing interview.

"piss on the old home town": Letter to E. J. Kahn, Jr., March 17, 1959 (courtesy E. J. Kahn).

"Otto Dietrich": "Nazi Sees Menace in America's Gum and Coca-Cola," *AJ*, Oct. 12, 1942.

"imported the germs": Albert "Red" Davis, 1966 notes, "Before the Iron Curtain Clanged Down on Coca-Cola." (Hunter Bell papers, CC Archives)

"jungle city": "Coca-Cola Found in Luxury Jap Headquarters in New Guinea," *RB*, March 1944, p. 40.

"Italian prisoners of war": "They Knew What They Wanted," *RB*, April 1944, p. 35.

"smaller children": Paul Madden, New Guinea, April 4, 1945, *T.O. Digest*, vol. 1, no. 5, p. 4. (CC Archives)

"Zulus, Bushmen": "One War Dance That Served a Good Purpose," *RB*, April 1944, pp. 33–34.

209 "Fuzzy-Wuzzy market": Sam Holden, New Guinea, March 10, 1945, *T.O. Digest*, vol. 1, no. 4, p. 5. (CC Archives)

"wearing crowncorks": "A King on His Wheelbarrow Throne," *RB*, Jan. 1945, p. 41.

"describe Kayo, a six-year-old": Lt. Robert G. Fisher, quoted in *RB*, Feb. 1944, p. 34.

"only increased": *T.O. Digest*, vol. 1, no. 8, frontispiece. (CC Archives)

"series of unpublished notes": George Downing notes, 1946, property of George Downing.

210 "soft pedal it": Paul Bacon interview with Hunter Bell, March 16, 1966, p. 23. (CC Archives)

"competed fiercely": *On the Up and Up*, April 2, 1946, p. 2; June 6, 1946, p. 3. (Courtesy George Downing)

"a war-time PT boat commander": Mladin Zarubica interview. Material mentioning Zarubica is based on this interview.

"Eisenhower introduced . . . drink": James Kahn, p. 34.

"his 1964 thriller": Zarubica, *The Year of the Rat*.

211 "Coca-Cola for sex": Maurice Duttera interview: Lew Gregg interview.

"Anything with sugar": Don Sisler interview.

"horniest individual": Gregg interview.

"added a little spice": Sisler interview.

212 "military presence . . . dwindling": H. K. Myers, *On the Up and Up*, Dec. 1948, p. 3.

"hang up their military uniforms": Many of the T.O.s went on to assume leadership positions in Coca-Cola, including Don Sisler, Burke Nicholson, Jr., John and Lee Talley, George Downing, Maurice Duttera, Pat O'Malley, and Paul Bacon. The wartime hustle and initiative they had learned proved to be a good foundation for their careers.

"almost universal acceptance": Hunter Bell, "It Had to Be Good to Become the Global Hi-Sign."

"Personally, I think": Pvt. Herbert H. Price, "A GI Opinion of Cooperation," *RB*, Nov. 1944, p. 41.

"poll of veterans": "Veteran's Preference," potential copy for *Red Barrel*, memo, CC Archives. Soon after the war, when the Army quizzed 650 recruits, twenty-one had never drunk milk, but only one soldier had never sampled a Coke. (Kahn, *Big Drink*, p. 7)

"25 years and millions": James Kahn, "Incidentally, It Paid," outline of his unpublished manuscript in CC Archives.

CHAPTER 13: COCA-COLA ÜBER ALLES

213 **"Ein Führer [ist] ein Mann"**: Claus Halle speech, quoting Coca-Cola pamphlet, "The Art of Leadership," *Max Keith: 30 Jahre Mit Coca-Cola*, Nov. 1963. (CC Archives)

"*One man* must": Hitler, *Mein Kampf*, p. 577.

"We are surprised": Kahn Notes, p. 2.

"Coca-Cola GmbH": GmbH stands for "Gesellschaft mit beschränkter Haftung," the equivalent to "corporation."

"Like many Germans": Shirer, *The Rise and Fall of the Third Reich*, p. 231.

"I was full of activity": Max Keith speech, *Max Keith, 30 Jahre Mit Coca-Cola*.

214 **"colorful, if shady"**: "I've done everything in the world except murder," Powers boasted. (Walter Oppenhoff interview; Allen, *Secret Formula*, pp. 197–201; Schutts, *Born Again*)

"American buffoon": Oppenhoff interview.

"villa in Florida": ibid.

"100,000 in 1933": "Coca-Cola in Germany," CC Archives file.

"in a state of chaos": Hamilton Horsey memo, 1935, quoted in Roy Stubbs, *Compilation on Germany*, pp. 252–257.

"fellow propagandist": Ray Powers to Robert Woodruff, Oct. 7, 1930, with enclosure by Viscount Rothermere, "My Hitler Article and Its Critics," *The Daily Mail*, Oct. 2, 1930; Powers to Woodruff, March 31, 1936, Box 70, RWW Papers; Louis & Yazijian, *Cola Wars*, p. 56.

215 **"quivered alarmingly"**: Claus Halle interview.

"chew you out": ibid.

"I was scared of him": Klaus Pütter interview. As he aged, Keith grew increasingly paranoid, firing subordinates he imagined were threats to his power, accusing them of betrayal and embezzlement. "I never knew when I went to work in the morning whether I would still have a job in the evening," Claus Halle remembers. (Halle interview)

"ruling thought . . . Über Alles": Pütter interview.

"They were mostly people": Max Keith interview with Hunter Bell, June 29/30, 1966, in CC Archives. Unless otherwise noted, all direct quotes from Keith and information on his activities in this chapter are from this interview.

"caused stomachaches": Oppenhoff interview.

216 **"endless repetition"**: Hitler himself learned valuable lessons from Western advertising techniques. "All effective propaganda has to limit itself only to a very few points and to use them like slogans," Hitler wrote. "It has to confine itself to little and to repeat this eternally." (Hitler, *Mein Kampf*, pp. 234, 238–240)

"over half the pubs": Oppenhoff interview.

"ten minutes of Keith": Pütter interview.

"lawyer usually procured": Oppenhoff interview.

"Autobahn system": Shirer, p. 118.

"one vast beehive": ibid., p. 259.

"kind of mini-dictator": ibid., p. 263.

216–7 **"a new hope"**: ibid., p. 231.

217 **"forty-three German plants"**: "Coca-Cola in Germany." (CC Archives)

"slapped his thigh": Mead, *Champion: Joe Louis*, p. 100; Hitler, p. 616.

"prestige for our race": *Das SchwarzenKorps*, quoted in Hart-Davis, *Hitler's Games*, p. 123. Two years later, however, the Brown Bomber was to knock the German out in the first round.

"thirty-six gold medals": Schaap, *An Illustrated History of the Olympics*, p. 217.

"in his private box": Hart-Davis, p. 174.

"We have no strikes": Mead, p. 144.

"elaborate parties": For a detailed description of one of Göring's parties, see Hart-Davis, pp. 205–206; Shirer, pp. 232–233.

"Coca-Cola entourage": Walter Oppenhoff to Mark Pendergrast, Nov. 22, 1991; E. J. Kahn, Jr., *RWW*, p. 110.

"more as an advertisement": Claus Halle interview; Oppenhoff interview.

218 "feeding itself on prejudice": John Sibley to RWW, Nov. 27, 1936. (Sibley Papers)

"I am not accustomed": Oppenhoff interview. Oppenhoff places this conversation in London, but it probably took place in Berlin.

"he was overwhelmed": Pütter interview.

"company lawyers agreed": Stephen P. Ladas, "Memorandum . . . on Ray Powers," undated, in Stubbs, *Compilation on Germany*, pp. 390–392. The actual agreement was finally signed in 1937.

"Four-Year Plan": Shirer, pp. 260–261.

"taken pains": Oppenhoff letter to Revenue Office, Feb. 6, 1936, in Stubbs, *Germany*, pp. 258–260.

"such as Walter Teagle": Just after the war began, Teagle wrote to Woodruff: "I am anxious . . . to exchange views with you on certain phases of the existing situation [in Germany]." Walter Teagle and Standard Oil continued to supply the Axis powers with badly needed fuel throughout World War II. (Walter Teagle to Robert Woodruff, Sept. 6, 1939, Box 84, RWW Papers. Higham, *Trading with the Enemy*, pp. 32–62; Sutton, *Wall Street and the Rise of Hitler*, pp. 67–76; "Walter Clark Teagle," Ingham, *Biographical Dictionary of American Business Leaders*, pp. 1438–41)

"Henry Mann, a German agent": Henry Mann had already demonstrated his close ties to the Nazi regime in 1933, when he facilitated a meeting between Hitler and Sosthenes Behn, the head of ITT. Mann also helped set up the first German Coca-Cola bottling plant in 1929. (1966 Keith interview; "American Visits Hitler," *NYT*, Aug. 4, 1933, p. 6; *Number Eight*, Dec. 1928, courtesy Citibank Archives; "Henry Mann, 78, World Financier," *NYT*, Aug. 26, 1968, p. 39; Higham, *Trading with the Enemy*, pp. 94–99)

"He accepts gifts": For Göring's larcenous habits and luxurious life-style, see Heiden, 728; Trevor-Roper, pp. 15, 86n.

219 "Some consideration": RWW to Sibley, Aug. 6, 12, 1936, (Sibley Papers, Box 1)

"pass fairly quickly": RWW to Sibley, Aug. 12, 1936; Aug. 6 letter has comment on sleep. (Sibley Papers, Box 1)

"complete rest": Sibley to RWW, Aug. 1, 1936. (Sibley Papers, Box 1)

"piece of veal": Oppenhoff interview.

"stimulating effect": Stubbs, *Germany*, pp. 98–99; 102–109; Walter Oppenhoff to Mark Pendergrast, Nov. 8, 1991.

"caramel coloring": Oppenhoff to Mark Pendergrast, Nov. 8, 1991.

"held 0.192 liters": Oppenhoff interview.

"Woodruff was traveling": Sibley to RWW, Aug. 6, 1936 (Sibley Papers); Sibley to RWW, July 16, 1938, (RWW Papers, Sibley file); Anonymous source; Joe Jones interview; Mladin Zarubica interview.

220 "Flach distributed": ibid.; Keith interview with Hunter Bell; Halle interview; Stubbs, *Germany*, pp. 43, 63–64, 164, 243.

"Nazi party headquarters": Kahn, Notes, p. 25.

"preliminary injunction": Oppenhoff interview; Stubbs, *Germany*, p. 243.

"any conception": Oppenhoff to Gwatkin, Feb. 1, 1939, in Stubbs, *Germany*, p. 243.

"Keith begged Woodruff": Halle interview; Oppenhoff interview. Halle asserts that Keith asked for Hirsch's removal from the board. Oppenhoff doubts Keith would have dared to ask such a thing.

"next generation": Keith interview with Hunter Bell.

"Hermann Göring paused": Oppenhoff interview; *Coca-Cola: A Quarter of a Century in Germany*, 1954 pamphlet, p. 9, Schaffendes Volk leaflet, courtesy Alfons Hilgers.

"Hitler . . . enjoyed Coca-Cola": Kahn Notes, p. 365; Kahn, *Big Drink*, p. 4; Kurtz interview.

221 **"three-fold 'Sieg-Heil'"**: *Coca-Cola, A Quarter Century*, p. 9; *Coca-Cola Nachrichten*, March 15, 1938, pp. 9, 27 (courtesy Alfons Hilgers, translated by Raul Hilberg & Ostara Bedo; see also Allen, *Secret Formula*, p. 247.

"Woodruff demurred": Stubbs, *Germany*, pp. 392–393.

"Powers was killed": ibid., p. 393. Powers died on Dec. 13, 1938.

"gratitude for our Führer": Max Keith speech, *10 Jahre Aufbau*, special issue of *Coca-Cola Nachrichten*, April 1939, pp. 17, 25 (courtesy Alfons Hilgers, translated by Raul Hilberg & Ostara Bedo). In the summer of 1939, when Hitler came to Munich to open the Day of German Art Exhibition, bottles of Coca-Cola were widely available. (Wistrich, *Weekend in Munich*, p. 70, 83)

"civil service men": Shirer, p. 262.

222 **"Supply . . . curtailed"**: Even after the war's 1939 commencement, Atlanta continued to ship Coca-Cola syrup to Keith. With the U.S. entry into the war, however, the syrup spigot was turned off. (H. B. Nicholson to RWW, Feb. 8, 1940, "Administration, Coca-Cola Export" file, RWW Papers; Charles Bottoms interview)

"left-overs": Ward Wells interview with Hunter Bell, March 18, 1966. (CC Archives)

"exempted from sugar rationing": For a good overview, see Mary Reagan, Aug. 22, 1949, report on Fanta in Stubbs, *Compilation on Switzerland*, pp. 381–385. See also Stubbs, *Germany*, pp. 241–242; Pütter interview; Halle interview; Keith interview; Oppenhoff interview.

"3 million cases": "Coca-Cola in Germany."

"soups and stews": Oppenhoff interview; Halle interview.

"included the phrase": Reagan report, Stubbs, *Switzerland*, p. 384; Stubbs, *Germany*, p. 242.

"wounded Nazi soldiers": Oppenhoff interview.

"Ford Motor Company": Keith interview with Bell; Higham, pp. 154–161.

"catastrophe water": Halle interview; Oppenhoff interview.

223 **"the war brought them"**: Keith interview with Bell.

"9 million *Fremdarbeiter*": "Forced Labor," *Encyclopedia of the Holocaust*, vol. 2, pp. 497–500.

"One false step": Pütter interview.

"killed in an air raid": Oppenhoff interview.

"Hitler shot himself": Trevor-Roper, pp. 201–205.

224 **"Send auditors"**: Pütter interview.

"Ladas returned": Oppenhoff interview.

"plant at Niedermendig": James Kahn speech, p. 12; Paul Bacon interview with Bell, p. 17; Paul Lesko interview.

"whatever remnants": Ward Wells interview with Hunter Bell, March 18, 1966, p. 7; John Talley speech, *Coca-Cola Nachrichten* 9/10, 1968, p. 50; Keith interview with Bell, p. 19.

"grea-a-at man": Don Sisler interview.

"even worse breakdown": Max Keith, *Max Keith: 30 Jahre*.

"de-Nazified": Higham, pp. 210–223.

"quite some discussions": Oppenhoff interview.

"a second Hitler": George Downing interview.

"curtailed his Fanta": Oppenhoff interview.

"Sales fell": "Coca-Cola in Germany"; Mary Reagan report in Stubbs, *Switzerland*, p. 385.

225 "native Coca-Cola men": Ansel Morrison, Aug. 21, 1945, *T. O. Digest*, vol. 1, no. 8, p. 6. (CC Archives)

"so *industrious*": Sisler interview.

"It was amazing": Henry J. Fleck, "Personal History," undated. (CC Archives) The Coca-Cola men weren't terribly interested in moral issues. During the War Crimes trials in Nürnberg, the prosecution provided a special Coca-Cola cooler for the refreshment of Göring and his fellow prisoners. (*On the Up and Up*, Sept. 5, 1946, p. 2; Oct. 3, 1946, p. 4; Albert Davis, "Before the Iron Curtain," CC Archives)

"this Kraut, Max Keith": Sisler interview.

"Lesko nearly dyed": Claus Halle relates this story, which he heard from Max Keith many times. Paul Lesko denies it, asserting that there was never any friction between Keith and him. (Halle interview; Paul Lesko interview)

"*wieder da!*": Keith interview with Bell.

"Bremen bottling rights": Halle interview; Lesko interview. Lesko used the profits from his Bremen plant to purchase the franchise in Costa Rica, where he moved in 1953 to make his *real* fortune from Coca-Cola.

226 "do what I tell you": Pütter interview; H. Burke Nicholson, Jr., interview.

"Super-Führer": Kahn Notes, p. 65. After several heart attacks, Keith retired in 1968, only to make life hell for employees at the bottling plants he continued to run until his death in 1974. (Halle interview).

"German hero contacted": Schmeling had played golf with Robert Woodruff and Bobby Jones in Atlanta in 1931, when, as heavyweight champion, he was on a U.S. tour. (Schmeling interview)

"boxer jumped at the chance": Schmeling interview; Hoy, pp. 113, 115.

"signed autograph of Hitler": Schmeling interview; Mead, p. 84; *Louis, Joe Louis*, p. 115; *Refresher*, July/Aug. 1967, p. 22.

PART IV: TROUBLE IN THE PROMISED LAND (1950–1979)

229 "he felt dizzy": This late 1979 scenario is based on an incident related by Virginia Moulder and Ian Wilson.

CHAPTER 14: COCA-COLONIZATION AND THE COMMUNISTS

231 "Apparently some of our friends": Quoted in Kahn, *Big Drink*, p. 5.

"relationships I established": Farley, "United Nations." (Farley Papers)

"rainbows flashed": 1932 *New York Times* quoted in "Sincerely, Jim," 1957 essay written for Columbia University Oral History Project, in Farley Papers.

"neither drank nor smoked": "James Aloysius Farley," *Current Biography*, 1944, pp. 196–200; Rowland, pp. 141–143.

"entirely divorced": Ralph McGill, "One Word More," AC, Nov. 16, 1941.

232 "prosecuted Alger Hiss": J. Ronald Oakley, *God's Country*, p. 6; Farley, "United Nations." While Coke officials could rely on powerful politicians, Pepsi had to woo more unsavory types such as Senator Joe McCarthy, dubbed the "Pepsi-Cola Kid" for his blatant lobbying. (Louis & Yazijian, pp. 83–84)

"look to the American nation": "World Is Looking to U.S., Farley Says," *NYT*, Dec. 8, 1946, p. 17.

"**When we think of**": Kahn, *Big Drink*, p. 164.

"**May Providence**": Louis & Yazijian, p. 78.

"**Key employees**": H. B. Nicholson, "Host to Thirsty Main Street" (NY: Newcomen Society, 1953), p. 18; "The Sun Never Sets on Cacoola," *Time*, May 15, 1950, pp. 30–31.

"**They are linked**": "A Unique Business," *CC Overseas*, Dec. 1952, p. 1.

"**Giovanni Pretti**": "Sun Never Sets," *Time*, May 15, 1950, p. 32.

233 "**I am Coca-Cola**": E. J. Kahn, Jr., Notes, p. 82.

"**four Pathy brothers**": "Sun Never Sets," p. 30.

"**WORLD & FRIEND**": ibid., *Time* cover, pp. 28–29.

"**speech to the American Trademark Association**": Farley, "Trademarks: America's Goodwill Ambassador," 1952, Farley Papers.

234 "**in Germany, it is**": Nicholson, "Host," p. 18.

"**a man with a soul**": Frank Harrold, "Bronxville to Bombay and Back," 1950–1953. (CC Archives)

"**degenerate capitalism**": H. B. Nicholson, "The Competitive Ideal," *Vital Speeches*, Dec. 15, 1952, p. 152.

"**its vile effects**": Nikita Khrushchev's son Sergei, a teenager in 1950, later recalled his eagerness to taste the imperialistic American soft drink, reputed to be poisonous and evil. (Sergei Khrushchev interview)

"**When China disappeared**": Robert Broadwater interview.

235 "**gave American multinational corporations**": Wachtel, *The Money Mandarins*, pp. 44–45.

"**bitter Englishman**": Denis W. Brogan in *As Others See Us*, p. 15.

"**Coca-Cola towns**": Kahn Notes, p. 153.

"**Thrifty Germans**": Peter von Zahn in *As Others See Us*, p. 97.

"**object held aloft**": Anthony Carthew, "Cold-Drink War: Kvass vs. Coke," *NYT Magazine*, July 12, 1964, p. 21.

"**gender of their drink**": Dr. Zimmerman to David N. Jones, Dec. 14, 1945, in Roy Stubbs, *Compilation on France*, 1951, pp. 397–399.

"**Frenchmen complained**": Kahn Notes, p. 20.

"**the largest party**": For more extended coverage of the French Coca-Cola affair, see Kuisel, *Seducing the French*, pp. 52–69, and Allen, *Secret Formula*, pp. 1–16. See also Pells, *Not Like Us*, pp. 199–201.

"**spy network**": "Letter from Paris," *New Yorker*, Jan. 21, 1950, p. 85.

"**Skull and cross-bones**": Harrold, "Bronxville to Bombay." (CC Archives)

236 "**Prince Alexander Makinsky**": Makinsky was typical of cosmopolitan Export men, many of whom spoke six or seven languages. (Kahn Notes, pp. 63–64; H. Burke Nicholson, Sr., "Competitive Ideal," 1952, p. 153; Allen, *Secret Formula*, pp. 1–2.)

"**innocent error**": Stubbs, *France*, p. 310.

"**sale of pharmaceuticals**": Kuisel, *Seducing*.

"**prejudicial to legitimate**": Acheson to Bruce, Dec. 2, 1949. (FDA Files, 475.11)

"**widespread and effective**": Bruce to Secretary of State, Dec. 18, 1949. (FDA Files, 475.11)

"**snooting our beverages**": All newspaper quotes from March 1950, French Scrapbook, vol. I, CC Archives. Quotes in following paragraph also from this source.

237 "**moral landscape of France**": French Scrapbook.

"**noblest product**": Raymond Aron quoted in Gregory Claeys, "Mass Culture and World Culture: On Americanisation and the Politics of Cultural Protectionism," *Diogenes* (Italy), vol. 136, 1986, p. 81; Kuisel, *Seducing the French*, p. 41; Rose, "Anti-Americanism in France," *Antioch Review*, Dec. 1952, p. 471.

"seven-hour filibuster": French Scrapbook.

"Mobs overturned": Eugene Tillinger, "The Cold War Against Coca-Cola," *Top Secret*, no date, p. 17. (Sibley Papers)

"French bicycle race": Kahn, *Big Drink*, p. 28.

"McCarthyism in reverse": Makinsky and wife quoted in Kahn Notes, pp. 64–65.

"when Frenchmen place": Ladas, July 24, 1950, in Stubbs, *France*, p. 333.

"Parisian temperance leader": French Notebook.

"gratuitous editorial mention": Nicholson, "Competitive Ideal," p. 152.

238 "a press agent's dream": Milton Bellis, "Bellis Returns to Paris," March 20, 1950, *Green Bay Press-Gazette*, in French Scrapbook. (CC Archives)

"emancipation": Makinsky in Kahn Notes, p. 64.

"Fantastic!": "Frenchmen Our Victims?" *Syracuse Post Standard*, March 3, 1950, French Scrapbook. (CC Archives)

"turned hair white": "Italian Invasion," *Time*, Aug. 22, 1949, p. 79; Kahn Notes, p. 26.

"Tremble!": "The Pause That Arouses," *Time*, March 13, 1950, p. 30. The feelings in Vienna ran so high that the Coke manager there was pulled from his car and beaten. (Allen *Secret Formula*, p. 6.)

"Coke nix gut": Tillinger, p. 18; Kahn Notes, p. 24.

"harmful laxative": James L. Wick, "Coca-Cola Flaming Issue in France and Belgium," *Niles* [Ohio] *Times*, April 18, 1950, French Scrapbook; Kahn Notes, p. 85.

"In Morocco": Tillinger, p. 18.

"In Cyprus": John Brinton interview.

"Labour Party member": *Wall Street Journal*, March 25, 1950, French Scrapbook.

"British satirist Nancy Mitford": Mitford, *The Blessing*, p. 152, 216–217; Allen, *Secret Formula*, p. 425, 472.

239 "Snake! Snake!": H. Burke Nicholson, Jr., interview; Dr. Blum to Dr. Ladas, May 12, 1949, in Stubbs, *Compilation on Switzerland*, p. 306; Makinsky to Ladas, May 12, 1949, in Stubbs, *Switzerland*, p. 307.

"loud propaganda": Dr. F. Kutter to Ladas, Feb. 19, 1949. (RWW Papers, Box 82)

"remaining patient": Brock to Ladas, May 15, 1950; Brock to Blum, July 13, 1950, in Stubbs, *Switzerland*, p. 22, 323.

"The winner": Kahn Notes, pp. 50, 77.

"campaign stopped": ibid., p. 80.

"made with pig's blood": Brinton interview.

"teeth fall out": Kahn Notes, p. 26.

"counter-rumor": ibid., p. 20.

"sterilized women": ibid., p. 24.

240 "men impotent": Harrold, "Bronxville"; Don Sisler interview.

"smooth wrinkles": Kahn, *Big Drink*, p. 26.

"In Trinidad": Annette Palmer, "Rum and Coca-Cola: The United States in the British Caribbean 1940–1945," *Americas*, 1987 43(4), pp. 441–451.

"dog medicine": Kahn Notes, p. 24.

"burnt comb": Sisler interview.

"foot's asleep": Letter to E. J. Kahn, Jr., undated (circa 1959), property of E. J. Kahn, Jr.

"sweet-and-bitter taste": Kahn Notes, pp. 10, 24, 224, 225.

"essence of capitalism": ibid., p. 1.

"every shopkeeper": J. Paul Austin, quoted in Kahn Notes, p. 52.

"workers' drink": Kahn Notes, p. 17.

"Italian Communists": ibid., p. 51.

"Isn't it a tragedy?": ibid., p. 64.

"Catholic priest": "Fun and Coca-Cola," *New Yorker*, Aug. 23, 1952, p. 16; "Cork, Eire, Dedicates Plant," *CC Overseas*, Aug. 1952, p. 2.

241 "Hindu priests": Kahn Notes, p. 22.

"governmental Muftis": "When the Ramadan Crescent Appears in Cairo, Egypt," *CC Overseas*, Aug. 1952, pp. 16–17.

"can't be offensive": Nicholson, "Competitive Ideal," p. 153.

"integral part": "A Unique Business," *CC Overseas*, Dec. 1952, p. 1. By the mid-fifties, the word "export" in the corporate title had become a liability, a reminder of the drink's American origin, and the Company seriously considered changing the name. (Lee Talley to H. B. Nicholson, Aug. 16, 1954, Sibley Papers, Box 1)

"Ah, but you must": "Sun Never Sets," p. 32.

"*pisco*, a native brandy": Kahn Notes, p. 22.

"with schnaps": ibid., p. 24.

"native corn liquor": Harrold, "Bronxville."

"Coexistence Cocktail": Albert Parry, "Calling Off the Cold War Against Coca-Cola," 1956, p. 1. (Sibley Papers)

"South African anniversary": Kahn Notes, pp. 62, 71, 72; "Miniature Case Campaign Staged by Lima Bottler," *CC Overseas*, April 1954, p. 6.

"blanketed Manila": "25 Million Cases in Their 25th Year," *CC Overseas*, Dec. 1952, p. 31.

"nearly identical": The Company distributed stencils or grids of various sizes to ensure the proper Coca-Cola logo. (Coca-Cola Export Booklets, 1954, 1957, CC Archives)

"Soviet athletes": Kahn Notes, p. 50.

"each Communistic gulp": Noel Finch and Gordon Christie, "XVI Olympiad, Melbourne, Australia, 1956," *CC Overseas*, Feb. 1957, p. 22.

242 "World Bank": Cook, *The Declassified Eisenhower*, p. vi.

"Don't forget": Zarubica interview.

"nephew Morton Hodgson": Throughout his career with Coca-Cola, Morton Hodgson was plagued by his relationship with Woodruff. "Everyone always assumed that I got where I did because of my uncle," he complained. Beginning in Canada in 1933, Hodgson worked in Europe, South America, the United States, and Japan in the course of his Coca-Cola career. (Hodgson interview)

"Joroberts Corporation": "Joroberts" was an amalgam of Jones and Roberts. The Americans owned 40 percent of the business, while locals owned another 40 percent, with Hodgson retaining the remaining 20 percent.

"heads of U.S. Steel": Hodgson interview.

"Bill Bekker, a Dutchman": Bekker, who refused to return to Holland during the war, remained fearful of arrest, avoiding flights on Dutch airlines for the rest of his life. (Sisler interview)

"considered them nonsense": Hodgson interview; William Solms interview; Sisler interview; Enrique Bledel interview.

243 "plowing the money back": Bledel interview.

"complete overthrow": Valdo Silveira, quoted in *As Others See Us*, *CC Overseas*, April 1954, p. 29.

"boy kings . . . sultan of Morocco": Kahn Notes, pp. 52, 54, 82–83.

"The leading commercial": Harrold, "Bronxville."

"Somoza's autograph": Farley, "Thirty-Five of the Most Pleasant Years of My Life," pp. 9, 13, Farley Papers.

"Salazar": Farley Papers, untitled, Box 70.

"United Fruit Company": Schlesinger & Kinzer, *Bitter Fruit*, pp. 65–117.

"blandly ignored": Henry A. Stephens, "Visiting United Fruit Company Banana Plantations," *CC Overseas*, June 1957, p. 18.

"Maharajah of Patiala": Frank Harrold to Woodruff, Dec. 13, 1956. (RWW Papers, Box 60)

244 "jewels have been estimated": Harrold to his wife, Feb. 10, 1953, "Bronxville."

"Harrold kept a diary": From 1948 to 1958, Frank Harrold—a tap-dancing Rhodes scholar—flew almost 500,000 miles, visiting 142 cities in sixty-two countries, checking on over 13,000 outlets. (E. D. Sledge Memo, Jan. 2, 1959, Administrative Files, CC Archives; Tom Law interview)

"a seething, boiling mass": Harrold, "Bronxville." All subsequent quotes from Harrold are from this source.

"second billion": CC Archives.

245 "more competitive": "Foreign Fizz," *Newsweek*, July 29, 1957, pp. 67–68. Imitation colas thrived in Coke's wake around the world, just as they had in the United States. (Stephen Ladas to Walter Oppenhoff, March 30, 1953, with affidavit, courtesy of Walter Oppenhoff)

"never drunk milk": Bill Robinson in Kahn Notes, p. 9.

"5-to-1": "Host With the Most," *Forbes*, Oct. 1, 1957, p. 15.

"bunch of wild daisies": J. Paul Austin, quoted in Kahn Notes, p. 54.

"measles rash": Turner, *Shocking History*, p. 260.

"No matter where": "A Unique Business," *CC Overseas*, Dec. 1952, p. 1.

"es perfecto": "An Interesting Story About Coca-Cola in Mexico," *CC Overseas*, April 1954, p. 26; "A True Story About the Cover Picture," *CC Overseas*, Dec. 1956, p. 28.

"billboard emerging": Kahn Notes, p. 54. Robert Woodruff's friend Bernard Gimbel taunted the Boss, asserting that his explorer son couldn't buy a Coke in the remote Andes. Woodruff subsequently arranged an airdrop to the young Gimbel, startled to find cases of Coca-Cola parachuted to his campsite. (Sisler interview)

CHAPTER 15: BREAKING THE COMMANDMENTS

246 "Any change": Arnold Bennett, *The Arnold Bennett Calendar*, and Robert Lynd, *The Blue Lion*, quoted in *Crown Treasury*, pp. 125, 126.

"as the Old Man": Robert Woodruff Speech, Oct. 28, 1940. (RWW Papers, Personal File 2)

"former government functionary": William J. Hobbs file, RWW Papers, Box 41; Allen, *Secret Formula*, pp. 268–272

"nomadic existence": Though devoted to his wife, Woodruff often avoided traveling with her, finding some excuse to stay with male friends. "You don't know how much I envy you," Nell told Edith Honeycutt just after World War II, "with your little home, a husband who comes home every day, and your children." (Joe Jones interview; Edith Honeycutt interview)

"amount of Scotch": Ralph McGill interview, Kahn Notes, p. 187.

"Delaware native": Joe Jones interview; Apparel file, Cigar file, in RWW Papers.

"without vacation . . . faithful retainer": Joe Jones interview.

"power base": Interview with Hughes Spalding, "Process Recording of Interview Atlanta Power Structure," in Floyd Hunter Papers, Box 16, Emory. Unless noted, all quotes from Mr. Spalding are from this source.

"fire extinguisher company": Harold Martin, *William Berry Hartsfield*, p. 8.

"I never made": Floyd Hunter Notes, Box 35, Hunter Papers; Kahn, *RWW*, pp. 123–124. Except for a brief period in 1941–1942, Hartsfield served as Atlanta's mayor from 1937 to 1962.

"$6,000 annual retainer": Pope Brock to Hughes Spalding, May 13, 1946; Lee Talley to Hartsfield, Dec. 11, 1961, Hartsfield Papers, Emory.

"The actions of the top leaders": Floyd Hunter, *Community Power Structure*, pp. 69, 195.

"lack of a quorum": Elliott, *Mr. Anonymous*, p. 29.

"never attributed to him": Woodruff's interest in medical research kindled in the 1930s when he discovered the prevalence of malaria at Ichauway. Due to his concern and money, the disease was eradicated in southwest Georgia within a few years. When his mother later died of cancer, Woodruff turned his money to fighting that malady. Throughout his life, the Boss commandeered the head Emory research doctor as his personal physician, a job which entailed much travel and little sleep. (Elliott, pp. 39, 197–201)

"Multimillionaire Nobody Knows": Joe Jones interview; Ralph McGill, "The Multimillionaire Nobody Knows," *Saturday Evening Post*, May 5, 1951, pp. 26–27.

247 **"abused his extraordinary power"**: Wilbur Kurtz, Jr, interview; Ian Wilson interview; anonymous source; Charles Bottoms interview.

248 **"white mob"**: In the 1920s, many prominent Atlanta businessmen belonged to the Ku Klux Klan, and Coca-Cola ads appeared in *The Searchlight*, the local Klan publication. (Jackson, *The Ku Klux Klan in the City: 1915–1930*, pp. 29–33)

"what the Negroes want": Spalding interview, Box 16; Mays interview, Box 35, Hunter Papers.

"wherever I am": Woodruff quoted in Floyd Hunter interview.

"they're the people": Makinsky quoted in Kahn Notes, p. 66.

"We sent him overseas": In 1948, Eisenhower became president of Columbia University. Three years later, he moved to Paris, as supreme commander of NATO troops. While there, he invited James Farley and Alexander Makinsky to lunch. (*Eisenhower Diaries*, p. 137; Brendon, *Ike*, pp. 199–207; Farley to Eisenhower, Aug. 28, 1951, Eisenhower Papers)

"Democrat or a Republican": Floyd Hunter interview.

"gang": Brendon, pp. 196, 209; Allen, *Secret Formula*, pp. 302–303

"business-bashing New Dealer": For Woodruff's anti-Roosevelt slant, see Woodruff speech, Oct. 28, 1940, Personal File 2, RWW Papers.

"wrote from Paris": Eisenhower to Roberts, Oct. 18, 1951. (Eisenhower Papers)

248–9 **"invited Eisenhower to Uruguay"**: Hodgson interview; Morton S. Hodgson Jr, to Eisenhower, July 21, 1949. (Eisenhower Papers)

249 **"twit the Boss"**: Joe Jones interview.

"reasonable protection": *Eisenhower Diaries*, p. 171; Louis & Yazijian, p. 151; Brendon, p. 202.

"with that puss": James Forrestal, quoted in Brendon, p. 202.

"complete spontaneity": Eisenhower to Cliff Roberts, June 19, 1952. (Eisenhower Papers)

"Dear Boss": Woodruff to Eisenhower, Dec. 7, 1954. (Eisenhower Papers)

"when I tip": Eisenhower to RWW, Dec. 26, 1959. (Eisenhower Papers)

250 **"modify his popular jingle"**: Milward Martin, *Twelve Full Ounces*, p. 126.

"Pepsi's profits plunged": Alvin Toffler, "The Competition That Refreshes," *Fortune*, May 1961, p. 127.

"a national expectation": Ralph Hayes to Ella Bell Carlton, Jan. 14, 1948; Hayes to Hobbs, July 26, 1948. (CC Archives)

"two Cadillacs": "The Nickel Drink Is Groggy," *Fortune*, Jan. 1951, p. 130.

"some relief": C. M. Brown to CC Co., Sept. 15, 1950. (CC Archives) "lobbied in favor": Charles M. Brown, "To All Bottlers in Tennessee," Sept. 12, 1950, quoted in Roddy, *75 Years of Refreshment*, p. 125.

"suing Coca-Cola": "Pepper Sues Coca-Cola," *NYT*, Jan. 25, 1951, p. 40.

"Senate committee": "Report of Senate Committee on Small Business, *Crisis in the Soft Drink Bottling Industry*, 1951. (CC Archives)

"medal instead of a lawsuit": "Coke's Valiant Fight," *Pittsburgh Post-Gazette*, Feb. 6, 1951. (CC Archives)

"he beseeched": Delony Sledge to Walter Thomas, May 15, 1950. (CC Archives)

251 "abortive coup": Ovid Davis interview; Nat Harrison interview; Veazey Rainwater file, RWW Papers, Box 72.

"Flattery is like": RWW to Ralph Hayes, May 3, 1963. (RWW Papers, Box 40)

"yessir, yessir": Ralph Hayes Speech, RWW Birthday Dinner, Dec. 6, 1959. (RWW Papers, Box 39)

"more depends": Spalding to RWW, Aug. 12, 1951. (RWW Papers, Box 80)

"Woodruff's hand-tooled . . . shoes": Joe Jones interview.

"brown parcel": Clifford "Randy" Barbee interview.

252 "Call me Al": "Pepsi's Double Trouble," *Forbes*, June 15, 1951, p. 15; "Pepsi-Cola's New Approach," *Tide*, May 18, 1951, p. 51; Kurtz interview; Allen, *Secret Formula*, pp. 273–277; 295–296; 318–319.

"talk the horns": Toffler, p. 126.

"sound system failed": ibid.

"publicly paged": Zarubica interview.

"stupid enough to get caught": Before Mladin Zarubica traveled overseas as a Technical Observer, for instance, Woodruff silently appraised him for a minute, then advised: "Young fella, you're a pretty handsome guy. Whatever you do, you do it back in the sugar bags where nobody can see it. Understand?" (Zarubica interview)

"doubled . . . salary": Rowland, p. 187.

"dramatic . . . board meeting": Toffler, p. 127.

253 "nigger drink": Walter Thomas interview. Similarly, in Canada, where low-wage-earning French-Canadians drank Pepsi, the Anglos contemptuously called them "Pepsis". (Irene Angelico interview.)

"out of the kitchen": Philip N. Schuyler, "Pepsi Reaches New Plateau," *Editor & Publisher*, March 26, 1960, p. 86.

"Light Refreshment": The Federal Trade Commission eventually halted the "reduced in calories" claim, since Pepsi still contained more sugar than Coca-Cola. Surprisingly, Coke and Pepsi were slow to create bona fide diet drinks, whose consumption increased 300 percent from 1952 to 1955. (Packard, p. 60)

"rushed to Tiffany's": Biow, *Butting In*, pp. 188–192.

"low-interest loans": "Pepsi's Double Trouble," pp. 15–16.

"You can conserve": M. Martin, p. 130.

"plunking down": "How Pepsi Bounced Back," *Sponsor*, Sept. 8, 1952, p. 62.

"copy Coca-Cola tactics": Toffler, p. 127.

"The whole trick": Louis & Yazijian, p. 80.

"goatskin pouch": Al Steele quoted by Jesse Meyers, *Future Smarts IV*, Dec. 16, 1986, pp. 4–5.

254 "Fox theater": Paul Snell to Steve Hannagan, June 23, 1950. (CC Archives)

"scalded cat": Toffler, p. 127.

"from 21 percent to 35 percent": "Host with the Most," *Forbes*, Oct. 1, 1957, p. 15; "Pepsi Calls Coffee, Tea Toughest Foes," *AC*, June 7, 1956; Toffler, p. 207.

"It's a tribute": "Pepsi Calls Coffee."

"slumbers peacefully": H. George Allen to President, Pepsi-Cola, Aug. 21, 1958. (CC Archives) "**modest, sedate**": Steve Hannagan to Delony Sledge, Oct. 27, 1952. (RWW Papers, Box 38)

"**prostate removed**": Spalding to RWW, May 27, 1948. (RWW Papers, Box 80)

"**debuted on TV**": Bateman & Schaeffer, "Edgar Bergen & Charlie McCarthy for Coca-Cola," *Cola Call*, April 1985, pp. 4–5, 11. By the mid-fifties, the average American viewer watched nearly five hours of television a day. (Oakley, *God's Country*, pp. 10, 97–98)

"**Christmas Day special**": Bateman & Schaeffer, "Edgar Bergen," p. 5.

"**long, slow decline**": In the early fifties, soda fountains disappeared at the rate of twelve hundred per year. (Visser, *Much Depends on Dinner*, p. 309)

255 "**take-home market**": "Coke: New Faces, New Bottles," *Business Week*, Feb. 12, 1955, p. 45.

"*Adventures of Kit Carson*": Bateman & Schaeffer, "Your Coca-Cola Bottler Presents 'The Adventures of Kit Carson,'" *Cola Call*, Sept. 1985, pp. 4–6.

"**1,535,406 people**": E. D. Sledge, "Advertising at the Point of Sale," May 19, 1952, p. 4. (RWW Papers, Box 79); Coke's advertising head Delony Sledge had a dry, self-deprecating wit, wore wrinkled old suits, hated New York, and displayed deep devotion to Coca-Cola, whose taste he would not attempt to define. "I don't think the words exist. What suffices for me is . . . to understand that the taste of Coca-Cola is the greatest taste ever invented by man—or God, either, for that matter." (Backer, *Care and Feeding*, pp. 235–237)

"**Eddie Fisher**": Bateman & Schaeffer, "Coke Time with Eddie Fisher," *Cola Call*, June 1984, pp. 4–7; Hoy, p. 127. There was also a radio version of "Coke Time."

"**the sort of face**": "Eddie Fisher," *Current Biography*, 1954, pp. 275–276; "Oh! My Sincerity," *Time*, May 26, 1961, p. 42.

"**In drugstores across America**": Fisher, *Eddie*, p. 85.

"**hypodermic shots of vitamins and amphetamines**": Fisher, *Eddie*, p. 2–8, 81–88, 96–98, 219–224, 236–239, 260–265; Greene, *Eddie Fisher Story*, pp. 16–19, 70–83, 108, 119; Hersh, *Dark Side of Camelot*, pp. 5, 234–237.

256 "**they spent their honeymoon**": Fisher, *Eddie*, p. 108.

"**reciprocal publicity**": "Tie-In Advertising," *Consumer Reports*, Jan. 1951, p. 44.

"**interim caretaker**": Hodgson interview.

"**it is faltering**": "Coke: New Faces," p. 44.

"**the only thing wrong**": ibid., p. 46.

"**ounce for ounce**": Coca-Cola's manager in Mexico took the unprecedented step of writing directly to the Boss in 1952, begging for a bigger bottle—to no avail. (Bill Solms interview)

"**One night at dinner**": Elliott, p. 29.

257 "**freckle-faced Alabama boy**": Lee Talley and his brother John inherited their missionary zeal from their father, a Methodist minister. Such an upbringing also produced "Preacher" Robert L. Franklin—a bishop's off-spring—who led Coca-Cola pep rallies known as "altar calls." (Kahn, *Big Drink*, p. 73; Rowland, pp. 153–159)

"**losing side**": Solms interview.

"**awesome scope**": "The Big Pause—Editorial," *Bottling Industry*, Oct. 26, 1954, p. 1.

"**Ed Forio noted**": Toffler, p. 128. Forio's speechmaking talents earned him the title, "Demosthenes of Coca-Cola." (Edgar J. Forio file, RWW Papers; Kahn Notes, p. 201)

"**long memo to the board**": Lee Talley, "Report to the Board of Directors

Covering Fourth Quarter, 1954, Operations, The Coca-Cola Export Corporation." (Sibley Papers, Box 1)

"dark, scuffed little bottle": The sturdy little recycled bottles even had nicknames to indicate their abused state. A "bum" could still be refilled, but looked disreputable. A "scuffie" sported a whitened ring around its waist from banging against other bottles. A "crock" had a chipped bottom. *The Coca-Cola Bottler* periodically ran articles such as "How to Prevent the Creation of Bums." (Kahn, *Big Drink*, p. 77)

"applied color label": Coke bottles finally received their applied color labels (ACL) for the first time in 1957. (William V. Seifert, "ACL," *Cola Call*, July 1983)

"prefer the standard": CC News Release, Jan. 28, 1955, CC Archives; Bill Robinson address to NY Society of Security Analysts, Jan. 12, 1956. (RWW Papers, Box 74)

"fun to be followed": "Change for Coke," *Time*, Oct. 24, 1955, p. 100.

"shift to larger sizes": In 1955, faced with new sizes, bottle manufacturers complained about the massive inventory needed to service different plants, their locations blown into the bottle base. When bottles were left anonymous, however, angry consumers complained that they were deprived of their favorite game, "Far Away," in which the bottle from the most distant point won. After a few years, the Company relented, but manufacturers simply blew random locations into the bottle bottoms. (C. W. Hodgson to Wilbur Kurtz, May 29, 1956; Charles Adams to Wilbur Kurtz, Oct. 27, 1964, CC Archives)

"available to 81 percent": June 10, 1958, CC Advertising Memo, Frank Harrold "Report on Imitator's 6½ Oz. Package," June 9, 1958. (CC Archives)

258 **"Coke archives are filled":** Lee Talley Memo, April 23, 1957 (RWW Papers, Box 83); Kahn Notes, p. 91; Harrold, "Report on Imitator," June 9, 1958; Warren Burns to J. D. Maclary, Dec. 5, 1958, "Poll Interview"; Harold Sharp to Lee Talley, Dec. 4, 1958, "Nielson Report on Carolina-virginia."

"second line": Talley, "Report to the Board," p. 12.

"trend is increasing": Joseph M. Collins to RWW, Jan. 29, 1957. (Sibley Papers Box 1)

"new line of Fanta": Bateman & Schaeffer, "The History of Coca-Cola, Part 3: 1950–1986," *Cola Call*, June 1986, p. 9.

"pre-mix machines": "Coke: New Faces," p. 46.

"free to negotiate": Talley, "A Statement Concerning the Differential in Price Between Bottler's Syrup and B-X Syrup," ca. 1955. (RWW Papers, Box 83)

"Tom Moore sued": Coca-Cola Bottling Co. of Minnesota vs. The Coca-Cola Co., U.S. District Court, Fourth Division, April 29, 1957. (CC Legal Library)

"wasn't an angel": Tut Johnson interview.

259 **"Harrison refused to sell":** Pope Brock to RWW, "Purchase of Coca-Cola Bottling Co. (Thomas), Inc." Sept. 21, 1959. (RWW Papers, Box 16); Gordon Bynum interview; Raymond Witt interview. At one point, Woodruff offered the presidency of The Coca-Cola Company to Dee Harrison in return for selling the Thomas Company. Harrison refused. (Sebert Brewer, Jr., interview; Pearl Ledoux interview)

"officially retired": Woodruff never really gave up ultimate authority at the Company. "Don't take this retirement business too seriously," he wrote to Max Keith thirteen years later. "However official it is, you'll learn that it doesn't mean much. I've been through it half a dozen times." (Woodruff to Max Keith, Aug. 7, 1968, RWW Papers, Keith file)

"switched ad agencies": "Overseas Expansion Cause of Coke Shift," *Business Week*, Oct. 22, 1955, p. 141; "Change for Coke," *Time*, Oct. 24, 1955, p. 100.

"Marion Harper, Jr.": Toffler, p. 128; Stephen Fox, *Mirror Makers*, p. 195;

"Interpublic Group Inc.," *International Directory of Company Histories*, vol. 1, pp. 16–18. Harper ruled McCann—and Interpublic, the umbrella agency he later formed with Marshalk, McCann and other subsidiaries—until 1967, when he was deposed by his board for financial mismanagement. (Neal Gilliatt interview)

"$15 million ad campaign": "Coke: New Faces," p. 46.

"in Punkin Center": Toffler, pp. 128, 200–202.

260 **"shot it"**: Brewer interview.

"drinking the wrong soda": Richard Trubo, "The Cola Rivalry," *Buffalo News Magazine*, Feb. 8, 1981. (CC Collection, Emory)

"Downey, the crooner": Kahn Notes, p. 92. In many ways, Morton Downey, Sr., took John Sibley's place as Woodruff's closest male friend. "It's too bad you are a man," Downey once wrote to the Boss. "If you were a woman, I might be able to show you how much I appreciate and love you." (Morton Downey to Woodruff, Nov. 16, 1970, RWW Papers, Box 24)

"Every week the Coke man": Morton Downey, Jr., interview; "The Odd Couple of Sensationalism," *Newsweek*, Nov. 14, 1988, p. 75. Morton Downey, Jr., had other reasons for his bitterness. His father sang "The Same Old Shillelagh," and he applied that rod unsparingly to his children, often drawing blood. None of the five offspring survived unscarred, but Lorelle, who had a nervous breakdown at fourteen, suffered the worst fate. Joe Kennedy, who had relegated his daughter Rosemary to an institution, advised Downey to do the same. Given a frontal lobotomy, Lorelle was ultimately smothered by a fellow patient. Morton Downey, Jr., tried to reverse his father's example: "While I have the outward image of the bastard, I'm the best father in the world to my three daughters." (Morton Downey, Jr., interview; "Morton Downey," *AC/J*, Oct. 25, 1985)

"Don't *ever*": Dick Halpern interview.

"*cut* the King Size price": Murray Hillman interview.

"Typically, Jewish consumers": ibid.

"the depth boys": Packard, *Hidden Persuaders*, p. 8.

"tender expert advice": ibid., pp. 22, 47.

"Delony Sledge explained": Delony Sledge, "Our 1955 Consumer Advertising," *CC Bottler*, Feb. 1955, p. 20. (Background on Sledge in Bill Mackey interview; Claire Sims interview; Mary Gresham interview)

"super hucksters": Ralph Goodman, "Freud and the Hucksters," *Nation*, Feb. 14, 1953, p. 143.

"bundles of daydreams": Packard, *Hidden Persuaders*, pp. 3, 7.

"red was 'hypnotic'": ibid., pp. 108–109.

"free samples in supermarkets": ibid., p. 110.

261 **"Poet James Dickey"**: Dickey interview.

262 **"visions, dreams, drives"**: Gay Talese, "Most Hidden Hidden Persuasion," *NYT Magazine*, Jan. 12, 1958, pp. 22, 59.

"turned out to be a hoax": Eric Clark, *The Want Makers*, p. 119. The claims of the Subliminal Projection Company, even when debunked, sparked an ongoing controversy, though there has never been proof that "subliminal" messages work. (N. F. Dixon, *Subliminal Perception*)

"consumerism is king!": Packard, *Hidden Persuaders*, p. 21.

"We must consume": ibid., pp. 19–20.

"Everybody liked Eisenhower": Mochtar Lubis in *As Others See Us*, p. 197.

"bland new world": Packard, *Hidden Persuaders*, p. 101; eight-ounce serving per capita figures from CC Company spokesman.

"Hi, Mom": "Johnny Remembers Something," 1958, composite advertising video (courtesy John Bergin).

263 **"the new jungle"**: Packard, *Hidden Persuaders*, p. 105.
"portable display racks": The author's father, J. B. Pendergrast, Jr., obtained a major portion of his living by designing display racks for Coca-Cola.
"The smart-ass said": Charles Bottoms interview.
"Ozzie got hopelessly confused": Hoy, p. 129; Ozzie and Harriet Coke commercial, McCann-Erickson files; Freeman, *Real Thing*, pp. 115–116.
"jump on the bandwagon": Charlotte Montgomery, "She Doesn't Have Brand Sentimentality," *CC Bottler*, Jan. 1955, p. 22.
"Fertile Acres": Oakley, *God's Country*, pp. 111–112, 121.
"so catered to": ibid., p. 123.
264 **"Kroc offered his customers"**: "McDonald's Golden Arches Mean Good Food, Quick Service and Coke," *Refresher*, July/Aug. 1967, pp. 8–10.
"*Automobilus Americanus*": Hillman interview.
"spying on over 20,000": Kahn Notes, p. 106.
"turned God into a friend": Oakley, pp. 319–325.
"urged Eisenhower": RWW phone call, 1955 White House memo, Eisenhower Papers; Farley to Eisenhower, March 31, 1955, Farley Papers.
"adjunct of man": "Culture from America?" *Time*, Jan. 23, 1950.
265 **"Clive M. McCay"**: See "Cola Drinks and Your Teeth," *Consumer Reports*, June 1950, p. 268.
"his allegations": *Time*, Sept. 29, 1950; Fred Othmer, AC, Oct. 21, 1950. (RWW Papers, Dental Caries folder)
"molar teeth of rats": Clive M. McCay "Prepared Statement," Select Committee to Investigate the Use of Chemicals in Food Products. (RWW Papers, Box 21)
"distorted picture": Orville E. May testimony, 1950. (RWW Papers, Box 21)
"The only way . . . harm children": Kahn Notes, pp. 102–103. Coke went to great lengths—and expense—to secure scientific support. Dr. Frederick J. Stare, a Harvard nutritionist, responded to Coca-Cola funding with 1954 articles in *McCall's* and *Ladies' Home Journal* suggesting Coke as an appropriate part of a healthy teenager's diet. Similarly, Dr. Glenville Giddings of Emory conducted research indicating Coke's harmlessness to teeth and health until his retirement in 1957, when he was put on a $12,000 annual retainer. (Dr. Frederick Stare, "Teen Agers Do Not Eat Right," *McCall's*, May 1954, and correspondence in Stare File; Orville May to Bill Robinson, Oct. 11, 1957, Giddings File, RWW Papers)
"women constituted": Oakley, pp. 298–299.
"consumers into hoodlums": "Youth Programs, 1953–1957." (RWW Papers, Box 95)
"Rock Around the Clock": Oakley, pp. 272–279.
266 **"economic pressure"**: Kahn Notes, pp. 14, 17. As early as 1950, a Harlem group called the National Fair Play Committee called for a boycott of Coca-Cola. (Allen, *Secret Formula*, pp. 284–288)
"Farley described opportunities": James Farley Speech, *CC Bottler*, May 1955, p. 51.
"strictly separate": Bateman & Schaeffer, "Black History and The Coca-Cola Company," *CC Collectors News*, Feb. 1987, pp. 9–11. Until this time, blacks had appeared in Coca-Cola advertising only as menials. (Bateman & Schaeffer, "Blacks in Early Advertising for Coca-Cola," *CC Collectors News*, Feb. 1987, p. 12)
"hosting a career conference": "The Coca-Cola Company and the Bottlers Cultivate the Negro Market," *CC Bottler*, Aug. 1954.
"Kendrix attended": Kahn Notes, p. 348; Rowland, pp. 181–182.
"hired . . . executives of color": "Cultivate Negro Market." Southern

bottlers only reluctantly changed, with white office managers like "Pop" Stewart routinely docking black employees' pay if they didn't like them. (Rowland, pp. 151, 178–180)

"Sure, we'll stand up": Delony Sledge interview with E. J. Kahn, Jr., Kahn Notes, pp. 348–349.

267 "mayor reduced their size": Harold Martin, *Hartsfield*, p. 49.

"betrayed his long-time ally": Sherrill, *Gothic Politics in the Deep South*, pp. 62–67, 134.

"master–slave relationship": Joe Jones interview.

"kindness, and condescension": In 1946, Mattie Heard, a black cook and singer at Ichauway, wrote to Woodruff thanking him "for the many nice things you do for me and my people." He endeared himself to the black community when he gave money—anonymously—for a new church to replace one which had burned at a crossroads near the plantation. (Mattie Heard to Woodruff, Jan. 31, 1946, RWW Papers, Box 40; Elliott, p. 38)

"right of a chimpanzee": RWW to Hayes, Nov. 22, 1960. (Sibley Papers, Box 1)

"agitation and strikes": "Strike Drying Up Coca-Cola Supply," *NYT*, June 21, 1955, p. 23; "Coca-Cola Strike Ended by Drivers," *NYT*, June 29, 1955, p. 33; "NLRB Overruled in Taft Act Dispute," *NYT*, Feb. 28, 1956, p. 22.

"Union men slashed": Roddy, *75 Years of Refreshment*, pp. 155–172.

"shoot for the belly": Carter, *Paul B. Carter*, pp. 115, 118.

"Black Friday": Bottoms interview.

267–8 "Troy Neighbors": Gresham interview.

268 "blood's not dry": Sims interview.

"drowned himself . . . shot herself": Bottoms interview.

"could have run naked": ibid.

"almost inconceivable": Joe Jones asserts, however, that Woodruff was unaware of Black Friday. (Joe Jones interview)

"Bill Robinson . . . kicked upstairs": Toffler, p. 200; Neal Gilliatt interview; Bottoms interview.

"aloof grandeur": "Resurgent Pepsi Gets New Boss," *Business Week*, May 30, 1959, p. 106; Toffler, p. 200.

"sign of good taste": "Coke Refreshes Ads to Regain Profit Norm," *Printer's Ink*, Feb. 13, 1959, pp. 44, 48.

"Party from Your Pantry": "Coca-Cola Promotion: More Gains for Grocers," *Printer's Ink*, Jan. 30, 1958, p. 22.

269 "d.j. would run out": Gilliatt interview.

"clubs in 325 cities": "Teenagers and Tastemaking," *Broadcasting*, June 1, 1959, p. 85; "How Coca-Cola Sways Youth with Music," *Editor & Publisher*, Dec. 5, 1959, p. 30; Gilliatt interview.

"visited twenty foreign lands": "Beverages: Refreshment with Pep," *Investor's Reader*, Aug. 21, 1957, p. 19; "Joan Crawford Finds Husband Dead," *New York Herald Tribune*, April 20, 1959; "Battle of the Bottlers Overseas," *Business Week*, June 15, 1957, pp. 131–138.

"she had bottles of Pepsi": Christina Crawford, *Mommie Dearest*, p. 199.

"she did not come cheap": ibid., pp. 205–211.

"Steele died suddenly": Toffler, p. 207; "Joan Crawford Finds Husband."

"highly valued assets": M. Martin, p. 136.

"over three million miles": Joan Crawford, *My Way of Life*, p. 124.

"Nixon loudly argued": "That Famous Debate in Close-Up Pictures," *Life*, Aug. 3, 1959, pp. 26–28; "Encounter," *Newsweek*, Aug. 3, 1959, pp. 15–18; Nixon to Farley, Aug. 20, 1959. (RWW Papers, Nixon File)

"he cajoled Khrushchev": Wisely, Kendall provided two versions of

Pepsi—one from the U.S., the other made with Russian water and sugar. Khrushchev loudly proclaimed the superiority of the Soviet Pepsi. (Don Kendall interview; Brodie, *Richard Nixon*, p. 385n)
"KHRUSHCHEV LEARNS TO BE SOCIABLE": Kendall interview.

CHAPTER 16: PAUL AUSTIN'S TURBULENT SIXTIES

271 **"a new generation"**: John F. Kennedy, "Inaugural Address," Jan. 20, 1961, *The Annals of America*, vol. 18, pp. 5–7.
"Eisenhower . . . complained bitterly": Eisenhower to RWW, Jan. 3, 1961. (Eisenhower Papers)
"Woodruff associate": Boisfeuillet Jones received the appointment through Vice-President Lyndon Johnson, who had served, like Jones, as a National Youth Administration executive. (Boisfeuillet Jones File, Box 53 & 54; Austin to Woodruff, Sept. 16, 1968. RWW Papers, Box 7)
"posing with him": 1961 photo, Ben Oehlert folder. (RWW Papers)
"available at any time": Farley to JFK, March 14, 1961, April 24, 1961. (Farley Papers)
"from a consumer": Frank Harrold, "40 Years with Coca-Cola," CC *Overseas*, Oct. 1963, p. 12.
"It was kind": Farley to JFK, Sept. 26, 1963. (Farley Papers)
"ambassadorship to England": Louis & Yazijian, p. 132.
272 **"franchise on the Moon"**: May 25, 1961, letter to CC Co. (CC Archives)
"when you're my age": Gus Grissom quoted in "Looking at the Moon," *The Refresher*, July/Aug. 1961.
"offering Sprite": The name for the new lemon/lime drink derived from Haddon Sundblom's war-era elf known as the Coca-Cola sprite—a silver-haired, ever-smiling boyish creature who wore a bottle cap for a hat. (Hoy, pp. 82, 100; Dec. 22, 1960, CC Co. memo, CC Archives)
"first non-returnable": "History of Non-Returnable Bottles." (CC Archives)
"buying Minute Maid": Minute Maid, established in 1946, dominated the market, owning 20,000 acres of Florida citrus groves, making Coca-Cola one of the world's largest orange growers. (The Coca-Cola Company, "Notice of Special Meeting of Stockholders," Nov. 21, 1960, Sibley Papers)
"expansionist mood": "This Is Coca-Cola?" *Business Week*, Oct. 8, 1960, pp. 80, 85.
"company hardly paused": "No Time for Parties," *Forbes*, Sept. 15, 1961, p. 24.
"he noted sternly": Lee Talley memo, "Policy of The Coca-Cola Company in Regard to the Sales of Bottle, Pre-Mix and Post-Mix Coca-Cola," Oct. 16, 1961. (RWW Papers, Box 83)
"post office complained": "Coca-Cola Co.," *Advertising Age*, Aug. 27, 1962, p. 105.
"born-again Christian": "Anita Bryant," *Current Biography*, 1975, pp. 56–57.
"air time for Bryant": "Filming a Livin' Doll, Our Lovely Anita," *Refresher*, 1962, p. 8.
273 **"ON A PEDESTAL"**: Lee Talley to J. Paul Austin, E. D. Sledge, Oct. 6, 1962. (RWW Papers, Box 83)
"pretty deep motivational": "Coke Tries New Ways to Refresh," *Business Week*, Aug. 24, 1963, p. 105.
"'in' enough to win": "Coke Meets Its Goal: 'In' Not 'Way Out,'" *Broadcasting*, June 29, 1964, p. 46. In 1963, Coca-Cola men's notion of "way out" included things that flabbergasted cinematographer Ed Vorkapich. At a

commercial's first screening, a Southern drawl welled from the rear: "There's a girl in there that doesn't have Coca-Cola length hair." Such hair should just brush the shoulder, and the pert blonde in question had a shorter bob. Such strictures soon drove Vorkapich to desert Coke for Pepsi, where he had a freer hand. (Ed Vorkapich interview)

"Things . . . was killing us": John Bergin interview.

274 **"Pepsi Generation"**: An elderly journalist in a retirement community complained of the "squeaky voiced female" who sang the Pepsi generation commercial. Further, he resented the implication that "if one doesn't drink her drink one is an old has-been, a fuddy-duddy." On the contrary, he insisted that "we're still full of beans, vinegar, and sometimes Coke." ("It's Not Our Generation," Scottsdale [AZ] *Daily Progress*, Jan. 20, 1966).

"seventy-five million": This "baby boom" figure includes Americans born from 1946 to 1964. (Johnson, *Sleepwalking*, p. 124)

"at the heart . . . Coca-Cola": It was around this time that Coke's ad men began searching for a fine balance between emphasis on *intrinsics*—product attributes such as taste, carbonation, and lift—and *extrinsics* such as popularity, sex, youth, and community. (Bergin interview)

"know the score": Hughes Spalding to RWW, Nov. 30, 1962. (RWW Papers, Box 80)

"J. Paul Austin": "Georgian Elected Coca-Cola Chief," *AC*, May 9, 1962; "Coca-Cola Elects New President," *NYT*, May 9, 1962; "J. Paul Austin, former head of Coca-Cola, dies at age 70," *AC*, Dec. 27, 1985.

"If you wanted to beat": Bill Mackey interview.

"imperious demeanor": Jack B. Weiner, "Why Things Go Better at Coke," *Dun's Review*, Oct. 1966, p. 72.

275 **"A certain degree"**: Anita Lands, "Profile . . . J. Paul Austin," *Hermes Exchange*, Oct. 1968, p. 21. (CC Archives)

"legs off the centipede": "Austin of Coca-Cola: The Uses of Adrenaline," *Forbes*, May 15, 1971, p. 70.

"Kennedy relished . . . tension": Chafe, *Unfinished Journey*, pp. 189, 191.

"Fidel Castro . . . nationalizing": Cuba file, Coca-Cola Archives; Louis & Yazijian, p. 169.

"former vice-president globe-hopping": Before going to work as Pepsi's lawyer, Richard Nixon approached Coca-Cola for a job. Recalling his role in getting Khrushchev to drink Pepsi during the Kitchen Debate of 1959, Coke executives objected, "We don't want that son-of-a-bitch on the payroll." Nixon circled the globe six times for Pepsi between 1962 and 1968, plus numerous shorter trips. (Brodie, *Richard Nixon*, pp. 385n, 478–481; Ambrose, *Nixon: Vol. 2, The Triumph of a Politician, 1962–1972*, pp. 17–18, 43, 68; Murray Kempton, Oct. 18, 1968, "How Nixon Endured," Austin folder, RWW Papers, Box 4; Louis & Yazijian, pp. 114–115; Allen, *Secret Formula*, p. 326.)

"Kendall, a savvy executive": Don Kendall, an aggressive, streetwise former Navy pilot and boxer, came to power in 1963.

276 **"optimistic 1959 survey"**: *Coca-Cola (Japan): The First Thirty Years*, pp. 20–24.

"almost fanatical desire": Murray Hillman to J. Paul Austin, July 18, 1961 (courtesy Murray Hillman).

"bottler Nisaburo Takanashi": *CC (Japan)*, pp. 16, 21.

"immediate sensation": ibid., p. 34; Bill Van Loan interview; Ron Sugarman interview.

"the Emperor": Roberts, like Al Killeen in Africa, Bill Bekker in Argentina, or Max Keith in Germany, maintained complete control in his region. "They ruled like absolute monarchs," a Company man recalls, "as long as they delivered the money." In the mid-fifties, James Curtis, the alcoholic president of the Export corporation, carried things too far, hosting a three-day debauch in Germany, replete with women and liquor. Max Keith blew the whistle, and Woodruff fired Curtis. (Bob Broadwater interview; Michael McMullen interview; Ian Wilson interview)

"direct distribution system": *CC* (*Japan*), pp. 26, 34.

"Much has been written": Aguayo, *Dr. Deming.*

277 **"skatto sawayaka"**: *CC* (*Japan*), pp. 33–39.

"nearly doubling": ibid., pp. 32, 36, 39.

"Esperanto of world business": W. F. Westerman, "Chalk Talks, a world-wide sales training program," *CC Overseas*, Oct. 1962, p. 22; *CC Overseas*, Feb. 1964, p. 5; "Sales Convention Reaches New Audiences," *CC Overseas*, June 1964, pp. 23–26; "Coca-Cola Advertised in 57 Languages," *CC Overseas*, Oct. 1960, pp. 14–15; "Our Readers Ask," *CC Overseas*, Oct. 1964; Paul Austin speech to American Federation of Advertisers, June 17, 1963, RWW Papers, Box 7.

"We used to be": Jack B. Weiner, "Why Things Go Better," *Dun's*, 1966, p. 76.

"management techniques": ibid., p. 73.

"bulging waistline": Bill Diehl, "Coca-Cola's Project Alpha," *Atlanta Magazine*, May 1963, p. 36.

"28 percent of the population": "Project Alpha," *New Yorker*, March 14, 1964.

278 **"Tom Law . . . argued"**: Tom Law interview.

"If God had wanted": Neal Gilliatt interview.

"elephantine labor": Diehl, pp. 36–40.

"How can just": Susan Whelan, "Increased Advertising," *Printer's Ink*, June 12, 1964, p. 33.

"Almost apologetically": "A Statement by the Coca-Cola Company Regarding . . . TAB," March 27, 1963. (Sibley Papers, Box 3)

"TaB was *not* Coca-Cola": The introduction of TaB caused a considerable uproar, particularly at the Thomas Company, which insisted that since the new drink was a dietetic form of Coca-Cola, the old contract applied. Without granting the validity of the claim, Paul Austin agreed to pay a "tribute" to the Thomas Company to assure its advertising cooperation. (RWW Papers, J. Paul Austin File, Box 5)

"a 10 percent share": John C. Maxwell, Jr., "Soft Drinks: Market on the Move," *Printer's Ink*, June 12, 1964, p. 27.

"Woolworth's lunch counter": Chafe, *Unfinished Journey*, pp. 165–171.

279 **"Guy Touchtone"**: Joe Jones interview; Charles Elliott interview.

"This nigger's coming": Branch, *Parting the Waters*, p. 528.

"languished in jail": Branch, p. 529. Ware was apparently never a field hand at Ichauway and was simply visiting on that fateful July Fourth. Nonetheless, it is surprising that Woodruff didn't intervene to help the wounded black man, since the incident began on his plantation. A case actually was brought against Gator Johnson for having beaten and shot Charlie Ware. In April of 1963, an all-white Columbus, Georgia, jury took less than ninety minutes to clear the sheriff. (Branch, p. 731; Joe Jones interview; Cal Bailey interview)

"three hundred acre farm": Joe Jones interview.

"We are appealing": Clarence Funnye, CORE program director to J. P. Austin, Sept. 5, 1963. (Sibley Papers, Box 3)

"first racial incident": "No. 6 Reports." (RWW Papers, Box 67)

280 **"blamed Harvey Russell"**: Six months after Harvey Russell became a Pepsi vice-president, the Ku Klux Klan circulated a picture of him and his wife, a light-skinned black, urging a white boycott of Pepsi because its "nigger vice-

president" was married to a white woman. Local Coca-Cola bottlers were rumored to have funded the brochures, but there was never any proof. (Harvey Russell reprints, Pepsi Collection)

"being a Southern institution": J. Paul Austin, "Memorandum to File," Sept. 10, 1963. (Sibley Papers, Box 3)

"syphilis was transmitted": Ambrose Pendergrast to Mark Pendergrast, Oct. 20, 1991.

"promised to hire blacks": "Ministers Declare War on Coca-Cola," *Atlanta Inquirer*, Aug. 10, 1963. (RWW Papers, Box 83)

"boycott loomed": In an audio clip from the early 1960s, Martin Luther King urged followers: "We're asking you tonight, to go out and tell your neighbors not to buy Coca-Cola." But as Coretta Scott King recalled, "We didn't have to go very far before the bottling companies . . . complied in upgrading black people and hiring new people . . . to our satisfaction." (*Cola Conquest*, Part 2.)

"business-orient, nonpolitical": Ivan Allen, Jr. *Mayor: Notes on the Sixties*, p. 30; Pomerantz, *Where Peachtree Meets*, p. 300–319.

"You are probably right": Ivan Allen interview.

"blacks comprised 11 percent": "Why Things Go Better at Coke," p. 76.

"full of blood": Charles Bottoms interview.

"resemblance to Martin Luther King": Bottoms interview.

"heart attack": Bottoms interview; Bob Oliver interview.

"desire for beauty": Chafe, p. 233.

"stable father figure": Ibid., p. 223.

"I'm sorry the vote": RWW to LBJ, Nov. 4, 1964. (RWW Papers, Box 52)

"Tell Bob to come see me": LBJ to RWW, undated. (RWW Papers, Box 52)

"there's Bob's boy!": Ovid Davis interview; for correspondence between Johnson and Woodruff, see RWW Papers, Boxes 52 and 53.

282 **"he favored the dinner"**: Allen, pp. 95–99; Pomerantz, *Where Peachtree Meets*, pp. 336–339

"Ray Charles, The Supremes": Freeman, **The Real Thing**, pp. 113, 117.

"white pop stars": "Historical List of Pop Performers, Coca-Cola USA," 9/19/91, CC Archives; Hoy, p. 130.

"negotiated with the Beatles": Murray Hillman interview. Coke adman Bill Backer encouraged the Beatles to buy their own Coca-Cola bottling franchise while they sang for Coke. (Backer, *Care and Feeding*, pp. 242–243)

"flower arranging": *Pause for Living*, Summer 1965. (CC Collection, Emory, Box 4)

"'typical' housewife": Freeman, pp. 117–118.

"Woodruff's real feelings about civil rights": Chafe, pp. 361–364; J. Edgar Hoover to RWW, Aug. 2, 1963. (RWW Papers, Box 40)

283 **"guards her man"**: Cameron Day, "With Coke Things Go Better & Better," *Sales Management*, April 16, 1965, p. 30.

"bottler convention skits": March 1964 *Refresher*.

"fussed and fretted": "Conversational Guidelines About Coca-Cola & Coke," 1965. (CC Archives) The vigilant trademark men were aghast when John Steinbeck published *The Wayward Bus*, which referred to "coke" and "Pepsi-Cola," asserting that "you can't tell them apart." When confronted with his error, Steinbeck sniffed: "Only the small need to capitalize." (Steinbeck, *Wayward Bus*, p. 182; Kahn, *Big Drink*, p. 122)

"per capita of 260": Ted Sanchagrin, "Battle of the Brands: Soft Drinks," *Printer's Ink*, April 9, 1965, p. 21.

"Duncan Foods": "Coca-Cola Goes Big for Food," *Printer's Ink*, Feb. 7, 1964, p. 10.

"**dynamic young Charles Duncan**": Wilson interview.

"**see to it the kiddies**": "Can Orange Juice Fill Pause That Refreshes?" *Business Week* July 25, 1964, p. 100.

"**introduced Chime**": Sanchagrin, p. 26.

"**It's a blizzard!**": Sugarman interview; Law interview; "Natural and Man-Made Blizzards," *Refresher*, March/April 1967, pp. 30–31.

"**joined Frito-Lay**": In fact, Paul Austin had wanted to purchase Atlanta-based Frito-Lay for Coca-Cola, but Robert Woodruff rejected the idea. ("Gulp, Munch and Merge," *Forbes*, July 15, 1968, p. 21; Louis & Yazijian, p. 118; Allen, *Secret Formula* p. 344).

"**gyrates with new products**": Cameron Day, pp. 28–30.

284 "**Growth is essential**": March 1964 *Refresher*.

"**vast, fickle, forgetful**": March 1965 *Refresher*, p. 7.

"***Walk-Up Hospitality***": Jan. 1965 *Refresher*.

"**joy in the fray**": March 1964 *Refresher*.

"**We'll fight 'em**": March 1965 *Refresher*.

"**Bulgar Cola**": "The Thaw That Refreshes," *Time*, Dec. 3, 1965, p. 98.

"**followed suit**": "Coke's Formula: Keep the Image Fresh," *Business Week*, April 25, 1970.

"**dispatched Boisfeuillet Jones**": Because of his Washington connections, Jones repeatedly served as a special Coke emissary. In the late seventies he flew to Hawaii to facilitate a top-secret project intended to produce a non-cocaine-bearing coca leaf. When word leaked to the Hawaiian press, however, the Company was forced to abandon the research. (Boisfeuillet Jones interview)

"**in the national interest**": W. Averell Harriman, "Memorandum for the Secretary," Jan. 3, 1967. (Harriman Papers, Box 499)

"**Farley approved**": Farley to Austin, Dec. 21, 1966. (RWW Papers, Russia File)

"**bottled in Moscow**": Austin to RWW, Jan. 5, 1967. (RWW Papers, Box 75)

285 "**help the Kremlin's pals**": *New York Daily News*, Jan. 23, 1967. (RWW Papers Russia File)

"**postponed the project**": Boisfeuillet Jones interview; Austin to Hughes Spalding, Dec. 29, 1966. (RWW Papers, Box 75)

"**refused . . . an Israeli bottler**": "Capping the Crisis," *Time*, April 22, 1966. For an overview of the crisis, see Feder, *U.S. Companies and the Arab Boycott of Israel*, pp. 38–44.

"**threw Coke coolers**": Dick Halpern interview.

"**Farley defended**": "Coca-Cola Moves to Franchise Israeli Bottler After Dispute," *Advertising Age*, April 25, 1966, p. 177.

"**No one bought**": "Restaurateur Bans Coca-Cola Products," *Advertising Age*, April 18, 1966, p. 54.

"**in the Arab countries**": "Two U.S. Firms Face Boycott by Arabs," *Washington Post*, July 19, 1966; "Arabs Vote to Bar Ford, Coca-Cola," *NYT*, Nov. 21, 1966.

"**the modern oasis**": Anthony Carthew, "Cold-Drink War: Kvass vs. Coke," *NYT Magazine*, July 21, 1964, p. 21.

"**Pepsi . . . avoiding Israel**": "Two U.S. Firms Face Boycott." Although never opening an Israeli franchise, Pepsi avoided a Zionist boycott. Inside sources suggest Pepsi's massive donations to Jewish organizations explain the mystery.

"**nothing is closer**": Mostafa Kamel to Ben Oehlert, Aug. 25, 1966; Oehlert to Austin, Aug. 22, 1966. (RWW Papers, Box 11)

"**Makinsky rushed around**": Makinsky material all from Makinsky to John Talley, July 9 and 11, 1966. (RWW Papers, Box 11)

286 **"not investing one cent"**: Lee Talley Rewrite, "Presentation—Egypt." (RWW Papers, Box 11)

"**boycott . . . finally commenced**": "Arabs Ban Coca-Cola for Keeps," *AJ*, Aug. 1, 1968.

"**They would have lost**": John Brinton interview. The Jewish market was so important to Coca-Cola that it was willing to reveal the secret formula to Atlanta Rabbi Tobias Geffen in 1935. If we are to believe Geffen's account, the Company made a slight modification to the formula to secure the kosher label. Later, the Company also unveiled its best-kept secret to Israeli Rabbi Moshe Landau, in charge of worldwide kosher certification. Company spokesmen deny revealing the precise formula while admitting that they have given rabbis detailed ingredient lists. (Tobias Geffen, "A *Teshuvah* Concerning Coca-Cola," in *Lev Tuviah*, pp. 117–121; Ralph Cipriano, "Passover, with Touch of Americana," *Philadelphia Inquirer*, April 17, 1992; "In the Know: Rabbi's Got a Secret," *JUF News*, Jan./Feb. 1992; "The Big Problem Is: If They Tell, That Wouldn't Be Kosher, Either," *WSJ*, April 29, 1992.)

"**Our Anita**": Jan. 1985 *Refresher*.

"**Danang and Qui-Nhon**": J. W. Jones to John R. Talley, Aug. 11, 1965. (RWW Papers, Box 83)

"**John Wayne movie**": "Coke Plays a Big Role in *The Green Berets*," *Refresher*, Nov./Dec. 1967, pp. 24–26.

"**seduce its way**": Tom Wolfe quoted in "The World Loves Coke—Official," *Financial Times*, Sept. 13, 1990; Japanese philosopher quoted in Dufty, *Sugar Blues*, p. 18.

287 "**unhesitating support**": LBJ to Farley, Aug. 23, 1965. (Farley Papers)

"**I am with you**": RWW to LBJ, June 1, 1965. (RWW Papers, Box 52)

"**turned to alcohol**": Elliott, *Mr. Anonymous*, p. 246; Martha Ellis interview; Charles Elliott interview; Joe Jones interview. Within a year, Woodruff found a surrogate wife in his niece, Martha Hodgson Ellis, whose husband died in the spring of 1969. Until the end of his life, Martha Ellis served as Woodruff's devoted companion. (Martha Ellis interview; RWW Papers, Ellis File, Box 26 Allen, *Secret Formula*, pp 352–354; Pomerantz, *Where Peachtree Meets*, pp. 379–380)

"**there together**": Davis interview; Califano, *The Triumph and Tragedy of Lyndon Johnson*, p. 273.

"**center of the universe**": Allen, *Mayor* p. 205; Ivan Allen interview.

"**dispatched the Windship**": Eugene Patterson interview.

"**in over a hundred . . . cities**": Chafe, p. 367. The same year, Coca-Cola began sponsoring the *Golden Legacy* series of comic books about famous blacks such as Harriet Tubman and Frederick Douglass. (Bateman & Schaeffer, "Black History and The Coca-Cola Company," *CC Collectors News*, Feb. 1987, pp. 4–8)

"**Someone's always makin'**": Freeman, p. 118.

288 "**elaborate take-off**": ibid., p. 153.

"**do your own thing**": ibid., p. 182–198. The subsequent discussion of "the real thing" lyric and ads owes much to John Paul Freeman's Ph.D thesis. See also Bill Backer, *The Care and Feeding of Ideas*. The "real thing" translated well in most places around the world, but not in Mexico, where it was initially translated as "*Esta es la verdad*," or "This is the truth." Mexicans didn't believe authorities when they talked about "truth," so Coke changed the slogan to "*La chispa de la vida*," or "The spark of life". (Oppenheimer, *Bordering on Chaos*, p. 269–270)

"**reflect Coke's awareness**": "Coke's Formula: Keep the Image Fresh."

289 "**eleven signs down there**": ibid., pp. 66–67.

"**'mod' look**": "Project Arden Gives Coke a New Look," CC press release, 1970, CC Archives; Ike Herbert interview.

"shorten her skirt": "Project Arden Gives Coke a New Look."
"flourish of trumpets": "Coke's New Image," *Time*, Oct. 10, 1969, p. 88.
"mushroomed to 1,500": Bottoms interview; *Refresher*, Nov./Dec. 1966, p. 16.
"drab and depressing": Mary Gresham interview.
"remarkably good shape": "Coke's Formula: Keep the Image Fresh."
290 "Coca-Cola's lack of vitamins": In 1966, when the FDA established standards of identity for cola drinks, the bureaucrats had actually made it *illegal* for Coca-Cola to contain vitamins or other nutrients, providing a convenient excuse for the Company.
"didn't like the taste": "The Pause That Nourishes," *Newsweek*, Feb. 19, 1968, pp. 73–74. Advertising for Saci emphasized that it made consumers "powerful" and healthy; macho Brazilian men interpreted this to mean that the drink would render them more virile. Consequently, Saci never reached many undernourished children. (Gilliatt interview; "Saci . . . A New Drink to Supplement Diets," *Refresher*, 1968; Michael McMullen interview)
"massive affliction": Ralph Nader, *Nutrition and Human Needs*, Hearings, Part 13A, July 15–18, 1969, pp. 3922–23.
"Austin rushed to testify": Paul Austin, *Nutrition and Human Needs*, Part 13C, July 28–30, 1969, pp. 4607–15.
291 "You'd drown before": "The Sweeteners Take Their Lumps," *Newsweek*, Nov. 3, 1969, pp. 73–74; "The Cyclamate Scare," *U.S. News and World Report*, Nov. 3, 1969, p. 7; "Cyclamates Sour Aftertaste," *Time*, Oct. 31, 1969, p. 79.
"obtained FDA approval": Richard F. Atwood, CC Attorney, to FDA, Nov. 21, 1969. (AF FDA Files)
"didn't hurt": Dec. 18, 1969, report, Dominick & Dominick. (RWW Papers, Box 20)
"Japanese consumers": *Coca-Cola (Japan)*, p. 56. Coca-Cola sales had doubled every year throughout the "Izanagi Boom" of unprecedented growth between 1966 and 1970. (*Coca-Cola [Japan]*, pp. 33, 42–43)
"force us to milk": Austin to RWW, June 16, 1968. (RWW Papers, Box 40)
"detailed memo . . . Woodruff": J. Paul Austin to RWW, Nov. 28, 1969. (RWW Papers, Box 8)

CHAPTER 17: BIG RED'S UNEASY SLUMBER

293 "Be careful": Cartha (Deke) DeLoach interview.
"Had we stood": Brian Dyson, "The Great Get-Together," June 12, 1979. (CC Archival Video)
"His next target": Austin to RWW, Sept. 19, 1969. (RWW Papers, Box 7)
"a bitch job": Bill Greeley, *Variety*, July 22, 1970, quoted in *Migrant and Seasonal Farmworker Powerlessness*, Hearings, July 24, 1970, Part 8-C, pp. 5867–69.
"$2 million worth": "Coke's NBC Buys," *Variety*, July 22, 1970, quoted in *Migrant and Seasonal*, p. 5870. Several months later, Coke transferred all of its ad dollars to CBS and ABC. (Louis & Yazijian, p. 144)
294 "major plan": "Coca-Cola Denies Link to Farm Ills," *NYT*, July 16, 1970, quoted in *Migrant and Seasonal*, pp. 5856–57.
"Nothing will change": *Migrant and Seasonal*, p. 5871.
"I would like to ask": Philip Moore, *Migrant and Seasonal*, Part 8-B, pp. 5502–7.
"National Alliance": The proposed Alliance for Agri-Business never materialized.

"Candor That Refreshes": "The Candor That Refreshes," *Time*, Aug. 10, 1970, p. 59.

294–5 "star interviewee": Willy Reynolds quoted in Phil Garner, "A New Life for Migrant Workers," AC Magazine Section, Jan. 23, 1972, p. 8f.

"most hostile hearing": Joseph Califano interview.

295 "Award for Business Citizenship": "Business Fights the Social Ills," *Business Week*, March 6, 1971, pp. 51, 61. Taking advantage of the publicity, Cesar Chavez's United Farm Workers (UFW) signed a contract for Coca-Cola migrant workers in January of 1972 without a hitch. Three years later, however, when the contract expired, the Company resisted its renewal. The UFW ultimately resorted to round-the-clock sit-ins at Coke's North Avenue head-quarters, and the Company capitulated. (Bob Hall, "Journey to the White House: The Story of Coca-Cola," *Southern Exposure*, Spring 1977, pp. 36–39; "The Power and the Story," *Forbes*, Dec. 15, 1975, p. 64)

"What's a sensitive man": Ralph Nader interview; Califano interview.

"40 percent of all": Louis & Yazijian, p. 143.

"protestors dumped mounds": "The Candor That Refreshes."

"bottle deposit bills": Coke and Pepsi banded together to fight the bottle deposit laws, but a few have been passed in states such as Michigan, Maine, Vermont, Iowa, Oregon, New York, California, and Connecticut, where each bottle carries a hefty nickel deposit. As a result, those states have succeeded in substantially reducing litter from cans and bottles, as well as providing a livelihood for scavengers. Coca-Cola officials argue that such laws turn them into garbage collectors; it would be more appropriate to recycle the cans and bottles along with other nondeposit products. Pat Franklin, head of the National Container Recycling Institute, called for *real* recycling—simply wash the bottle out and refill it, as in the old days. "It's as if we were a nation of dukes and earls," Franklin said, "pitching our brandy snifters at the hearth." (Louis & Yazijian, pp. 325–326; Franklin quote in *Masks of Deception*, p. 118)

"1971 survey": Louis & Yazijian, p. 143.

"If you love me": "Company Fights Litter with People-Involvement Pro-grams," *Refresher*, May 1970.

"Bend a little": "Austin of Coca-Cola: The Uses of Adrenaline," *Forbes*, May 15, 1971, p. 70.

"Harvard-run seminars": Bob Broadwater interview.

"leading company": "Aqua-Chem, Inc. Pollution Fighters," *Refresher*, Nov. 1972.

296 "$150 million in cash": "The Pause That . . .?" *Forbes*, Oct. 1, 1974, p. 55.

"It's fascinating": "Austin's Orphans," *Forbes*, July 15, 1970, p. 36.

"apocalyptic 1970 address": Paul Austin, "Environmental Renewal or Oblivion . . . Quo Vadis?" *Vital Speeches*, May 15, 1970, pp. 470–475.

297 "function simultaneously": Richard J. Walton, "The Carter Connection: Why Things Go Better with Coke," *The Nation*, March 31, 1979, p. 333.

"Big Name Bingo": "Things Go Wrong for Coca-Cola," *Consumer Reports*, Oct. 1970, pp. 578–579; "A Prize Snafu in the Coke Game," *Business Week*, July 18, 1970, p. 32; "Contests: $100 Misunderstanding," *Newsweek*, July 20, 1970, p. 70.

"misleading Hi-C advertisements": FTC Complaint and Proposed Order, April 14, 1971. (CC Legal Library)

"Company defended itself": "Answer of the Coca-Cola Company [to FTC Complaint about Hi-C commercials]," May 24, 1971. (CC Legal Library)

298 "commissioners agreed": FTC Docket No. 8839, Final Order, Oct. 5, 1973. (CC Legal Library)

"my humble feeling": Jim Jordan, *The Coca-Cola Company*, p. 85A.

"wired to . . . Nixon": Ovid Davis to RWW, Sept. 20, 1972. (RWW Papers, Case 65)

"it would seem": John Talley to RWW, Sept. 20, 1972. (RWW Papers, Box 83)

"Pepsi . . . ten-year exclusive": Stephen Aris, "How Pepsi Beat Coke to Moscow." Because of foreign exchange problems, Pepsi had to take its profits out of Russia by bartering for Stolichnaya vodka. ("Profiting from Pepskis," *Time*, Jan. 31, 1977, p. 39; Chafe, *Unfinished Journey*, pp. 402–403; Don Kendall interview)

"will be available": Aris, "How Pepsi."

"over twenty trips": Broadwater interview. In 1974, Coca-Cola and the Soviets signed a "long-range scientific and technical cooperative agreement" which, although it made splashy headlines, did not actually amount to more than a foot in the door. (Sam Hopkins, "Soviets, Coke Agree," AC, June 27, 1974; Paul Troop, "No Profit in Coke's Red Pact," AC, June 30, 1974)

299 **"Kent State"**: Chafe, pp. 405–406.

"clustered at love-ins": ibid., pp. 408–412.

"Bridge Over Troubled Waters": Nite, *Rock On Almanac*, pp. 231, 234.

"quirky collection": Freeman, *Real Thing*, pp. 205–218.

"leaned for comfort": ibid., pp. 218–229, 492–494.

"You've Got a Friend": Nite, p. 244.

"composing the music": Roger Greenaway and Roger Cook also contributed to the song "I'd Like to Buy the World a Coke."

"hilltop in Italy": The famed Hilltop commercial was very nearly a complete disaster. During the first take, 1,200 Italian orphans waited in steaming buses in the rain for their appearance. Eventually, they rioted, threw Coke bottles at the director, and began to rock a Coke truck, trying to turn it over. As Bill Backer recalled, it demonstrated the exact opposite of what was intended—"lack of harmony and understanding between diverse peoples." (Freeman, pp. 245–256, 495–496; Backer, *Care and Feeding*, p. 200–204.)

300 **"over 100,000 letters"**: Hoy, pp. 134–137.

"sure-fire form": "Have a Coke, World," *Newsweek*, Jan. 3, 1972, p. 47.

"advent of *Grease*": Nite, p. 252.

"Munsey wrote": Munsey, *Illustrated Guide*.

301 **"center of attention"**: Wilbur Kurtz, Jr., interview.

"Dottie West wrote": Billy Davis co-wrote Country Sunshine.

"raised on country sunshine": Freeman, pp. 513–514.

"handsome hometown boy": The boyfriend was a serendipitous last-minute addition to the "Country Sunshine" commercial. While shooting on location, the boy from the farm next door came over in an old truck just to watch the commercial. The director had a brainstorm and told the non-actor: "Look this is a beautiful girl, you've loved her all your life. Now we've got about two more takes before sundown . . . Jump out of that truck like you've been waiting for her all your life." It worked. (*Cola Conquest*, Part 1.)

"You in the striped shirt": "Take One!" *Refresher*, Oct. 1972, p. 2.

302 **"liberation movement"**: Bill Solms to RWW, Aug. 18, 1972. (RWW Papers, Box 79)

"Chilean Coca-Cola": John Talley to RWW, July 14, 1972, (RWW Papers, Box 83); W. O. Solms to RWW, Aug. 18, 1972. (RWW Papers, Box 79)

"Argentinean Coke officials": Coke paid a million dollars to free the first Argentinean manager, but when others were taken, they dispatched Mitch Werbell, the self-styled "Wizard of Whispering Death," to Argentina, where the Georgia anti-Communist publicly informed the kidnappers, "We will kill you. We'll go after your wife. We'll kill her." His threats having no noticeable effect, he departed. The affair ended with a dramatic shoot-out, as local police rescued the final Coke man from a dugout cell under the kidnappers' home. ("How Coke Runs a Foreign Empire," *Business Week*, Aug. 25, 1973, p. 41; Louis & Yazijian, p. 175; Bill Solms interview; Leo Conroy interview)

"It may be serious": "Italy: Let Them Drink Pepsi," *Newsweek*, Oct. 18, 1971, p. 98.

"wagging the dog": Ian Wilson interview.

"commerciogenic malnutrition": Barnet & Müller, *Global Reach*, p. 184; Louis & Yazijian, p. 182. In 1976, the Company responded to criticism by hiring an outside investigator, whose research revealed $600,000 in "questionable foreign payments." (Wilson interview; Frederick Allen & Sallye Salter, "Coca-Cola Probing Foreign Payments," AC, Oct. 9, 1976; Sam Hopkins, "Coke Admits to $600,000 in Payments," AC, Dec. 7, 1976)

"Dufty blamed": The *Refresher* countered Dufty's accusations with a spirited defense of sugar. "According to Hindu legend," the article began, "sugar cane was part of a concept of earthly paradise and a heavenly gift to mortals." (Ellis Hughes, "Sugar: Nature's High Performance Food . . . History's White Gold," *Refresher*, Nov. 1, 1977, p. 10)

302–3 **"The sugar pushers"**: Dufty, *Sugar Blues*, p. 25.

303 **"profiled Carol Hinkey"**: "Carol Hinkey, Tech Rep," *Refresher*, April 1973, pp. 10–11. The Company's residual sexism wasn't too hard to locate. A 1972 *Refresher* article on Company women received the headline "Girls Girls Girls Girls"—including an older woman who had joined the Company in 1963 after fifteen years with a trucking firm. (*Refresher*, July 1972, pp. 4–6)

"considerable progress": "Social Audit—Seeking Facts for Action," *Refresher*, July 1973, pp. 4–5; "The Way to Work," *Refresher*, July 1973, pp. 6–8.

"all-women's seminar": Mary Gresham interview.

"Diane McKaig": "Consumerism," *Refresher*, July 1973, pp. 14–16, 29–30.

"Duncan's resignation": Wilson interview; Virginia Moulder interview; Broadwater interview; Charles Duncan interview. Duncan denies that his resignation was forced.

"like two cats": Wilson interview.

304 **"50,000 or fewer"**: Crawford Johnson testimony, *Exclusive Territorial Allocation Legislation*, pp. 16, 29.

"Thomas bargaining position": Walter "Bud" Randolph interview for this entire section.

305 **"null and void"**: *Exclusive Territorial Allocation Legislation*, Part 2 (Appendix), p. 180 (Luke Smith to Bottlers, June 23, 1972); William Pope Taft testimony, p. 675.

"Through the grapevine": J. Guy Beatty, Jr., to Trustees of the Benwood Foundation, Sept. 12, 1974, Memorandum, property of Bondurant, Mixson & Elmore, Atlanta.

"I'll have your balls": Clisby Clark interview.

"Vietnam War": Chafe, p. 430.

"portrayed the Liberty Bell": Freeman, pp. 525–529.

306 **"It's up to . . . us"**: Don Keough, quoted in Freeman, p. 372.

"Nixon . . . resignation": Freeman, p. 375.

"Broadway show": "Why Would Coke 'Put on a Show'?" AC, Sept. 25, 1975, p. 7-A.

"felt chest pains": Broadwater interview; Wilson interview.

"fled his native land": In the 1940s, when Roberto Goizueta was an upper-class Cuban teenager attending the prestigious Colegio de Belen, he probably looked up to Fidel Castro, four years ahead of him at the same school. Castro was an exceptional athlete and brilliant, if erratic, scholar, in contrast to Goizueta, who was always a serious, studious, quiet boy. The two Cubans were both destined to find their place in history as virtual monarchs of their respective realms. Goizueta's kingdom—the worldwide Coca-Cola empire—was certainly the more impressive. Yet in a way, he owed it all to Castro for nationalizing American companies. (Greising, *I'd Like the World to Buy a Coke*, pp. 8–22.)

307 **"Roberto is now"**: Joe Jones to RWW, Feb. 7, 1974. (RWW Papers, Box 78)
"I was afraid": Broadwater interview. The normal cassia importation process is, of course, legal, but Broadwater knew that individuals were forbidden to bring any plant material into the United States. He could picture the scene: "Oh, so you're a Coca-Cola official, and this is part of the secret formula?"
"Shillinglaw recovered": Broadwater interview.
"administrative mishandling": "Japan: An Old Coke Hand Tries to Rev Up Profits," *Business Week*, March 1, 1976, p. 32. When Coca-Cola was accused of "donating" more than $300,000 to Japanese retail outlets in return for exclusive contracts, forcing competing firms into bankruptcy, Hal Roberts refused to apologize or acknowledge a problem. ("Japan: Things Go Bitter," *Newsweek*, Oct. 13, 1969, p. 86)
"complex mind": Wilson interview.
"a few of them exploded": In Japan, housewives shopped late each afternoon for the evening meal, bringing home a sun-warmed family-sized Coke bottle—typically stacked outside shops on the street to conserve space—and putting it into the freezer for a quick chill. Not surprisingly, some of the bottles exploded at eye level. (Michael McMullen interview)
"wasn't about to say": Broadwater interview.
"protective plastic": *Coca-Cola (Japan)*, p. 57.
"snowstorm in the bottle": Bill Van Loan interview.
"Tokyo Bay purple": Wilson interview; Broadwater interview; Morton Hodgson interview; Claus Halle interview.

308 **"I'm in big trouble"**: Hodgson interview. The rest of the Japanese story comes from this interview.
"American . . . youth joyously imbibing": *Coca-Cola (Japan)*, pp. 62–67. The Japanese ads were influential in ways that astonished Coke men. "Coca-Cola became a kind of standard for how Japanese youth should act," one veteran recalls. "If we put commercials on the air showing kids wearing Madras shirts, the next day the stores swarmed with teens looking for Madras shirts." (McMullen interview)
"commercial spoof": Ron Sugarman interview.
"late in 1975": Broadwater interview.
"multimillion-dollar tower": "Company Reveals Plans for Expanding Headquarters Complex in Atlanta," *Refresher* No. 2, 1975, p. 27.

309 **"reorganized the company"**: Sam Hopkins, "Coca-Cola Splits into Three Groups," *AC*, Sept. 24, 1976.
"ailing Canadian business": Woodruff crony Eugene Kelly refused to delegate authority or to loosen the purse strings in his later years. In failing health, Kelly shot himself, and the following manager failed to turn the business around, so Wilson, brought from Africa in 1973, consolidated plants and bottlers, modernizing the facilities. (Wilson interview)
"man from Plains would win": Glad, *Jimmy Carter: In Search of the White House*, p. 157.
"tea with the Queen": Richard J. Walton, "The Carter Connection," *The Nation*, March 31, 1979, p. 333.
"Austin laughed": Wilson interview.
"Coca-Cola men squired him": Meyer, *James Earl Carter*, p. 192.
"prestigious Trilateral": The Trilateral Commission, a think tank of Americans, Western Europeans, and Japanese initiated at the behest of David

Rockefeller in 1972, was planned as "a marriage of the intellectual and the influential," as one journalist put it. (Meyer, *James Earl Carter*, pp. 192–193; Mazlish & Diamond, *Jimmy Carter*, pp. 238–239)

"built-in State Department": Louis & Yazijian, p. 285; "Carter's Chum From Coke," *Newsweek*, Feb. 7, 1977, p. 58.

310 "I will be a friend": Lasky, *Jimmy Carter: The Man and the Myth*, p. 265.

"Schwartz explained": Meyer, p. 153.

"behaved as an outsider": Chafe, p. 452–453.

"You know, ma'am": "Carter's Chum from Coke," p. 58.

"National Gallery": Richard J. Walton, p. 336.

"Anderson pointed out": Jack Anderson, "Coke Has Things Its Way Under Carter," *AC*, Sept. 13, 1979.

311 "call in a few chits": ibid., Richard J. Walton, p. 337; Louis & Yazijian, pp. 308–313.

"meetings with Fidel Castro": DeWitt Rogers and Maurice Fliess, "Secret Mission: Coke's Austin, Castro Meet," *AC*, June 10, 1977.

"Havana cigars": Woodruff to Castro, June 1977. (RWW Papers, Castro File)

"nefarious scheme": William Safire, "Coke's Connection with Carter Paying Off," *AC*, July 8, 1977. It isn't surprising that Safire, a former Nixon speech-writer, attacked the Carter/Coke connection. (Louis & Yazijian, p. 93)

"Portuguese permission": Richard J. Walton, p. 336; "Once-Banned Coca-Cola to Sell in Portugal in '77," *AC*, Dec. 30, 1976.

"reason for our conversation": "Carter's Chum," p. 57. To secure permission to bottle Egyptian Coke again, the Company promised to convert 15,000 acres of desert into orange groves. The project foundered, however, when the Egyptian Air Force, resentful of the Agriculture Department's intrusion, commenced bombing practice on adjacent property, and terrified laborers fled. Sadat's intervention failed—an early warning signal of the military discontent that resulted in his assassination in 1981. Coca-Cola lost $10 million on the project, but the back of the Arab Boycott had been broken. (Sam Ayoub interview)

"exception of India": In 1977, the nationalistic Indian government demanded that *all* of the soft drink must be manufactured inside India—which meant turning over the secret formula. Coke balked, and the Company reluctantly withdrew, abandoning twenty-two bottling plants. ("India May Swallow Coke," *Time*, Aug. 22, 1977, p. 44; "Sweet Stuff," *Nation*, Sept. 17, 1977, pp. 228–229; Edward A. Gargan, "A Revolution Transforms India: Socialism's Out, Free Market In," *NYT*, March 29, 1992, p. 1)

"Eastern Bloc sports festival": "Coca-Cola and Fanta Orange Go on Sale in the Soviet Union," July 25, 1979, Coca-Cola Press Release. (CC Archives)

"Moscow Olympics": Bob Broadwater interview; "Things Go Better," *AC*, May 20, 1978; DeWitt Rogers, "Coke Maneuvering for Growth in Russia," *AC*, May 28, 1978.

"hammered out an arrangement": Wilson interview; "Coke Goes to China," *Newsweek*, Jan. 1, 1979, p. 42.

"the opiate of the running": Mao Tse-tung quoted in Arthur Hoppe, "Battle of the Supercolas," AC, Dec. 28, 1978.

312 "scooping Coke": "Pepsico, Inc." *International Directory of Company Histories*, vol. 1, p. 278.

"Broadway production . . . folded": Sam Hopkins, "Coke Fizz-le: Broadway Musical Lays an Egg," AC, May 7, 1976.

"hopeless mission": Dick Alven interview with Scott Ellsworth, Pepsi Collection; Peter H. Reader, "Pepsi Takes Coke Head-On in Television Taste Tests," *Broadcasting*, Feb. 20, 1978, p. 14.

"drastic measures": Sculley, *Odyssey*, pp. 42–44.

"little bitty sips": Louis & Yazijian, p. 352; *Cola Conquest*, Part 2.

"did prefer Pepsi": Dick Alven interview, Pepsi Collection.

"Challenge commercials were airing": "Pepsi Pushes Coke in Soft-Drink Fray," AC, July 29, 1980, p. 3-C.

313 **"just over $24 million"**: Elliot Wendt, "Pepsi Reaches Total Ad Parity with Coke," *Beverage World*, Aug. 1978, p. 18.

"Nielsen market figures": While Nielsen tracks soft drink sales in super-markets, it does not research fountain or vending machine usage.

"strange numbers": "Pepsi Takes on the Champ," *Business Week*, June 12, 1978, p. 90.

"saccharin ban": The Calorie Control Council, a pro-saccharin lobbying organization, maintained an Atlanta address near Coke, its largest single contributor. The Company need not have worried; the moratorium on a saccharin ban has been routinely extended ever since, in large part because of prudent nurturance of politicians. Coke also supports two other corporate lobbying fronts: the American Council on Health and Science and Keep America Beautiful, Inc. (Louis & Yazijian, pp. 141, 270; Megalli & Friedman, *Masks of Deception*, pp. 23–28, 45–49, 116–123; Earl T. Leonard, Jr., to Roberto Goizueta, March 9, 1981, RWW Papers, Case 246)

"gloomy future": "The Graying of the Soft-Drink Industry," *Business Week*, May 23, 1977, pp. 68–72.

"welter of new beverages": "Brand Report 44: Soft Drinks," *Marketing and Media Decisions*, Aug. 1979, p. 140.

"John Denver country": "Brand Report 44," p. 145.

"Coke quickly responded": In his landmark study, *New and Improved: The Story of Mass Marketing in America*, Richard S. Tedlow discusses the rise of Coke and Pepsi in addition to three other case studies. He identifies three "phases" of marketing, culminating in market segmentation targeting specific demographic groups. To a large extent, however, brand Coca-Cola itself has resisted segmentation, since it still appeals to a broad range of consumers. (Tedlow, pp. 4–9, 22–111)

"insisted on his shrimp farming": Elizabeth Cronin, "But Is It the Real Thing?" *Forbes*, Sept. 18, 1978.

314 **"Baptist stockholders"**: Charles Bottoms interview.

"Pepsi . . . much more diversified": "The New Sparkle in Soft-Drink Stocks, *Financial World*, Oct. 15, 1975, p. 14; "Pepsi Takes on the Champ," *Business Week*, June 12, 1978, p. 88.

"Khomeini handed over": Claus Halle interview.

"Calero continued bottling": "Adolfo Calero," *Current Biography*, 1987, pp. 77–78.

"brief, untroubled": Kahn, *Big Drink*, p. 144.

"Sister Gartland lamented": Frundt, *Refreshing Pauses: Coca-Cola and Human Rights in Guatemala*, pp. 72, 84; Frundt to Mark Pendergrast, Jan. 31, 1992.

"introduced Israel Marquez": Frundt, pp. 84–86; "Coke and the Death Squads: Guatemala, The Next Nicaragua?" *Nation*, Aug. 25, 1979, pp. 140–141.

315 **"Trotter . . . resorted . . . bribes"**: From here until Austin bangs his gavel, Frundt, pp. 4–27, 48, 61–71, 82, 85. See also Jonathan Fried, "In Guatemala, Things Go Worse With Coke," *Multinational Monitor*, April 1984, p. 8; "Silencing Workers: Guatemalan Army Decimates Unions," *Multinational Monitor*, Oct. 1986, pp. 8–9, Alan Riding, "Coca-Cola Caught in Latin Storm," AJ/C, June 8, 1980, p. 35–A.

"killings . . . proliferated": One of Trotter's managers was wounded and his bodyguard killed in apparent reprisal. Subsequently, the police arrested a union member's sixteen-year-old daughter, taking her to the adult prison, where she was beaten, repeatedly raped, and permanently blinded when a plastic bag full of pesticide was placed over her head. (Frundt, p. 97)

316 **"never even entered"**: Leo Conroy interview.

"I value my life!": Conroy quoted in Frundt, p. 88.

"We have revulsion": Keough quoted in Frundt, p. 88.

"allegations . . . import taxes": Jeff Nesmith, "Coke Caught in the Middle of a Bloody Fight in Guatemala," AC, June 3, 1979, p. 6-C; Frundt, p. 50.

"Company yearned": Anonymous Company source.

"Congressman Donald Pease": Frundt, p. 98.

317 **"just opened a museum"**: Schmidt, *The Schmidt Museum Collection of Coca-Cola Memorabilia*, pp. 7–9.

"it just boiled up": Bill Schmidt interview.

"split men whose forebears": ibid.

"Why don't you get": Brian Dyson interview.

"Pepsi utterly dominated": In Venezuela, the powerful Cisneros family bottled Pepsi.

"two huge outfits": Bill Schmidt interview; Dyson interview; Bottoms interview; Bud Randolph interview; Oliver, p. 30; Louis & Yazijian, p. 345.

318 **"decade's disasters"**: Dyson Speech, "The Great Get-Together," June 12, 1979, from Video, CC Company.

"Coke causes the smile": Bill Van Loan Speech, "Great Get-Together."

319 **"demanding . . . release"**: Van Loan interview. When Roger Mosconi, the ad's creative co-director (with Penny Hawkey) first presented the storyboard, the Company wanted to use white quarterback Terry Bradshaw. Mosconi insisted on Joe Greene, who had earned his "mean" nickname not only for ferocious on-field action, but for assaulting officials and hecklers. The shooting required 128 retakes due to lighting problems and the boy's muffed lines. One executive complained, "Where do you get off having a white boy kowtow to a nigger?" Before the Great Get-Together, rumors flew through the ad industry that McCann was about to lose the Coke account to Kenyon & Eckhart. The bottlers' enthusiastic reaction to the Mean Joe Greene ad saved the account and Mosconi's career. (Roger Mosconi interview; Blount, *About Three Bricks*, pp. 41, 91, 180, 299, 322–325)

"made-for-TV movie": Hoy, p. 138.

"playing Othello": Tom Mattingly, "Mean Joe Greene and Coke!" *Refresher* No. 1, 1980, pp. 2–4; Richard Trubo, "Pepsi-Cola, Coca-Cola: The Cola Rivalry," *Buffalo News Magazine*, Feb. 8, 1981; John Bergin interview. The McCann men quickly replicated the Mean Joe commercial around the world, using a soccer player for Spanish, Brazilian, Argentine, and Thai ads. In Thailand, for instance, it was Mean Joe Niwat who threw the kid his sweaty jersey. (Sugarman interview)

"retiring for personal reasons": "J. Lucian Smith Retires as President," *Refresher* No. 3, 1979, p. 27.

"Greene threw up": Mosconi interview; Scott Fowler, "Hey Kid! Catch!" *Miami Herald*, Feb. 16, 1992.

320 **"Paul wants you out"**: Virginia Moulder interview.

"refusing to allow the video": Dick Halpern interview; Roy Stout interview.

"forgot why he was there": Moulder interview; Wilson interview.

"named six men": The six men were Roberto Goizueta, Claus Halle, Ike Herbert, Don Keough, Al Killeen, and Ian Wilson. Killeen, who had followed Wilson up the chain through South Africa, ran the Wine Spectrum. Ike Herbert, a soft-spoken advertising man, had switched to Coca-Cola from the McCann agency. Don Keough had come to the Company along with Duncan Foods. Later, financial man John Collings was added to the list, resulting in references to the "Seven Dwarves."

"privately told him": Wilson interview.

"thinking of retirement": "Succession at Coke Is a Horse Race Again," *Business Week*, Sept. 10, 1979, pp. 33–34.

"raised the hackles": Bottoms interview.

"D-plus or F": John Huey & John Koten, "Former Coke Chairman Reasserts His Power, Shaking Up the Troops," *WSJ*, June 10, 1980.

"crumbled to make way": Stephen Hesse, "Park Plan Is Lights Out for Historic Coke Sign," AC, July 20, 1979.

320–1 **"crusaded against homosexuals"**: "Anita Bryant's Crusade," *Newsweek*, April 11, 1977, pp. 39–40; "Battle Over Gay Rights," *Newsweek*, June 6, 1977, pp. 16–22; "Gay Rights Showdown in Miami," *Time*, June 13, 1977, p. 20; "The Gaycott Turns Ugly," *Time*, Nov. 21, 1977, p. 33.

321 **"was worth less"**: "KO Stock," CC Co.

"unimpressive 5.4%": Rob Chambers, "After the Austin Era, Coke's Coming Home," AC, 1981, in Box 5, CC Collection, Emory.

"hostage crisis": Salinger, *America Held Hostage*.

"Get out of my office!": Sam Ayoub interview.

"near death from pneumonia": Edith Honeycutt interview.

PART V: THE CORPORATE ERA (1980–1999)

325 **"What have you done?"**: Quotes and scenario from Oliver, *The Real Coke*, p. 153, and Jesse Meyers interview with Roberto Goizueta, *Beverage Digest*, Sept. 30, 1988, p. 5.

CHAPTER 18: ROBERTO GOIZUETA'S BOTTOM LINE

327 **"Two vultures"**: Roberto Goizueta, quoted in "Look Beyond Chance, Coca-Cola Chief Urges," *Food Business*, May 6, 1991.

"I am speaking for": C. Dianne Smith to J. Paul Austin, May 6, 1980, courtesy Dianne Smith Nau; Nau interview.

"Grumman Aircraft": Charles Bottoms interview.

"$100 million debt": John Huey & John Koten, "Former Coke Chairman Reasserts His Power, Shaking Up the Troops," *WSJ*, June 10, 1980.

328 **"now summoned"**: The exact timing of events during the spring of 1980 is difficult to pin down, since there is no documentation other than memory. In interviews, some Coca-Cola men placed Woodruff's ultimatum to Austin in April rather than May. The scenario in the text follows the logic of events more closely, however.

"concerned executives . . . role": Exactly who got to Woodruff may never be known. Around this time, Bob Broadwater recalls running into Roberto Goizueta, who told him, "We almost had a real disaster. We almost had Ian Wilson as the next CEO." Goizueta denies speaking directly to Woodruff about Wilson. Luke Smith secretly met with Woodruff in the afternoons and may have poisoned him against Wilson. Whatever the truth, there is no doubt that Goizueta played a "grand game of corporate chess," as one anonymous source commented. (Bob Broadwater interview; Ian Wilson interview; Sam Ayoub interview; Morton Hodgson interview; Claus Halle interview)

"read from the phone book": Wilson interview.

"It seemed strange": "Vying Among the Vice Squad," p. 34.

"**Insiders**": Many commentators later asserted that Goizueta's 1979 earnings of $488,000 compared to Keough's $361,000 clearly indicated their relative standing. (CC 1979 annual report)

"**attention of his grandfather**": Goizueta interview with Jesse Meyers, *BD*, Sept. 30, 1988.

"**pigeons in the park**": "Vying Among the Vice Squad," *Fortune*, June 1, 1981, p. 34.

329 "**knew little English**": Greising, *I'd Like the World to Buy a Coke*, p. 5, 11.

"**My professor said**": Goizueta, "Commencement Address," *Cheshire Academy Quarterly*, July 1982, p. 4.

"**valedictory address**": Goizueta interview; "Coke's Man on the Spot," *Business Week*, July 29, 1985, p. 57.

"**every grain of sand**": "Coke's Man on the Spot," p. 58.

"**quality of one's compromises**": Gene Griessman, "Giant Steps: An Interview with Roberto Goizueta," *Atlanta Magazine*, Nov. 1982, p. 82.

"**pretty good bet**": Goizueta, "Commencement Address," p. 5.

"**emotions under . . . control**": One hint of how Goizueta dealt with issues beyond his control was his response to a question about whether he missed Cuba. "I have drawn kind of a curtain in that regard." Unlike Austin, Goizueta made no overtures to Castro, whom he regarded as a usurper and thief, since Goizueta's grandfather's house now served as headquarters for the Cuban National Academy of Science. For one thing, however, Goizueta was grateful to Castro. If it had not been for the revolutionary leader, Goizueta would probably have risen to direct Cuban Coke affairs, but he would never have become the company's CEO. ("Roberto's World," *Southpoint Magazine*, Oct. 1989, p. 96; Goizueta interview)

"**piece of crystal**": "Coke's Man on the Spot," p. 59.

"**country music**": Goizueta to Pendergrast, June 24, 1991.

"**teacher in a business school**": Neil Shister, "The Man Who Changed Coke," *Atlanta*, June 1986, p. 134.

"**I'm very persistent**": ibid., p. 86.

"**uneasy year**": There was, in fact, one final drama in the struggle for power. In early July 1980, Robert Woodruff asked Joe Jones to contact the ousted Luke Smith in London to offer him the board chairmanship without being the CEO. At the same time, rumors flew that Charles Duncan, Jr., was being brought back as both chair *and* CEO. Goizueta supposedly confronted Woodruff, threatening to resign unless he were made both chairman and CEO, with Keough as his president. Woodruff relented, and Joe Jones called Smith to withdraw the offer. A broken man, Luke Smith died of a heart attack a few weeks later. Charles Duncan *was* summoned, but only as a board member. (Anonymous sources; Virginia Moulder interview; July 20, 1980, CC memo on Luke Smith's death, RWW Papers, Box 79)

330 "**Chief Operating Officer**": In February of 1980, before Goizueta had been named as president, he and Keough made a pact that if either were chosen as head man, the other would assume a key secondary position. By that time, Keough must have realized that Goizueta had a far better chance than anyone had recognized. Only months earlier, Keough had privately told Ian Wilson, "I'll never work for the Cuban. What about you?" (Note: Keough denies the quote, attributed to him by Wilson.) Once Keough took the supporting position, however, his public stance was impeccable. "I have learned," he once said, "that when the boss speaks, the arguing time is over. And I have survived almost forty years." An anonymous insider, however, said that Keough maintained a "simmering rage" under his well-mannered exterior. (Jesse Meyers, "A Talk with Roberto Goizueta," *BD*, Sept. 30, 1988, p. 3;

Wilson interview; Don Keough deposition, July 30, 1987, Diet Coke Case, pp. 358, 365)

"Ed McMahon of Coca-Cola": Keough looks and sounds a bit like McMahon—not altogether surprising, since Keough and Johnny Carson befriended one another as fellow television personalities in Omaha. (John Huey, "Secrets of Great Second Bananas," *Fortune*, May 6, 1991, p. 68)

"There was never any doubt": "Vying Among the Vice Squad," p. 34.

"twisting in the wind": Wilson interview; Rob Chambers, "Coke Exec Listed in FBI Sting," *AJ*, June 10, 1980.

"he was framed": Wilson interview.

"appropriated his locker": ibid.

"questions and questions": Sam Ayoub interview.

331 **"liquidating itself"**: "He Put the Kick Back into Coke," *Fortune*, Oct. 26, 1987, pp. 48, 50.

"high-fructose corn syrup": Initially, Coca-Cola was sweetened with 50 percent HFCS, 50 percent cane sugar. Beginning in November of 1984, 100 percent HFCS sweetened U.S. Coke, although cane and beet sugar remained in the formula outside of America.

"20 percent savings": "Coke Strikes Back," *Fortune*, June 1, 1981, p. 34.

"Remember when we": Goizueta interview. The colas' sweetener switch caused huge economic ripples. Between 1980 and 1988, the United States cut its cane sugar imports from 3.8 million to about 1 million tons. (Katherine Isaac, "Tate & Lyle: The Grandaddy of Sugar," *Multinational Monitor*, April 1989, p. 22)

"Bondurant had decimated": Vincent Coppola & Jeffry Scott, "The Equalizer," *Atlanta Magazine*, June 1989, pp. 65–87. The following material on Bondurant comes from this article.

"lost your damn mind!": ibid., p. 86.

332 **"gory picture"**: Frundt, *Refreshing Pauses: Coca-Cola and Human Rights in Guatemala*, p. 107.

"clattered to a halt": *Soft Drink, Hard Labour*, p. 18.

"Ted Circuit assured": For a detailed account of this period in Guatemala, see Frundt, pp. 107–172.

"four more . . . killed": Alan Riding, "Coca-Cola Caught in Latin Storm," *AJ/C*, June 8, 1980.

"Chispa de la Muerte": Information from here to footnote about four years later from *Soft Drink, Hard Labour*, pp. 19–35. For more information on the 1984 plant occupation, see also: Jonathan Fried, "In Guatemala, Things Go Worse With Coke," *Multinational Monitor*, April 1984, pp. 8–10; "We Will Neither Go Nor Be Driven Out," 1984 booklet, IUF, Geneva.

333 **"negotiating situation"**: "Did Coca-Cola 'Negotiate' with International Labor?" *Business Week*, Nov. 24, 1980, p. 133.

"passed both houses": "Soft Drink Interbrand Competition Act," Public Law 96–308, *Weekly Compilation of Presidential Documents*, vol. 16, No. 28, July 10, 1980.

"repeatedly vowed": "Coke Strikes Back," p. 35.

"stop this madness": Sculley, *Odyssey*, p. 48. John Sculley fulfilled the worst Pepsi nightmare when he took the taste test himself, choosing Coke as the better-tasting drink. Fortunately, the media never got wind of it, and he avoided any such future gaffs. (Sculley, p. 49)

"go out and kill you": ibid., pp. 49–51.

"Project David": Oliver, *Real Coke*, pp. 51–52; Roy Stout interview.

334 **"young Mexican"**: "Corporate Culture," p. 8; Don Kendall interview; *Business Week*, Oct. 27, 1980, p. 154; Enrico, *The Other Guy Blinked*.

"**Bottler Productivity Study**": Ramsey, *Corporate Warriors*, p. 73.

"**Over the last few years**": Sergio Zyman to Brian Dyson, Feb. 14, 1980, Plaintiff's Exhibit 16; Diet Coke Case.

"**cryptic April telegram**": Ramsey, p. 66; Oliver, *Real Coke*, p. 89.

"**The TaB Company**": Goizueta interview.

335 "**Goizueta was elected**": "Austin, Goizueta Moves Announced," *Refresher* III, 1980, p. 26.

"**looked like a movie star**": ibid.

"**the go-ahead**": Zyman to Dyson, Aug. 16, 1980, Plaintiff's Exhibit 25, Diet Coke Case.

"**Austin . . . finally diagnosed**": Joseph Califano interview; Neal Gilliatt interview.

"**accounting for 30 percent**": "After the Austin Era, Coke's Coming Home," AC, 1981, undated clipping, CC Collection Box 5, Emory; "Coca-Cola Elects Austin President," *NY Herald Tribune*, May 9, 1962.

"**earned $422 million**": 1980 Coca-Cola Annual Report.

"**Paul was too big**": Ian Wilson interview. After leaving Coke, Wilson moved to California to start another business venture, but Pepsi hired him in 1994 to go back to South Africa, where he failed to boost Pepsi's lagging market share. ("Pepsi Fights Back with Ex-Coke Exec," *AJC*, Oct. 2, 1994, p. P1.)

"**vision was too broad**": Consequently, Austin found an outlet as chairman of the board of the Rand Corporation, the California think tank, from 1972 to 1981 (Tom Bennett, "J. Paul Austin, former head of Coca-Cola, dies at age 70," AC, Dec. 17, 1985)

"**something had to be done**": Ayoub interview; Oliver, *Real Coke*, pp. 58–59.

336 "**no sacred cows**": Oliver, *Real Coke*, pp. 60–62.

"**our consumer image**": "Strategy for the 1980s: The Coca-Cola Company," March 1981, CC Company.

"**ruthlessly weeded**": Ayoub interview.

"**blew . . . to bits**": Richard Trubo, "Pepsi-Cola, Coca-Cola: The Cola Rivalry," *The Buffalo News Magazine*, Feb. 8, 1981, p. 5; "We Can't Let Pepsi Outflesh Us!" *Forbes*, Nov. 27, 1989, p. 272. In 1981, a Coca-Cola man in Thailand took his aggressive training too literally. Enraged when he found a Pepsi man tacking up posters in his territory, he pulled his truck alongside his rival and killed him with a shotgun blast. Back at Atlanta headquarters, the macho attitude sometimes translated into illicit office sex, according to several anonymous sources. When a Coke veteran discovered that a conference table had been the site of one such passionate session, he wisecracked, "Well, that's probably the best use that table has ever served." ("Bloody Bottlers," *Time*, Aug. 3, 1981, p. 53)

"**placate disaffected bottlers**": "Coke's New Program to Placate Bottlers," *Business Week*, Oct. 12, 1981, p. 48.

"**rainfall in Japan**": 1980 CC Annual Report.

337 "**pipsqueaks**": Ayoub interview.

"**30 percent equity position**": "The Risk That Wasn't," *Journey*, June 1991, pp. 6–8.

"**Wearing Army fatigues**": Neville Isdell interview.

"**overtaken Pepsi**": 1983 CC Annual Report.

"**command 71 percent**": "The Risk That Wasn't," p. 7.

338 "**24 percent**": Thomas Oliver, "Black Ministers Ignore Call for Attack on Coke," *AJ/C*, July 18, 1981; Bob Ingle, "Coca-Cola's Responsibility to Blacks," *AC*, July 24, 1981.

"**withdrawal of enthusiasm**": Oliver, "Black Ministers."

"**Fooling no one**": Oliver, "Coke and PUSH Make Covenant for $34 Million," *AC*, Aug. 11, 1981.

"show of spinelessness": Lewis Grizzard, "'Push' Against Coke Too Far," *AC*, Aug. 1981. (CC Collection, Box 12, Emory)

"*Barron's* . . . chided": Hal Gulliver, "On Coca-Cola and Jesse Jackson," *AC*, Sept. 8, 1981.

"blackmail pressures": Tennessee businessman to RWW, Aug 19, 1981; Keough reply, Aug. 25, 1981. (RWW Papers, Box 67)

"he had made a mistake": "Coke Chief Admits Error on Black Covenant," *Florida Times-Union*, 1981. (CC Collecton, Box 12, Emory)

339 "limp-wristed": John Bergin interview. In 1974, when Bergin was unaccountably passed over as creative director at BBDO, he quit, moving to SSC&B, another New York agency. In September of 1979, Interpublic bought SSC&B/Lintas, ostensibly because it had key accounts such as Johnson & Johnson and Lipton Tea. When Coca-Cola promptly stole Bergin to head McCann's team, one insider joked: "That's a hell of a price to pay for Bergin."

"Coke is it!": Working with Tony DeGregorio, Ken Schulman wrote the original lyrics, including the main slogan, "Coke Is It." Ginny Redington rewrote most of the lyrics to fit her tune, and John Bergin finally fiddled with them as well, replacing "the biggest taste in Canada" with "the biggest taste you've ever found" and other modifications. (Ginny Redington interview; Ken Schulman interview; John Bergin interview)

"egg all over us": Bergin interview.

"all three networks": Ramsey, *Corporate Warriors*, pp. 75–76. Ramsey got the date wrong, however, placing it in 1981 instead of 1982.

"new marching song": Tom Walker, "Battle Cry for '80s: Coke Is It!," *AC*, Feb. 5, 1982.

"sighing with relief": Video of "Coke Is It" commercials, courtesy McCann-Erickson.

"strong, assertive message": "'Coke is it!' Says It all!" *Refresher*, March 1982, pp. 8–9.

340 "periods of addiction": Cosby remarks, "1979 Great Get-Together" Video, CC Co.

"This is real refreshment": Cosby commercials courtesy of John Bergin.

"Cosby with killing": It is likely that the Challenge was halted because of a combination of factors. Aggressive Pepsi USA president John Sculley left to head Apple early in 1983, and Don Kendall, never comfortable with the Challenge, killed it.

"I don't think": Cosby quote from "Great Get-Together" 1979 video.

"inconceivably arrogant": Bergin interview.

"bought part ownership": Thomas Oliver, "Blacks to Purchase First Major Share of a Coke Bottler," *AJ/C*, March 11, 1983.

341 "$750 million": Oliver, *Real Coke*, p. 77.

"We're doing absolutely": Walker, "Battle Cry for "80s."

"unbelievably sweet deal": Oliver, *Real Coke*, pp. 78–83.

"studio's new researcher": "Coke Tries Selling Movies Like Soda Pop," *Fortune*, Dec. 26, 1983. The idea that movies could sell soft drinks wasn't new. During the filming of *Lawrence of Arabia* in 1961, Peter O'Toole asked a colleague why they were making the film. The story of a man's spiritual quest? The story of the decline of the British Empire? No, O'Toole said. "It's soft drinks. Most people don't know it, but the profit center in movie theaters is the concession stand. It's impossible to spend three hours watching a film that takes place in the desert without getting incredibly thirsty." (Wapshott, *Peter O'Toole*)

"two blue Pepsi": Miller, *Seeing Through Movies*, pp. 190–192.

"70 percent sales jump": Michael Schudson, *Advertising: The Uneasy Persuasion*, p. 102.

342 **"most carefully developed"**: "Diet Coke: Time Is Right," *Refresher*, Aug. 1982, p. 2.

"scores of stars": "1984 Get-Together" Video,. CC Co.; *People*, Fall 1989, p. 24.

"$2.5 million": Ramsey, *Corporate Warriors*, p. 78.

"perfumy and lacy imagery": Jack Carew, "Advertising Position for Tampa," May 29, 1981, Plaintiff's Exhibit 1353, Diet Coke Case.

"when Stout dispensed": Oliver, *Real Coke*, p. 88.

"twenty-eight overseas markets": 1983 CC Annual Report. In foreign markets, diet Coke was often renamed Coca-Cola Light, since many European countries taxed any item with the word "diet" as if it were a medicine.

343 **"temporary contract"**: Coca-Cola Bottlers' Association to All Coca-Cola Bottlers, Aug. 1982, Plaintiff's Exhibit 297, Diet Coke Case. Company officials point out that no bottler received diet Coke without signing a temporary contract and that transhipment of product into their territory was forbidden by their exclusive contract. Nonetheless, TV ads recognized no territory, and consumers expected to find diet Coke in their local stores. Consequently, local bottlers had little choice but to sign up.

"file suit over diet Coke": Schmidt's group decided to sue after an ad hoc committee of the Bottlers' Association proposed a January 1983 version of the diet Coke contract which they considered unsatisfactory. Schmidt accused the committee members of working in secret sessions against most bottlers' best interests; in return, the ad hoc members complained that the renejgades pursued a "sue first, talk later" course of action. (Schmidt interview; CC Bottlers' Association, "Highlights of the 1983 Amendment," April 28, 1983)

"E-Town, the nickname": The original case was called E-Town because Bill Schmidt's bottling plant is located in Elizabethtown, Kentucky.

"earned $91 million": 1983 CC Annual Report.

"unveiled Pepsi Free": Ramsey, p. 79.

"caffeine constituted a health hazard": "Coke's Big Market Blitz," *Business Week*, May 30, 1983; Jacobson, *The Complete Eater's Digest and Nutrition Scoreboard*, pp. 255–261.

344 **"once the giant finally stirred"**: By the eighties, the market leaders such as Coke and Pepsi didn't crawl out on any unnecessary limbs. If a trend manifested itself, they could use their enormous advertised budgets and efficient distribution systems to dominate with their own brand. "Show me a company that's a product innovator," said one industry analyst, "and I'll show you a company that's going downhill." (George Thompson in "Hold the Gloom," *Beverage World*, Jan. 1991)

"opted for 100 percent": "Now With NutraSweet!" *Refresher*, Sept./Oct. 1983, p. 12.

"Memorial bricks": Wayne Estes, "Closing the Plum Street Doors," *Refresher*, July/Aug. 1983, pp. 15–18.

"giant has awakened": Mark Potts, "Coca-Cola Giant Has Awakened," *Washington Post*, Nov. 27, 1983.

"marketer of the year": "Coke's Roberto Goizueta: A Dreamer and a Doer," *Adweek*, Aug. 1983, pp. M.R.6–8; "Coca-Cola Shows Who's Boss," *Dun's Business Month*, Dec. 1983.

"1984 Summer Olympics": Rhonda Ogelsby, "Meeting an Olympic Challenge," *Refresher*, March/April 1984, pp. 8–12.

"Reagan . . . Pepsi man": Reagan cabinet member Casper Weinberger was on the Pepsi board of directors. Actually, Reagan had Coca-Cola ties as well. From 1954 to 1962, he had served as the host of TV's *General Electric Theater* and toured GE plants. Almost certainly, Reagan would have befriended Robert Woodruff, a longtime GE board member. In addition, Reagan's older brother,

Neil "Moon" Reagan, worked for McCann-Erickson in Los Angeles for many years (1943 to 1973), where he cultivated the Hollywood crowd for Coke. (Louis & Yazijian, p. 367; Johnson, *Sleepwalking Through History*, pp. 47, 56; J. Neil Reagan interview)

344–5 **"cola wars"**: Enrico, p. 12; Don Kendall interview.

345 **"image manipulators"**: Johnson, *Sleepwalking*, p. 139.
"fast-food commercial": Chafe, *Unfinished Journey*, p. 476.
"I'm always going": "Ads with the Dusenberry Touch," *NYT*, Nov. 16, 1986.
"$5,000 went to Reagan": Federal Election Commission 1983/84 printout, "Coca-Cola Company Nonpartisan Committee for Good Government."
"profile . . .Coca-Cola": Sergio Zyman to Mike Beindorff, Oct. 15, 1984, cover letter on report, "Diet Coke Personality Statement" and "The Coca-Cola User," by SSC&B Lintas Worldwide, Plaintiff's Exhibit 234, Diet Coke Case.

346 **"*Ghostbusters*"**: CC 1984 Annual Report, p. 25; Kathryn Harris, "Coke to Market Taped Films Through Bottlers," *Los Angeles Times*, Oct. 17, 1984.
"Coca-Cola USA tower": "Building for Growth," *Refresher*, Jan./Feb. 1984, p. 19.
"Coca-Cola Foundation": "Information, Please," *Refresher*, Jan./Feb. 1984, pp. 26–27; "Company Establishes Philanthropic Foundation," *Refresher*, Nov./Dec. 1984, p. 25.
"leap-frogged past 7-Up": "Thank You, America," *Refresher*, March/April 1984, pp. 3–5.
"Julio Iglesias": "20 Questions: Sergio Zyman," *Refresher*, July/Aug. 1984, p. 11; "Would Class: Julio Iglesias and Coke," *Refresher*, May/June 1984, p. 29.
"whopping 63 percent": Tim Davis, "The Coke Enterprise: Out Front and Pulling Away," *Beverage World*, July 1984, p. 25.
"Ready, Fire! Aim": Brian Dyson, "1984 Get-Together" Video, CC Co.
"repurchasing six million": 1984 CC Annual Report, pp. 2, 5.
"We live nervous": Herb Greenberg, "King Coke Widens Realm," *Chicago Tribune*, Aug. 19, 1984.
"There is a danger": William E. Schmidt, "Putting the Daring Back in Coke," *NYT*, March 4, 1984.

CHAPTER 19: THE MARKETING BLUNDER OF THE CENTURY

347 **"To the Master Dodo"**: Letter to CC Co., May 12, 1985. (CC Archives)
"Pepsi-Cola gained": "Silver from All Sides: Coca-Cola's Goizueta," *Financial World*, April 3–16, 1985, p. 24. Pepsi USA president Roger Enrico was convinced that his new Michael Jackson commercials were the catalyst for Pepsi's surge in market share. ("Pepsi's High-Priced Sell Is Paying Off," *Business Week*, March 5, 1985, p. 34; Oliver, *Real Coke*, p. 99; "Michael Jackson," *Current Biography*, 1983, pp. 197–201; "Bringing Back the Magic," *Time*, July 16, 1984, pp. 64–67; Bruce Horovitz, "It May Be Hard to Swallow Some Endorsements," *LA Times*, Feb. 11, 1992; Clark, *The Want Makers*, p. 23; Roger Enrico, *The Other Guy Blinked*, pp. 2, 12)
"11 percent": Oliver, *Real Coke*, p. 103; Roy Stout interview.

348 **"Goddam it"**: John Bergin interview.
"they wavered": Oliver, p. 104.
"six-point margin": ibid., p. 105.
"it's a nice thing": Scott Ellsworth interview with Dick Alven, Nov. 16, 1984. (Pepsi Collection)
"take the heat off": Weil interview. Roberto Goizueta once told John Bergin

that New Coke did not contain coca leaf. (Bergin interview; Clifford D. May, "How Coca-Cola Obtains Its Coca," *NYT*, July 1, 1988, p. 25; "Coca: An Ancient Herb Turns Deadly," by Peter T. White, *National Geographic*, Jan. 1989, pp. 3–51)

349 **"On New Year's Day"**: The date of Goizueta's fateful visit to Ichauway is actually uncertain. In an interview with the author, Goizueta placed it in November of 1984, but in subsequent correspondence amended his memory to the beginning of January. During the press conference announcing New Coke in April of 1985, however, he said that the date was late in February. The January 1 date seems reasonable, since it came shortly after the corporate decision to go ahead, and just before the advertising men were informed.

"stopped eating": According to Edith Honeycutt, Martha Ellis, Joe Jones, and Cal Bailey, Woodruff stopped eating around the beginning of the year.

"Honey, where am I?": Edith Honeycutt interview.

"Predicted . . . bankruptcy": Kahn, *RWW*, p. 44.

"neighboring parent": Robert Woodruff's mentor was Harrison Jones' father, who, Woodruff asserted, "liked me better than he did his son Harrison."

"wealth, power": Robert Woodruff Speech, April 7, 1953. (RWW Papers, Box 54)

"Goizueta and Woodruff were alone": Anonymous sources; Wilbur Kurtz interview; Jack Tarver interview; Bob Broadwater interview.

350 **"really knew him"**: Joe Jones interview.

"every penny of it": Wilbur Kurtz interview.

"style rose": Kahn, RWW. p. 11.

"$230 million to Emory": Ann Hardie, "Money's No Object as Emory Heads Up the Academic Ladder," *AC*, Feb. 13, 1991.

"when he couldn't sleep": Examining the lives of Woodruff's two younger brothers only adds to the mystery of a strange family heritage. George Woodruff committed his second daughter, Frances "Tut" Woodruff, to a Florida mental institution, and she won her freedom in a bitter lawsuit only after years of detention. The youngest Woodruff brother, Henry, was "never quite right." In a burlesque of his father's obsession with wasted time and money, Henry wore four watches and left dollar tips for $40 meals. He committed suicide. (Frances "Tut" Woodruff interview; Emma Edmunds, "The Trials of Tut Woodruff," *Atlanta Magazine*, Jan. 1989, p. 52–54; Lois Troutman interview)

"administering Ichauway": Joe Jones interview.

351 **"the Bunker"**: Oliver, pp. 107–108.

"no one could brainstorm": Bergin interview; Marcio Moreira interview.

"recently modified": Bergin interview.

"It's a new tin": Moreira interview.

"impatient Sergio Zyman": Bergin and Zyman, formerly good friends, now barely spoke to one another. (Bergin interview)

"Soviet citizens": "Soviet Union Opens Door to Coca-Cola," *Refresher*, Jan./Feb. 1985, p. 24.

"cherry Coke": "Wrapping Up Something New," *Refresher*, March/April 1985, p. 12.

"Enrico's open letter": Oliver, p. 128.

"Lincoln Center": ibid., p. 131.

352 **"the best soft drink"**: "Coca-Cola USA Press Conference Satellite Downlink," April 23, 1985, transcript, Plaintiff's Exhibit 78, Diet Coke Case. All ensuing quotes from this press conference are from this source.

353 **"every glitzy thing"**: "Battling It Out," *Time*, May 13, 1985.

"No one would have listened": Oliver, p. 123.

"bought 110 cases": Dan Lauck interviw; Oliver, pp. 7–9.

"world is immutable": Zyman to Beindorff, "The Coca-Cola User," Oct. 15, 1984, Plaintiff's Exhibit 234, Diet Coke Case. In September 1979, Coke marketer Peter Sealey wrote a memo about then-tentative plans for New Coke. He observed that there were two distinct types of consumer product—utilitarian items such as soaps and detergents, for which "new and improved" made sense, and complex, emotionally laden items such as beer, cigarettes, perfume, and soft drinks. As for Coke, he wrote: "The brand cannot be made new or improved, for to do so would destroy the mystique, mystery, and lore that surround the brand and constitute its heritage. In the minds of our consumers, be brand cannot be improved." Obviously, no one paid much attention to his memo. (Peter Sealey interview.)

354 "Bob Greene . . . mourned": Oliver, pp. 144–145.
"it sucks": "Coke Tampers with Success," *Newsweek*, May 6, 1985, p. 50.
"Coke *Was* It": Oliver, pp. 11–12.
"96 percent of all Americans": Hoy, p. 150.
"inexplicably clumsy": New Coke commercial video, from McCann-Erickson. Quotes and examples are from this video.
"enormous popularity": *Facts on File*, 1985, p. 312; *People*, Fall 1989, p. 101.
"Television Quotient": Bergin interview; Jeffry Scott, "Consumer Survey Puts Cosby at Top of Chart in Popularity," *AC*, Oct. 14, 1989.
"stressed the tart taste": Oliver, p. 114.
"words I'm about to say": Cosby New Coke Commercials, McCann-Erickson video.

355 "Goizueta was shaken": Oliver, pp. 153–155.
"Fidel Castro": *AC*, July 12, 1985, untitled clipping, (CC Collection, Box 9, Emory)
"beginning of June": For these loyal Coca-Cola drinkers, all other news from late April until mid-July of 1985 was immaterial. Ronald Reagan visited a Nazi cemetery and endured a cancer operation. Death squads terrorized Guatemala, 10,000 died in a Bangladesh cyclone, and Lebanese Shiites hijacked a TWA airliner. None of these events compared to the tragedy of the altered Coca-Cola formula. (*Facts on File*, 1985, pp. 299–521)
"failed to identify": Oliver, pp. 159–162.
"second class-action": Keith Herndon, "The Old Coke Is Back," *AC*, July 11, 1985.
"universal conversation topic": "All A fizz Over the New Coke," *Time*, June 24, 1985, p. 60.
"limited supply": "Saying 'No' to New Coke," *Newsweek*, June 24, 1985, p. 32.
"chic to dump": "Classic Comeback for an Old Champ," *U.S. News & World Report*, July 22, 1985.
"elixir of the gods": Oliver, p. 163.
"40,000 letters": ibid., p. 157.
"our latest research": CC Consumer Affairs Dept. files.
"consulting psychologist": Oliver, p. 163.
"Most letters": All letters from CC Consumer Affairs Dept. files unless otherwise noted.

356 "There are only two things": Quoted from "Coca-Cola's Big Fizzle," *Time*, July 22, 1985, p. 49.
"social pariahs": Oliver, pp. 166–167; Charles Schifilliti interview.
"You bastard": Jesse Meyers interview.
"sleeping like a baby": Jimmy Williams interview.
"June's sales plummeted": Oliver, pp. 169–172.
"only real argument": Oliver, p. 175–76. Company officials deny that the

name "classic" had anything to do with the lawsuits. Chicago journalist Bob Greene claims credit for the Coke Strategy. In his June 9, 1985 column, he suggested a "face-saving gesture": the Company should distribute cans of the old Coke, marked with the words "Original Formula," to be sold alongside New Coke. Gradually, he predicted, the original would predominate, and the Company could "quietly let the old Coke resume its place as the only Coke." (Bob Greene interview; "The New Coca-Cola Should Be Canned," *Chicago Tribune*, June 9, 1985)

357 **"scientific study"**: "The Pause That Represses," *Science Digest*, Aug. 1986, p. 15.

358 **"meaningful moment"**: Thomas Oliver, "Coke Wants to Kiss, Make Up with America," *AC*, July 12, 1985; "Coca-Cola's Big Fizzle," *Time*, July 22, 1985, p. 48.

"lovely American enigma": Oliver, *Real Cola*, pp. 178–181.

"*Si mi abuela*": Jesse Meyers, *BD*, July 19, 1985, p. 3.

"sprawled in a bathtub": "Here's to Gay Mullins," *People*, July 29, 1985, p. 95.

"small airplane": Maureen Downey, "Coke Fans Rejoice About 'Classic': How Sweet It Isn't!" *AC*, July 12, 1985; Lauck interview.

"Eighteen thousand calls": Oliver, *Real Coke*, p. 181.

"better is sex!": Ramsey, *Corporate Warriors*, p. 91.

"cure for cancer": Oliver, *Real Coke*, p. 181.

"We love you for caring!": All letters from CC Consumer Affairs Dept. files.

359 **"marketing blunder"**: "Coke's Man on the Spot," *Business Week*, July 29, 1985, p. 56.

"pride still blinded": One Coca-Cola man saw the situation quite clearly, as excerpts from his July 1985 diary indicate: "We were sucked into believing that taste was the only dimension . . . consumers will ask for old Coke just as a way of expressing their . . . anger at Company." Later, in August, he wrote: "Atmosphere is becoming Orwellian. Management insists that there can be only one Coke, when in fact there are two." (Anonymous 1985 diary)

"term he despised": Roberto Goizueta deposition for E-Town Case, July 5, 1985.

"formidable megabrand": Goizueta to Shareholders, July 11, 1985. (CC Collection, Box 9, Emory)

"whatever he . . . *said*": Roberto Goizueta deposition, July 5, 1985, Diet Coke Case.

"flexible pricing . . . future": Charles L. Wallace to Bottlers of Coca-Cola, July 24, 1985, Plaintiff's Exhibit 1664, Diet Coke Case.

"Wonderland thinking": Emmet Bondurant interview.

360 **"When *I* use a word"**: Carroll, *Through the Looking-Glass*, in *The Annotated Alice*, p. 269.

"reveal the secret formula": Scott Kilman, "Coca-Cola Is Told to Disclose Secret of Coke Formula," *WSJ*, Aug. 21, 1985.

"Company has never disclosed": William O. LaMotte III to Judge Murray M. Schwartz, Sept. 9, 1985, Plaintiff's Exhibit 1899, Diet Coke Case.

"brazen defiance": "Businesses Struggle to Keep Their Secrets," *U.S. News & World Report*, Sept. 23, 1985, p. 59.

"reportedly incapacitated": Jesse Meyers, *BD*, Nov. 27, 1985, Green Sheet Supplement.

"walking billboards": "Licensing a Legend," *Refresher*, March/April 1984, pp. 19–21.

"cried foul": Bateman & Schaeffer, "Coca-Cola Clothes," *Cola Call*, Sept. 1985, pp. 7–8; "Tempests in a Pop Bottle," *Time*, Aug. 26, 1985, p. 45.

"soft drink in space": "Coke to Be First Soft Drink in Outer Space," *Refresher*, May/June 1985, p. 23.

"lukewarm cola": "Tempests in a Pop Bottle," p. 45.

"pedantic corrections": Oliver, *Real Coke*, p. 58.

"How boring": Roberto Goizueta, "Press Credibility: A Businessman's View," address to The Associated Press Managing Editors, Oct. 29, 1985. (Pamphlet, CC Co.)

361 "quick gloss": As it struggled with all of its problems, the Company finally allowed the Cola Clan to use the Coke name, since the shaken soft drink giant now needed all the goodwill it could muster. In the fall of 1985, the organization was renamed the Coca-Cola Collectors Club International and proudly began using the telltale script in its logo. (Randy Schaeffer, Bill Bateman interview; Thom Thompson to Mark Pendergrast, Oct. 16, 1991)

"*Newsweek*'s headline": "Hey America, Coke Are It!" *Newsweek*, July 22, 1985, p. 42.

"May we now expect": CC Consumer Affairs Dept. files for all quotes.

"the same affection": Jesse Meyers, *BD*, Sept. 20, 1985, p. 2.

"fell slightly *below*": Meyers, *BD*, Jan. 24, 1986, p. 1.

"calls weren't returned": Thomas Oliver interview.

"addresses the visionary": "Advertising's New Wave," *Refresher*, March/April 1986, p. 2.

"shape of the curve": One of these commercials officially broke the long-standing taboo against children under twelve drinking Coke.

"Horizontal Pour": "Coke 'Defies Gravity' In New Commercial," *Refresher*, March/April 1986, pp. 4–5.

362 "a castaway": McCann video archives.

"Cokeologists": ibid.

"commercials debuted": Jesse Meyers, *BD*, Feb. 14, 1986, p. 1.

"Red, White & You": ibid.

"Classic had fizzed": Meyers, *BD*, May 7, 1986, pp. 1–2.

"McDonald's switched": "Brian Dyson Takes the New Coke Challenge," *Business Week*, May 26, 1986, p. 81; Pamela G. Hollie, "Keeping New Coke Alive," *NYT*, July 20, 1986; Meyers interview.

363 "Latin mass": See "Coca-Cola's Big Fizzle," *Time*, July 22, 1985, p. 49; "Here's to Gay Mullins," *People*, July 29, 1985, pp. 95–97; "New Coke's Fizzle—Lessons for the Rest of Us," *Sloan Management Review*, Fall 1986, pp. 71–76.

"token American": Oliver, *Real Coke*, p. 66.

"Whenever things": June 4, 1985, letter to Coke from Austin, Texas. (CC Consumer Affairs archives)

"commercial coup": In a blind taste-test, the author of this book sipped Coca-Cola Classic, New Coke, Pepsi, and A&P Cola. He chose Classic as his favorite taste, followed by New Coke, correctly identifying both. His third choice was A&P Cola, which he thought was Pepsi.

CHAPTER 20: THE BIG RED MACHINE

364 "Can Big Red": Jeffry Scott, "With New Launches, Coke Is It," *Adweek*, Dec. 12, 1988.

"$23 million centennial bash": Facts on the Coke Centennial celebration come from the following sources: BBC TV 1989 special; Video of events provided by CC Co.; "Fizz, Movies and Whoop-De-Do," *Time*, May 12, 1986; Jesse Meyers, *BD*, May 7, and 10, 1986; Articles from *Atlanta Constitution* and other papers, May 9–11, in CC Collection, Box 11, Emory; Russell Shaw, "100 Years of Coca-Cola," *Sky*, May 1986, pp. 62–70; *Refresher*, May/June 1986, pp. 20–30.

365 **"one family"**: Ike Herbert, "Heritage" videotape, 1986, CC Co.

"almost everyone in Atlanta": Only the Candlers seemed miffed. Not invited to take part in the Company celebration, over 200 Candler descendants rented Callan Castle, Asa's 1903 mansion, for their own birthday party. ("Going Steady: Atlanta and Coca-Cola," *AC*, May 3, 1986; Lewis Grizzard, "Y'all, It's Not Soda, It's Co-Coler," *AC*, May 9, 1986, Howard Pousner, "Mayor Makes a Bubbly Pitch for Coca-Cola Party Monday," *AC*, May 2, 1986; Thomas Oliver, "Mr. Coke Civilized Atlanta," *AC*, May 9, 1986; Martha Woodham, "Candlers Gather, Pay Tribute to Pop," *AC*, May 9, 1986)

"exchanged marriage vows": Chris Elliot interview.

"product of the future": Jesse Meyers, *BD*, May 10, 1986, p. 4.

"Stomp on": "Coke and Pepsi Stomp on the Little Guys," *Fortune*, Jan. 7, 1985, pp. 67–68.

"FTC intervened": "Coke Cries 'Checkmate'," *Newsweek*, March 3, 1986, p. 53.

"embarrassing flops": Timothy K. Smith and Laura Landro, "Profoundly Changed, Coca-Cola Co. Strives to Keep on Bubbling," *WSJ*, April 24, 1986; "Hollywood's Big New Mogul," *U.S. News & World Report*, June 23, 1986, p. 58.

366 **"Flat in Hollywood"**: "Coke: Flat in Hollywood," *Newsweek*, Oct. 28, 1985, p. 61; "Columbia Pictures: Are Things Really Better with Coke?" *Business Week*, April 14, 1986, pp. 56–58.

"annual return of 24%": 1985 CC Annual Report, p. 3. In June of 1986 the stock split 3-for-1.

"My job is": "Fizz, Movies and Whoop-De-Do," *Time*, May 12, 1986.

"Doug Ivester": Facts in this section from Stuart Mieher, "Things Go Better with Debt," *Georgia Trend*, March 1986, pp. 42–49.

367 **"dollar peaked"**: "The Dollar Takes a Dive," *Newsweek*, July 22, 1985, p. 44.

"70 percent of its top value": Pendergrast, *Practical Ways*, p. 1.

"ordinary tap water": Roberto Goizueta address, May 7, 1986, videotape, CC Co.

"As population centers": Keough, quoted by Jesse Meyers, *BD*, May 10, 1986, p. 4.

368 **"This is the world"**: Donald R. Keough, "The New Century Begins," May 9, 1986, CC Co.

"alliterative slogan": "Three A's Spell Global Success," *Journey: The Magazine of The Coca-Cola Company*, May 1987, pp. 5–11.

369 **"Think globally"**: "New Coke," *Chief Executive*, May/June 1988, p. 39.

"supervise Germany": Neville Isdell interview.

"Beatrice Foods": Kohlberg Kravis Roberts and Company took over Beatrice Foods in a record-breaking $6.2 billion leveraged buy-out in 1986, then sold off chunks such as the Coca-Cola bottler. (Johnson, *Sleepwalking*, p. 433)

"Coca-Cola Enterprises": The Company also created a new Master Contract for CCE, providing unlimited flexibility in pricing syrup. Whenever Big Coke took an equity position in larger bottlers, it insisted on their signing what Bill Schmidt derisively called the "Master-Slave Contract." By the end of the decade, bottlers covering 70 percent of U.S. volume had signed up. (Bill Schmidt interview; "The New Coca-Cola," *Financial World*, p. 34)

"fine guerrilla fighter": Roy Stout lost his position as head of U.S. research in 1988, though Don Keough rehired him on the corporate level. (Keith Herndon, "Coca-Cola Co. to Create New Bottling Firm," AC, July 15, 1986; Charles Bottoms interview; Roy Stout interview)

"CCE was embarrassed": "A New Coke Has Birthing Pains," *Georgia Trend*, Feb. 1987, p. 20.

370 "syrup pump": Emmet Bondurant interview.

"packaged . . . entertainment holdings": "He Put the Kick Back into Coke," *Fortune*, Oct. 26, 1987, pp. 48, 50.

"poison pills": Betsy Morris, "Coke's Strategy Is to Divide and Conquer," *WSJ*, Oct. 8, 1987.

"gratuitous tail fins": Roberto Goizueta, "The Emerging Post-Conglomerate Era," Jan. 1988, supplement to 1987 Annual Report.

"disinvest in South Africa": "Company Sells Holdings in South Africa," *Refresher*, Sept./Oct. 1986, p. 23; Connie Green and Keith Herndon, "Coke to Sell Its Assets in South Africa," AC, Sept. 18, 1986; Carl Ware interview.

371 "leader Albert Luthuli": Chief Luthuli won the Nobel Peace Prize in 1961 and was assassinated in 1967.

"They are so visible": Tandi Gcabashe interview.

"Tutu, visiting Atlanta": "Archbishop Tutu Visits Atlanta Headquarters," *Journey*, Aug. 1988, p. 23.

"196,000 acres of Belizean": David A. Kyle, "Transnational Politics: Coca-Cola Foods in Belize," *Belizean Studies*, vol. 16, no. 3, 1988, pp. 14–31. All material on Belize from this source unless otherwise noted.

"Calero . . . Coca-Cola bottler": "Adolfo Calero," *Current Biography*, 1987, pp. 77–80.

372 "a natural preserve": William Branigin, "'Save the Rain Forest' Rings Out in Belize," *Los Angeles Times*, Oct. 15, 1989. The Company sold the last of its Belizean land in 1992.

"rainforest generation": Denise Voelker, "In Belize, Coke Goes Better," *Sierra*, Sept./Oct. 1987.

"Schwartz stopped short": Murray Schwartz, Diet Coke Case opinion, May 23, 1986.

"this case was a pleasure": Murray Schwartz decision, E-Town Case, Aug. 8, 1986.

"projected $7 million": Because the number of unamended bottlers dropped soon afterward, the actual annual cost to the company was $4 million rather than $7 million.

"We underestimated": Bondurant interview.

373 "coercive tactics": Bondurant to Charles L. Wallace, CC Co., April 9, 1987, E-Town Case, Plaintiff's Exhibit 1401.

"window of opportunity": E-Town Case, Consolidated Pre-Trial Order, p. 147. On Jan. 6, 1987, the Company informed non-amended bottlers that they had until May 1, 1987, to sign the amendment.

"fell from sixty-four to twenty-nine": Bill and Jan Schmidt interview.

"gorgeous plant . . . 'double-bottoming'": Robert Lindsey interview; Skey Johnston interview.

"Schifilliti serviced Vermont": Charles Schifilliti interview.

374 "life itself": Jesse Meyers, *Future Smarts VIII*, Dec. 12, 1988, pp. 6, 11, 13.

"Nanni, the litigation chief": Anthony Nanni, *Future Smarts/Legal Smarts*, May 20, 1991, pp. 1–6.

"*60 Minutes* . . . revealed": Andy Panztor & Larry Reibstein, "Cola Sellers May Have Bottled Up Their Competition," *WSJ*, Dec. 9, 1987, p. 6.

"twenty-nine separate legal actions": Department of Justice files.

"we were street-fighters": Jim Harford, *Future Smarts/Legal Smarts*, May 20, 1991, pp. 101–117. Harford, a staunch conservative, was transformed by his jail experience. He also learned that there was life outside the cola wars. "Even if I may not sell flavored, colored, sugar-charged water again," he told a group of bottlers, "life thereafter looks good to me. I've had more time with my family."

"lock-out agreements": Panztor and Reibstein, "Cola Sellers"; Jim Wallace, *Future Smarts VI*, Dec. 14, 1987, p. 16.

375 **"kiss my ass"**: Allen Peacock interview. A Coca-Cola Consolidated spokesman denied some of Peacock's allegations, including extraordinary work hours and the 260 percent turnover ratio. The bottler refused to permit an interview with a current route salesman, however, and did not disclose the actual turnover ratio. (Bob Pettus interview)

"That's a sin": Bottoms interview.

"Dual-income families": Melissa Turner, "Soda Fountain War Bubbles Up," AC, Aug. 23, 1987; Johnson, *Sleepwalking*, pp. 151, 451.

"3 billion drinks": "Selling More Than Syrup," *Journey*, March 1990, pp. 2–7.

"Kentucky Fried Chicken": "New Reality," *Refresher*, Dec. 1987, p. 2.

376 **"Wendy's switched"**: "A New Line from Wendy's: Where's the Coke?" *Newsweek*, Oct. 27, 1986, p. 88.

"Domino's Pizza": Melissa Turner, "Pepsi Food Push Soured Some," AC, Aug. 23, 1987.

"introduced the BreakMate": "The Third Wave Rolls In," *Journey*, Sept. 1989, pp. 14–16.

"within *wrist's* length": Jesse Meyers, *Future Smarts VII*, Dec. 12, 1988, p. 3.

"Perhaps coming years": Goizueta quoted in *Beverage Digest*, 15, 1992, p. 5.

"special relationship": "Consumers Create New Ad Campaign," *Journey*, May 1987, p. 17.

"refused to abandon New Coke": Melissa Turner, "New Coke: Time to Pull Plug?" AC, Oct. 30, 1988.

"Phil Dusenberry": Jeffry Scott, "Pepsi's Ad Man Thrives," AC, Dec. 4, 1989.

"America's Choice": "Pepsi Wins in Taste; Coke Tops in Sales," AC, June 15, 1987.

377 **"Ike Herbert replaced"**: "Has the Coke Cart Hit a Ditch?" *Georgia Trend*, Jan. 1989, p. 20; "The Cola SuperPowers' Outrageous New Arsenals," *Business Week*, March 20, 1989, pp. 162–163; "An Interview with Ike Herbert," *Refresher*, Feb. 1989, p. 3; Bottoms interview; Ike Herbert interview.

"diet Coke attack ads": Melissa Turner, "Coca-Cola Tries to Make Diet Coke No. 2 Soft Drink," AC, Nov. 2, 1987.

"Project Manhattan": "Surprise Attack on a New Front," *Journey*, May 1989, pp. 20–21.

"doesn't express anything": "Coca-Cola Plans a New Ad Campaign in Its International Marketing Effort," *WSJ*, Dec. 12, 1988.

"minor change": John Bergin interview; "Coca-Cola Decides It's 'The Real Thing' Again," AC, Oct. 20, 1989.

"love with a black saint": Roger Mosconi interview; "The Cola Super-Powers," *Business Week*, p. 162; King, *Madonna: The Book*, pp. 170–176.

378 **"1987 internal memo"**: Don Keough, "The Power of Presence," Dec. 28, 1987, CC Co.

"We reach into": "The Power of Prestige," *Journey*, May 1989, p. 12.

"Disney account": "Mickey Mouse and Coca-Cola Create Magic," *Journey*, Aug. 1987, pp. 2–7.

"thousands of theaters": Marcy Magliera, "Coke Ads Plunge into Movie Videos," *Advertising Age*, Nov. 20, 1989; "Wide-Screen Ads Coming Soon to Theater Near You," *AC*, Jan. 31, 1990.

"standard 80 percent mark-up": Susan Spillman, "Concession Stands Get Top Billing at Theaters," *USA Today*, March 21, 1990.

"*Ishtar*'s dismal performance": *Ishtar* lost $25 million. ("He Put the Kick," *Fortune*, p. 50)

"synergies between": "Selling Soft Drinks & Celluloid," *Journey*, Nov. 1987, pp. 4–8. The information and quote in the next paragraph are from this article.

379 "audience *hated* it": Andrew Yule, *Fast Fade*, p. 332.

"film failed utterly": Kipps, *Out of Focus*, p. 324.

"*MAC and Me*": MAC supposedly stood for "Mysterious Alien Creature," but it was more obviously a McDonald's plug. Much of the movie's action took place under the Golden Arches where, of course, everyone drank more Coke. (Mark Crispin Miller, *Seeing Through Movies*, pp. 194–195)

"I am the future": McCann-Erickson videotape.

"nineteen different languages": Marcio Moreira interview. The final "General Assembly" cuts appeared to have been filmed and sung entirely in the appropriate language by all thousand youths. In fact, only the soloists and small groups singing "tomorrow," "*mañana*," or "*demain*" were depicted in close-ups. With clever editing, no one could tell that the hordes had originally sung in English only.

380 "Machu Picchu": Moreira interview.

"I Feel Coke": Michael J. McCarthy, "Coca-Cola Plans a New Ad Campaign," *WSJ*, Dec. 12, 1988.

"policing women's nipples": Moreira interview.

"First Time": "Europe Gets Fifth Coca-Cola Hit with 'First Time,'" *Journey*, Feb. 1989, p. 27.

"contravening any major": Moreira interview.

"Rock in Rio": "Rio Rocks the World," *Journey*, March 1991, p. 20.

"Lulu Santos": "Brazil Rocks with Coca-Cola," *Journey*, Feb. 1989, p. 28.

"groomed local rock": "Where There's Music, There's Coca-Cola," *Journey*, Aug. 1988, pp. 8–12.

381 "college teams to Tokyo": "Coca-Cola Bowl Scores in Tokyo," *Journey*, Feb. 1989, p. 26.

"Sawayaka . . . Clinics": "A Natural Double Play," *Journey*, Aug. 1988, p. 20.

"The visual effect": "Brazilian Football," *Journey*, May 1988, pp. 8–11.

"World Cup venues": "Pouring Coca-Cola into the World Cup," *Journey*, Sept. 1990, pp. 28–30; "Looking Ahead with FIFA," *Journey*, Dec. 1991, p. 28.

"famed bicycle race": "A Marketing Tour de Force," *Journey*, Dec. 1990, pp. 10–11.

"Regardless of the sport": "Youth Athletics Promoted in Argentina," *Journey*, Dec. 1989, p. 28; "Number One on the Street," *Journey*, Dec. 1988, p. 16.

"hot marketing opportunity": "Can't You Feel It?" *Journey*, Feb. 1988, pp. 28–29.

"scrawled gaudily": "Olympic Ties Most Visible in History," *Journey*, Nov. 1987, p. 31; "Coca-Cola in Clear View at Summer Olympics," *Journey*, Dec. 1988, p. 15.

"$80 million": Melissa Turner, "Coca-Cola Running Hard in Olympics," *AC*, Feb. 9, 1988; "A Powerful Presence," *Journey*, May 1988, p. 13.

"vast world map": 1988 CC Annual Report.

382 "bribed . . . into the USSR": Melissa Turner articles in *AC*, June 11, June 30, July 2, Aug. 6, Aug. 14, 1988. The Coca-Cola venture in Russia commenced with a 1985 agreement between Don Keough and Mikhail Gorbachev, pleased to make one more nonalcoholic beverage available to his vodka-swilling countrymen. The complex agreement essentially allowed the Russians to pay for their Coke with Lada automobiles exported to England.

"**Neither . . . disturbed**": The extensive coverage given to the grand jury investigation by the *Atlanta Constitution* did irk Roberto Goizueta, however. When Pulitzer Prize-winning Bill Kovach became editor of the *Constitution* in 1986, he vowed to convert it into a hard-hitting investigative paper. When Goizueta invited Kovach twice to his home for dinner, the editor was impolitic enough to decline. Thus, when Kovach was fired late in 1988, many critics pointed the finger at Coca-Cola. After all, paper owner Anne Cox Chambers sat on the Coca-Cola board. According to inside sources at the paper, however, Kovach's departure had little to do with pressure from the soft drink company. (Wendell Rawls interview; Melissa Turner interview)

"**his cocked smile**": John Huey, "Secrets of Great Second Bananas," *Fortune*, May 6, 1991, p. 68.

"**I was the bad cop**": Roberto Goizueta interview.

"**You'll never spend**": John Huey, "Second Bananas," pp. 68–70.

"**heaven . . . for a soft drink**": Don Keough interview.

382–3 "**fourth EC Group**": "Regrouping the World," *Journey*, Dec. 1988, p. 2.

383 "**William Hoffman**": "Coke Gets Off Its Can in Europe," *Fortune*, Aug. 13, 1990, pp. 68–73. The ensuing stories and quotes are from this source unless otherwise noted.

"**marketing blitz**": "Painting Bordeaux Red," *Journey*, Feb. 1989, pp. 8–13.

"**welcome part . . . landscape**": "Painting Bordeaux Red," p. 11.

"**He's so *American!***": "Coke Gets Off Its Can," p. 69.

"**café operators mobilized**": Bruce Crumley, "Bordeaux to Coke: 'Non' on Machines," *Fortune*, July 30, 1990.

"**anti-fascist drink**": "Coke Is It for European Socialists," *USA Today*, July 26, 1989.

384 "**plant at Wakefield**": The Company often played hardball with union representatives where it provided much-needed jobs. In Wakefield, the union signed a contract promising not to strike under any circumstances. (Philip Bassett, "AEU Signs Strike-Free Deal at Bottling Plant," *Financial Times*, Aug. 13, 1988)

"**EC Group contributed 29 percent**": "Coke Gets Off Its Can," pp. 69–70.

"**Japanese loved vending**": "All Day, All Night, All Year," *Journey*, Dec. 1990, p. 8; James Sterngold, "Why Japan Is in Love with Vending Machines," *NYT*, Jan. 5, 1992; "Drink Coca-Cola . . . With a Card," *Journey*, Feb. 1989, p. 28.

"**5,000 different flavors**": Ford S. Worthy, "Japan's Smart Secret Weapon," *Fortune*, Aug. 12, 1991; David Thurber, "Japan Soft Drink Wars," *Associated Press*, June 5, 1991.

"**over 700,000 . . . Coca-Cola**": "All Day, All Night," p. 8.

"**hard to overstate**": "Heritage," *Journey*, Aug. 1987, p. 26.

"**reaped more profits**": 1987 CC Annual Report, p. 7; "Heritage," *Journey*, Aug. 1987, p. 26. Japan was Coke's number-one profit center, even though only the fourth-largest market by volume. In the United States, the Company earned 11 cents on the concentrate used to fill a case of Coke. In Japan, it made four times as much for the same concentrate. (Maria Saporta, "To Coke, Worldwide Growth Is the Real Thing," *AC*, July 29, 1990)

"**per capita stalled**": Bergin interview; Dick Halpern interview.

"**Japanese health drinks**": In Japan, patent medicines found a ready market—not too dissimilar from the American boom of 1885 that spawned Coca-Cola. Japanese consumers spend 40 percent more than Americans on cancer drugs and antisenility pills—largely placebos which would never gain FDA approval in the U.S. ("The Strange Ways of Japanese Medicine Makers," *Fortune*, June 29, 1991, p. 63)

"drink Pokka's Mucos": "Japanese Down Drinks with Fiber and Calcium," *WSJ*, Nov. 16, 1989.

"Pocari Sweat": Thurber, "Japan Soft Drink Wars."

"Can you fight": "Jingle Single Jangles Japan," *Time*, Feb. 12, 1990, p. 53.

"for indolent youth": Bergin interview.

"Typical Japanese employees": Sterngold, "Why Japan Is in Love with Vending Machines"; Ron Sugarman interview; Bergin interview.

385 **"entire train"**: "Coca-Cola Train Rolls in Japan," *Journey*, Nov. 1987, p. 31; "MOBOTRON Hits the Streets," *Journey*, Feb. 1988, p. 31.

"sociological study": Bergin interview; Stout interview.

"piece of America's soul": Kester, *Japanese Takeovers*, pp. 118–123; "Japan Goes Hollywood," *Newsweek*, Oct. 9, 1989, p. 62.

"four times the value": Betsy Morris, "Coke's Windfall from Expected Sale Is Likely to Go to Overseas Operations," *WSJ*, Sept. 26, 1989.

"David Puttnam affair": Puttnam's dubious achievements included commissioning a movie about a talking penis, which was never released. (Yule, *Fast Fade;* Sealey interview.)

"cash from the sale": The Company also used the money to repurchase more stock.

"There's a perception": Michael J. McCarthy, "As a Global Marketer, Coke Excels," *WSJ*, Dec. 19, 1989.

386 **"tell me something"**: Anthony Ramirez, "It's Only Soft Drinks at Coca-Cola," *NYT*, May 21, 1990, p. D1.

"Sage of Omaha": "America's Number One Fan of Cherry Coke?" *Journey*, Nov. 1987, p. 30.

"Buffett plunked down": "Use of Corporate Assets," Fortune, Jan. 29, 1990, p. 48; Stan Luxenberg, "Are Soda Stocks Recession-Proof?" *NYT*, July 16, 1989; "Financial Soundness," *Fortune*, Jan. 29, 1990, p. 46.

"another undisclosed illness": Information and quotes for this section from: Ann Woolner, "De Novo Coke: Bottlers' Suit Recycled," *Fulton County Daily Report*, July 17, 1989; "Cola Warriors Return to Delaware," *FCDR*, Sept. 28, 1989; Peter Applebome, "No Doves Around as Coca-Cola, Bottlers Restart Long Battle," *The State Journal* (Frankfort, KY), Sept. 24, 1989; "The New Coca-Cola: No More Mr. Nice Guy," *Financial World*, July 25, 1989.

"rumors circulated": Jan and Bill Schmidt interviews. Schwartz may also have left the bench because of a heart condition.

"complete disdain": Emmet Bondurant interview.

"the cases ended in a whimper": "Coca-Cola Wins Battle With 30 Bottlers," *WSJ*, Feb. 19, 1993, p. B4; Schmidt interview.

"confusing star wars": The two colas also went to war late in 1989 on another front, when Pepsi college recruiters defamed Coke's Atlanta home, where cow-tipping—sneaking up on a sleeping bovine and pushing it over—was purportedly the favorite sport. The nasty dig exploded in Pepsi's face when outraged Atlanta editorials, political cartoons, and letters to the editor forced a public apology. (Philip Stelly, Jr., "Grits Hit the Fan After Pepsi Quiz," *Adweek*, Nov. 11, 1989; Ron Tidmore, "Open Letter to Atlanta-Area Residents," AC, Nov. 23, 1989)

387 **"who stands for what"**: Thomas R. King, "For Colas, the Fault Is in Too Many Stars," *WSJ*, Jan. 24, 1990; "Star-Struck Advertisers Lean on Celebs" *USA Today*, June 20, 1990.

"Ray Charles": Like Michael Jackson, Ray Charles didn't even drink the product he promoted, rejecting a young woman's offer of a diet Pepsi: "Honey, I don't drink that diet stuff. I just drink sweet, whole milk." ("Unless It's Milk, Hit the Road, Jack," *AC*, Sept. 17, 1990) "detective hunt": Scott Seltzer interview; Skip Wollenberg, "Coke's Ad-makers Went on Detective Hunt for 'Hilltop,'" *AP*, Dec. 22, 1989.

"it was nothing": Hilltop Reunion Videotape, World of Coca-Cola Museum, Atlanta.

"reading lesson": ibid.

"burst into tears": Seltzer interview.

388 "Landor & Associates": "Name That Brand," *Fortune*, July 4, 1988, p. 9.

"735% during the Eighties": 1989 CC Annual Report, p. 6; Roberto Goizueta to NY Society of Security Analysts, May 29, 1991.

"revised strategy statement": Roberto Goizueta, "Coca-Cola, a Business System Toward 2000: Our Mission in the 1990s," Feb. 1989. **CC Co.**

"Shirley Batista da Silva": Melissa Turner, "Coca-Cola's Brazil Push," *AC*, Aug. 13, 1989; "Building from Scratch," *Journal*, May 1989, pp. 16–19.

"Valentin Lachica": "Measuring the Day in Cases," *Journey*, May 1989, pp. 22–23.

"*spazas*": "Informal But Important," *Journey*, Sept. 1989, pp. 8–12.

"burro, gondola": "Stretching to Reach Arm's Length," *Journey*, Feb. 1989, pp. 20–23.

"southernmost city": "Ushuaia: Doing Business at the Very End of the World," *Journey*, June 1990, pp. 12–13.

"Arab Boycott . . . eroded": "Coca-Cola: Foreign Fizz," *The Economist*, July 15, 1989.

"gigantic new neon": "Coke Lights Up a Sign of the Times in Moscow," *USA Today*, Nov. 30, 1989.

"East German soldier": "Bottlers Greet East Germans," *Journey*, March 1990, p. 32.

389 "become the benchmark": Jeffrey Scott, "Coca-Cola Calls Itself the Bench-mark," *AC*, Nov. 16, 1989.

"impossible . . . to escape": Roberto Goizueta letter to editor, "Coke's Blocking and Tackling," *Fortune*, Sept. 10, 1990.

CHAPTER 21: GLOBAL FIZZ

390 "perpetual motion machine": J. P. Donlon, "The Eight-Nine Billion Dollar Man," *Chief Executive*, July 1996, p. 42.

"spigot that has a C": Joan Holleran, "The King of Coca-Cola," *Beverage Industry*, Nov. 1996, p. 34.

"efficient Coca-Cola juggernaut": CC 1993 Annual Report, p. 2.

"Ivester and Heinz Wiezorek": Ferdinand Protzman, "Coke's Splash in Eastern Germany," *NYT*, May 3, 1991; Patricia Seller, "Coke Gets Off Its Can in Europe," *Fortune*, Aug. 13, 1990, p. 72.

"'Just ship the product'": Greising, *I'd Like the World*, p. 185–186.

"our gut feelings": *Journey*, June 1991, p. 3; Baghai, *Alchemy of Growth*, p. 8–10, 172–173.

391 "East Germans gulped Coca-Cola": WSJ, March 16, 1990; "How Coke Is Invading East Germany," *Fortune*, Aug. 13, 1990, p. 72; *Journey*, June 1990, p. 6.

"Company upped the ante": Protzman, "Coke's Splash."

"Eastern Europe and Russia": Greising, *I'd Like the World*, p. 188; *Journey*, Dec. 1992, p. 28.

"Company invested directly in Poland": *Journey*, June 1993, p. 2, Sept. 1993, p. 18–20; Huey, John, "The World's Best Brand," *Fortune*, May 31, 1993, p. 44; Pell, *Not Like Us*, p. 200–201.

"Ukrainian joint venture": *Journey*, Dec. 1991, p. 27–28; March 1992, p. 2–3, Dec. 1992, p. 2.

"round metal kiosks": *Journey*, March 1992, p. 19, June 1993, p. 20; Siobhan Darrow, "U.S. Companies Find Fertile Ground," *CNN*, June 1, 1993, Transcript #372–4.

"bottling plant in St. Petersburg": *Journey*, June 1993, p. 2.

392 "former physicist": *Journey*, June 1993, p. 10.

"It's just like Pepsi-Cola!": Bob Edwards, NPR *Morning Edition*, July 1, 1993.

"joint ventures with the Chinese government": *Journey*, Sept. 1993, p. 8–17; Mark L. Clifford, "Coke Pours into Asia," *Business Week*, oct. 21, 1996, p. 22.

"embraced Western culture": *Cola Conquest*, Part 3.

"world's tallest bottling plant": *Journey*, Sept. 1993, p. 14.

"annual Chinese per capita": 1993 CC Annual Report.

"Coca-Cola returned to India": *Journey*, March 1992, p. 20.

"Goizueta salivated": *Journey*, Jan. 1994, p. 8–11.

"nature abhors a vacuum": *Journey*, March 1992, p. 12.

"Coke returned to any country": *Journey*, Dec. 1991, p. 28.; *Journey*, Dec. 1992, p. 28; Cynthia Mitchell, "Coca-Cola Extends Its Reach," *AJC*, July 20, 1993, p. C3.

393 "Operation Desert Storm": *Journey*, Sept. 1990, p. 32.

"Stormin' Norman Schwarzkopf": *Journey*, June 1991, p. 26.

"average Mexican drank": 1993 CC Annual Report.

"Sandinista regime ended": *Journey*, Dec. 1992, p. 20–21; Americas Watch Report, *Messengers of Death: Human Rights in Guatemala, Nov. 1988-Feb. 1990*, p. 20–23, 57–58.

"Apartheid is good business": "ANC Won't Let Coke Cash in on Mandela Visit," *UPI*, June 13, 1990.

"soft drink was banned": Laurence Jolidon, "Divestment, Sanctions Not Always Simple," *USA Today*, June 19, 1990, p. 5A; Donna Britt, "Mandela, The Man in Demand," *Washington Post*, June 21, 1990, p. E1; Clarence Johnson, "ANC's Oakland Headquarters," *San Francisco Chronicle*, June 27, 1990, p. A9; Deborah Scroggins, "Mandela in Atlanta: Regular Folk to Coke Elite," *Atlanta Journal/Constitution*, July 11, 1993, p. A1.

"Carl Ware . . . befriended Mandela": Juan Williams, "Getting Mandela's Ear," *Washington Post*, April 1, 1990, p. C1.

"Ware assured Mandela": Scroggins, "Mandela in Atlanta: Regular Folk"; John Blake, "Mandela in Atlanta: Visit is Low-Key," *Atlanta Journal/Constitution*, July 12, 1993, p. C1; Ernest Holsendolph, "Coca-Cola in Position For Success in S. Africa," *Atlanta Journal/Constitution*, July 14, 1993, p. E1.

394 "to break $2 billion": Coca-Cola Co. 1993 Annual Report, p. 2–3.

"Coke stock split two-for-one": Greising, *I'd Like the World*, p. 189–190.

"Coke shares languished": 1990, 1991, 1992 and 1993 CC Annual Reports.

"$15 million museum": Ron Alexander, "A Pause to Refresh Memories," *NYT*, Nov. 24, 1991.

"spectacular in Times Square": *Journey*, Dec. 1991, p. 26; March 1992, p. 16–17; "Broadway's Big Bottleneck," *Time*, Jan. 13, 1992, p. 45.

"barely two percent": 1991 and 1992 CC Annual Reports.

395 "Coke II": Eventually, Coke II's market dwindled until by the year 2000 it was available only in the Chicago area. (CC Co. Answer Line)

"foul-smelling and tasting liquid": Greising, *I'd Like the World*, p. 199–200.

"saturation point": Laurie M. Grossman, "Slimmer Diet-Cola Sales," *WSJ*, Nov. 19, 1991.

"mere commodities": Greising, *I'd Like the World*, p. 225.

"private-label colas": "Cheers!" *Globe and Mail*, Feb. 21, 1992; Michael J. McCarthy, "Soft-Drink Giants Sit Up and Take Notice," *WSJ*, March 6, 1992.

"Coke and Pepsi are passé": *Cola Conquest*, Part 3; Greising, *I'd Like the World*. p. 225.

"blind taste tests": "Who's Got the Right One, Baby?" *Consumer Reports*, July 1991.

"baiting fish-hooks": *Cola Conquest*, Part 3.

396 **"a hipper source,"**: Greising, *I'd Like the World*, p. 195–196.

"Ike Herbert . . .called": Ike Herbert retired at the end of 1991 at the age of 63.

"I was blissing out": Laura Zinn, "For Coke's Peter Sealey, Hollywood Is It," *Business Week*, March 15, 1993, p. 84.

"cheap, phony, patronizing": Joanne Lipman, "To Remember '91 Ads Is Human," *WSJ*, Dec. 30, 1991.

"Uh-huh": Greg W. Prince, "Uh-Huh!" *Beverage World*, Dec. 1991; "Best of 1991 Advertising," *Time*, Jan. 6, 1992, p. 69.

"smarmy rendition": Joanne Lipman, "Ads for Elderly," *WSJ*, Dec. 31, 1991; "M. C. Hammers Coke," *Atlanta Constitution*, Dec. 11, 1990.

"staring at a loss": Greising, *I'd Like the World*, p. 194–195, 203–204.

"Coke/CAA partnership": "Coke-CAA Deal Shakes Agency Role," *Advertising Age*, Sept. 9, 1991; Marcy Magiera, "My Meeting with Ovitz," *Advertising Age*, Dec. 9, 1991; Melissa Turner, "Coca-Cola Turns to a Star-Maker," *Atlanta Constitution*, Sept. 5, 1991.

397 **"soft drink ad blitz continued"**: Bob Garfield, "Diet Coke Raises the Dead," *Advertising Age*, Dec. 2, 1991.

"first truly global ad": Martha T. Moore, "Games Vie For Bowl Advertising," *USA Today*, Jan. 24, 1992; Melissa Turner, "Coca-Cola Goes Global," *Atlanta Constitution*, June 24, 1992.

"'Gotta Have It'": Bob Garfield, "Nike Leads Way to Super Bowl," *Advertising Age*, Jan. 20, 1992.

"suspicion, jealousy, resentment": The following section relies on these sources: Greising, *I'd Like the World*, p. 204–215; John Bergin interview; Noreen O'Leary and Richard Morgan, "The Real Story," *Adweek*, Feb. 8, 1993.

398 **"each of the disparate spots"**: Bob Garfield, "Coke Ads Great," *Advertising Age*, Feb. 15, 1993, p. 1.

"underwhelmed by the CAA efforts": Rance Crain, "Ovitz or No Ovitz, Coke Still Adrift," *Advertising Age*, Feb. 22, 1993, p. 22; Jeffrey Wells, "Is It the Reel Thing?" *Los Angeles Times*, Feb. 17, 1993, p. 1; Greising, *I'd Like the World*, p. 216.

399 **"a love fest"**: Larry Jabbonsky, "Coke Take Incomparable Route," *Beverage World*, Feb. 28, 1993, p. 1; Peter Sealey interview; Laura Zinn, "For Coke's Peter Sealey, Hollywood Is It," *Business Week*, March 15, 1993, p. 84; Noreen O'Leary, "Advertising Driven by Client Choice," *Adweek*, Feb. 15, 1993.

"Don Keough retired": Cynthia Mitchell, "Coca-Cola's 'Heart and Soul' Keough," *Atlanta Journal*, April 11, 1993, p. H1.

"Saturday mornings with Sergio": Greising, *I'd Like the World*, p. 212–224.

"failed to rejuvenate diet Coke": Eric Sfiligoj and Greg W. Prince, "Diet Coke's 'Taste' Is Altered," *Beverage World*, Jan. 31, 1993, p. 1; Cynthia Mitchell, "New Coke Classic Ad Blitz," *AJC*, May 28, 1993, p. G7; Cynthia Mitchell, "Coca-Cola Takes a New Look At Diet Coke Ads," *AJC*, July 14, 1993, p. E3.

400 **"isn't working out"**: Michael McCarthy and Andrew Jaffe, "Sealey's Ouster," *Mediaweek*, July 26, 1993, p. 8; Cynthia Mitchell, "Architect of Coke's 'Always' Campaign Quits," *AJC*, July 22, 1993, p. G1; Peter Sealey interview.

"resurrection of Sergio Zyman": John N. Frank, "Zyman Seen Quickly Shaking Up," *Beverage Industry*, Aug. 1993, p. 13; Cynthia Mitchell, "Coca-Cola Looks to Marketing Exec," *AJC*, July 23, 1993, p. H1; Greg Farrell and Jennifer Comiteau, "Big Red Machine," *Adweek*, Nov. 6, 1995.

"I have no desire": Cynthia Mitchell, "Selling the Image: Coca-Cola's Sergio Zyman," *AJC*, April 14, 1994, p. E1.

"Get Used to Sergio.": Greising, *I'd Like the World*, p. 230; Anonymous source.

"create hip products": Greising, *I'd Like the World*, p. 224–228; Cynthia Mitchell, "Coca-Cola Plans Quicker Response on New Products," *AJC*, Nov. 18, 1993, p. E3.

401 **"alternative drinks had grabbed"**: Maria Mallory, "Behemoth on a Tear," *Business Week*, Oct. 3, 1994, p. 54; Cynthia Mitchell, "Coca-Cola Taking Aim at Alternative Market," *AJC*, March 2, 1994, p. G1.

"creation of Tab Clear": Peter Sealey interview; Zyman, *End of Marketing*, p. xv, 35, 48.

"Marlboro Friday": Gerry Ghermouch and Fara Warner, "Reports of the Demise of Brands," *Brandweek*, April 12, 1993, p. 8; Huey, "World's Best Brand," *Fortune*, May 31, 1993, p. 44.

"Neff advised shorting": "Barron's Roundtable 1994, Part 1," *Barron's*, Jan. 17, 1994, p. 12.

"advanced only $4.50 per share": 1993 CC Annual Report, p. 52–53.

"Fruitopia and OK Soda": Larry Jabbonsky, "A Fruitopian Vision," *Beverage World*, March 1994, p. 6; Cynthia Mitchell, "Coca-Cola Taking Aim at Alternative Market," *AJC*, March 2, 1994, p. G1; Wellman, David, "Fruity as a Nutcake," *Food & Beverage Marketing*, April 1994, p. 46; *Journey*, Aug. 1994, p. 11.

402 **"ultra-hip retro-sixties image"**: John N. Frank, "Analysts, Bottlers Give Fruitopia Benefit of Doubt," *Beverage Industry*, April 1994, p. 19.

"a brash effort": *Journey*, Aug. 1994, p. 11–13; Cynthia Mitchell, "OK: Coke Targets New Product," *AJC*, April 21, 1994, p. F1; Larry Jabbonsky & Greg W. Prince, "Things Are Going to Be OK," *Beverage World Periscope Edition*, April 30, 1994, p. 1; "Coke Targets Young Men," *Marketing News TM*, May 23, 1994, p. 8; Noah Adams, "Coke Hopes to Sell New Drink," *All Things Considered*, May 27, 1994.

403 **"Teenagers weren't . . . as disaffected"**: Becky Eblen, "Kids Taste Test Coke's New Product," *AJC*, July 11, 1994, p. E3; Maria Mallory, "Behemoth on a Tear," *Business Week*, Oct. 3, 1994, p. 54; Roush, "Coca-Cola Drops OK Soda Line," *AJC*, Sept. 12, 1995, p. 1D.

"Tangerine Wavelength": *Journey*, Feb. 1995, p. 18; Cynthia Mitchell, "Surreal Thing," *AJC*, Aug. 5, 1994, p. F1.

"Coke–Nestlé partnership": Richard Greer, "Coca-Cola, Nestlé Decide To Scale Back Partnership," *AJC*, Aug. 30, 1994, p. D2.

404 **"loved the new ads"**: Michael Clark, "Bomb Factory Trio Lenses 'Hypnosis' for Coke," *Shoot*, April 22, 1994, p. 11; Cynthia Mitchell, "Marketing Coca-Cola," *AJC*, Feb. 8, 1994, p. D2; Garfield, "CAA Casts Perfect Spell," *Advertising Age*, Feb. 14, 1994, p. 40.

"Zyman began to farm out": Greising, *I'd Like the World*, p. 230–231; Alex Benady, "Coke and IBM's Globe Message," *Marketing* (UK), June 2, 1994, p. 8; Chris Roush, "Marketing a Classic," *AJC*, Feb. 11, 1996, p. F1.

"contour bottle": Matt Walsh, "Coke Goes Better With Contour," *Forbes*, April 11, 1994, p. 20; 1994 CC Annual Report, p. 17–19, 30; Ray Morgan interview; Susan McWhorter interview; *Journey*, Aug. 1994, p. 7–9; *Journey* Feb. 1995, p. 16; "The Contour," *Beverage World Periscope*, May 31, 1994, p. 1;

Larry Jabbonsky, "Coca-Cola Trots Out 26 New Spots," *Beverage World Periscope Edition*, Feb. 28, 1994, p. 1; *Journey*, Feb. 1995, p. 16.

"resurgence of Sprite": 1994 CC Annual Report, p. 22–23.

"tiny Polar Corporation,": Jacqueline Adams, "Coca-Cola and Polar Beverage," *CBS Evening News*, Dec. 29, 1994; Chris Reidy, "Ruling Could Come in Cola TV Ad War," *Boston Globe*, Dec. 30, 1994, p. 69; "Bear Ad Must Change," *Marketing News TM*, Jan. 30, 1995, p. 1.

405 **"Diet Coke . . . a problem child"**: Bob Garfield, "What Taste? Diet Coke Ads Gulp Down Attitude," *Advertising Age*, Jan. 17, 1994, p. 46; Michele Ingrassia, "Hunk-Ogling Babes Reverse Roles," *Montreal Gazette*, March 12, 1994, p. C7; Greising, *I'd Like the World*, p. 231; "Lucky Vanous," *People*, May 9, 1994, p. 58; Jeannie Williams, "Lucky Fans Will Lunch With Diet Coke Hunk," *USA Today*, June 21, 1994; Richard L. Eldredge, "Women Crowd Mall To Glimpse TV Hunk," *AJC*, Aug. 19, 1994, p. D2; DeQuendre Neeley, "Thirsty Women Get Lucky," *Newday*, Sept. 11, 1994, p. 5; Frank DeCaro, "Getting Lucky for New Year's," *Newday*, Dec. 27, 1994, p. B2.

"now it slipped": Larry Jabbonsky, "With Diet Segment In Need of a Boost," *Beverage World*, Jan. 31, 1994, p. 1; "Is This Refreshment?" *Beverage World*, Jan. 31, 1994, p. 4; Eccke Raymond, "Tarsem-Directed Coca-Cola Spot," *Shoot*, July 22, 1994, p. 8.

"recommended Doug Ivester": Cynthia Mitchell, "Ga. Native Is Coca-Cola's New President," *AJC*, July 22, 1994, p. A1; Cynthia Mitchell, "Hard Work an Ivester Hallmark," *AJC*, July 22, 1994, p. B9; Maria Saporta, "Goizueta Proud to Have Groomed Likely Successor," *AJC*, July 22, 1994, p. B1; Cynthia Mitchell, "Likely Successor Is a Cola Warrior," *AJC*, Oct. 19, 1997, p. C6; Betsy Morris, "Doug Is It," *Fortune*, May 25, 1998, p. 74.

406 **"a driving ambition"**: Stephen Dowdell, "Coke President Knocks Store Labels," *Supermarket News*, Nov. 7, 1994, p. 1; Kristine Portnoy Kelley, "Ivester: Squash Parasites," *Beverage Industry*, Dec. 1994, p. 40; Cynthia Mitchell, "Likely Successor Is a Cola Warrior," *AJC*, Oct. 19, 1997, p. C6.

"Get a live hose": Patricia Sellers, "How Coke Is Kicking Pepsi's Can," *Fortune*, Oct. 28, 1996, p. 73; Cynthia Mitchell, "Likely Successor Is a Cola Warrior," *AJC*, Oct. 19, 1997, p. C6.

407 **"marketing blitz"**: Maria Mallory, "Behemoth on a Tear," *Business Week*, Oct. 3, 1994, p. 54; *Journey*, Aug. 1994, p. 19; *Journey*, July 1995, p. 5; "Coca-Cola, NRA Foundation Form Forum," *Nation's Restaurant News*, June 5, 1995, p. 83; Cynthia Mitchell, "It's Hard Work," *AJC*, Oct. 23, 1994, p. Q1; Cynthia Mitchell, "Big Bottler: CCE Overhaul Bearing Fruit," *AJC*, Oct. 23, 1994, p. Q1.

"New Age threat receded": Cynthia Mitchell, "Soft Drink Shake-Up," *AJC*, Nov. 3, 1994, p. E1; Greg Burns, "Tea and Synergy?" *Business Week*, Nov. 14, 1994, p. 44; Chris Roush, "New Ads Make a Case for Coke," *AJC*, Feb. 14, 1995, p. D1.

"Marketer of the Year": "Two Reasons Why Coke Isn't Bearish," *Beverage World*, Jan. 1995, p. 10; 1994 CC Annual Report, p. 1–6.

"on a roll": Chris Roush, "New Coke's 10th Anniversary," *AJC*, April 11, 1995, p. 1D; *Journey*, July 1995, p. 9.

"increased volume everywhere": Chris Roush, "Things Go Better With Risk," *AJC*, July 30, 1995, p. 1R; *Journey*, Aug. 1994, p. 3; *Journey*, Feb. 1995, p. 5; *Journey*, July 1995, p. 24, 29; *Journey*, Jan. 1996, p. 15, 21; Tim O'Brien, "Coca-Cola's New Cool Zones," *Amusement Business*, Aug. 7, 1995, p. 6; 1995 CC Annual Report, p. 29, 32; Marcia Kunstel, "Touch of Home," *AJC*, May 12, 1995, p. 1D; Nikhil Deogun, "Pop Culture: A Coke and a Perm?" *WSJ*, May 8,

1997, p. A1; Nikhil Deogun, "Can His Successor, Douglas Ivester, Refresh Coca-Cola?" *WSJ*, Oct. 20, 1997, p. B1.

408 **"infiltrate schools"**: *Journey*, July 1995, p. 4, 25; "Coke's Polar Bears Going BTS," *Supermarket News*, Dec. 11, 1995, p. 72.

"Patrick Leahy proposed": "Mouse for the War on Cancer," *U.S. News & World Report*, May 9, 1994, p. 18; Patrick Leahy, "Testimony, May 15, 1994," *Federal Document Clearing House*; Christopher Seward, "Group Wants Coke Out of Schools," *AJC*, Sept. 3, 1994, p. B3; "Healthy Meals for Healthy Americans Act of 1994," PL103–448, Sec. 203.

409 **"University administrators"**: Tony Kennedy, "Coke Squirts Past Pepsi at U," *Star Tribune*, Dec. 23, 1995, p. D1; Kathy Hoke, "Coke, Pepsi Pour It On," *Business First-Columbus*, April 3, 1998, p. 1.

"anchor bottlers": 1995 CC Annual Report, p. 40; Scott Weeks, "Always Panamco," *LatinFinance*, Dec. 1995, p. 59; Havis Dawson, "Anchors Swell the Tide," *Beverage World*, Dec. 1995, p. 6; Chris Roush, "Things Go Better With Risk," *AJC*, July 30, 1995, p. 1R; Chris Roush, "Coke's Ivester Gets Good Marks," *AJC*, July 30, 1995, p. 5R.

"Champ of Wealth Creation": Terence P. Pare, "The New Champ of Wealth Creation," *Fortune*, Sept. 18, 1995, p. 131.

"Red Hot Summer": *Journey*, Aug. 1994, p. 10; *Journey*, July 1995, p. 5; Greg Farrell and Jennifer Comiteau, "Big Red Machine," *Adweek*, Nov. 6, 1995; Chris Roush, "Soda Fountain for Space," *AJC*, Jan. 24, 1995, p. F3.

"The dispenser": "Things Go Better in Orbit," *AJC*, May 24, 1996, p. B1.

"Coke bought Barq's": Karen Benezra, "Taking Stock," *Adweek*, Nov. 6, 1995; *Journey*, Jan. 1996, p. 14; Bob Garfield, "Barq's Keeps Its Cool in Stink-n-Stare Promotion," *Advertising Age*, Aug. 21, 1995, p. 3.

"end of 1995": 1995 CC Annual Report, p. 1–40; *Journey*, Feb. 1995, p. 13.

410 **"Billy Payne had decided"**: Greising, *I'd Like the World*, p. 246–254; Jennings, *New Lords of the Rings*, p. 133–149.

"Atlanta had won": Edward Neilan, "Atlanta's Olympic Gold Not Cheered by Sore Losers," *Washington Times*, Sept. 19, 1990, p. A1; "Selection Took Many by Surprise," *USA Today*, Sept. 19, 1990, p. 2C.

"all manner of special favors": Jennings, *New Lords of the Rings*, p. 58, 124, 138–141; Kathy Lohr, "Records Kept by Atlanta's Olympic Organizers," NPR, May 8, 1999; Melissa Turner, "Coke Puts Olympics on Notice," *AJC*, Jan. 12, 1999, p. 1A; Melissa Turner, "IOC Official Vows to 'Clean House,'" *AJC*, Jan. 14, 1999, p. 1A.

411 **"Goizueta and Juan Antonio Samaranch"**: Greising, *I'd Like the World*, p. 251–257; Jennings, *New Lords of the Rings*, p. 15, 138; Andrew Jennings email, May 19, 1999.

"marketer's dream": *Journey*, July 1996, p. 1, 10.

"activate our sponsorships": Greising, *I'd Like the World*, p. 264–265.

"Experiential event marketing": Mark Driscoll interview.

412 **"came from the Nazis"**: Greising, *I'd Like the World*, p. 267; Bryant, John, "Bogus Tradition Is Burning Brightly," [London]*Times*, April 11, 1996.

"sponsor the torch": Thomas Heath, "Olympic Torch Relay's Path Paved with Gold," *Washington Post*, March 16, 1996, p. A1.

"masterfully planned": Glenn Collins, "Coke's Hometown Olympics," *NYT*, March 28, 1996, p. D1; Elizabeth Lee, "Sites Carry Torch for Olympics," *AJC*, April 28, 1996, p. 4H.

"rolling street party": Michael Ollove, "On the Road with the Torch," *Baltimore Sun*, June 19, 1996, p. 1E; Mark Driscoll interview; Jim Auchmutey, "Whose Party Is It, Anyway?" *AJC*, May 9, 1996; Henry Unger, "Coke's Games Plan," *AJC*, June 2, 1996, p. 4H.

"**pins, jackets**": John Masson, "Despite Cola Hype, Torch More Than Passing Fancy," *Indianapolis Star*, June 6, 1996, p. C1.

413 "**like hosting the Olympics**": Amy Rinard, "Torch Gets Olympic Welcome," *Milwaukee Journal Sentinel*, June 1, 1996, p. 3.

"**a harder edge**": Donna Glenn and Mike Lafferty, "Cola War Flares Up During Torch Run," *Columbus Dispatch*, June 8, 1996, p. 2A.

"**draping the Pepsi**": Anne Hart, "Have a Coke and a . . . Pepsi?" *AJC*, June 27, 1996, p. 3M.

"**91-page guidebook**": Greising, *I'd Like the World*, p. 267.

"**Coca-Cola carnival**": James Langton, "Pop Go the Olympics," *Sunday Telegraph*, June 30, 1996, p. 1; Bruce Venner interview.

"**children out of school**": Dan Hulbert, "Behold the Flame," *AJC*, July 4, 1996, p. 1C; Howard Pousner, "Small Town Gives Big Welcome," *AJC*, April 30, 1996, p. 4E.

"**Even in big cities**": Mark Gleason, "Coca-Cola Co. Looked to Better Integrate," *Advertising Age*, March 17, 1997, p. S1; Mark Driscoll interview; Michael Ollove, "On the Road with the Torch," *Baltimore Sun*, June 19, 1996, p. 1E.

"**genuine emotion**": Susan McWhorter interview; Bruce Venner interview; Jon Gailmor interview.

"**cheered, cried, and drank**": "Coke Is First Off Blocks," *Marketing Week*, Aug. 2, 1996, p. 24–25; Mark Driscoll interview.

414 "**Coke Here, There,**": "Atlanta Games Keepsake Edition," *AJC*, Aug. 6, 1996, p. 13; Henry Unger, "Stationing Olympic Promotions," *AJC*, March 28, 1996, p. 1G; Bill Glauber, "Welcome to the Coca-Cola Games," *Baltimore Sun*, July 19, 1996, p. 2A.

"**Coca-Cola Olympic City**": Kate Fitzgerald, "Events & Promotions," *Advertising Age*, March 25, 1996, p. 16; Tim O'Brien, "High-Tech, Interactive Attractions Focus of Coca-Cola Olympic City," *Amusement Business*, April 15, 1996, p. 20; Chris Roush, "Visitors Put Olympic City to the Test," *AJC*, May 17, 1996, p. 3H.

"**promotional campaign**": "Coca-Cola Designs Olympic Zone Merchandising," *Supermarket News*, May 13, 1996, p. 40; Chris Roush, "Red-Hot Olympic Giveaway Campaign," *AJC*, May 16, 1996, p. 1D.

"**pressured Atlanta organizers**": Judann Pollack, "A-B's Olympic Snack Deal," *Advertising Age*, April 1, 1996; "Coke Signs Lease Deal," *Reuters Financial Service*, April 9, 1996; Larry McShane, "Coke is It in Atlanta at Olympic Games," *Burlington Free Press*, July 21, 1996; Greg W. Prince and Nick Christy, "Cold Fun in the Summertime," *Beverage World*, May 1996, p. 30.

"**displaced subsidized Techwood housing**": Preston Quesenberry, "The Disposable Olympics Meets the City of Hope," *Southern Changes*, Summer 1996, p. 3–14.

415 "**For the Fans,**": Chris Roush, "Tribute to Sports Fans," *AJC*, March 6, 1996, p. 1E; Chris Roush, "Commercials Spotlight Spectators," *AJC*, June 2, 1996, p. 5H.

"**Coke as the star**": Chris Roush and Henry Unger, "Coke's Game Plan," *AJC*, June 2, 1996, p. 1H; Chris Roush, "It's Around the World," *AJC*, June 2, 1996, p. 5H; Chris Roush, "Coca-Cola to Air 100 Ads," *AJC*, July 16, 1996, p. 17S; "Coke is First Off the Blocks," *Marketing Week*, Aug. 2, 1996, p. 24–25.

"**very economic buy**": Greg W. Prince and Nick Christy, "Cold Fun in the Summertime," *Beverage World*, May 1996, p. 30; Glenn Collins, "Coke's Hometown Olympics," *New York Times*, March 28, 1996, p. D1.

"**Coke's Olympic efforts**": Greising, *I'd Like the World*, p. 264; Patricia

Sellers, "How Coke Is Kicking Pepsi's Can," *Fortune*, Oct. 28, 1996, p. 80; "Atlanta Games, Keepsake Edition," *AJC*, Aug. 6, 1996, p. 20, 22.

"Gustavo Cisneros": Chris Roush, "Coca-Cola Pulls Rug From Under Pepsi with Deal in Venezuela," *AJC*, Aug. 17, 1996, p. 1G; Greising, *I'd Like the World*, p. 272–278; Patricia Sellers, "How Coke is Kicking Pepsi's Can," *Fortune*, Oct. 28, 1996, p. 70–84; David Swafford, "Coca-Cola's Sweet Formula," *LatinFinance*, July 1997/Aug. 1997, p. 75.

416 **"victory in Russia"**: Chris Roush, "Coca-Cola Claims Victory in Russia," *AJC*, Aug. 27, 1996, p. 1B.

"Pepsi two black eyes": Roberto Goizueta interview.

"monarch of soft drinks": "Roberto Goizueta, the Man Atop the No. 1 Brand," *Fortune*, March 4, 1996, cover; "Pepsi's Enrico: Bottled Up By Coke," *Fortune*, Oct. 28, 1996, cover.

"his greatest challenge": Patricia Sellers, "Pepsico's New Generation," *Fortune*, April 1, 1996, p. 110; David Swafford, "The Fizz That Couldn't Last," *Latin Finance*, Nov. 1996, p. 36; Patricia Sellers, "How Coke Is Kicking Pepsi's Can," *Fortune*, Oct. 28, 1996, p. 70–84; Bill Saporito, "Parched for Growth," *Time*, Sept. 2, 1996, p. 48–49; "Pepsi-Cola's International Focus Looks Sharp," *Beverage Industry*, May 1998, p. 8.

"Minute Maid Company": David Wellman, "Dairy Maid," *Food & Beverage Marketing*, July 1996, p. 29; "Coca-Cola Offers New Single-Serve," *Supermarket News*, July 1, 1996, p. 21; Chris Roush, "Juice Unit's Big Push," *AJC*, Sept. 18, 1996, p. 1D; Chris Roush, "Coca-Cola Juices Up a Name," *AJC*, Oct. 15, 1996, p. 1B; Chris Roush, "Coca-Cola Tweaks the Taste of Minute Maid Orange Juice," *AJC*, Nov. 21, 1996, p. 3D; Judann Pollack, "Minute Maid Ad Budget Will Triple," *Advertising Age*, Nov. 25, 1996, p. 29; Nicole Harris, "It's Zero Hour for Minute Maid," *Business Week*, Dec. 2, 1996, p. 87.

417 **"By year's end"**: 1996 CC Annual Report, p. 1–7; David McNaughton, "Coca-Cola-Related Stocks Do Better," *AJC* Jan. 4, 1997, p. 23S.

"I'm having fun": Patricia Sellers, "How Coke Is Kicking Pepsi's Can," *Fortune*, Oct. 28, 1996, p. 72–73; Maria Saporta, "Coca-Cola's Jaunt to Delaware," *AJC* April 18, 1996, p. 1B; Maria Saporta, "Always Full of Spirit," *AJC* Oct. 22, 1997, p. F3.

"billion hours ago": 1996 CC Annual Report, p. 10; Edward Robinson, "America's Most Admired Companies," *Fortune*, March 3, 1997, p. 68.

418 **"Caught Red Handed"**: Mark Gleason, "Coke Creates Prize-Laden 'Red Crew,'" *Advertising Age*, Jan. 6, 1997; Chris Roush, "Big Push," *AJC*, Jan. 11, 1997, p. 1E; p. 2; Mark Driscoll interview; Chris Roush, "Cashing in on Summer," *AJC*, March 29, 1997, p. 1C; Karen Benezra, "Coke Kicks Off Summer Campaign," *Adweek*, June 9, 1997.

"interactive marketing": Chris Roush, "Coca-Cola aims Super Bowl Events at Fans," *AJC*, Jan. 14, 1997, p. 6F; Chris Roush, "Coca-Cola's Bigger Game Plan," *AJC*, Feb. 23, 1997, p. G1; Chris Roush, "Coca-Cola Goes to Bat," *AJC*, March 22, 1997, p. 4E.

"museum in Las Vegas": Chris Roush, "Coke's Vegas Store Raises Ante," *AJC*, May 2, 1997, p. 2H; John McIntosh, "A Las Vegas Story," *MacWeek*, Aug. 11, 1997, p. 18.

"introduced Surge": Scott Hume, "Marketer of Dr. Rush and Other Beverages Sues Coca-Cola," *Adweek*, Feb. 24, 1997; "Judge Orders Mom & Pop 'Surge' Makers to Accept Coca-Cola Offer," *Intellectual Property Today*, Oct. 1998, p. 13; Chris Roush, "Teens Have Urge For Surge," *AJC*, Jan. 11, 1997, p. 2E; Mike Reynolds, "Citrus Clash," *Food & Beverage Marketing*, Feb. 1997, p. 10; Havis Dawson, "Caffeine and Kids," *Beverage World*, Feb. 1997, p. 8; Greg W. Prince, "Is Coke Building the Next Great Brand in Surge?" *Beverage*

World, March 1997, p. 30; Jeffery D. Zbar, "Marketing 100: Surge," *Advertising Age*, June 30, 1997, p. S35.

419 **"introduced Citra"**: Mark Gleason and Pat Sloan, "Coke's New Citra," *Advertising Age*, Jan. 13, 1997, p. 1; "Coca-Cola Plans Grapefruit-Flavored Drink," *AJC*, Jan. 14, 1997, p. 3F; Chris Roush, "Another Citrus-Flavored Soft Drink," *AJC*, Feb. 27, 1997, p. 4F.

"Obey Your Thirst": Chris Roush, "Sprite Moves Up in Rankings," *AJC*, Feb. 5, 1997, p. 1C; Chris Roush, "Shootout at the Fairgrounds," *AJC*, Aug. 3, 1997, p. 2H.

"Cool Nestea": Chris Roush, "Coca-Cola Dropping Last Two Fruitopia Teas," *AJC*, Feb. 18, 1997, p. 1E; "Shakeup on Horizon in 'New Age' Segment of Beverage Market," *Chain Drug Review*, July 28, 1997, p. 28.

"long-delayed contour can": Chris Roush, "Coca-Cola Ready to Test New Curvy Can," *AJC*, Feb. 19, 1997, p. 3F; "Coke Throws a Curve at Can-Making Technology," *Packaging Digest*, March 1997, p. 3; Chris Roush, "Trying to Shape a Success," *AJC*, April 4, 1997, p. 8F; Chris Roush, "Improved Cola Taste?" *AJC*, May 23, 1997, p. 1E.

"Overseas, Coke sales bounced": Chris Roush, "Rebound Overseas Fuels Coca-Cola Profit," *AJC*, Feb. 1, 1997, p. 1E; "Coca-Cola Outsells Pepsi 2 to 1," *AJC*, Feb. 14, 1997; Chris Roush, "Earnings Reports Positive," *AJC*, April 15, 1997, p. 1B; "Coca-Cola Invests $360 Million," *Jet*, March 31, 1997, p. 33.

"buy and sell bottlers": "Coca-Cola Designates 9th 'Anchor,'" *AJC*, March 26, 1997, p. 2F; Cynthia Mitchell, "Bottler Deals Hurt Coca-Cola Earnings," *AJC*, Oct. 17, 1997; Chris Roush, "Coca-Cola Consolidation of Its Bottlers Paying Off," *AJC*, July 18, 1997, p. 1F.

"Coke stock surged": Robert Luke, "Barron's Is Down on 'Extravagant' Coca-Cola Shares," *AJC*, March 4, 1997, p. 4F; "Fidelity Investments' Flagship," *Washington Times*, March 9, 1997, p. A12; Cynthia Mitchell, "Bottler Deals Hurt Coca-Cola Earnings," *AJC*, Oct. 17, 1997; Robert Luke, "Habitual Naysayer Once Again Hurls Barb at Coca-Cola," *AJC*, July 2, 1997, p. 4E.

"David Greising,": Chris Roush, "The Word on Coke," *AJC*, March 6, 1997, p. 1E; Greising, *I'd Like the World*, p. v–ix.

"Hillary Rodham Clinton praised": Maria Mallory, "Carbonating a Continent," *U.S. News & World Report*, May 5, 1997, p. 55.

420 **"thinking about his legacy"**: Maria Saporta, "Coca-Cola's Jaunt to Delaware," *AJC*, April 18, 1996, p. 1B.

"he began to reach out": Roberto C. Goizueta, "It's a Bold Program," *AJC*, May 21, 1996, p. 6D; Chris Roush, "Goizueta Pops Top on $38 Million Gift," *AJC*, June 13, 1997, p. 1F; Maria Saporta, "Goizueta's Indirect Philanthropy Was Vital," *AJC*, Oct. 19, 1997, p. C2.

"to create value": Roberto C. Goizueta, "The Real Essence of Business," *Vital Speeches*, Jan. 15, 1997, p. 199; Chris Roush, "Coca-Cola's Guiding Light," *AJC*, Nov. 24, 1996, p. 1H; Chris Roush, "Coca-Cola Chief: Layoffs Not a Part of Growth Strategy," *AJC*, Sept. 4, 1996, p. 3E; William J. Holstein, "Drink Coke and Be Nice," *U.S. News & World Report*, June 9, 1997, p. 50.

421 **"strategic philanthropy"**: Maria Saporta, "Coca-Cola, Other Companies Offer 'Strategic Philanthropy,'" *AJC*, April 26, 1997, p. 3E.

"Financially strapped tight schools": Irene Cherkassky, "Exclusive School Contracts," *Beverage World*, Oct. 1998, p. 96; Michael Jacobson, "How Much Soda Pop?" *NYT*, Nov. 15, 1998, p. C36.

"Goizueta's enthusiasm": J. P. Donlon, "The Eight-Nine Billion Dollar Man," *Chief Executive*, July 1996, p. 42; Joan Holleran, "The King of Coca-Cola," *Beverage Industry*, Nov. 1996, p. 34.

"asked about his successor": J. P. Donlon, "The Eight-Nine Billion Dollar

Man," *Chief Executive*, July 1996, p. 42; Chris Roush, "Looking Ahead at Big Red," *AJC*, July 13,1997, p. 1D.

"the soul of their companies": Maria Saporta, "Goizueta Takes Cue From Marcus," *AJC*, May 31, 1997, p. 1E.

"I'm a little fatigued": Greising, *I'd Like the World*, p. 300–304; "Hospitalized: Goizueta," *AJC*, Oct. 11, 1997; Cynthia Mitchell, "Goizueta 'Gravely Ill' at Hospital," *AJC*, Oct. 14, 1997; Cynthia Mitchell and Tom Eblen, "Funeral Tuesday for Coca-Cola CEO," *AJC*, Oct. 19, 1997.

422 **"funeral ceremony"**: Cynthia Mitchell and Maria Saporta, "A Classic Tribute to Goizueta," *AJC*, Oct. 22, 1997, Cynthia Mitchell, "With His Dying Breath," *AJC*, Oct. 22, 1997; "Business and Politics Merge To Mourn Coke's Chairman," *NYT*, Oct. 22, 1997, p. A21.

"outpouring of tributes": *AJC* Perspective section, Oct. 19, 1997, p. C1–C8; Cynthia Mitchell and Tom Eblen, "Funeral Tuesday for Coca-Cola CEO," *AJC*, Oct. 19, 1997.

"Goizueta left an astonishing legacy": Patricia Sellers, "Where Coke Goes From Here," *Fortune*, Oct. 13, 1997, p. 88; Tom Eblen, "It Was His Passion," *AJC*, Oct. 19, 1997, p. C3; "Coca-Cola's Driving Force," *AJC*, Oct. 19, 1997, p. C7; Nikhil Deogun, "Coke's Impact on Atlanta," *WSJ*, Oct. 21, 1997, p. E1; Greg W. Prince, "Goizueta's Legacies," *Beverage World*, Dec. 1997, p. 42; Nikhil Deogun, "Ivester Alert," *WSJ*, March 9, 1998, p. A1.

423 **"remained an enigma"**: Greising, *I'd Like the World*, p. xvi.

"day he fled Castro's Cuba": Scott Thurston and Cynthia Mitchell, "He Was the Real Thing," *AJC*, Oct. 19, 1999, p. C1.

"a group of immigrants": Roberto Goizueta, "Opportunity Always Comes Accompanied by Obligations," *AJC*, Oct. 19, 1997, p. C1.

CHAPTER 22: IVESTER INHERITS A WORLD OF TROUBLE

424 **"*One of the virtues*"**: Constance L. Hays, "Worldwide, Things Are Not Going Better for Coke," *NYT*, March 2, 1999, p. C1.

"pick as his No 2": Cynthia Mitchell, "Where Will Coke Go Without Him?" *AJC*, Oct. 19, 1997, p. C6; Cynthia Mitchell, "Challenges Await Ivester," *AJC*, Oct. 26, 1997, p. 6G; Louise Kramer, "Coke Mum on Who'll Take President's Post," *Advertising Age*, Oct. 27, 1997, p. 66.

"Zyman soon departed": Louise Kramer, "Frenette Has Local Agenda," *Advertising Age*, March 23, 1998, p. 3; "Coke Marketing Chief Zyman Departs," *Adweek*, March 23, 1998, p. 34; Nikhil Deogun, "Advertising Coke's Marketing Chief, Sergio Zyman, to Quit," *WSJ*, March 19, 1998, p. B1; Nikhil Deogun, "Will Coke's New Marketing Chief Cut Back?" *WSJ*, March 23, 1998, p. B6.

"Neville Isdell, arguably": 1997 CC Annual Report, p. 7; Nikhil Deogun, "Coke Overseas Bottler to Split Into Two Firms," *WSJ*, Feb. 5, 1998, p. A3.

"what it would take": Hedy Halpert, "The Big Picture," *Beverage World*, Nov. 1998, p. 36; Betsy Morris, "Doug Is It," *Fortune*, May 25, 1998, p. 84.

"direct calls and e-mails": Nikhil Deogun, "Can His Successor, Douglas Ivester, Refresh Coca-Cola?" *WSJ*, Oct. 29, 1997, p. B1; Nikhil Deogun, "Ivester Alert," *WSJ*, March 9, 1998, p. A1.

"an odd couple": Peter Sealey interview; Chris Roush interview.

425 **"signs of trouble"**: Nikhil Deogun, "Coke CEO's Strategy, Not Illness, Causes Jitters," *WSJ*, Sept. 21, 1997; Cynthia Mitchell, "Bottler Deals Hurt Coca-Cola Earnings," *AJC*, Oct. 17, 1997, p. 1F; Albert J. Meyer and Dwight M. Owsen, "Coca-Cola's Accounting: Is It Really the Real Thing?" *Accounting Today*, Sept. 28, 1998.

"smashed Coke can": Karyn McCormack, "Losing Fizz," *Financial World*, July/Aug. 1997, p. 28–32.

"look back at 1997": Cynthia Mitchell, "Looking for French Fizz," *AJC*, Dec. 23, 1997, p. 1E; Nikhil Deogun, "Coca-Cola May Purchase Orangina," *WSJ*, Dec. 22, 1997, p. B1; Nikhil Deogun, "Coca-Cola's Orangina Deal Likely to Face Protests," *WSJ*, Dec. 23, 1997, p. B4; Nikhil Deogun, "Ivester Sees Rise in Sales," *WSJ*, Dec. 22, 1997, p. A4; 1997 CC Annual Report, p. 5; *Journey*, May 1998, p. 12; Randy Boswell, "How the World Caught the Asian Flu," *Ottawa Citizen*, Oct. 7, 1998, p. A1.

"a significant challenge": 1997 CC Annual Report, p. 1–5.

"rippling out from Asia": *Journey*, May 1998, p. 14–25; Martha M. Hamilton, "In Asia, Things Go Better With Coke," *Washington Post National Weekly Edition*, Sept. 7, 1998, p. 19

426 **"bottom dropped out"**: David Barbarzo, "Stocks Gain Slightly," *NYT*,, May 29, 1998, Jonathan Fuerbringer, "Crucial Week for a Frayed Global Safety Net," *NYT*, Sept. 27, 1998, p. C7; Randy Boswell, "How the World Caught the Asian Flu," *Ottawa Citizen*, Oct. 7, 1998, p. A1.

"third quarter dropped": Michael Shari, "Everything Was Totally Destroyed," *Business Week*, June 1, 1998, p. 33; Nikhil Deogun, "Can Coke Rise to the Global Challenge?" *WSJ*, Sept. 24, 1998, p. C1; Nikhil Deogun, "Coca-Cola's Net Income Fell by 12%," *WSJ*, Oct. 16, 1998, p. A4; "Markets Plunged," *News 4 Texas At Five*, Aug. 27, 1998; Chris Rivituso, "Hanging Tough in Russia," *Advertising Age*, Sept. 7, 1998, p. 3; "Inchcape Limits Russian Damage," *Corporate Money*, Oct. 14, 1998, p. 2; William C. Symonds, "Why No Company Is Immune," *Business Week*, Sept. 14, 1998, p. 38; Constance L. Hays, "Coca-Cola's Earnings Down by 12.2% in Third Quarter," *NYT*, Oct. 16, 1998, p. C2; Constance L. Hays, "Global Crisis for Coca-Cola," *NYT*, Nov. 1, 1998, p. 1; Nikhil Deogun, "Burst Bubbles," *WSJ*, Feb. 8, 1999, p. A1.

"outwardly unflappable": Nikhil Deogun, "Ivester Alert," *WSJ*, March 9, 1998, p. A1; Constance L. Hays, "Global Crisis for Coca-Cola," *NYT*, Nov. 1, 1998, p. 1.

427 **"meeting on December 11"**: "Coca-Cola Abruptly Calls Analyst Meeting," *NYT*, Dec. 11, 1998, p. C7; Lauren Thierry and Rhonda Schaffler, "NYSE Update," *Trading Places, CNN*, Dec. 11, 1998; Constance L. Hays, "Coke Warns of Poor Foreign Results," *NYT*, Dec. 12, 1998, p. C2; Nikhil Deogun, "Coke to Buy Cadbury Brands," *WSJ*, Dec. 14, 1998, p. A3; Nikhil Deogun, "Coke Hastily Schedules Analyst Meeting," *WSJ*, Dec. 11, 1998, p. A4.

"share price ended 1998": 1998 CC Annual Report, p. 1–19.

"a recharged Pepsico": Chris Roush, "Pepsi, Coke At It Again," *AJC*, June 12, 1997, p. 3G.

"spun off Pepsi's restaurants": "A Pepsico History," 9/2/98, from Pepsico, Purchase, NY;

"struck deals": Mary Ellen Kuhn, "Taking on Goliath," *Food Processing*, Sept. 1997, p. 22; Louise Kramer, "Coke Makes Fast-Food Gain," *Advertising Age*, Nov. 17, 1997, p. 85; Kent Steinriede, "Fountain War Heats Up," *Beverage Industry*, Oct. 1, 1998, p. 32; Constance L. Hays, "To Increase Sales, Burger King Plans," *NYT*, April 15, 1999, p. C10.

"Pepsi sued Coke": Larry Light, "Litigation: The Choice of a New Generation," *Business Week*, May 25, 1998, p. 42; "Cola Wars Open Distribution Front," *ID*, July 1998, p. 17; Caroline Perkins, "Soft Drink/Software Power Struggle," *ID*, July 1998, p. 13; "Big Suits," *American Lawyer*, July/Aug. 1998, p. 101; "Coca-Cola Inquiry in Italy Is Extended," *WSJ*, Jan. 6, 1999, p. C2; "Coca-Cola Must Answer Charges in India," *AJC*, April 18, 1998; Cynthia Mitchell, "Pepsico Striving to Reignite Cola Wars," *AJC*, May 8, 1998; Mickey

H. Gramig, "Pepsi Sues Coke over Sales Tactic," *AJC*, May 8, 1998; "Pepsi May Face Uphill Challenge," *AJC*, May 8, 1998; Mickey H. Gramig, "Pepsi Suit Ultimately About Larger Market Slice," *AJC*, May 10, 1998, p. R1.

428 **"offer or acquire new drinks"**: "Pepsi OKs Pepsi One," *Advertising Age*, July 6, 1998, p. 21; "Marketers Seek, Find Opportunities," *Chain Drug Review*, Aug. 10, 1998, p. 90; Sarah Theodore, "Sweeteners Put to the Test," *Beverage Industry*, Dec. 1998, p. 32; Nikhil Deogun, "New Sweetener," *WSJ*, July 1, 1998, p. B1.

"Mountain Dew continued": Stuart Elliott, "Coca-Cola Prepares a New Campaign for Surge," *NYT*, Feb. 10, 1999, p. C8.

"introduced Storm": Louise Kramer, "Pepsi Moves New Storm Into Broad Battlefield," *Advertising Age*, July 13, 1998, p. 1; Louise Kramer, "Coca-Cola Not Concerned by Surge Supermarket Dip," *Advertising Age*, July 20, 1998, p. 30.

"Pepsi bought Tropicana": "Pepsico Buys Tropicana," *Advertising Age*, July 27, 1998, p. 25; "Beverage Wars Intensify As PepsiCo Acquires Tropicana," *Chain Drug Review*, Aug. 10, 1998, p. 6; Constance L. Hays, "Pulp Friction," *NYT*, May 19, 1999, p. C1.

"Pepsi Stuff campaign": Kate Fitzgerald, "Pepsi Stuff," *Advertising Age*, June 30, 1997, p. S22; Michael J. McDermott, "Coke & Pepsi: Still At It," *Food & Beverage Marketing*, Aug. 1997, p. 12.

"playing catch-up ball": "Pepsi Plays Ball," *Marketing News TM*, April 14, 1997, p. 1; Chris Roush, "Pepsi Swinging for the Fences," *AJC*, March 20, 1997, p. 1F.

"battle for soda supremacy": David Greising, "Cola Wars on the Mean Streets," *Business Week*, Aug. 3, 1998, p. 78.

"Pepsi sharpened its focus": "Pepsi-Cola's International Focus Looks Sharp," *Beverage Industry*, May 1998, p. 8.

"India was sputtering": George Skaria, "Can Coca-Cola Bottle Up the Chauhans?" *Business Today*, Aug. 22, 1998, p. 38; Nikhil Deogun, "For Coke in India, Thums Up Is the Real Thing," *WSJ*, April 28, 1998, p. B1.

429 **"In Venezuela"**: Constance L. Hays, "Coca-Cola Is Battling . . . in Venezuela," *NYT*, Dec. 18, 1998, p. C3.

"Brian Swette resigned": Louise Kramer, "Pepsi Revamps Marketing Staff," *Advertising Age*, May 4, 1998, p. 4; Mickey H. Gramig, "Pepsi's Challenge," *AJC* May 24, 1998.

"uncharacteristically lame": "Pepsico History," Pepsico, 9/28/98; Gramig, Mickey, "Pepsi-Cola Marketing Chief Quits," *AJC*, May 1, 1998.

"marketing chief Dawn Hudson": Sally Beatty, "Coke, Pepsi Gear Up for Ad Wars," *WSJ*, March 22, 1999, p. B9; "Pepsi Looks for a New Generation of Ads," *Bloomberg News*, Jan. 27, 1999, p. C13.

"stressed the synergies": Frank Gibney Jr., "Pepsi Gets Back in the Game," *Time*, April 26, 1999, p. 44–46.

"Pepsi Bottling Group": Michael Ozanian, "Numbers Game," *Forbes*, Aug. 24, 1998, p. 52; Constance L. Hays, "Pepsico's Latest Strategic Move," *NYT*, Jan. 26, 1999, p. C11; Edward Wyatt, "Pepsi Bottling Is a Giant Offering," *NYT*, March 31, 1999, p. C13.

"ducks in a row": 1998 Pepsico annual report, cover, p. 2.

"Coke continued to dominate": Chris Roush, "Coca-Cola Plans Better Sales Data," *AJC*, Sept. 13, 1996, p. 1F; Charles Elliott in *Cola Conquest*, Part 2; Betsy Morris, "Doug Is It," *Fortune*, May 25, 1998, p. 70–84; Nikhil Deogun, "Ivester Alert," *WSJ*, March 9, 1998, p. A1; Nikhil Deogun, "Australia Blocks Coke's Bid," *WSJ*, April 9, 1999, p. A3; "Coke Expands Its Lead in U.S.," *NYT*, Feb. 13, 1999, p. C14.

430 **"business jargon"**: Betsy Morris, "Doug Is It," *Fortune*, May 25, 1998, p. 74; Hedy Halpert, "The Big Picture," *Beverage World*, Nov. 1998, p. 36; Dyan Machan, "There's Something About Henry," *Forbes*, Oct. 5, 1998, p. 82; Nikhil Deogun, "Pop Culture," *WSJ*, May 8, 1997, p. A1; *Journey*, May 1998, p. 8–9, 28–29.

"do the right thing": *Journey*, Nov. 1998, p. 20, 23.

"a relentless force": Betsy Morris, "Doug Is It," *Fortune*, May 25, 1998, p. 73; Ray Morgan interview; Jim Stevens interview; Terry Neill interview.

431 **"arrogant?"**: *Journey*, Aug. 1997, p. 7; *Journey*, May 1998, p. 2.

"Ivester's imprint": Cynthia Mitchell, "Bribery Trial," *AJC*, Dec. 2, 1997, p. 1E; Cynthia Mitchell, "Key Witness Tells of Payoffs," *AJC*, Dec. 4, 1997, p. F1; Cynthia Mitchell, "Prosecution Rests Case," *AJC*, Dec. 8, 1997, p. F5; Cynthia Mitchell, "CCE Executives' Final Witness," *AJC*, Dec. 10, 1997; Cynthia Mitchell, "Bribery Trial of CCE Executives Goes to Jury," *AJC*, Dec. 12, 1997; Matt Kempner, "CCE Managers Acquitted," *AJC*, Dec. 16, 1997, p. C1.

"non-apple sources": "In Re The Coca-Cola Company Apple Juice Consumer Litigation," *Business Wire*, Dec. 17, 1997.

"against its own distributors": Constance L. Hays, "Distributor Accuses Coca-Cola Enterprises of Fraud," *NYT*, Jan. 7, 1999, p. C2; Constance L. Hays, "When Your Bottler Is Your Rival," *NYT*, Jan. 21, 1999, p. C2; Nikhil Deogun, "Antitrust Suit Against Big Coke Bottler," *WSJ*, Jan. 2, 1999, p. B1; Henry Unger, "Consolidation Sweeping Coca-Cola Bottlers," *AJC*, March 23, 1999, p. D1; Constance L. Hays, "Distributor Settles Fraud Case," *NYT*, May 20, 1999, p. C3; Nikhil Deogun, "B. K. Miller Co. Antitrust Lawsuit Settled," *WSJ*, May 21, 1999, p. B2.

"used child labor": Cynthia Mitchell, "Coca-Cola Unit Target of Protest, *AJC*, Jan. 14, 1998.

432 **"class action suit"**: Steven A. Holmes, "Blacks, Citing Bias at Work, Sue Coca-Cola," *NYT*, April 23, 1999, p. C3; David McNaughton, "The Lawyer Taking on Coke," *AJC*, May 2, 1999; David McNaughton, "Coke Debate: Fight or Settle?" *AJC*, May 9, 1999, p. H5; Henry Unger, "Coke, Plaintiffs in Court Today," *AJC*, May 10, 1999, p. C1; Ernest Holsendolph, "Judge Allows Recruiting in Coke Suit," *AJC*, May 14, 1999, p. C1; Henry Unger, "Coke Free to E-mail View on Suit," *AJC*, May 18, 1999, p. F1; Nikhil Deogun, "A Race-Bias Suit Tests Coke," *WSJ*, May 18, 1999, p. B1; Nikhil Deogun, "Coke Was told in '95 of Need for Diversity," *WSJ*, May 20, 1999, p. A3; "Amended Complaint, Abdallah et al. v. The Coca-Cola Co., U.S. District Court, Northern District of Georgia, Civil Action No. 1–98-CV-3679; Dan Morse, "Coke Says It Will Form Diversity Panel," *WSJ*, May 27, p. A8; "Coca-Cola Diversity Group," *NYT*, May 27, 1999, p. C21.

"catastrophic health scare": Constance L. Hays, "A Sputter in the Coke Machine," *NYT*, June 30, 1999, p. C1; Henry Unger, "Coke Fights to Redeem Its Good Name," *AJC*, June 27, 1999, p. A1, A9; Henry Unger, "CCE's Share of Tab Rises Sharply," *AJC*, July 13, 1999, p. 1E.

433 **"rumours that rat poison"**: Neil Buckley, "Rat Poison Probe Under Way At French Coca-Cola Plant," *Financial Times*, June 24, 1999, p. 1; Henry Unger, "Coke Recalls Bottled Water," *AJC*, June 30, 1999, p. 13D; "Lab: BonAqa Bacteria Not Hazardous," *AJC*, July 6, 1999, p. 4F: Russ Bynum, "Pepsi Plays Soft-Drink Hardball," *Burlington Free Press*, July 24, 1999, p. B1; Henry Unger, "Australia Investigates Coca-Cola Bottler," *AJC*, July 29, 1999, p. D1.

"Pepsi . . . syringes": Tom Mashberg, "FDA Backs Pepsi; Hoaxes Revealed," *Boston Globe*, June 18, 1993, p. 1.

434 **"Belgians . . . already spooked"**: Bert Roughton, "Scientists: Blunders Abound in Coke Flap," *AJC*, July 3, 1999, p. 1A; Luisa Dillner, "A Case of Mass Hysteria," *Guardian*, July 6, 1999, p. 16; Maria Saporta, "Going It Alone," *AJC*, June 27, 1999, p. D1.

"what better victim": In the wake of the Belgian health disaster, much of the old French animosity towards Coke surfaced again. Because the Europeans refused to buy U. S. hormone-fed beef, the United States imposed 100 percent tariffs on a variety of European food and luxury products, including Roquefort cheese. In retaliation, a French village imposed a 100 percent "tax" on Coca-Cola. Why Coke? "It is a symbol of the American multinational that wants to uniformize taste all over the planet," explained the mayor. (Anne Swardson, "When Cheese and Coke Go to War," *Washington Post National Weekly Edition*, Aug. 30, 1999)

"beset with worries": Nikhil Deogun, "Coca-Cola Net Income Fell 13%," *WSJ*, April 22, 1999, p. A4; Constance L. Hays, "A Once-Sweet Bottling Plan Turns Sour for Coke," *NYT*, May 5, 1999, p. C1; Henry Unger, "Profit Down at Soft Drink Maker," *AJC*, July 16, 1999, p. F1.

"vaunted anchor bottler program": Constance L. Hays, "Global Crisis for Coca-Cola," *NYT*, Nov. 1, 1998, p. C1; Constance L. Hays, "A Once-Sweet Bottling Plan Turns Sour for Coke," *NYT*, May 5, 1999, p. C1; Constance L. Hays, "$1.2 billion Bill at Coke Raises Eyebrows," *NYT*, March 17, 1999, p. C2; Constance L. Hays, "Coca-Cola Bid for Orangina Rebuffed by French Court," *NYT*, April 10, 1999, p. C14; "Europeans to Look at Coke-Cadbury Deal," *NYT*, April 29, 1999, p. C5.

435 **"Ivester appeared unfazed"**: Nikhil Deogun, "Coca-Cola Net Income Fell 13%," *WSJ*, April 22, 1999, p. A4.

"its implacable world conquest": Coca-Cola Company 1999 press releases; "Peru's National Soft Drink Challenging Coke's Lead," *CNN*, Sept. 26, 1995; Nikhil Deogun and Amy Barrett, "Coke Signs Amended Letter to Acquire Orangina," *WSJ*, May 5, 1999, p. B4; Nikhil Deogun, "Most of Cadbury's EU Beverage Business is Excluded," *WSJ*, May 25, 1999, p. A20.

"Japanese bottlers merged": Coca-Cola Co. 1999 press releases; "European Coca-Cola Bottlers to Complete $2.9 Billion Merger," *Bloomberg News*, Aug. 19, 1999.

"relentless marketing initiative": Coca-Cola Company 1999 press release; Matthew Rose, "Coke Chief's Strategy is to Gulp, Not Sip," *WSJ*, Feb. 1, 1999, p. B9; "Coca-Cola Opens $100M Soft Drink Plant in Ukraine," *Dow Jones News Service*, Feb. 2, 1999; "Pepsi, Coca-Cola to Vie Through 'Live Concerts,'" *Business Standard*, Feb. 8, 1999, p. 6; "Coca-Cola Launches Campaign," *Jakarta Post*, Feb. 8, 1999, p. C12; "Have a Coke and a Cell Phone," *Bloomberg News*, Sept. 16, 1999.

436 **"memorabilia on the road"**: *Journey*, Jan. 1996, p. 3; *Journey*, Feb. 1996, p. 7.
"Coca-Cola Wear": "Coke Clothes to Be the Next Real Thing," *Financial Times*, Jan. 21, 1999, p. C12.

"Charles Frenette took over": Louise Kramer, "Frenette Has Local Agenda for Coke," *Advertising Age*, March 23, 1998, p. 3; Louise Kramer, "Coca-Cola to Boost Local Efforts," *Advertising Age*, April 6, 1998, p. 3; Beth Snyder and Louise Kramer, "AT&T, Coca-Cola Team," *Advertising Age*, Nov. 9, 1998, p. 32; Louise Kramer, "Coke, Pepsi: Don't Look for Shifts in Ad Strategy," *Advertising Age*, May 18, 1998, p. 10; "Coke's Wall of Speed," *Potentials in Marketing*, Sept. 1998, p. 20; Kat Fitzgerald, "Coca-Cola Takes Wanna-be Race Drivers," *Advertising Age*, July 6, 1998, p. 20; Patricia Sellers, "How Coke Is Kicking Pepsi's Can," *Fortune*, Oct. 28, 1996, p. 73; "Breaking: Coca-Cola Big Screen Laughs," *Advertising Age*, March 9, 1998, p. 44; Patricia Riedman, "P&G

Plans Pivotal Ad forum about Net," *Advertising Age*, May 11, 1998, p. 4; Louise Kramer, "Cola Wars May Get Ferocious," *Advertising Age*, Oct. 5, 1998, p. S6; Bob Garfield, "Coca-Cola Classic Loses Its Former Edge," *Advertising Age*, May 5, 1997, p. 69; "Briefs," *Advertising Age*, April 1, 1996, p. 56; Kathy DeSolvo, "Digital Domain Throws One Trippy Diet Coke Party," *Shoot*, April 4, 1997, p. 14; John Bergin interview.

"*Pagliacci*": Karen Benezra, "Edge Fills Coca-Cola's Summer Pool," *Adweek*, July 13, 1998, Laurie Freeman, "Marketing 100: Sprite," *Advertising Age*, June 29, 1998, p. S33; Edge Creative retrospective video, 1999.

437 **"Frenette initially floundered"**: Stuart Elliott, "Looking for a Jolt," *NYT*, June 22, 1998, p. D9; Madeline Brand, "New Diet Coke Promotion," *NPR Morning Edition*, Oct. 26, 1998; Hank Kim and Sloane Lucas, "Lowe Ain't Lucky on Diet Coke," *Adweek*, Jan. 4, 1999; Doreen Carvajal, "Cross-Media Deals Mean Bonanza for Publishers," *NYT*, Jan. 25, 1999, p. C1; Mickey H. Gramig, "A Heavy Diet of New Ads," *AJC*, Dec. 30, 1998, p. D1; Hillel Italie, "Coke Packages Prose, Pop," *Chicago Sun-Times*, Feb. 2, 1999, p. 41; Denise Gellene, "Diet Coke's Message," *Los Angeles Times*, Jan. 7, 1999, p. C5; "Rest Stop" and "Video Dating" 1999 Diet Coke ads.

"to penetrate schools": *Journey*, May 1998, p. 9; Irene Cherkassky, "Getting the Exclusive," *Beverage World*, Oct. 1998, p. 96; "District 11's Coke Problem," *Harper's*, Feb. 1999, p. 26–27.

"veritable feeding frenzy": "Huntington Beach Opts for Real Thing," *AJC*, Feb. 20, 1999, p. D2; Marc Kaufman, "Pop Culture," *Washington Post*, March 23, 1999; Julie Flaherty, "With Schools the Battleground, a New Kind of Cola War Breaks Out," *NYT*, Feb. 3, 1999, p. C26; Anna White, "Coke and Pepsi Are Going to School," *Multinational Monitor*, Jan. 1999; Constance L. Hays, "Today's Lesson: Soda Rights," *NYT*, May 21, 1999, p. C1; Manny Gonzales, "Will School Go Better With Coke?" *Denver Rocky Mountain News*, Jan. 22, 1999, p. 31A; Manny Gonzales, "Schools Seal Sweet Deal With Coke," *Denver Rocky Mountain News*, Feb. 3, 1999, p. 25A.

438 **"give away soft drinks"**: Patrick Leahy, "Statement," May 7, 1999; 1998; *Congressional Record*, May 11, 999, p. S5038–S5041; "Better Nutrition for School Children Act of 1999 Official Statement," ASFSA web site.

"Several new Coke ads": Edge Creative retrospective video, 1999.

"water called Dasani": Matt Kempner, "And Now . . .Dasani," *AJC*, Feb. 20, 1999, p. D1; Patricia Guthrie, "Critics Tap Bottled Water," *AJC*, Feb. 20, 1999, p. D2.

439 **"that's the idea"**: Mickey H. Gramig, "Coca-Cola's Ivester Sees World of Opportunity," *AJC*, Jan. 12, 1999, p. F5.

"Ivester . . . would retire": McKay, Betsy and Nikhil Deogun.

"After Short, Stormy Tenure, Coke's Ivester to Retire." *WSJ* Dec 7, 1999, p. B1, B4; anonymous ex-Coke executive.

CHAPTER 23: WORLD WITHOUT END?

440 **"You can run from it"**: Michael Konik, "On Not Getting Away From It All," *NYT* Feb. 24, 1991.

"Mecca": Kahn, *Big Drink*, p. 50.

"a million people": Don Keough interview; 1991 CC Annual Report.

"shift on its axis": Dick Halpern interview.

441 **"missionaries"**: Some Coke men have been married in their uniforms, while others have chosen to be buried in them. (Kahn, *Big Drink*, p. 49)

"incredible mobilization": Bob Hall, "Journey to the White House: The Story of Coca-Cola," *Southern Exposure*, Spring 1977, p. 33.

"never be boring": Carol Moog, quoted in "The Cola Wars: Who's Got the Right One?" *Consumer Reports* Aug. 1991, p. 520.

"dark-coloured medicine": "Elixir of Life," *Man, Myth & Magic*, p. 809.

442 "dispensed holy water": Clairmonte, *Merchants of Drink*, p. 185–186.

"reverence towards the product": Dick Halpern interview. My first cousin worked briefly for Coca-Cola in 1967, when he wrote: "These people are fanatics! I mean, I drink the stuff but, my God, I never knew it would be like this. If you took a poll, I bet 9 out of 10 Coke executives would maintain that it could supplant altar wine, undergoing with ease the profundities of transubstantiation." (Robbert Schwab III to Nan Pendergrast, Oct. 1967)

"It's a religion": Robinson, Edward, "America's Most Admired Companies," *Fortune*, March 3, 1997, p. 68.

"If all the Coke ever produced": 1995 "Refreshing Facts"; 1991 "Fabulous Numerical Facts," CC Co.

"defines religion": Clifford Geertz, "Religion as a Cultural System," in *Anthropological Approaches to the Study of Religion*, p. 4.

"universal brotherhood": Coca-Cola also shares less glorious traits with organized religions—tedious hair-splitting rules and rituals, rigid militaristic hierarchy, and holier-than-thou condemnation of the Enemy.

"worshipful' moods": Geertz, pp. 11.

"a drug-laced drink": "Drink," in *Man, Myth & Magic*; Pendergrast, *Uncommon Grounds*, p. 6, 411.

443 "man is a discontented animal": "Drugs," in *Man, Myth & Magic*, p. 712.

"almost irresistible": Ann Nietzke, "The American Obsession With Fun," *Saturday Review* Aug. 26, 1972, p. 35. The best Coca-Cola commercials can touch the most obdurate heart. Even a hardened ad man like John Bergin told me he still sometimes weeps at his own commercials. (John Bergin interview)

"pitiful creatures": Dostoevsky, *The Brothers Karamazov*, p. 267–269.

"7X of the soul": The Reverend Howard Finster, a folk artist whose Paradise Garden attracts tourists to rural Pennville, Georgia, paints Coke bottles replete with Biblical sayings and fantastic creatures. "Religious people drinks Coca-Cola," he explained. Finster's first Coke made as strong an impression as his first vision. "I was just a little fellow," he recalled. "They bought me a nickel drink that was pretty good size and I drunk all of that. I thought that was the best thing I ever drunk, you know, and directly I belched and it come through my nose and it like to knocked the top of my head off." (Howard Finster interview; Eileen M. Drennen, "The Reverend's Real Thing," *AC* Dec. 7, 1989, *Cola Conquest*, Part 1.)

"modern discoveries": Drew Jubera, "Tibetan Monks Tour Shrine To A Soft Drink," *AC* Feb. 7, 1992.

"this church of consumption": Sidney Mintz in *Cola Conquest*, Part 1.

"great love affairs": Ike Herbert at 1990 Fountain Meeting in San Francisco, CC Co. videotape.

"We're selling smoke": Dick Halpern interview.

444 "of brimstone": Jean Stafford, "Coca-Cola," *Esquire* Dec. 1975, p. 96.

"Jacobson, founder": Bea Lewis, "Michael Jacobson," *New York Newsday*, June 12, 1991; *Eating Well*, Jan/Feb. 1991, p. 22; Jacobson, *Safe Food*, p. 33; Jacobson, *Liquid Candy*.

"three times more likely": Jacobson, *Liquid Candy*; Don Colburn, "Overweight Children Are More Likely in Poor Families," *Washington Post* Jan. 14, 1992.

445 "like you're in civilization": Alix M. Freedman, "Deadly Diet: Amid Ghetto Hunger, Many More Suffer Eating Wrong Foods," *WSJ* Dec. 18, 1990; "Habit

Forming: Fast-Food Chains Play Central Role in Diet of the Inner City Poor," Dec. 19, 1990.

"When advertised": Sidney Mintz, "Food and Culture: An Anthropological View," in *Completing the Food Chain*, p. 119–120.

"caffeinism": Jacobson, *Safe Food*, p. 160–161, Pendergrast, *Uncommon Grounds*, p. 413.

"doesn't think . . . danger": Michael Jacobson interview. Scientists disagree about caffeine's possible contribution to heart disease. (Ludwik J. Bukowliecki et al, "Effects of Sucrose, Caffeine, and Cola Beverages on Obesity, Cold Resistance, and Adipose Tissue Cellularity," *American Journal of Physiology* April 1983, p. R500; Jacobson, *Liquid Candy*; Pendergrast, *Uncommon Grounds*, p. 339–341, 411–418; Braun, *Buzz*; James, *Understanding Caffeine*)

"sooth upset stomachs": Plain Coca-Cola syrup used to be sold as medicine at drug stores throughout America and can still be purchased (for $1 an ounce) at a few Atlanta pharmacies.

"Some studies . . . kidney stones": Jacobson, *Liquid Candy*.

446 **"drinking through a straw"**: William Bowen interview. Dental researcher Dr. B. G. Bibby concluded that Coke's sugar content actually offers *protection* from the acidic effect on teeth. He also discovered that scrupulous tooth-brushing can cause *more* demineralization, since the acid then works immediately on the clean tooth surface, while plaque acts as a buffer. (Bibby, *Food and the Teeth*, p. 108–111.)

"law of the cynical elite": Roberto Goizueta, "Globalization: A Soft Drink Perspective," *Vital Speeches* April 1, 1989, p. 361.

"Alabama woman": Kahn, *Big Drink*, p. 7–8.

"Have a Coke!": Alfred C. Andersson, "In the Past 50 Years Luke Kingsley Has Downed 25 Cokes Per Day!" *Memphis Press-Scimitar* June 8, 1954 (courtesy E. J. Kahn).

"nice white sugar": Mintz, *Sweetness and Power*, p. 103.

"a defect": ibid, p. 134.

"Drink of Health": ibid, p. 251.

"I sometimes shudder": Kahn, *Big Drink*, p. 35.

447 **"British social ritual"**: Mintz, *Sweetness and Power*, p. 120, 181.

"tiny amount of cocaine": Cocaine, too, was used as a cheap, short-term method of getting more work out of Southern black laborers.

"Watching the Cowboys": ibid, p. 202–203.

"We are what we eat": ibid, p. 211.

"25-year-old financier": Matthew C. Vita, "Busy Britons Skipping Proper Tea For Fast Coffee Breaks," *AC* Oct. 28, 1990.

448 **"American's fuel"**: Klaus Liedtke, "Coca-Cola Über Alles," *Atlas* October 1978, p. 37.

"With the supermarket": Adlai Stevenson quoted in Corwin, *Trivializing America*, p. 65.

"movie industry": Without making such an overt political statement, artists such as Andy Warhol, Salvador Dali, and Robert Rauschenberg have painted Coca-Cola bottles as evocations of materialistic capitalism, while academic folklorists have created a thriving sub-specialty appropriately labeled "Coke-lore." (Paul Smith, "Contemporary legends," *Contemporary Legend*, vol. I, 1991, p. 123–152; Mike Bell, "Cokelore," *Western Folklore* 1976, vol. 36, p. 59–65; Gary Alan Fine, "Cokelore and Coke-Law," *Journal of American Folklore* 1979, vol. 92, p. 477–482.)

"You have entered": Klaus Liedtke, p. 37.

"truly global brands": "The Tomato That Ate Chicago," *The Economist*, June 9, 1990.

"Everywhere people learn": Ted Levitt, "The Pluralization of Consumption," *Harvard Business Review* May/June 1988, p. 8.

"People around the world": Goizueta, "Globalization," p. 361. Unquestionably, Coca-Cola's marketing blitz has directly affected local drinking habits. In the Philippines, indigenous beverages such as *kalamansi* (lime juice) and *buko* (coconut water) have virtually disappeared except for ceremonial use. An interesting thing happened in Indonesia, however, indicating how adaptable cultures can be. When Coca-Cola made inroads on the traditional tea market, a local business put sweetened jasmine tea in red-and-white labeled bottles, calling it *Tehbotol* (tea bottle) and underpricing Coke. Tehbotol proved so popular that Coke had to introduce its own Hi-C tea product as a competitor. (Clairmonte & Cavanagh, *Merchants of Drink*, p. 13, 171–172; John Hunter interview.)

449 "From infancy to adulthood": Barbara Tuchman, quoted in Corwin, *Trivializing America*, p. 176–177.

"opulent, imaginary would": "Advertising," *International Encyclopedia of Communications*, v. 1, p. 11.

"global teenager": "World Youth," *Richmond Times-Dispatch*, Aug. 19, 1990.

"Benjamin Barber argues": Barber, *Jihad vs. McWorld*, pp. 67, 71.

"hearts and souls": Barber in *Cola Conquest*, Part 2.

"world that is coming": Barber, *Jihad vs. McWorld*, pp. 11, 14.

"Although Coke unquestionably exerts": *Cola Conquest*, Parts 2 and 3; Watson, Julie, "In Chiapas, Cola Wars Take New Twist," *Miami Herald*, March 3, 1997.

450 "The worldwide spread": Haviland, *Cultural Anthropology*, p. 395.

"terrifying giant step": Kuisel, *Seducing the French*, p. 228–229, 233. "To a considerable extent, Europeans resisted the standardization and homogeneity allegedly inflicted on them by their American masters," observed Richard Pells in *Not Like Us: How Europeans Have Loved Hated, and Transformed American Culture Since World War II*. "Instead they adapted America's products and culture to their own needs, 'Europeanizing' and domesticating most of the items and images they received from the United States." (Pells, *Not Like Us*, p. 279)

"The differences among races": Robert Hughes, "The Fraying of America," *Time* Feb. 3, 1992, p. 47.

"You'll find plenty": Don Keough interview.

"would conjure romance": Ann Nietzke, "The American Obsession With Fun," *Saturday Review* Aug. 26, 1972, p. 35.

"very, very comforting": "Many Memories Reflected in Familiar Green Bottle," *AC* Aug. 16, 1990. The warm, nostalgic place that Coca-Cola has secured in the American heart may diminish in time, as memories of the cute little green bottle, old-fashioned ice chests, and small-town soda fountains give way to childhood experiences with computerized vending machines shooting out cans. In his book *The Great Good Place*, sociologist Ray Oldenburg lamented the passing of the American soda fountain, one of the few peaceful public gathering places for all ages. So, he argued, we feel increasingly isolated, fractured, lost. (Oldenburg, *The Great Good Place*, p. 3–11; 111–115)

451 "roots, remembrance": Ted Levitt, p. 7–8.

"Corporations are not": Roberto Goizueta, "Commencement Address," *Cheshire Academy Quarterly* July 1982, p. 5.

"We believe": Don Keough, "To Serve The Customer With A Passion," *Journey* May 1988, p. 6.

"We *do* have": Weldon Johnson interview.

"Fulbright . . . devoted to Coca-Cola": J. W. Fulbright interview.

452 "they bring something new": *Cola Conquest*, Part 3.

"new consumerism": *Journey*, May 1998, p. 3; Cui, Geng, "The Different Faces of the Chinese Consumer," *China Business Review*, July 17, 1997, p. 34.

"corporate shuttle diplomacy": Carl Ware, Coke's brilliant black executive, spearheaded the South African diplomatic effort. Ware rose to head the company's entire African Division.

"In the perfect world": Edwards, Bob, *NPR Morning Edition*, Jan. 6, 1995, Transcript 1515–5.

"As Roberto Goizueta used to say": J. P. Donlon, "The Eight-Nine Billion Dollar Man," *Chief Executive*, July 1996, p. 42.

"For much of the world": "Global Markets' Lethal Magic," *NYT*, Feb. 21, 1999, p. D16.

"It would be nice to think": Greenway, HDS, "The Refugee Century," *Boston Globe*, April 4, 1999.

"More and more multinational companies": McGee, Suzanne, "Fund Managers Faced Off in Debate," *WSJ*, May 28, 1999, p. C14.

454 **"an elephant's ass"**: Harrison Jones quote from Jimmy Sibley interview.

"Coca-Cola is more durable": James G. Peck to Mark Pendergrast, April 2, 1992.

"When Hurricane Georges struck": *Journey*, Nov. 1998, p. 3, 22.

"Civic Action Network": *Moving Forward: The Soft Drink Industry, Bottle Bills and Waste Management*, National Soft Drink Association, n.d.; *Journey* Jan. 1996, p. 3; *Journey*, Nov. 1998, p. 16.

"Even in normal times": *Journey*, July 1995, p. 17–19; *Journey*, Nov. 1998, p. 21; Clifford, Mark L, "Coke Pours Into Asia," *Business Week*, Oct. 21, 1996, p. 22; Nolan, Peter, "Coke Didn't Interfere With This Study," *Business Week*, Jan. 13, 1997, p. 6.

APPENDIX I: THE SACRED FORMULA

464 **"story behind this formula book"**: E. D. Murphy, "No One Knows His Name," *Sunday Ledger-Enquirer Magazine*, Dec. 24, 1967 (Pemberton Archives File No. 144).

"apprentice . . . final few years": W. C. Woodall to Franklin Garrett, Jan. 24, 1955, Pemberton files, CC Archives; "J. P. Turner to be Laid to Rest," *Columbus Ledger*, Jan. 13, 1943; W. C. Woodall, "From Here to Everywhere," *Columbus Ledger*, Nov. 19, 1969.

465 **"kola nuts are not mentioned"**: The "Turner formula" corresponds closely to an unpublished version written by Frank Robinson, the man who named Coca-Cola, wrote out its tell-tale script, and manufactured and marketed the drink, according to his great-grandson Frank Robinson II, who owns it. Neither formula mentions kola nuts. The Turner formula does not appear to be written in the inventor's handwriting, it may have been copied over by his apprentice.

"Merck in Darmstadt": Pemberton Speech from Minutes of the Eleventh Annual Meeting held in Savannah, GA, April 1886. (Sherman Collection)

"That wasn't the only formula change": According to another Coke history, there have been over a dozen alterations to the Coke formula over the years. (Allen, *Secret Formula*, p. 17)

"fiddled around": CHC, "True History of Coca-Cola," p. 10. CC Collection. Asa Candler abandoned the expensive caffeine extracted from kola nuts, relying instead on stems and droppings from tea manufacturers. He added only enough kola nut to avoid accusations of misbranding.

"accurate guestimate": Poundstone, *Big Secrets*, p. 42–43.

      "they did speak to Frederick Allen:" Allen, *Secret Formula*, p. 432.

467 **"sworn testimony"**: Third Affidavit of Dr. Anton Amon, Plaintiff's Exhibit 195, Diet Coke Case.

      "fell by the wayside": Bob Broadwater interview.

      "herbal lore surrounding": Krutch, *Herbal*, p. 140; Duke, CRC *Handbook of Medicinal Herbs*, p. 319–320, 505; Duke and Ayensu, *Medicinal Plants of China*, vol. 2, p. 388.

      "senior psychometrician": Harry Waldrop interview.

APPENDIX 2: COCA-COLA MAGIC

463 **"If Pepsi didn't exist"**: Chris Roush, "Coca-Cola's Guiding Light," *AJC*, Nov. 24, 1996, p. 1H.

Bibliography

MANUSCRIPT COLLECTIONS

Bateman, William E., and Randy S. Schaeffer Private Collection. Reading, PA.

Candler, Asa G. Papers. Special Collections, Robert W. Woodruff Library, Emory University, Atlanta.

Candler, Charles Howard Papers. Special Collections, Robert W. Woodruff Library, Emory University, Atlanta.

Candler, Warren, Papers. Special Collections, Robert W. Woodruff Library, Emory University, Atlanta.

Center of Military History. U.S. Department of the Army, Washington, D.C.

Coca-Cola Collection. Special Collections, Robert W. Woodruff Library, Emory University, Atlanta.

Coca-Cola Company, The, Archives. North Avenue, Atlanta.

Coca-Cola Company, The, Legal Library. Atlanta.

Department of Justice Files. Anti-Trust Division, Legal Procedures Unit, Washington, D.C.

Dun, R. G. & Company, Collection. Baker Library, Harvard University Graduate School of Business Administration, Cambridge, MA.

Eisenhower Papers. Eisenhower Library, Abilene, KS.

Farley, James Papers. Library of Congress Manuscripts Division, Washington, D.C.

Harriman, Averill Papers. Library of Congress Manuscripts Division, Washington, D.C.

Hartsfield, William B. Papers. Special Collections, Robert W. Woodruff Library, Emory University, Atlanta.

Hollingworth Papers. Harry Hollingworth Collections, Nebraska State Historical Society, Lincoln, NE.

Hunter, Floyd Papers. Special Collections, Robert W. Woodruff Library, Emory University, Atlanta.

Jacobs, Joseph Papers. Atlanta Historical Society.

Kahn, E. J., Jr. Notes made 1958–1959 for *Big Drink*. Courtesy of E. J. Kahn, Jr., *The New Yorker*, New York, copies in Pendergrast collection.

National Archives, Washington, D.C. AGO Document File #1239224.

Pemberton Archives. Monroe King Private Collection, Douglasville, GA.

Pendergrast, Mark, Collection. Special Collections, Robert W. Woodruff Library, Emory University, Atlanta. (Mark Pendergrast has donated his taped interviews, transcripts, notes, court cases, and other research material used to write this book).

Pepsi-Cola Advertising History Collection. Collection of Advertising History, National Museum of American History, Smithsonian Institution, Washington, D.C.

Robinson, Frank II, Private Collection, Atlanta. (Collection of materials relating to Frank Robinson.)

Sherman, Ernestine, Private Collection. Albany, GA. (John Pemberton material.)

Sibley, John Papers. Special Collections, Robert W. Woodruff Library, Emory University, Atlanta.

Sizer, J. B., Correspondence. Schmidt Museum, Elizabethtown, NJ.

Thomas, Benjamin, Correspondence. Benwood Foundation, Chattanooga.

Thompson, Thom, Collection. Versailles, KY.

Toner Collection. Library of Congress, Washington, D.C.

U.S. Food and Drug Administration Files. Rockville, MD.

White, William Allen, Papers. Library of Congress Manuscript Division, Washington, D.C.

Wiley, Harvey W., Papers. Library of Congress Manuscript Division, Washington, D.C.

Woodruff, Robert W., Papers. Special Collections, Robert W. Woodruff Library, Emory University, Atlanta.

SELECTED COURT CASES

(Most are in the CC Legal Library)

Barrels Case: U.S. vs. Forty Barrels and Twenty Kegs of Coca-Cola, Supreme Court, Oct. Term 1915, No. 562.

Blood Balm Case: "The Blood Balm Company vs. Cooper," *Georgia Supreme Court Records*, vol. 83, Oct. Term, 1889.

Bottler Case: The Coca-Cola Bottling Co. vs. The Coca-Cola Co., District Court, Delaware, Nov. 8, 1920. No. 389.

Byfield Case: Candler vs. Byfield. Byfield vs. Candler. Supreme Court of Georgia, July 16, 1925. *Southeastern Reporter*, vol. 50, p. 57.

Chero-Cola Case: Coca-Cola Company vs. Chero-Cola Company, Opposition No. 1662, U.S. Patent Office, Before the Examiner of Interferences.

Cleo-Cola Case: Cleo Syrup Corp. vs. The Coca-Cola Company, U.S. Circuit Court of Appeal, Eighth Circuit, No. 12,592 Civil. 1943.

Coca-Cola: Opinions, Orders, Injunctions et al. Atlanta: Coca-Cola Co. vol. 1: 1923; vol. 2–3: 1939, in CC Legal Library and other libraries.

Daniel Case: The Coca-Cola Co. vs. John B. Daniel, Fulton Country Superior Court, Spring Term 1901, #8577.

Diet Coke Case: Shreveport Coca-Cola Bottling Co., Inc. et. al. vs. The Coca-Cola Co., U.S. District Court, Delaware. Civil Actions No. 83–95 MMS, 83–120 MMS. 1991 (one opinion—it would be unwieldy to list all opinions, depositions, and other court records).

Dixi-Cola Case: The Coca-Cola Company vs. Dixi-Cola Laboratories, U.S. Supreme Court, Oct. Term, 1940.

E-Town Case: Coca-Cola Bottling Company of Elizabethtown, Inc., et al. vs. The Coca-Cola Company. Civil Action Nos. 8—48/87–398-JJF Consolidated, U.S. District Court, Delaware. 1991 (one opinion—it would be unwieldy to list all opinions, depositions, and other court records).

Fulton County Superior Court Records, Atlanta.

Hudgins Case: Hudgins v. Coca-Cola Bottling Co., Supreme Court of Georgia, May 10, 1905, *50 Southeastern Reporter*.

Husting Case: E. L. Husting Co. vs. Western Coca-Cola Bottling Co., State of Wisconsin Supreme Court, Jan. Term, 1931.

Kent Case: Coca-Cola Company vs. Berman vs. Kent. Opposition No. 15,753 in U.S. Patent Office (records destroyed).

Koke Case: The Coca-Cola Company vs. The Koke Company of America, Supreme Court of the United States, Oct. Term, 1920, part of the *Briefs and Records of the United States Supreme Court*.

My-Coca Case: My-Coca Co. vs. Baltimore Process Co., In the Circuit Court of Baltimore, Sept. 2, 1924.

Nehi Case: The Coca-Cola Company vs. Nehi Corporation, Supreme Court of Delaware, No. 4, Sept. Session, 1942 Term.

Pre-Mix Case: Coca-Cola Bottling Co. of Minnesota, Inc., vs. The Coca-Cola Company, Civil No. 5269, U.S. District Court, District of Minnesota, Fourth Division, April 29, 1957.

Queens Case: Pepsi-Cola Company vs. Coca-Cola Company, Supreme Court of the State of New York, County of Queens, 1938.

Rucker Case: Henry A. Rucker vs. Coca-Cola Company, U.S. Circuit Court of Appeals, Fifth Circuit, No. 1161, Original Record filed May 12, 1902.

BOOKS AND VIDEOS

Acts and Resolutions of the General Assembly of the State of Georgia, 1902. Atlanta: Franklin Printing & Pub. Co, 1903.

Adams, Samuel Hopkins. *The Great American Fraud.* NY: P. F. Collier & Son, 1907.

Aguayo, Rafael. *Dr. Deming: The American Who Taught the Japanese About Quality.* NY: Simon & Schuster, 1990.

Aliber, Robert Z. *The International Money Game.* 3rd ed. NY: Basic Books, 1979.

Allen, Frederick. *Secret Formula.* NY: Harper Business, 1994.

Allen, Ivan, Jr. with Paul Hemphill. *Mayor: Notes on the Sixties.* NY: Simon & Schuster, 1971.

Ambrose, Stephen E. *Nixon: Vol 2, The Triumph of a Politician: 1962–1972.* NY: Simon & Schuster, 1987.

Anderson, Oscar E., Jr. *The Health of a Nation: Harvey W. Wiley and the Fight for Pure Food.* Chicago: U. Chicago Press, 1958.

Annals of America, The. Chicago: Encyclopaedia Britannica, 1968.

Anthropological Approaches to the Study of Religion. Ed. by Michael Banton. NY: Praeger, 1966.

As Others See Us: The United States Through Foreign Eyes. Ed. by Franz M. Joseph. Princeton: Princeton U. Press, 1959.

Ashley, Richard. *Cocaine: Its History, Uses and Effects.* NY: Warner Books, 1975.

Atkinson, Ruth de Forest Lamb. *The Devil's Candle.* Vassar College Library, 1946, unpublished.

Backer, Bill. *The Care and Feeding of Ideas.* NY: Times Books, 1993.

Baghai, Mehrdad, Stephen Coley, and David White. *The Alchemy of Growth: Kickstarting and Sustaining Growth in Your Company.* London: Orion Business Books, 1999.

Barber, Benjamin. *Jihad Vs. McWorld: How the Planet is Both Falling Apart and Coming Together.* NY: Ballantine, 1996.

Barnet, Richard J., & Ronald E. Müller. *Global Reach: The Power of the Multinational Corporations.* NY: Simon & Schuster, 1974.

Barry, Iris, & Eileen Bowser. *D. W. Griffith: American Film Master.* NY: Garland, 1985.

Bauman, Mark K. *Warren Akin Candler: The Conservative as Idealist.* Metuchen, NJ: Scarecrow, 1981.

Beard, George. *American Nervousness: Its Causes and Consequences.* NY: G. P. Putnam's Sons, 1881.

Bell, Hunter. "History of Coca-Cola." Unpublished manuscript. Atlanta: Coca-Cola Archives.

Bibby, B. G. *Food and the Teeth.* NY: Vantage, 1990.

Biow, Milton H. *Butting In: An Adman Speaks Out.* Garden City, NY: Doubleday, 1964.

Bletter, Rosemarie Haag. *Remembering the Future: The New York World's Fair from 1939–1964.* Flushing, NY: Queens Museum, 1989.

Blount, Roy, Jr. *About Three Bricks Shy of a Load.* NY: Ballantine Books, 1974, 1980.

Blum, John Morton. *V Was for Victory.* NY: Harcourt Brace Jovanovich, 1976.

BNA Tax Management Portfolios. 7th ed. Bureau of National Affairs, 1988.

Bowers, Q. David. *The Moxie Encyclopedia.* NY: Vestal Press, 1985.

Branch, Taylor. *Parting the Waters: America in the King Years 1954–63.* NY: Simon & Schuster, 1988.

Braun, Stephen. *Buzz: The Science and Lore of Alcohol and Caffeine.* NY: Oxford U. Pr., 1996.

Brendon, Piers. *Ike: His Life and Times.* NY: Harper & Row, 1986.

Brodie, Fawn M. *Richard Nixon: The Shaping of His Character.* NY: Norton, 1981.

Califano, Joseph A., Jr. *The Triumph and Tragedy of Lyndon Johnson.* NY: Simon & Schuster, 1991.

Campbell, William T. *Big Beverage.* Atlanta: Tupper & Love, 1952.

Candler, Charles Howard. *Asa Griggs Candler.* Atlanta: Emory University, 1950.

———. *Asa Griggs Candler; Coca-Cola & Emory College.* Atlanta: Emory, 1953.

Candler, Warren. *Great Revivals and the Great Republic.* Nashville: Publishing House of the Methodist Church South, Smith & Lamar, 1904.

———. *Wit and Wisdom of Warren Akin Candler.* Ed. by Elam Franklin Dempsey. Nashville: Cokesbury Press, 1922.

Carroll, Lewis. *The Annotated Alice.* NY: Bramhall House, 1960.

Carson, Gerald. *One for a Man, Two for a Horse.* Garden City, NY: Doubleday, 1961.

Carter, Paul B. *Paul B. Carter: His Family, Friends and Great Adventures.* Chattanooga: Ray McDonald, 1977.

Chafe, William H. *The Unfinished Journey: America Since World War II.* NY: Oxford, 1986.

Clairmonte, Frederick, & John Cavanagh. *Merchants of Drink: Transnational Control of World Beverages.* Penang, Malaysia: Third World Network, 1988.

Clark, Eric. *The Want Makers: Inside the World of Advertising.* NY: Penguin, 1988.

Clarke, E. Y. *Atlanta Illustrated.* 3rd ed. Atlanta: Jas. P. Harrison & Co., 1881.

Coca-Cola Company: An Illustrated Profile. Atlanta: The Coca-Cola Company, 1974.

Coca-Cola (Japan): The First Thirty Years. Japan: Coca-Cola (Japan) Co., 1987.

Cola Conquest, The. 3-hour documentary in 3 parts. Montreal, Quebec: DLI Productions, 1998.

Collective Testimony of the Benefit and Virtue of the Famous French Tonic Vin Mariani. NY: Mariani & Co., 1910.

Committee on Science and Technology, U.S. House of Representatives. *Subliminal Communication Technology,* Aug. 6, 1984. Washington, D.C.: GPO, 1985.

Completing the Food Chain. Ed. by F. M. Hirsehoff. Washington, D.C.: Smithsonian Institution Press, 1989.

Cook, Blanche Wiesen. *The Declassified Eisenhower: A Divided Legacy.* Garden City, NJ: Doubleday, 1981.

Corwin, Norman. *Trivializing America.* Secaucus, NJ: Lyle Stuart, 1983.

Crawford, Christina. *Mommie Dearest.* NY: William Morrow, 1978.

Crawford, Joan. *My Way of Life.* NY: Pocket Books, 1972.

Crown Treasury of Relevant Quotations. Edited by Edward F. Murphy. NY: Crown, 1978.

Crunden, Robert M. *Ministers of Reform: The Progressives' Achievement in American Civilization*. NY: Basic Books, 1982.

Davidson, Elizabeth H. *Child Labor Legislation in the Southern Textile States*. Chapel Hill: UNC Press, 1939.

Dietz, Lawrence. *Soda Pop*. NY: Simon & Schuster, 1973.

Dimond, E. Grey. *The Reverend William W. Whitehead, Mississippi Pioneer: His Antecedents and Descendants*. Kansas City, MO: E. Grey Dimond, ca. 1983, pp. 43–44.

Dining in America 1850–1900. Ed. by Kathryn Grover. Amherst: U Mass Press, 1987.

Disease and Distinctiveness in the American South. Ed. by Todd L. Savitt & James Harvey Young. Knoxville: U of TN Press, 1988.

Dixon, N. F. *Subliminal Perception: The Nature of a Controversy*. London: McGraw-Hill, 1971.

Dixon, Sarah Robertson, & A. H. Clark. *History of Stewart County Georgia*. Vol 2. Waycross, GA: 1975.

Donovan, Robert J. *Eisenhower: The Inside Story*. NY: Harper & Brothers, 1956.

Dostoevsky, Fyodor. *The Brothers Karamazov*. NY: Macmillan, 1919.

Dufty, William. *Sugar Blues*. NY: Warner, 1975.

Duke, James A. *CRC Handbook of Medicinal Herbs*. Boca Raton, FL: CRC Press, 1985.

Duke, James A., & Edward S. Ayensu. *Medicinal Plants of China*. NY: Reference Publications, 1985.

Eisenhower, Dwight D. *The Eisenhower Diaries*. Ed. by Robert H. Ferrell. NY: Norton, 1981.

Elliott, Charles. *Mr. Anonymous: Robert W. Woodruff of Coca-Cola*. Atlanta: Cherokee, 1982.

Ellis, Harry E. *Dr Pepper: King of Beverages*. Dallas: Taylor Publishing Company, 1979.

Encyclopedia of the Holocaust. NY: Macmillan, 1990.

English, John W., & Rob Williams. *When Men Were Boys: An Informal Portrait of Dean William Tate*. Lakemont, GA: Copple House Books, 1984.

Enrico, Roger, with Jesse Kornbluth. *The Other Guy Blinked: How Pepsi Won the Cola Wars*. NY: Bantam, 1986.

Exclusive Territorial Allocation Legislation. Hearings Before the Subcommittee on Antitrust and Monopoly. Washington, D.C.: GPO, 1973.

Fast, Howard. *Being Red*. Boston: Houghton Mifflin, 1990.

——. *The Howard Fast Reader*. NY: Crown, 1960.

Feder, Holly L. *U.S. Companies and the Arab Boycott of Israel*. Ann Arbor: UMI Dissertation, 1988.

Fisher, Eddie. *Eddie: My Life, My Loves*. NY: Harper & Row, 1981.

Fowler, Nathaniel C. *Fowler's Publicity*. NY: Publicity Publishing, 1897.

Fox, Stephen. *The Mirror Makers: A History of American Advertising and Its Creators*. NY: William Morrow, 1984.

Freeman, John Paul. *The Real Thing: "LifeStyle" and "Cultural" Appeals in Television Advertising for Coca-Cola, 1969–1976*. Ann Arbor: UMI Dissertation, 1986.

Freud, Sigmund. *Cocaine Papers*. Ed. by Robert Byck. NY: Stonehill, 1974.

Frundt, Henry J. *Refreshing Pauses: Coca-Cola and Human Rights in Guatemala*. NY: Praeger, 1987.

Fucini, Joseph J., and Suzy Fucini. *Entrepreneurs: The Men and Women Behind Famous Brand Names and How They Made It*. Boston: G. K. Hall, 1985.

Garrett, Franklin. *Atlanta and Environs*. 2 vols. NY: Lewis Historical Publishing, 1954.

Garrison, Webb. *A Treasury of Civil War Tales*. NY: Ballantine Books, 1988.

Gershman, Michael. *Getting It Right the Second Time*. Reading, MA: Addison-Wesley, 1991.

Gilded Age: America, 1865–1900. Ed. by Richard A. Bartlett. Reading, MA: Addison-Wesley, 1969.

Glad, Betty. *Jimmy Carter: In Search of the White House*. NY: Norton, 1980.

Goldman, Jonathan. *The Empire State Building*. NY: St Martin's Press, 1980.

Graham, Elizabeth Candler and Ralph Roberts, *The Real Ones: Four Generations of the First Family of Coca-Cola*. NY: Barricade Books, 1992.

Greene, Myrna. *The Eddie Fisher Story*. Middlebury, VT: Paul S. Ericksson, 1978.

Greising, David. *I'd Like the World to Buy a Coke: The Life and Leadership of Roberto Goizueta*. NY: John Wiley, 1998.

Griffith, D. W. *The Man Who Invented Hollywood: The Autobiography of D. W. Griffith*. Louisville: Touchstone, 1972.

Griffith, Sally Foreman. *Home Town News: William Allen White and the Emporia Gazette*. NY: Oxford, 1989.

Haden-Guest, Anthony. *The Paradise Program*. NY: Morrow, 1973.

Hart-Davis, Duff. *Hitler's Games: The 1936 Olympics*. NY: Harper & Row, 1986.

Haviland, William A. *Cultural Anthropology*. 5th ed. NY: Holt Rinehart & Winston, 1987.

Hechtlinger, Adelaide. *The Great Patent Medicine Era*. NY: Grosset & Dunlap, 1970.

Hersh, Seymour M. *The Dark Side of Camelot*. Boston: Little Brown, 1997.

Higham, Charles. *Trading With the Enemy*. NY: Delacorte, 1983.

Historical Abstracts of the United States. Part I. Washington, D.C.: U.S. Dept. of Commerce, 1975.

Hitler, Adolf. *Mein Kampf*. NY: Reynal & Hitchcock, 1939.

How It Was in Advertising. Chicago: Crain Books, 1976.

Hoy, Anne. *Coca-Cola: The First Hundred Years*. Atlanta: The Coca-Cola Co., 1986.

Hunter, Floyd. *Community Power Structure: A Study of Decision Makers*. Garden City, NY: Anchor Books, 1953, 1963.

——. *Community Power Succession: Atlanta's Policy-Makers Revisited*. Chapel Hill: UNC Press, 1980.

Ingham, John N. *Biographical Dictionary of American Business Leaders*. Westport, CT: Greenwood Press, 1983.

International Encyclopedia of Communications. NY: Oxford U. Press, 1989.

Jackson, Kenneth T. *The Ku Klux Klan in the City: 1915–1930*. NY: Oxford U. Press, 1967.

Jacobson, Michael F. *The Complete Eater's Digest and Nutrition Scoreboard*. NY: Doubleday, 1985.

Jacobson, Michael F., & Sarah Fritschner. *The Completely Revised and Updated Fast-Food Guide*. NY: Workman, 1991.

Jacobson, Michael F. *Liquid Candy: How Soft Drinks are Harming Americans' Health*. Washington, D.C.: Center for Science in the Public Interest, 1998.

Jacobson, Michael F., et al. *Safe Food; Eating Wisely in a Risky World*. Los Angeles: Living Planet Press, 1991.

James, Jack E. *Understanding Caffeine: A Biobehavioral Analysis*. Thousand Oaks, CA: Sage, 1997.

Jennings, Andrew. *The New Lords of the Rings: Olympic Corruption and How to Buy Gold Medals*. London: Pocket Books, 1996.

Johnson, Haynes. *Sleepwalking Through History: America in the Reagan Years*. NY: Norton, 1991.

Jones, Sam. *The Life and Sayings of Sam P. Jones, by His Wife*. Atlanta: Franklin-Turner Co., 1907.

Jordan, Jim. *The Coca-Cola Company: A Chronological History*. Unpublished, 1977. Property of Alice Fisher, Atlanta.

Justices of the United States Supreme Court, The. NY: Chelsea House, 1969.

Kahn, E. J., Jr. *The Big Drink: The Story of Coca-Cola.* NY: Random House, 1960.

——. *Robert Winship Woodruff,* Atlanta: Coca-Cola Co., 1969.

Kennedy, Joseph. *Coca Exotica: The Illustrated Story of Cocaine.* Rutherford, NJ: Fairleigh Dickinson U. Press, 1985.

Kester, W. Carl. *Japanese Takeovers.* Boston: Harvard Business School Press, 1991.

Khrushchev, Nikita. *Khrushchev Remembers.* Ed. and commentary by Edward Crankshaw. Boston: Little Brown, 1970.

King, Norman. *Madonna: The Book.* NY: William Morrow, 1991.

Kipps, Charles. *Out of Focus.* NY: William Morrow, 1989.

Knight, Lucian Lamar. *A Standard History of Georgia and Georgians.* Chicago: Lewis Publishing Co., 1917.

Krutch, Joseph Wood. *Herbal.* Boston: David Godine, 1976.

Kuisel, Richard F. *Seducing the French: The Dilemma of Americanization.* Berkeley, CA: U. California Pr., 1993.

Lasky, Victor. *Jimmy Carter: The Man and the Myth.* NY: Richard Marek, 1979.

Lev Tuviah: On the Life and Work of Rabbi Tobias Geffen. Ed. by Joel Ziff. Newton, MA: Rabbi Tobias Geffen Memorial Fund, 1998.

Lewis, W. David, & Wesley Phillips Newton. *Delta: The History of an Airline.* Athens, GA: UGA Press, 1979.

Life History of the United States, The. NY: Time-Life Books, 1964.

Louis, J. C., & Harvey Yazijian. *The Cola Wars.* NY: Everest House, 1980.

Louis, Joe, with Edna and Art Rust, Jr. *Joe Louis: My Life.* NY: Berkley Books, 1981.

Lutz, Tom. *American Nervousness, 1903.* Ithaca: Cornell U. Press, 1991.

Mack, Walter. *No Time Lost.* NY: Atheneum, 1982.

Man, Myth & Magic: The Illustrated Encyclopedia of Mythology, Religion and the Unknown. NY: Marshall Cavendish, 1983.

Marchand, Roland. *Advertising the American Dream: Making Way for Modernity, 1920–1940.* Berkeley: U. Cal. Press, 1985.

Mariani, Angelo. *Coca and Its Therapeutic Applications.* NY: J. N. Jaros, 1886.

Marquis, Alice G. *Hopes and Ashes: The Birth of Modern Times 1929–1939.* NY: Free Press, 1986.

Martin, Harold H. *Three Strong Pillars: The Story of Trust Company of Georgia.* 2d. ed. Atlanta: Trust Co., 1981.

——. *William Berry Hartsfield: Mayor of Atlanta.* Athens: U. Ga. Press, 1978.

Martin, Milward W. *Twelve Full Ounces.* NY: Harper and Row, 1962.

Matthews, J. B., and R. E. Shallcross, *Partners in Plunder: The Cost of Business Dictatorship.* NY: Covici, Friede, 1935.

Mazlish, Bruce, & Edwin Diamond. *Jimmy Carter: A Character Portrait.* NY: Simon & Schuster, 1979.

McCarthy, J. Thomas. *Trademarks and Unfair Competition.* Rochester, NY: Lawyers Co-operative Publishing Co., 1973.

Mead, Chris. *Champion: Joe Louis, Black Hero in White America.* NY: Charles Scribner's, 1985.

Megalli, Mark, & Andy Friedman. *Masks of Deception: Corporate Front Groups in America.* Washington, D.C.: Essential Information, 1991.

Meyer, Peter. *James Earl Carter: The Man and the Myth.* Kansas City: Sheed Andrews and McMeel, 1978.

Migrant and Seasonal Farmworker Powerlessness. Hearings Before the Subcommittee on Migratory Labor. Washington, D.C.: GPO, 1971.

Miller, Mark Crispin. *Seeing Through Movies.* NY: Pantheon, 1990.

Mintz, Sidney. *Sweetness and Power: The Place of Sugar in Modern History.* NY: Penguin, 1985.

Mitford, Nancy, *The Blessing.* NY: Carroll & Graf, 1951, 1989.

Morgan, H. Wayne. *Drugs in America: A Social History, 1800–1980*. NY: Syracuse U. Press, 1981.

——. *Yesterday's Addicts: American Society and Drug Abuse 1865–1920*. Norman: U. of Oklahoma Press, 1974.

Mortimer, W. Golden. *Peru: History of Coca, "The Divine Plant" of the Incas*. NY: J. H. Vail, 1901.

Munsey, Cecil. *Illustrated Guide to the Collectibles of Coca-Cola*. NY: Hawthorne, 1972.

Musto, David. *The American Disease: Origins of Narcotic Control*, expanded edition. NY: Oxford, 1987.

National Dispensatory: Containing the Natural History, Chemistry, Pharmacy, Actions, and Uses of Medicines, The. Ed. by Hobart A. Hare, Charles Caspari, and Henry H. Rusby. Philadelphia: Lea Brothers & Co., 1905.

Nineties, The Ed. by Oliver Jensen. NY: American Heritage, 1967.

Nite, Norm N. *Rock On Almanac*. NY: Harper & Row, 1989.

Nostrums and Quackery. Chicago: American Medical Association, 1911.

Nutrition and Human Needs. Hearings Before the Select Committee on Nutrition and Human Needs. Washington, D.C.: GPO, 1969.

Oakley, J. Ronald. *God's Country: America in the Fifties*. NY: Dembner Books, 1986.

Oldenburg, Ray. *The Great Good Place*. NY: Paragon House, 1989.

Oliver, Thomas. *The Real Coke, The Real Story*. NY: Random House, 1986.

Oppenheimer, Andres. *Bordering on Chaos: Guerrillas, Stockbrokers, Politicians, and Mexico's Road to Prosperity*. Boston: Little, Brown, 1996.

O'Reilly, Bernard. *Life of Leo XIII*. NY: Charles L. Webster & Co., 1887.

Packard, Francis R. *History of Medicine in the United States*. NY: Hafner Press, 1931, 1973.

Packard, Vance. *The Hidden Persuaders*. NY: David McKay, 1957.

Pells, Richard. *Not Like Us: How Europeans Have Loved, Hated, and Transformed American Culture Since World War II*. NY: Basic Books, 1997.

Pendergrast, Mark. *Practical Ways to Buy, Sell and Profit from Foreign Currencies*. Phoenix: Aden Research, 1991.

Pendergrast, Mark. *Uncommon Grounds: The History of Coffee and How It Transformed Our World*. NY: Basic Books, 1999.

Petretti, Allan. *Petretti's Coca-Cola Collectibles Price Guide*. Hackensack, NJ: Nostalgia Publications, 1989.

Pierce, Alfred M. *Giant Against the Sky: The Life of Bishop Warren Akin Candler*. NY: Abingdon-Cokesbury Press, 1943.

Pierce, Phyllis S., ed. *The Dow Jones Averages 1885–1980*. Homewood, IL: Dow Jones-Irwin, 1981.

Pomerantz, Gary M. *Where Peachtree Meets Sweet Auburn: The Saga of Two Families and the Making of Atlanta*. NY: Scribner, 1996.

Popular Culture & Industrialism, 1865–1890. Ed. by Henry Nash Smith. Garden City, NY: Doubleday, 1967.

Poundstone, William. *Big Secrets*. NY: Quill, 1983.

Presbrey, Frank. *The History and Development of Advertising*. Garden City, NY: Doubleday, 1929.

Ramsey, Douglas K. *The Corporate Warriors*. Boston: Houghton Mifflin, 1987.

Reform Medical Practice: With a History of Medicine, by the Faculty of the Reform Medical College of Georgia. Macon: Georgia Telegraph Steam Power Press, 1857.

Reports of the President's Home Commission. Washington, D.C.: GPO, 1909. Senate document no. 644.

Revenue to Defray War Expenses, Hearings and Briefs Before the Committee on Finance, United States Senate . . . on HR 4280. Washington, D.C.: GPO, 1917.

Riley, John A. *A History of the American Soft Drink Industry*. NY: Arno, 1958, reprint 1972.

Rios, Merlene Dobkin de. *Hallucinogens: Cross-Cultural Perspectives*. Albuquerque: U of New Mexico Press, 1984.

Roddy, Pat, Jr. *75 Years of Refreshment*. Knoxville: J. P. Roddy, Jr., 1983.

Rowland, Sanders, with Bob Terrell. *Papa Coke: Sixty-Five Years Selling Coca-Cola*. Asheville, NC: Bright Mountain Books, 1986.

Russell, James Michael. *Atlanta, 1847–1890: City Building in the Old South and the New*. Baton Rouge: Louisiana State U Press, 1988.

Salinger, Pierre. *America Held Hostage*. Garden City, NY: Doubleday, 1981.

Schaap, Dick. *An Illustrated History of the Olympics*. 3d ed. NY: Knopf, 1975.

Schaeffer, Randy & Bill Bateman. *Coca-Cola: A Collector's Guide to New and Vintage Coca-Cola Memorabilia*. Philadelphia, PA: Courage Books, 1995.

Schlesinger, Stephen, & Stephen Kinzer. *Bitter Fruit: The Untold Story of the American Coup in Guatemala*. Garden City, NY: Anchor, 1984.

Schmidt, Bill, & Jan Schmidt. *The Schmidt Museum Collection of Coca-Cola Memorabilia*. Elizabethtown, KY: Schmidt Books, 1983.

Schudson, Michael. *Advertising: The Uneasy Persuasion: Its Impact on American Society*. NY: Basic Books, 1984.

Schutts, Jeff R. *Born Again in the Gospel of Refreshment: Coca-Cola in Germany and the Making of History*. Unpublished colloquium paper, European History Research Seminar, Georgetown University, Spring 1996.

Sculley, John. *Odyssey: Pepsi to Apple*. NY: Harper & Row, 1987.

Shavin, Norman, & Bruce Galphin. *Atlanta: Triumph of a People*. Atlanta: Capricorn Corp., 1982.

Sherrill, Robert. *Gothic Politics in the Deep South*. NY: Grossman Publishers, 1968.

Shirer, William L. *The Rise and Fall of the Third Reich*. NY: Simon & Schuster, 1960.

Silverman, Milton. *Magic in a Bottle*. NY: Macmillan, 1941.

Simson, Vyv and Andrew Jennings. *The Lords of the Rings: Power, Money and Drugs in the Modern Olympics*. London: Simon & Schuster, 1992.

Smith, T. E. *The History of Education in Monroe County*. Forsyth, GA: Monroe Advertiser, 1934.

Soft Drink, Hard Labour: Guatemalan Workers Take on Coca-Cola. London: Latin American Bureau, Transport and General Workers Union, 1987.

Spalding, Hughes. *The Spalding Family of Maryland, Kentucky and Georgia from 1658 to 1965*. 2 vols. Atlanta: Hughes Spalding, 1966.

Stamps, Thomas P. "A History of Coca-Cola." Unpublished thesis, ©1976, property of author, Atlanta.

Steinbeck, John. *The Wayward Bus*. NY: Viking, 1947.

Stoddard, Bob. *Pepsi-Cola: 100 Years*. Los Angeles, CA: General Publishing Group, 1997.

Stubbs, Roy. *Compilations* on various countries. Atlanta: Coca-Cola Company Legal Library, various dates.

——. *The Confessions of a Country Lawyer*. Atlanta, 1961, property of George Mitchell, Atlanta.

——. *Letters from Latin America*, Atlanta 1941–1942, property of George Mitchell, Atlanta.

Sullivan, Mark. *Our Times: Pre-War America*. NY: Charles Scribner's Sons, 1930.

Superculture: American Popular Culture and Europe. Ed. by C. W. E. Bigsby. Bowling Green, Ohio: Bowling Green U Popular Press, 1975.

Sutton, Antony C. *Wall Street and the Rise of Hitler*. Seal Beach, CA: '76 Press, 1976.

Taylor, Norman. *Plant Drugs That Changed the World*. London: George Allen & Unwin, 1965.

Tedlow, Richard S. *New and Improved: The Story of Mass Marketing in America*. NY: Basic Books, 1990.

Tocqueville, Alexis de. *Democracy in America*. Ed. by Phillips Bradley. NY: Random House, 1945.

Trademark Reporter. NY: U.S. Trademark Association, 1981.

Treseder, Ross C. *As I Remember*. Atlanta: Coca-Cola Co., 1973.

Trevor-Roper, H. R. *The Last Days of Hitler*. NY: Macmillan, 1947.

Turner, E. S. *The Shocking History of Advertising!* London: Michael Joseph, 1952.

Twain, Mark, & Charles Dudley Warner. *The Gilded Age: A Tale of To-Day*. NY: Harper & Brothers, 1873.

Vaughn, Charles L. *Franchising: Its Nature, Scope, Advantages, and Development*. 2d ed. Lexington, MA: Lexington Books, 1979.

Visser, Margaret. *Much Depends on Dinner*. NY: Macmillan, 1986.

Wachtel, Howard M. *The Money Mandarins: The Making of a New Supranational Economic Order*. NY: Pantheon, 1986.

Walton, Francis. *Miracle of World War II*. NY: Macmillan, 1956.

Wapshott, Nicholas. *Peter O'Toole: A Biography*. NY: Beaufort Books, 1984.

Watters, Pat. *Coca-Cola: An Illustrated History*. Garden City, NY: Doubleday, 1978.

Webster's New International Dictionary. 2d ed., unabridged. Springfield, MA: G. & C. Merriam, 1935.

Weil, Andrew. *The Marriage of the Sun and Moon*. Boston: Houghton Mifflin, 1980.

Wells, Della Wager. *The First Hundred Years: A Centennial History of King & Spalding*. Atlanta: King & Spalding, 1985.

——. *George Waldo Woodruff: A Life of Quiet Achievement*. Atlanta: Mercer University, 1987.

While You Were Gone: A Report on Wartime Life in the United States. Ed. by Jack Goodman. NY: Simon & Schuster, 1946.

White, William Allen. *The Autobiography of William Allen White*. NY: Macmillan, 1946.

Wiley, Harvey W. *Harvey W. Wiley: An Autobiography*. Indianapolis: Bobbs-Merrill, 1930.

——. *History of a Crime Against the Food Law*. Washington, D.C.: Harvey W. Wiley, 1929.

Wistrich, Robert S. *Weekend in Munich: Art, Propaganda and Terror in the Third Reich*. London: Pavilion, 1995.

Wolfe, Thomas. *Look Homeward, Angel*. NY: Grossett & Dunlap, 1929.

Woodward, C. Vann. *Tom Watson: Agrarian Rebel*. NY: Oxford, 1963.

Yallop, David A. *The Day the Laughter Stopped: The True Story of Fatty Arbuckle*. NY: St Martin's Press, 1976.

Young, James Harvey. *The Medical Messiahs*. Princeton: Princeton U. Press, 1967.

——. *Pure Food: Securing the Federal Food and Drugs Act of 1906*. Princeton: Princeton U. Press, 1989.

——. *The Toadstool Millionaires*. Princeton: Princeton U. Press, 1961.

Yule, Andrew. *Fast Fade: David Puttnam, Columbia Pictures and the Battle for Hollywood*. NY: Delacorte, 1989.

Zarubica, Mladin. *The Year of the Rat*. NY: Harcourt, Brace & World, 1964.

Zyman, Sergio. *The End of Marketing As We Know It*. NY: HarperBusiness, 1999.

PERIODICALS AND NEWSPAPERS

See Endnotes. Within each chapter, the full information is given only for the first citation of a particular article.

INTERVIEWS

Michael Aldrich, September 17, 1991
Miles Alexander, September 30, 1991
Ivan Allen, Jr., May 20, 1991
Irene Angelico, December 1998
Brad Ansley, April 16, 1991
J. Arch Avary, Jr., July 29, 1989
Sam Ayoub, April 1, 1991; February 7, 1992
Cal Bailey, February 13, 1992
Christel Balzer, November 10, 1988
Clifford Randolph "Randy" Barbee, May 7, 1991
Bill Bateman, April 6, 1991
John Beach, July 11, 1989
Mae Beach, July 12, 1989
Dorothy Benjamin, April 1999
John Bergin, August 13, September 10, 1991; January 28, February 21, 1992, June 1999.
Enrique E. Bledel, April 18, May 21, 1991
Emmet Bondurant, March 1, May 6, 1991.
Charles Bottoms, April 2, November 15, 1991; February 7, 1992, April 23, 1992, April 1999
James K. Boudreau, May 6, 1991
William Bowen, April 16, 1992; Sept 1999
Sebert Brewer, Jr., April 8, October 2, 1991
John Brinton, August 12, 1991
Robert Broadwater, May 17, June 4, 1991; May 1, 1992
Tim Brown, September 1, 1991
Gordon Bynum, March 21, 1991
Dorothy Caldwell, June 1999
Joseph Califano, February 20, 1992
Asa G. Candler V, February 18, 1991
Jac Chamblis, April 8, 1991
G. Clisby Clarke, May 14, 1991
Dudley Clendenin, March 2, 1991
Leo Conroy, January 12, 1992
Ralph Cooper, May 28, 1991
Emilio Cordova, February 11, 1992
Carlton Curtis, March 25, May 21, November 15, 1991
Ovid Davis, March 21, May 29, December 20, 1991
Tony DeGregorio, February 20, 1992
Cartha D. "Deke" DeLoach, July 16, 1989

Nikhil Deogun, May 1999
James Dickey, October 19, 1992
Sean Morton Downey, Jr., March 30, 1991
George Downing, July 27, 1989
Mark "Dill" Driscoll, April 1999
Charles Duncan, Jr., June 17, 1991
Maurice Duttera, July 28, 1989
Brian G. Dyson, June 4, 1991
Emma Edmunds, April 9, 1991
William Effinger III, October 7, 1991
Chris Eliot, April 10, 1992
Charles Elliott, April 6, 1991
Martha Ellis, March 16, 1991
Arthur Ferguson, Jr., April 1, 1992
Pierre Ferrari, March 1999
Gary Fine, June 22, 1992
Howard Finster, July 30, 1989
Alice Fisher, April 15, 1991
Charlotte Fortune, April 18, 1991
Jonathan Fried, December 16, 1991
Henry J. Frundt, October 30, 1991
J. W. Fulbright, Nov. 18, 1992
Jon Gailmor, February 1999
Franklin Garrett, July 13, 1989
Tandi Gcabashe, March 8, 1991
Phil Geier, January 7, 1992
Neal Gilliatt, June 27, 1991; January 16, 1992
John Gillin, April 30, 1991
Marion Glover, May 1999
Roberto Goizueta, June 4, 1991
Susan Gordon, January 15, 1992
Vera Shea Gordon, March 15, 1991
Marc Grauer, May 16, 1991
Bob Greene, Nov. 4, 1992
Tom Greenwood, March 15, 1990
Lewis Gregg, December 9, 1989
Arthur Gregory, May 28, 1991
Mary Gresham, May 29, 1991
Joy Anne Grune, September 13, 1991
Claus Halle, March 13, 19, December 15, 1991
Dick Halpern, March 3, 4, 6, 1992
Garth Hamby, May 20, 1991
Nat Harrison, April 16, 1991
Carlton Henderson, May 11, 1991
Ira Herbert, April 29, 1991; March 12, 1992
Neil Herring, March 9, 1991
Robert Hester, April 29, 1991

Raul Hilberg, December 5, 1991
Alfons Hilgers, April 28, 1991
Murray Hillman, August 6, 1991
Morton Hodgson, March 15, September 30, October 9, 1991; February 12, 1992
Stephen Holtzman, March 7, 1991
Edith Honeycutt, May 19, 1991
Floyd Hunter, July 3, 1991
John Hunter, May 29, 1991
Gerald Imlay, June 7, 1991
E. Neville Isdell, May 1, 1991
M. Douglas Ivester, May 21, 1991
Michael Jacobson, March 3, 1992
Richard Johnson, March 20, 1992
Weldon Johnson, May 3, 1991
William T. "Tut" Johnson, July 12, 1989
Summerfield "Skey" Johnston, Jr., May 1, 1991
Boisfeuillet Jones, May 2, 6, 1991
Joseph W. Jones, August 1, 1989; May 2, 1991; January 7, 27, 1992
Donald Kendall, March 20, 1992
Donald R. Keough, May 16, 1991
Bill Key, July 12, 1989
Sergei N. Khrushchev, February 18, 1992
Dudley King, Jr., July 14, 1988
Monroe King, March 9, April 21, July 25, 1991
John Knox, July 16, 1989
Cliff Kuhn, March 20, 1991
Wilbur Kurtz, Jr., July 29, 1989
Marshall Lane, March 12, 1991
James Langford, February 1999
Dan Lauck, February 2, 1992
Tom Law, June 2, 1991
Pearl Ledoux, April 11, 1991
Paul Lesko, November 6, 1991
Robert Lindsey, February 10, 1992
Hamilton Lokey, May 20, 1991
Julius Lunsford, March 21, 1991
Bill Mackey, February 10, 1992
James Manley, June 4, 1991
Randy Mayo, March 18, 1991
Frank McGuire, April 20, 1991
Alex McLennan, May 1, 1992
Michael McMullen, April 8, 9, 10, 1992
Charles H. "Pete" McTier, May 4, 1991
Susan McWhorter, April 1999
Jesse Meyers, November 22, 1991
Mark Crispin Miller, February 21, 1992
George Mitchell, April 14, 1991

Russell Mokiber, January 23, 1992
Betty Molnar, Summer 1991
Philip F. Mooney, Spring 1991
Marcio Moreira, June 14, 1991
Ray Morgan, April 1999
Al Morrison, April 27, 1992
Jack Morrison, January 24, 1992
Roger Mosconi, January 30, 1992
Clinton Moses, April 14, 1991
Virginia Moulder, October 9, 1991
E. D. Murphy, November 3, 1992
Vince Murphy, December 18, 1991
Ralph Nader, January 18, 1992
Dianne Smith Nau, April 9, 1991; February 5, 1992
Terry Neill, May 1999
H. Burke Nicholson, July 6, 1989; March 27, 1991
Steve Norcia, March 1999
Robert L. Oliver, March 13, 1991
Thomas Oliver, March 11, 1991; February 12, 1992
Charles O'Neal, June 3, 1991
Steve Oney, April 9, 1991
Walter Oppenhoff, April 20, 1991
Eugene Patterson, April 14, 1991
Allen Peacock, April 10, 1991; February 15, 1992
Bill Pecoriello, June 1999
Bert Pelletier, August 20, 1989
Ambrose Pendergrast, Spring 1991
J. B. Pendergrast, Jr., Spring 1991
Nan Schwab Pendergrast, Spring 1991
Bob Pettus, June 29, 1992
Faith Popcorn, February 26, 1992
Klaus Pütter, September 12, 1989
Walter R. "Bud" Randolph, April 18, 1991
Wendell "Sonny" Rawls, March 10, 1991
J. Neil Reagan, March 9, 1992
Ginny Redington, February 14, 1992
Frank Robinson II, March 15, 1991
William Ross, May 8, 1991
Chris Roush, April 1999
Bruce Ruff, April 19, 1991
James Michael Russell, April 9, 1991
Jim Ruwoldt, June 4, 1991
Maria Saporta, March 18, 1991
Randy Schaeffer, April 6, 1991
Charles & Lillian Schifilliti, July 1, 1989
Max Schmeling, May 2, 1991
Bill & Jan Schmidt, April 10, 1991; March 5, 1992; April 1999.

Ken Schulman, March 11, 1992
Robert W. Schwab III, Spring 1991
Tony Schwartz, January 29, 1992
Peter Sealey, February 1999
Scott Seltzer, January 30, 1992
Bill Sharp, March 28, 1991
Ernestine Sherman, May 26, 1991
Gus Shubert, January 9, 1992
James Sibley, May 22, 1991
John Sicher, May 1999
A. B. Simms III, April 23, 1991
Bob Simonton, April 6, 1991
Claire Sims, May 23, 1991
George W. Singleton II, May 2, 1991
Donald Sisler, August 2, 1989; February 11, 1991
Jacobus "Smitty" Smit, April 16, 1991
William O. Solms, April 5, 1991
Jack Spalding, March 16, 1991
Thomas Paty Stamps, May 22, 1991
C. Preston Stephens, June 2, 1991
James Stephens, February 1999
Cecil R. Stockard, October 5, 1991
Roy Stout, March 10, 1992
Ron Sugarman, February 4, 1992
Jack Tarver, November 7, 1991

Bernice L. Thomas, February 16, 1992
Ken Thomas, March 9, 1991
Walter & Mary Thomas, March 10, 1991
Thom Thompson, August 21, 1991
Lois Troutman, January 24, 1992
Melissa Turner, March 18, 1991
William Turner, May 16, 1991
Bill Van Loan, February 6, 1992
Bruce Venner, February 1999
Ed Vorkapich, March 13, 1992
Harry Waldrop, May 31, 1991
Carl Ware, May 7, 1991
Teena Watson, March 2, 1991
Andrew Weil, September 28, 1991
Billy Wilder, January 28, 1992
James F. Williams, May 14, 1991
Jimmy Williams, May 29, 1991
Ian Wilson, January 18, 23, 1992
James W. Wimberly, July 18, 1989
Raymond Witt, April 12, May 15, 1991
Frances "Tut" Woodruff, May 10, 1991
Jasper Yeomans, March 24, 1991
James Harvey Young, March 2, 14, 1991
Mladin Zarubica, January 7, 1990; April 27, 1992

Acknowledgments to First Edition

It's hard to know where to begin to express my gratitude to all the people who made this book possible. First, I must thank Phil Mooney, Joanne Newman, and Laura Jester at the Coca-Cola Archives for allowing me access to the private collection, not normally open to the public. Their assistance and insights truly made this book possible. I had been told that officials at The Coca-Cola Company were impossible to deal with—"suspicious" and "paranoid" were the words I heard most often. On the contrary, I found them to be gracious and open, once they were convinced I would write a well-researched, objective book.

Similarly, I cannot adequately thank all of the current and retired Coca-Cola men and women who spoke with me so willingly and at such length. They are listed at the end of the book in the interviews section of the bibliography. I would particularly like to thank Joe Jones for his insights into Robert Woodruff, and Charlie Bottoms for his rapid-fire repartee. I am also deeply indebted to Claus Halle, who not only spent a great deal of time talking with me, but helped with other contacts. At McCann-Erickson, the primary Coke ad agency, John Bergin performed a similar service. Kentucky bottler Bill Schmidt and his wife, Jan, allowed me the run of their excellent Coca-Cola museum and provided insights and anecdotes into their protracted lawsuits with the company. Their lawyer, Emmet Bondurant, gave me office space and copying privileges for boxes of nonrestricted court records. King & Spalding, the main law firm for The Coca-Cola Company, was also helpful.

I found Linda Matthews and her reference staff (Ellen Nemhauser, Beverly Bishop, Kathy Knox) at Special Collections in the Robert W. Woodruff Library at Emory University eager to help with my project, as they patiently brought box after box to my table. Other libraries and librarians went beyond the call of duty, including Julie Pickett at the Stowe Public Library in Stowe, Vermont, Sue Miller at the Brownell Public Library in Essex Junction, Vermont, Joyce Miller and Mara Siegel at the Trinity College Library in Burlington, Vermont, and Mark McAteer and Diane Boisnier at St. Michael's College Library in Cochester, Vermont. I also conducted research at the Atlanta Historical Society, Fulton County Superior Court, the Benwood Foundation in Chattanooga, the Bailey Howe Library at the University of Vermont, the University of North Carolina Library, the Center for Advertising History at the Smithsonian, the Library of Congress, and the Baker Library at Harvard Business School—at every facility, I received professional, able assistance. Jesse Meyers, publisher of *Beverage Digest*, not only provided an industry insider's perspective but a complete run of his magazine and seminar booklets.

I was extremely lucky to find Mrs. Emestine Sherman, John Pemberton's grandniece. Despite her frail health and misgivings, she opened a treasure trove of family letters and documents which proved invaluable for a reassessment of Pemberton's legacy. The same goes for Monroe King and his self-styled "Pemberton Archives." For years, King has systematically collected esoteric documents on Pemberton, and his insights were vital to my understanding of the inventor. Frank Robinson II, the great-grandson of the man who named Coca-Cola, was generous with his time and knowledge, providing me with a vital clue to the amount of cocaine in original Coca-Cola.

My contacts through the Coca-Cola Collectors Club International proved extremely helpful. Bill Bateman and Randy Schaeffer, two Pennsylvania computer professors, have painstakingly researched not only memorabilia, but the history behind it, in a series of articles printed in the club newsletter. They were kind enough to help me on my way whenever I requested specific information. Thom Thompson, a Kentucky architect, spent untold amounts of time at the photocopy machine, sending me reams of interesting material and giving me insight into the history of Coca-Cola memorabilia hounds.

My work builds on previous books on Coca-Cola by E. J. Kahn, Jr., Brad Ansley, Hunter Bell, Franklin Garrett, Lawrence Dietz, Sanders Rowland, Pat Roddy, Jr., Pat Watters, J. C. Louis, Harvey Yazijian, Henry Frundt, Richard S. Tedlow, Anne Hoy, and Thomas Oliver. I am personally indebted to E. J. Kahn, Jr., for his humanity and encouragement. At the outset, he allowed me to forage through his files at *The New Yorker* and copy over four hundred pages of meticulously indexed notes, which not only gave me concrete information, but served as an exemplary role model. Brad Ansley, who ghost-wrote the biography of Asa Chandler, provided frank background information on the Candlers. I never met Hunter Bell, but his unpublished history of Coca-Cola in the company archives deserves much credit. Franklin Garrett, who anonymously penned the only "official" company history and is a legendary walking encyclopedia of Atlanta and Coke lore, was kind enough to answer my detailed queries. Pat Watters cheerfully shared his knowledge and library, while Henry Frundt added details to his book on Coke in Guatemala. Thomas Oliver willingly talked about his more recent experience in researching the New Coke story. Thomas P. Stamps was kind enough to share his unpublished master's thesis on Coca-Cola, which was especially valuable because Stamps had access to Harold Martin's biography of Robert Woodruff before it was sealed from public view.

Scholars from various fields gave of their expertise and insights. I am particularly indebted to James Harvey Young, the world's leading authority on patent medicines, for sharing his time and knowledge. Sidney Mintz, an anthropologist who specializes in the effects of sugar on history and culture, gladly discussed his writings and ideas through our correspondence. John Flynn, a psychologist, and Andrew Weil, a physician, helped considerably with their experience with coca and cocaine, while biochemists Stephen Holtzman and Roland Griffiths were invaluable resources on caffeine issues, with Susan Schenk combining a knowledge of cocaine *and* caffeine. Michael Jacobson offered a broad overview of nutrition and health issues. Floyd Hunter, a sociologist who wrote about the Atlanta power structure during the Woodruff era, reminisced about his interviews, while historian James Michael Russell provided most of my background on Atlanta. Without the aid of Suzanne White, the historian at the U.S. Food and Drug Administration, I would never have gained access to the FDA files on Coca-Cola and Harvey Wiley. Her enthusiasm and comments were an unexpected bonus.

I recruited anyone who was stupid enough to express any interest in this project. The most outstanding example is my long-suffering uncle, Ambrose Pendergrast, who patiently waded through the extensive Robert Woodruff papers at Emory University and wrote highly entertaining notes—many of which called on his own life experience. He recalls, for instance, that Bishop Warren Candler declined a Coca-Cola once while visiting his parents, preferring buttermilk. My parents, Britt and Nan Pendergrast, were also hauled in to help with the Woodruff papers. In addition, my father became intimately familiar with microfilm machines and various Atlanta archives, while my mother used her social network to ferret out information unavailable in printed form. My lawyer brother Craig helped out with an esoteric legal case, while another brother, Scott, made several trips to the World of Coca-Cola Museum.

My thanks to Jennifer Harrington and the other work-study students who found and photocopied articles, to my former colleague Mark Yerburgh for spotting the Howard Fast World War II story, to Fritz Moore for his computerized flow charting, to Henry Lilienheim for his one-man clipping service, and to my underpaid transcribers: Gail Reid, Jan Clark, Andrea Hall, Cindi Iacono, Marian Saunders, and William Folmar. Jim Peck, playwright/actor extraordinaire and my former teacher, read the manuscript in progress, making unsparing and incisive comments, as well as serving as my grammatical mentor. Irene Angelico brought her filmmaker's perspective to my work, as well as sensitive literary antennae. In addition, Abbey Neidik, Suzanne White, Jeff Potash, Gill Deford, John Pendergrast, and David Galland also read portions of the book and made useful suggestions.

Thanks to Helen Pfeffer for spotting the book proposal and to Peter Miller for representing it.

Without Charles Scribner III and his overwhelming interest in this project, this book would never have been written. Without Hamilton Cain, my primary editor, it wouldn't read so smoothly. For their patience, advice, and encouragement, I am eternally grateful.

Finally, to Betty Molnar, my apologies for this obsessive venture and my thanks for her vital assistance and input.

Acknowledgments to Revised Edition

I am much obliged to journalists Chris Roush and Nikhil Deogun for sharing their background knowledge with me, and particularly to Nik for reading over the new material. It was a pleasure to renew acquaintance with John Bergin, father of both the Pepsi Generation and Coke Is It. Shelly Hochron was kind enough to send a retrospective video of Edge Creative Coke Classic ads, suggesting I watch it while sipping a fine port. Peter Sealey, former head of Coca-Cola marketing, offered many interesting insights. Others who shared their views and memories in interviews are in the list of interviewees, unless they wished to be completely off the record. For her invaluable help with interlibrary loan, I thank Ginny Powers of the Brownell Library in Essex Junction, Vermont. And to Martin Liu of Orion Publishing in the United Kingdom, and Tim Bartlett of Basic Books in the United States, I am grateful for support of this effort.

Acknowledgements to Revised Edition

Index